S0-BBM-818

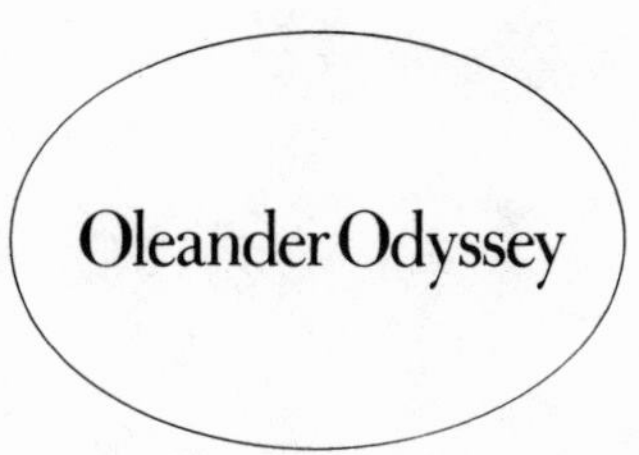

NUMBER SIX

Kenneth E. Montague Series in Oil and Business History

·

Joseph A. Pratt

GENERAL EDITOR

Oleander Odyssey

THE KEMPNERS OF GALVESTON, TEXAS, 1854-1980s

By Harold M. Hyman

TEXAS A&M UNIVERSITY PRESS
COLLEGE STATION

Manufactured in the United States of America

First Edition

The paper used in this book meets the minimum requirements
of the American National Standard for Permanence
of Paper for Printed Library Materials, Z39.48–1984.
Binding materials have been chosen for durability.

LIBRARY OF CONGRESS CATALOGING-IN-PUBLICATION DATA

Hyman, Harold Melvin, 1924–
Oleander odyssey : the Kempners of Galveston, Texas, 1854–1980s / by Harold M. Hyman.
p. cm. — (Kenneth E. Montague series in oil and business history ; no. 6)
Includes bibliographical references.
ISBN 0-89096-438-6
1. Kempner family. 2. Jews—Texas—Galveston—Biography. 3. Galveston (Tex.)—Biography.
I. Title. II. Series.
F394.G2H96 1990
929′.2′089924073—dc20 89-20622
CIP

To my pride of grandchildren:
Joshua, Rebecca, Eric, Daniel, Hannah, Sarah, and Andrea.
And to the late Fannie Kempner Adoue,
Sara Kempner Weston, and Harris Leon Kempner,
whose recollections flavor this account.

The Odyssey of the Oleanders . . . need take
second place to . . . the annals of few American cities.

Arthur A. Brackman,
Houston Gargoyle, May 5, 1929

·

Tropical plants were imported from the West Indies.
One in particular, the oleander, when stuck in sandy soil,
grew like a weed and flowered through half the year.

Anne Nathan and Harry I. Cohen,
The Man Who Stayed in Texas

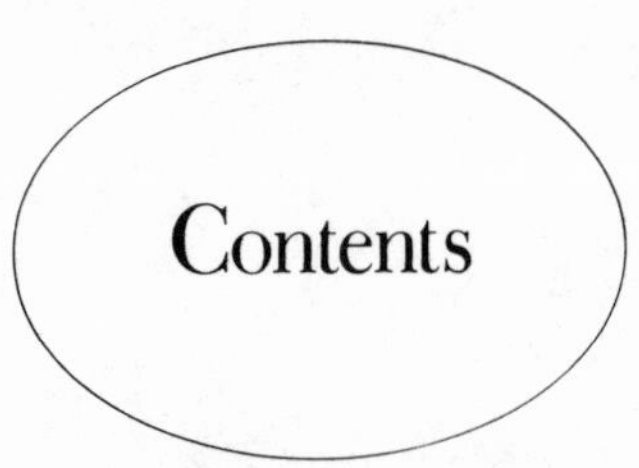

Contents

Illustrations

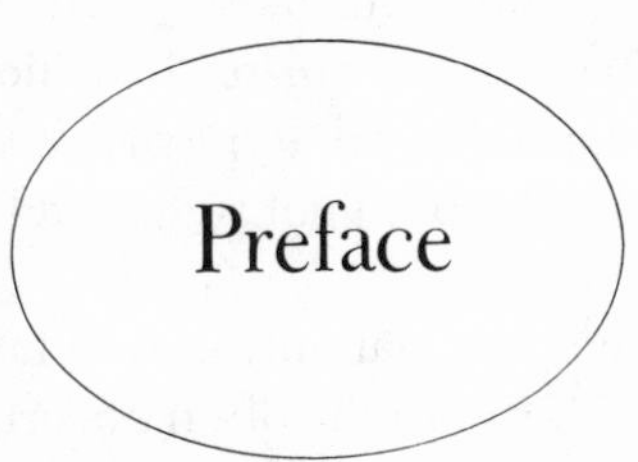

Preface

ALMOST A DECADE AGO I agreed to attempt a history of the Kempner family of Galveston, from the 1850s, when its American pathbreaker immigrated, to as close to the present as I think a historian should venture. The lures were considerable. As originator of Rice University's Center for the History of Leadership Institutions (acronymically, CHLI, a welcome name in Texas), I have tried to interest regional business leaders in preserving and opening the records of their firms and families for historical scholarship. The Kempners had deposited at Galveston's Rosenberg Library Archives several hundred boxes of their family business records dating from the mid-nineteenth century to the recent past. Some documents remain missing. For example, in 1918 Robert Lee Kempner was an applicant for an Army commission, but no Texas county court clerk could locate his late father's naturalization papers in order to verify the son's citizenship. Texas counties were commonly subdivided between 1855 and 1870, as populations grew, and fires were frequent in county courthouses. Another missing item was the 1924–29 volume of Daniel Kempner's rich scrapbooks. He lent one in the early 1940s to writer Donald Day, whose "The Americanism of Harris Kempner" appeared in the *Southwest Review* (Winter, 1945) but who apparently never returned the scrapbook.

On invitation from the Kempner family I conducted a preliminary survey of these records. I was convinced that they are a rich source for a history, or, better, for several kinds of history, including business, family, urban, southern, and Jewish. Generations of Kempners involved themselves collectively and individually in numerous businesses. Equal attention to all these diverse businesses would have required a volume at least equal in size to this one. Therefore I elected to slight two major Kempner businesses, banking and insurance, in favor of larger attention to enterprises in which Kempners essayed novel techniques and/or achieved atypical successes or failures. The exclusions or diminutions should not suggest a lack of importance of these endeavors.

The family has been very patient, particularly since many of its members were unfamiliar with the often uncertain paces and scheduling pitfalls that afflict many if not most historians. Family members have also been gratifyingly forthcoming about being interviewed, even when some interviewees were aged and ill, especially Sara Kempner Weston and Fannie Kempner Adoue. They were both in their nineties when interviewed, yet their recollections proved to be illuminating and basically in harmony with other evidence. Transcripts of these interviews became major sources, as the documentation will suggest. Of interviewers, Dr. Louis Marchiafava was especially productive as oral historian. In addition, Kempner family members were candid critics, and I benefited from their reactions to drafts. At the same time, however, I exercised the right of final judgment in matters of interpretation. When irreconcilable views persisted, I elected to suggest the alternatives, often in footnotes, and leave it to readers to opt for one view or another. At no time did any family member seek to override the historian's research imperatives. Walter Buenger and Joseph Pratt (*But Also Good Business: Texas Commerce Banks and the Financing of Houston and Texas, 1886–1986* [1986]) developed an agreement in an analogous research enterprise that deserves to be a model. Through a cooperative third party, the Galveston Historical Foundation, for whose assistance I am grateful, the Harris and Eliza Kempner Fund subvented research expenses and thus eased the task while economic relationships remained at arms length. I add to the catalog of the Kempners' aids their dredging up of private photographs, some of which appear in this volume. For photographs I thank also Robert Armstrong and the Imperial Sugar Company, and Joan Golden.

I am indebted also for photographs, books, and manuscripts to Galveston's Rosenberg Library, especially the former director of its splendid archives, Jane Kenamore, and its present assistant archivist, Casey Greene; the Houston Metropolitan Research Center of the Houston Public Library and its director, the aforementioned Dr. Marchiafava; Rice University's Fondren Library and its associate librarian, Ferne B. Hyman; the Eugene C. Barker Texas History Center, University of Texas at Austin, and its director, Dr. Don Carleton; the American Jewish Archives, Hebrew Union College, Cincinnati; Galveston's Temple B'nai Israel and its records-keeper, Helen Levy; the Baker Library of Harvard University's Graduate School of Business Administration; and the National Aeronautics and Space Administration. Several then–Rice University history graduate students, including Barbara Guidry, Kenneth DeVille, and Charles Zelden, assisted in this research, and their help was welcome. Sylvia Ross, Marta Gonzalez, Sandy Perez, and Irene Zisek labored typing drafts, and I greatly appreciated their patience. Rice University afforded an agreeable environment for research, writing, and thinking, and I heartily acknowledge its numerous supports.

Now to the work.

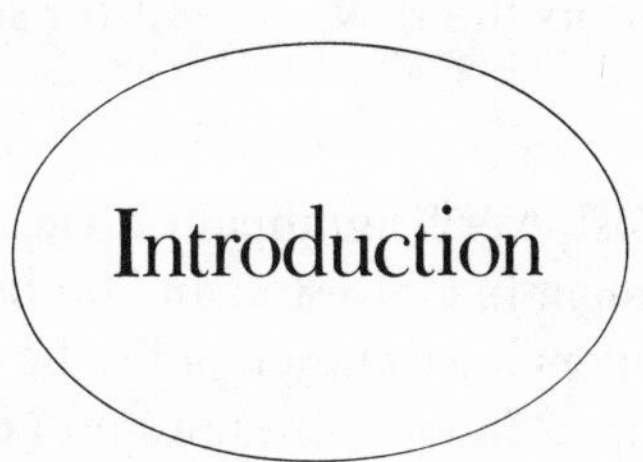

Introduction

"CAPITALISM is not just a matter of technical practices. It's a mentality, an attitude," remarked one historian, excited at news of the recent discovery of nearly complete business and personal records of generations of a merchant and banking family of Renaissance Italy.[1] I felt analogous appropriate excitement upon gaining access to the generations-spanning (1850s–1980s) business and family papers of the Kempner family of Galveston, Texas, an island city whose roots are deep in Texas' past.

Multitudes of Americans have shaped and shared the capitalist "attitude" since colonial times, but scholars have concentrated on relatively few barons of business and captains of industry. Few historians or biographers evaluated the numerous but lesser victors in America's marketplace wars. In part because southern rural life and race-centered politics dominated scholars' agendas, they gave relatively little attention to southern urban capitalists. Of this last overlooked category, southern urban business families of Jewish origins formed a further minuscule fraction.

But the availability of research collections like the Kempner family papers makes timely the admonition of the president of the Southern Historical Association in 1988: "[T]he time has come when the South can and should claim, in the generic sense of the term, an economic history of its own." He noted further that regional businessmen created enterprises of significant scale as measured not only in the South but nationally and globally.[2] There are, in short, interwoven

1. *New York Times*, Nov. 24, 1988.
2. Wall, "What Is *Not* Southern History," *Journal of Southern History*, pp.

business, social, family, urban, and religious "sunbelt" stories to be told. This book attempts the task, at least for several generations of one family in one city.

Prominent in almost every significant civic, cultural, charitable, and business development in Galveston and far beyond, from the 1870s to the present, Kempners have chosen not to be part of the statewide political "establishment." They were not and are not among the nation's super-rich lords of creation. The Galveston Kempners apparently produced no unsavory, ruthless business barons or sleazy market manipulators and were not and are not one of the unhappy, often cruel business dynasties that, in addition to scalping society, so abused their youth as to drive some to social and business ineffectiveness, mental instability, or even suicide.

Instead, the Kempners constitute a business clan, a family. Its generations retained close business and community ties without smothering younger members, nurtured humanitarian sensibilities without blunting capitalism's acquisitive urges, and amassed impressive wealth without outraging civic virtue—indeed, by nurturing that elusive attribute. Rather than "manufacture evil," the family developed a "company culture" that encouraged considerable civic contributions. An analyst of the understudied company culture phenomenon suggested that "a historical approach to company culture begins with the guiding beliefs of the founders [who] define the . . . 'primary task' of an enterprise, the task that it was created to perform. . . . [T]he test of a company culture is how principles are enacted and modified in practice."[3]

Generations of Kempners blended capitalist and humanitarian imperatives in ways that only recently have received close scrutiny.[4] These blendings shaped the Kempners in the context of a family that kept

3, 10; see also Grantham, "The Twentieth Century South," in *Writing Southern History*, esp. pp. 41–44.

3. For studies focusing on unsavory aspects of some business families, see Tiger, *The Manufacture of Evil*, Allen, *The Founding Fathers*, Green, *The Establishment in Texas Politics*, and Bainbridge, *The Super-Americans;* Delheim, "The Creation of a Company Culture," *American Historical Review*, pp. 13–14.

4. Cf. Haskell, "Capitalism and the Origins of Humanitarian Sensibility," *American Historical Review;* Ashworth, "The Relationship between Capitalism and Humanitarianism," *American Historical Review;* Lapham, *Money and Class in America*, passim.

its capital pooled and its business interests diverse, largely to ensure both profits and places for future generations. Without ruinous feuds, each generation produced one or more heirs apparent for top management positions. Decency prevailed in the family's dealings with customers, clients, workers, and neighbors. Overall, this business family of many businesses retained a vigorous sense of social responsibility. It became an inextricable part of the culture of their central company and of its diverse spin-offs.

A Kempner family history is part also of the American Jewish story in the South. This experience was long overlooked, although it began with the first settlements. Except for sporadic spectacular offenses committed against these thin, isolated cadres, the Jews were virtually without a place in the region's history, which seems to have been the way most southern Jews wanted it.[5] As Jews, the Kempners, as well as their history, fit this pattern. Yet generations of Kempners meshed their religion with their business, legal, and social arrangements.

The essentially biographical question of what drives business leaders has long been asked. In our time, characterized by often uncomfortable mixtures of capitalism, industrialization, and urbanization, some business managers wonder if they owe society only the responsibility to compete without fraud or deception. Otherwise, their sole duty is to generate profits for shareholders, some argue.[6]

Disagreeing, Kempners reconciled large-scale enterprise with social and civic responsibility. Alienation from America's values, including the acquisitive, was never part of the Kempners' situation. Educated and aware of society's warts, Kempners retain a high sense of social responsibility, proficiency in commerce, and warm allegiance to nation and community. Combined with the family's welcome habit of preserving both business and personal records and willingness to open them to research, these attitudes offer both a kind of road map of their world of wealth and a key to its meanings.

The Kempners' diverse business enterprises and their innovations in urban government entitled them to be called "Titled Texans," wrote the dean of the state university medical school campus on Galveston Island. Kempners were "an inspiration to family, neighbors, commu-

5. Dinnerstein and Palsson, eds., *Jews in the South*, p. 3. See also Chafets, *Members of the Tribe*, and Ashkenazi, *The Business of Jews in Louisiana*, passim.

6. (London) *Economist* 33 (June 19, 875): 722–23; Wardell, "The Corporation," in *A New America?*, p. 109.

nity, and country," he declared. Learning in the later 1950s that some Kempners were writing their memoirs, the dean expressed his pleasure at the news and offered advice: "Let yourselves go, and really enjoy it."[7]

Some did both. Their reminiscences, in both published and manuscript forms, plus the family's voluminous pool of private letters and ancillary documents and the willingness of individuals to be interviewed, made possible this family history.

Specialist family historians have noted both the fact of Americans' extraordinary mobility and some families' exceptional ability to resist the moving tide and remain content and stable in a shared community. The Kempner "founder" or "dynast" who came virtually penniless to America in 1854 and died a millionaire in 1894, exploited this blessed privilege of mobility. But by his middle age he might well have agreed with a contemporary who worried that "the one great defect in our progressive and migratory people is that they have preserved no authentic trace of their ancestry and but little of its traditions." Because the Kempners were exceptional and preserved authentic traces, this account will try to do what modern specialists in family history urge be done, that is, "present a realistic and interesting . . . means of crossing the bridge between history and life, between one generation and the next, between families, communities, and the nation."[8]

Scholars have studied intently America's elites and workers, leaving the business leaders and professionals who first yearned to rise to the middle class and then, for the lucky and able, to transcend it, in Mary Ryan's phrases, "largely a residual category in American historiography, the assumed, but largely unexamined, context for much of the writing about popular culture and reform movements. . . . Historians have hardly begun to analyze middle Americans as a class unto themselves." But they have begun. Among their early conclusions is one that an increasingly self-conscious business and professional class developed early in America's history and ballooned in size

7. Dean Chauncy Leake to Daniel Webster Kempner (hereafter, DWK), Oct. 26, 1957, file K, Box K9-1957, Personal Papers file, #80-002, Kempner Papers, Rosenberg Library Archives (hereafter, this collection cited as Kempner Papers, and this depository as RLA).

8. Kaler, comp., *History of the [David and Cornelia] Kerr Family*, p. 1; Clark et al., *Three Generations in Twentieth Century America*, p. xiii.

and significance in the nineteenth century, leading to its present eminence. It was self-conscious about what Burton Bledstein called "the advantage of being middle class."[9]

For whites at least, high among these advantages was the absence of constraints against the pursuit of happiness – property.[10] When in 1854 Harris Kempner reached America, although large ironies were inherent in the spectacle of slave-owning democrats running the society they intended further to democratize, whites, including immigrants Jews, pursued "happiness" in the sense of property in ways forbidden or chokingly curtailed in Europe. The self-conscious urban American bourgeois class tended to coalesce around broad values of industry, thrift, family, sobriety, social order, and civic duty. And, concluded Stuart Blumin, "family organization and 'strategy' . . . contributed to middle class formation." Domestic values and family practices, elements in historical biography familiar to Herodotus and Plutarch, are thus again deemed central in evaluating businessmen, their families, and the histories of their urban communities.

Blumin asserted further that, "once implemented, these [self-perpetuating] strategies [of capital accumulation and retention] would succeed in gaining or securing each family's position in the middle class, and established middle-class families would be ones most likely to pursue the same strategies in subsequent generations."[11] Kempners retained many middle-class characteristics to the present, although their elevation to wealth was achieved by the 1880s. Using it to build numerous and diverse family businesses and literally to rebuild two cities, Kempners embraced veritable catalogs of social commitments.

Elements of the Protestant ethic, translated into terms acceptable to, or rather, eagerly sought after by acculturating American Jews, were and are part of their tale. Long part of what one analyst calls "old money," Kempners never let their funds decay into mere remittances for posterity. Mobile risk-takers, Kempners both shaped some contours of America's past and were shaped by them. Not only the

9. Ryan, *Cradle of the Middle Class*, pp. xiii, 13; Bledstein, *The Culture of Professionalism*, p. 334 and passim; Fussell, *Class*, is irreverent and insightful.

10. Appleby, *Capitalism and a New Social Order*, pp. 4, 50, 85, 104.

11. Blumin, "The Hypothesis of Middle-Class Formulation in Nineteenth-Century America," *American Historical Review*, pp. 336–37; and see Baritz, *The Good Life;* Diggins, "Comrades and Citizens," *American Historical Review*, p. 614.

story of multinational corporations, robber barons, economies of scale and routinized bureaucracies, business history is also the stories of diverse enterprises, almost always in cities and often of individuals organized as families.[12]

An effort to re-create American business history so perceived requires the historian both to tell the subjects' story and to explain their history. Still another essential context exists: that of these southern "urbanites'" urban history. Galveston is the city that is central to the family's life. After exploring techniques in collective biography, Richard Jensen concluded that "no satisfactory history of urban America is possible without knowledge of the business and professional leaders in the cities." In local and regional business history, including that of the South, a possibility exists to enhance efforts toward a national synthesis because small producers like the Kempners made worldwide commercial connections.[13]

In the 1980s, leading urban sociologists wondered if they could make both historical and theoretical breakthroughs in studies of interactions between capitalism and cities.[14] This book attempts only an improved history, yet with some yearning on my part toward providing improved illumination of complex processes. This improvement—if improvement results from a reading—derives from the book's focus on adversary actors on a city stage, who build and rebuild their personal lives and urban environments as parts of both capitalist and democratic political imperatives.

What follows strives to attend to such contextual elements and concerns in this history of the Harris Kempner family since its American founder reached these shores a century and a third ago. To that history this account now turns.

12. Aldrich, *Old Money;* see Drucker, *Innovation and Entrepreneurship;* Cochran, *Challenges to American Values;* Miller, ed., *Men in Business;* Wyllie, *The Self-made Man in America.*

13. Jensen, "Quantitative Biography," in *Quantification in American History*, p. 389; see also White, *The Urbanists, 1865–1915;* Watson, "U.S. Local History and the Possibility of National Synthesis" (Southern Historical Association, 1985), pp. 11–12.

14. See Castells, *The City and the Grassroots* and *The Urban Question;* Harvey, *Social Justice and the City* and *The Urbanization of Capital;* Lefebvre, *La révolution urbaine.*

Oleander Odyssey

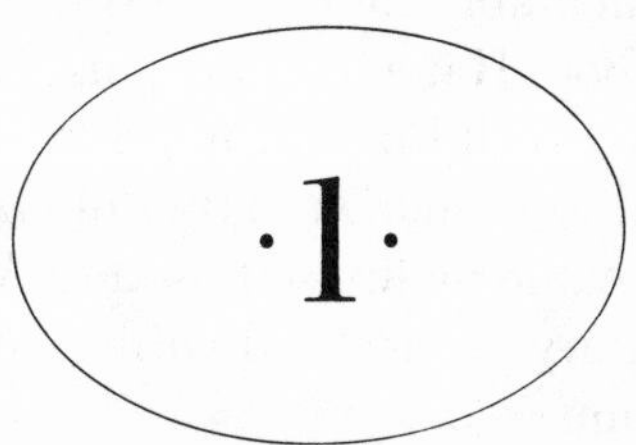

Harris Kempner in America

"ANOTHER FACE in a boatland of Polish immigrants," Harris Kempner reached New York City in 1854, during one of history's most massive voluntary movements of people. With respect to many details of his life, "one is on a safari, searching for facts but encountering many mirages," as his oldest son lamented a century later, ". . . so estimates or even shadowy recollections must be used."[1] Nevertheless these sources both permit and invite efforts to traverse this engaging biographical and historical terrain.

They describe Harris Kempner's unheralded arrival in New York City, seventeen years old, alone, one of a crowd of largely German-speaking Polish immigrants eager to disembark from their ship's crowded steerage. A refugee from the czar's brutal military conscription policy with its particular threats to Jewish draftees of forced religious conversions, Kempner had been born and raised in a succession of rural hamlets (*shtetls*, in Yiddish) in Russian Poland of the sort *Fiddler on the Roof* glamorized. With perhaps $100 as his total capital (although some accounts give his wealth on landing as only $1.75), he entered this strange new world at a time when the American economy would soon be enduring one of its periodic "panics" or depressions and when its political parties and governing institutions were breaking up from ultimately intractable slavery-centered regional tensions. It was a hard time for a Jewish immigrant to adjust from

1. First quotation in I. H. Kempner (hereafter, IHK), "I. H. Kempner Testimonial Dinner" (n.p., n.d.), unpaginated. Second quotation in IHK, "H. Kempner: The First One Hundred Years," 1 *Gulf Coast Historical Association Publications*, p. 1.

rural origins to urban living and from a stratified society to a relatively, or rather, incalculably more open one.

Another question about Harris concerns his given name in English. Even when writing to his children or to relatives in Europe, Kempner signed himself "H. Kempner" and thus offers no help in the matter. But Harris is the name he himself used in America for all other purposes such as military service and voting, and so it is employed throughout this account.[2]

Other biographical details are firmer. Already upon his arrival in America the youth was unusually muscular and tall, standing five feet, ten inches high, and these physical characteristics he passed on to many male descendants. Strong-featured, young Harris was also aggressive, ambitious, thrifty, and hard-working, attributes he shared with many newcomers. He took jobs as a manual laborer, first as a hod carrier at twenty cents an hour, and spent his evenings studying English, perhaps in one of the numerous East Side adult institutes that synagogues, labor unions, and fraternal associations sponsored.

Family tradition has it that his diligence in learning, love for books, and lifelong envy of persons who enjoyed the luxury of a formal education derived from his childhood and that in Poland a grandparent who was reputed to have been a learned and prominent rabbi had instructed him secretly in the Old Testament and the Talmud, the

2. Various accounts suggest that his birthplace was Krzepice, in Russian Poland, or Jaskrow, or Dzialozyn, the last reported a half century later to Galveston rabbi Henry Cohen by John Chapman, a senior English rabbi. But Kempner's oldest son, Isaac H. ("Ike") Kempner (IHK), heard that it was Jaskrow. Probably Harris Kempner's father moved to Jaskrow sometime after the son left for America. Rabbi J. Chapman, letter to Henry Cohen, June 26, 1894, Box 3M218, Cohen Papers, Eugene C. Barker Texas History Center, University of Texas at Austin (hereafter cited as Cohen Papers); cf. IHK, *Recalled Recollections*, p. 14. The London rabbi, according to details supplied in 1894 by the family's Polish relatives, referred to him as "Herman." Kempner's father, on news of the son's death, mourned "Herschell," a Hebrew given name commonly transliterated in America as Herman, Harris, or Harold, especially by Jews acculturating in American ways, but one more likely to have been rendered as "Herman" in a German-speaking region. IHK, "My Memories of Father," *American Jewish Archives*, p. 41, specifies "Herschell" as his father's name in Hebrew; see also Harris Kempner, letter to "My Dear Aunt," May 23, 1880, (trans. from the Yiddish by Alex Schwartz) in Daniel Webster Kempner (hereafter, DWK) Scrapbook, vol. 1, Kempner Papers; see *Galveston Daily News*, Apr. 14, 1894, on wealth on arrival.

study of which was discouraged by Russian authorities.[3] Many transplanted Jews from German-language regions made similar claims of high rabbinical status for their ancestors. Whatever the validity of this suggestion for Kempner, he had, as a youth preparing for his *bar mitzvah*, necessarily mastered written Hebrew to a degree. In New York, young Harris learned spoken and especially written English quickly and well, in later years preferring to carry on correspondence in English, even with persons who had written to him in Yiddish, responding in one instance, "You will pardon me for answering . . . in English . . . [I]t is quite hard for me to write in . . . [Yiddish]." Indeed it was. His written Yiddish remained crabbed, convoluted, and difficult to translate.[4]

Once in the United States, Kempner's concentration on English may well have reflected also the fact that by the 1850s English and Dutch Jews dominated Jewish life in New York, having outnumbered the Sephardic Jews from Spanish- and Portuguese-language areas. As a result, English proficiency tended to ease the entrance into American society of newcomers like Kempner, a forerunner of the Ashkenazi (German-language) immigration to come.[5]

Gone to Texas

Building on what he learned as a bricklayer's assistant, sometime in 1855 young Kempner tried his hand as a very minor independent brick subcontractor. Then, probably because of the catastrophic decline in building activity resulting from the panic of 1857, and also perhaps because of the itchy loneliness of a young bachelor, he decided to head westward. Somehow, by what prodigies of parsimony, self-denial, and labor remain unknown, Kempner had saved between four and five thousand dollars, a substantial amount for that time.

Texas was then a distant magnet to a generation of adventurous American youths. Once arrived, probably after a coastal voyage to New Orleans, then one overland to the west, Harris chose ("I never

3. IHK, "H. Kempner," p. 5; DWK, "Historical Record" (manuscript), Kempner Papers, p. 1.

4. Tinsley, ed., "Select Letters of Harris Kempner," *Gulf Coast Historical Association Publications*, p. 28. On Yiddish, see H. Kempner, letter to "My Dear Aunt," May 23, 1880, in DWK Scrapbook, vol. 1.

5. Rosenwaike, *On the Edge of Greatness*, passim.

knew why or exactly in what year," his son was to write) to settle in the tiny town of Cold Springs (now Coldspring) in what became San Jacinto County, a cotton-growing and timbering region between the San Jacinto and Trinity rivers in southeast Texas. Dense stands of pine, oak, and cedar still shaded the area, although the cotton cultivators had already had their slaves cut great swaths through the forests. Most farmers also cut timber for added income. Perhaps Cold Springs reminded Kempner of the minute Polish village of his boyhood or was, as his grandson and namesake recalls, the first place he came to which did not already have a backpack peddler, the trade that Kempner had apparently already decided to pursue. He boarded at first with an "old citizen" of Cold Springs, then rented private quarters.[6]

From these beginnings Kempner was to build himself a millionaire's fortune by the time of his death in 1894. But there was more in Harris Kempner's amassing of wealth than a rags-to-riches, self-help tale. As we shall see, a Tocquevillian mix of unfettered individualism and ethics was involved.

Kempner's early techniques of accumulating capital were common to hard-driving young immigrant males of his generation and the next who ventured from eastern cities to rural areas of the South and West. As a base for his itinerant peddling operations Kempner opened a very modest general store in Cold Springs, on credit apparently. Initially he spent little time there. Leaving a hired youth in the shop, he shouldered a heavy pack and peddled varied goods door-to-door at farms throughout the region's lush river valleys.

Peddling was the usual business pursuit open to immigrant Jews of little capital. It was already familiar to many newcomers and was a first step toward greater sufficiencies offered by a modest retail store or, even more daring as a dream, wholesaling. Back in Europe, almost all governments, guilds, and societies excluded Jews by law and custom from trades and professions. Therefore, both in absolute numbers and in percentages of other immigrant groups, far more Jews became peripatetic petty entrepreneurs than did Irish or Germans, for example.[7]

6. IHK, *Recalled Recollections*, p. 14; E. R. Thompson, Jr., "History of H. Kempner" (manuscript), Kempner Papers, pp. 1–2; Danhoff, "Business Leadership in the South," *Journal of Business*, pp. 130–37; G. I. Turnley, letter to Leon Blum, Apr. 17, 1884, in DWK Scrapbook, 1894–1915.

7. Howe, *World of Our Fathers*, pp. 76–79. See also Handlin, *Adventure in Freedom*, passim.

But if an applied freedom, peddling in rural areas was a sometimes hazardous and always backbreaking way to squeeze out a living and to accumulate some capital. For bachelors like Kempner, loneliness on the road only increased upon returning to rented rooms or boardinghouses. Towns were small and isolated, their residents often mean in appearance and spirit. In many poor hamlets time itself seemed to have stopped with the first settlers. But other communities bustled with prosperity, with outlying farms fat from lush staple crops and owners eager for consumer comforts.

Extremes of weather in much of America surprised and dismayed most European immigrants. Texas was life at America's edge, a vastness added to vastnesses. Southeastern Texas' endless, torrid, humid summers and often shockingly severe winters were especially wearing. Roads, ferries, or bridges were few and primitive. The newest arrivals were the least habituated to domestic carriers of dreaded epidemics, and traveling salesmen seemed to be peculiarly vulnerable to a host of afflictions, including cholera, yellow fever, and malaria.[8]

Bachelor cooking on campsite fires and the dubious quality of much river and well water must have increased susceptibility to diseases, an inclination compounded when obstreperous riding horses and other draft animals, voracious insects, and sometimes dangerous reptiles added to the trials of a peddler's life. Injuries and infections were calamities. Door-to-door salesmen calling on outlying plantations learned to avoid thieves and deadbeats if possible and to resist them if not. Precisely because they traveled through cotton counties, most peddlers received careful surveillance by edgy constables, sheriffs, and tavernkeepers. The quality of law-and-order protections was often uncertain for a Jew peddling in overwhelmingly Baptist areas of Texas. Non-Jewish merchants could call on local sheriffs or constables. But an owner of a "Jew shop" in a village or the peddler circuiting farms (often, as in Kempner's case, the same person) was usually on his own, at least until he earned enough goodwill from his neighbors and customers to insulate himself from assault and insult. "It is hard, very hard indeed, to make a living this way," a Jewish peddler of the 1840s confided to his diary: "I must stop this business, the sooner the better."[9]

8. Davis, "Life at the Edge," *Southwestern Historical Quarterly*, p. 451.
9. Silberman, *A Certain People*, p. 44. See also Friedman, "The Problems

Just starting in "this business," still unsure of his spoken and written English, Kempner had chosen to live in a community where speakers of that forbidding language used an accent as strange to him as his must have been to them. Probably he was the only Jew in Cold Springs. But he possessed the large assets of educability, determination, and charm. Although Kempner burdened himself with a motley array of saleables, including corset stays and yard goods, like many other peddlers he dressed formally, in the manner of circuit-riding Protestant ministers in America or central European burghers, in a black broadcloth suit, beaver hat, and white cravat, perhaps to enhance his standing in the estimations of his customers. As his trade grew, Kempner bought a horse and wagon and expanded his portable stock to include quinine and other medications, brandy, shoes, hosiery, bolts of cloth, and kitchenware. Unfailingly formal and courteous, he never omitted "Very respectfully" from notes he tacked to doorframes for an absent housewife or from bills he sent to cotton farmers. He also attended systematically to news of local births, deaths, and other events, paying congratulatory or condolence calls on the families concerned. This recent hod carrier from eastern Europe was soon welcomed at the front doors of lonely farmhouses after his forthright greeting: "Good morning. My name is Harris Kempner. I have here some things which you will like."[10]

Not even this muscular young man could carry everything consumers wanted on his back or, later, in his wagon or in his Cold Springs shop. "I have no Bl[ac]k alpaca," he admitted to a customer: "Plenty delaicie[?] and other Bl[ac]k worsted goods." High sales volume soon justified Kempner in hiring a Cold Springs youth to travel to wholesalers in Galveston or Houston to replenish stock, although Kempner increasingly preferred to undertake those tasks himself, perhaps enjoying urban amenities away from censorious villagers. On one such occasion, in Houston, a magistrate fined Kempner five dollars for racing on horseback, that is, exceeding the speed limit of five miles an hour. When he was off mining his expanding territory or in Galves-

of Nineteenth Century American Jewish Peddlers," *American Jewish Historical Publications*, p. 1; Marcus, "Trailblazers of the Trans-Mississippi West," *American Jewish Archives*, p. 59; Light, "Immigrant Entrepreneurs in America," in *Clamor at the Gates*, p. 170.

10. Thompson, "History," p. 2; Trammell, *Seven Pines*, p. 230; IHK, *Recalled Recollections*, p. 14.

ton at wholesalers, he saw to it that the young clerk was on hand in Cold Springs to receive orders and stock. But Kempner himself attended diligently to all other orders. A $7.75 account for one bottle of brandy ($1.75), one of quinine ($2.50), one ounce of "Blue pill" ($0.25), one pair of women's shoes ($1.75), and four pairs of wool hose ($1.50) showed his careful handling, as did larger orders for barrels of "very fine flour." Soon Kempner added less utilitarian items to his stock, including delicate giftware suitable for brides.[11]

Kempner was also quickly known as a man of sound judgment, and this reputation was a key to his quick successes and more so for his survival as a merchant. Even the modest things that Kempner could carry required capital. Except for one in New England, and another in New York City, banks did not make personal loans to small entrepreneurs like Kempner until well into the next century. Most immigrants starting modest businesses had to obtain capital from friends and relatives and by working for others and having sidelines to augment wages. Kempner had no access then to the small coterie of elite German-Jewish financiers already established as private international bankers, principally in New York City, and years would pass before he elevated himself to a level of wealth that intruded upon their horizons. By then Kempner no longer needed their resources. Had he been able to shift time to fifty years after his arrival in America, he would have found a network of Hebrew Free Loan Societies developing, especially in the eastern cities. To seemingly worthy immigrants they lent at least a portion of the capital necessary to begin enterprises, interest free. But such advantages did not exist in the 1850s.[12]

Landsmanschaftn (grass-roots mutual aid organizations composed chiefly of immigrants from the same European village or region) did exist.[13] But Kempner cut himself off from such cohesive societies by his decision to head westward where few coreligionists lived and by his intense drive to acculturate into American secular society. He was one of that undoubtedly small number of immigrants who accumu-

11. Trammell, *Seven Pines*, pp. 230–31, 234.

12. Cf. Carosso et al., *The Morgans;* Supple, "A Business Elite," in *The American Jewish Experience*, pp. 73–77; Tenebaum, "Immigrants and Capital" (American Historical Association, 1985), pp. 1–2.

13. Kliger, "Traditions of Grass-Roots Organization and Leadership," *American Jewish History*, p. 25.

lated enough capital himself to launch the petty business on which he had set his heart.

In addition to risking a portion of the small store of dollars he had brought to Texas from New York, Kempner had established before his departure a modest line of credit (perhaps twenty-five dollars) either in the New York bank or with a goods wholesaler. Either way, the favor shown him by banker or wholesaler was uncommon for the time. He added to that credit line the profits from his peddling and store sales and became known in Galveston and Houston, where he ventured to replenish stock.

Traveling the rural wagon traces, Kempner came to understand his farmer-customers' chronic complaints. Themselves often as lonely as he, these isolated rural residents, almost all of whom cultivated cotton, confided in the hard-working, attentive young man. What historian Gilbert Fite calls "the agricultural trap in the South" was rigged with credit snares, especially in these years of ongoing economic depression. Nature imposed rigid rhythms on farmers that made them peculiarly vulnerable to exploitative local merchants and usurious money lenders. Virtually every Texan was a farmer, and they all needed credit roughly at the same time every year, for seed, livestock, slaves, and fertilizer. The gougings they endured from the 1850s through the early 1900s generated the farmers' anticapitalist rhetoric that would permeate the Granger, Redeemer, Alliance, and Populist movements, Coxey's Army, and the "free silver" crusade, all of which included elements of anti-Semitism.[14]

Though perhaps no Jew could wholly escape bigotry, Kempner managed to accommodate his behavior to his neighbors' ways in order to minimize discriminations. "He found that everybody liked him," wrote one chronicler.[15] Kempner quickly established among the residents of the Cold Springs region a reputation for honesty and fair dealing and prospered enough that by decade's end he was no longer only an itinerant peddler and shopkeeper but also an attractive local source of credit. Using perhaps most if not all of his credit and capital, Kempner lent money to trusted regional customers at slightly lower than prevailing market rates. He would repeat this process on a larger

14. Fite, "The Agricultural Trap in the South" (Southern Historical Association, 1985); Fehrenbach, *Lone Star*, p. 107. Only 2 percent of Texans are agriculturalists in the 1980s (Davis, "Life at the Edge," p. 454).

15. Trammell, *Seven Pines*, p. 230.

scale in future decades, in Galveston, and it became a base for his fortune. But in Cold Springs merchandising remained his primary occupation.

Kempner's life is illustrated in a retrospection involving a local cotton grower named Robertson, a "feudal lord" of antebellum East Texas. Out peddling, Kempner visited the Robertson cotton plantation (in Texas, called a "farm" only out of earshot of the grower). The proprietor insisted that he stay the night, a common practice among isolated agriculturalists. But next day, Kempner, stopping for a drink at a spring, discovered that the pack containing his entire portable stock of goods had been stolen. He returned to Robertson's. The two men scoured the area but failed to find either thief or goods. Kempner was almost "at his wit's end," but Robertson insisted on staking him to a full replacement of stock. "From this low point," the reminiscence continued, "Mr. Kempner went on to amass a substantial fortune. For years thereafter, Mr. Robertson did business with H. Kempner, shipping . . . cotton and drawing drafts on the concern without knowing the value of his shipments. At the end of the season, Mr. Robertson might owe H. Kempner or vice versa, and settlement would be made then. This arrangement based on mutual trust continued [for] many years."[16]

Merchants and Storekeepers

Specialist historians assert that peddlers and shopkeepers using merchandising methods of the sort Kempner employed were more important than their modest capital and local horizons suggest. These minuscule bucolic businesses, selling everything from cowbells to coffins, coupled farms to cities, regions to nation, and nation to nations.[17]

When Kempner developed his modest merchandising network in semifrontier Texas, cotton was "king" both there and in America's international trade. Britain's ballooning textile industry depended on raw cotton from Dixie for more than 80 percent of its essential inflow, and American mills were competing increasingly for larger shares of domestic output. Even in tiny Cold Springs, the advantages and

16. A. Harrel Blackshear, letter to DWK (?), undated (ca. 1936), in DWK File, 1918–1954, Box 41, Kempner Papers.

17. Davis, "Life at the Edge," p. 454; Beverley, *Cowbells and Coffins*, passim.

risks of concentrating on cotton growing became quickly apparent. Costs for land, seed, tools, draft animals, and slave labor were high. Increasingly, local merchants and itinerant peddlers became central participants in what would be called the transaction sector of the cotton economy, the sector devoted to facilitating the exchanges rather than to the production of the commodity itself.[18] As a peddler-storekeeper Kempner was one of many "nodal points through which many goods passed to and from rural households," Christopher Clark concluded. Kempner, as did many petty merchants who lent money and extended credit, accepted payments in the form of claims on future crops or in kind, and many southern merchants handled cotton as agents of farmer-debtors.

In economic terms the country shopkeepers who offered alternative sources of credit eased the farmers' chronic cashlessness, thereby helping to swing exchanges more toward credit than cash bases. In so doing, such merchant–money lenders, even if unwittingly, connected local agricultural producers and consumers to regional, national, and, in the case of cotton, even international markets. And merchandising, at least as Kempner practiced it in the later, Galveston phase of his career, according to Clark, "became a self-reproducing occupation, with sons and other relatives carrying on and enlarging the founder's work."[19]

In 1856, just as Kempner began his rural merchandising, *Hunt's Merchants Magazine* editorialized that traders "really rule." By the turn of the twentieth century, soon after Kempner's death, Thorstein Veblen argued that storekeepers had usurped the place of Jeffersonian yeoman farmers and become America's true "independents," the new paradigm of community respectability and republican worth.[20] Kempner enjoyed an ascending place in the Cold Springs social structure as the result of the reputable means he evolved to carry on his business.

By 1860 Kempner was clearly accepted by his white neighbors as

18. Pusateri, *A History of American Business*, p. 99; North and Wallis, "Measuring the Transaction Sector in the American Economy," in *Long Term Factors in American Economic Growth*, pp. 95–161.

19. Clark, "Taking Stock of the Nineteenth Century Store" (Organization of American Historians, 1985), pp. 1, 9, 13, 24; Jones, *Middlemen in the Domestic Trade of the United States, 1800–1860*, and Atherton, *The Southern Country Store*, both passim.

20. *Hunt's*, quoted in Clark, "Taking Stock," p. 25; Veblen, "The Country Town," *Freeman*, p. 420.

a trustworthy citizen and businessman. He neither exhibited nor recorded any conscience-stricken agonies about slavery. Kempner always kept his own counsel about the "peculiar institution," perhaps letting his silence signify his acquiescence in this exploitative system. He never bought a slave himself, although he could have afforded one or more by the time the Civil War altered events. Odds are that Kempner had taken on the ways of the white South in all appropriate respects, and accommodation specifically to human slavery and to white supremacy generally was one of them.

Although the only Jew in an overwhelmingly Gentile, agricultural society, Kempner prospered in part because he charged less for goods or credit than competitors did. But on a deeper level he throve because of the respect he earned in the community and region. For example, San Jacinto County officials deposited county funds with him. Indeed, Kempner may have been the county's sole depository. With the onset of the Civil War, wealthier planters placed funds in trust with him.[21]

Just what Kempner did to safeguard these moneys, or his own, during the Civil War is unclear, but his methods succeeded. Although he volunteered for the Confederate army and was severely wounded in combat, Kempner bought no substantial amounts of Confederate bonds. Instead, he probably kept almost all the funds at his command in "hard" form such as gold or sheltered them in safe securities, in real estate in Mexico, or perhaps even in the northern banks he dealt with. He may have also speculated, through agents, in the widespread Texas-Mexican smuggling and black marketeering, or the so-called "Matamoros trade" that developed soon after Sumter and continued until Appomattox.

With funds sheltered, Harris Kempner, who never spoke against secession, went off to war as the ultimate expression of his accommodation to the society that nourished him. As a soldier in the Ellis County "Blues," a local militia unit that eventually, as part of W. H. Parsons's 12th Texas Cavalry Regiment, failed to keep Union soldiers out of New Orleans and southern Missouri, Kempner survived his combat experiences. During one fierce if obscure skirmish in Louisiana, an eyewitness among his comrades reported that "a cannon-ball struck

21. IHK, *Recalled Recollections*, p. 4; Lucy McMurrey, letter to IHK, June 18, 1935, DWK Scrapbook, 1935–1940.

. . . [Kempner's] horse, . . . and cut through the horse's neck, . . . then the horse ran a short distance . . . before falling; Mr. Kempner was so shocked and stunned, he also fell and was unconscious, and his comrades thought he was dead and . . . carried him off the battlefield; but after a time he revived, but it was some time before he got over the effects of it. They all say no braver or true man ever drew a [sword] blade or fired a gun."[22]

The common assumption then was that most wounded men would die, if not immediately from injuries then because the crude surgical and postoperative procedures of the time would finish them off. But robust Kempner recuperated and immediately volunteered again for combat. Superiors refused the application—an indication of the seriousness of his wound, considering the manpower needs of the trans-Mississippi rebel forces. Kempner accepted still-active noncombatant service as a quartermaster sergeant, and Appomattox may have interrupted the procedures that would have given him an officer's commission.[23]

Kempner always treasured his memories of wartime comradeship. He had bought a single thousand-dollar Confederate bond in 1864, thereafter preserving the worthless note. Later he stood surety for another former CSA soldier who wished to become a river and coastal pilot, and when a chapter of the United Confederate Veterans formed in Galveston, Kempner became an early member. In 1885, a new, nominally military organization, the Kempner Rifles, organized there. Kempner's oldest son was second lieutenant, and the father and his partner subsidized the unit. More social than martial, its roster was heavily Jewish. A non-Jewish Galvestonian, the prominent lawyer and Confederate military veteran D. Charles Hume, reflecting on these matters, years later wrote that "the loyalty of Jews to this country has not escaped even my limited personal observation. In the Confederate War there were many Jews on our side distinguished for devotion to soldierly duty in all forms."[24]

22. Quotation from G. I. Turnley, letter to Leon Blum, Apr. 17, 1894, DWK Scrapbook, 1894–1915; Buenger, "Secession Revisited," *Civil War History*, p. 293, on analogs to individuals like Kempner.

23. DWK, "Historical Record," p. 1; IHK, *Recalled Recollections*, p. 14; Thompson, "History," p. 4.

24. Hume, letter to Rabbi Henry Cohen, Apr. 27, 1893, Box 3M218, Cohen Papers; other details in DWK Scrapbook, 1894–1915.

When the Boys Came Marching Home

Settling in again at Cold Springs, the wisdom of Kempner's safeguarding of capital became apparent. His own assets and those entrusted to him by others were largely intact at a time when many Southerners were suffering severely from the war's physical destruction, the loss of investments in slaves, and the worthlessness of Confederate paper. He reopened his store, profiting quickly and substantially by satisfying his neighbors' accumulated wants for consumer goods and credit. Within a few years he had replaced his original ramshackle shop with a large structure. Less than two years after Appomattox a field agent for the credit-reporting firm R. G. Dun (since, Dun and Bradstreet), although given to variant spellings of Kempner's surname, concluded confidentially that he was "a German who has recently commenced business. No visible means other than his shop. Has a large stock of goods. Is doing a . . . [sharp?] business. Has bought a large stock of Cotton for cash and paid better prices than anyone else."[25]

Already intrigued by possibilities in the cotton trade but necessarily carrying on eclectic merchandising, Kempner continued saving. "Young, energetic, and clearheaded, [this] excellent business man owes no one here . . . considered honest & reliable," the Dun reporter confided. Unlike many other subjects of these reports, Kempner was never known to drink to excess or carouse (news of his offense in Houston for speeding on horseback apparently did not reach bucolic Cold Springs). Instead, the continuing view there was that Kempner was "an enterprising businessman. Doing a large business. No visible judgements against him. Of good business habits."[26]

Dun's reports were written anonymously, in this instance undoubtedly by some Cold Springs professional acquaintance of Kempner's, probably a fellow merchant, lawyer, banker, cotton grower, teacher, or journalist serving the company for fees. Circulating nationwide to subscribers, the Dun rating helped Kempner to borrow money in the Northeast both to replenish stock and to relend to Texas clients at rates slightly lower than they could obtain locally. Subsequent Dun

25. Dun Reports, Texas vol. 25, p. 160, R. G. Dun and Co. Collection, Baker Library, Harvard Graduate School of Business Administration. Used with permission.

26. Ibid.; IHK, *Recalled Recollections*, p. 14.

reports remained uniformly positive. Kempner, an 1869 report stated, was worth a "clear $9 or 10 thousand . . . with prospects for further success very flattering."

But Kempner himself was finding personal prospects in tiny Cold Springs less flattering. His wartime quartermastering had taught this observant young man about the marketplace economies and profits of wholesaling. The year 1869 was one of sharp economic downturn nationally. Kempner suffered one of his rare setbacks; he had invested some of his own funds in a Galveston cotton brokerage that failed. Even so, in early 1870 a Dun reporter described Kempner as still "perhaps the strongest merchant in the township" and predicted that he "will succeed anywhere."[27]

Less than a year later Kempner was ready to test the prediction. After studying alternatives carefully with friends in Cold Springs, Kempner and they agreed that Galveston had the brightest business prospects of any place in the region for a young man on the go. To a close friend Kempner confided that as soon as he had fifty thousand dollars saved he would move to Galveston and try to become a wholesaler. In 1871 Kempner sold his Cold Springs shop and stock advantageously and made the move. He hoped not only to enjoy a larger scale of operations but also to search for a wife. Though he was "popular among the young people . . . [of Cold Springs and] not a few of the young ladies were beginning to cast their nets in his direction," the town offered no eligible Jewish women.[28] He was to find a business partner in Galveston before he found a wife.

27. Dun Reports, Texas vol. 25, p. 160; see also Norris, *R. G. Dun & Company, 1841–1900.*

28. Quotation from Lucy McMurrey, letter to IHK, June 18, 1935, DWK Scrapbook, 1894–1915; Trammell, *Seven Pines*, p. 231.

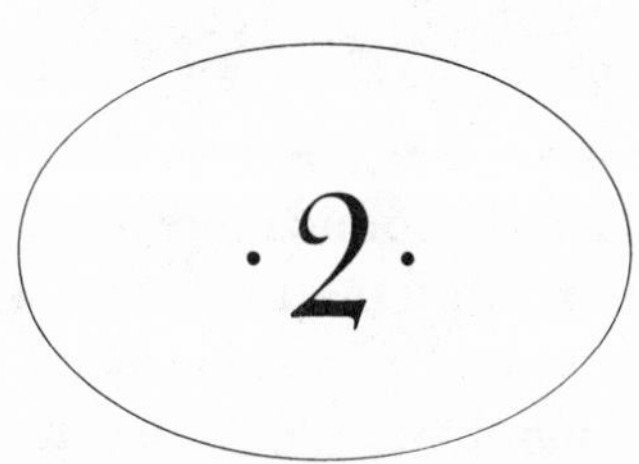

Galveston, Grande Dame of the Gulf

By the early 1870s Galveston was no longer the crude, foul-smelling settlement of prewar years. Instead it had become what one Jewish visitor described as a large, beautiful island city of perhaps twenty thousand inhabitants, making it Texas' largest community. In this "New York of Texas," fine shops carried choice imported carpets, pianos, fabrics, and wines. Many Galvestonians, like Kempner, prospered during the war. The accumulated wealth of leading residents was reflected in what the same visitor described as "mammoth business houses, [an] extensive and most beautiful cotton exchange (the handsomest in the United States) . . . magnificent churches, schoolhouses, and places of amusement."[1]

Perhaps news of an active Jewish community in Galveston helped Harris Kempner to decide on a move to the Island City. In 1868 Galveston Jews numbered well over a hundred individuals, and in 1853 Galveston had elected a Jew, Michael Seeligson, as mayor. Since 1852 Galveston's Jews had had a consecrated cemetery. Because they had no permanent place for worship, however, they assembled in various temporary locations for religious services, meanwhile organizing Temple B'nai Israel (Sons of Israel). In 1870 the congregation laid the cornerstone for a permanent building, the first synagogue in Texas, completing it the following year.[2]

Coming to Galveston from tiny Cold Springs, Kempner had been happily impressed by his new home, and he never lessened his affec-

1. De Cordova, *Texas*, p. 64.

2. Henry Cohen, unpublished typescript on Galveston, in Box 3M326, Cohen Papers; Schmeier, ed., *Reflections of Southern Jewry*, pp. 80–81 and n. 53; Dreyfus, comp., *Henry Cohen, Messenger of the Lord*, p. 13.

tion for it.[3] On his earlier visits he had seen about him the amenities of this well-planned, large city: paved streets, uniform sidewalks, grand residences, a mule-drawn street railway with nine miles of track, thirteen hotels, three markets, an opera house, two theaters, and three concert halls. Perhaps now he found more interesting the several iron foundries, machine shops, illuminating gas works, and meat-packing plant. To serve commerce, Galveston boasted two national banks, another only for savings, two of mixed banking and insurance functions, four insurance firms, and more than twenty joint stock companies. The combined capital worth of these private companies, totaling well over $12 million, could only have impressed young Kempner.[4]

The city's economic pace and health improved markedly in the wake of Appomattox. Unlike much of the defeated South, Galveston's mercantile operations surged to match those of the booming North. Still "Old South" in its manners, the Island City was determinedly "New South" in its business ways. The former Confederate states as a region failed to develop bourgeois society, but Galveston embraced those values with affection bordering on lust. It was indeed a frontier of opportunity for a hustling merchant. The major local newspaper reported that since Appomattox, "All is bustle and activity, the wharves are crowded with shipping, the stores filled with goods, buyers from the country are in force and our merchants jubilant."[5]

Young Kempner must have been impressed also by the city's numerous pleasures for socially accepted residents, especially for marriageable males with good prospects. True, working hours were long, from 7:00 in the morning until 9:30 or 10:00 at night through the week, with stores and offices closing at noon on Sundays. But heavy schedules were nothing new to Kempner or the other young men of his age and financial situation with whom he associated. Demanding work calendars seemed not to interfere with their dedication to busy social lives. Kempner was hardly a rare commodity, however. Long since an international port, Galveston's heavy overseas traffic justified foreign governments in establishing consular offices there. Among the

3. Rabbi L. J. Stillpass, "Our Temple Highlights & Sidelights" (manuscript), Kempner Papers.

4. Nunn, *Texas under the Carpetbaggers*, p. 238; Burka, "Grande Dame of the Gulf," *Texas Monthly*, p. 164; McComb, *Galveston*, chaps. 1–3.

5. *Galveston Daily News*, Sept. 8, 1865; Wright, *Old South, New South*, passim.

representatives of American and European mills, banks, and shipping firms were many bachelors like Kempner—good company but tough social competition.

Men's clubs proliferated. Englishmen established the Aziola Club soon after Kempner's arrival. The Galveston Garden Club, initiated by Frenchmen but thereafter dominated by Germans who renamed it the Garten Verein, surpassed the Aziola, becoming the social mecca of Galvestonians in the late nineteenth century. Kempner's oldest son reflected his father's pleasures in the club's niceties, coming as they did after poverty, toil, and austere bucolicity:

> The club's regulations were enforced with German thoroughness. The membership was limited and normally maintained at 500. . . . Wonderful affairs were staged here—six and seven course banquets; dining rooms completely changed by hanging colored materials decorated with flowers and greens; often bowling parties with beautiful silver prizes were given; many a debutante or bride-elect was so honored; chaperones were always present and no well brought up young lady wandered off into the garden beyond a certain walk. At one time a miniature or at least embryo zoo obtained in the north corner of the garden; at night it was definitely out of bounds. Excellent tennis courts were available for members' use.[6]

New Orleans was Galveston's major Gulf antagonist in commerce. But New Orleans's reputation as a sinful city, one susceptible also to epidemic diseases, made it less attractive than Galveston. True, the Louisiana city had a venerable Jewish community with offshoots branching from the Mississippi River highway that connected the Crescent City directly to the continent's interior. Substantially through the influence of Galveston rabbi and Kempner family friend Henry Cohen and because railroad trunk lines through Houston soon after Appomattox linked Galveston to the nation's middle and west, Galveston's Jews identified with Cincinnati and other upper Mississippi urban centers more than did the Louisianans.

Galvestonians did, however, have to bear to some degree the unsavory reputation weighing on residents of almost all coastal and river-

6. Quotation in [IHK], "Their Hearts Were Young and Gay," *Guide Magazine to Galveston and the Mainland* (Oct., 1947): 2-3, 14 (typescript in Kempner Papers). Other data in A. Stanley Dreyfus, "Hebrew Benevolent Society" (manuscript), Kempner Papers.

port cities, mining towns, and other near-frontier communities. Folklore populated Galveston with rogues, whores, deserters from coastal shipping, and evaders from the criminal laws of other American states and Mexico who allegedly had "GTT" ("Gone to Texas") in order to avoid private debts, public justice, or both. But the sheer weight of the commerce moving in this sometimes hostile environment suggests more laboring than roistering.

The outgoing transshipment of bulk crops, especially cotton, grains, sugar, coffee, tobacco, potables, and rice, was the island's major business. Local wood and metal manufactures were to remain minor. Commercial opportunities had been growing, however, since Texas' incorporation into the United States. By the late 1850s, when Kempner had arrived in Texas, Galveston's population and business growth already distinguished it from all other communities built on myriad barrier islands flanking America's shorelines from Chesapeake Bay and the Florida Keys to Corpus Christi on the Gulf Coast. Indeed, until shortly after Kempner's death in 1894, Galveston, in addition to being the state's largest city, was its chief port of entry.

True, the Texas city, unlike New Orleans, could tap nothing like the Mississippi River's vast navigable river systems leading into the continental heartland's swelling populations. To balance, Galveston Bay was a magnificent, protected maritime expanse on a coastal fringe. But Galveston's development as a port was relatively sluggish until in the late 1880s the national government subsidized the dredging of a reliable deepwater channel through sandbars that formed Galveston Bay. Until then incoming goods were "lightered" onto a raffish "mosquito fleet" of wind-driven barges for transfer to the wharves and warehouses that were altering the Island's northeastern face. This transshipping was a slow operation that increased costs and exposed the goods to theft, breakage, and spoilage. Less easily improvable, regional rivers were only erratically navigable and thus attracted sparse populations, although investors sparked sporadic efforts to develop rail links that, in the boosterish imagery of that time, would make Galveston Denver's deepwater port as well as the terminal for other developing inland cities.[7]

The city's land area, like that of New Orleans, was severely lim-

7. Kelly, " 'Twixt Failure and Success" (MA thesis); Axelrod, "Galveston: Denver's Deep Water Port," *Southwestern Historical Quarterly*, p. 220.

ited. A true island, it spanned only three miles at its widest point and was roughly thirty miles long, and nature constantly reshaped its landforms and the Gulf's shallow channels of navigation. In 1837 a storm, perhaps of hurricane ferocity, blew away nearly every structure on Galveston Island.[8] Fears of monstrous storms had long since subsided, but nature's strength revealed itself to residents every day of every year.

Galveston shared with all the low-lying, tropical Gulf regions a reputation for disagreeable, Bombay-like summers when it was "an awful humid place," although other seasons were attractive. Travelers worried about contagious diseases, especially the dreaded yellow fever, cholera, and malaria. Yellow-fever epidemics inspired what a local humorist described as "a great deal of interest" and some early but futile efforts at "strict cleanliness." Reliance on medical doctors was futile, Islanders professed to believe. One dominant branch of medicine, the "allopathic," killed the patients; the other branch, the "homeopathic," let them die. But Galvestonians knew also that in addition to the human pains and tragedies involved in mass diseases, their economic costs hurt everyone. For example, in 1867, shortly before Kempner's arrival there, a yellow fever epidemic took one thousand lives on the Island. But anytime a single case was diagnosed there, competitors in other ports quarantined Galveston imports and exports, or so Galveston's business leaders alleged as a reason for their city's ultimately intractable economic limitations.[9]

Galvestonians had indeed been notoriously inattentive to elementary urban concerns, including sewage disposal. Records of the Island City's Hebrew Benevolent Society "insist that Jewish immigrants found it very difficult to endure the rigors of the Galveston climate. They were very susceptible to the dread and often fatal scourge of yellow fever."[10] But young Kempner did not succumb. Perhaps his Cold Springs years had immunized him against such ills. But all Galvestonians had to endure the floodings from frequent heavy rainfalls that drew rank odors from the soaked soil. The hot sun magnified these miasmas, then, generating a blanketing humidity, mixed them with emissions from decaying fish and oysters and the droppings of draft animals until the atmosphere sometimes assumed almost solid qualities.

8. Hayes, *Galveston*, 1:277–79; Eisenhower, ed., *Alexander Sweet's Texas*, p. 16 n.

9. Eisenhower, ed., *Alexander Sweet's Texas*, pp. 60–62.

10. Dreyfus, "Hebrew Benevolent Society."

Cleansing sea breezes were also common and frequently created beautiful conditions. By raising homes and shops on high foundations and creating as much shade and ventilation as possible, residents who could afford the costs adapted housing styles to seaside humidity and regional heat. Nature limited the amount of available real estate, however, and living costs were high. Drinking water, food except for the sea's bounty, most building materials, and fuel had to be imported from the mainland. With conditions so different from those obtaining in vast mainland Texas, it is unsurprising, a journalist has suggested, that residents there developed attitudes that were "as alien to the rest of Texas as those of New England. . . . Of the mythic elements that shaped Texas — the endless expanse of land, the frontier, the quest for water, rugged individualism, cultural isolation, cattle, oil — not one applies to Galveston."[11]

Actually, some do. Galvestonians shared with mainland Texans certain attitudes toward races, genders, government, and livelihoods. Granting these commonalities, Texas was yet penultimately a post-Enlightenment society in which, according to an impressive analysis, "individualism, religious freedom, social egalitarianism, and local autonomy [was] its tradition."[12]

The Marx and Kempner Partnership

In this bustling city Kempner discovered, or rediscovered, Marx Marx. He was an established wholesale grocer, a man described by a contemporary as possessing "all the elements of a popular and successful merchant, genial, warm hearted, energetic and honorable . . . [who] makes friends wherever he goes. He is a boon companion . . . [who] gives hearty and enthusiastic support to every measure inaugurated to enlarge the commercial scope of Galveston." In 1872 Marx and Kempner, who had met during the latter's frequent trips to Galveston, became partners in a wholesale grocery and liquor importing business.[13]

A native of Prussia born in 1837, Marx had upon immigrating set-

11. Burka, "Grande Dame," p. 160.

12. Davis, "Life at the Edge," *Southwestern Historical Quarterly*, pp. 451–52.

13. Quotation from Brown, *Indian War and Pioneers of Texas*, pp. 279–80. Marx's mother "liked the name so much she named him [with it] twice. . . . [Although] it is spelled many different ways . . . it should really be 'Marx Marx,'"

Marx Marx, business partner to H. Kempner, ca. 1880
(Courtesy Joan F. Golden)

tled first in New Orleans and clerked in his father's modest grocery store. Dissatisfied with this dead end Marx sought quick fortunes in Central America and gold-rush California, but these fabled places denied him success. He later amassed a sizable fortune in the British Columbia fur trade, in Nevada silver strikes, and in quieter wholesale grocery ventures in Utah and Montana. While in Utah merchant Marx had Brigham Young among his customers, and the Jewish shopkeeper charmed the Mormon elder. Delighting in Marx's wit and "broad, round face and genial disposition," Young took to calling him "Bishop." The nickname stuck and most Galvestonians continued to call Marx by the title, except for his intent, sober young new partner, Harris Kempner, who also probably thought unfunny any sug-

a Marx descendant stated (H. L. Kempner, interview with Joan Frenkel Golden, Sept. 1, 1987; quoted with permission).

gestion that his partner shared genealogy or ideas with Karl Marx, as was sometimes suggested in jest.[14]

Like Kempner, by the late 1860s Marx was ready for city life and matrimony. He married a socially prominent New Orleans woman and resettled in Galveston. An unusually energetic entrepreneur even for the Old West, later a regent of the University of Texas, Marx would likely have been delighted by the designation "capitalist" on his death certificate in 1909.[15] Affable and accommodating, Marx would be Kempner's senior partner and in many ways the perfect "outside man." Perhaps Kempner's habit of deference to his senior associate derived in part from Marx's greater wealth when they became partners. He already owned three commercial buildings in Galveston and had earlier been associated with the auctioneer turned wholesale grocer and dry-goods merchandiser, Sampson Heidenheimer. In March, 1868, the latter put twenty thousand dollars in cash into the new alliance and Marx, ten thousand dollars—large sums for that time and place. A Dun credit reporter doubted their claim of so much capital: "Their statement is not entirely disbelieved but several [Galvestonians] think it improbable. We think they are straining every point to establish a large credit, and when it is obtained, to . . . go under—securing themselves at the expense of their creditors."

The anonymous reporter was alleging that Marx and Heidenheimer were "milking" their company, a technique commonly attributed then to unscrupulous businessmen, especially Jews and Germans. But even the unknown accuser soon admitted that his canard was baseless. His June, 1869, analysis described the partners as "energetic good businessmen [who] speculate [in cotton?] and thus far successful . . . [but] any reverse might embarrass [them]. . . . They have good cr[edit] with some of the leading Jew houses here."[16]

Marx's association with Heidenheimer ended in 1870, and Marx, looking for a new venture and partner, found Kempner. Of the latter, a contemporary noted that

> in many respects Mr. Kempner is the opposite of his partner. He is business all over, is a cool calculating man, full of ready resources,

14. Hayes, *History*, 1:974–75. See also IHK, *Recalled Recollections*, pp. 4–5.
15. Details in Marx's obituary, *Galveston Daily News*, June 26, 1909; H. L. Kempner interview with Golden, Sept. 1, 1987; Brown, *Indian Wars*, pp. 279–80.
16. Heidenheimer entry, Feb. 2, June [?] 1869, Dun Reports, Texas vol. 13, p. 156, R. G. Dun Collection.

> thoroughly posted in the markets, has no time for pleasure, but is wholly and entirely engrossed in his business affairs. A man of few words, and those directly to the point. Quick to see a change in the market, and to take advantage of it. Pushing, driving, energetic, he has no time for the pleasant amenities of life. He thrusts these all on to his jolly good-natured partner. While Marx looks after the outside business of the house Kempner directs and manages the inside affairs.[17]

With Marx as senior, his and Kempner's stock on the first day of trade consisted of "three barrels of flour, three barrels of whiskey, a dozen boxes of crackers, a barrel of syrup, [and] a few cases of eggs. . . . The entire stock was sold out that [opening] day." The wholesaling of foodstuffs and potables proved to be both engaging and profitable to these diligent, enthusiastic, and energetic young men, and their advertisements for homely items, including "Appolinaris Water [and] German Seltzer; Just received a fresh supply," dot the pages of Island City newspapers.[18]

"Kempner could hardly have picked a more opportune time than the 1870s or a more likely spot than Galveston to enter the wholesale business," judged historian James Tinsley. A contemporary visitor marveled at this city so "full of life, bustle, activity" and its spectacular role as "commercial outlet for . . . Texas." Every decade marked a 25 to 50 percent rise in population. By the time Kempner settled there, Galveston, recovering from its wartime constraints, was becoming the terminus of scheduled shipping companies, including the Morgan Star Line, the Galveston-Bremen Line, and the Texas and New York Line. Now commerce, whether coastal or foreign, no longer depended on itinerant waterborne "tramps." Cargoes could be anticipated on the Island and scheduled dependably for reshipment inland or outward. By 1870 a canal linked Sabine Pass and the mouth of the Brazos River. Ferries and stagecoach lines plus a new railroad bridge connected Galveston itself to the mainland. To be sure, Houston, fifty miles inland, though still smaller and less affluent than Galveston, appeared destined to be the regional hub of the growing network of transcontinental railroad lines. But in the 1870s that network was still

17. Hayes, *History*, 1:975.

18. E. R. Thompson, Jr., "History of H. Kempner" (manuscript), Kempner Papers, p. 5; "Advertisers 50 Years Ago" columns, undated, unidentified clippings in DWK Scrapbook, 1929–1935, Kempner Papers.

incomplete and Galveston, as Houston's port, continued to profit from its dominance of waterborne trade.[19]

As a former inland retailer, Kempner had already endured an intensive on-job education about Galveston wholesaling. Virtually all retailers across vast Texas, including petty merchants of the sort Kempner had been in Cold Springs, received their goods from Galveston wholesalers like Marx and Kempner, who in turn acquired their boatloads from the East Coast, England, and Europe. But depite improved water transportation facilities and the railroad bridge, communications and other transportation facilities were not keeping pace with the vigorously improving Galveston commercial scene. Rail links to trunk lines and navigable inland waterways remained few. In many ways all Texas was in a colonial relationship to the nation's centers of capital, industry, culture, and education, in part because it chose to be.[20] Republican-dominated national administrations gave only grudging appropriations for internal improvements to southern states, and the latter, dominated by rural lawmakers, were usually ill-disposed to cities and to marketplace interventions by government for nonfarmers. Both before and after the Civil War, Galveston merchants, especially those dealing in bulk commodities, as we shall see, felt impelled themselves to develop and improve navigation, wharfing, and warehousing facilities on the Island.

In October, 1871, Marx and Kempner, after only two months of wholesale grocering, were so encouraged that they had a "mercantile store" built for their "large stock of goods," noted a Dun reporter, adding that the mortgage was unusually light and decreasing quickly as the partners repaid the debt. Both men were already also homeowners, and Kempner was investing in rural real estate across Texas. The partners could call up $100,000 worth of credit at almost any time because they "are regarded as good business men." Six months later the praise was even higher: "They are both splendid businessmen, careful & . . . provident . . . and we regard them [to be] safe for their contracts." The partnership's books showed a six months' profit of $34,000. Even divided, this was an impressive capital gain. By June,

19. Tinsley, ed., "Select Letters of Harris Kempner," *Gulf Coast Historical Association Publications*, p. 38; Schmeier, *Reflections of Southern Jewry*, p. 80; Kelly, " 'Twixt Failure and Success," pp. 14–19; McComb, *Galveston*, p. 47.

20. Fehrenbach, *Lone Star*, p. 675.

1872, the Dun reporter reaffirmed the achievements of these "energetic businessmen." They had "many warm friends, are cautious and regarded [as] good [risks?]. They are well spoken of by their Banker & in high credit."[21]

By late 1872 a worsening regional credit picture was constraining most Galveston merchants. But Marx and Kempner were "all right . . . [and] doing a large business," according to the Dun writer. Even the early tremors of what in 1873 became a nationwide economic depression did not inhibit them. "They lately lifted a mortgage on their store. . . . Are reliable, honest men," and though the panic deepened, "So far through this crisis they have met everything promptly and have got two men out collecting & claim they will be able to [with]stand the pressure unless it lasts longer than is generally thought it will. . . . Kempner is a close shrewd man & considered to be one of our best business men. They have done a good business & made money," stated Dun's correspondent in July and October, 1873.[22]

The Dun agent was impressed also by the fact that unlike some merchants and professionals, Marx and Kempner unhesitatingly opened their books to him. In late 1873 the firm showed stock on hand worth "fully" $120,000. It owned its own storehouse and store worth $40,000, and each of the partners' homes was valued at $20,000, "all unencumbered, besides which they own some stocks & personal property. Their Bank speaks well of them & says they carry an average balance of about $6,000 to their credit, & that they have not been known to owe any bank for a long time." The first entry for 1874 repeated this happy theme of exceptional prosperity despite depressed trade: "Do a large & prosperous business and making money. Capital of $60–70,000 & very good credit." A year later (January, 1875): "Ditto. . . . Are very hard workers & good businessmen." Guessing now that the partners had increased their total worth to $125,000, the Dun reporter noted that the baled cotton Marx and Kempner had

21. Dun Reports, Oct. 23, Dec. [?], 1871; Apr. [?], June [?], 1872, Texas vol. 13, pp. 215, 229. Sometime in 1872, Morris Lasker joined the firm to take over collections and sales, in return for a one-fifth partnership. But the Dun agent concluded that Lasker added no strength. It appears that Marx recruited the young Texan because of Lasker's "extensive acquaintanceship," perhaps reflecting obstacles in the way of the two immigrant senior partners (ibid., p. 215).

22. Ibid., pp. 215, 261.

contracted for that year as sales agents for mainland growners had suffered unusually severe physical shrinkage. Therefore the partners "will not make much money this year." But by May, 1875, the partnership's achievements and prospects had improved: "[Marx and Kempner] Is one of our heaviest dealers in their line and carry a very large stock. . . . Have capital in business of $250,000 and own real estate . . . besides insurance & other stocks. Are regarded very safe & conservative & good businessmen, & worth $200,000 or more."[23]

At least partly, Marx and Kempner's quick and enduring prosperity resulted from the fact that the partners had both paid their dues as rural retailers. They understood the needs of both country merchants and cotton growers better than their competitors did. The quick prosperity reflected also the fact that a very large number of cotton farmers were cash poor, particularly at planting and harvesting seasons. Quickly minimizing their retail operations, Marx and Kempner adapted their business practices to the fact that their inland customers could pay bills only seasonally, after selling harvests, and then often in kind. Crop-sharing and crop liens were becoming increasingly common adaptations to these situations, but Marx and Kempner did not find these devices attractive. Instead, digging deeply into their own capital resources and exploiting willing third parties, the partners involved themselves increasingly with cotton (and to a lesser extent with sugar) exports as well as with importing wholesale tobacco, groceries, coffee, and liquor.

Cotton set the rhythm of all businesses. As a Kempner descendant recalled, "Marx and Kempner sold goods on credit to the wholesalers and big retailers throughout Texas . . . and ultimately the farmers and they [inland wholesalers and retailers] paid when the [cotton] crops came in. . . . [T]hey made substantial profits because it was a very risky business."[24] Losses resulted when the promised crops did not come in. Aware of the risks, Marx and Kempner extended credit to retail merchants inland and to farmers, their security being their interest as agents in the sale of future crops. The partners had to find purchasers for the commodities pledged to them as payments for debts and, if cotton was the security, also to adjust selling prices to cover

23. Ibid., p. 261.
24. H. L. Kempner interview with Golden, Sept. 1, 1987.

the costs of grading, compressing, bagging, and warehousing the commodities.

Galveston's already-extensive port facilities existed to move commodities, chiefly cotton, sugar, and rice, from the interior onto outbound ships and to shift to the mainland the imports that ships brought in. Wholesale grocering naturally involved the entire chain of commerce and finance. Inland, Marx and Kempner traveling agents called on retail grocers in established towns and on "railhead merchants," who operated in the instant communities that developed at the ends of railroad lines. In the 1870s and 1880s these new rail lines were taking commercial travelers where slow oxcarts and shallow-draft barges had never penetrated and were making the export of cotton and grains more certain and inexpensive than before.

Marx and Kempner agents quickly established reputations for unusual aggressiveness and inventiveness. Especially at railheads that promised to become permanent communities, the wholesale grocery "drummers" (salesmen) competed with those of other firms to tie retailers to their employers, commonly by extending credit to them. Some of the more adventurous grocers and a few favored cotton farmers became local bankers by re-extending to growers in need of foodstuffs, seed, labor, and tools, the credit granted to them by Marx and Kempner, and, later, by Kempner alone. Growers consigned future crops to the local lenders, who would sell them for a fee or percentage to apply against loans. Some number of these inland banker-cotton agents then committed these assets to Marx and Kempner as agents for either the grower or businessman, or both.

Almost inevitably the partners' interest in wholesale comestibles became mixed with excitement about commodities, an excitement justified by the firm's ledgers. But profits did not come easily and were never free of risks.

In order to reach the communities that sprouted at successive rail extremities and that survived as agricultural centers when construction crews moved on, Marx and Kempner's sales agents came quickly to be served by a chain of wagon drivers, stablemen, blacksmiths, and feedlot operators that stretched across much of Texas. The partners reserved storerooms for their merchandise in transit and stables for livestock, while haggling spiritedly with railroad and stagecoach officials on rates, rebates, and standards. This increasingly complex organization kept groceries moving to distant retailers and their farmer-customers, and cotton and other commodities moving to Marx and Kempner.[25]

Ambitious Galveston wholesalers like Marx and Kempner had to devote time, thought, and energy to the shifting winds of commerce. Junior partner Kempner was the more devoted. He observed major shifts in sugar and cattle exports through Galveston as the amount of outgoing cotton increased, a change caused both by the Civil War and by the opening of vast new competing areas for the other commodities. Southeast Texas' economy was becoming ever more dominated by cotton and, to a smaller degree, by sugar and grains. As a result of this observation and because rural consumers of Marx and Kempner's grocery stock ultimately had to pay inland retail merchants with proceeds from the sales of their cotton and rice crops, Marx and Kempner entered into the cotton trade as middlemen. Further impelling the firm toward involvement in cotton was Galveston's vigor as a city and port. From the 1870s to 1900 Galveston enjoyed a happy, seemingly endless cotton export boom. The city came to depend on the export of cotton and its by-products, chiefly cottonseed oil and cake, for economic health, a formula that to contemporaries seemed to be all but perfect but that contained elements of economic frustration.[26]

Unforeseeably, frustration developed because Galveston's growing dependence on exporting cotton, which Kempner and many others encouraged, in effect cast the city in a colonial role from which it was unable to emerge. Galveston shipped goods in and out, increasingly out. It developed splendid port and associated service facilities for banking, warehousing, and insurance. But it never developed enough mass-employing, capital-creating smokestack industries to maintain citywide prosperity should the cotton trade wither, although, to their credit, successive generations of Kempners perceived the problem and tried to remedy it. What did develop were profitable light-service industries, especially those associated with the cotton traffic, such as cotton compressing, baling, and grading facilities, and broker-

25. Details on Marx-Kempner operations in DWK Scrapbook, 1894–1915, passim; see also Max London letters from the field, 1873–1880, Sampson Heidenheimer Collection, Eugene C. Barker Texas History Center, University of Texas at Austin.

26. McComb, *Galveston*, chaps. 1–2, passim.

ages. The chief servitors of cotton such as the Kempners became wealthy, but they were able to extend prosperity over generations by diversifying their interests, though retaining a large commitment to cotton.

As a community, Galveston did not—perhaps could not—protect itself as well. "To a large degree . . . the port of Galveston developed as a conduit whereby much more went out, in terms of value, than came in," wrote a noted Galveston historian. "Galveston was able to remain one of the important cotton ports [of the United States]," he concluded, "but it lost everything else."[27] Facts visible in the decades from 1870 through the 1890s, however, justified increasing concentration on the cotton and grains trade, at least in the opinions of perceptive middlemen like Kempner.[28]

Substantial credit resources were essential for a middleman in the growing cotton trade. New York merchant bankers extended short-term loans and longer credit lines only to some Galvestonians. Kempner's good standing with fellow Confederate army veteran Charles Fry, soon to be president of the Bank of New York, gave him and Marx substantial and enduring advantages. Soon after arriving in Galveston, Kempner had opened an account with that bank. It was to remain active through three generations of his family.[29] But more than credit was needed. Wholesalers like Kempner also had to master local small-loan and international financial operations, especially as the region's major commodity became cotton.[30]

Probably because of competition from other food wholesalers who were serving farmer-customers as small loan bankers, Marx and Kempner entered that risky arena as a sideline. Unlike state or federally chartered private banks, they issued no paper notes. Like chartered banks, however, general purpose merchants with banking sidelines

27. Ibid., p. 47 and chaps. 1–2, passim.

28. Sitterson, *Sugar Country*, pp. 41–43, 49–50; Kelly, " 'Twixt Failure and Success," p. 24 and n.

29. Tinsley, ed., "Select Letters," p. 38; IHK, *Recalled Recollections*, p. 17. Bank president J. C. Traphagen, letter to IHK, Apr. 21, 1944, DWK Scrapbook, vol. 3, bk. 1, sketched the antiquity of the Kempner account, but misdates its initiation as 1868 or 1869 and erroneously indicates that the account was established by Harris's wife.

30. DWK, "Historical Record" (manuscript), Kempner Papers, p. 2; Tinsley, ed., "Select Letters," pp. 3–4; Thompson, "History," p. 5; Clark, "Taking Stock of the Nineteenth Century Store," pp. 22–25.

accepted deposits, lent money, traded in foreign currencies, and discounted letters of credit and other commercial paper. The unincorporated status of such private banks shielded owners from a duty to report on profits, losses, or operating procedures or to submit to state or federal inspections. Typically, unincorporated private banks were back-room operations of middlemen in commodities like cotton, and the Marx-Kempner duo fit the pattern.

The most successful among them might associate as borrower with one of the now well-established large banking houses that since 1800 had come into being on both sides of the Atlantic.[31] By the early 1870s, several of these dominant firms were already being run by sons of founders. They advanced money to cotton middlemen (factors and merchants) in the South in return for promises to consign shipments to the lender, issued letters of credit to importers of British industrial products, and served as a market for foreign bills of exchange. Long before the Civil War, private merchant-bankers in the South had found association with a northeastern bank to be essential to the success of their own operations.[32]

Association incurred hazards, however, especially for neophytes like Marx and Kempner. Competition was fierce not only between the giant banking houses but at every level from farm to mill. If grocery wholesaling competitors were aggressive, cotton adversaries were predatory. Marx feared the greater risks in cotton. His partner Kempner welcomed and enjoyed them and tried to aim the partnership toward the alluringly greater profits and stimulations of the cotton trade.

Among these risks was the fact that agents of foreign and domestic textile spinning mills and other commodity buyers, unlike Marx and Kempner, could shop among worldwide producing regions for favorable prices. Profits and losses in Galveston depended on the wisdom, good fortune, and hard bargaining of Marx and Kempner and their agents in Texas' interior in contracts with farmers. Both partners were intelligent and tough-minded men who were generally lucky in their

31. Carosso, "American Private Banks in International Finance, 1870–1914," *Business and Economic History*, p. 1926.

32. Pusateri, *A History of American Business*, pp. 100–101; Carosso, *Investment Banking in America*, chap. 1; Schweikart, "Antebellum Southern Bankers," *Business and Economic History*, pp. 79–103; Jones, *International Business in the 19th Century*, chaps. 1–5.

estimates and fortunate as well in their possession of on-hand capital plus unusually adequate credit sources in Kempner's connection to New York banker Fry. They also had a solid and rising base of profits from their grocery wholesaling business. Such advantages enabled Marx and Kempner to undercut many competitors in both grocery and cotton operations. A traveling salesman for a competing wholesaler, the prominent and long-established Heidenheimer firm of Galveston, complained in 1880 that "Marx and Kempner offer . . . salt at 90" as against Heidenheimer's 92½ rate, a differential that required him to seek preferential rebates from freighting companies, "thinking the rebate may help us out."[33]

As a result of such advantages Marx and Kempner had enough liquid assets, even in the conditions attending the panic of 1873, to mesh their growing trade with national and international commodity and capital networks. They lent inland retailers money to carry farmer-customers at rates lower than Texas banks demanded. An approximately 2 percent differential adhered to the Galveston partners, allowing repayment of the New York bank's loan and attesting to the Texans' creditworthiness there and abroad. Keeping aside enough to repeat the process in the next growing season, Marx and Kempner invested a portion of the surplus in other commodities and enterprises that were bubbling around them, including sugar, wharves, railroads, and banks. Thereby they increased their capital assets, which served in turn as additional collateral for larger loans from New York, still at favorable rates. And the more borrowed, the more that was lendable at attractive rates. Alternatively, Marx and Kempner lent directly to farmers who pledged them the handling of their crops at agreed-upon prices.[34] Meanwhile, the partners continued their general merchandising operations.

In 1877 a fire burned through Galveston's compact business district, consuming the Marx and Kempner buildings on the south side of the Strand—Galveston's "Wall Street of the South." They at once rented two large rooms in a building across the street from their destroyed quarters, and testing now all their connections, telegraphed

33. Max London, letter to Heidenheimer Co., Nov. 24, 1880, 3P57, AR 81–155, Heidenheimer Collection.

34. Thompson, "History," pp. 5–6; Johnson, "A Short History of the Sugar Industry in Texas," *Texas Gulf Historical Association Publications*, esp. chap. 3; IHK, *Recalled Recollections*, p. 17; Tinsley, ed., "Select Letters," p. 38.

suppliers and bankers in New York, Cincinnati, Chicago, and New Orleans with requests for more credit and entire new stocks. Goods poured in. Before the ruins had cooled, Marx and Kempner were selling and buying again. They decided to move to better quarters, first on the corner of the Strand and Twenty-fifth Street, then back to the Twenty-first Street location which they bought and on which they erected a handsome three-story building, a journalist noting that "the casting for the rebuilding will be made in this city."[35]

But the very foundry that cast the structural members of the new Marx and Kempner building, probably the Vulcan works, was to be the source of another, greater conflagration. On a cold, windy predawn in November of 1885, a fire started in the Vulcan property perilously near the Marx and Kempner shops. The blaze swept Galveston from the bay to the Gulf. Uncheckable because of a scandal-producing failure in the city's water supply, the blaze consumed all buildings, plus furnishings and stocks, on more than forty square blocks. At least twenty-five hundred Islanders were suddenly homeless. Hotels, including one then owned by Marx and Kempner, sheltered many of them. Prominent citizens, the Kempners undoubtedly among them, donated funds to tide over some of the victims. Concerning such attention to civic responsibility, a contemporary chronicler noted of Marx and Kempner: "This house has shown by its actions and the large outlay they have made in public improvements and costly buildings their abiding faith in the future greatness of Galveston. Few firms have done as much, none have done more, to advance the city by the erection of buildings and aiding public enterprises, of practical utility, than Marx & Kempner."[36]

Kempner's home was among those destroyed. He rented a temporary residence, contracting to extend a private sewer line and then electric lights to the house.[37] Meanwhile, he labored to repair the damage to Marx and Kempner from the fire and to improve further his own wealth through unremitting attention to the partnership.

Such diligence paid off. Along with other vigorous mercantile houses, Marx and Kempner ordered consumer goods, including co-

35. "50 Years Ago" column, *Galveston Daily News*, Dec. 19, 1928; IHK, *Recalled Recollections*, p. 5.

36. Hayes, *History*, 1:975. On the 1885 fire, *Galveston Daily News*, Nov. 17, 1935. IHK, *Recalled Recollections*, pp. 7–8, misdates the fire as 1886.

37. IHK, *Recalled Recollections*, p. 8.

mestibles and potables, in such quantities "when trade is lively" as to exceed the capacities of warehouses and freight yards and to necessitate storing the imports on flat rooftops, more or less protected under tarpaulins. Downstairs the aisles and sheds burst with saleables as the business sections of the growing city rocked with the noises and smells of trade. It was only marginally an exaggeration for a visitor in the 1870s to suggest that at the height of the cotton exporting season "the town is so crowded with eager purchasers that some of them have to roost on poles stuck out of second story windows" and that Galveston's streets were made wide in order "to accommodate the vast crowds of buyers."[38]

Despite the partners' profits, Kempner was restless. He was originally attracted to Marx, and Marx to him, by their complementary personalities. Marx's effervescence drew business to the firm. When in the late 1870s he and Kempner bought the Tremont Hotel, Texas' largest and grandest, it was Marx who was "mine host" and who, Kempner wrote, toured East and West Coast states for "pleasure and observations of major hostelries there."[39]

Marx's frequent absences from Galveston, even in the firm's interest, sometimes irritated Kempner. During one particularly hot July when Marx was away, Kempner complained that he had hoped to visit Cincinnati relatives, "but my partner Mr. Marx left here about a month ago for Va. and N.Y., and has not yet returned." Such peevishness was rare. Kempner and Marx usually got on well, with Kempner addressing him formally in correspondence and to third parties as "Mr. Marx." Indeed, Kempner came to encourage Marx's traveling, as in 1884–85, to France and other European textile centers where customers for Texas cotton were located. Writing to Marx in Paris in late August, 1884, Kempner advised him that the cotton crop would be short because of drought and credit that was tighter than ever in memory. But, perhaps adverting to earlier indiscretions by his loquacious partner, he also pleaded with Marx to say nothing about the firm's financial situation to bankers there or in New York when returning. Kempner and the bankers, after "much correspondence," now "fully understood each other . . . and you not being acquainted with

38. Eisenhower, ed., *Alexander Sweet's Texas*, p. 64.

39. Kempner, letter to Abe Seinsheimer, July 6, 1883, no. 4, Kempner Letterpress Book, AJA/HUC (hereafter, Kempner Letterpress Book).

it [credit commitments?] you must necessarily do us harm . . . if you now undertake to make any arrangements at all."[40]

Although less the "front man" than his ebullient partner, Kempner did his share of promoting Marx and Kempner. Accepting a partial crop from a grower, Kempner asked him thereafter to "ship all your crop to us. We are willing and ready to do all we can and all you ask us in reason." Exploiting his special sources on the partnership's behalf, by the 1880s Kempner was accustomed to dealing in large lines of credit. "Would you lend me $10,000 to be secured by Marx & Kempner?" he asked banker Fry in December, 1883, in one of many such inquiries. No refusals by Fry are in the records.[41]

Together, Marx and Kempner "were two yokes . . . who were men indeed—big brained, broad-gauged, [and] farseeing," estimated a contemporary. But by the early 1880s Marx's very virtues had bred business problems. Seemingly the perfect outside man, Marx, according to an 1879 description, "whether 'neath fortune's favor or her frown, remained always the same . . . hopeful optimist."[42]

These "virtues" had become faults in Kempner's eyes. In one instance, Marx's uncriticality about third parties entangled Marx and Kempner in a contract dispute that threatened to generate a lawsuit against the partnership. Through an agent resident in Galveston, an out-of-state food-packing house persuaded Marx to buy its product. Marx failed to notify Kempner. Billed, Kempner refused to pay. Threatened with a lawsuit, the partners learned that the complainant's agent, lacking his principal's authority to contract, had "overreached." Marx and Kempner took the position that they "were no partners to it [the contract] and can not be held liable." But though this tremor passed, it helped to build in Kempner an edginess about his sometimes careless partner and a lifelong distaste for lawsuits.

Although Kempner remained fond of Marx, he grew impatient with the man. More than personality differences were involved. Kempner's ambitions were outstripping those of Marx. Kempner wanted to concentrate all but exclusively on cotton factoring. Marx was reluctant.

40. Aug. 26, 1884, no. 197, Kempner Letterpress Book.

41. On the grower, Kempner, letter to Capt. Norsworth, Apr. 11, 1883; letter to Fry, Dec. 30, 1883, nos. 25, 69, and 71, respectively, all in Kempner Letterpress Book.

42. *Houston Chronicle*, June 25, 1909; see also Marx obituary, *Galveston Daily News*, June 26, 1909.

Back in 1833 Kempner had persuaded him to sell off a portion of their wholesale liquor and grocery operations, thereby titillating regional commercial circles. Henceforward, Marx and Kempner concentrated more on cotton factoring but maintained grocery wholesaling. Kempner continued to carry on numerous side investments. At the same time, however, he enlarged his credit lines with Fry and other bankers, securing their risk with his bonds, stocks, real estate, and commercial paper. "I have plenty of good bills of credit and stocks," he advised Fry in March, 1886, adding: "You doubtless know what I want it [more credit] for."[43]

Fry did know. The shared confidence was that Kempner was determined to buy Marx out. Kempner not only wanted to concentrate on cotton factoring more than did Marx, he wanted to do it solo. Whatever Marx's virtues, he lacked a capacity to say no to his greedy relatives, some of whom maintained extravagant residences in Paris and New York as well as in Texas. Marx paid many of their bills. Perhaps his softness in this matter plus Kempner's own developing ambitions persuaded the latter that the association should end and that Kempner relatives should not play similar roles.

Kempner's wisdom in severing the partnership became manifest as Marx, who joined Aaron Blum (whose daughter would marry Kempner's oldest son) as partner in a large Galveston wholesale shoe firm, failed to stem the drain of capital to spendthrift relatives, some of whom Marx and Blum employed and others who were virtual remittance men. Bankrupted in the 1907 panic, Marx and Blum, now "blind poor, went bust" and sold out.[44]

Still retaining his good personal reputation, Marx died in 1909. Kempners were prominent among the funeral mourners. Harris Kempner's oldest son was pallbearer for Marx's interment in the Hebrew cemetery. But drenching seasonal rains prevented burial, and Marx's body was stored temporarily in an aboveground vault. Still exhibiting the deepest trust in the Kempners (Harris had died in 1894), Marx had named Isaac Kempner, the oldest son, an executor of his estate, perhaps to guard his widow against further depredations by spend-

43. Kempner, letter to Fry, Mar. 31, 1886, no. 389, Kempner Letterpress Book; and see IHK, *Recalled Recollections*, pp. 4–5.

44. Henrietta Blum Kempner, "The Blum Saga" (manuscript), Kempner Papers; H. L. Kempner interview with Golden, Sept. 1, 1987, in her possession, quoted with permission.

thrift relatives. Ike Kempner bore the burden responsibly and without complaint from impatient Marx heirs. Marx's widow died in 1913. She too had named Ike an executor of her estate. He saw to the division of the Marx wealth among the heirs, again without recorded acrimony.[45]

This amiability in part reflected the fact that in 1887 Marx and Kempner had dissolved their sixteen-year-old partnership with none of the vicious squabbling or costly litigation that often attended such divisions. Harris Kempner emerged with what he wanted: a solo cotton factoring and private banking business that he named simply "H. Kempner."

But if the dissolution was amiable, Kempner had soon discovered that the unsystematic ways of his former partner had left enduring traces on his solo venture. Marx's recordkeeping had been occasionally defective, and apparently the meticulous Kempner accepted the blame and consequences for substandard files. Soon after taking wing the fledgling sole proprietor requested a cotton merchant to "send me a list of all [Marx and Kempner] contracts which you have for my account. . . . I have mislaid my book in which these contracts were registered." And Kempner assured his trusting correspondent that his own financial resources were wholly "adequate for your protection."[46]

Indeed they were. H. Kempner's success as solo factor was immediate and large, he confided proudly to banker Fry in 1888. Since his decision to go solo he had "made clear of office and private expenses $160,000. . . ."[47] Clearly, Harris Kempner was able to go it alone.

H. Kempner: Solo Cotton Factor and Married Man

Alone only in business, however. The 1879 chronicler who described Kempner as a man without time for life's amenities or frivolities was wrong. As noted earlier, Kempner was arrested and fined for racing

45. On the estate, Folder 54, Box 14, #80-002, Kempner Papers. Marx's obituary, *Galveston Daily News*, June 26, 1909, offers other details.

46. Kempner, letter to Lehman and Goodrich, Mar. 11, 1887, no. 411, Kempner Letterpress Book.

47. Tinsley, ed., "Select Letters," p. 38. See also Thompson, "History," p. 7; IHK, *Recalled Recollections*, p. 5; "50 Years Ago" column, *Galveston News*, Feb. 27, 1933.

on horseback in Houston, and he later risked $3.50 on a lottery ticket, without success, it appears.[48] But by 1871 he had weightier purposes in mind. Marriage was now his highest priority, and he took time for life's premier amenity. He courted and wed, with, to be sure, his customary decisiveness.

Family tradition has it that Kempner went to New York City to buy groceries and tobacco for the then-new partnership with Marx. He took rooms in a Jewish-run hotel noted for its generous meals and modest rates. Seated across from him at the dining table was vivacious, handsome young Eliza Seinsheimer, "Lyde" to her family and friends, not yet twenty years old, from a well-to-do German-Jewish Cincinnati family. She was in New York to visit relatives. Her appetite for food matched his own, and this meant, Kempner always insisted, "that such a girl must be vigorous and healthy." He arranged to meet her. On his next buying trip from Texas, Kempner found reason to shift Marx and Kempner wholesale liquor purchases from New York to Cincinnati, to which Eliza had returned. There, Kempner, "without calling on any stimulation from his whiskey purchase, proposed, was accepted, the wedding date fixed and [on March 6, 1872] marriage followed."[49]

The birth of their first baby neared a year later. Eliza, like Harris, still new in Galveston, and herself only twenty-one years old, wanted it to occur in familiar Cincinnati with her parents around her. The whole of Texas could not claim one trained obstetrician or specialist obstetrical nurse. Now far advanced from his immigrant near-pauper past, his backpack peddling, and "little rich" Galveston merchant status,[50] quiet, grave, studious Harris Kempner, secure in the new dignity of his thirty-five years and of his ascending wealth and prospects, indulged his lovely young bride.

They traveled the "great distance" from Galveston to the Ohio city "in the best accommodations," and their son was born there on January 14, 1873. Named Isaac Herbert (later called Isaac by his fond father only when the parent was angry, Ikey when he was pleased, and Ike by his contemporaries), Ike was to be the first of eleven children. All following him were "born on the island" (BOI, in local shorthand),

48. IHK, *Recalled Recollections*, p. 14; Harris Kempner, letter to A. Pellers, June 27, 1883, no. 1, Kempner Letterpress Book.

49. IHK, *Recalled Recollections*, pp. 3–4.

50. Fehrenbach, *Lone Star*, p. 646.

even Ike becoming credited with enough good taste to arrange his return there within weeks after his birth.

In local slang Ike, though not a BOI, had "sand between his toes," a lesser, provisional status requiring such a person to prove worthy of a BOI's respect. Sojourners found Galveston to be almost a "closed, all-business" society. A journalist complained of the "Standard of Respectability" there in 1881:

> In Galveston the man who sighs to be looked up to with awe and reverence has to be an old inhabitant. The longer he has been on the Island the more he is regarded as a saint, although he may otherwise not be a fit person to associate with the inmates of the penitentiary. If a man has lived on the Island five years, they say: "We can't tell anything about him until he gets here." If he has lived on the Island ten years they say: "He only got off the cars yesterday. Give him a chance to vindicate himself." After a man has lived in Galveston fifteen years the boys quit throwing brickbats at him and tying dead cats to his gate, but he is not yet looked upon as anything better than a Houston emissary. . . . The man who does not go to Galveston before he is born might as well stay away afterwards.[51]

Joining Ike but with BOI status, with their mother attended by local general practitioners and black midwives, were Abraham, who arrived on December 6, 1874; Daniel Webster, on March 28, 1877; Sidney, on January 2, 1879; Hattie, October 10, 1880; Robert Lee, January 21, 1883; Stanley Eugene, April 7, 1885; Joe Clarence, December 25, 1886; Fannie, March 18, 1888; Sara, July 7, 1890; and Gladys, March 18, 1893. In the sad pattern of the times, Abe, Sidney, and Joe Clarence died in infancy or early childhood from then-deadly diseases such as diphtheria, the first two succumbing only two weeks apart, in 1879.[52]

Kempner advanced his business interests while retaining closeness with his growing family. Because of the naturally compact character of Island life, Galveston then had no "streetcar suburbs." In the 1870s and early 1880s, before electrification, mules pulled twenty-passenger streetcars through the major downtown thoroughfares. Galveston's

51. Eisenhower, ed., *Alexander Sweet's Texas*, pp. 68–69.
52. "I. H. Kempner Testimonial Dinner" (transcript), RLA; IHK, *Recalled Recollections*, p. 6.

commercial life, centering on the Strand and on the wharves facing the bay, was well within walking distance of most merchants' homes.

The first Kempner post-marriage residence sprawled across seven city lots, an impressive spread in light of the relatively high cost of the developed urban real estate, but one necessitated by the mixed family and commercial uses to which Harris put the property. The main house was a spacious frame structure on the corner of Twentieth and M streets. It featured all regionally evolved attempts to cope with the summer heat and humidity. The house faced northward. It rested on brick piers, and both its floors were shaded by wide porches leading to broad hallways from which main rooms branched. Rooms were large—perhaps eighteen by twenty feet, Harris Kempner's oldest son remembered across three-quarters of a century—with high ceilings and many windows to catch the Gulf breezes and to dissipate heat and humidity. Laundry, cooking (on wood stoves; gas was used only for illumination), and the storage of bulk foodstuffs and wine were attended to by servants in an "annex" connected to the main house by a latticed walkway covered with flowering vines. The domestics came to include maids, cooks, and a coachman-butler. Their rooms were on the other side of the annex, except for the children's black governess, who shared a room with the youngest Kempners. This governess, "Aunt" Eveline, remained with the Kempners for decades. Her presence attested to Harris's visibly growing prosperity, as did Eliza's growing participation in community and congregation affairs. A white tutor took over from the governess as each child reached grade-school age.

Even in this "Redemptionist" phase of southern history, race relations seemed to be neither a topic nor a problem to the Kempner children. Ike never abandoned the conviction that "many of those who had been slaves found sudden freedom a great disappointment," a judgment that is susceptible to considerable disproof. But it is undoubtable that in the 1870s and 1880s "a plethora of servants sought positions, but above all maintenance of themselves and their children." Black women servants earned ten dollars a month, and men, fifteen dollars. All servants were "bountifully fed," Ike recalled, and "their numerous children, whether legitimate or 'source unknown,' crowded into the quarters assigned their mothers and were fed by our household without question." The resident black men not employed as house servants or on outside maintenance worked for Marx and Kempner before the dissolution of the partnership and for H. Kempner after, principally as wagoneers (called "hostlers").

The mules and horses in backyard stables and sheds perfumed the household. Every morning, long before sunrise in winters, drivers and handlers crowded the rear yard to prepare draft animals and to check orders assembled the night before. The Kempner children played among the three-hundred-pound sacks of fragrant mocha and java coffee, barrels of wine from France, mounds of rice from South Carolina, and mountains of mainland cotton waiting for export to New England and European textile mills. Handlers' shouts and animals' sounds and smells were the youngsters' common memories. So were games played with wagon wheel hoops, dusty adventures in haylofts, footraces down streets paved with ground oyster shells, ritual twilight convoys for the lighter of the gas streetlamps, awed applause for the novel electric streetlights that replaced gas in 1883, excited observations of ships flying flags from exotic lands, "rusticating" family vacations on a ranch near Mexia, Texas, rides on placid horses, daredeviltry for the boys on piers, jetties, and bridges, and beachfront picnics for all.[53]

Especially during the long hot summers the endless beaches were natural centers of fun for adults and children. Residents and visitors enjoyed daily drives on the miles of firm sands washed by the Gulf of Mexico. Sun worshipers rented little changing houses that lined the beaches, structures "so lightly built that they could not stand much of a mortgage," quipped a humorist. Emerging from these "perpendicular coffins," young men dressed in short, striped bathing suits reminded an onlooker of escaped felons. Proletarians of both races employed the Gulf for racially separated family cleansings, although black maidservants accompanied white charges into the water, where riptides, stinging jellyfish, and barbed ray fish had to be avoided. Everywhere on the beaches and in the Island City, black peddlers shouted and sang their wares in ritualized shorthand chants that strangers found incomprehensible but yet were clear to disdainful locals: "Afreshigess" (fresh eggs) or, without spacings, "Here'syourpotatusses . . . green corn O!" In 1866 Gen. Phillip Sheridan said that if

53. IHK, *Recalled Recollections*, pp. 2, 3, 6, 9; DWK, "Historical Record," p. 2; H. Kempner obituary in *Galveston Daily News*, Apr. 14, 1894; "I. H. Kempner Testimonial Dinner," p. 42; Tinsley, ed., "Select Letters," p. 3; Schmeier, ed., *Reflections of Southern Jewry*, p. 80.

he owned Texas and hell, he would rent out the former and live in the latter; in 1880, revisiting Galveston, he apologized.[54]

Deep Water and Wharves

Kempner needed no other imperatives to maintain his extraordinary pace of business than his growing family and his memories of poverty. He devoted more time than ever to mixed civic-business projects. If done well they might add to his prosperity. But if left undone or done poorly, they would diminish Galveston's overall economy. As his capital increased and his reputation grew, Kempner joined the inner circle of Galveston entrepreneurs who were trying to improve the Island's port facilities and rail links to major national trunk lines and to isolated Texas and regional areas.

Galveston had to fulfill many needs if it was to preserve its commercial leadership over upstart Houston and other Gulf competitors. Though Houston still lacked a commercially usable waterway to the Gulf, it did not suffer Galveston's vulnerability to storms, naturally limited land area and resultant high land costs, total lack of on-site drinking water, or uncertain water supply for industrial purposes. By the 1870s Houston merchants had encouraged Charles Morgan's Direct Navigation Company, a private firm, to construct a narrow, shallow, but relatively dependable sheltered barge canal from near Galveston on the Gulf to within six land miles of Houston. Offloading and lightering still had to occur at Galveston's terminals for all but the smallest, shallow-draft ships. Nevertheless, Morgan had made Houston's practicality as an inland port at least arguable. In the 1870s and 1880s Galveston retaliated by trying to make itself the terminal of a Galveston, Harrisburg, and San Antonio Railway Company, and then of a Gulf, Colorado, and Santa Fe railroad, and Kempner invested substantially in both.[55]

In 1881, Galveston cotton factors and merchants, with allied bankers, land developers, and lawyers, impatient at the failures of jetties to prevent silting of the channel into the bay, formed the Deep Water

54. Eisenhower, ed., *Alexander Sweet's Texas*, pp. 62, 65–67, 76–77, 88–89.

55. Dugas, "A Duel with Railroads," *East Texas Historical Journal*, pp. 118–27; McDonough, comp., "Building the Santa Fe" (unpublished manuscript), RLA; DWK, "Historical Record," pp. 1–2. On the Texas Pacific Railway, see Hearden, *Independence and Empire*, p. 55.

Committee, a parallel to the Houston-based Direct Navigation group. As its name suggests, the committee's purpose was to ensure, through lobbying, the navigability of the bay and access to Galveston's urban and port amenities and inland commerce.

A port was a complex organism. Galveston's precious channel and all its feeders required unremitting dredging, a costly chore that, as noted earlier, the federal government had already begun subsidizing in part. Buoys, a lighthouse, and other markers also required maintenance. The quality of pilots was a recurring concern. And no city was a viable port without a complex infrastructure of financial institutions, wharves, warehouses, and attendant facilities such as steam-powered derricks, hoists, and shovels, plus armies of trained stevedores and draft animals, and relevant urban facilities such as police, fire, information and sanitation services, and by no means least, paved streets.[56] Only when these worked in unison and with reliability could commodities become commerce.

Deep Water Committee members became expert lobbyists in Washington and Austin. Membership in the committee was a sure sign of political influence and high social status in Galveston. Kempner became a member in the early 1880s, remaining one almost until his death in 1894, and his oldest son then took the father's place, entering into close working and social relationships with the Island's commercial elite. Other members included, from time to time, Bertrand Adoue (with whom the Kempners would be related by marriage), enormously wealthy enterpreneurs George Sealy and William L. Moody, influential lawyer William Pitt Ballinger, and prominent congressman Walter Gresham. Later Kempner's son Ike described this "self-constituted, self-perpetuating entity" as one that "had been originated by a group of successful citizens who gave their time and their services without compensation toward capitalizing underlying sentiment in the . . . trans-Mississippi section . . . favorable to the development by the [national] government of a needed port for the southwest."[57]

An ongoing concern of members of the Deep Water Committee was

56. Rosen, "Infrastructural Improvement in 19th Century Cities," *Journal of Urban History*, p. 221, and see p. 250.

57. Quotation in IHK, "The Drama of the Commission Plan in Galveston," *National Municipal Review*, p. 410; *Galveston News*, Oct. 30, 1885, on Kempner's place in the Deep Water Committee; other data in Ellis, "The Revolution-

the private company, the Galveston Wharf Company, or "Wharves" in Island shorthand. Several committee members were also Wharves directors at one time or another, and most had financial interest in Wharves operations.

The Galveston Wharf Company began out of land sales by Texas in 1838 to Galveston's original developers, J. M. O. Menard and Associates, who formed the Galveston City Company and assigned to it all its lands. In 1840 Texas incorporated the City of Galveston and in 1851 authorized it to lay out streets leading to the protected bay side of the island and to build wharves at the bayshore. But meanwhile, in 1845, Menard had organized the Galveston Wharf and Cotton Press Company, and it, not the city, built the large majority of the Island's wharves, dockside railroad, warehouses, and related terminal facilities. Galveston officials later claimed that these important amenities were on municipal land. Menard won the resulting litigation; his company had legitimate title to the waterfront "flats."[58]

The Civil War intervening, in the 1867–69 years Galveston again sued the Galveston Wharf Company, claiming municipal ownership of the street ends that led to the developed waterfront. An out-of-court settlement (the so-called "Brazoria Decrees") merged all the docks, relevant waterfront land, and connecting street ends into the Wharf Company, with the City of Galveston being declared owner of an undivided one-third of all the company's assets and with that number of non-voting seats on its board. In effect the Wharves' directors remained spokesmen more for the private than the public interests. The Wharves, or "Octopus of the Gulf" as Houstonians soon called it, now semipublic in ownership, was usually profitable to both the public and private holders of its securities. Occasionally, however, the Wharves' directors, including the political representatives, were also classic spoilsmen who took advantage of their monopoly of Galveston's docking and carting facilities. Other times the private board members simply overrode the public ones and instead of being partners in progress, set extortionate rates that victimized the ship, lighter, and barge companies that embarked cargoes from offshore merchantmen for reshipment to Houston and made corrupt

izing of the Texas Cotton Trade, 1865–1888," *Southwestern Historical Quarterly*, pp. 478–79; McComb, *Galveston*, pp. 58–60.

58. Galveston *v.* Menard, 23 Texas, 343 (1859).

bargains with mayors, aldermen, and wharf officials, complainants charged.[59]

Price gougings gave Houston's lobbyists in Washington reasons to justify exploratory federal grants for a navigable Houston-Gulf waterway deep enough to float large vessels without the costs and delays of off-loading at Galveston. Island City spokesmen fought against its development until, in 1900, as will be seen, nature itself took sides against Galveston.[60] The price gouging and other exploitative practices, along with exposures of corruption in the city governments of Houston and Galveston, became occasional concerns of the Deep Water Committee, although its members preferred to retain an apolitical posture.

Everywhere, American municipalities were governed by the propertied for the propertied, to exploit Edward Pessen's relevant phrases. Long before the Civil War, the real estate of the wealthy was underassessed. "Water grants" enriched inside-trading real estate speculators, as allegedly occurred with the Wharves. To be sure, the beneficiaries of favoritism and deals saw themselves in different, sometimes idealistic terms. Often their interests did not prevail. Individualists, they were seldom monolithic.[61] But neither the Wharves nor the Deep Water Committee were arenas of stark differences of opinion.

To seemingly unresting, meticulous, expense-paring businessman Kempner, that was the proper mode of public business. He was becoming one of the Island City's commercial elite. Its members exhibited what to Kempner were happy blends of both the "Old" and the "New" South. Like him, they were inventive and aggressive large-scale merchants and professionals. In other southern seaport cities, notably Charleston and Mobile, leaders of commerce maintained a notably relaxed life-style commonly characterized by post-luncheon afternoon-long relaxations in barrooms and gentlemen's clubs. By contrast, inland railway centers including Atlanta, Nashville, and Hous-

59. Details in Galveston Wharf Company *v.* Galveston, 63 Texas, 14 (1877); C. G. Dribbell, "A Short History of the Galveston Wharves" (manuscript), in IHK, letter to J. McCullough, Apr. 24, 1957, Box 146, Kempner Papers; Sibley, *The Port of Houston*, p. 77; McComb, *Galveston*, p. 56.

60. Sibley, *Port of Houston*, pp. 79–120, passim; Kelly, " 'Twixt Failure and Success," p. 102 and passim. In 1881, Kempner tried unsuccessfully to lease the "flats" and to build his own wharf facilities (*Galveston News*, Aug. 16, 1881); Barker, "Partners in Progress" (Ph.D. diss.), pp. 1–4.

61. Pessen, *Riches, Class, and Power before the Civil War*, pp. 292–304.

ton were recruiting into elite ranks numbers of more sober, industrious, ambitious young men of Kempner's sort. As it did in so many matters, Galveston mixed these characteristics and produced its particular pattern. Though a seaport, it followed more the ways of the interior commercial centers in recruiting youthful successes into the arenas of privilege and influence. Yet Galveston's often hectic commercial pace was leavened by some of the softer Deep South ways of South Carolina, Alabama, and Louisiana.[62]

The southern tradition extolled reciprocal loyalty between institutions, employers, and faithful workers. Kempner had learned as Marx's partner the need to find and keep expert, honest, and reliable employees. Some were to remain with Kempner and his sons for more than fifty years. For example, with respect to the Tremont Hotel, neither he nor Marx knew the hotel business or was inclined to learn it. Instead, on Kempner's urging they hired "a thorough hotel man" to run it, one who stayed on for decades. The hotel added to their profits (plus providing an observation post for little Ike and many celebrating Galveston blacks to use in 1880 during Ulysses Grant and General Sheridan's visit to Galveston and festive parade in their honor). But the increased profits could not balance the fact that for Kempner, wholesale grocering, however inclined toward the cotton trade or leavened with other investment opportunities like the hotel, necessarily involved relatively petty dealings. He simply disliked, for example, the occasional need to resort to lawsuits. Apparently this prejudice of Kempner's against litigating was well known by the early 1880s, a defendant in a garnishment action noting that "I don't think that I stand any risk by it." He didn't. Plaintiff Kempner and he settled out of court.[63]

Even in the early 1870s when much of his capital was committed to the partnership with Marx, Kempner remained alert for new opportunities. In addition to the Tremont Hotel, Kempner invested locally in the Galveston Shoe and Hat Company, in the Island City Manufacturing Company (wholesale clothing), in a cotton compress (baling) plant, and, as we shall see (chapter 8), in furniture manu-

62. Doyle, "Urbanization and Southern Culture," in *Toward a New South?*, pp. 11–36.

63. IHK, *Recalled Recollections*, pp. 5–6; DWK, "Historical Record," pp. 2–3, on hotel. On lawsuit, Max London, letter to firm, Jan. 10, 1881, Heidenheimer Collection, 3P7AR155, Barker Texas History Center.

facturing on the mainland using prison labor. A Cold Springs lawyer friend his own age looked Galveston over as a site for a practice and came to Kempner for advice. Kempner encouraged him, agreeing to give the attorney some of Marx and Kempner's legal business. But he also wanted to send the lawyer at once to Mexico on a land deal, and before long the two former Cold Springers, now Galveston neighbors, shared financial interests as charter investors in the Gulf, Colorado, and Santa Fe Railroad. Kempner encouraged its evolution toward the Atchison, Topeka, and Santa Fe combination. As that line extended its track through Lampasas County, railroad and county officials named a town after Kempner and in 1888 Nolan County cotton growers, reached earlier by Marx and Kempner agents, with some ceremony consigned their first bale of cotton that year to H. Kempner by this railroad.[64]

Kempner and Leon Blum were original incorporators of the Galveston Steamship and Lighter Company in 1881. In 1885 he, Blum, and his wife's brother Joseph Seinsheimer (who had moved to Galveston), among other Jewish merchants and prominent Islanders, subscribed to a $100,000 capital stock offering in order to rescue the undercapitalized Island City Savings Bank, which was withering in the face of the bank president's suicide. Though a stranger to banking save as it was incidental to merchandising, Kempner quickly discerned that the bank needed fresh sources of funds to cover immediate withdrawals, else the uninsured savings of hundreds of Island residents would be lost. Kempner recruited Seinsheimer and Blum to join him in lending enough money to the bank to tide it over. Accepting an executive officership in the bank, Kempner reformed its practices. He became its president the following year, his grandson and namesake, Harris L. Kempner, noting that "the stockholders took a beating but the depositors were paid off [in full]. He [the first Harris Kempner] refused to accept any payment. . . . This [incident] started my grandfather's interest in banking."[65]

Kempner's success resulted in part also from his valued connection

64. Trammell, *Seven Pines*, p. 234; DWK, "Historical Record," pp. 2–3.

65. Harris L. Kempner, "The Kempners of Galveston and Sugar Land" (manuscript; Address to Harvard Business School Club of Houston, Sept. 27, 1981), RLA, p. 2. The younger Kempner noted also that his grandmother, who survived his grandfather by fifty years, kept the silver service that grateful depositors gave Harris Kempner, willing it to her great-grandson, Harris L. ("Shrub") Kempner, Jr.

with Charles Fry of the Bank of New York. "The Island City Bank will require some accommodations for the present," he advised Fry in late 1885. "I have instructed . . . the [Galveston Bank's] Cashier to request . . . credit [for] the bank's note and other securities. . . . The bank may need more in the near future but of this I will again speak."[66]

Fry's cooperation and the bank's success encouraged Kempner to invest in at least ten banks across Texas, including those in Athens, Ballinger, Belton, Gatesville, Groesbeck, Hamilton, Marble Falls, Mexia, Temple, Velasco, and Wichita Falls, and he became a director of more than a dozen. Later, his solo cotton brokerage functioned also as a private bank. Irrigation and real estate projects in arid West Texas areas, where he had interests in cattle grazing and cotton acreages, also appealed to him. True, a recession in the mid-1880s "very much depressed" land investments, but he was still willing to buy. Sometimes nearby acreage lured him. In one instance in 1884 he authorized a nephew, Ike Markowitz, to serve him as agent at an auction, but, Kempner warned, "Do not pay over $30 for the whole tract [10 acres] in Galveston County."[67]

By the early 1880s Kempner's name appeared with increasing frequency in newspaper announcements of varied joint ventures with the Island City business elite. These investments included barge operations, insurance, banks, and, increasingly, railroads.[68] Odds are that few if any of their numerous risk-takings were mere "wallpaperings" (selling speculative stock) for quick profits. Instead, as in the Santa Fe instance, Kempner had goals transcending but never ignoring profits. He aimed also at far-reaching security for Galveston's economy by developing rail links that might overcome Houston's advantages as a hub and feed Galveston freight imports to redress the export imbalance. Deep Water Committee member Kempner contributed much money and time to its efforts to have the federal government maintain the dredged channels into Galveston Bay from the

66. Thompson, "History," p. 8; DWK, "Historical Record," p. 3.

67. Quotations, respectively, from Kempner, letters to G. W. Norsworth, June 28, 1883 [?], no. 2; to W. L. Thulemeyer, Mar. 23, 1885, no. 266; and to Markowitz, Mar. 20, 1884, no. 119, all in Kempner Letterpress Book.

68. Kempner, letter to Fry, Dec. 18, 1885, no. 345, Kempner Letterpress Book. See also DWK, "Historical Record," p. 3; Thompson, "History," p. 8; undated "50 Years Ago" clippings, DWK Scrapbook, 1929–1935.

Gulf. He understood clearly that the port, while still the premier entry point for Texas, was destined to contest that primacy with Houston once the latter city developed as a hub of the great transcontinental railroads. But until then Galveston retained the advantage of being a working port 700 miles closer to the products of the West than any on the Atlantic, and 350 miles closer to grain-producing centers than was New Orleans.

Like New York and Chicago, Galveston had existed from its beginnings as a commercial conduit. Galveston's harbor would profit its servitors so long as the transit of water-borne bulk goods in and out of the port profited both shippers and the port's owner-investors. Nature had blessed Galveston (and, as we shall see, hexed it as well). A maritime complex requiring endless and expensive maintenance and modernization, Galveston could and did outpace all Gulf port rivals, but only until cheaper, more certain, and swifter avenues of transshipping competed for trade.

Kempner's efforts to augment Galveston's natural advantages as a port city with rail links northward and westward, were, therefore, primarily defensive in nature. The recurring hope was that the Santa Fe venture would make such far-inland markets as Denver look to Galveston as their "seaport."[69]

What Kempner and almost all of his contemporaries, however farsighted, failed to see was that the shift toward concentration on cotton that they favored was to contribute to the city's decline. As, in a sense, cotton became their new "king," the earlier pattern of a diverse local economy changed. In 1870 Galveston was a major port city of mixed economy, with its light manufactories outnumbering Houston's and outvaluing the products of that competing city. But by 1890 only Galveston's shoemaking and light-iron foundry fabricators remained significant on the Island. Cotton had subsumed almost all else. Talent shifted from low-profile and lower-paying jobs to jobs in cotton firms. Year after year through the 1880–1900 decades, Galveston handled increasing percentages of the Texas cotton crop but less and less of other products. Galveston's numerous and varied small manufactories of the shoe, hat, and furniture sorts, and the local barge operations, in which Kempner had invested in his earlier

69. Axelrod, "Galveston: Denver's Deep-Water Port," p. 217; Barker, "Partners in Progress," pp. 7–8.

years in Galveston, gave way to cotton and to railroads as the essential conduit for cotton.

Perhaps Kempner understood that Galveston's natural superiority as a seaport would not of itself attract adequate external capital, especially from railroad companies, to sustain the Gulf city's economy. He appears to have believed that capital would have to come from Galveston itself, and so he put some of his risk capital where his perceptions were. But he also offered to his generation a vivid spectacle of the rich rewards available in cotton merchandising. Many talented, aggressive, and ambitious young Galvestonians must have been influenced by his increasing affluence to follow the cotton trail rather than to attend to the less swift enrichments offered by a more diversified Island economy, a better balance between imports and exports, and an improved inland transportation network. Both Kempner and cotton enjoyed the advantages that Galveston's magnificent bay offered, but, to repeat, those very advantages contained seeds of the city's enduring problems.[70]

70. Angell, "Vantage on the Bay," *East Texas Historical Journal*, pp. 14–16; McComb, *Galveston*, chaps. 2–3; Shore, *Southern Capitalists*, passim.

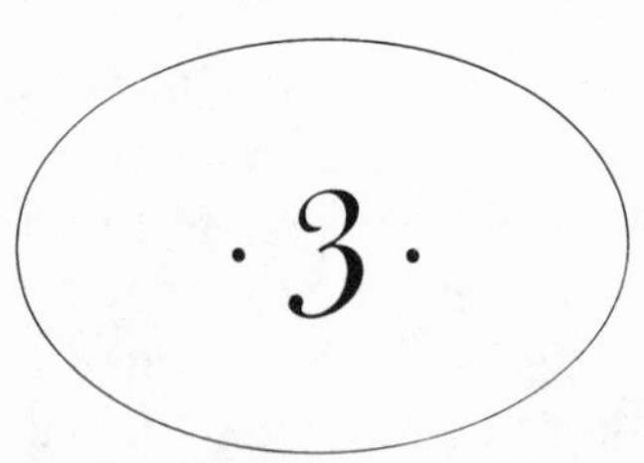

In the Land of Cotton

KEMPNER HAD PREPARED HIMSELF WELL to be a solo cotton dealer, or factor: a commission-earning middleman who served growers as agent and spinners as a source of the commodity. A new kind of middleman, factors took cotton from growers on consignment and sought to sell it for the planters at the highest possible prices, receiving from the growers a commission, usually from 2.5 to 5 percent, for their service. Inland factors, some of whom were agents of port grocery merchants like Marx and Kempner, scouted mainland plantations at harvest time, meanwhile having provided growers with credit and supplies. The inland agents sent the commodity on to specialized port factors in coastal cities like Galveston. Only rarely did factors themselves become owners. When they did, they were known as "cotton merchants," who themselves bought cotton and resold it to spinners.[1]

Not all wholesale grocers became cotton factors; fewer became merchants. But to Kempner the temptation first to extend wholesale grocering into cotton factoring, and then to phase out grocering in favor of the cotton trade, became as intense as his urge to escalate his Cold Springs peddling to wholesaling.

For his solo operation Kempner retained the aggressive Marx and Kempner grocery drummers, who contributed to the firm's reputation for advantageous rates and honest dealing. Through them and from his own increasingly frequent business trips, usually by rail, across Texas, Kempner improved his understanding of the needs of the in-

1. Blackford and Kerr, *Business Enterprise in American History*, p. 107. See also Pusateri, *A History of American Business*, pp. 127–29.

land growers and retail shopkeepers who were the customers and clients of Marx and Kempner and now of H. Kempner.

An ever-enlarging percentage of his farmer-customers were cultivating cotton. Kempner's connections with these farmers, plus those he enjoyed with eastern credit sources, generated substantial and quick profits for him. Further, as a later arrival among cotton middlemen concluded, it was still the case then that American cotton dealerships typically "were modest concerns, with modest capital and modest credit. In general, financial and credit limitations compelled them to confine their activities to a rapid-turnover type of business, since they could not finance the carrying of large stocks."[2]

Additional lures to the cotton trade derived from the fact that amassed information on cotton marketing was available to novices through the medium of the Galveston Cotton Exchange, and Kempner was a quick learner. Created in 1871, almost simultaneously with Kempner's arrival in Galveston, the exchange, an association of middlemen and agents, quickly became a balance-wheel of the cotton trade and a symbol of the community's rising importance as a cotton-exporting port and of its members' high standing in the community.[3] During the years when Kempner was establishing himself in the cotton trade, the pre–Civil War business network was breaking down. Changing textile manufacturing processes and more sophisticated communications, transportation, and money markets created by new technologies, including the steam engine, railroad, telegraph, and telephone, made the newcomer's task infinitely more intense. The cotton exchange provided procedures and some standards.[4]

Well that it did, on two counts. First, because cotton was such a wealth-earning asset, the factor was becoming one of the nation's most important middlemen. Second, the cotton trade was bewilderingly

2. Lamar Fleming, Jr., "Growth of the Business of Anderson, Clayton & Co.," ed. James Tinsley, *Texas Gulf Coast Historical Association Publication Series*, pp. 1–2.

3. "In the largest port cities, . . . yet another specialized institution developed, the brokerage house [or exchange]. For a fee brokerage houses brought together buyers and sellers of cotton. An elaborate credit system based on advances from one middleman to the next, using the traditional financial instruments of promissory notes and bills of exchange, grew up to service the cotton trade" (Blackford and Kerr, *Business Enterprise*, p. 107).

4. Porter and Livesay, *Merchants and Manufacturers*, p. 8 and passim; Harris L. Kempner, interview with B. Guidry, Aug. 6, 1982, RLA.

complex and exotic even to a new factor like Kempner who had dabbled in it as an all-purpose wholesale grocer.

In that association with Marx, Kempner had mastered business practices requiring little specialized knowledge of the many commodities with which the partnership dealt. But specialization as a cotton middleman required swift mastery of highly technical farm-to-factory processes and of the domestic and international money markets. By tying themselves to a single commodity, cotton middlemen might win large profits, but the risks multiplied. No longer able to spread the risks across a "shopping list" of commodities, the factor was vulnerable to fluctuations in the cotton cycle, from seed to finished textiles.

A sense of the Galveston Cotton Exchange's capacity to bewilder neophytes to the trade emerges from an 1880 local colorist's reaction to a day spent in that handsome new building. The swiftly altered chalked hieroglyphics that agile clerks were scrawling on huge blackboards mesmerized and confused the comic writer, who wrote, "[I]f you don't understand the technical terms, you might as well stand on your head and try to glean late information . . . from . . . advertisements in a Chinese newspaper, turned bottom upwards."

It was likely that young Kempner, a newcomer to the exotic business life-style carried on in the exchange, obeyed the unwritten "Rule for Strangers": be silent, learn, and "never undertake to instruct any of the [more senior] members of the exchange. . . . Let them find out for themselves."[5]

By the time Kempner read these popular satirical descriptions when they appeared in the *Galveston Daily News* in the late 1870s and early 1880s, he was an exchange veteran and acknowledged expert in its arcane ways. And he knew that "things are not what they seem at the cotton exchange. It was all bona-fide business."[6] And a risky one at every step.

Exchange members included sellers (growers or their agents, commonly the fee-earning factors), buyers (the purchasing agents of spinning mills), and commodity-owning merchants (middlemen). They conducted business on the basis of procedures, contract forms, and standards of the exchange. By the 1870s commodity dealers in cotton commonly engaged in "to arrive" or future contracts negotiated through

5. Eisenhower, ed., *Alexander Sweet's Texas*, pp. 70–72.
6. Ibid., p. 72.

the cotton exchanges, a development that was greatly to accelerate in the 1890–1930 decades. Contracts for future sale or purchase were either by individual negotiation or auction.

For the middlemen, particularly merchants, membership in an exchange offered opportunity to protect ("hedge") their contracts against adverse price shifts by subcontracting to speculators, who, as we shall see, assumed this risk and hoped for favorable marketplace variations. Merchants, bound by the set commitment, made or lost money not only on their skill in anticipating fluctuations but also on their own and their staff's proficiency in buying, grading, recompressing, baling, and warehousing the cotton they and their staffs bought. By contrast, the cotton factor, a true middleman, owned nothing except his claims on farmers' promises to consign future crops through him, claims often secured by money advances that factors made to farmers, and his intuitions of the needs and, especially, of the probable timing of the needs of merchants and buyers for spinning houses here and abroad.

Another feature of exchange membership that Kempner found congenial was its service as mediator in disputes between growers and middlemen. Mediation offered a happy alternative to litigation, that bugaboo of Kempner's. Disputes arose frequently. Rascals existed among both farmers and businessmen. If higher ethics or good intentions prevailed, standards of bookkeeping, weighing, and grading were still rudimentary or sloppy. Many farmers were appalled at their unshrinking debt to middlemen. Yet the advances to them did not overwhelmingly favor the lenders, specialist scholars concur. Many chronic debtors resorted to nonpayment or delayed payments. Some defaulters accepted new advances then shipped through other middlemen. Resultant disputes came to the exchange for resolution.[7]

The exchange charged fees and dues for membership. Exchange standards had no equivalent in grocery wholesaling or liquor importing. To a man of Kempner's temperament and ambitions, the exchange's relatively rationalized functions and procedures encouraged a civility he treasured, plus greater certainty in contract relationships. Exchange rules redefined what in other situations were no-holds-barred contests for profits into gentlemanly interactions, especially in unprofitable or break-even seasons. Kempner's son Ike, who succeeded his father in the work, wrote: "The basic theory of future exchanges

7. Pusateri, *History*, pp. 128–29.

is that the conglomerate of all private demands and offers, meeting in a central trading place, will determine and reflect the price which truly reflects the consensus of supply and demand and informed opinion at any given time." Always "the motive[s] of all buyers and sellers . . . [are] motives of gain, which [at the Exchange] are scrutable by third parties." And, Ike concluded, back when his father made his decision to be a factor, "cotton was merchandised from farm to mill with the smallest merchandising toll of any farm product in terms of percentage of value. This was possible because the middlemen had excellent means of limiting their price risks through hedges in the cotton futures markets, enjoyed cheap credit because of their limitation of price risk, and had built up experience, expertness, and efficient organizations through . . . trial and error."[8]

All of which suggests that there was more to Harris Kempner's commitment to cotton than the simple pursuit of profits. Even in atypical, nonplantation Galveston, cotton's servitors were the community's social leaders. Despite all predictions about natural limits to cotton cultivation imposed by labor, rainfall, or soil types, it was proving to be surprisingly and profitably adaptable and movable.[9]

When the Civil War started, cotton was entrenched from the rich if tiring river valleys of the Atlantic seaboard to the quickly deforested fields of eastern Texas. By the mid-1870s the center of its cultivation was in Arkansas, Mississippi, and eastern Texas, where rainfall still averaged at least thirty inches per year. The plant was already being worked farther westward to far drier but irrigable areas of the Texas Panhandle, and to New Mexico, Arizona, and California. Total production in these newer areas still lagged behind those east of the Mississippi. But as the Indian tribes retreated and their last strongholds in Oklahoma opened for white settlement, the differentials increasingly favored the newer regions that the Galveston middlemen were tapping.[10]

Through their inland travelers and from scientific reports, the cotton middlemen of the port were well aware of Texas' enormous variations in rainfall, from fifty inches a year in the east to less than fif-

8. IHK, "Cotton Marketing" (manuscript), ca. 1950, Box IHK, A–W, #80-002, Kempner Papers.

9. Cf. Fite, *Cotton Fields No More;* Woodman, "How New Was the New South?" *Agricultural History,* p. 529.

10. Ellis, "The Texas Cotton Compress Industry" (Ph.D. diss.), pp. 409–13.

teen in the west. The humid, low-lying coastal prairies and the higher, quickly clearable forest lands of East Texas were similar to the familiar lands of the Old South. A more westerly region of extensive blackland prairies experienced slightly less precipitation than East Texas but was still suitable for good cotton production. Westering farther, middle Texas from the Panhandle to the Rio Grande had occasional rain and slim forestation, with a topsoil of decayed grasses that was also to prove itself splendid for growing cotton. The most western regions were to remain dedicated largely to cattle grazing until after the century's turn, when they too exhibited their value for the cotton enterprise.[11]

Galveston dealers had to keep up with these mobile cotton frontiers. One method, already noted, fit Kempner's experience: personally enticing railhead storekeepers, petty bankers, and peddlers with loans and investments. Kempner's agents traveled even more extensively and aggressively than had been true for the Marx and Kempner firm, throughout Texas, Oklahoma Territory, and northern Mexico, to assess the size, grade, and value of a current crop. Then at harvest time they tried to outbid other factors' agents but at the lowest winnable level. After acquiring the cotton and seeing to the necessary ginning, an agent then arranged for its processing and shipment to Galveston by the common carrier of lowest cost. Always the drummers stressed H. Kempner's connections to essential facilities for reconcentrating the consigned, graded, and stapled cotton, for selling it as advantageously as possible, and for providing the grower with all these and other services in an honest manner.

From Field to Commodity

Endless opportunities existed for sharp dealing. Once the cotton was picked, ginned, and hauled to a freight line, the grower rarely if ever retained physical control over this property, depending thereafter on a paper trail left by agents of freight companies and cotton middlemen. Early in this initial phase the first of many gradings occurred. A grader or classer (a Kempner employee if Kempner had contracted for the crop) cut a sample from each bale of ginned, baled cotton from a single grower. The grader determined the color of the

11. Ibid., pp. 409–27.

cotton and the number of seed pieces left in the ginned commodity, these factors determining its grade. A determination of the average length of fibers in a sample (stapling) followed. Then lots from a single grower were concentrated for compressing by grade and staple. The values assigned to a crop were entered onto H. Kempner's books as credits to the grower's account, in the form of points above ("on") or below ("off") the exchange's "middling inch" standard, a level to which the commodity traders paid close attention.

As the cotton moved from gin to Galveston, it endured several further gradings and staplings by representatives of every interest involved. Reconcentratings followed as consignments from diverse growers flowed from tributary freight lines toward main carriers who carried the cargo to Galveston. At each noisy, dusty, busy, labor-intensive step, concerns about a shipment's grade, cleanliness, strength, fiber length, and weight (absorption of rain affected weight and bulk) offered opportunities to the unscrupulous to slant evaluations and records.

Freight agents had their own interests to serve. The movement of cotton from farms to port or rail trunk hub involved repeated reshufflings from wagons to barges to freight rail cars or ships. The condition, weight, and bulk (water-swollen or dry) of cotton bales affected freight charges, and Kempner's agents kept close watch on these third-party verdicts.

Compressing, the forcing of concentrated or reconcentrated cotton into bales, was essential for the economical use of the limited number of available wagons, rail cars, barges, and ships. All growers in a region shipped at once in harvest season. Great traffic jams of hauling vehicles, called "blockades," inevitably and frequently developed at junctions as the baled cotton flowed riverlike to Galveston. Railroad representatives grumbled that the compressed, baled cotton in their "blockaded" freight cars was enjoying free warehousing and so demanded higher rates.

Until the 1880s, Galveston had the only facilities in Texas capable of systematically delivering ready-for-milling cotton onto waiting freighters. Basically, these facilities consisted of huge compressing machines and enormous warehouses. Cursed still with high costs and tentative technology, the Galveston "presses" performed the last in the bulk reductions the cotton had endured since it was picked, a series that began at the low-powered press near the farm of its growth or at the first freight station. This initial compression and tying produced a relatively loosely packed bale. Another compression of greater vigor occurred at rail junction points, resulting in smaller bales that were more economical for rail carriage, better tied, and more completely covered with cloth for protection against rain and insects. But ties often broke and cloth bagging ripped. Recompression, rebagging, and retying were then necessary.

Finally, H. Kempner or a like firm exhibited samples in their offices or warehouse to agents of American and European spinning mills. Then delicate, swift-paced price negotiations ensued. Once orders were in hand, H. Kempner's warehouse workers (later, compress workers as well) saw to another round of appropriate concentrations, compressions, rebalings, retyings, and recoverings. Then the bales were delivered to waiting ships or railcars for haulage to New England or Europe, H. Kempner following through with billings to millers and payouts to farmers, house agents, freighting companies, and suppliers of baggings, twine, and other necessaries, and to H. Kempner house agents and staffs of the company's warehouse and office and, later, compress.[12]

In addition to possessing superior pressing and warehousing facilities, until the century's turn the Galveston middlemen were able to exploit their city's advantages as an oceanic port. Oceangoing ships at the wharves served as cheap, temporary warehouses into which cotton factors and merchants could assign bales, thus saving on storage costs and keeping capital liquid and overhead low. And so, if presses were becoming increasingly large, powerful, and costly, the rich yields of cotton each year were resulting in declining unit prices of the commodity with resulting increases of profits to alert brokers. H. Kempner was both honest and alert. Unlike other growth industries of the time, the Galveston cotton dealers were able to increase greatly the flow of the commodity through their hands without suffering giant increases in costs or becoming dwarfed by the producers they served or the market they fed.[13]

Agents of American and European (and, later, Latin American and Asian) spinning mills who resided in Galveston bid for the ware-

12. Ibid.; H. L. Kempner, letter to author, Sept. 1, 1987.

13. Fleming, "Anderson, Clayton," p. 4; Atack, "Firm Size and Industrial Structure in the U.S. during the 19th Century," *Journal of Economic History*, p. 464.

housed cotton if immediate delivery was wanted or for future stock. The Galveston factors were usually able to book sales of cotton consigned to them as fast as it was available or committed. The bills of lading resulting from these commitments connected the Galveston middlemen to Texas growers and domestic and foreign cotton spinners and to international money markets.[14]

Kempner soon involved himself in both "spot" and "future" operations. The spot, or actual, market was the result of a mill's immediate need for cotton. The mill's agent usually approached H. Kempner directly, in person, or by telephone, telegram, or cable, or sometimes through an agent, and arranged to buy a specified number of bales of certain quality with a set cash payment due on delivery. To facilitate his participation in spot sales, H. Kempner acquired "seats" on local-regional cotton exchanges not only in Galveston, but also in Houston, New Orleans, and Memphis, and had access through "seated" brokers to the two national exchanges, in New York City and Chicago.[15]

On school vacations and in summer, Kempner's son Ike, as he reached his mid-teens, "had a ringside seat as large matters of finance with banks in New York . . . [and abroad] were transacted by his father." What made these extracurricular experiences in the H. Kempner offices even more engaging for the maturing youngster was his father's capacity to monitor the smallest detail in his cotton-focused regional, national, and international concerns, and numerous local and statewide investments.[16]

Young Ike and, decades later, his own son Harris in turn were endlessly fascinated by the transcontinental and transoceanic magic practiced by the Galveston cotton factors and merchants. The letters of credit provided to them by the purchasing agents of American and European spinners allowed the Galveston middlemen to draw upon the buyer's bank even if it was in Europe, through selling the commercial paper at discounts to local speculators or bankers, thus almost immediately recouping credit advanced to farmers months ear-

14. Ellis, *The Texas Cotton Compress Industry*, chaps. 1–3.

15. *Galveston Daily News*, Apr. 14, 1894; and see Waller, "Overland Movement of Cotton," *Southwestern Historical Quarterly*, p. 137.

16. "I. H. Kempner Testimonial Dinner" (transcript), RLA; Tinsley, ed., "Select Letters of Harris Kempner," *Gulf Coast Historical Association Publications*, p. 37.

lier, plus costs, fees, and profit. The Galveston factors and merchants then paid the farmers, minus agreed advances, fees, and other costs.

How different all of these crisp procedures were from the tedious stock control and longer-term credit illiquidities in wholesale grocering. Though elaborate, this hierarchy of discounted bills of exchange and promissory notes was not difficult for an aspirant such as Kempner to master. He also grasped quickly the fact that the Galveston factors enjoyed a favored situation of rapid turnover, low inventories, and opportunity to liquidate debt at the close of every crop year and concluded that they should not modify it casually. One constant was that both cotton farmers at one end and spinners and bankers at the other would contract only with "the American [factor or merchant] firms of their confidence."[17] Harris Kempner's first task was to make H. Kempner a cotton factor worthy of confidence.

A Firm of Their Confidence

Kempner was responsible for the grading and packaging of a crop, and after the sale, for making an account of the proceeds to his clients. Kempner's interests and those of his grower-clients were the same—to get the best price—and Kempner's income was a percentage, usually from 2 to 5 percent of that price. The fact that his clients tended to borrow from "his" bank for advances on future sales added to his returns.[18] Quickly prominent, competing with such established rivals as the Hutchins and Sealy group and W. L. Moody through traveling agents on the supply side and through Galveston's Cotton Exchange on the distributive side, H. Kempner handled cotton from farmers who grew and owned it and from ginners (sometimes the same person), and then sold it to agents of spinning firms on the farmers' or ginners' accounts. Since factors were middlemen, they hazarded less than cotton merchants, who themselves purchased cotton from producers and thereafter resold on their own accounts to spinners.

Spinners were elusive elements in the market equation. They bought

17. Fleming, "Anderson, Clayton," pp. 2–3.

18. Harris L. Kempner, "The Kempners of Galveston and Sugar Land" (manuscript; Address to Harvard Business School Club of Houston, Sept. 27, 1981), RLA, pp. 4–6; IHK, *Recalled Recollections*, p. 16; Schweikart, "Entrepreneurial Aspects of Antebellum Banking," in *American Business History, Case Studies*, pp. 122–29.

as and when they pleased. Their rewards or losses depended on their capacity to buy raw cotton from middlemen like H. Kempner at a price spread that was adequate to cover the manufacturing and distribution costs at their mills. Only rarely could cotton producers, factors, merchants, and spinners completely balance their operations. A futures market developed in order that shortfalls and overyields, either long or short term, roughly balanced out.

The futures market arose to permit spinners to assure themselves a steady supply of raw cotton without maintaining large on-hand stocks. A spinner, having anticipated the needed amount of cotton, would purchase incrementally rather than buy and store the entire amount, and in hope also of a drop in prices. Spinners contracted with cotton factors like H. Kempner to purchase raw cotton at a fixed price during the five harvest months – March, May, July, October, and December – only resorting to the spot market when need exceeded supply. In the interim, H. Kempner was readying the cotton for resale by lots based on quality. Generations of Kempners insisted that the firm's involvements in the swings and roundabouts of the cotton market did not involve speculation either for grower-clients or for H. Kempner's own account. Instead, these involvements were part of inescapable risk-taking.

Yet Kempner knew well that speculators were indispensable to the entire complicated process. As in many commodity markets, speculators chanced large windfalls and swift losses. They bought futures contracts and at their maturity sold them to spinners in need of additional supplies beyond the capacity of the spot market to provide, at whatever prices current conditions allowed. Especially when selling "short," cotton traders like Kempner exposed themselves to imputations of speculating.

Kempner and most other cotton middlemen insisted that commodity trades were separable from speculation and gambling and that efforts toward market efficiencies were not steps toward monopolies (a theme linked to that of speculation to which this account will return). Among agricultural entrepreneurs in the New South, cotton dealers were both economically self-interested in fending off restrictive public policies demanded by anti-speculation forces, and, so far as Kempner was concerned, he was consistent in denying that he speculated, as well as self-conscious of his social roles. "I do not speculate but watch my business," Harris advised then-teenaged Ike, who worked in the H.

Kempner offices weekends and on school holidays, learning first to aid and then to succeed his father.[19]

As risks increased, new, small, financially unstable cotton dealers were replaced by a decreasing number of larger middleman firms. Kempner's capacity to survive these trends testifies to his ability and reputation as factor and later of his son Ike's ability as a merchant. In part because it became widely known that he did not speculate on his own account, many farmers authorized Ike to act for them in all their financial transactions involving marketing. "His name," recalled Daniel Webster Kempner in a memoir of his father, "was known to every large planter in the State, many of whom came to Galveston in the spring of the year to make their financial arrangements, and then shipped their cotton to Mr. Kempner in the fall." H. Kempner also had "hard credit" in New York and abroad, listing Lazard Frères in Paris, Crédit Suisse in Geneva, and Kleinworth in London among others in his treasured private file of credit sources. Kempner, as noted earlier, in addition to serving grower-clients as a private banker, developed several banks in Texas, becoming a director of the Citizens Loan Company in 1883 and president of the Texas Land and Loan Company in 1890.[20]

Even a man committed to close surveillance over his many diversified investments occasionally found himself in a speculation. Becoming aware of the unwelcome speculative element in one venture, Kempner declined to endorse any notes that the participants had pooled, writing that "I assure you that no enterprise would induce . . . [me] to . . . put my name to any paper as I am determined to pull out."[21]

In order to increase H. Kempner's advantages, Harris labored to develop something akin to a linked cluster of businesses essential to the crop-to-factor-to-spinner process. In addition to banks and insurance companies, he invested in and/or became a director of rail-

19. "I. H. Kempner Testimonial Dinner"; IHK, *Recalled Recollections*, p. 7; E. R. Thompson, Jr., "History of H. Kempner" (manuscript), Kempner Papers, p. 7; Fabian, "The Metaphysics of Money Making" (Organization of American Historians, 1988); Hearden, "Agricultural Businessmen in the New South," *Louisiana Studies*, p. 146.

20. DWK, "Historical Record," p. 3; "50 Years Ago" columns, *Galveston Daily News*, Apr. 13, 1933, Apr. 19, 1940.

21. Letter to Sampson [probably Heidenheimer], Aug. 27, 1883, no. 30, Kempner Letterpress Book.

roads, lighters, a cotton compress, and bagging-cordage firms. Rarely a merely passive investor, Kempner became versed in these manifold operations and sometimes ran noncotton enterprises.

Success required the development of swifter, more reliable, and cheaper mass transportation, especially for the underserviced counties of northern and western Texas. As a member of the board of the Gulf, Colorado, and Santa Fe Railroad, Kempner spearheaded efforts to encourage the railroad's development by himself investing in the line and thus inspiring mainland interests. Kempner was fascinated also by the investment opportunities that raw rural real estate offered and probably in the late 1880s or early 1890s risked some savings in such ventures. He made few wrong choices. Some part of his good fortune resulted from the improving economic environment as Texas recovered from the severe recession of the 1880s. Concerning urban real estate, for example, a form of investment Kempner usually eschewed in favor of agricultural land, he profited substantially from what a reporter of the *Galveston Daily News* described (Mar. 15, 1890) as "the boom [that] struck the vicinity of Postoffice and 20th Streets, . . . and the Kempner building on Strand . . . [selling] for $26,000."

His augmenting wealth resulted also from careful attention to detail. Ike recalled his father demanding to know from a ranch manager: "[H]ow is the grass on the ranch at Mexia—are the cattle in good condition to go into the winter . . . how many calves have you branded this fall?" And, on another occasion, Harris enjoyed reporting happily, "plenty of rain . . . spring grass fine."[22]

Business Ethicist

Young Ike, barely into his teens, came to realize from his vacation-time work in his father's office that principles established in Cold Springs and Galveston governed the most distant venture. His father's contemporaries later estimated that these principles included especially the mutual interdependence and "integrity of men who managed railroads and banks and plantations, and . . . the strength of a complex fabric of agriculture and banking [interests] throughout . . . Texas." Ike's insight that his father assumed the "integrity of men who managed that 'complex fabric'" was more than the uncritical

22. "I. H. Kempner Testimonial Dinner"; Tinsley, ed. "Select Letters," p. 37.

estimate of an admiring son. The senior Kempner's vexations and even outrage at duplicity or shady dealing are illuminated in a story that Ike passed on to his own son:

> One day my Grandfather got a letter from someone up country saying will you advance me so and so much on so many bales of cotton? And he wrote back yes he would. The draft came in with the bill of lading attached, it was paid, and the shipment arrived; but instead of being cotton it was linters which is what is left over after they have ginned the cotton and [it] has vastly inferior value to cotton. . . . So my Grandfather went immediately to his lawyer and said. . . . The railroad issued a forged bill of lading—it says cotton and it isn't cotton. The man who drew the draft was obviously deceiving me. I understand the cottonseed oil mill up there was an accessory to this thing because they certainly knew the difference. . . . So the lawyers said to him, "My goodness, Mr. Kempner, you must think all cotton men are thieves." And my Grandfather is supposed to have replied, "No, no, no, I don't think that, but I do think that a lot of thieves have gotten into the cotton business.[23]

Another illustration concerned insurance for the Tremont Hotel. Kempner insured it with the New York Life Insurance Company through its Detroit agent, who, it appears, neglected to forward premiums to his home office. Kempner received due bills, then past-due notices for premiums he had already paid. A large, increasingly heated, and extended correspondence grew between Galveston and Detroit. Kempner finally won his point by providing his own documentation for records that the insurance company could not or would not dredge up from its files. He admonished the agent: "It does you no good [and] the company no good to take advantage of me and impose on me . . . and I do not believe you will allow it." Kempner also had bank president Fry exert his influence on the insurance executives.[24]

He was both disappointed and surprised that others, especially relatives or close friends, failed to meet his own standards. In 1884, for example, in the nationwide economic depression during which many businesses failed, Kempner informed a co-investor in a large-scale cattle feedlot and meat-processing speculation that was collaps-

23. "Complex fabric" quotation in "I. H. Kempner Testimonial Dinner"; anecdote in HLK, "Kempners of Galveston and Sugar Land," pp. 6–7.

24. Letter to J. H. McDonald, Mar. 28, 1884, no. 129, Kempner Letterpress Book; see also no. 68, 88, 94, 261.

ing of his suspicions about having been deceived by the scheme's promoters.[25] Once the facts were before him, he agreed that a simple misapprehension on a contract rather than a swindle had occurred.

Although in the late 1880s and early 1890s Kempner invested personally in varied enterprises, including Central American coffee and banana plantations, Ohio real estate, and a New England paper manufactory, he came to prefer more local investments, especially in cotton. "I have already got too much money invested in outside matters and not enough . . . in my legitimate business [cotton]," he wrote Abe Seinsheimer, his wife's brother, whom Kempner trusted and always addressed as "Dear Brother Abe."[26]

Kempner worked hard to enhance the area's capacities to produce, transport, process, and market high-grade cotton. The crop was, arguably, no longer "king" among America's agricultural commodities. But it still reigned in Galveston and required faithful, inventive middlemen. Kempner encouraged ready financing, adequate transportation, and stable labor even to the point of using contract prison labor (see chapter 8), and, along with others of like drive and vision, helped to make the whole work adequately as a system.[27]

Business Managers

Kempner came early to believe in the wisdom of using specialist-managers to run investments that involved technicalities with which he was unfamiliar and of keeping such valuable employees as contented as possible in their work. For example, when considering the manufacture of inexpensive wooden furniture, he requested from an Illinois acquaintance in that line some information on woodworking techniques, patents, and standards, and opinions on subcontracting components as opposed to a raw material–to–finished product operation. Kempner asked also for recommendations for a manager to "give special attention to the business, to act with us, counsel with us, and carry out the ideas we may agree upon." Such a person, Kempner continued, should be a "man of good judgment and scope of mind who can see what is needed and recommend it." Then he stipulated

25. Tinsley, ed., "Select Letters," pp. 19–20.
26. Oct. 6, 1887, no. 434, Kempner Letterpress Book.
27. Woodman, *King Cotton and His Retainers;* DWK, "Historical Record," p. 3.

that the most desirable manager would also invest his own money in the venture, "not that we need capital, on the contrary we do not need a dollar, . . . but we would like his money in it as it would be sure to make him feel more interested in the business."[28]

That statement suggests that Kempner was maintaining currency with emerging practice among large-scale corporate enterprises, at least during his sons' minorities. One response to mass industrialization was and would continue to be the hiring of specialists without ownership interests. This managerial evolution reflected, partly at least, the fact that new industrialists, distrusting nepotism or finding among their family members and close associates too few qualified successors for top positions, were hiring professional managers to fill gaps.[29] Never distrusting nepotism, Kempner both adopted this practice then modified it by having long-term employee-managers become investors (a practice widely engaged in by major corporations after World War II). And after his death his sons, as we shall see, then some of their sons, became manager-owners of H. Kempner.

In the early 1880s Kempner ventured into furniture and wagon manufacturing in Huntsville in southeast Texas, where both lumber and labor were cheap. But the hot, humid climate caused even seasoned wood to reject glues and to repel fasteners, so that wagon wheels loosened and veneers peeled. He circularized manufacturers of industrial dryers for information on these machines' effects on various woods.[30]

Public Issues and Private Self-Education

This very private individual, so filled with enthusiasm for the opportunities that America offered him, "was always known as simply a plain man of business . . . [who] never sought office, and took but little interest in partisan politics," concluded a contemporary biographer of prominent Texans. The writer was only superficially correct. By the 1880s Kempner was well on the road to large wealth,

28. Tinsley, ed., "Select Letters," p. 10.

29. Ibid., pp. 8–11; Hays, *Response to Industrialization, 1885–1914,* chap. 1; Chandler, *The Visible Hand.*

30. H. Kempner, letter to Beaumont Lumber Co., July 28, 1883, no. 17, Kempner Letterpress Book. The Kempners' use of convict labor began with this investment in furniture manufacturing. See chap. 8, below.

and he now allowed himself to be deeply interested in many non-business matters, including politics. To feed his mind and to find a substitute for formal education he exploited opportunities that his manifold business and social associations made available. Kempner's office, clubs, temple, and home sometimes took on the atmosphere of the classroom. In these private arenas he gathered information about public issues and made decisions to assist "whatever would elevate, adorn, or improve the society in which he moved or the country in which he made his home," the biographer asserted. For example, after discussing the unsettling "silver question," which Kempner's old friend, banker Charles Fry, condemned as an immoral monetary heresy, Fry asked him to circulate their shared views among Galvestonians. Kempner saw to it that the *Galveston News* ran an article on the burning question, telling Fry that he hoped it might "have some effect eventually among our Representatives."[31]

Kempner distinguished his distaste for litigation from his respect for the law as the basic element in America's impressive yet ever-fragile social stability. Beginning in the late 1870s he initiated at his home what was to become an annual dinner party, with the honored guests including politicians, federal and state judges, and regionally famous attorneys. Other invitees came from among the Island City's elite, a status to which the Kempners now belonged. Such occasions were more than social climbing to the graying, now heavy-set, mustachioed, almost archetypically Victorian *pater familias* at the head of the long dining table. In addition to winning insights into the legal and political life of this huge, complex, and diverse state, Kempner was simply happy to share in the company: "It was always a source of amazement to . . . [him] that he could talk freely and without fear and on a level of equality with men in such high office," wrote a family member.[32]

Kempner circulated comfortably among Galveston's other merchants, Jews and non-Jews alike. Few "5 o'clock curtains" separated prominent Galveston Hebrews from Gentiles. The white residents of the Island City who worked together all day went off to the same residential streets and frequently intersected socially, their families

31. Brown, *Indian Wars and Pioneers of Texas*, p. 297; on search for ideas, IHK, "H. Kempner," p. 5; on Fry, Tinsley, ed., "Select Letters," p. 16.
32. IHK, "H. Kempner," p. 67. Other data in Thompson, "History," p. 9.

even more so. Galveston had no exclusive housing tracts where deed restrictions excluded Jews as purchasers. The city's social clubs appear to have been open to Jews, at least to those of Kempner's status. Perhaps Galveston's ease with its diverse white populations resulted partly from its insular nature. Little space existed for exclusivity. Perhaps also, in this superheated commercial environment, the dominant members of Galveston's society and economy shared enough beliefs to warrant interacting beyond those daily occasions required for business. In this sense Galveston's physical confinement, when combined with the very large and swift increase in the wealth of many Islanders like Kempner, may have been a factor in liberating Jewish residents from ghettoizing tendencies prevailing elsewhere.[33]

Kempner and the area's other business successes exchanged many at-home parties. As a member of several select retreats, including the Artillery, Harmony, and Garden clubs, and active in numerous civic improvement associations, by the late 1880s, Kempner had a social and business circle that included George Ball, William Moody, Henry Rosenberg, Julius Runge, and George Sealy, his former partner Marx, and Leon Blum. The Kempners' new residence on a spacious lot at the corner of fashionable Post Office and Eighteenth streets adjoined their fine homes.[34] These palatial structures opened onto paved streets illuminated by electric lights. Galveston's excellent shops offered valued customers selected imported and domestic goods. Kempner's Tremont Hotel was the grandest hostelry between New Orleans and San Francisco, and in its gilded public rooms an annual Mardi Gras Ball became increasingly lavish. Most of the Island's 125 or so Jewish families of 1880–90, while clustering both religiously and socially around their temple, B'nai Israel, felt welcome also at the secular festivities and facilities the Island now offered its leadership. As if in return, Galveston's Jews made their annual Purim Ball a keenly awaited social event for all the Island's white elite. In short, Galveston was a pleasant and stimulating place for Kempner and his family to live and work in. Even nature seemed to conspire both to enhance its charm and to increase its prosperity, the latter by unleashing a savage storm on a competing Texas port city, Indianola, in 1875, virtually leveling

33. McGerr, "Confinement, Liberation and Social Class" (American Historical Association, 1986), esp. pp. 1–5.

34. This home was destroyed in the 1885 fire that leveled almost two thousand residences (IHK, *Recalled Recollections*, p. 7).

it, yet sparing Galveston. In fact, since 1867 Galveston had escaped serious damage from hurricanes or other storms, and residents blamed that one on the Lincoln Republicans.

Born of geography and shaped by commerce, Galveston had the first bank, telephones, typewriters, opera house, golf course, country club, law firm, and YMCA in Texas. In addition to the railroad bridge that since 1860 had connected the Island to the mainland and to Houston, with connections there to rail trunk lines, in the early 1890s an insubstantial wooden bridge accommodated light wagon and pedestrian traffic across the bay, encouraging an infant tourist industry to grow. Orphanages, public and parochial schools, a refuge for distressed women and other victims of epidemics and like natural disasters, and the John Sealy Hospital for the indigent, which in 1890 became an institutional base for the University of Texas Medical College, all of which Harris Kempner supported generously, suggest the bent toward public benefactions as well as private enrichment that moved Galvestonians.

Kempner knew that these accumulating amenities resulted from hard, unremitting toil, risky private investments, and unending charitable bequests by people like himself. If the contributions of labor to economic growth and to the community were essential, he felt that every advance derived from risk capital – a common view of his time and class. Concerning organized labor, Kempner was both hostile and unperceptive. Of the tumultuous 1885–94 decade of the Pullman strikes and "Coxey's Army," Ike remembered a local strike against the Santa Fe Railroad and "the strange sight of his father and other directors of the railroad manning the locomotives and riding with rifles atop the freight cars in a desperate effort to keep the port alive."[35]

Although the Kempners enjoyed all the amenities of a city that deserved the label "grande dame of the Gulf," Galvestonians of their standing increasingly looked eastward for models of desirable lifestyles. A culture of aspiration was growing in bourgeois America that linked opportunity to elite education. Sharing in this perception, Islanders like the Kempners were sending their sons, and some, their daughters, to prestigious East Coast prep schools and colleges and

35. "I. H. Kempner Testimonial Dinner"; Thompson, "History," p. 10; IHK, *Recalled Recollections*, p. 8.

to Europe for "grand tours" upon graduation.[36] Kempner, as will be shown, determined that his children would benefit from these niceties, and the sons could expect college educations in the East.

Still bemused at times by his own swift rise from horny-handed immigrant hod carrier Kempner sometimes flaunted his wealth, primarily in terms of his ever-more luxurious homes and their appurtenances, a common Victorian form of what Peter Gay has described as "the bourgeois experience" and Thorstein Veblen labeled "conspicuous consumption." Other times Kempner tried to assume a less financially exalted posture. An aunt in Europe had written him and requested financial aid. "I hope that God will help you," Kempner replied in a seeming refusal. But he wrote to his own parents, still in Europe, and arranged for the poor relative to receive funds then, with additional amounts to follow as a sort of pension.

As news of Harris's growing affluence reached Europe through the network of relatives, of rabbis, and of Kempner's commercial agents, people in Germany, Russia, and Poland claimed close or distant relationship and requested money or other favors. Even if kinship was unclear, Kempner, though often brusque in the tone of his reply, tended to be an easy mark, which may have prompted other European relatives or claimants to kinship to seek similar help.[37] In 1885 he replied to one such request:

> In reply I beg to state that I owe a duty to [do] all in my power for my parents sisters & their children—beyond this I do not feel it my duty. I have my own family to provide for. I live here and this community is intitled to my charity—we have plenty of poor people here. I am forced to draw a line of duty to my relations in Europe—I get from 5 to 10 letters every week and every one of these letters contain the same pleading—I am absolutely unable to respond to all of these notwithstanding some are doubtless deserving and need my aid but as before stated I am doing all that I ought to do and feel able to do.[38]

36. Burka, "Grande Dame of the Gulf," *Texas Monthly*, p. 164; Eliza Kempner, letter to Rabbi H. Cohen, Oct. 13, 1897, Box 3M220, Cohen Papers; Levine, *The American College and the Culture of Aspiration, 1915–1940*.

37. Kempner, letter to "My Dear Aunt" (trans. from the Yiddish by Alex Schwartz), May 23, 1880, in DWK Scrapbook, vol. 1. See also Hyman Block, interview with L. Marchiafava, June 6, 1981, RLA.

38. Tinsley, ed., "Select Letters," p. 28.

Kempner brought to Galveston for annual seashore picnics several black families from Cold Springs who had worked for him there. Both for them and for numerous relatives in Germany and Poland he offered advice, loans, and, sometimes, outright money gifts. Kempner quietly supported numerous community charities, but he made the temple his major local benefaction and a quiet conduit of charity for persons needing aid, without regard for race or creed. Rabbi Henry Cohen remembered that he served as Kempner's "chief almoner to the needy and distressed. To him [Kempner] charity was synonymous with justice – a definition which was . . . the incentive and . . . background of Harris Kempner." Ike stated that there were three things his father guarded zealously: "his religious heritage, his American citizenship, [and] his responsibilities to society in general as well as to his family in particular."[39]

Harris Kempner: Patient Goad

When replying to the numerous appeals that came to him for advice and, commonly, financial aid of some form, Harris Kempner was rarely reluctant to preach his own work ethic and belief that every American white man was master of his fate. He was surprised that "there are comparatively few who do prosper."[40] And he was sometimes disturbed that even those like himself, who through hard work and risk-taking did prosper, could be laid low by uncontrollable marketplace vagaries.

One such victim was Isaac Heidenheimer of Galveston, a commercial rival but a personal friend. His business devastated by the lingering depression of the late 1880s, Heidenheimer appealed to Kempner for large loans. Himself squeezed for funds, Kempner had to refuse:

> It is absolutely painful to me to have to say I cannot accommodate you. I want to do it. I would do it if I could. But I am positively unable to do it. The demands on me today have been unusually heavy and have been for some time. My account in the bank is largely

39. IHK, *Recalled Recollections*, p. 18; Thompson, "History," pp. 5, 13; Scoufelis, "The Public Views and Charitable Contributions of American Big Businessmen toward Learning, Culture, and Human Welfare, 1910–1932" (Ph.D. diss.).

40. Tinsley, ed., "Select Letters," p. 43.

> overdrawn and I have to make it good on Monday. . . . I have a portfolio of . . . bills receivable from which I am receiving nothing. Very few if any are paying me and it is a drain and a strain . . . to meet the drafts . . . for customers who have established claims on me. I confess this to you only because I want you to feel how anxious I am to assist you, and how cheerfully I would do it if in my power.[41]

Proud of but rarely boastful about his own affluence—"I have done reasonably well" was his self-description in 1887 to a long-absent former neighbor—he was capable of descending to "I-told-you-so" levels and of refusing requests for financial aid, even in good times, at least from nonrelatives. "Had you consulted with me before parting with your money you would have lost nothing," Kempner wrote a victim of a soured investment. And to an appeal from a New York woman on behalf of her tailor-husband for a loan aimed at starting a custom clothing shop in Galveston, Kempner replied, "Your husband could find no employment here as this town needs no cloak designers or gentlemen dressmakers. I have no money to lend. I need all I have and more too to help my own relatives in Europe as well as here in Texas."[42]

True. A succession of Kempner's nephews and young cousins, having emigrated from Europe to America, won his assistance, advice, loans to start businesses, and, a few, jobs in Kempner enterprises. He sometimes deeply regretted the last expedient.

Kempner tried to apply to family members something like the strict tests of his usual business procedures. To a relative of dismal business history who wished to open a retail shop, Kempner decided that "I have no objection to lending you a few hundred dollars to further your business. But I am not willing to take your judgment in the matter. You will have to wait until I . . . convince myself . . . that the business you propose to invest this money in is the proper business. Whilst I am anxious to assist you I am altogether adverse of putting my money in jeopardy. Again I will advise you to work [at what] you are doing for at least six months longer.[43]

Another relative-applicant for a loan (twenty-five thousand dollars

41. Letter to Heidenheimer, Oct. [?], ca. 1890, no. 486, Kempner Letterpress Book.

42. Letters to J. W. Hall, Dec. 18, 1890, and to Mrs. P. Widman, July 11, 1890, nos. 4867, 484, Kempner Letterpress Book.

43. Letter to "Dave," Sept. 12, 1884, no. 215, Kempner Letterpress Book.

this time) with which to start a wholesale business received his uncle's flat negative response. The nephew, Kempner wrote the youth, had "altogether inadequate [experience] for a wholesale business . . . Yet I am will to help you to do something for yourself whenever you find a small country business which is already established say to the extent of [$]15,000."[44]

Kempner admired young male relations who, like himself, were willing to learn trades and businesses, to open "an apple stand or [carry] a bundle on your shoulder" in order to accumulate enough capital for the next upward steps. And Kempner, who wrote of a troublesome nonrelative business associate, "If he is honest he will act honest," also expected of relatives no lower ethicality in dealing with the world in general but especially with himself.[45]

To the deep distress of this intensely family-oriented, principled businessman, not all of his young relatives shared his own standards. The most troubling to Kempner were nephews Jake Cohen (not related to the rabbi) and Isaac and Julius Markowitz.

Cohen emigrated from Germany to Galveston in the late 1870s. Kempner's sponsorship won him quick entrance into moneyed business and social circles, but accusers charged that Cohen exploited these connections for dishonest ends. Exposed and indicted by Galveston County for obtaining money under false pretenses, Cohen fled to Germany.

Kempner's distress was acute. In tight Galveston society the miscreant's deeds, he wrote Cohen, were "dark clouds . . . which you have placed upon your character here . . . painful wounds which you have so cruelly inflicted in [the] bosoms of your most near and dear." He counseled Cohen to write to every Texas victim with promises to repay all relevant sums, and he committed himself to provide Cohen with up to 50 percent of the considerable total, but with a stipulation: Cohen must keep Kempner's generosity secret. "I do not wish anyone here to know that I am helping you," he wrote.[46]

Kempner helped this engaging but disturbing relative primarily by making him a resident agent in Germany for cottonseed-oil cakes.

44. Letter to Julius Markowitz, Feb. 26, 1886, no. 384, Kempner Letterpress Book.

45. First quotation in Tinsley, "Select Letters," p. 35; second in Kempner, letter to W. Simpson, Mar. 13, 1885, no. 265, Kempner Letterpress Book.

46. Letter to Jake Cohen, Mar. 17, 1884, nos. 113–15, Kempner Letterpress Book.

Once Cohen drew large sums (thirty-five hundred dollars or more) on his uncle's name without prior consultation with Galveston. To Kempner's dismay and slow anger, his frequent and lengthy exhortations to the unstable youth to reform elicited only expressions of hurt surprise from Germany. "Really," Kempner replied in turn, "your letter deserves no answer. You seem to be surprised that [I] have doubted your veracity. You certainly do know that I have cause for such."[47]

Then in early 1886, Kempner learned that Cohen had been reverting to practices in Germany like those that had forced him to flee Texas. Reciting the facts, Kempner, still with seemingly endless patience and with added sadness, advised him now "to close up your affairs and get ready to go to America, England, France or any other country that you decide upon" but not to Galveston or anywhere in Texas, where the fraud indictment pended. Its mere existence condemned Cohen "in the estimation of the respectable people." If again in Texas, Cohen and his wife would at best be ostracized socially. Kempner could not face the foreseeable strains on himself:

> I am getting old and gray, have my family to bring up and I cannot allow them [to be] sacrificed and disgraced. Under these circumstances you must look for a new country and rely on yourself. America is a large territory. . . . This you will doubtless consider poor advice and consultation from an uncle. Under the circumstances it is all I can do. I am trying to do my duty toward my near relatives and if I fail to do so, it is an error of my head not of my heart.

But if at last convinced of Cohen's perfidy Kempner could still not cast him off. "I think I have done my duty," the older man concluded, "and might be persuaded to do more if I could see how it would do you good without [further] injury to myself and my family."[48]

While Kempner wrestled with Cohen in distant Germany (in the early 1890s Cohen settled down in a German importing firm not connected to H. Kempner), he endured also the distasteful habits of other nephews resident in America, the brothers Markowitz (one of the latter not to be confused with Kempner's oldest son, also nicknamed "Ike"). He employed both Markowitzes in Saint Louis as salesmen for the Marx and Kempner partnership during its last years, complaining re-

47. July 30, 1884, no. 180, and see nos. 172, 202, 277, and 279, Kempner Letterpress Book. Tinsley, ed., "Select Letters," p. 21, omits the quoted sentences.
48. Entry, Feb. 26, 1886, no. 382, Kempner Letterpress Book.

petitively about their swollen expense accounts and Ike Markowitz's quick temper, which antagonized subordinates and customers. Ever attempting to keep peace in the family, Kempner wrote in mid-1883: "Just got a letter from Dave [another Kempner relative on the Markowitz staff] stating that he was forced to quit you. What is the cause[?] Now Ike are you not acting hastily with Dave[?] . . . I know your disposition. Please reconsider and do what is good. No hurt feelings ought to dictate."[49]

Matters worsened. The Markowitzes were persistently sluggish in repaying personal loans and business bills. "*You [must] pay . . . your notes as they mature[!]*" Kempner exploded to them in May, 1884. Subsequently, Ike Markowitz placed his patient uncle in what Kempner worried was "a fearful predicament." Kempner had to cover Ike's note for two thousand dollars, almost without notice. "God knows where this $2,000 is to come from," Kempner scolded in August, 1884; "You are treating me shamefully to place me in this hot water." Then, in early 1886, just as Kempner was buying out Marx, Ike Markowitz requested a loan of ten thousand dollars. It was the worst possible time, Kempner grumbled, but, as the nephew had foreseen, he extended the money.[50]

But even Kempner's avuncular forbearance had limits. In early 1887 as Kempner was completing negotiations that brought him the Marx interests and the solo entity of H. Kempner, Kempner's bank presented him with a note on himself that Ike Markowitz had signed, for five hundred dollars, apparently to allow the younger man to indulge in a speculation. "I will not pay it," the angry uncle informed his nephew. but the younger man peppered Kempner with repeated pleas to back this now-overdue note. Kempner's growing irritation shadowed his response:

> You ought not to expect me to stay here [to] work continuously and honor your debts — at random. You ought not to be in any such condition; you ought to be able to be worth $75–100,000 today. [You] are young and more able to work than I am and yet I do more work in a week than you do in 12 months. This is a free country and you

49. To Ike Markowitz, July 28, 1883, no. 16, Kempner Letterpress Book. On Cohen, Tinsley, ed., "Select Letters," p. 43.

50. Letters to Ike Markowitz, May 9, Aug. 20, 1884, nos. 145, 159; to Julius Markowitz, Feb. 26, 1886, no. 384, all in Kempner Letterpress Book.

are doing as you please. . . . So far as I am concerned I have done all I could to help you out of the present condition you are in. . . . I have a wife, 6 children, and my parents, 3 sisters with their children to care for and many others which I do not care to enumerate. This [is] enough.[51]

But despite his strong words, Kempner was incurably vulnerable to family pressures and relatives' demands, however outrageous and overextended. He covered Markowitz's note after all. Kempner could only have been more vexed and saddened when the barrage of demands from the brothers resumed. Nevertheless, in a sad letter a few months later Kempner returned to a favored theme: Cohen and the Markowitzes were more victims than offenders. The latter two men had developed "habits and poisend [*sic*] ideas . . . in St. Louis." Therefore, he recommended relocation to frontierlike California, a place in a state of development analogous to eastern Texas when he arrived there. In such a region strivers could still start with a peddler's pack or a modest produce cart. But his nephews must abandon notions of "an easy position such as drum[m]er" and of "silk lined clothes without a dollar in your pockets."

Perhaps this locational rationale calmed Kempner, for he offered both Markowitzes summer jobs in Galveston with his now-solo cotton house, H. Kempner. They could solicit cotton consignments and keep relevant books, but under his supervision. "My reasons for offering you this was to keep you doing something instead of staying at the . . . Hotel as I know you are not able to support such life . . . [N]either am I able or willing to sup[p]ort my nephews who are more able to work than I am in such fine style. You can come [to Texas] if you want to." And he enclosed two hundred dollars.[52]

For whatever reasons the Markowitzes remained in Saint Louis, becoming coffee wholesalers, surely with Kempner's aid. H. Kempner did buy some of that commodity annually from them for its ongoing if diminishing wholesale grocery operations. Perhaps only these erratic relatives kept Kempner in the food business. But as always with the Markowitzes, the course of commerce ran anything but smoothly. In the spring of 1892 a new recession slowed the pace of

51. Letter to Ike Markowitz, Feb. 10, 1887, nos. 409–10, Kempner Letterpress Book.

52. To Ike Markowitz, May, 1887, in Tinsley, ed., "Select Letters," pp. 34–35.

business nationally. H. Kempner found itself burdened with more than eight thousand sacks of coffee, for Harris had helped his nephews out by overstocking. Much of the surplus would have to be sold at a loss, he reported.

Just at this unpropitious time when Kempner's health was also seriously declining, the Markowitzes popped up again with a proposal to establish a coffee-roasting business in Galveston. Not a bad idea, Kempner replied, but wrong in timing and proposed location. "Business is really bad . . . All southern states are in [a] no good fix," he wrote. Furthermore, the Markowitz brothers were shipping him low-grade coffee, which did not sell. "[Y]ou do not follow instructions," he complained. But Kempner concluded resignedly that "of course, we must take things as they come."[53]

Kempner's evident sense of weary resignation concerning his few rarely-do-well relatives may have reflected his failing health. To balance, he knew also that in less than a decade since he had gone solo, H. Kempner was well structured, soundly financed, and very profitable. Even in the backwash of the economic depression of the late 1880s he was able proudly to decline offers of loan funds from distant bankers who now sought his accounts.[54] What a long way he had come since Cold Springs!

And if Kempner sometimes felt old and, increasingly, fatigued, in the late 1880s he still impressed outsiders as a vigorous and handsome man. At least one woman perceived him so in excessive terms, in his opinion. "I cannot accept your kind invitation to call on you neither can I sanction your calling on me at my office for the purpose of bringing me flowers," he wrote his admirer. "I am a married man and you madam [are] a married lady."[55]

Wholly and happily married, Kempner's immediate family came first among his concerns. Perhaps his bitter, recurring disappointments in some relatives inspired him to hold his older sons to stern schedules

53. Tinsley, ed., "Select Letters," pp. 43–44, plus additional paragraphs he did not reproduce, nos. 501–506, in Kempner Letterpress Book. Even in 1929, the Kempners were still aiding the Markowitzes, by "straightening out tax matters in re Ike Markowitz Estate" (J. Seinsheimer, letter to Rabbi Cohen, July 10, 1929, Box 3M247, Cohen Papers).

54. Letter to L. Fellman, Nov. 2, 1891, no. 497, Kempner Letterpress Book.

55. To Mrs. J. O. Hyman (no known relation to the author), Jan. 21, 1889, no. 463, Kempner Letterpress Book.

of schooling and working vacations. He preached individual responsibility to them at every opportunity. Kempner wanted no indolents among his children! And how pleased he must have been by his older sons' evident industry, intelligence, attractive features and personalities, and responsiveness to parental guidance.

His wife and children, boys and girls alike, knew him to be a far less unbending person than outsiders perceived from his public demeanor. The news of his mother's death, in Europe, in 1888, evoked his "patent and intense" grief, which his wife tried to assuage. At home "he relaxed his iron grip over his environment, permitting Eliza to construct her own matriarchal domain," family lore suggests. And it was as a homebound matriarch that Eliza, who was to live until 1947, was remembered by her children and intimates as a combination "Jewish mother" and Southern lady.[56]

Both Harris and Eliza had long since settled in as lifetime residents of the Island City. They had found it and all America to be an open community, one that allowed Harris to wrest material well-being from his labors. They did not live on America's margins, become entrapped in the South's often choking webs of social relationships, or choose between identities as Americans or Jews.[57] Prosperous and content, the Kempners were a happy family as the 1890s advanced.

56. Thompson, "History," p. 10.
57. Greene, *American Immigrant Leaders*.

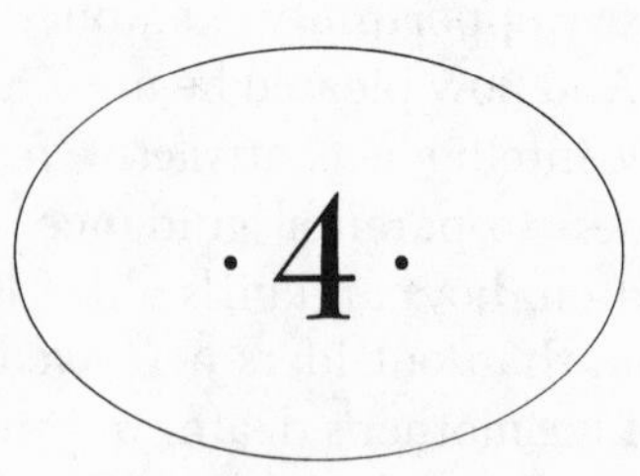

Tradition and Assimilation

UNLIKE OTHER JEWISH EX-CONFEDERATES, such as Judah Benjamin, who remained determinedly uninvolved in traditional Jewish religious life yet who would not convert to Christianity, Harris Kempner was ever faithful to his religion. His chosen residence of Galveston was sophisticated and unhostile to his family and coreligionists, so Kempner had no need to put his pride in being a Jew to the test.

Many new Jewish immigrants had, like Kempner, chosen to settle far from the crowded northeastern cities that were the primary ports of entry. This dispersal made both necessary and easier the immigrants' adaptation to American life.[1] Everywhere in America Judaism faced challenges from the effects of immigrants' spectacular career successes and from Enlightenment-generated rationality that weakened the attractions of Orthodoxy. In Europe rabbis were little concerned with non-Jewish political or social issues. Externalities were unimportant; ritual was preeminent. By 1860–61, however, when young Harris Kempner was hearing rebel muster-drums in Texas, Rabbi Isaac Mayer Wise of Cincinnati was already emerging as a proponent of "Reform" Judaism, one that invited externalities and change into Jewish life. Wise helped to establish Hebrew Union College in Cincinnati, and he and its graduates became major evangelists among the American rabbinate for cultural adaptation and secular assimilation, a position that in America came to be known as Reform Judaism.

Wise's devotees spread the message that American Jews needed to "reform" Judaism in order to win emancipation from ghetto ways.

1. Mayer, "German-Jewish Identity in 19th Century America," in *The American Jewish Experience*, p. 45.

They should embrace secular, natural-rights views and laissez-faire ideas. "The Jew must become an American in order to gain the proud self-consciousness of the free-born man," Wise preached on one occasion. On another, he argued that "we must be not only American citizens but Americans through and through outside the synagogue."[2]

Orthodox and Conservative critics of Reform Judaism argued that assimilation would result in apathy, apostasy, and marriages of Jews to non-Jews. And indeed such drifts from Judaism were occurring, not only in New York and Cincinnati but in minute Galveston as well. In 1898 Galveston lawyer Leon Levi mourned about coreligionists who were marrying Unitarians, in effect settling with the Lord "at fifty cents on the dollar."[3] The secular benefits of wondrously open American society were softening religious cohesion.

Eliza and Harris held their children to their Jewish heritage, by the late 1880s opting for the Reform approach to rituals. Kempner found the Reform appeal increasingly strong because it seemed to fit with and dignify the facts of his own life. Although he always admired Europe's culture, Kempner never forgot how even in its most secularized and defeudalized nations, including Germany, Jews were kept on the margins of society. The American South, despite its reputation for racial and religious bigotry, in idiosyncratic situations provided at least its most favored Jews with a warm and elastic environment. Galveston was one such idiosyncrasy.[4]

When Harris Kempner settled on the Island in the late 1860s, the city's boosters boasted of the diverse religions of its residents. Jews, who since before the Civil War had been meeting in private homes for religious services, determined to build a synagogue, and their fund-raising activities and other events became popular, secularized activities. Construction of Temple B'nai Israel began in 1870, but for some years the congregation continued to be without a resident ordained rabbi. Elected presidents of the temple officiated at ceremonies until Rabbi Abraham Blum assumed charge.

2. Wise quoted in Silberman, *A Certain People*, p. 43; and see Jick, *The Americanization of the Synagogue, 1820–1870*, chap. 1; Gurock, "The Emergence of the American Synagogue," in *The American Jewish Experience*, p. 193.

3. Levi, letter to Cohen, July 29, 1898, Box 3M220, Cohen Papers; and see Kraut, "Reform Judaism and Unitarian Challenge," in *The American Jewish Experience*, pp. 89–97.

4. Marcus and Peck, eds., *The American Rabbinate*, passim; and Proctor and Schmeier, eds., *Jews of the South*, p. 78 and passim, are invaluable.

During Blum's tenure temple politics became increasingly disruptive. Tensions flared over the question of whether the congregation should support a Sunday school or mixed choir and whether Blum should give English lectures rather than Hebrew sermons. The abandonment of Hebrew was as large a step for Jews to take in the 1870s as the one Roman Catholics had to face about abandoning Latin in the 1960s.

The move toward Reform Judaism hastened. In 1875 the congregation argued the permissibility of men praying without wearing hats or skullcaps. Unable to resolve the question pacifically, the congregation's board president, a canny pro-Reform tactician, referred it to Cincinnati's Rabbi Wise, who offered a persuasive doctrine favoring hatlessness. Temple B'nai Israel records state that "at this same meeting, it was voted that this congregation should join Wise's American Hebrew Congregation [of Reformed Temples], thus becoming one of the first members of . . . [Cincinnati's Hebrew Union] College affiliates."[5]

The unrest in the Galveston congregation was not limited to issues of reform. Rabbi Blum was apparently both undiplomatic and quarrelsome. The self-governing lay board of the temple heard complaint after complaint about Blum, finally admitting in 1883 "that there is a great aversion amongst many of the members to Mr. Blum's reelection as a minister and that this would create further dissention." In 1888, fresh from advanced rabbinical studies with Wise in Cincinnati, Rabbi Henry Cohen assumed charge of the Galveston temple. Cohen and his Reform proclivities meshed well with the Galveston congregation, including the Kempner family. He was to be a significant figure in their lives for more than half a century. Hyman Block, cotton traffic manager for H. Kempner for six decades, came to the heart of the matter: "You can hardly get into the Kempners without talking about Dr. Cohen."[6]

The "Jewish Archbishop"

London-born in 1863, Henry Cohen, like Harris Kempner, had to claw his way upward from poverty, though he used different means.

5. L. J. Stillpass, "Our Temple Highlights and Sidelights" (manuscript, 1952), Kempner Papers.

6. Hyman Block, interview with L. Marchiafava, June 6, 1981, RLA.

Rabbi Henry M. Cohen, ca. 1950s (Courtesy Rosenberg Library Archives, Galveston, Texas)

A youthful "almoner" (clerk) of London's Jewish Board of Guardians, a charitable association, Cohen distributed tickets for bread and other necessities to the poor, in evenings attending "Jews' College" classes to prepare himself to be a rabbi. After ordination in England's rigidly Orthodox rabbinate, in 1883 Cohen went to a rural South African synagogue set in the midst of the chaotic diamond rush. Seriously wounded in one battle with Zulu warriors, Cohen recovered and went to a small congregation in the West Indies. Though smitten by Kingston's ocean-girt beauty, Cohen grew restive about the endless quarrels about ritual between factions of the congregation.[7]

7. Nathan and Cohen, *The Man Who Stayed in Texas*, pp. 8–11, 39–53; see also Henry Cohen, letter to Rabbi S. Woolf, July 10, 1946, Box 3M288, Cohen Papers.

The Reform movement in America began to attract his attention as the disputes in his Kingston congregation increased and as he considered the prospect of a lifetime as a rabbi in England, where he would be under the thumb of the theologically standfast chief rabbi in that country. After a year in Kingston Cohen accepted a rabbinate in Woodville, Mississippi, in the heart of the Deep South's "cotton kingdom." Good reports about Cohen's diplomacy (he engineered a compromise on Saturday business closings in Woodville) reached Texas via the cotton brokers' communications network. After leaving Woodville and undertaking advanced studies in Cincinnati, Cohen made the move to Galveston. Upon his arrival in 1888, he put his deft diplomacy and passion for justice into action, action that continued well into the next century. From Woodrow Wilson he earned the accolade "first citizen of Texas," and the Roman Catholic archbishop of Galveston, J. M. Kirwin, called Cohen "the archbishop of Texas."[8]

In Galveston Cohen found a relatively sophisticated congregation. Substantial numbers of influential younger members, like Harris Kempner, were disposed to Reform approaches, but most were still fence-sitting. Cohen perceived accurately that excessive pressure or speed toward Reform would rend the little Jewish community. And so the patient, learned, and swiftly educable immigrant moved prudently, a manner deeply pleasing to Kempner.[9]

Among his Galveston congregants, Cohen especially liked and cultivated the Kempners, who became one of Cohen's primary sources of financial support. Eliza was to lend the temple money to buy a Galveston residence for Cohen, holding the generous mortgage herself, and in 1899 she presented the property to the temple as a gift. Both Eliza and Cohen lived well into the twentieth century, and the latter maintained a near-avuncular attitude of affection and concern for the Kempners.[10]

8. Nathan and Cohen, *The Man Who Stayed in Texas*, p. 74, and see pp. 53–73; Wise, letter to Henry Luce, Mar. 16, 1933, Box 3M255, and Cohen, letter to Woolf, July 10, 1946, Box 3M288, Cohen Papers.

9. Nathan and Cohen, *The Man Who Stayed in Texas*, p. 74.

10. For some reason Eliza's 1899 deed to Congregation B'nai Israel was unrecorded, probably because of defective municipal archival practices. Lawyer Marion Levy discovered the flaw in 1943, and he notified Ike Kempner of the clouded title. Ike searched H. Kempner office files, found the original deed, and recorded it, half a century late, in early 1944. See Levy's memo to Ike Kempner, Apr. 11, 1945, attached to a copy of the 1899 warranty deed, in DWK Corre-

Rabbi Cohen's Sunday school class, 1895 (Courtesy Temple B'nai Israel, Galveston, Texas)

Cohen's large influence in Galveston, particularly but not exclusively on Island Jews, stemmed in part from his view of Reform Judaism. He saw in it the call for the greatest possible degree and frequency of interaction between Gentiles and Jews on both secular and religious occasions. Through his numerous enduring friendships with Protestant ministers and Archbishop Kirwin, he worked indefatigably toward that end, while maintaining what Harris Kempner's son Ike described in 1908 as "the thorough harmony and sympathy that prevails between Rabbi and congregation."[11]

---

spondence, 1919–1957, Box 41, File #80-003, Kempner Papers. See also, Stillpass, "Our Temple Highlights." On the loan, Box 8, and see File #61, Kempner Papers; on avuncularity, Rabbi E. Calish, letter to Cohen, Feb. 14, 1901, and IHK to Cohen, July 19, 1902, Box 3M222 and 223, respectively, Cohen Papers.

11. Quotation in Ike Kempner, letter to Cohen, Apr. 10, 1908, Box 3M228, Cohen Papers. Other details, Cohen, letter to Rabbi J. L. Levy, Sept. 10, 1894, Box 3M218, and J. Koen to Cohen, July 17, 1900, Box 3M221; Police Chief John Rowan, letter to same, Feb. 27, 1903, Box 3M223, Cohen Papers.

Nevertheless, Cohen consistently refused to officiate at marriages of Jews to non-Jews, being willing only to give his "tacit consent after I have begged and implored" against the cross-sectarian union. Combined with apostasies, intermarriages would obliterate Judaism in only a few generations, he worried. "The Jews have a mission in the world. . . . They live for a purpose," Cohen preached, to protest "against everything unjust."[12]

Assimilation and Southern Race Traditions

Race inequality was not labeled as "unjust" on either Kempner's or Cohen's agendas. White-on-top race hierarchy was not even a dilemma to the great majority of white Texans and white Americans in general. If Kempner or Cohen saw a contradiction between the sweet and wide access to opportunity that he and other Jews enjoyed in America, and the reshrunken, sour, narrow paths that blacks could traverse, they were untroubled in mind about it and left the perception unrecorded.[13] Kempner practiced an "American creed" that glorified opportunity, but not yet for everyone.

In tolerating and sometimes profiting from race inequalities, Kempner continued a long tradition among southern Jews. A few prominent Jews had been substantial slaveowners, finding justification in the Old Testament for their ways. Since emancipation, Jews in Dixie had helped to readjust state and local laws and customs to keep blacks substantially less equal in their freedom. However paternalistic toward their black employees, Harris Kempner and Rabbi Cohen unquestionably were, like many other southern Reform Jews, comforted by the consistently critical attitude of Rabbi Wise against activist race-equalitarians. Wise feared that Jewish civil liberty advocates in the South would trigger outbreaks of anti-Semitism there, where their small numbers left them particularly vulnerable.[14]

More to his credit, however, Cohen did define contract prison labor (see chapter 8), a system afflicting mostly blacks, as unjust. And through the writer "O. Henry," also a Texas resident in Cohen's early days, the rabbi first became interested in rehabilitating paroled and dis-

12. Cohen, undated letter to editor of *Jewish Exponent* (typescript), Box 3M325, Cohen Papers.
13. Litwack, "Trouble in Mind," *Journal of American History*, p. 317.
14. Shankman, "Friend or Foe?" in *Turn to the South*, pp. 105–109.

charged prisoners, a concern which he would develop over a half century and one in which he would involve the Kempners.[15] Although Harris and later Ike Kempner would disagree with Cohen on the subject of contract prison labor, the Kempners did not become alienated from their energetic minister.[16] Instead, the rabbi infected the Kempners with his passion for social justice, which Wise had helped implant in him.

Developing the Tradition of Social Justice

With the Reform imperative of expanding the synagogue from a weekend resort for ritual to a center of daily beneficent interactions, Cohen initiated in Galveston programs whereby first he and then members of his congregation visited the city's poor, jobless, sick, homeless, and prisoners. Early becoming convinced that lengthy prison sentences only corrupted salvageable felons, Jews among them, Cohen exploited all connections in efforts to place in stable jobs parolees and convicts who had completed their sentences. The relentlessly job-seeking rabbi made Kempner's capitulatory phrases well known in Galveston: "He [Kempner] thought that he could find a place for the man," or "in about a week they'd need to put on some more night watchmen."

Sometimes the rabbi stormed about injustices that Harris and Ike Kempner simply could not see. In one instance Cohen railed about "prison shoes" the state gave to prisoners upon release. The rabbi argued that the shoes signaled to every police officer that a miscreant was loose and bore watching and that they prevented the wearers from finding employment. Worst of all were the "state farms" where inmates toiled like slaves for the state or as leased labor for private contractors like the Kempners. At a non-Kempner site Cohen had personally observed "bull whip[s] . . . dipped in wet sand to inflict additional pain." And child marriages! In the 1880s when Cohen arrived in Texas a girl of ten or twelve could legally "consent" to marriage. "That was a terrible thing," Cohen insisted. Such children "ought

15. Stephen Wise, letter to Henry Luce (cc: H. Cohen), Mar. 16, 1933, attached to biographical sketch of Cohen, Box 3M255, Cohen Papers.

16. With one exception. In the 1940s, a lasting coolness developed between Dan Kempner and Cohen over the latter's recommendations of third parties for Kempner jobs. See their exchanges, Oct., 1942, Box 3M382, Cohen Papers.

to be playing with dolls." Cohen and the Kempners lobbied successfully to raise the age of consent to eighteen, an effort they had to extend over years.[17]

A Talmudic scholar of some note, having published several books and many sermons, Cohen had a command of foreign languages that was a special asset in cosmopolitan, commercial Galveston. Welfare agencies often referred to Cohen stranded foreign tourists and jailed sailors, and visiting foreign dignitaries usually found the rabbi in company with Harris and later, Ike Kempner, acting as masters of ceremonies in their honor.

Such demands on Cohen tore him away from his books and Kempner from his ledgers. The rabbi's library constituted one of Texas' three largest private collections, and Kempner borrowed and used many volumes. But if the two men shared significant areas of interest, their visible differences were extreme. Kempner always clad himself as a gentleman of property and standing; Cohen grew increasingly careless of his appearance. He favored white suits but spoiled the traditionally elegant southern costume by using the cuffs of his shirt and coat for recording memoranda, overstriking each reminder of his crowded daily agendas-to-the-distressed as he completed an errand. Kempner walked sedately along Galveston's downtown streets. Cohen raced perilously on his wobbling bicycle through the bustling vehicular traffic, quickly becoming a widely known and admired "character" of the city.

And not only there. In the wake of the cataclysmic Great Storm of 1900 that all but devastated Galveston (chapter 6), Cohen would achieve national prominence as a major organizer of relief and rehabilitation without regard to the sufferers' creed or race, a distinction applicable also to Ike Kempner, who worked in closest concert with the rabbi. Rabbi Stephen Wise noted later that Cohen was also "a close friend of the late [philanthropist] Jacob H. Schiff and [in 1907–14] was largely responsible for the success of . . . [the] Galveston Immigrant experiment." In that "experiment," as will be shown (chapter 9), Cohen, again in concert with Ike and other Kempners, would exploit all available sources of emergency and long-term good

17. Nathan and Cohen, *The Man Who Stayed in Texas*, pp. 102–103, 128–29, 231–32, 261–78.

works in an extraordinarily ambitious effort in humanitarian social engineering.[18]

Rabbi Wise frequently invited Cohen to lecture at the Hebrew Union College and the Synagogue and School Extension Center of the Union of American Hebrew Congregations. Cohen's visits to Cincinnati coincided so often with those the Kempners made to family reunions that officials of the college and center came to expect the rabbi to appear there with the cotton merchant. Whether in Ohio or Texas, the Kempners proudly applauded news of the distinctions their rabbi earned. For example, Cohen's sermon-essay, "A Call to Justice," probably delivered initially in the late 1880s, was still eliciting commendations when it reappeared in expanded form in the early 1930s. The Hebrew Union College awarded Cohen an honorary doctorate (1924), and in 1930 he was named the most outstanding American rabbi and the only Jew on a "big ten" list of the most important American theologians. In 1933 Rabbi Stephen Wise advised *Time* publisher Henry Luce that Cohen "is first among the men of my calling in America, a singularly interesting being and genuine through and through. I know of no one alive who more abundantly deserves the title of friend to all men."[19]

In sum, the lives of the rabbi and the cotton factor's family became mutually supportive. Because they did, in their case at least, it is arguable that Mark Twain's picturesque descriptions of selfish, grasping, "Gilded Age" America may have obscured the coexistence of contrary elements in the late nineteenth and early twentieth centuries. Reform rabbis like Cohen enlisted enthusiastically in the many manifestations of a search for social justice that characterized those hectic years, and brought with them moneyed congregants like the Kempners who were bent that way in any event.

For Cohen, as for both Eliza and Harris Kempner, social justice reflected a vision of America as liberator and secularizer. Cohen expressed this view in his popular sermon on Americanism, which he defined as a credo "that spends itself in righteous living." Righteous, not riotous, living was the secular face of merit, a sentiment most

18. All details in Stephen Wise, letter to Henry Luce, Mar. 16, 1933.

19. Ibid.; for "big ten" list, see *Galveston Daily News*, Sept. 23, 1930; on visits, see Rabbi George Zepin, letter to Cohen, Nov. 10, 1915, Box 3M234, Cohen Papers; Cohen, "A Call to Justice," *Texas Jewish Herald*, Sept. 18, 1930.

agreeable to Kempner. Cohen pressured men and women like him and Eliza to exhibit civic virtue both by example and by active support of secular good works.

For example, in the early 1890s the Galveston Chamber of Commerce called on Cohen to press for passage of a pure milk law, which he did by writing a newspaper article on the subject and recruiting the female auxiliaries of a dozen Christian churches and the Jewish temple, Eliza among them, as lobbyists "in the interest of humanity and the protection of the homes in Galveston." Fifty years later he was still a gadfly of community uplift, telling journalists that Galveston slums were worse than any he remembered in London's Dickensian ghetto: "I cannot prescribe the remedy for this state of affairs, but the condition should be taken in hand by practical citizens, landlords among them, to the end that this unsavory status be wiped out."[20]

Kempner, who rarely invested in urban real estate, had little leverage among fellow Galvestonians who were slum landlords. But beginning around 1905 his sons and grandsons would begin to replace leased convict labor with Cohen-nominated parolees, and start also greatly to improve the quality of housing, workplace, and community in an entire small city, at Sugar Land, Texas. Common to Cohen, to Harris Kempner, and to Kempner's wife, children, and grandchildren, was the conviction that property incurred responsibilities to mitigate human suffering, not to increase it. Senseless accumulation of things denigrated the purpose of laboring for them. Ownership involved loving use of what one held.

To be sure, the careers of many self-made persons suggest that noble doctrines gave way easily to selfish denials of social responsibility. But preachers like Cohen who equated property with humanitarian sensitivity were not naive or hypocritical, and their disciples like Kempner were not merely minor Hebraic Carnegies or Pullmans. Instead, the evidence suggests the genuine dedication of the Galveston rabbi and the rising cotton trader, and the validity of these teachings in their particular time and place for both private and public values. Cohen sermonized to the Galveston congregation in 1893 that "the

20. Galveston Chamber of Commerce, letter to Cohen, May 1, 1893, and Americanism address, May 30, 1921 (draft); press release on slums, Mar. 21, 1940, all in Box 3M236, Cohen Papers; and see Mervis, "The Social Justice Movement of the American Reform Rabbis, 1890–1940" (Ph.D. diss.); Pollack, *The Just Polity*, passim.

Jew who is faithful to his creed and is governed by its laws is respected by every educated non-Jew [and] is the peer of every other citizen."[21]

This irrepressible rabbi and the formidable financial and civic resources of his faithful adherents headed long catalogs of Jewish and non-Jewish welfare agencies, educational institutions, and cultural associations. For Eliza and Harris Kempner, Cohen's tenure in Galveston began so to enrich the place that they came to dream of generations of their descendants retaining lifelong residence there.

The Vision of Family Cohesion

By the 1870s and 1880s Americans' mobility was a staple element in commentators' warnings about the impending erosion of family and society. One contemporary analyst concluded unhappily that "the American people are so restless that scarcely a generation can be traced in a single state. Few men or women reaching the noonday of life die within half a thousand miles of their birthplace. Brothers and sisters leave the parental threshold and are at once completely lost to each other, their children scarcely able to say their parents had brother or sister." But a reaction against this rootless diffusion was also growing; family and community values were being weighed against the value of mobility.

Harris Kempner's and Rabbi Cohen's careers reinforce historian Timothy Smith's argument that "studies of immigrants in cities [should] concentrate more upon the life histories of families who settled in multiethnic neighborhoods and passed rapidly into associations and activities geared to interest rather than ethnicity." As Smith surmised, families like the Kempners "later exercise[d] a mediating role among newcomers of the father's nationality."[22]

Unconsciously preparing his wife and oldest son for this role, by the late 1880s Harris Kempner, inspired by most of Cohen's preach-

21. On the sermon, Moses Dropsie, letter to Cohen, May 1, 1893, Box 3M218, Cohen Papers. See also Haskell, "Capitalism and the Origins of Humanitarian Sensibility," *American Historical Review*, p. 547; Justice Stephen Field in Butchers' Union *v.* Crescent City Co., 111 U.S. 746 (1884).

22. First quotation, Kaler, comp. *History of the [David and Cornelia] Kerr Family*, p. 1; second quotation, in Smith, "New Approaches to the History of Immigration in Twentieth-Century America," *American Historical Review*, p. 1268.

ments and by his pride in his own successes, developed aspirations that were to shape their lives and those of their descendants to the present. Chief among these aspirations was Harris Kempner's hope that the children not become expatriates from his adopted city and region, much less nation, as he and so many other Jews had been forced to do. Concerning educations, however, he saw no excuse "for a provincial training," but he wanted the children to "return to Galveston after their educations" and become a part of the community he was helping to construct.[23]

Rabbi Cohen encouraged Kempner's ambition for his male children: lifetime residence in their Island City, devoted civic responsibility as a reflection of religion, and humanistic educations, the better to appreciate the fruits of diligent business successes. Of these goals, that of family cohesion in a culturally sophisticated civic polity would dominate not only Harris but every succeeding Kempner to the present.

Assimilating the New Generations

Eliza and her husband shared the responsibility of directing their sons' religious and secular educations in line with Harris Kempner's ambition for them. They attended zealously to the boys' preparation for their bar mitzvahs and were confident that all were impressed with "the duties of the Jew to his fellow man." Seven decades after his bar mitzvah Ike remembered that some business crisis made his father miss the key ceremony, to the amusement of the congregation. Eliza was not amused.[24]

Always regretting Harris's own lack of formal education, the Kempner parents determined in gender-prejudiced manner that the boys must have the best available secular and religious educations. The parents and Rabbi Cohen closely monitored Ike's progress through the Galveston public schools, coming to fear that it was more rapid than thorough. Out of this concern, the Kempners, with Cohen's advice and support, enrolled Ike in a Catholic preparatory school, Saint Mary's, in Galveston. In Europe it was common for "emancipated"

23. E. R. Thompson, Jr., "History of H. Kempner" (manuscript), Kempner Papers, p. 11.

24. Ibid.; and see DWK, "Historical Record" (manuscript), Kempner Papers, p. 4; IHK, *Recalled Recollections*, p. 9; "I. H. Kempner Testimonial Dinner," unpaginated.

Isaac H. ("Ike") Kempner, ca. 1885 (Courtesy Leonora K. Thompson)

Jews to have their children educated in Catholic schools, which in some countries were the best available to anyone and in others were the only ones open to Jews. But the practice was and is rare among Jewish Americans.

Ike recalled that the nuns at Saint Mary's taught well but that godliness ranked too far above cleanliness. The school's bathing and toilet facilities "were ancient . . . even for the 1880s. [They] offered the temptation and excuse of my frequently skipping the compulsory weekly bath." Becoming aware of Ike's reasons for avoiding baths at school, Harris had Saint Mary's rework the boy's schedule so that between school, temple, and visits home he received adequate doses of personal hygiene as well as learning and religion. The nuns had Ike every Monday through Friday. Each Saturday, accompanied by the aging black governess "Aunt" Eveline or the family's coachman, Ike went first to Temple B'nai Israel and then "for a thorough cleansing . . . at the Turkish baths." Excused from Saint Mary's religious services, Ike returned to the temple for Sunday school classes.

When Ike's graduation from Saint Mary's neared, his parents decided to send him to board at Bellevue High School in Virginia. By reputation it had a pipeline into a southern "ivy league" of colleges, especially William and Mary and the University of Virginia. Ike received competent instruction at Bellevue, but the physical facilities were even less comfortable than those at the Galveston school. Four Bellevue students shared each log cottage. Only a wood stove heated each cabin in the often-bitter winter months, a trial to a boy from the semitropical Gulf Coast. Each youth took his turn stoking the fire. Baths were optional, and the facilities consisted of large wash tubs. Ike was often lonely and homesick, especially when learning of the deaths of two of his infant brothers and of Aunt Eveline and also at Passover and the Christmas holiday season if distance prevented him from enjoying family reunions, a deprivation mitigated only partly by visiting instead his mother's Cincinnati family. But summers meant Texas, close family, and beach parties, plus, as the boy advanced through his teens, increasingly responsible office work at Marx and Kempner and then at H. Kempner. There Ike felt the excitement of communication with distant and therefore romantic places and of complex contracts involving what seemed to the boy to be incredibly large sums of money.[25]

By the early 1890s both Ike and Dan were old enough to indicate their high academic capabilities and, in working vacations in their father's office, their aptitudes for commerce. The decades-long trouble Harris had endured with unruly and grasping younger relatives concerning their undisciplined work habits and unethical business practices was affecting the Kempner boys in the form of their father's enhanced determination to instill higher standards in his children.

As the oldest son, Ike received the fullest share of parental surveillance, trust, and also pressure about fundamental approaches to life

25. IHK, *Recalled Recollections*, pp. 7–10.

and labor. An example of the trust the father offered Ike in order to encourage the youth's sense of responsibility, just when problems caused by the troublesome relatives were greatest, was the extraordinary privilege, at Bellevue, of a credit line on H. Kempner with merchants in Lynchburg. His father entrusted him also with cash and checks with which to pay the school, to reimburse one of the faculty for small amounts advanced to the boy, and to purchase rail tickets and deal with other expenses for vacation trips home.[26]

Concerning surveillance, during their secondary school and college years Ike and Dan (the latter followed Ike's educational route to Virginia) were unaware that their father regularly and comprehensively monitored both their classwork and extracurricular behavior through their teachers and through Rabbi Cohen's connections with Virginia ministers. In later years all the Kempner children were to treasure belatedly acquired evidence of their father's unfailing love and concern. The warm, unharassing quality of this monitoring emerges in a letter of December, 1888, that Harris wrote to the Bellevue School's headmaster.

> I . . . note that his [Ike's] course of instruction includes only the following, viz: Latin, German, mathematics, orthography, and Bible lessons. . . . Does he not study Geography, History, Rhetoric, or Composition, etc.? Please let me know everything he studies even to the books he is using. I want to know what my boy is doing. I know he is at a good school and believe you are taking all pains with him; still you will appreciate a father's interest and anxiety and advise me fully about my son. Above all things I want him to have a good substantial foundation, plenty of useful knowledge, and [be] well prepared and fitted for the practical duties of life.[27]

Ike graduated from Bellevue in 1889 and entered Washington and Lee University. He did well in classes, organized a Texas Club (with only a dozen members) at the college, and came to enjoy especially the company of fellow students Newton D. Baker, John W. Davis, and Miles Poindexter, youths who became, respectively, Woodrow Wil-

26. Harris Kempner, letters to Ike, Jan. 5, 1887, Mar.[?], 1888, nos. 411, 473, Kempner Letterpress Book.

27. "I. H. Kempner Testimonial Dinner"; Tinsley, ed., "Select Letters of Harris Kempner," *Gulf Coast Historical Association Publications*, pp. 33–34; Rabbi E. Calish, letter to Cohen, Feb. 14, 1901, Box 3M222, Cohen Papers.

son's secretary of war, United States solicitor general and a presidential candidate, and Oregon's United States senator.

In his junior year Ike advised his father that he was thinking about studying law. Harris sought the counsel of one of Ike's professors in a letter reflecting the father's overall purposes combined with his respect for the subject expert. It is a letter of a sort that academics welcome but too rarely receive, and it offers further insight into this seemingly narrow-focused businessman.

Kempner informed the teacher that he preferred Ike to receive first a broad general education before plunging into the vocational curriculum of the law. "When . . . [Ike] comes out to take his place among men I want him fitted for any position to which he may aspire or be called," Harris wrote. "I prefer that he read law, but at the proper time. He seems to think for himself that he is now ready. What is your opinion? Is his general education now finished?" Kempner assured the professor that adequate funds existed to support Ike though further studies of whatever nature. "I want your plain views on the subject & your careful recommendation," Kempner continued: "If Ikey were your son, under the circumstances, what would you wish him to do? . . . I ask of you that after you have concluded what to say to me that you take him aside, show him this letter, or not, as you think proper, and tell him what you shall have advised me, . . . and induce him to your way of thinking about it."

The professor's response reassured Kempner. Ike entered the law school, enjoying especially the classes taught by constitutional specialist John Randolph Tucker.[28]

While Ike labored in the law, his younger brother Dan entered nearby Bellevue High School in turn, and their father now maintained caring oversight of both boys' progress and welfare. Dan, reporting to his father on his improving academic progress in the fall, 1893, semester, received this Thanksgiving Day response: "Very glad to hear from you and especially today. I trust that you will turn out to be such a man as will justly cause me to Thank God for blessing me with such a son as you are—We are all well and hope that you will keep good health and strength to enable you to do your full duty. I will

28. Letter to Prof. G. W. C. Lee, May 22, 1891, in Tinsley, ed., "Select Letters," p. 41. See also IHK, *Recalled Recollections*, pp. 11–13.

advise Ikey not to leave Virginia for the holidays but remain there [perhaps to tutor Dan?]." And, characteristically, Harris signed this warm letter, "Your father, H. Kempner."

Two months later, Dan learned from his father that the parent had "ordered made for you a spring suit – nothing of interest to report – we are all well. Please write often and do your full duty." But Harris, perhaps aware now of his own declining health, closed this letter more warmly: "With love I am your father H. Kempner."[29] As Ike anticipated his twenty-first birthday and graduation from college in early 1894, Harris solemnized the occasion, writing at impressive length and with warmth to this soon-to-be "man among men" of his hopes for Ike's longevity, success, moderation, and ongoing learning: "Not only in years, but in education you are at the threshold of man's estate. Preparatory textbooks are to be laid aside for advanced culture and the experience and responsibilities of life. You have our hopes and prayers that you may be a useful man always honorable and distinguished in your day and generation."[30]

Ike was homesick. The fact that his father had arranged an interview for him with President Grover Cleveland at the White House in 1893 did not lessen the young man's unease. He replied that except for summer vacations spent mostly working in the father's office he had been away from home and family for eight years, missing all Christmas holidays and Passovers. Besides, he understood that his father was unwell and needed him at work.

Last Requests

Kempner responded in his patient manner, making ever more clear his goal of persuading the children to choose lifetime residences in Galveston and vicinity and to pursue careers there that might perpetuate what he was building. He appreciated his son's motives for wanting to return home at once upon graduating. But he assured Ike that he could manage the firm without his aid "for the next 2 or 2-1/2 years." Better that Ike, upon completing law school, travel abroad

29. Nov. 30, 1893, and Feb. 15, 1894, respectively, in DWK Scrapbook, 1894–1915.

30. IHK, *Recalled Recollections*, pp. 18–19.

Ike Kempner (*standing, far left*) as a student at Washington and Lee, ca. 1893–94 (Courtesy Leonora K. Thompson)

with Dan to Germany and France, remaining there until they had mastered both languages plus Spanish if possible. And then Harris restated his desire first set down on paper in the late 1880s, and now, in 1894, repeated in more specific terms: that his children, or the boys at least, find their lifelong destinies in Galveston, there to enjoy careers, marry, and raise their own families.

In his 1894 letter to Ike, Harris argued further that the sons, once returned multilingual and generally more cultured to Galveston, would therefore be more helpful in the H. Kempner business and also "the pride and honor of your parents." He wanted the boys to meet their paternal grandfather (Harris's mother had died in 1888) and aunts in German Poland and, dredging up memories from his own youth, recommended Göttingen for the German leg of the projected trip. It was, he wrote, "a beautiful city . . . [with] one of the finest universities in Europe, plenty [of] Americans residing there, and only the purest of German used there." The boys should also travel widely around Europe, he urged, to the Low Countries, Switzerland, and Great Britain: "I will gladly furnish you the means. . . . I want you educated[,] accomplished[,] refined[,] & honorable. . . . I will trust you alone that you will act like a gentleman. No one will exercise control over you."[31]

Perhaps Harris Kempner was clinging to a conviction that he would regain his former vigor and that he could spare Ike for "the next 2 or 2-1/2 years." Obviously, the father was almost desperately intent on seeing to it that Ike enjoy what his own young manhood had lacked: both formal education and a cultural "finishing."

Ike heard from Galveston that his father was concealing a serious decline in health, so he wrote home to insist on abandoning the European trip. The father, not the son, needed a vacation, Ike argued. Replying, Harris tried to reassure the young man and, perhaps, himself:

> I am now thank God in fine health[,] need no recreation, and cannot consistently leave my office for any length of time, even if you were here. I will do all in my power to meet you in New York to see you off – and if possible will bring mama and some of the children with me. You say you fear that constant work will in the course of a few years undermine my health. Now my son I am not working hard. I take very good care of myself and assure you I feel better stronger and by far more satisfied when I am at my own home and [doing] something to occupy my time. I am having more comfort . . . [in Galveston] than I can possibly get at any Hotel in the U.S. or Europe. I know you . . . will do all you can to behave yourself physically and mentally to take charge of my affairs and let . . . your mother and I have a pleasant and good time after you will have finished. I am not an old man. I am in the very prime of life strong and healthy and can very well wait until you are 24 years old. . . . [G]o to Europe.

Perhaps because the depth of his son's concern required the further effort, Harris returned to the reasons why the projected trip was so important:

> The object of my desire to send you to Europe is simply that you are quite young now. I can easily do without your aid for the next three years. During this time I want you to enjoy yourself by seeing something of the world and at the same [time] educate yourself[,] polish up, so as to enable you after you are 24 or 25 years old to

31. Ibid., pp. 10–11; "IHK Testimonial Dinner."

> help me to take care [of] what I now own and so that I can with confidence leave matters in your charge when I go away during the summer months.

It was time to close. "I know of nothing more to write. We are all well. Business bad [and cotton] shrinkage heavy. With love I am y[ou]r father H. Kempner."[32]

That was Harris Kempner's furthest concession to his physical problems – a grudging willingness to schedule long vacations away from Galveston's grueling summer weather once Ike, perfected by exposure to Europe, could be deemed mature enough to take seasonal charge of H. Kempner's complex operations.

Meanwhile, Harris was not ignoring son Dan. In mid-March, 1895, he sent the high school student, also in Virginia, a ten-dollar check plus another of many admonitions to "do your full duty" and "graduate with honors." Later that month, anticipating by a few days the boy's seventeenth birthday, Kempner congratulated Dan, praying also that God would grant him "a good old age, not only in years but in Education. You now have good health, and if you will take care of yourself, pursue the happy medium, you have every reason to hope that you will make a good and useful man, always honorable and distinguished in your generation."[33]

Ill health had little place in these essentially cheery if didactic messages. But the father had admitted to a Seinsheimer relative in Cincinnati back in 1887 when Ike, unable to make Texas during a brief school holiday, was to visit there, that "[Y]our brother Kempner is getting old. He needs a good man to take charge of his affairs – I wish to make a good man out of Ikey." And, typically, Kempner begged the Ohioan not to spoil the boy, in another instance writing, "I am indeed glad . . . that you are satisfied with Ikey."[34]

Whether or not Kempner sensed the seriousness of his own physical decline, it came faster than his planning allowed. Only three months after he sent the optimistic letters about the European tour, while Ike was busily preparing for his final exams in law and Dan

32. H. Kempner, letter to Ike, Feb. 21, 1894, in DWK Scrapbook, 1894–1915.

33. Letter to Dan, Mar. 15, 1894, DWK Scrapbook, 1894–1915; ibid., Mar. 23, 1894, no. 524, Kempner Letterpress Book. Note repetition of phrases in this letter to Dan, used in one of Jan. 10, 1894, to Ike (IHK, *Recalled Recollections*, pp. 18–19).

34. Letter to Abe Seinsheimer, Dec. 19, 1887, in Tinsley, ed., "Select Letters," p. 38.

was still a college freshman, the sons received telegrams. Their father was so seriously ill as to justify the dread command: "Come home at once." Communicating with each other and with Galveston by telephone and telegraph the two apprehensive youths left their respective campuses, met in Richmond, and shared a miserable, endless rail journey to the southwest. An unavoidable layover in New Orleans was brightened by a telegram delivered to their hotel: "Papa still resting easy. He asks for apples. None here. Bring some apples with you."[35]

Fruit could not cure what afflicted Harris Kempner. His enemy was Bright's disease, an acute and chronic kidney ailment for which no remedy existed. The day following the two oldest sons' arrival in Galveston from Virginia, April 13, 1894, Harris Kempner died. His obituary in the *Galveston Daily News* for April 14, 1894, was headlined, accurately enough: "Galveston Millionaire Passes Away."

Kempner *was* a millionaire, leaving an estate of almost one and a half million dollars. Proud of this accumulation, Harris Kempner had sometimes boasted a bit about it. "The recent financial difficulties did not affect me any further than to contract the volume of my business," he had written to his cooperative New York banker friend in December, 1893, a time of deepening economic depression nationwide. "I have every reason to think that my [annual] profits net up to Dec[ember] 1st will amount to 60,000 doll[ar]s."[36]

Harris Kempner would have welcomed also the description of his career that Ike was to offer sixty years later. Harris's American adventure, Ike wrote, "is in retrospect a saga of personal achievement, a demonstration of the potentialities and rewards of individual initiative, intellectual honesty, and free enterprise."[37]

The Entrepreneurial Tradition

Enterprise. Entrepreneur. Ike had hit the essence of his father's life and, indeed, of his own life and those of his male siblings and many of their children and some grandchildren. Harris had won his victories as an individual entrepreneur, a self-perceived taker-of-risks

35. Telegrams in DWK Scrapbook, 1894–1915.
36. Tinsley, ed., "Select Letters," p. 45.
37. IHK, *Recalled Recollections*, p. 14.

who braved many marketplaces and created venture capital. Kempner was a rare phenomenon, an essentially unfettered explorer in the still-unfolding and perilous interstices of capitalism. His career testified to and helped to define upwardly mobile, upper-middle-class practices and standards.

As old as history, entrepreneurs are only recently becoming the focus of serious scholarly attention. Perhaps the first meaning of the word was literally the person beginning a small enterprise, as peddler Kempner did in the 1850s. A newer meaning is also illuminated by his later career. This newer meaning leans heavily on insights from history as well as psychology, ethics, economics, and sociology, with connectives to relationships between Reform Judaism and social responsibility. Entrepreneurs of Kempner's type are incurable addicts of odds, and are often individuals of large talent and implacable drive. To such persons reverses are inevitable but less important than seeking new goals.[38] Like timid Willy Loman's shadowy but successful brother in "Death of a Salesman," entrepreneurs must venture and reventure, for they are happy only when taking risks.

Respectful of marketplace customs and their own capital, entrepreneurs see these customs as keys for releasing energies rather than as constrictions. Such owner-managers are notably proud more of their families than of themselves and, like Harris Kempner, commonly want their children to emulate the parents' careers. Indeed, many fathers of that time encouraged promising offspring to match or even outdo the senior.[39] This "encouragement" often produced generational tensions, however, frequently of such severity as to result in children rejecting parents' vocations. On this crucial point of estrangement between fathers and sons and even grandsons, and of brothers, sisters, and their spouses fighting one another, the Kempners, as we shall see (chapter 7), were uncommon. Their rarity in this sense reflects the passion of Harris Kempner's goal of family cohesion as inherited, accepted, and implemented by his widow, children, and their children.

Other hazards exist for winning entrepreneurs. As with victorious combat troops, especially members of elite corps, the entrepreneur's self-confidence can edge perilously close to excessive belief in one's infallibility, can fertilize bigotry, and may lead to use of dubious means.

38. Dethloff and Bryant, *Entrepreneurship*, pp. 1–2.
39. Goldwasser, *Family Pride*, passim.

The ego-itch to win generates intolerance of those who differ or contradict. When combined with resistance to external constraints or even contempt for ethical and social standards of behavior, these attributes can breed distrust of all external monitoring. But neither Harris nor his descendants succumbed to these tendencies.

In more general terms, Kempner's happy conviction was that life, at least his own life in his adopted land, was far more a fulfilled promise than a dreary trap. This type of conviction helped to feed a wider intellectual premise of his own time, a complex of ideas since labeled "social Darwinism," which was extrapolated from evolutionary biology. To Harris Kempner and his family it was a reality that made Rabbi Cohen's preachings about social responsibility more than a Sabbath convention. By the 1880s, social Darwinist idealizations of the bootstrapping, successful, acquisitive solo entrepreneur had gained currency across American society. Sometimes individuals like Cohen were able through supporters like Kempner to soften the sharp edges of unfettered individualism. In subtle and complex ways, leading theologians like Cohen, plus jurisprudents, economists, and historians, incorporated social Darwinian ideas into prevailing universes of knowledge and climates of opinion. So incorporated, these ideas confirmed propositions equivalent to a "millionaire mystique": that individuals' successes were essential for general social progress. Useful government aids such as dredging the channel into Galveston were wholly desirable; external interventions, especially by government, that constrained, no matter how benign in purpose, were not.

In many instances social Darwinism merely added self-serving justifications for often-ruthless exploitations of labor, land, and resources. But such ideas involved also perceptions like Kempner's and Cohen's, about democracy, federalism, history, and ethics.[40] Ideas of these sorts already circulated in Galveston when Kempner settled there in the late 1860s. They flourished far more mightily by the time of his death in 1894. His own career bore witness to their apparent validity, seeming to justify the pretensions of this self-consciously bourgeois, privatistic, emerging entrepreneurial class. Its members embraced the gospel of success and were eager to wrest profits from swiftly chang-

40. Hofstadter, *Social Darwinism in American Thought;* Weiss, *The American Myth of Success;* Welter, "The American Money Mentality after the Civil War" (Organization of American Historians, 1985), p. 3; Haskell, "Capitalism," p. 547.

ing matrixes of agriculture, industry, and commerce. By stressing the need for improving banking, transportation, and communications facilities, the swelling entrepreneurial class fostered regional and then national markets and other elements essential for continental cohesion. Its values veneered the earlier American liberal tradition even in the South until concerns over race hierarchies obscured regional and even individual self-interests.[41]

Harris Kempner's life exemplified also the upwardly mobile quality of the successful American entrepreneur of the post–Civil War decades. As peddler, wholesale merchant, and cotton factor he, though a Jew, had found few doors barred to him or the members of his family. The vocation of merchant had become one of the widest avenues of mobility for otherwise disfavored immigrant groups, including the Irish and Jews. True, most petty shopkeepers remained forever in "mom-and-pop" subsistence trade. But those few who burst upward to larger endeavors, with some major exceptions, enjoyed widespread esteem.[42] This remarkable mobility for the few was the aspiration of the many. Those who carried the mobility banner dramatically upward from the peddler's level inspired others with similar drive and ambition, as Harris Kempner inspired his sons.

41. Daniel, *Breaking the Land*, passim; Blumin, "Hypothesis of Middle-Class Formulation," p. 299.

42. Whitfield, "American Jews," in *The American Jewish Experience*, p. 284.

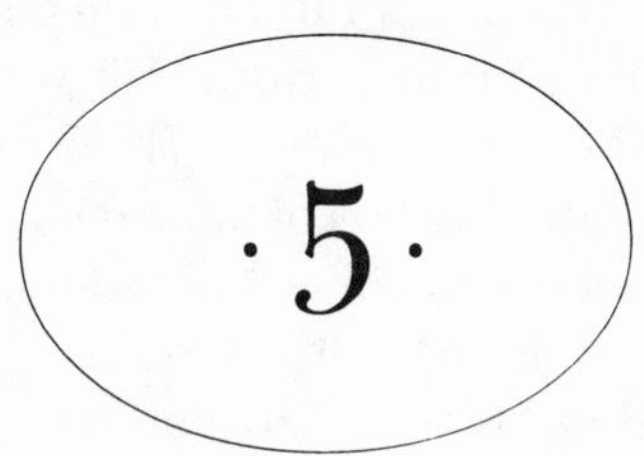

Ike Kempner's Proving Years

From Darkest Night

IN THE PREDAWN QUIET the day after his father died, Ike, barely twenty-one years old, "alone and disconsolate," depressed by his mother's rending grief, went to the second-story porch of their home, looking "into a sky of darkness." The oldest child and son, deeply emotional, sensed the responsibilities that were now to become his and that he never even tried to evade. Ike found himself, though alone, talking aloud about "how hopeless was the future for my Mother and her eight children and made a vow that as I could not help the dead, I would always seek to help the living." His then six-year-old sister Fannie remembered eight decades later how overwhelmed he was, "called home [from college] to take over this brood of people, and, [only] with mother's help, . . . to [try to] raise us."[1]

Ike assumed unquestioningly that, as he understood Jewish custom to demand and as his own predilections confirmed, he, the oldest son, would shoulder responsibility not only for himself but for his mother and seven younger siblings. Notwithstanding these assumptions, in the first dark days after Harris's death Ike, sitting in his father's swivel chair before the old roll-top desk, frequently doubted his own capabilities, sometimes to the point of near panic.

He did not know then that his mother and close family friends also felt "grave doubts" and "outright fears" about him as head of family

1. IHK, *Recalled Recollections*, pp. 13–14; Fannie Kempner Adoue, interview with L. Marchiafava, Aug. 1, 1981, RLA.

and breadwinner.[2] They masked their concerns. He could barely mask his. Ike's work experience in his father's office had been limited to three or four summer vacation periods. He was fully aware of his minimal knowledge about the complex H. Kempner enterprises. A fearfully destabilizing nationwide economic depression was then front-page news. Ike almost lost control at the thought of having to select among options in the chaotic and hazardous business climate. But no alternatives existed to his trying to step into his father's business role. In stereotypical masculine manner, Ike presumed that his mother "had no knowledge of the business," a presumption echoed in Texas inheritance law, as we shall see. Ike felt himself to be too inexperienced. He asked of the unresponsive night: "And what to do?"[3]

There was a great deal to do. Aided immeasurably by his father's faithful office manager, Uncle Joseph Seinsheimer; by cashier Benjamin Reading, a holdover from Marx and Kempner years who was destined to remain in Ike's employment for over a half century; and by equally durable and trustworthy Galveston business leaders, Ike applied himself to the intricacies of H. Kempner's operations. He pored over the firm's ledgers. Perhaps for the first time Ike realized that Harris Kempner's estate might well reach over $1.5 million.[4]

Ike learned, however, from his volunteer tutors that H. Kempner's assets were dismayingly illiquid. "Only a fraction . . . was cash in the bank," a family intimate recalled: "Assets other than cash were threatened by disaster in the depression year of 1894, a year that saw panic in Wall Street. . . . The great bulk of the family enterprises were subject to the [uncontrollable] elements of nature and the financial state of the country." H. Kempner needed large sums of cash quickly. Commodities his father had contracted for were coming in. Payrolls must be met. Interest on loans was due. What other obligations might pop

2. IHK, "H. Kempner," p. 8; "I. H. Kempner Testimonial Dinner" (transcript), Kempner Papers, unpaginated.

3. IHK, *Recalled Recollections*, p. 13; Harris L. Kempner, "The Kempners of Galveston and Sugar Land" (manuscript, Address to Harvard Business School Club of Houston, Sept. 27, 1981), RLA, p. 7.

4. On Reading, see *Houston Press*, July 1, 1929, p. 1. The *Galveston Tribune* (Apr. 20, 1894) compared the Kempner estate to those of George Ball ($1.4 million), John Sealy ($1.7 million), R. S. Willis ($1.6 million), and Henry Rosenberg ($1.2 million).

out of the ledgers' still-unturned pages and the firm's other files, Ike could only guess.[5]

But neither Ike nor his family's true friends anticipated one jarring fact. His father, belying his otherwise deserved reputation as a meticulous businessman, and probably reflecting the debilitating seriousness and suddenness of his terminal illness, had made what is properly described as "one conspicuous oversight. . . . [He had] failed to execute a will."[6]

This unhappy news decided Ike's course of action. He withdrew from his university although he was only six weeks away from the final examinations that would have given him a law degree.[7] Almost-lawyer Ike understood how serious was this omission of a valid will. Inheritance law concerned itself particularly with the estates of persons of property like Harris Kempner, especially those who died intestate. "The death of [such an] individual creates a hole in the special fabric which society must fill," wrote a specialist on inheritance history: "At the highest levels of wealth, what testators are passing on is not just economic security and . . . comfort, but significant power."[8]

As a recent senior law student, Ike knew also that the American legal profession was then almost passionate — near-hysterical by later evaluations — on the subject of stabilizing substantial property accumulations, especially in intestacy situations.[9] Behind these passions and fears among legalists, uncertainties festered about economic class tensions. More immediate to Kempner interests, a "New South" was developing, but its configurations were unclear and its stability uncertain. Scholars have recently modified an interpretation that the

5. "I. H. Kempner Testimonial Dinner." Of course, Ike's advisors shared his burdens if not his "sole responsibility."

6. Barbara Guidry, "Twisted Threads" (Ph.D. diss.), p. 21. Harris Kempner had completed a draft of a will but had not signed it.

7. Ike later passed the Texas bar examination but applied professional insights only in family business matters. He never earned a university degree, however.

8. Dahlin, "Old Age Policy, the Family, and Inheritance in 20th Century America" (Organization of American Historians, 1985), pp. 1, 11; J. D. Claitor, "Personality Sketch of Isaac Herbert Kempner" (manuscript), Kempner Papers, p. 4.

9. Howe, *Justice Oliver Wendell Holmes*, p. 201.

Civil War so weakened the old planter class as to make it give way by the 1880s to bourgeois industrialists and their coattailers. The revisionists suggest that by the 1880s rising cotton entrepreneurs like Harris Kempner and planters across the south contrived political coalitions among businessmen, lawyers, and bankers. In these coalitions the merchants and the legal fraternity played increasingly important roles. Coalition members stabilized marketplaces advantageously and came to dominate southern society for many decades.[10] A near-member of the legal fraternity and now head of a cotton-factoring firm that was tied by business links to all the other components of this evolving galaxy of interests, Ike would be an enthusiastic player in several guises.

Where There's No Will There's Still a Way

Ike's immediate concern was the fact that his father's failure to execute a will threatened the capital of the firm, and, ironically, considering Harris Kempner's aspirations for family cohesion, exposed the widow and children to the consequences of a dispersal of that capital, a dispersal governed by state laws in the absence of a valid will. In effect, family disruption and dispersal, not cohesion and community, might result from Harris's failure to perfect a will. Complicating the matter further was Texas' Married Women's Property Act of 1879. Written and interpreted by male legislators and judges, these statutes, typically patronizing toward women, assumed that bereaved widows required special state protection against unscrupulous male opportunists. Therefore, these laws apportioned shares of estates of survivors in intestacy situations and monitored the division.

Since no prenuptial contract existed to govern the intestate estate of Harris Kempner, under Texas' 1879 law what Eliza owned before the marriage remained hers. Because Texas was one of the few "community property" states, the law did not perceive Eliza as the heiress of all they had accumulated during the marriage. Instead, the statute depicted this community property as having been tenanted jointly: as undivided halves of the total. Now she was the "survivor in com-

10. Cf. O'Brien, *The Legal Fraternity and the Making of a New South Community, 1848–1882;* Woodward, *Origins of the New South, 1873–1913.*

munity," which meant that the law allowed her to keep as widow what was already hers as wife.[11]

Of assets accumulated during the marriage, she would receive title to one-third of the personal (i.e., non–real estate) property and a life estate (i.e., a lifetime right to use but not to sell) in the real estate. The children could share equally and immediately the remaining two-thirds of both the real and personal property, and they enjoyed a residual title to the one-third of the real estate in which Eliza had a lifetime right of usage. An exception was homestead land (i.e., that used for a primary residence) in which the children would inherit equal shares upon their mother's death, but the law stipulated no immediate partition.[12]

Of all the children, in 1894 only Ike was legally, if barely, an adult. Odds were high that the county court would respond to the estate's size and lack of a will by appointing a "caretaker trustee" from outside the family. The only immediately acceptable "outsider" was Eliza's brother Joseph Seinsheimer. He had taken up residence in Galveston and, as noted earlier, at Harris's death had already been H. Kempner office manager for some years. Certainly he was no "stranger."

But though trusted, and rightly, by everyone concerned, Seinsheimer himself nevertheless advised against any court-appointed caretaker trustee. Perhaps his reluctance was a matter of personality. Seinsheimer was relatively unambitious. Additionally, he advised against a caretaker trustee in order to have H. Kempner avoid the large fees that such a court appointment entailed. Instead Seinsheimer joined with other business tutors to Ike and Eliza and advocated that she become the survivor-in-community while Ike served as the H. Kempner executive.

The legal status of survivor-in-community was awardable by a probate judge, upon petition, allowing the named administrator of an intestate estate to do so in undivided form, on behalf of all legal beneficiaries. All of which suggests that Seinsheimer already shared the family cohesion aspirations of his late brother-in-law, aspirations

11. Shammas et al., *Inheritance in America from Colonial Times to the Present*, p. 100 and passim.

12. Texas Revised Civil Statutes, 1879, Articles 1645–53, in *Vernon's Civil Statutes of . . . Texas Annotated*, vols. 17a, b (Probate Court Appendix); Guidry, "Twisted Threads," pp. 21–24.

that the widow and oldest son were, apparently, ready to extend to this trusted relation. "Without Joe [Seinsheimer] there would have been no survivorship," Ike's son Harris Leon Kempner would recall decades later.[13]

The prospect of any other outsider becoming privy to family matters bothered Eliza, Ike, Seinsheimer, and the prominent contemporaries of his late father who gathered around Ike during those dark days. They knew that caretaker trusts existed to protect vulnerable widows, minors, orphans, the senile, and other "incompetents." But, notoriously, some trustees had feathered private nests more than protected their charges; so much so that *fin de siècle* melodramatists made stock figures of the self-aggrandizing trustee and the innocent, financially despoilable female ward. Further, it appears that Ike, though young and untested, was nevertheless already his father's heir in another sense. That is, he inherited his father's vision of family cohesion. A division of the estate imperiled all chances of realizing this vision. Therefore, Ike and his intimates hurriedly evolved an alternative to the unwelcome third-party presence.

The upshot was that the traditional week of mourning required by Jewish custom was barely ended when Eliza filed in the county court a petition that she administer the entire estate as the survivor-in-community. To become administratrix she supplied an affidavit legally confirming her husband's death, identifying each heir and attesting that a community estate existed. She stipulated that within ninety days she would submit a detailed inventory of the liabilities and assets of the estate. Next, she posted a performance bond equal to twice the estimated value of the personal property of the estate plus "a reasonable amount" to be determined by the judge that would equal roughly the incomes and rents from the estate's real property. The bond posted, the county judge authorized Eliza to act as community administratrix. She promised the court faithfully to administer the still-undivided estate "as a prudent man would take care of his own property." Once empowered, she could "control, manage, and dispose of the community property . . . as fully and completely as if . . . she were the sole owner thereof; to sue and be sued . . . [and]

13. H. L. Kempner, letter to author, Sept. 1, 1987, in possession of author. Seinsheimer not only supported the "survivor" resolution, he supplied bond for Eliza and for many decades afforded Ike essential advice on H. Kempner policies.

carry on as a statutory trustee for the owners of the community estate, investing and reinvesting the funds of the estate and continuing the operation of the community enterprises until termination of the trust."[14]

Now proceeds from all H. Kempner operations went into the survivor-in-community estate in which all the heirs shared equally. Ike took additionally only what amounted to reimbursements for out-of-pocket expenses pertaining to H. Kempner business rather than a prevailing or higher level of reward for managing. As his younger brothers came into the firm in conformity with their father's hopes, Ike and they agreed to continue this unusual practice for each newcomer, and it was to prevail for decades.

Texas' cumbersome probate and survivor-in-community procedures had evolved since colonial days in order to inhibit the tendencies of family firms to fragment in consequence of absent or inadequate testamentary behavior by the deceased owner or owners. The use of these procedures in Texas of the 1890s, nominally by Eliza Kempner, suggests that the required maneuverings were undertaken in order to advance the legal fiction that she would administer the undivided estate. Instead, everyone knew that she, her relatives and friends, and Ike himself had decided to take a chance on his ability to grow up without delay to the job of replacing his father as businessman.

What had to be coped with at once was the matter of the required bond. The million-dollar–plus estate required a huge bond even if the actual money posted was only a percentage of the assets for which it was surety. As a firm, H. Kempner possessed nowhere near the bond amount in liquid form. The money, Ike recorded, came from "individual friends . . . [who] generously and without compensation . . . [gave] bond for over a million and a half dollars to cover an estate whose continued solvency and or liquidation would be dependent on the integrity and ability of a twenty-one-year-old with no business experience beyond that gained by three or four summers' casual work in his Father's office."[15]

Nothing was casual now to Ike. His gratitude to the older, estab-

14. Guidry, "Twisted Threads," pp. 23–24; Claitor, "Isaac Herbert Kempner," p. 4. See, in general, Lazarou, *Concealed under Petticoats;* cf. Basch, *In the Eyes of the Law,* both passim.

15. IHK, *Recalled Recollections,* p. 13, on "individual friends." Shammas, *Inheritance,* pp. 81–122.

lished Galvestonians, many of them business competitors, who rallied to his side so swiftly, relevantly, and repetitively in this dark time was large and lasting. Identifying with them as never before, Ike was soon to join them in city government and politics as well as in many interweaving business ventures. He emerged from these manifold experiences convinced about the essential goodness of these community benefactors and of community itself. It was to take a lot for his conviction to erode.

Senior H. Kempner office and field staff taught Ike another enduring lesson about business survivorship in crises: the need for uninterrupted operations and faithful service by longtime employees. H. Kempner's veteran field and office workers indulged in no panicky exodus from the firm. The highly skilled, irreplaceable graders and others who actually handled the commodity stayed on the job. H. Kempner's confidential pricing and grading codes and terms of contracts with farmers and spinners did not filter from agents out to competitors. This spectacle of fidelity and of overtly calm transition was engineered in part by trusted uncle Seinsheimer, and it seemed to Ike to prove also the inherent virtue of the family ethic in H. Kempner's business.

On coming into the firm, Ike and then his brothers in their turn exhibited the fact that they learned well from their uncle, and he was to have a long time to teach. Seinsheimer would manage H. Kempner's office until his resignation in 1932. Meanwhile he trained Dan, who in turn would oversee the business educations of next-generation Kempners plus the rise of a nonrelative, A. H. Blackshear, to the near-to-the-top job of H. Kempner office manager until his death in the mid-1950s. Blackshear was succeeded in turn by A. M. Alpert, whose service extended into the 1980s.[16]

Little wonder then that Ike was long grateful to his benefactors. There were, he remembered fifty years later of those uncertain days and weeks, always those people at home depending on him, people who "had abiding faith in him." And so, in this crucial decade, Ike "began a lifetime of justifying that faith," a contemporary concluded.[17]

16. A. M. Alpert, letter to Leonora Kempner Thompson, undated, ca. July, 1988, copy supplied to author; H. L. Kempner, letter to author, Sept. 1, 1987. Blackshear and successor office manager/trustees served under the 1948 trust agreement, Alpert, under the 1948 and 1981 agreements.

17. "I. H. Kempner Testimonial Dinner."

Ascending the Island City's Hierarchies

The successful Galvestonians of his father's generation not only coped with his immediate cash-flow crisis by becoming his bondsmen, thus freeing H. Kempner's cash reserves for business operations, but also eased his way swiftly into relevant business and social hierarchies. Thereafter he had to prove himself, and did.

Ike became a director of the Galveston Cotton Exchange in 1895, by far the youngest man to hold that position, and joined the elite Deep Water Committee wielders of power and influence, including its chairman, George Sealy, plus Kempner family intimates Seinsheimer, Leon Blum, Bertrand Adoue, and Walter Gresham.[18] Henceforward Ike, an honorary "BOI" as well as his father's son, moved on terms of equality and ease with this roster of the region's influential and wealthy. That committee, it will be recalled, was nominally a division of the unofficial chamber of commerce, an advisory body appointed by Galveston's mayor, although it was actually self-perpetuating. The committee's primary task had been to acquire federal aid for systematic dredging of the vexatious sandbars that otherwise blocked big ships from the Gulf. The committee did far more than its formal charge because of the prominence of its membership and their intertwinings with that mixed public-private entity, the Galveston Wharf Company. By setting its rates, the Wharves was the primary determiner of costs for all Galveston maritime traffic, and therefore for every farmer, factor, and merchant, and for everyone in the cattle or lumber industries and virtually all other interests in the entire vast region. Because the City of Galveston had a non-voting one-third ownership interest in the Wharves, its rates were involved in politics.

Probably nine of the fifteen Deep Water Committee members owned Wharves stock. Non-Wharves stockholders on the committee included the owners or managers of major cotton and noncotton enterprises whose businesses depended on Wharves operations. Ike reinforced the cotton and private banking interests in the committee.

In the decades to follow, such cozy mixes of private and public con-

18. From 1895 through 1945 Ike was, successively, exchange vice-president, president, a director again, and then another turn through these and similar posts (E. R. Thompson, Jr., "History of H. Kempner" [manuscript], Kempner Papers, p. 15. IHK, *Recalled Recollections*, p. 24).

cerns would appear to be unwholesome and undesirable, perhaps illegal conflicts of interests. But in the late 1890s the shared perceptions and influence represented by the simultaneous devotions of these men both to private gain and, as proclaimed, to the public interest, were generally seen as a rational, efficient way to achieve progress.[19]

Odds are that these favors to Ike would have stopped flowing were he not exhibiting impressive competence in the business context. State judges began to name him as trustee for the assets of Island merchants who were succumbing to the effects of the persisting economic depression. He exhibited his father's habit of respect for specialists: Ike, a local journalist stated, "consulted with experts for four months before taking hold of . . . [a new Galveston fuel distributing venture] finally." Further pleasing tradition-minded business leaders, Ike rejoined the Kempner name with that of Marx Marx. As co-investors they gained control of a large Galveston wholesale shoe and hat company in which Harris Kempner had risked funds and which Marx had let slide into bankruptcy.

Harris had largely avoided investing in Galveston real estate save for the substantial commitments of his own residences and shops, choosing instead cotton or cattle-grazing acreage on the mainland. While retaining for H. Kempner most of these rural mainland properties, except at Sugar Land (see chapter 8), in the early 1900s Ike added few others. Instead he showed what a family friend called a "greater emphasis on Galveston and its future; an interest which ultimately the entire family was to share and support."[20] This series of actions is translatable into that enlarged sense of community that Ike cherished as the essential context of his family's cohesion.

Like Galveston, Ike seemed to be doing almost everything right. By the late 1890s the city's economy was booming again due in part to military traffic generated by the Spanish-American War. Shortly before that conflict began, Galveston's Deep Water Committee celebrated the opening of the federally subsidized ship channel that its lobbying in Washington had procured. Now navigation across the vex-

19. "Partners in Progress" (Ph.D. diss.), chaps. 1–4 and passim.

20. Thompson, "History," pp. 15–16, on "greater emphasis." Other data in "50 Years Ago" columns of *Galveston Daily News*, respectively, Oct. 4, 1945, Feb. 17, 1948, July 19, 1947 (for the quoted sentence on experts), May 4, 1948, all in DWK Scrapbook, 1894–1915.

ing sandbar existed without lightering, from Gulf to bay. The pace of business increased, and H. Kempner shared in it.

The firm's prosperity redounding to his credit, Ike took time to pass the Texas bar examination, which was generally considered undemanding. Unlike his father, Ike entered politics in 1899. He openly supported a Republican candidate for Congress, serving as ultimately successful campaign manager in Galveston. Even such regional party apostasy did not crack the crust of esteem that was building around Ike.

Further enhancing his luster, Ike discovered in himself both a liking and a talent for public speaking. Fellow business leaders began to exploit his skills, and he did not protest. Tourism-minded promoters of a Galveston convention center and summer garden fête charged him with raising subscriptions for such projects, and he helped to achieve initial fundraising goals by making a series of talks to private associations. By the late 1890s the annual Artillery Club Ball, the opening night of the opera house, or the launching of a new hotel was likely to have I. H. Kempner on the speakers' list. Less publicly, Ike accepted membership in the elite Harmony Club, it boasting much the same economic and social leadership of Island and region that Ike knew on the Deep Water Committee. It held regular one-dollar limit Saturday night poker parties capped by midnight dinners featuring shellfish, fowl, steaks, and pies. Even more fun were the frequent evening beach parties Ike attended, the women "all garbed in [Mother Hubbard] bathing suits and long stockings—positively 'de rigueur'—covering and touching every part of the human frame from neck to ankle."[21]

Ike made business mistakes in these learning years, as in an East Texas investment to develop lignite coal resources. He recalled the episode ruefully: "With inadequate capital and decided ignorance of geology [among both investors and project managers] the venture was doomed to prompt financial failure." He also speculated in cotton on his own account, quickly losing two thousand dollars. "I have since been rather wary of gambling or speculation," he remarked, again rather wistfully.[22] The H. Kempner firm, therefore, continued its rare

21. Quotation in "I. H. Kempner Testimonial Dinner"; other details in IHK, *Recalled Recollections*, pp. 21–25.

22. IHK, *Recalled Recollections*, pp. 26, 22, respectively.

reputation for not speculating on its own account and never for its grower-clients.

He learned from his errors not only to respect experts and to avoid speculations, lessons that his father had observed, but also that cotton was H. Kempner's central concern. He began to divest the firm of its last lingering connections to non-cotton wholesaling. Most important, Ike commenced a systematic effort to modernize and enlarge not only H. Kempner's role in the industry but also the industry itself. His first step was to transform H. Kempner from cotton factor to cotton merchant, a step signaling to the Texas business community that the job of the second Kempner generation transcended the traditional one of preserving assets. Instead, Ike was bent on enlarging them, yet with a purpose beyond enrichment.

From Cotton Factor to Cotton Merchant

Cotton factoring as H. Kempner had been practicing it energetically and effectively was essentially a nonownership, middleman function. Ike hoped to shift the operation from commission-earning middleman factoring to a role as an "integrated merchant" with ownership interests.

A cotton merchant offered farmers a direct market, buying and handling the picked, graded, baled, and shipped cotton and reselling it to spinners' agents. After buying cotton from a farmer or factor, the merchant saw to the compressing of the ginned stock, classifying it into standard grade, color, and staple characteristics that determined prices. Upon receiving orders from mills, the merchant selected appropriate materials from stocks to fill the demand, preparing shipments for domestic and foreign purchasers, repeating the process many times during a season.[23]

The merchant had greater risks and potential profits than a factor because a merchant was an owner, not a middleman. Theoretically, "hedging" would cover the merchant against usual major market risks and produce profit or loss on the difference between the price paid for specific lots of raw cotton (figured as points on and off the market) and the price at which the merchant sold that particular quality

23. Woodman, *King Cotton and His Retainers*, pp. 15–29; H. L. Kempner, interview with L. Marchiafava, June 6, 1981, RLA.

or lot of the commodity. Nevertheless a merchant also incurred risks. The cotton bought one day at a certain price might rarely match the orders that came in at that price or above or below, on the next day. Therefore the merchant had to resort to other dealers (the "spot" market) in order to cover promises.

The merchant might still be unable to deliver as per contract even by recourse to the spot market, thereby risking fines and other penalties set by the exchange and/or by judgments in lawsuits. A merchant always exerted every effort to "cover"; one's reputation depended on fulfilling commitments. Immediate losses were preferable to the long-term consequences of a flaw in that reputation.

Ike found the whole process endlessly fascinating but the tensions sometimes nearly unbearable. Credit and cotton were often not available at decent rates. Other times, "the ups and downs of the market could be laid off [balanced] through the hedges on the future exchanges."[24]

The merchant was responsible to all parties, having to pay the grower at the agreed price, then press, bag, and warehouse the cotton in certain grades until it was purchased, and finally deliver it at the agreed price and condition. And many of all these complex and quick commercial exchanges were made on the basis of a nod, handshake, or other informal sign of commitment.

Another kind of risk the merchant endured over the factor was that of loss of the commodities, which the merchant owned rather than the client, through fire. In 1897, for example, H. Kempner suffered a loss of five hundred bales of cotton, valued at ten thousand dollars, that had been stored at the Gulf City Compress yard on Twenty-eighth Street and the Strand.[25] Ike was willing to shoulder such enlarged risks because increased profits for H. Kempner seemed likely from the hazarding, and also because of the vision of family cohesion he was implementing even as he was transforming the inherited business from factor to merchant.

The vision required a better-rationalized cotton industry to lessen the subservience of American growers to fluctuations in the world

24. The quotation about market risks is in IHK, undated typescript in File IHK: Cotton Marketing, Box IHK-A, #80-002, Kempner Papers, and see Thompson, "History," pp. 16–17; H. L. Kempner, letter to author, Sept. 1, 1987, in possession of author.

25. *Galveston Daily News*, Apr. 13, 1897.

market and to decrease advantages possessed by agents of foreign spinners. These foreign agents were privy to their principals' actual needs for the commodity and money resources. American cotton farmers, factors, and merchants did not, however, possess analogous information and so competed globally with merely partial knowledge of market factors.

Ike's first step toward a solution for H. Kempner was to eliminate as much as possible the foreign spinners' advantages from the equation. He would replace spinners' agents, especially those resident in Galveston, with H. Kempner's own agents. They would be residents of foreign countries with substantial spinning industries; persons adept in local languages and knowledge of those countries' business procedures, cultural history, and laws—a probable reflection of his father's insistence that all the Kempner boys prepare for business and life in part by residence abroad. So reinforced, the American cotton merchant would compete better.[26]

Ike also proposed closer concert between American bankers and lawyers on the one hand, and cotton farmers, factors, and merchants on the other. He became an evangelist of the need for the "commercial bodies of the state to take action looking to the judicious marketing of the cotton crop," as a journalist summed up Kempner's plea to this effect. Ike wanted H. Kempner, with its advantageous connections to New York banks, to enlarge its private banking operations as a step toward better-stabilized cotton merchant procedures. Then H. Kempner could help to enlarge the flow of credit through inland Texas banks. All parties would benefit from the reduced interest payments, and H. Kempner could anticipate enhanced commitments from growers attracted to these banks. Soon put into effect, this arrangement, Ike wrote a half-century later in a serio-comic tone, was "a species of banking which was sufficiently precarious to wipe out any profits to the lenders."[27]

26. Corrosive consequences followed from having H. Kempner agents abroad; see chap. 12, on the spinners' litigations. But such results of the widespread enthusiasm for vertical integration, one so strong as virtually to reshape American capitalism, were unforeseeable. See Sklar, *The Corporate Reconstruction of American Capitalism, 1890–1916,* passim.

27. "Fifty Years Ago" column, unidentified clipping, probably *Galveston Daily News,* June 7, 1950, in DWK Scrapbook 1948–1951; Ike's statement, of July 5, 1949, to W. P. Andrews, Vice-President, Mercantile National Bank, Dallas, in File A, M–Q #80-002, Kempner Papers.

Ike's early successes among his seniors of the Galveston Cotton Exchange derived in part from what one impressed intimate was to describe as Ike's "power of persuasion." The young man "had a way with people."[28] But more than his communication talents swayed auditors. Many rising young entrepreneurs were champions then of better rationalized industrial and commercial processes coalescing into larger, presumably more efficient and profitable entities, yet with decent sharings of gains with labor and with responsibility to consumers. For Ike, an early (1898) example was his acquisition for H. Kempner at advantageous terms of a substantial Galveston cotton press. In part, he intended the acquisition partly to assure H. Kempner's farmer-suppliers with in-house compressing and warehousing. But the very name that Ike gave it—the Merchants and Planters Compress and Warehouse Company (M&P for short)—reflects his goal of a vertically integrated crop-to-manufacturable commodity process. Rounding out Ike's purposes, in a few years Dan would take charge of M&P's operations.[29]

Innocents Abroad? . . .

To emancipate H. Kempner from dependence on agents of European spinners, in 1899 Ike "vacationed" in England, France, the Low Countries, and Germany. This trip, he wrote later, "was really the first step in transition of our family firm from a cotton factorage to a cotton [merchant] exporting buisness." Dan had graduated the year before from the University of Virginia (Dan being the only first-generation American-born Kempner to earn a degree). Almost in a reprise of their late father's role, Ike sent Dan to Europe for study and touring. Accompanied by their sister Hattie and an aunt, Ike met Dan in England. Whereupon the two young Kempner men proved, as a family chronicler noted, that "their plans were not exclusively devoted to pleasure; indeed, a most important step [toward H. Kempner becoming a cotton merchant] was taken on this trip." The brothers reached agreement with a prominent London firm to act as agent for H. Kempner in the direct sale of cotton to British spinners. Simi-

28. "I. H. Kempner Testimonial Dinner."

29. Thompson, "History," p. 16; IHK, *Recalled Recollections*, p. 26. Fuller details on M&P are in chap. 8.

lar agreements followed with firms in Liverpool, in Havre, in Ghent, and, with others in Germany, Austria, and the Low Countries.[30]

Concerning this trip, Ike later depicted himself as being "decidedly ignorant of either the conditions or consequences of [the] export cotton business." In long articles about their 1899 tour that Dan sent to Galveston newspapers, the two Kempner men described themselves as "Innocents Abroad." But if they were innocents, that Edenic condition quickly ended as market information of sorts earlier unavailable to American exporters commenced to reach Galveston from H. Kempner's new agents in Europe. Ike wrote later that "strange to relate, [my] ignorance paid off, as practically all sales made, necessarily more or less speculative, turned out profitably [for H. Kempner]."[31]

Ike's successes suggest that he had studied carefully the people, places, and institutions affecting his market. His initial foray abroad convinced him further of the wisdom of his decision to turn H. Kempner into a cotton merchant selling directly to spinners through its own resident agents abroad.

Not-so-innocent young entrepreneurs, Ike and Dan returned to Texas filled with optimism that this analysis was proving itself in its first marketplace tests. Again in Galveston, Ike announced his decision to modify further his father's ways, and not only in business.

. . . and Politician at Home

Ike in 1899 determined to play roles in Galveston politics and government, a decision complementing his simultaneous efforts to rationalize H. Kempner operations and to advance the family cohesion goal. As an elected city official—the office of Galveston's treasurer was the one he chose to pursue—he would guard the city's pocketbook in order to enhance the community's attractiveness for that posterity of his special concern, his family, and of all Island residents.

Ike's generation of young, optimistic, upwardly mobile "Progres-

30. Thompson, "History," p. 16, which noted also that in 1957 the 1899 pattern of associations persisted; see also Harris L. Kempner, "Beneficiary Interest Report, 1963," p. 2.

31. IHK, *Recalled Recollections*, p. 27. The "Innocents Abroad" articles appeared in the *Galveston Tribune*, Feb.–Mar., 1899.

sives" saw the American city, their particular city, as not the last but the first vital level of the federal system requiring purification and regeneration. Ignored in the 1787 Constitution that spoke only of nation, states, and territories, cities had long been catspaws of tight-fisted, unsympathetic rural constituencies and grasping urban spoilsmen. Ever-vulnerable to budgetary and functional checkreins held by "rings" at county courthouses and state capitals, as the new century dawned cities were exhibiting increasing distaste for such tenaciously inhibiting regimes. But the federal and state constitutions were high obstacles to changes in the status of cities.[32]

To overcome these higher-level obstructions urbanites must first clean their own municipal houses, Progressive leaders insisted. "Civic virtue" was the label that city reformers commonly applied to the cleaning medium as they attempted to realize their urban visions.[33] Individuals exhibited civic virtue by active participation in reform politics aimed at purified public administration. The silk-stockinged youths who were trying to elbow rascals out of municipal offices across the country insisted that corrupt spoilsmen must give way to business-minded rationalizers who would replace wasteful graft with efficient administration and neutral policy-making. This dream was particularly appealing to young Ike Kempner, who, with his goal of family cohesion, wanted neighborhood-like Galveston to be a decent place for residence over several generations.[34]

What urban reformers needed were qualities that Ike and others like him possessed: energy, ambition, and, in Galveston, unimpeachable credentials, including what one analyst has described as "Southern ways in . . . household routines and attitudes . . . [and a persistent] admiration for ancestors." Regional routines, attitudes, and the appropriate drawl and pace of speech were essential to gain hearings before Texas audiences. Ritual and intimacy proved to be as essential for leadership on the urban frontier as among rural planters. Yet reform, especially perhaps urban reform, was more alike everywhere than other political crusades of the time. Urban improvers exhibited

32. Williams, "The Constitutional Vulnerability of American Local Government," *Wisconsin Law Review*, p. 83.

33. Bender, *Toward an Urban Vision*, passim.

34. Brownell, "The Urban South Comes of Age, 1900–1940," in *The City in Southern History*, p. 152; Melvin, *The Organic City*, passim.

"eerily constant" dependence on arguments aimed at community well-being as a product of bourgeois private interest and public morality.[35]

Galveston was one of the few southern cities of a pace and sophistication comparable to other major urban centers where coalitions of merchants, lawyers, ministers, architects, and politicians were redefining the very nature of the city forms. If cities were America's valuable orphans, they were also the sources of its wealth and culture, insisted upward climbers like Kempner in both political parties.[36] They were convinced that their commercial interests and community values were frustrated by the unwillingness of the South's politicians to repair and improve the commercial facilities of the region's cities. Therefore the region suffered especially from inadequate credit and transportation facilities (the drag of institutionalized race prejudice was not yet acknowledged). Few southerners—certainly not Kempner—desired to transform their communities into monster metropolises. In any event Galveston Island had natural barriers to physical expansion. But reasonable population increases and improvements in the city's infrastructure were essential for it to retain and increase prosperity.[37]

Even among specialist academics and government officials the concept of infrastructure barely existed in the 1890s and is none too precisely comprehended a century later. Infrastructures are the fundamental frameworks of urban economic and social organizations. The concept describes a city's interwoven physical assets and economic, social, and political institutions and facilities: roads, power transmission systems, and governing arrangements for health, education, police, entertainment, and communications—in short, the entire urban environment of a functioning city.[38]

Since its incorporation by legislative acts in 1840, until 1895 Gal-

35. Wyatt-Brown, *Southern Honor*, pp. viii–ix; Walker, *Reform in America*, p. 180; see also Stowe, *Intimacy and Power*, passim.

36. Wright, *Old South, New South*, chap. 1 and passim; Larsen, *The Rise of the Urban South*, and Schuyler, *The New Urban Landscape*, both passim.

37. One specialist on this matter of contemporary awareness of urban infrastructure concluded that while emphasis on economic matters is justified, the "historical examination . . . must incorporate such noneconomic, nonpolitical factors as the influence of cultural values and the harsh but simple reality of the finitude of urban space" (Rosen, "Infrastructural Improvement in 19th Century Cities," *Journal of Urban History*, p. 250).

38. Konvitz, *Urban Millennium*, pp. 130–33.

veston was governed—and often misgoverned—by an elected mayor plus ward aldermen who together formed the city council. The council determined urban functions and the condition of commercial facilities by their control over city finances, contracts, and patronage, while affecting Wharves operations through the city's minority ownership of that private company. Good citizens, a prominent muckraking Progressive wrote about Galveston, "went about their own business and disregarded . . . [the corrupt city government]."[39] Charles A. Beard and Harvard's William B. Munro, among others, summarized opinions that Galveston had one of the nation's most corrupt and inefficient city governments, one that not only seriously impeded the channels of commerce but also degraded the quality of community life.[40] Many educated business leaders like Ike Kempner were embarrassed by the opinions of such social critics.

In 1895, just when Harris Kempner's death had thrust heavy family and business responsibilities onto young Ike, Galveston's mayor and aldermen went too far. Again to quote a contemporary chronicler, they "did not even trouble themselves to steal in a quiet and businesslike way." Reformers won a partial change in 1895, substituting aldermen-at-large for the old ward leaders. But the changes proved to be largely cosmetic.[41]

By 1899 Galveston's mayoral-aldermanic excesses were bringing the city, the business owners' primary sources of income, and their hopes for a more rational, improved community to frustration if not disaster. In January, 1899, Ike's mother hosted a dinner, perhaps her first major reemergence into society since Harris's death five years earlier. Ike made it his stage from which to throw his hat into the political ring.

First reviewing the existing condition of Galveston public life, he noted that city finances, records, and tax rates were chaotic. The municipality was paying its employees and suppliers with scrip that merchants and bankers discounted heavily when they accepted it at all. An antitax revolt was brewing among owners of Island real estate. Default on the city's bonded indebtedness was seemingly imminent, and the municipal government's involvement in the Wharves, from

39. Turner, "Galveston," *McClure's Magazine*, p. 611.

40. Munro, *The Government of American Cities*, p. 205; Beard, *American City Government*, p. 93. See Bradley R. Rice, "The Galveston Plan of Government by Commission," *Southwestern Historical Quarterly*, pp. 363–75, 378 n. 18.

41. Turner, "Galveston," p. 611.

which all Galvestonians ultimately derived sustenance, made default a general disaster.

On Galveston's positive side, Ike sketched a "New South" future: a "glorious panorama and grand theatre of action wherein commerce, navigation, trade and finance will play the leading roles." He outlined his city's basic needs. They were, first, to expand imports to match exports, chiefly cotton; and, second, to develop diverse Island City industries in order the better to balance the trade flow and to attract large numbers of new permanent residents and so broaden the tax base. The city could attract imports only by improving transport and dock facilities. But granting this improved infrastructure, America's and Canada's industrial and agricultural producers would funnel their products southward to the Island City. Looking northward, Galveston should also be "the most successful and convenient port" for Latin American and Caribbean producers as well as for Europe's, Kempner asserted.

None of this was self-executing, however. Galveston had to overcome allegedly discriminatory rate structures imposed by lobbyists for northeastern ports and for Houston, where hub rail lines were proliferating. Railroad trunk lines were needed instead to bridge Galveston Bay, with spurs leading to Bolivar Island on the east and across San Luis Pass on the west, and, on Galveston itself, to modernized deepwater docks and efficient warehouses. All would entwine the interests of major capital entities nationwide with Galveston enterprises. His were not mere boosterish vaporings but realistic ways for Galveston to ascend to its "rightful position." No passive policy will avail, he continued. Rather, "progressive steps are necessary in order to revolutionize the channels of trade."

Undergirding Kempner's catalog was the assumption that Galveston's primary disadvantages in the competition for commerce were inefficiency and corruption in city government, especially in municipal operations affecting port functions. These functions included the Wharves' roads, rail spurs, docks, warehouses, derricks, and other essential land adjuncts to oceanic commerce that the city partly owned and at least nominally helped to manage, or mismanage. Thieving stevedores were colluding with grafting dock police and dishonest or inefficient higher-ranking city officials at almost every point in this commercial stream, snagging progress or sometimes even completely blocking it, thus discouraging shippers and investors.

Corruption in the city's financial offices was one source of these ills, so Ike volunteered as a candidate for city treasurer. The city treasurer had—or could have with honesty, energy, and independence—a finger on the very pulse of the community's infrastructure. Urban tax rates and derivative commercial facilities not only determined a city's efficiency as a port but also affected its cultural attractions.[42] Ike's concern for Galveston's quality of life and efficiency in the conduct of city business led him into the sordid world of municipal government.

Goals and Interests

Was Ike Kempner's motivation in declaring for office a true devotion to good government or a mask for self-interest? It is impossible to separate the pecuniary interests of a businessman who was turning to elective politics from simultaneous concerns about the quality of governance and community. Perhaps the very effort at separation may be misleading. The Kempners' enterprises depended on the reliable movement of goods from ships to shore and thence inland, as well as the reverse flow. Young Kempner and his college-educated peers shared faith in the applicability to selected social problems of the then-new "socially scientific" disciplines that they had studied, including history, political science, economics, and sociology. In what has come to seem a charming mix of abstract theory, hard research, and unacknowledged romanticism about "commonwealth," advocates of these disciplines believed in the inevitable improvability of institutions, including the political.[43]

These disciplines commonly linked the health of government and business, and taught also that municipal corruption threatened not only commercial relationships but also the entire constitutional and political process. Civic virtue and other ethics were inseparable. Applied locally, these assumptions had since 1895 been leading to conclusions that Galveston, like other cities, was suffering because venal politicians were eroding bedrock virtues by fostering class, ethnic, racial, and religious divisions in order to manipulate voting blocs and

42. *Galveston News*, undated, ca. Jan., 1899, in DWK Scrapbook, 1894–1915.

43. Cf. Lane, *Political Life*, pp. 299–303; Pessen, *Riches, Class, and Power before the Civil War*, pp. 292–93.

by profiting from protected graft in the urban services essential to rationalized port commerce.[44] If permitted to continue, the "shame of the cities" would transform both native youth and new immigrants into cynics about American values and the promises of American life.

Kempner, in short, was buoyed by many Progressive ideas and ideals then flourishing in white America. An attitude more than a political affiliation, a creed rather than a platform, a compelling urge to harmonize labor and capital and to contest with spoilsmen in their own muddy waters rather than sneer uselessly at them, Progressivism required the participation in politics of allegedly incorruptible "mugwumps" like Kempner.[45]

Members of the Galveston commercial-civic elite like Kempner who were themselves plunging into the hurly-burly of elective politics believed that the urban South must come of age. Overrepresented agricultural interests in Congress, state legislatures, and county courthouses must no longer fatten on wealth the cities generated. Rationalized urban public finance, not earlier thought to be exciting or central to goverment operations, was a high Progressive priority.

Few Progressives were antistatist dogmatists, although their public discourse often made them sound that way. Intelligent government interventions monitored by men of their own mind and useful to risk-takers of their Progressive kind were better than the class lures of labor union organizers, the demagogic rural appeals of William Jennings Bryan's sort, or the predatory practices of rapacious new smokestack industrialists and their corrupt political allies.[46]

Father and sons, the Kempners understood that discretionary federal tax and commerce-clause policies on navigable waterways, tariffs, interstate and local freight rates, and union labor shaped all marketplaces; and that states' innate "police powers" regulated local ways of life and labor. The Wharves always interested both Galveston ship-

44. IHK, "The Drama of the Commission Plan in Galveston," *National Municipal Review*, pp. 409–12; and see Steffens, *The Shame of the Cities;* Grantham, *Southern Progressivism.*

45. "Mugwumps" was a term coined by spoils politicians in the 1870s to deride reformers as timid birds with "mugs" on one side of political-party fences and "wumps" on the other.

46. Benedict, "Laissez-faire and Liberty," *Law and History Review*, p. 293; Cochran, *Railroad Leaders, 1845–1890*, p. 181.

pers and Texas politicos, the latter being the ones who decided on state aid. In short, strict logic could not govern public policy.[47]

Good government was no abstraction when considered in this intimate light. Ike was not merely masking the self-interests of a capitalist. He was cleaning his nest, not feathering it. Historian Edward Chase Kirkland suggested concerning Andrew Carnegie's analogous visions, that "the picture of the millionaire as constituting one of an ascetic order toiling in the public service borders on the laughable." But, Kirkland continued, "it had its sober truth, however."[48]

Ike Kempner was no Carnegie. His father was the one who had traveled the rags-to-riches route, but Ike was emulating his father in continuing capital accumulation by ongoing devotion to business. The established Kempner family way was one of rewards through toil and of sharing the rewards within the family, if not yet among labor that sustained the flow of wealth. Self-help included the duty of direct participation in politics in order to turn rascals out and provide better leadership — a duty that birth and success imposed on the diligent fortunate.

Galveston versus Houston

Hardly idle, Ike was particularly anxious that Galveston retain commercial leadership over its aggressive neighbor. Only fifty miles away, Houston was a growing threat to Galveston's middleman profits deriving from the latter's oceanic situation and port operations. Galvestonians attributed Houston's growth to corrupt politics in Island government, in Washington, and in Austin. Houston business leaders were also upset by inefficient urban government conducted by elected aldermen whose horizons rarely transcended wards, and by consequent reluctance of northern bankers, investors, wholesalers, and administrators to take the city seriously. Houston's business and civic leaders had been making their city government both cleaner and more efficient, suggesting that they were coping with and benefiting from the rapid changes that were occurring in technology, com-

47. Brownell, "The Urban South Comes of Age," p. 152.

48. Kirkland, *Dream and Thought in the Business Community, 1860–1900*, p. 157. See also Van Tassel and Grabowski, eds., *Cleveland*, pp. 5–6.

munications, and production.[49] As a result, the city's attractiveness to large business interests increased.

Although enjoying splendid connections to capital, H. Kempner's cotton trade was affected increasingly by Houston's growing domination of railroad hubs. Rationality, a preeminent Progressive trait, called for Galveston to improve its waterborne facilities in order to compete with railroad-rich Houston. Galveston's need for waterfront efficiency and Houston's root-and-branch improvements were factors in Kempner's decision to contest for the city treasurer's office.[50]

Kempner enjoyed the support of a "good government" coalition of civic, business, and cultural organizations adequate to overcome the ward aldermen's manipulations of district lines and ballots and claims on bloc voters' loyalties. Even so, when on August 30, 1899, the reform coalition nominated Kempner to be city treasurer, the placeholders rallied. A rancorous deadlock developed in the city council. Then arguing suddenly stopped: "In the midst of the balloting two loud reports of a gun were heard and most of the spectators decamped to see what happened," a journalist wrote. Returning to the council rooms, the relieved crowd learned that "the guns were fired [as a salute] by a ship leaving the port." Whereupon the council deadlocked again. A week later, on September 7, 1899, they succumbed to coalition pressures and, still reluctantly, named Kempner city treasurer, as he recalled, "by a bare majority as a compromise choice."[51]

City Treasurer Kempner

Once installed, only twenty-seven years old, Ike brought swift order to the chaotic bookkeeping he inherited. Cooperating with exposé-hungry journalists, Kempner confirmed reformers' suspicions that city offices were major sources of bribes and graft for venal politicos and shoddy contractors. He issued contracts for long-deferred sewers and paved streets. His monitoring of contractors' performances was visible proof of Galveston's new probity, and therefore, a means of im-

49. Dugas, "A Duel with Railroads," *East Texas Historical Journal*, pp. 119–27; Platt, "City Building and Progressive Reform," *The Age of Urban Reform*, p. 28.

50. IHK, *Recalled Recollections*, p. 27; clipping, "50 Years Ago: City Council Deadlocked, June 28, 1899," source unidentified, DWK Scrapbook, Box IV.

51. "50 Years Ago" column, *Galveston Daily News*, Aug. 30, 1949, Sept. 7, 1949; IHK, *Recalled Recollections*, p. 27.

pressing investors with the city's advantages and reliability. Ike successfully negotiated new issues of city bonds to pay for the sanitary and repaving projects at favorable interest rates. He utilized old H. Kempner ties with New York and Cincinnati bankers, then publicized the new loans to other money sources, some of whom rather nervously held earlier Galveston bonds. Kempner's message was that essential sewer lines would be laid and roads would be built and that his office would oversee tax rates and collections and ensure prompt payment of interest and principal on bonds. The new city treasurer "is a good officer and a man who understands his business," judged a Cincinnati banker who bid successfully for the bonds.

Kempner's arrival in the council coincided with conspicuous improvement in all its procedures. Debate lessened, and full agendas were more regularly transacted. Kempner caught journalists' attention by initiating a long-overdue property tax reassessment on residences and businesses and by personally lending twenty-five thousand dollars without interest until taxes were collected the following autumn, so that the street paving might proceed until money came in from the new bond issues. The council accepted.[52]

Impressive initial improvements in urban governance would likely weigh little against the fact that in Galveston as elsewhere, most good-government amateurs in politics quickly lost interest after a triumphant skirmish, mistaking it for a final victory. Indeed, the very voters that made Kempner city treasurer also elected a machine politician as mayor. Once attention shifted away from Ike's success with the bond sale, the mayor connived with some council members to seize control of the reassessment and expenditures.[53] Kempner publicly condemned this deviation from the politics of civic virtue.

As in other cities, Galveston's reform coalition was composed of business leaders, lawyers and other professionals, and ministers, with support from voteless middle- and upper-class white women. Unlike most other cities, however, Galveston had a potential standing watchdog institution, the Deep Water Committee, considered "ancient" in Texas' relatively brief history as a state. That private association of merchants, shippers, bankers, lawyers, and cotton brokers in 1899

52. Quotation from *Galveston Daily News*, Aug. 17, 1900; on loan, ibid., May 8, 10, 1950, letter to editor. See also *Galveston Tribune*, July 26, 1900; IHK, "Drama," p. 410.

53. Turner, "Galveston," p. 611.

abandoned its traditionally neutral political posture and supported Ike's candidacy and his policies once he was in office.

As of the spring and summer of 1900 Galveston's civic affairs appeared to be improving. Houston's commercial threats were still largely prospective, although the 1900 census showed that Galveston was no longer the state's largest city.

In March, 1900, the battleships *Texas* and *New York*, plus escorts, anchored at the wharves. Special trains from Waco, Dallas, and Houston, and coastal steamers from Beaumont and New Orleans, brought thousands of visitors to see the squadron, and Kempner joined the local elite at breakfast with its commodore in his cabin.[54] Then in April, ten thousand residents and visitors gathered on Broadway to commemorate San Jacinto Day. City officials, Kempner among them, unveiled a monument to Texas heroes that the benefactor to the public library, Henry Rosenberg, had given to the city. Now even the bigger ships could navigate through the new federally subsidized deepwater cut between protective stone jetties from Gulf to bay, substantially lessening shipping costs. Local investors announced that day plans to replace a hotel that had burned down in 1898 with a large, new beachfront structure that would reassert Galveston's claims on tourism.[55]

Sharing in this optimism, Ike had bought for H. Kempner a three-story brick building at Twenty-second and Market streets, with the intention of remodeling it into a large retail store for a family venture. Also optimistic, the Galveston Wharf Company had spent $2 million since 1893 to improve its landside facilities, adding thirty-three miles of tracks connecting them to warehouses capable of holding one million bales of cotton and other transiting merchandise. Foreign exports jumped to $86 million in the 1899–1900 fiscal year, and total port business reached $220 million. Still Texas' only natural port, Galveston attracted Collis P. Huntington, president of the Southern Pacific Railroad. In 1899 he bought the Galveston, Houston, and Northern Railroad, plus two hundred acres on Galveston's western end at the San Luis Pass, and announced plans to create there the eastern

54. "Galveston Fifty Years Ago," unidentified clipping, Mar. 27, 1950, in DWK Scrapbook, 1948–1951.

55. *Galveston Daily News*, Apr. 11, 1900, on ceremonies; "50 Years Ago" column, unidentified clipping, June 13, 1950, DWK Scrapbook, 1948–1951, on building.

hub of a rail line tying the Gulf to the West Coast. Kempner's pet, the Gulf, Colorado, and Santa Fe, had its general offices on Galveston's Strand. Field offices of the Sunset-Central Line, the Cotton-Belt Route, and the Galveston, Houston, and Henderson Railroad (the last a subsidiary of the Great Northern) offered connections from the Great Lakes to San Francisco. Cotton, wheat, corn, and cattle flowed out of Galveston in volume and value to rival New Orleans, and no end seemed in sight.[56]

Little wonder that in the summer of 1900 the Kempners were optimistic. Confidence was the mood of white America in this new century. An unceasing flow of immigrants and inventions promised cheap labor, unprecedented consumer comforts, large profits for merchants, markets for farmers, and new jobs, especially in the burgeoning smokestack industries. With the federal government all but abandoning efforts to protect the civil rights of blacks, sectional tensions, on the surface at least, along with class strains and fiscal heresies, appeared to be declining. The overwhelming American victories in the war against Spain had seemingly further reconciled North and South. Keenly sensitive to the commercial opportunities in the new American Pacific and Caribbean empires, Galvestonians approved the progress toward peace and stability represented by international conferences at the Hague. Like most Galveston Jews, Ike Kempner added to this happy catalog the comfortable situation of his family and of coreligionists on their island, where troublesome divisions between Orthodox, Conservative, and Reform factions seemed on the way to adequate resolutions. But catastrophe intervened.

56. Barker, "Partners in Progress," pp. 1–10; Bradley R. Rice, *Progressive Cities*, chap. 1; Ousley, ed., *Galveston in Nineteen Hundred*, p. 180.

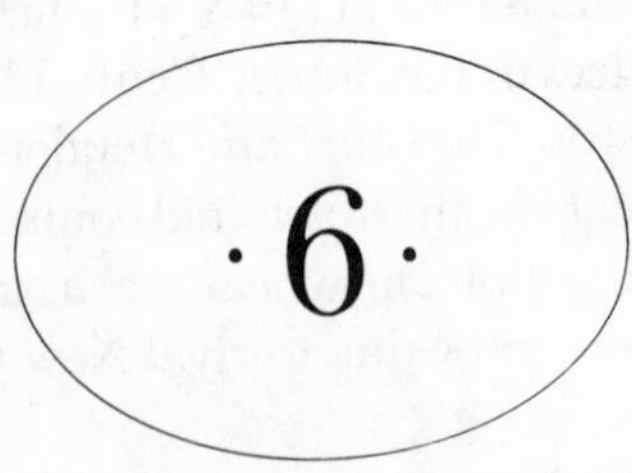

After Havoc and Agony

The Great Storm of 1900

On September 8, 1900, a hurricane-spawned storm surge smashed Galveston Island. Perhaps like every mature survivor, Ike Kempner, who was to live keen of mind past his ninety-fourth birthday in 1967, never forgot its nightmarish elements and everyone's helplessness before the shattering wind and crashing water. That cataclysmic "Great Storm" of 1900 became history's pivot to its survivors. Thenceforward Islanders dated events as either before or after the Great Storm, almost like Christians setting up their calendar or like combat veterans subdividing all things into prewar and postwar terms.[1]

Ike and the community were to learn also that the storm, in addition to creating innumerable immediate individual tragedies and group catastrophes, had severe and adverse long-range economic and political consequences. Among the latter, it became the clinching proof that the existing city government was incapable and the Island City's export imbalance undesirable, and so the dour catalog of hurts and reverses had some leavening. Soon after the storm passed, Kempner, as we shall see, in addition to safeguarding his family's economic interests, also played a central role in imagining, initiating, and implementing basic improvements in the governance and physical safety of the community.[2] For Kempner these improvements, made possible perhaps only because of the magnitude of the storm's ravages, increased

1. Sibley, *The Port of Houston*, pp. 125–26. On analogy to wartime heroism, see Holmes, *Acts of War.* An earlier version of this chapter appeared in *Houston Review* 10, no. 2 (1988): 56–85.

2. IHK, "The Drama of the Commission Plan in Galveston," *National Mu-*

the odds favoring civic virtue and urban survival, and with them, family cohesion.

Nothing in that hot, cloudy, breezy morning in September, 1900, warned Galvestonians that in less than two early-evening hours they would suffer the worst natural disaster in America's history. Although a federal weather station operated at Galveston, weather predicting was then hardly more useful than farmers' almanacs. Galvestonians knew from regional folklore and history that, as previously noted, a storm in 1837 had destroyed the few flimsy structures then forming Galveston, and that Indianola, a Texas Gulf Coast community that once competed commercially with Galveston, had been a ghost town since an 1875 hurricane. Although Galvestonians had been spared direct major blows from weather, Indianola's spectral condition since 1875 had inspired them to lobby periodically in Austin for the state's permission for the city to issue bonds to pay for a protective "breakwater, seawall, or other improvement as will protect the said city . . . against all injury and danger from the waters of the Gulf Coast." In 1875 a provision to this effect had almost become part of a revised state constitution. But conservative rural Texans successfully opposed favors for urban Galveston, and the legal and investment communities looked suspiciously then on municipal bonds because numerous cities repudiated bonded indebtedness.[3] And so the opportunity was lost, like others, in the seas of state politics. Still, as decades passed and massive storms bypassed Galveston, Islanders assumed for themselves a kind of deserved exemption from basic hurt equivalent to Indianola's.

But the usual benign Gulf breezes swiftened on that morning in September, 1900. Heavy rains began to fall. By noon keening winds made work difficult in the Kempner offices. Employees became tense. The weather station flew warning flags. During the early afternoon the sky darkened. Ike tried to appear unruffled. But, increasingly nervous about the comfort and safety of his own family, at 4 P.M. he dismissed his help and closed up shop. When he reached the street he found salt water already two to three feet high in some low areas. Sloshing through it, Ike, like other veteran Islanders, was still more annoyed than worried by seemingly minor inconvenience. Strong wind

---

nicipal Review, pp. 409–10; and see Weems, *A Weekend in September;* Mason, *Death from the Sea;* Eisenhower, ed., *Alexander Sweet's Texas*, p. 16 n.

3. *Austin State Gazette*, Sept. 28, 1875; 1876 Texas Constitution, Article XI, sec. 7; Moretta, "William Pitt Ballinger" (Ph.D. diss.), p. 284.

gusts were sending whitecapped waves down Galveston's major streets, but these were part of Gulf life. Most Galveston dwellings and shops were elevated on pilings to avoid damage from high water. Slatted wooden shutters protected doors and windows from wind and airborne debris. What residents could not foresee was the frailty of any such defenses and the vulnerability of all institutions against the unprecedented combined fury and force of wind and height of water that would soon assault the island.

The oncoming storm surge, a liquid wall, was driven on its murderous course by an unrelenting wind, a deadly combination. Even as Kempner plodded homeward through the inundated streets, that combination neared Galveston. An eerily early summertime twilight began to fall as he reached his house. Ike saw no injured people, domestic animals, or damaged property while on his wet trek. But three hours after he arrived at home, coal-pit darkness suddenly replaced the lingering murk of that strange evening. A maniacal blast of wind and then a colossal wave suddenly submerged much of Galveston Island.

At once electric and gas supplies failed. The quick darkness became more intense until kerosene lanterns and candles, hurriedly retrieved from closets and attics, relieved the gloom. Now there was plenty of damaged property, injured people and beasts, plus corpses of both, to observe, although days were to pass before the unbelievable extent of the disaster emerged from the wreckage that nature created in a few hours that night.

No wind meter on Galveston could measure the wind velocity. Every gauge on the island broke, their air scoops strained beyond the capacity of metal. Dwellings and warehouses, almost all built of wood, literally exploded. Buildings faced with brick or stone collapsed. Unknowable numbers of huddled inhabitants lay trapped under debris. Many hundreds died quickly from the impact or compression. But many less fortunate persons drowned in the rising liquid rage or suffered slow deaths from the awful artilleries created by the wild wind and swirling water.

The very lumber that had been buildings, slates that had faced roofs, great timbers that were wharves, ties that had aligned streetcar and railroad tracks; whole rail- and streetcars, wagons, ships, uprooted trees, utility poles, baled cotton (some of it H. Kempner's), rolls of barbed wire, chimney bricks, firewood, interwoven mats of

Galveston residences destroyed by the 1900 hurricane (Courtesy Rosenberg Library Archives, Galveston, Texas)

branches and other vegetation, struggling people and animals, and—everywhere—corpses abraded each other on the grinding edges of the cataclysmic wall of water that, wind-built to ten or twelve feet, rasped across the city and Island. A half century later Ike remembered vividly the storm's brief yet seemingly endless fury, and how, blessedly, the wind suddenly slackened. The water quickly receded "yet leaving a trail of havoc and agony," he wrote.[4]

During the shocking, numbing height of the storm, Ike, Dan, Hattie, Lee, and Stanley, protected the family, servants, and some refugee neighbors. By good fortune and the solidity of their home all there escaped physical hurt although the lower floor of the house was "gutted," Ike noted later. But as it became apparent—or possible to hope—that the peak of the storm was passing, Ike exhibited a restlessness that in other situations, especially wartime firefights, men displayed before performing acts of bravery.

He was self-convinced that his passive hospitality in sheltering neighbors was somehow inadequate. Dangerously if commendably soon after the wind softened enough (at about 9 P.M.) for him to feel

4. IHK, *Recalled Recollections*, p. 28, and "Drama of the Commission Plan," p. 409.

Public buildings damaged by the hurricane (Courtesy Rosenberg Library Archives, Galveston, Texas)

reasonably confident of his family's safety yet long before he could have been certain that the rushing air and ramming waves were ended, Ike became one of the many heroes of the storm.

He tied a long rope around his chest, entrusting the other end to a neighbor, Safford Wheeler, now a refugee in Ike's home, who secured the line to the Kempner back porch. Ike then swam first to the stables, or, as he discovered to his dismay, to where the stables had stood. He found neither structure nor beasts nor the coachman whose room had been in the loft of the vanished building.[5] Only opaque water filled with whirling debris covered the Kempner yards. Everywhere, the flood carried snagging tree branches, entangling fishing nets, splintered shards of uprooted fencing and house siding, sparking electric cables and escaping flammable gas from destroyed utility lines, jungles of barbed wire from livestock corrals, irritated snakes, sewage dislodged from cesspools and privies, and a grim cargo of injured or dead humans and animals. Anything and everything could trap who ventured out and add them to the long list of dead, injured, and missing.

Nevertheless, through that forbidding night Kempner swam, then, as the water receded he waded, crawled, and splashed from house to house in his neighborhood to check on relatives, friends, associates, and anyone else he encountered. He found few, heartbreakingly few, persons to assist. Too often he discovered only "death and disorder," Ike told a Houston journalist only a few days after the storm.[6]

Six decades later he portrayed his own role during that awful night and its immediate aftermath in strikingly different, self-deprecatory terms. The difference between his forthright, intensely dramatic, and convincing on-scene description of 1900 to the journalist, and another, near slapstick version of 1961 suggest that Ike's way became one of understatement, perhaps to gloss over horrible memories.

In his long-after-the-fact reminiscence, Ike asserted that on that ghastly 1900 night, upon returning from the tethered exploration, he agreed with anchorman Wheeler that they deserved "a stiff drink" to celebrate the moderating weather. They had several. Then, Kempner alleged, the two now stimulated men determined to spread the happy word of the diminished crisis. Welcoming the night's first good news, neighbors tendered further "spiritual courage" to the two stinking, dripping, filth-encrusted messengers. Progressing from house to house, each time rewarded with liquor, Kempner and Wheeler began to feel in "high fettle." So befuddled, at least according to Ike's 1961 reconstruction, the two befouled young men saw through the darkness, upper-story windows ashine with welcome light from oil

5. The coachman was safe "on the back porch (about ten feet high) of an irate neighbor" (IHK, *Recalled Recollections*, p. 29). On the "gutted" home, IHK, telegram to his mother, Sept. 12, 1900, in DWK Scrapbook, 1894–1915.

6. All details in undated interview with IHK, ca. Nov. 1900, unidentified clipping, probably *Houston Post*, in DWK Scrapbook, 1894–1915.

lamps, the city's biggest structure, the Tremont Hotel, apparently undamaged or at least undemolished. It drew them like a magnet, as it did many other Galvestonians that night. Finally reaching the hotel, they found all doors and low windows sheathed in planks of wood and could rouse no one to admit them.

Debris lay all around. The two exhausted yet exhilarated men, using unseated wooden street-paving blocks, "began smashing [upper floor] windows [of the hotel] to . . . [satisfy] our philanthropic desire to advise alarmed guests that the storm was over," Ike wrote in 1961. Perhaps the hotel's watchman thought them to be looters, for many human scavengers were already busy. In any event, Ike asserted, the guard marched him and Wheeler to the police station five blocks away only to find that facility itself destroyed, its pieces scattered along several streets, and no police officers anywhere. There the matter apparently ended, if, indeed, it ever occurred in the self-demeaning manner that Kempner offered six decades after the event. Tongue-in-cheek, he concluded by noting that "No charges as yet . . . have been filed against me."[7]

Odds are that Ike Kempner's 1900 statement reflected the facts far better than the reminiscence of 1961. Ike's Island peers knew of and applauded his bravery. Kempner's storm-night daring merged into desperate, but ultimately successful attempts by him and many others to initiate crisis management and then to apply lessons from the emergency to long-range improvements in their seemingly crippled city's governance.

Relief

In the bright sun-filled morning of September 9, Ike, at the Tremont Hotel, found there Mayor Walter Jones, several members of the Deep Water Committee, Wharves executives, ministers (including Rabbi Cohen), and some relatives, neighbors, friends, and business associates. Not a single department of city government was functioning. Jones formed these haggard men into ad hoc central relief and public safety committees. He delegated police powers to them, especially to suppress looters who within hours after the storm were stripping corpses, ransacking shops, banks, and warehouses, and worse.

7. IHK, *Recalled Recollections*, pp. 28–29.

No official mass disaster organizations existed then. The central relief committee members, becoming aware of the gigantic problems facing them, joined the mayor in declaring martial law to be in effect, and created a city militia composed of volunteers and the slim roster of available though undependable police officers. The militia implemented committee orders forbidding and punishing looting and price-gouging, closing saloons, and confiscating scarce essentials including potables, foodstuffs, medical supplies, tenting, and lumber for redistribution in some still unestablished order of need. Committee members tried to get the wounded hospitalized on the Island and the mainland, but the human misery and property destruction far exceeded facilities. As an antiepidemiological necessity hastened by the return of the tropical sun and heat, within two days after the storm the committee organized mass funeral pyres on isolated sections of the island, quick burials of anonymous heaps of dead people and animals, and the dumping of bargeloads of weighted bodies far out in the now-quiet Gulf. For months to come remains surfaced and littered the shore, requiring quick mass cremations or reinterments in mainland graves.[8] The collapse of government and private institutions was shockingly apparent in this matter of identifying and disposing of the dead from the tropical moraines on the island. In light of the huge number of fatalities and saturated ground, mass cremations, burials, exhumations, reinterments, and disposals at sea were perhaps the only practical emergency measures. But these grisly policies deeply offended many survivors, particularly women, who were considered the traditional guardians of the dead and whom the 1900 Great Storm converted into civic activists.[9] So too were many men, and in the predictable quicker pace and more visible manner that prevailing double standards allowed.

Galveston Women before and after the 1900 Storm

The storm so overtasked the existing Galveston "ol'-boy network" of merchants, bankers, and lawyers as to give the associated women

8. Bradley R. Rice, "The Galveston Plan of City Government by Commission," *Southwestern Historical Quarterly*, pp. 365–78.

9. Turner, "From Benevolent Ladies to Civic Women" (Southern Historical Association, 1986), pp. 10–12.

Corpses at a temporary morgue prior to mass burial at sea or cremation (Courtesy Rosenberg Library Archives, Galveston, Texas)

both influence and place, if not yet power.[10] Until the 1900 storm, access to the government offices, business boardrooms, professional and fraternal associations' assemblies, and private clubs that afforded habitués environments for exercising clout, were male domains. Eliza's pre-storm benefactions were largely personal and private, echoing her late husband's ways. As Sara Kempner Weston recalled, her father, "even after he was very influential . . . every Saturday morning after going to the Temple . . . went from house to house [of poor people] with baskets of foods. Mother . . . did the same thing." After Harris's death Eliza had continued many discreet individual benevolences. On learning of the widowhood and poverty suffered by a co-congregant, she ordered Lee, by then a banker, to secretly and regularly draw a check from her account in favor of the bereaved woman, "but nobody else ever heard of that," Sara stated.[11]

10. Belkin, "Lace over Steel" *New York Times Magazine*, p. 41.
11. Sara Kempner Weston, interview with L. Marchiafava, Aug. 29, 1981, RLA.

In 1898 Eliza had helped to organize a private Galveston refuge for distressed females, the Women's Home. Until 1935 she served uninterruptedly on its Board of Lady Managers, then as president and president emeritus.[12] Before the 1900 storm her service involved primarily genteel fundraising. Hard decisions and administration were in male hands. But since the storm overbusied surviving males, women's erstwhile white-glove benevolences changed to bared-hands-on daily implementation and, necessarily, to ongoing involvement in municipal politics.

In like manner that dreadful event diverted two generations of Galveston women from unsystematic private charity and cultural activities into urgent, sustained, and coherent involvement in and responsibility for numerous relevant civic policies. As recent wars have done, the storm crisis impelled and legitimized women's shouldering of distasteful, "unfeminine," yet still family-centered duties, as when hurriedly organized women saw to the identification and reburial of decomposing corpses. Thereafter these women escalated from crisis management to civic rehabilitation, then to gain the vote, and then to wield ballots effectively. In effect the storm created women's "boot camps" in the administration of large-scale relief and community rehabilitation efforts, some of which became women's long-term responsibilities.[13]

Remaining organized, women brought to political discourse topics long unspeakable for females, such as sewage disposal, privy-contaminated drinking water, and vice control. Relocating the homeless, finding the missing, disbursing funds for the injured, and lobbying for state-mandated inoculations and hot lunches for black as well as white schoolchildren plus special grants for restoring education facilities, required metaphorical replacement of white gloves with work gloves. Donning the latter, managing females saw to the repair, maintenance, staffing, and operation of asylums, orphanages, libraries, schools, and church or temple charities.[14]

12. See numerous obituary accounts, Sept. 27–30, 1947, in DWK Scrapbook, 1945–1948, Kempner Papers.

13. Turner, "Benevolent Ladies," and "Women, Religion, and Reform in Galveston 1880–1920" (Texas State Historical Association, 1987), both passim.

14. Ibid. Evans and Boyte, *Free Spaces*, esp. chap. 3, affirm that the "free social spaces" voluntary associations offered to activist women often became seminars about political institutions and procedures.

Manning Relief and Recovery Efforts

In the immediate wake of catastrophe, Kempner and his haggard committee colleagues sought from any sources the ways and means to reestablish order. On the night of September 10, Texas militia and federal regulars reached Galveston by sea. These better-disciplined troops quickly suppressed looters and restored order. Thereafter the committee members, overcoming their increasing fatigue, concentrated on tasks transcending immediate survival.

These tasks led to the more enduring phase of Kempner's post-storm activities. They included allocating the money and supplies that generous private individual and group benefactors throughout America and some foreign countries were sending to the Gulf (neither the United States nor the Texas governments provided relief funds) and then trying to restore nonemergency municipal government while also fundamentally reforming it.[15]

The Red Cross sent Clara Barton to supervise distribution of its relief shipments. But Kempner handled all other independent distributions. In England, Cuba, and Canada special theatrical benefits generated money for Galveston. Shipping lines, railroads, and breweries donated money, cargo space, and products. Labor unions passed hats. Even middle- and upper-class Galvestonians accepted handouts, for storm insurance was virtually unknown.

Only the muscles of many could dent the appalling strata of debris. The city council ordered that all able-bodied residents desiring relief must work, and labor gang numbers swelled briefly to a maximum of thirty thousand.[16] Kempner assumed charge of accumulating and distributing emergency housing, especially tents, confiscating some tenting from local shops and sail lofts. Soon surplus tents from the Spanish-American and Civil wars arrived from armories, and labor gangs erected whole tent communities.

Kempner and his committee colleagues, exhausting themselves in

15. IHK, "Drama of the Commission Plan," p. 410, and *Recalled Recollections*, pp. 30–31. No complaints by black citizens or their leaders about racially discriminatory relief distributions came to light. Race segregation undoubtedly prevailed, but it appears that Kempner oversaw these allocations in an even-handed manner that was noteworthy for that time.

16. Barker, "Partners in Progress" (Ph.D. diss.), pp. 10–20; McComb, *Galveston*, chap. 4.

A biracial work force clearing the littered streets (Courtesy Rosenberg Library Archives, Galveston, Texas)

these dour tasks, were among the first to realize that the storm had killed at least seventy-five hundred Galvestonians, fully one-fourth of the Island's population. Probably as many more residents were injured. A substantial additional number of the walking wounded and the uninjured abandoned Galveston permanently within days and weeks after the storm and many others were threatening to leave. The city's population, its ultimate source of survival if not progress, was evaporating. For example, in 1980 the then-nonagenarian John McCullough recalled that his family lived elsewhere until 1915, ironically returning to Galveston just after a far-less destructive storm of that year. During those fifteen years Galveston lacked the presence of this talented family, plus the jobs and taxes its activities generated.[17] No one knows how many such accounts could be told. Was Galveston to be another Indianola?

17. John McCullough, interview with R. L. Jones, Dec. 4, 1980, RLA; IHK, *Recalled Recollections*, pp. 53–56, on 1915.

Kempner assumed correctly that his mother, who with all the younger children had been vacationing in Colorado, was anxiously reading the newspaper descriptions of the Galveston carnage. He nevertheless waited his turn for access to the restored telegraph, and on the twelfth he wired Eliza: "Loss and damage cannot be exaggerated, death lists fifteen hundred [a gross underestimation, perhaps made to comfort her], none [of them] your friends [but the Kempner] house gutted, stable destroyed, condition[s] appalling. All churches destroyed, also water works, [the Kempner] cotton compress, and city railroad. No trains for several days, [but] don't worry we are all well and have ample food supplies."[18]

As weeks passed in committee work, Ike came to fear that the city's tax base, economy, and society were all but destroyed and that the morale and health of the storm's survivors were declining dangerously. Its economy dependent on shipping, the Island's very topography and geography were altered by storm erosion threatening its essential functions as a port. Who knew what changes had occurred under water, to that precious deepwater channel? The entire urban infrastructure serving waterborne commerce, so laboriously accumulated over many decades, lay ruined. Wharves, piers, and breakwaters had disappeared. Buoys, channel-markers, and lighthouses no longer existed, or, if surviving, were distorted or inoperable. Warehouses lay flattened or roofless, their stored merchandise or machinery exposed to the elements to rot or rust. Streets and sidewalks were washed away, eroded, buckled. Electric, gas, and water lines were ruptured, power poles down, and sewers plugged with vegetable and animal debris, including corpses. Water wells were blocked, broken, or contaminated from privies and cesspools, and seawater, sifting through the Island's sandy soil, was perhaps forever blighting possible sources of potable water. Trolley and railroad tracks lay buried under mountains of debris or were twisted into abstract sculptures. Trains, marooned ships, and dray wagons intricately barricaded downtown streets. Hospitals, the orphanage, churches, the home for derelict women, and other Kempner benefactions, along with police and firefighting facilities, lay in untidy heaps. The new Southern Pacific docks and connecting spur tracks had largely disappeared. Great Northern Railroad estimated a $6 million loss in tracks, depots, warehouses, and wharves, while

18. Telegram, IHK to Mrs. Kempner, DWK Scrapbook, 1894–1915.

the Gulf & Interstate registered a more modest $80,000 loss. But all twenty-seven miles of rail track on Bolivar Peninsula, east of Galveston, were gone and the roadbed washed away.

First estimates from insurance officials were that more than thirty-six hundred residences, stores, and warehouses worth $5 million had disappeared, and additional private property losses were at least $50 million, mostly uninsured. Public buildings, including schools, hospitals, and churches, were not included in this doleful estimate. Floodwaters had inundated the gas and electric works as well as major cotton presses and bagging companies.[19]

In this awful context the committee and Ike Kempner managed not only quick and effective immediate relief but enduring improvements in urban governance. Far from undercutting his belief in reason and moral order, beliefs his father's career and mother's ways seemed to him strongly to affirm, the Great Storm tested them. More than ever now, Ike believed that Galveston must attack the intertwined obstacles to recovery in broad, rational ways if it was to re-create a viable infrastructure in time to stave off commercial death. Not the only dreamer of a rebuilt, improved Galveston, his vigor, efficiency, and incorruptibility in the long-range work and results of the committee helped give form to the dream and to win a substantial if ultimately impermanent success.[20]

Rehabilitation

By a month after the Great Storm, Ike found himself responsible less for immediate alleviation of distress than for what he called "largely economic" and potentially more permanent rehabilitation. For example, he now controlled large relief accumulations of "tools and equipment [ranging] from axes to sewing machines, [from] hammers and saws, [from] . . . cooking stoves to trowels." He could have chosen to distribute these homely resources unsystematically in response to individuals' requests and politicians' pressures. Instead he undertook the more arduous and less popular task of rationing supplies in ways to encourage the beneficiaries of these basics "to more quickly become self-sustaining in their trades and in their domestic activi-

19. Barker, "Partners in Progress," pp. 15–17.
20. Turner, "Galveston," *McClure's*, p. 610.

ties." Kempner tried to match carpentry tools with carpenters, sewing machines with dressmakers and tailors, and lumber and timbers with housebuilders and shipwrights. "The amount of detail was terrific," he was to write later, reflecting the pressures that, in a democratic society, rationing officials experience in emergencies.

A reward and a lesson existed. The reward: "the practical success by cooperation was inspiring. The term 'Galveston Spirit' became a byword in the press of the nation." The lesson: "effective work of this relief committee was not susceptible to political interference or personal influence. . . . [O]ur municipal political situation was recognized to be, in the hands of a mayor and aldermen, incompetent to deal with the city's problems and some suspicion [existed] that incompetency was accompanied to no little extent by dishonesty."[21]

When by year's end the Relief Committee disbanded without scandals despite the huge sums of money and the passions involved, Kempner and others decided to reap further rewards by applying the lesson. "A group of our more prominent attorneys and businessmen determined that the recovery and future of the city and port, politically, economically, [and] morally required efficiency and integrity in administration of its municipal affairs," he wrote.

Reform: Commission Government

Ike's increasingly pressing concern and his primary duty as an elected fiscal official was financing Galveston's payroll and bills. The latter had grown mountainous with emergency expenditures added to the city's long-term bond obligations, at a time when the tax base was derelict and investor confidence nil.

Out of closed sessions in the 1900–1901 winter of the Relief and Deep Water committees (with some members like Kempner wearing both hats) came the proposal that Galveston adopt the so-called "commission form of city government."[22] Other cities had recently suffered catastrophes. Their experiences guided the Galveston survivors who, like Kempner, had networks of commercial data available. Chicago, for example, was just Houston's age, also a major port,

21. IHK, *Recalled Recollections*, pp. 30–31.
22. Ibid.; and see Bradley R. Rice, *Progressive Cities*, pp. 7ff; Barker, "Partners in Progress," p. 24.

and a survivor of a catastrophic fire in 1871, and a year later another huge conflagration almost obliterated Boston's downtown. Once basic relief efforts were in hand in both cities, reformers, especially local business leaders, gathered evidence indicating that the fires had spread far and quickly because Topsy-grown, politics-ridden public works departments were simply inadequate to defend people and places. Haphazardly built water "systems" did not match hydrants to hose couplings; narrow streets and unmaneuverable pushcarts and freight wagons blocked police vans and ambulances; unlicensed retail stands impeded passages already too narrow for pedestrians; fire alarm apparatuses were faulty. In short, the accumulated lessons from these pre-Galveston disasters were that slapdash urban contrivances of governance and trade invited worst-case situations to arise from future afflictions.[23]

Rather than reproduce history, a rebuilding city should systematically plan for contingencies in its infrastructure. Such planning had necessarily to begin with the replacement of the old corrupt city government by some less corruptible form, one capable of initiating and managing a better rationalized modern metropolis.

Some cities not afflicted by disasters, like Washington, D.C., had nevertheless adopted various forms of reformed governance, chiefly of the commission type. Memphis, Tennessee, its taxable population shrunken after a yellow fever epidemic, announced bankruptcy and surrendered its municipal charter to the state, which, in turn, organized and supervised city taxes as part of the encompassing county. Houston's business leaders had sporadically raised the commission proposal only to have the idea dissipate. Dallas had established a hybrid government involving an elected mayor and council plus a supervisory commission with control over administration, finances, and franchises, and with the governor choosing the commission members in charge of the police and fire departments.[24]

Kempner and other reformers thought of allowing Galveston to default on its obligations and go into receivership as Memphis had done. Instead, they determined to essay beyond the Houston-Dallas expedients and to try to restore the confidence of residents, expatri-

23. Bradley R. Rice, "Galveston Plan of City Government," p. 388.

24. Rosen, "Infrastructural Improvement in 19th Century Cities," *Journal of Urban History*, p. 214 and passim.

ates, and investors in their Island City by introducing the commission in unalloyed form.[25]

The Commission Innovation as Part of a Reform Agenda

For Kempner the commission reform was a vital first step in a three-point agenda. These points were: first, the initiation of commission government to rationalize the city's administration and attract private businesses and worker-residents; second, the floating of a new bond issue to cope with Galveston's pre-storm bonded debt and the swollen, unfunded debts since accruing; and third, with funds from new bond issues and private subscriptions plus aid from Texas primarily in the form of remissions of state and county taxes for Galvestonians, the financing and the mounting of three massive public works projects. These three projects were the raising of the grade level of the ravaged southeastern portion of the city, the building of a seawall on the city's exposed Gulf face, and the construction of a new multi-use causeway bridge the better to link Galveston to the mainland. Only people who felt relatively confident about the capacity of the three imagined public works projects to protect them would risk themselves, their families, and their money on Galveston. Similarly, the new bond issues would depend for success on investor confidence nationwide. Kempner was convinced that no rational entrepreneur would build a factory on Galveston Island or buy a bond issued by the existing government.

To effect change, Galveston voters had first to signify to the state legislature a wish for an appropriate revision of the city charter. Then the lawmakers must provide enabling legislation, thereafter approving what the Galvestonians contrived. In early 1901 Kempner and his associates initiated the first step. Their appeal to the public was that the existing government was inept in the Great Storm crisis because its basic structure was innately inefficient, adversarial, and corrupting, with much evidence offered, especially from Treasurer Kempner's records, of incumbents' fiscal irresponsibility.[26]

One historian has concluded that although these arguments had

25. It is unknowable what effect the unprecedented photographic coverage of the destruction had on possible investors. However static by modern standards of instant replay TV, photographs of Galveston's destruction shocked America.

26. Bradley R. Rice, "Galveston Plan of City Government," pp. 378–408.

"a blush of truth," they were also hyperbolic and opportunistic, asserting further that the commission activists, in order to discredit the incumbent government, exaggerated its "past extravagance and carelessness" and the nearness of the city to bankruptcy and "civic death." The existing government was guilty mainly of irregularities, not of basic defects or felonies. Yet this same analyst acknowledged also that an independent audit of city ledgers in 1895 indicated that no remotely adequate bookkeeping had occurred during the preceding five years. But, he concluded, "There was no fraud, just procrastination, laxity and error."

Accumulated malfeasances and misfeasances seem to justify more than a "blush of truth" to Kempner's accusations. The same writer suggests further, nevertheless, that would-be reformers exploited the Great Storm crisis for selfish purposes primarily to place "the elite in temporary control to carry out their plans for long-range recovery of the city and protection of their economic base."[27]

Much depends on how one weighs those phrases. If they equal lust for power and private gain, proof is needed to justify the charge. Alternative analyses fit better the tyranny of facts and contours of context.

Facts and context support a conclusion that the existing government had indeed failed to perform adequately in pre-storm years and had utterly abandoned governing responsibilities in the wake of the storm. Deep Water Committee members led in relief and recovery efforts not because of a coup but because the mayor and aldermen were unable to cope with crisis. Kempner was perhaps more familiar than any other Galvestonian with both the pre- and post-storm pictures. On the pre-storm side, he had helped to expose delinquent fiscal ways in the city administration. To his dismay, he found that the storm had taught that administration little if anything. For example, on the very day the storm hit Galveston, the Cincinnati buyer of city bonds that Kempner had helped earlier to float had paid for them in a letter of credit to a New York bank. Kempner therefore recommended that the Ohioan not be held to his purchase since the tax base undergirding those bonds was now somewhere in the Gulf. But, he recalled, "In spite of cries of distress, act of God, and unforeseen contingency, the [Galveston] . . . aldermen insisted on . . . not cancelling the transaction. The financial consequences to the [Cincinnati] bond firm were

27. McComb, *Galveston*, p. 135.

serious as the bonds were virtually unmarketable for several years."[28]

Kempner's evident disgust at the ineptitude and insensitivity on the part of his fellow city officers is understandable if his idea of family cohesion is kept in mind. He had power and influence as matters stood, with places in city government, the Deep Water Committee, and the Cotton Exchange. The affairs of H. Kempner needed careful direction. He could have made much more money for himself by using the time and inventiveness he was expending and would expend on city business, in any of a hundred investments. Kempner determined instead to try to restore the faith of residents and investors in the city by reforming its fiscal base and government.[29]

Means toward Ends

Would-be reformers like Kempner accepted degrees of bureaucratization and regulation as necessary means of joining democratic politics with business practices and ethics.[30] Were such techniques relevant to Galveston's damage? No one knew. Ten years after Galveston's Great Storm, America's preeminent city planner, Frederick Law Olmsted, who never had to deal with a crippled city, admitted that he was almost overwhelmed by "the complex unity, the appalling breadth and ramification of real city planning . . . [involving] enormously complex forces which no one clearly understands and few pretend to."[31]

Kempner and his fellow businessmen and professionals who championed commission government did not pretend to understand precisely how to revive and repair Galveston. What they understood—or believed that they understood—was the management of large enterprises. Contrasting dramatically with the ditherings of most incumbent city officials, many Galvestonians, including Dan Kempner and Uncle Joe Seinsheimer in temporary charge, were operating their businesses again one week after the storm, with shops open, streets

28. IHK, *Recalled Recollections*, p. 31.

29. Ibid., p. 32; "[I. H.] Kempner Addresses [Tulane University] Economics Society," undated (ca. 1907) copy in DWK Scrapbook, 1894–1915; Platt, *City Building in the New South*, pp. 204–205; McComb, *Galveston*, pp. 135–37.

30. Cochran, *Challenge to American Values*, chaps. 5, 7; Konvitz, *Urban Millennium*, chap. 5.

31. Quoted in Konvitz, *Urban Millennium*, p. 142.

cleared, orders delivered. Kempner provided an interest-free indefinite loan to Temple B'nai Israel for rehabilitating its roof and similar benefits to several Catholic and Protestant churches, an orphans home, and the library. Rabbi Cohen, now, like Ike, busier than ever, served as a conduit for H. Kempner relief and rebuilding funds.[32]

In this pantheon of self-help, the Galveston Wharf Company held a lead role. Its managers performed heroically in the storm's wake. Despite serious damage to docks and silting of channels, large ships were using Wharves facilities within two weeks after the blow. With the resumption of oceanic traffic Galveston breathed again as a port city. Company directors coped with the extraordinary costs of reviving business but resumed paying dividends and interest on its securities.[33]

The 1901 Charter

Kempner and other spokesmen for a redefined public sector exploited this evidence of vitality to win state lawmakers' authority for a new city charter. Most Texas legislators reflected the overrepresented rural constituents' values. Some were linked to "rings" in the counties embracing Galveston that were entwined in turn with that city's aldermen. Kempner and his associates in reform had to sever these lucrative links between hardened Texas spoilsmen.[34]

City officials and the Deep Water Committee (Kempner in both guises) by January, 1901, had prepared a draft revision of the city's charter and, with Wharves allies, were lobbying for its passage at the state capital, meanwhile employing the revision in Washington to persuade Congress to accelerate federal funds for fully restoring the navigability of Galveston waters. Part of their argument rested on the impressive private-sector rebuilding efforts already under way. But lobbyists revived talk of the Wharves as a monopolizing octopus in its pricing policies, reminding lawmakers that the city of Galves-

32. Congregation B'nai Israel Executive Board Minute Book, 1889–1902, AJA/HUC, p. 90, and see "Relief" files, Cohen Papers.

33. Barker, "Partners in Progress," pp. 34–38.

34. "Kempner Addresses [Tulane University] Economics Society"; IHK, "The Galveston Commission Form of Government" (Address to the Galveston Historical Society, Feb. 12, 1946).

ton was a minority owner of the company, in this way entangling questions of charter reform with state or federal assistance. Galveston spokesmen, including Ike, retorted that such reports were exaggerated and prejudiced accounts, especially those given by proponents of competing port cities. Wharves stockholders had averaged only 4 percent annual return on investments in the preceding quarter-century, a rate hardly reflecting monopolistic price-gouging. In Congress and the Texas legislature lawmakers nevertheless chose to mark time on all Galveston requests for aid and reform.

So for revenue commissioner Kempner, problems increased as the immediate post-storm crisis lessened. The reluctance to act in both Austin and Washington indicated that Galveston might indeed be another Indianola, an economically dead entity. Investments in Island City bonds and enterprises dried up and the tax base eroded further because many former residents who had returned to the Island since the storm now migrated inland, often attended by hurtful publicity. By year's end the city council had cut employees' salaries and then suspended them. The manager of the private electric light plant warned the council that the cost of coal was soaring nationally because of the unusually bitter winter and might exceed the company's budget, already strained by repair expenses and delinquent accounts. When the City of Galveston offered to buy the coal, vendors refused to sell, fearing the municipality's insolvency.

Through these wearying weeks Kempner scrambled for revenue. His proposal for a root-and-branch revision of property tax rates fell afoul of the council's entrenched ward interests. Forced to look to palliatives, Ike won authority to license taverns, to tax, ironically, peddlers, and to impose hook-up charges for restored sewer connections to residences and shops. Galveston journalists described bickering and ineffectiveness in the city council, reserving praise for a few incumbents, including Kempner. Like old men of the sea, the mayor and council were dragging the city to death.[35]

If only by contrast, the reform proponents appeared to be both efficient and effective. A popular presumption in their favor existed when the draft revision of the city charter appeared in Galveston's

35. Barker, "Partners in Progress," pp. 34–38; cf. McComb, *Galveston*, pp. 135–37.

newspapers on January 1, 1901. It, and the justifications for it that accompanied the draft, bore Kempner's stamp. The justifications embraced his agenda: government reorganization to purify politics and rationalize governance, tax exemptions, and the three great public works (the grade-raising, seawall, and bridge), the further to encourage long-term investors and new taxpaying residents.

But from opponents, these questions: Did not the 1876 Texas Constitution (Article VIII, sec. 10) stipulate against the proposed tax exemption for stricken Galveston, stating that the legislature "shall have no power to release the inhabitants of, or property in, any county, city or town from the payment of taxes levied for State or county purposes, unless in case of great public calamity in any such county, city or town, when such release may be made by vote of two-thirds of each House of the Legislature"? Perhaps Galveston had not really suffered a "great public calamity." If Galveston enjoyed exemption from state taxes might not other Texas cities claim similar immunities, perhaps with less need? The Deep Water Committee itself stressed the large steps already taken toward economic recovery under existing governing arrangements. Was all the agitation for charter reform and state aid inspired by the committee in concert with the Wharves management?

Arguments continued into 1901. Then Texas' governor approved a waiver bill that for two years only, not the requested fifteen, abolished property and poll taxes for Galvestonians. Whereupon Galveston renewed its increasingly sophisticated lobbying efforts. Special trains brought hundreds of ardent Islanders to Austin. Leading reform advocates, Kempner prominent among them, addressed business, fraternal, religious, and social clubs statewide, and cultivated legislators, journalists, and members of professional associations. It worked. Texas lawmakers extended the tax exemption for Galveston rate-payers to fifteen years. In March, 1901, the legislature approved the new charter over the crumbling opposition of those Galvestonians and others who decried the apparent diminutions of self-government allegedly involved, but who, Kempner believed, were really those "to whom politics has become a revenue bearing profession."[36]

36. IHK, *Recalled Recollections*, p. 32; cf. McComb, *Galveston*, pp. 135–37; Barker, "Partners in Progress," pp. 35–39.

Form Finding Function

Kempner's ability, and that of his coadjutors, to improve city governance in storm-wracked Galveston has parallels in the ways that businesses were transforming industry at this time by encouraging bureaucratization, employing specialist-managers, and routinizing work. This reform process involved a new phase of relationships between business and politics, one that even in the absence of a crisis like Galveston's Great Storm exalted frank marriages between the two.[37]

Under the new state charter, Galveston's government would be a commission. Unlike the nation's and state's tripartite arrangements for check-and-balance separation of functions, Galveston would merge executive, legislative, and administrative operations. An elected mayor was to have no veto power. Replacing the ward aldermen, a board of at-large commissioners would be the city's only elected officers. At the price of diminished democracy the Galveston mode allowed a short ballot and less obfuscation, corruption, and irrelevant emotionalism in elections and administration, according to reform advocates. The mayor and commissioners would be elected for two years. Elections would be in May, a month as far removed as possible from the traditional state and national ballotings, on the premise that workaday city issues had little to do with broader policy alternatives.

Majority votes of the commission were to determine all city policies, the mayor having only one vote. However, in emergencies (the 1900 storm was not forgotten), the mayor could act alone. In effect the mayor was to become a figurehead, a general manager of specialist-managers, the commissioners, who possessed all municipal powers within each commissioner's sphere of operations. Responsibility would be centralized. Each commissioner's performance and those of all appointees would be judged by easily visible results in a short list of intimate, homely, essential urban functions: finance and revenue, police and fire, streets, public property, and water and sewerage. Now citizens seeking particular city services or with particular grievances knew where to turn, lessening spoilsmen's roles and encouraging accountability. Policies would result from deliberate exchanges of views

37. Cochran, "The History of a Business Society," *Journal of American History*, p. 5; Jacoby, *Employing Bureaucracy*.

by the commissioners, not from partisan disputes and claims during election campaigns or from hidden trades after ballotings. Commissioners would be part-time, low-paid city servants who carried on their private businesses. Professional subordinates would implement policies, thus presumably preventing conflicts of interest and minimizing corruption and patronage.

Annual salaries for mayor and commissioners were set at two thousand dollars for the mayor and fifteen hundred dollars for the rest, all but guaranteeing that only individuals with adequate external incomes could participate. Economic status was supposed to be immaterial to a commissioner's function.

Reform, Race, and Labor Unions: At-Large Districts

Race relations, especially as they concerned labor unions, were part of the southern urban Progressive equation, and they led Kempner and the other 1901 charter-makers to adopt a device undertaken in other cities: the at-large district. Although it has since been properly described as favoring white elites rather than racial minorities or blue-collar majorities, the at-large arrangement was for decades after the century's turn defended by Kempner as a general benefit. It led to more even-handed citywide services, he insisted. Other southern cities, including Mobile and Jackson, had established at-large elections in their commission governments. In those cities, whites' desire to exclude blacks' representation and the business elite's desire to perpetuate its rule did indeed impel the at-large innovation.[38]

While not wholly different, the Galveston situation was dissimilar. Unghettoized if only by the nature of Island living, a predominantly black ward with many registered voters among its residents, had nevertheless long existed in Galveston. Republican presidents like McKinley and Theodore Roosevelt sometimes appointed a few blacks to high-visibility local federal positions, often as postmasters, thus annoying southern whites already upset by Congress's flirtations in the 1890s with new civil rights laws. Local blacks' occasional success at levering jobs and other patronage out of city officials, often in ex-

38. Bradley R. Rice, "Commission Government Adoption in Jackson, Mississippi," and Alsobrook, "Bosses and Businessmen" (Southern Historical Association, 1985).

change for kickbacks or other graft, seemed to Kempner to be part of the corrupt old order that required purification.

Many white Galvestonians were unsettled by the militancy of labor unions during the turbulent 1880–1900 decades, and union leaders were upset by the question of admitting black members. Employers who took on black strikebreakers found that some Galveston blacks proceeded to form their own unions, even on the treasured docks. Perhaps Galveston makeweights, including Kempner, and white unionists contrived the at-large reform as a means of further relegating blacks to political oblivion.[39]

Could Galveston's reformers have fought off Jim Crow in 1900? Race segregation was a mighty force. Ike would oppose it only on a relatively minor though public matter, that of segregation on Island streetcars. Otherwise, the charter-crafters cloaked any racist imperatives in the vocabulary of reform, as with the at-large innovation.[40]

Galveston blacks did not then or for years to come request reinstatement of the old ward arrangements. True, some Galveston blacks were to nurse exaggerated traditions about the extent of black power during the aldermanic decades, even in 1980 criticizing the displacement of the aldermen by city managers and commissioners. But one such critic, though still preferring a strong mayor-alderman government, admitted that in other southern cities with city managers, whites "wouldn't even let . . . [blacks] have an audience. We never had anything like that here in Galveston. [Its] City Managers have always been reasonable and fair to most of us when we go up there [to City Hall]."[41]

Finance Commissioner Kempner

On April 18, 1901, city treasurer Ike Kempner became Galveston's first commissioner of finance and revenue under the reformed charter. He would serve the new mayor, or, more precisely, the president of

39. Allen, *Chapters in the History of Organized Labor in Texas*, pp. 136–37; Morrison, ed., *The Port of Galveston and the State of Texas*, pp. 9–10, on blacks' unions. See also Hinze, "Norris Wright Cuney" (MA thesis), p. 46; Bradley R. Rice, "Galveston Plan of City Government," p. 372.

40. Isaac, "Municipal Reform in Beaumont, Texas, 1902–1909," *Southwestern Historical Quarterly*, p. 430.

41. John H. Clouse, interview with R. L. Jones, Apr. 22, 1980, RLA.

the board of commissioners, in this capacity for the next fifteen years. The commissioners of 1901, wrote economist-lobbyist George K. Turner five years later, "came into . . . [Galveston's] service it is true under the pressure of a great calamity; but they still remain . . . in Galveston, where the office of commissioner is [now] a high honor, and an absorbing personal interest for its holder."[42]

By agreement, the sitting mayor, council (Kempner included), and aldermen remained in office until mid-September, 1901, to allow both the new commissioners and the lame-duck aldermen to locate and move relevant records to their offices in a storm-worn building on Twentieth and Market streets and to master them, to appoint subordinates, and to set up new procedures. Some records never surfaced. Others did, sometimes to the dismay of the new incumbents as the latter discovered overdue bills, cronyism, or worse. Then on September 19, the outgoing mayor and board of ward aldermen met in special session and administered official oaths to their successors, each of whom had filed thirty-five-thousand-dollar bonds.[43] The old order had changed—but in time?

Staffing the new departments came first, and Kempner's choices proved also to be durable, wrote Turner in 1906: "This force [except for mayor Austin] still remains intact . . . form[ing] an administration as continuous as that of any business concern. Galveston, instead of changing managers every two years, has been governed by trained and experienced men. . . . It has ceased to be an experiment. It has had ample time to prove itself. Its brilliant success is best shown by its financial record."[44] Kempner made that success possible.

The pre-storm assessed value of Galveston property was $28 million (a much lower figure, of course, than the market value). The storm destroyed or seriously depreciated perhaps $15 million worth, plus the projected loss of future revenues represented by deceased, injured, or departed taxpayers and shrunken real estate valuations. Bonded debt exceeded $2.8 million, plus a $200,000 floating debt (i.e., immediate calls on city funds for past-due salaries and the like). In effect, Galveston was worse than bankrupt. But it was alive.

Kempner was determined to keep it so. Exploiting his banking and

42. Turner, "Galveston," p. 613.

43. All details in "50 Years Ago" newspaper columns, unidentified and undated, in DWK Scrapbook, 1894–1915.

44. Turner, "Galveston," p. 613.

other business connections, Ike, in the phrases of an admiring journalist, "though an amateur politician . . . was by no means an amateur financier, when he started to put the bankrupt city on a firm financial basis."[45] Ike proved himself to be skilled at politicking as well. In Houston only weeks after the storm, Kempner told journalists that his public optimism was more than a façade, that he was reviving all Kempner enterprises to pre-storm levels or beyond.[46]

Firm in his conviction that responsible civic polity and a positive business environment were inseparable and that Galveston's salvation must come primarily from its own resources of people and capital, Ike was to retain this principle throughout his long life. His well-publicized commitments of family money in 1900–1902 for rebuilding H. Kempner properties, although clearly involving self-interest, aimed also to illuminate reform of the city's government as the likeliest way to its economic recovery.

Kempner reached this conclusion about the primacy of community self-help in part from his disappointments about private external relief sources. He had flirted briefly with a notion that Galveston's distress afforded American millionaires nationwide an opportunity to participate financially in "some of the noblest far reaching and practical charity the world has ever seen." Moneyed men should endow on a large scale programs for the systematic pairing of relief with recipients' talents, of the sort he had initiated in the first weeks after the storm. Such continuing donations, Ike asserted, "would be charity in its broadest sense . . . [and] a grander monument than all the liberal endowments of colleges or libraries or what not."[47]

But Ike's appeal failed to convince moneyed contemporaries. Once observing the noneffect of this trial balloon, he abandoned further appeals of that nature. Instead, he returned to less grandiose efforts simultaneously to advance the interests of Galveston's government and community in the context of his hope to maintain his family's residence there. A fusion of community and private concerns was central in Ike's successful efforts to restore Galveston's public credit.[48] Once Texas remitted to Galveston all property taxes collected in its

45. "Kempner Addresses [Tulane University] Economics Society."
46. For H. Kempner business revival, see chap. 8.
47. Undated *Houston Post* clipping, DWK Scrapbook, 1894–1915.
48. For details, see undated clippings, DWK Scrapbook, 1894–1915; Barker, "Partners in Progress," chap. 1.

county, this assured income allowed him to begin paying off the dismaying floating debt, which was in the form of pre-storm bills and city scrip, to meet some part of the interest due on outstanding bonds, and to initiate a huge (ultimately approximately $7 million on a remaining tax base of approximately $20 million) new issue of Galveston city bonds.[49] If the city could market this indebtedness, then, as per Kempner's agenda, Galveston would build that protective seawall, raise the municipality's grade, and construct a multiuse bridge to the mainland.[50]

Reverses and accumulating weariness sometimes eroded Ike's confidence in these interweaving elements. After lobbying city voters to approve the issue of these municipal bonds, Kempner learned that their interest rate (4 percent) was too low ("a cheap rate at that time," he admitted) and the backing too uncertain (the bonds had behind them only the "scant and impaired credit of the city and the state tax remission," he noted) to attract skittish buyers. To spur sales, H. Kempner and other major Galveston merchants and bankers themselves bought substantial blocks of the issue, Ike ensuring that the purchases were attended with due publicity. He professed to find aspects of politicking unpalatable but discerned no way to avoid this added weight.[51]

To create more capital, Ike and Deep Water Committee members conducted another successful lobbying campaign, this one in Galveston's county, whose thin cadres of voters approved a $1.25 million bond issue. But that amount, though more than doubled by the private subscriptions of Galvestonians, including H. Kempner, still did not reach the needed total for the seawall, grade raising, and bridge.

Kempner was increasing city income substantially by collecting long-delinquent taxes and fees, thus cutting costs and increasing income. To fund traditional city services as well as the seawall, grade raising, and bridge, Kempner searched for further cost savings in city opera-

49. IHK, "Galveston Commission Form." The city-county distinction was quite nominal. County population was so sparse that the city government performed almost all public functions on the Island, and the burden of all the new bonds fell primarily on city taxpayers.

50. Undated, unidentified clipping, probably *New York Times* (ca. June, 1902), DWK Scrapbook, 1894–1915.

51. He recorded later that the issue was not only ultimately "entirely subscribed" but also that "no [Galveston] subscriber who held these bonds for a few years suffered a loss" (IHK, *Recalled Recollections*, pp. 32–33).

tions that had long been spoilsmen's fiefs, and for reservoirs of city funds that may have escaped his own earlier scrutinies. He saved Galveston $1 million in economies while adding no new floating debt in this category. The vehicle tax alone, long unenforced, now yielded an average of $5,000 a year, an insignificant sum by itself. But it helped to swell totals.[52] Despite the attenuated property-tax base, in 1901 Kempner's tax collectors brought in $500,000 more than his pre-storm predecessor, plus savings in collections costs. He assigned $200,000 of this windfall to retiring old debts and $300,000 to permanent improvements. Fellow commissioners acceded to his view that the fire, police, and electric light departments should reduce their personnel (many were still patronage hangovers) and thereafter recruit only merit appointees under more objective methods of public administration. Kempner gained $100,000 annually for Galveston from this economy. He lowered police salaries and the size of the force while requiring it to enforce old ordinances prohibiting bordellos and gambling houses. Long-entrenched lotteries, policy and "numbers" games, and slot machines were no longer immune from police interference. Police officers now enforced midnight closing hours for saloons and arrested prostitutes, pimps, and vagrants, steps that pleased business owners, professionals, and Island religious leaders, including Rabbi Cohen.

Kempner gave spending priority for the installation of new electric streetlights for the business district and many residential streets. It was all intended to prove that Galveston was not only reviving but would do so decently both fiscally and morally, that all residents and their families could live there unafraid of a New Orleans–type environment and that money wasted on gambling might become available for consumer goods.

A non-Island commentator admired Kempner's "great pressure and ingenuity to add to the sources of [city] revenue," noting also that previous city treasurers, presumably while logrolling, "by an extraordinary piece of carelessness," had commonly deposited Galveston funds in non-interest-paying "pet" banks. Now bankwise Kempner moved these funds to interest-bearing accounts elsewhere, generating $60,000 in new annual income for the city. Accounting and billing efficien-

52. Bradford, "Financial Results under the Commission Form of City Government," *National Municipal Review*, p. 374; Turner, "Galveston," p. 610; Munro, "Municipal Government by Commission," *Nation*, p. 322.

cies in water-supply operations squeezed out $105,000 more, and at Kempner's insistence the city attorney shifted $7,500 in previously collected fees to the general treasury.[53]

Ike was particularly aggressive when negotiating with applicants for new or renewed public utility franchises, especially streetcars. The Great Storm had scraped tracks off many streets and made the routes of others obsolete. An unprecedented opportunity existed for either honest franchising and greater efficiency in utility routings, or for mass corruption. Kempner rebuffed spoilsmen and as a result the streetcar franchises alone (not counting electric, gas, or telephone) immediately added $40,000 to the rebuilding pot.

Kempner faced resistance to his unrelenting collection of delinquent property taxes. Some ward aldermen had made property valuations and tax collections their particular hunting grounds for bribes and favors. "Nothing could have been looser than the methods of collection [of taxes] under the ward alderman regime," economist Turner reported: "Delinquent taxes were let go of not merely for a few years; a great share of them were lost forever." Kempner's tax assessors and collectors, following ethical procedures, managed even on the diminished valuation base to collect within $175,000 of the pre-storm best, and dependably rather than spasmodically. "There is no miracle about all this," concluded Turner. "It means simply that for the first time Galveston is operated by businessmen on a business basis."[54]

Galveston in general and Kempner in particular received praise from Theodore Roosevelt and Woodrow Wilson and were soon known in municipal reform circles nationwide. Most important to Kempner, his policies nourished investor confidence in Galveston bonds.[55]

Municipal bonds were not then commonly held by individuals. Banks and specialist investors, concentrated in northeastern centers of capital, acquired them. Such investors held most of Galveston's pre-storm debt. Bondholders' nervousness about Galveston made prospects for the new issue doubtful. The storm had wrecked so much taxable property that holders of pre-storm bonds, chiefly banks and trust firms, had formed a "protective committee," in effect signaling their apprehension that Galveston would default. Sharing this fear,

53. Turner, "Galveston," pp. 613–14.
54. Ibid.
55. IHK, "Galveston Commission Form."

Kempner proposed that holders of the existing securities should defer at least part of the interest due to them without litigation or repudiation by the city. Either bankruptcy or lawsuits would likely scuttle the prospects of selling the new bonds.

Galveston's commissioners assigned Kempner to negotiate with the bondholders' protective committee. He recruited a delegation of prominent Islanders, including fellow Deep Water Committee members George Sealy and banker Bertrand Adoue, to go with him to New York. But Sealy died en route. Canceling the meeting, the Galveston delegates became a funeral escort back to Texas.

In early 1902, Kempner arranged for a special train to bring New York City business and banking leaders to Galveston. He kept them busy almost every hour of their days-long stay with hard looks at balance sheets mixed with land tours and Gulf voyages in glorious weather and with rounds of lunches and dinners. From then till midsummer Ike, again accompanied by Adoue, conferred several times in New York with the bondholders' representatives. He stressed to them Galveston's efforts since the storm to pay interest on its bonded debt, a spectacle so rare in that period of numerous municipal bond repudiations as to evoke from Judge Sidney Dillon, a noted law scholar and critic of defaulting cities and now bondholders' counsel, high praise for the city's good faith, "luck and courage in this period of disaster." Dillon agreed publicly with Ike's proposition that if the bondholders insisted on full and immediate payment of interest, they risked their capital.

In mid-1902 these negotiations produced agreement. For five years the interest rate Galveston had to pay on its obligations lessened, from 5 to 2 percent, without penalties, and with possible further concessions thereafter, ultimately saving the city well over $1 million plus strengthening the immediate market for its other bond issues.[56]

Ike exploited interviews by New York and Texas journalists to broadcast nationwide news both of Galveston's augmenting if still precarious fiscal stability and of his vision for the city. Even Ike's seemingly inexhaustible store of confidence and resiliency must have been strained when in mid-1901 Galveston suffered another flood, one far milder

56. Telegram, May 20, 1902, and IHK interview in *New York Times*, undated (ca. Feb., 1902), both in DWK Scrapbook, 1894–1915. See also "50 Years Ago" columns in *Galveston News*, Apr. 26, Oct. 23, Nov. 19, 1951; IHK, *Recalled Recollections*, p. 34.

than the terrible inundation of 1900. Yet in its six-foot height and capacity to rekindle memories of its gargantuan predecessor, the 1901 storm surge, though causing little destruction, upset residents, insurers, potential investors in Galveston bonds, and, as we shall see (chapter 8), money-heavy beneficiaries of a new oil boom centered in nearby Beaumont.[57] Nevertheless, good auguries abounded.

The 1900 and 1901 cotton crops were large and of fine quality. Internationally the price of cotton was rising. Cotton-related exports (cottonseed cake and meal) through Galveston exceeded $20 million in 1901; wheat exports transcended the pre-1900 volume and value by approximately 8 percent, as did lumber, finished wood products, and minerals. Only livestock exports and imports generally showed declines, and these were modest. Economic indicators reflected Galveston's increased coastal oceanic trades since the deepwater channel was cut from the Gulf into the bay, and now new talk was heard about a canal across Central America to give the Gulf favored access to the Pacific trade as well.[58] But then, from the most trivial-sounding circumstance, a lawsuit threatened to undercut every achievement of the young city official.

One of Kempner's seemingly least abrasive innovations, aimed at improving both public health and the aesthetic appeal of the reviving city, made a felony of cleaning privies during prohibited hours. A violator, fined twenty-five dollars, sued, claiming that the three city commissioners the governor had appointed (a trio that included Kempner) held office in violation of the state constitution requirement calling for popular elections of all officials who implemented felonies. The intended results of the taxes, bond issues, and reformed administration were suddenly rubbery.

A Texas appellate court sustained the allegation of unconstitutionality. Whereupon the state legislature, happily then in session, hastily amended the new city charter so that all the commissioners would be elected, a method of selection the Deep Water Committee had suggested years earlier. The special city election took place in 1903 and voters returned all five incumbent commissioners, including Kempner, to office.[59]

57. Barker, "Partners in Progress," pp. 39–40.

58. Ibid., p. 40.

59. "Ex parte Lewis," *Southwest Reporter* 75 (1903): 811; cf. Barker, "Partners in Progress," pp. 43–44; McComb, *Galveston*, p. 137.

The Seawall, Raised Grade, and Bridge

Ike and his commission colleagues had still to decide on types of construction for the seawall, grade raising, and causeway and to choose contractors. These were forbiddingly large-scale urban engineering projects in terms both of costs and complexity. What a cornucopia for the unreformed government and corrupt builders these projects would have been! In mid-1902, Kempner, the other commissioners, and then the public, in mass meetings on which Kempner insisted and that he helped to arrange, underwent crash courses in at least some technical aspects of seawalls. The commissioners approved finally the proposals of a Dutch firm experienced in reclaiming its flood-prone homeland. The federal government would ultimately supply some rebuilding funds for the small frontage (Thirty-ninth through Fifty-third streets) of Fort Crockett, a military installation on the Island. But the nation had clear constitutional jurisdiction over all the coastal fringe because of the navigability of Galveston Bay. Army and civilian engineers clashed on seawall design. Galveston's commissioners defused the situation by appointing a three-man board of experts, including Henry M. Roberts, a retired chief of the Army's Corps of Engineers. This nice mixture of respect for both experts and politics was Ike Kempner's new political style. Yet Galveston's financial situation was still so desperate that he was unable at once to pay more than half the fees ($750 each) of the three engineer-consultants.[60]

Construction

Despite hosts of uncertainties about the financing of the seawall project and its ultimate capacity to contain the Gulf, work on the wall began in December, 1902. Eighteen months later, in July, 1904, the massive structure defied the Gulf along what would finally be almost five miles of the Island's seaward side. The seawall became a fifteen-to-seventeen-foot-high barrier of granite and concrete blocks reinforced by steel rods, bound together with ties of the same hardy alloy, all set atop pilings driven thirty to forty-five feet into the ground to prevent lateral shifting of components. Sixteen feet wide at its base,

60. *Galveston Daily News*, Jan. 26, 1902; Cheesborough, *Galveston's Commission Form of Government* (reprinted in *Galveston Tribune*, Dec. 31, 1909); IHK, *Recalled Recollections*, p. 32.

the seawall narrowed to a generous walkway at its top, creating a splendid asset for generations of tourists and residents, one since widened to serve additionally as a multilane auto roadway on the flat lip of the ramp that, on the wall's landward side, sloped (the slope being the raised grade) from it to the old ground level at Broadway. The seawall's Gulf side curved in a concave arc to turn incoming waves back on themselves, thus diffusing wave impacts vertically and directing incoming swells to smash on an outer perimeter of "rip-rap" (a reinforcing mosaic of randomly intermixed rocks ranging in size from great blocks to small boulders, placed in front of the seawall to break up waves and diminish undercutting of the wall from currents and tides).

Great concrete pilings and granite blocks were imported by rail or on ships from the mainland, then laboriously hauled on mule-drawn wagons from either the train depot or bayside wharves to the work site. "Little Susie," the repaired Galveston rail utility, built tracks to the Gulf to carry bulk materials. At the beach huge steam-driven pile drivers, of types recently perfected for building monumental bridges, tunnels, and mines, and brought to Galveston disassembled, opened huge holes in the sandy soil down to the clay subsurface. Work gangs followed the pile drivers, mixing enormous vats of concrete and pouring it around steel-reinforced rods set into the new holes. When the mix hardened, great cranes positioned pre-shaped stone blocks onto the foundations. Workers then attached concave forms into which more mountains of concrete were poured to assume, when hardened, the desired contour. Once rip-rap defended the wall's foundations along the Gulf reaches, that section of the seawall was finished. Then the battalions of workers with machines and animals moved on to the next section a few hundred yards westward. The seawall soon proved itself an effective buffer against the angriest seas and winds, proving the validity of Ike's decisions, and has become an integral, essential part of Island life for residents and visitors alike.[61]

61. Roberts, "Curbing the Sea at Galveston," *Scientific American*, p. 268; Hudson, "The Great Sea Wall at Galveston," *Scientific American*, pp. 163–64. (In July, 1904, the major portion of the wall, to Thirty-ninth Street, was finished, and its extension to Fifty-third Street was celebrated a year later. Eastward extensions of the wall in the 1920s reached Sixth Street, and in the 1960s the wall was doubled in length to shield the land westward from Fifty-third to 103rd streets, increasing its length to ten miles.) *Galveston Daily News*, Oct. 28, 1902, Jan. 23, 1903.

The seawall under construction (Courtesy Rosenberg Library Archives, Galveston, Texas)

The Galveston commissioners advanced simultaneously the grade-raising effort. By contrast to free-standing walls like the ancient ones of China or Jerusalem, Galveston's ramplike raised grade was to make the land side of the lofty seawall almost invisible, and the seawall is therefore most physically impressive when viewed from the sea. The wall justifies a rhapsodist's description of it as "one of the greatest engineering works of modern times."[62]

From landside, however, the raised grade impresses when one stands on the wall's top. The gradually angled earth buttress formed by the raised grade is the foundation for a new gridiron of south-north streets and abutting houses. It extends from the wall's crown to the old street level at Broadway, the Island's major east-west avenue. The ramp thus obscures the substantial height and breadth of the wall structure in order to realize its primary function.

Grade raising proved to be a much more complicated source of legal, political, and human-relations problems than the seawall, and its first phase was not completed until 1910. (A second phase took place

62. Turner, "Galveston," p. 615.

The seawall after completion of the initial phase (Courtesy Rosenberg Library Archives, Galveston, Texas)

after a major storm in 1915, to drain Galveston areas adjoining the city center.) The seawall grew primarily on vacant public beaches. By contrast, the grade-raising had to take place in the heart of the city. The property and the legal rights of virtually every landowner and tenant in numerous Galveston buildings (ultimately, well over two thousand) were affected by odors, noises, mud, dust, and dislocations.

The commissioners decided after careful consideration to accept the proposal by an engineering firm with offices in New York and Germany. Their project included a canal across the Island from the south jetty to Third Street. It would serve two purposes. The first, long yearned for by Galveston merchants irked by flood-prone roads and muddied goods, was better drainage through the new canal (which would be covered over after the grade-raising was completed). The second involved using the excised earth from the canal plus silt pumped from the bay bottom to create the inclined and raised grade embankment on the land side of the rising seawall along the entire length of the latter.[63] In this manner the grade of the entire southern section of the city most vulnerable to floods would double, to sixteen feet above mean sea level. The embankment would also buttress the seawall, its partner in protection and its Gulfside anchor.

63. Ibid., pp. 614–16. Details concerning the seawall are derived also from numerous clippings in DWK Scrapbook, 1894–1915; and Bates, "Galveston," *Scientific American*, p. 64.

The raised grade. Shorings and new foundations on the old level can be seen at left. (Courtesy Rosenberg Library Archives, Galveston, Texas)

But, all this angled area was relatively densely tenanted and intensively used; the affected streets were filled with homes, shops, and a few light industries, plus schools and hospitals. All owners and lessees had legal rights. Outright confiscation was too arbitrary for serious consideration even in post-storm Galveston. But the need for the grade increase was also clear, and Galveston's commissioners freely used "eminent domain" powers of the state, powers delegatable by Texas to its subordinate constituent governments such as counties and cities, to advance the general good against property owners who were unwilling to sell to the city or to grant rights of access. After prescribed hearing procedures such owners received market value compensation from the city or county. These estimates were appealable to courts. Few were.

Work on the canal began in the summer of 1904. It was to be twenty feet deep and three hundred feet wide. Advancing methodically one or two city street-lengths at a time, laborers took apart all viable houses and commercial buildings in manner to allow reassembly. Structures too decrepit to raise or to move, including many abandoned since the storm, were destroyed, and the materials usually salvaged for some reuse. In a trade-off that bears Ike's stamp, the property owners involved paid the moving expenses and the city remitted taxes for the duration of the relocation. Then, with the drainage canal filling with bay water behind them (to the joy of a generation of Island youths who swam, sometimes riskily because of the unstable, unreinforced canal walls), workers advanced to an adjoining section. Behind them, other crews laid down earth from the diggings and from bay silt.

City officials, on notice from the construction supervisors, gave affected residents two weeks in which to prepare their property for removal, elevation, or destruction. Other than structures in the canal excavation area, few buildings were moved. Instead, workers jacked up almost 2,150 buildings onto piers higher than those on which they were originally constructed. The height to which a particular structure needed to be raised depended on its site in relationship to the planned ramp to the seawall—a theoretical height in early stages, leading to future irritations for those owners whose buildings perched ridiculously high on piers, or so low as to be below the new grade level.

Section by section beginning at its highest point just behind the seawall and descending gradually toward Broadway, where commerce proceeded as usual, for six years work on the inclined plane made every successive section of south Galveston resemble a combined military camp and contractor's yard. Smoke-belching steam engines powered pile drivers, derricks, hoists, and industrial saws. The noise was frightful. The vigorous language of workers offended gentlefolk. Rains made muddy bogs of cleared areas. Vegetation cleared from affected sites was commonly buried under the fill, producing offensive stenches as decomposition progressed. In dry spells, dust rose in great clouds, especially from layered oyster shells that were formerly roads. Miles of wooden sidewalks offered residents, and shoppers, and tourists, precarious access to affected homes, shops, and warehouses.[64]

As the pace of work increased, contractors for materials and labor had to revise many estimates upward. Kempner accommodated seem-

64. E. R. Thompson, Jr., "History of H. Kempner" (manuscript), Kempner Papers, pp. 19–20.

An index to the scale of the raised grade: a fire hydrant at the old level (Courtesy Rosenberg Library Archives, Galveston, Texas)

ingly legitimate overbudget requests and denied others. But granting proper petitions meant unanticipatable, spasmodic searches for more city income, and this at a time of still-attenuated tax bases and of a citizenry almost all of whose personal budgets were stretched by the storm.

In 1910, five years after the seawall's first phase challenged the sometimes militant Gulf, the primary grade-raising project was completed. It was only half complete when construction began on Kempner's third pet project, the multiple-use bridge or causeway across Galveston Bay to the mainland.

To finance the causeway, Kempner negotiated with Galveston

County so that it issued the requisite bonds. Intensive consultations with bridge architects, Army Corps of Engineers, and railroad and shipping executives led to public meetings that resulted both in approvals for another bond issue and for a "bascule" (i.e., counterweighted) drawbridge, ultimately the world's largest span to be lifted by a roller pivot or counterbalance to a height sufficient for tall-masted or funneled ships to pass through. The bridge carried not only railroad tracks but also a roadway for motor vehicles and wagons and a pedestrian walkway. For all preceding decades, Galvestonians had resorted to boats for this lifeline until the Santa Fe had built a single-track railroad bridge. In a further example of Kempnerian cooperation, the railroad companies installed on the new bridge modern signaling devices for train traffic. Ninety-nine years later the bridge is still operative.

The causeway opened for traffic in 1915. Now mainland farmers had a sure, swift, and cheap way to reach the Island, and Galveston merchants enjoyed reciprocal benefits concerning mainland markets. The old, picturesque but raffish "mosquito fleet" that for decades had ferried people, livestock, and produce across the bay, began to disappear. Houston's growing population quickly exploited the causeway as the vacation route of choice leading to the beachfront pleasures of Galveston, and tourism increased on the Island. And in all this recovery from the terrible 1900 storm, Ike Kempner played a central role.[65]

Retrospection

Galvestonians have celebrated the protective measures and policies in which Kempner played central roles after every severe storm and each good tourist year from then to now. Many other cities, including San Francisco, Toronto, Des Moines, and Columbus, Ohio, plus communities along much of Mississippi's Gulf shore, were to pay him and Galveston the compliment of adapting the commission form to their needs and ways. A long list of academics saw Galveston's commission reform as the crowning reform achievement of the time. Woodrow Wilson, for example, in 1911 stated that "no single movement of reform in our governmental methods has been more signifi-

65. Barker, "Partners in Progress," pp. 50–52.

cant than the rapid adoption of the . . . commission form of government in the cities of the country." This "Texas Idea" received praise by business groups, the National Municipal League, and Harvard president Charles W. Eliot, the last stating that Galveston's successes were lights piercing the "dark days" of civic corruption.[66]

In subsequent decades, in strikingly different situations and moods from those of 1900–1901, Galvestonians themselves were to alter their turn-of-the-century, post–Great Storm innovation in public governance, the commission form. Some analysts suggest that the changes measure defects that should have been visible in 1902, and that Kempner's Herculean recovery and reform efforts were part of a plot by elitists to halt rather than spur Galveston's economic progress.[67] To such suggestions this account now turns.

66. Wilson quoted in *Galveston Daily News*, May 22, 1911; Eliot quotation and other data in Bradley R. Rice, "Galveston Plan of City Government," pp. 365, 407–408.

67. McComb, *Galveston*, p. 135 and chap. 4.

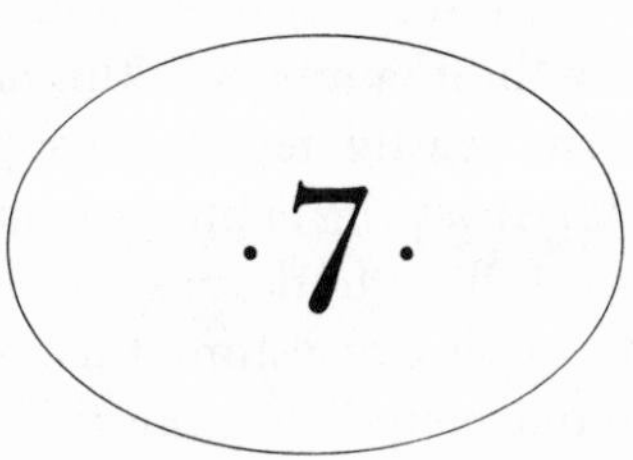

The "Fly in Amber" Controversy

Accusations

"The Sealys, Kempners and Moodys ran the Galveston economy, ruled society, and directed politics until after World War II," concluded David McComb in his 1986 history of the Island City. McComb also wrote that "they reigned because the economy was stagnant and the population grew but slowly. There was no new blood, no one to rock the boat, and people of vitality went to Houston." This is a hardened tradition. Proceeding backward to review it, in 1987 Galveston mayor Jan Coggeshall was accused of "kowtow[ing] to special interests, old-money families, developers, the tourist industry and others."[1] In 1975 historian Ruth Kelly asserted that since the 1900 Great Storm the Island's oligarchs obstructed Galveston's economic progress because of their "overweaning [*sic*] pride of accomplishment and arrogant optimism," producing flawed public policies and marketplace practices. Journalist John Gunther argued similarly in 1960 that the "seignorial" families, in order "to hold . . . [Galveston] within their grip, deliberately sought to keep it from expanding and competing with Houston, which presently began to grow rapidly. . . . Today . . . [Galveston is] a fly in amber—not decayed, but arrested."[2]

Historian–lawyer–political scientist Earl Fornell of Rice University in 1956 attributed Houston's triumph over Galveston to the fact that the leading Islanders were "primarily mercantile-Southern gentle-

1. McComb, *Galveston*, p. 174; *Houston Chronicle*, June 15, 1987, p. 1.
2. Kelly, " 'Twixt Failure and Success" (MA thesis), p. 100. See also IHK, *Recalled Recollections*, p. 44; and Gunther, *Taken at the Flood*, p. 18.

men, remarkably cultured men, who, . . . [b]ecause they loved a conservative way of life, . . . lost control of an empire to the 'plungers of Houston.'" Including the Kempners in this allegedly shortsighted and indolent breed, Fornell castigated them for preferring immediate profit-taking instead of reinvesting capital to modernize the port and city, most especially for failing to develop a "fanlike" rail system of north-south trunk lines with Galveston at its apex as an alternative to the east-west transcontinental that nourished Houston.[3]

Frank Goodwin's breezy but more reasonable 1955 overview of "Lone-Star Land" hit closer to the mark. Formidable natural obstacles impeded Galveston's growth after 1900, Goodwin perceived. These included the Great Storm itself, limited high-cost land, uncertain water supply for industry and residences, and, even after the causeway, inadequate vehicular connections to the mainland. Ranging from fear of more Great Storms and concerns about epidemics, human responses compounded nature's suppressive effects and throttled Galveston's efforts to compete with Houston for trade and manufacturing. Essentially correct, Goodwin nevertheless also concluded that an additional cause of the Island's torpidity was the major families' shortsighted selfishness since the crucial early decades of the century.[4]

Ike's son Harris, who, born in 1903, grew up in the backwash of the Great Storm and carried on his father's and family's efforts to resurrect and reform the city, challenged the "oligarchy" and "fly in amber" theses. "I don't think there has ever been a time when Galveston . . . has been controlled by the old interests," he asserted in 1980. "In the first place, they didn't agree about anything themselves. The Sealys and ourselves were very close friends and saw each other socially constantly . . . [but] had practically no business dealings and differed about a great many things." Over the decades Harris had been troubled enough by the resilient accusations to demand that persons offering it "give me one specific instance of [a Kempner] running anybody off [Galveston] or trying to prevent somebody from coming here with . . . a home or business or . . . industry or anything. . . . I don't think they [the alleged instances] exist, but if they do they must be damn few because no one has furnished me with one. . . . It's a nice

3. Fornell in *Houston Post*, Sept. 30, 1956.
4. Goodwin, *Lone-Star Land*, pp. 160–62.

way to excuse all the things you find wrong—that somebody else caused it to happen. I don't believe it."[5]

Should anyone?

The very meaning of "oligarchy" has become an imprecise near-epithet. A specialist on Houston's history has concluded that "much work and reconsideration needs to be done . . . [on] the conception of a 'business oligarchy.' . . . [It] . . . distracts as much as it helps, largely because it tends to minimize the complex relationship between business and government over the course of the city's history."[6] So, too, for Galveston.

Later pages will attend to some of the "complex relationships between business and government" that both affected the Kempners and that they helped to shape. But attention goes first to reasons why Kempners continued efforts to develop, not throttle, Galveston both economically and as a community.

Family Cohesion

The scholar's task, according to one reevaluation, is "to grasp and to analyze . . . [an individual's emotions and interests] reciprocally in order to understand the forces which shape inter-familial relationships, determine the level upon which exchange takes place and create conflict and tensions which need to be resolved or which bring about severance of connections."[7] Ike's almost three-quarters-of-a-century career at the helm of H. Kempner and the roles also of his brothers, sisters, mother, and then of some of their children, justify this call to grasp and analyze.

His late father's aspirations attracted Ike in the pre–Great Storm years 1894–1900. Then that dramatic event escalated the earlier allure to an irresistible impulsion, one that his mother encouraged in all her children, especially the boys as they matured. Beginning in the early twentieth century Ike and then Dan, Lee, and Stanley searched for ways to translate their father's shadowy goals of the

5. Harris L. Kempner, interview with Robert L. Jones, June 17, 18, 1980, RLA.

6. Fisher, "Houston, Texas" (Southern Historical Association, 1985), unpaginated [1–3].

7. Medick and Sabean, eds., *Interest and Emotion*, pp. 10–13.

1890s into appropriate lifetime family policies. In so doing, the Kempners accommodated individual selfishness with larger sensibilities while addressing family and community interests.[8]

Considered this way the 1900 Great Storm was both an encouragement for Kempners to essay large projects and a threat to their father's dream for them as a family in a community, a perception better explaining Ike's enormous activity on behalf of Galveston's regeneration. Thereafter Kempners linked emotions and interest about family and community to the crisis context of the Great Storm. Ike's simultaneous efforts to restore Kempner business activities, to reform Galveston's government, and to create a small model community at Sugar Land (see chap. 8) were devotions both to emotion and to interest, a death-to-regeneration cycle with regeneration remaining uncertain for a wearyingly long time.

H. Kempner Properties

H. Kempner properties were another reason the Kempners sought to move the city forward. First estimates after the storm were that all was dismal about Kempner interests, second looks, less so. "The sheds of Merchants and Planters Compress were totally destroyed," a journalist reported, "the loss between $25,000 and $30,000." A happier note: "Machinery not injured." Less happy: The Kempners' Island City Manufacturing Company (wholesale clothing) "lost on stock . . . $20,000, which absorbs the profits of the year." Happier note: "Otherwise the company was not injured and its capital was not impaired." The Kempner-owned Galveston Shoe and Hat Company building was a ruin, the upper three stories strewn across Twenty-fourth Street "together with the stock of the goods." Happier note: No injuries to persons in any of these buildings. Soon Kempner's employees were readying the usable merchandise for salvage sales and advising brewers about bargains in soaked grains. To journalists, politicians, suppliers, investors, and brokers outside Galveston, businessman Kempner constantly stressed his confidence in the city as an environment

8. Suttle, "The Passion of Self-Interest," *American Journal of Economics and Sociology*, p. 459; Hareven, "Family History at the Crossroads," *Journal of Family History*, pp. ix–xxiii.

for profits. He told a Houston gathering that "I am ambitious to be among the first who will start reconstruction. The Merchants and Planters Compress will be among the first, if not the very first, press to resume business in the city."[9]

By the end of 1901, Ike, in addition to his city work, with Seinsheimer's and Dan's essential full-time assistance, especially with the rehabilitation of the Merchants and Planters (M&P) Compress, and with tutoring Lee and Stanley about H. Kempner enterprises, had overseen the restoration of all the family's storm-damaged businesses to pre-disaster scale and vigor. These years became intense, compacted, urgent on-job apprenticeships for all the younger Kempner brothers. Dan especially proved to be an able tutor and overseer, and before the end of 1901 Kempner salesmen were on the road again, taking orders, a journalist reported, "and . . . meeting with success."[10] The M&P was working "on a larger scale than before" after a technologically adventurous fuel conversion from coal to oil. H. Kempner and other major stockholders of the Galveston Shoe and Hat Company, the stock value of which had been halved by the storm, were making up the company's operating deficit so that it "resumed its business with unimpaired capital." And the quasi-private Wharves, as noted earlier, was reconstructing its piers, grain elevators, and storage sheds in a partnership between it and city government that seemed to contemporaries to place Galveston on the crest of the modernity wave.[11]

Ike's Leadership

Looking back to Harris Kempner's death, Eliza and the younger children had depended on "Brother Ike," as they called him all their lives. His early head-of-family leadership status is evident in his monitoring of his siblings' educations. True to prevailing gender attitudes, Ike attended more to his brothers' schooling than to his sisters'. In order to oversee Dan's progress at the University of Virginia and Lee's at the same nearby prep school that he and Dan had attended, Ike

9. Undated *Houston Post* clipping, DWK Scrapbook, 1894–1915.
10. All details in undated, unidentified clippings, DWK Scrapbook, 1894–1915.
11. Ibid.; Barker, "Partners in Progress" (Ph.D. diss.), chap. 1.

Dan Kempner, ca. 1910 (Courtesy Leonora K. Thompson)

exploited the rabbinical network through Rabbi Cohen. Also like his father, Ike encouraged his brothers to excel as students, avoid excessive indulgence in sports, and to explore the widest possible cultural horizons, first as students and then as travelers abroad. Despite Ike's wishes, Dan returned to Galveston upon his graduation and began a procession of younger brothers into eclectic Kempner enterprises that Ike and they developed.

In decades to come, Great Storm or no, Ike and all Kempners developed his ideas of a family business based on an intact estate and on the spread of profits and losses equally among family members.

The result of these ideas was a planetary system of diverse local and regional businesses.[12] Some of these enterprises, the sugar operation, for example, were to grow to great size. Others (banking and insurance) were of more modest scale, and some (oil and real estate) became primarily investments. H. Kempner's cotton and private banking operations formed the hub. All served the goal of family cohesion in complementary if differing ways.

The Business of Family Cohesion

All H. Kempner enterprises provided Ike's brothers, when and if qualified, with access to lifetime executive careers. These enterprises also gave all the Kempners, males and females alike, equal shares in the pooled profits or losses of all the linked businesses, including those that cotton merchant Ike rang up at H. Kempner. Appropriate spin-off businesses, especially the bank and the insurance company, themselves became credit sources for both H. Kempner as private banker and cotton merchant, and for other diverse ventures that were creditworthy, thus offering attractive alternatives to external money markets.

Ike ran H. Kempner, and he influenced—not controlled—all the family interests. Substantial collegiality in decision-making would develop, especially among the males, but also engaging the females as equal shareholders in calendared meetings of the family in Galveston. The result: reasons for the males, especially, to establish lifetime residences in or near Galveston, while providing for the financial well-being of all the family, while yet encouraging both independence and concert. Ike encouraged cohesion also by casting himself, his brothers, and Seinsheimer as a board of directors, and all his siblings (and later their spouses) as a collegial assembly of equal beneficiaries in what became the H. Kempner conglomerate, a term not yet in use during Ike's young manhood.[13]

They developed this structure gradually while struggling simultaneously to repair and reform the storm-abused city, while experimenting with the generation of a livable company town at Sugar Land, and while transforming H. Kempner to a cotton merchant operation.

12. The Kempner ideas about family cohesion, or sense of family, are known as *Familengefühl* in German. See Birmingham, "*Our Crowd*," p. 386.

13. "We were conglomerates before the word was invented" (Harris L. Kempner, interview with L. Marchiafava, June 6, 1981, RLA).

Somewhat perilously, H. Kempner and its affiliates remained legally under widow Eliza's control as executrix of the survivors-in-community estate. Then in 1920 the family substituted an unincorporated trust in its place. Trust shareholders, still Eliza and all her children, owned equally the much-enhanced pooled value of H. Kempner and the several closely held family businesses that became tied to it.[14]

Perils of Business Dynasties

Today generation-spanning family businesses such as Harris and Ike dreamed of are known to possess great hazards for their intended beneficiaries. Specialized consultants and psychologists exist now to blunt the hazards of family businesses destroying the family, and vice versa.[15] But Harris and Ike Kempner, unserved by specialist counselors or prescience, seem to have apprehended few if any of the difficulties in passing on not only their money but also their purposes.

Ike's life would have been simpler and he wealthier had he struck out on his own, contrived to be H. Kempner's solo head and chief beneficiary, or incorporated the firm and left its management to professional executives. In a sense, he was operating in an unusual fashion, for there was in his day a cult favoring efficiency, corporate forms, and professional managers.[16] Even if of large scale, family businesses were notably inefficient. Ancient family feuds and new jealousies inspire conspiracies, coups, and sellouts to strangers. Heirs or rival beneficiaries of institutionalized nepotism struggle so mightily to control or to dispose of business estates as to evoke analogies with Greek tragedies, Old Testament preachments, King Lear, and Hamlet.

Nepotism was one particularly serious plague of family businesses. In novelist Garson Kanin's acerbic account of the early years of the motion picture industry, his heroine, the young descendant of a Jewish Hollywood pioneer, described her own occupation as that of an

14. H. L. Kempner, "Beneficiary Interest Report," Jan. 21, 1986.

15. Muson, "Generations," *New York Times Magazine*, Nov. 29, 1987, p. 25. See also Bork, *Family Business, Risky Business*.

16. Collier and Horowitz, *The Fords;* Brenner, *The Bingham Family of Louisville;* Chandler, *The Binghams of Louisville;* Lacey, *Ford;* on the Sakowitz family, see *Houston Chronicle*, Feb. 22, 1988, sec. 2, p. 3; Clark, "Authority and Efficiency," *Journal of Economic History*, p. 1069; Hawley, "The Corporate Component of America's Quest for National Efficiency, 1900–1971" (Organization of American Historians, 1986), pp. 2–3.

agent "with my uncle's company. Our family is not religious," she continued, "but we do believe in nepotism."[17]

Nepotism's great ill was that it elevated incompetents and trapped abler veteran staff in dead ends, often forcing their defections to rivals. Ike and his brothers worked out ways both to provide male Kempners with executive positions, if they trained for them and exhibited effectiveness once in place, and yet retain longtime devoted, able non-Kempner managerial staff. Nepotism became an accepted fact of Kempner family life over generations for many purposes, as suggested in a 1959 letter from Ike's grandson to the then–H. Kempner office manager: "I must get out of the habit of using my family."[18]

But the family wanted to be used. As an example, in 1960 Ike wanted urgently to recruit his grandson, Isaac Kempner III ("Denny," b. 1932), for future top management of the family-owned Imperial sugar refinery. He could start as "understudy, or sub-executive" to the incumbent manager. "There would be no nepotism involved," Ike wrote, "nor in placing you on the road to earn promotions in the Sugar Co. — if that is preferred [in the future by you]." If the younger man refused, however, the situation "could easily become a matter of urgency, which could defeat the great pride we should have in the efforts and success of another Kempner at Sugarland."[19] Of course nepotism was involved.

In addition to the perils of nepotism, few family businesses attracted adequate fresh capital or adapted production to changing technology or markets. Minefields multiplied in unincorporated enterprises like H. Kempner. Their owners were subject to unlimited personal liability for adverse legal judgments, and rancorous family businesses often spawned lawsuits.

Succession in Jewish Family Businesses

Succession was and is "one of the most difficult challenges facing any family business," concluded the chroniclers of the DuPonts' for-

17. Kanin, *Moviola*, p. 29.

18. Edward ("Tim") Thompson, letter to A. M. Alpert, Nov. 27, 1959, "Alder-Alpert" folder, Box 158, #80-002, Kempner Papers.

19. Oct. 12, 1960, Box "I.H.K. Personal, 1960," #80-002, Kempner Papers. The incumbent Imperial manager, Bill Louviere, did not retire until 1964, meanwhile holding to a policy that there was no room in top management. Robert Arm-

tunes.[20] Especially in Jewish families, founders' businesses that lubricated social mobility often bred generational discontinuities. Often, the younger generation's choices for careers in the professions or other white-collar fields resulted in fierce family factionalizations that commonly alienated adult children from both their family and its religious tradition. Expensive and protracted litigations led to the permanent estrangements of siblings and diffusion of the founders' estates.[21]

With the full support of his mother and siblings, Ike nevertheless chose the rocky family business route that led to the goals the father had sketched and that Ike developed. As developed gradually, H. Kempner became a galaxy of family-run businesses in which Ike would long be the first among equals in policy-making. Nurturing collegiality, cohesion, and consensus and keeping roughly equal all heirs' shares in profits, H. Kempner's entrepreneurial astronomy perpetuated mutuality across generations. Yet Harris Kempner and then Ike had created conditions that in other families invited frictions, discontinuities, frustrations, and litigations.

Long before the century's turn German-Jewish financiers, especially in New York, some of whom had resettled there after reaping rich rewards from entrepreneurship in the American South and West, had their lawyers and accountants devise suitable transgenerational transfers.[22] What set Kempners apart was their durable commitment to community, to neighboring family residences in the region where the founder had won his first large prosperity, to the mixing of further acquisitions of wealth with impressive devotion to civic improvements, and to the maintenance of mutually respectful interfamily relationships over generations.

Probably as a result of his endless troubles with ne'er-do-well young nephews and cousins, their father had left as a heritage to his sons the mandate to bring outsiders into management if qualified family members, whether blood or in-law kin, were not available. The Kemp-

strong became president in 1964 and encouraged Denny's move to Imperial (R. M. Armstrong's memorandum, in Leonora K. Thompson, letter to author, Aug. 18, 1988, in possession of author).

20. Chandler and Salsbury, *Pierre S. DuPont and the Making of the Modern Corporation*, p. 301.

21. Wayne, "Brothers at Odds," *New York Times*, Dec. 7, 1986, p. 102.

22. Langbein, "The Twentieth-Century Revolution in Family Wealth Transmission," *Michigan Law Review*, pp. 722–51; Supple, "A Business Elite," in *The American Jewish Experience*, pp. 73ff.

ners' success is measurable by others' failures, as, often attended with embarrassing publicity, heirs carried on costly litigations to break restrictive wills or trusts, or to deny one particular heir, often the oldest sibling, control over inheritances. In Galveston, prominent neighbors who perhaps rivaled Ike in business acumen proved to be less able than he to keep family ties from unraveling, often very publicly. "I have watched with embarrassment while other [Galveston] families battled in court over their estates," Ike mused in 1957.[23]

Recruiting in the Family

Ike's younger sister Sara recalled decades later that "when each one of the boys finished college and came home, Brother Ike would ask them what branch of the family's interests would you like to go into? And it was Lee's turn . . . and he said, I think I'd like to start in the bank. And Brother Ike said, all right, tomorrow morning at 7:30 you go down and sweep it out. That's how he began, and he ended up as president. You had to work for what you got."[24]

And work they did. Ike was not creating sinecures for unproductive placeholders. Nepotism had limits. So beginning with their forced-draft labors in the Great Storm's wake, as noted earlier, Ike's brothers endured rugged apprenticeships under his, Seinsheimer's, then Dan's tutelage in H. Kempner itself before moving on to whatever affiliated enterprise interested them. To achieve management they had to be effective. Ike retained and advanced only those who exhibited commitment and achievement, later sometimes preferring talented outsiders, including incumbent managers of newly acquired companies.

"Isaac Kempner demanded the best of everyone . . . and he had the power," longtime H. Kempner cotton traffic manager Hyman Block reported. Ike encouraged Block and other long-tenure, trusted non-Kempner office staff to monitor everything and everyone, including his brothers as they came on board. Block himself remained in H. Kempner employment for more than forty years, rising to middle manager rank; Benjamin Reading and his assistant, Betty Goldstein, stayed

23. IHK, interview in *Houston Post*, Oct. 20, 1957, sec. 1, p. 9; and see Train, "Rejuvenating Old Money," *New York Times Magazine*, June 8, 1986, pp. 90, 128ff.
24. Sara K. Weston, interview with L. Marchiafava, Aug. 28, 1981, RLA.

more than thirty years. Fidelity and long service reaped rewards in H. Kempner's associated businesses as well. Robert Armstrong graduated from high school in 1926 and started in a menial capacity at Imperial Sugar. Himself the son of a Kempner salesman who had worked at Imperial for long periods of time since 1908, Armstrong would retire as president of Imperial Sugar in 1973, and in 1987 remained a member of the board of directors.

Persons like these understood that "you would get up [only] so far then you hit the bottom rank [of managers] and a lot of that was Kempner," according to Block. But most stayed on with H. Kempner or its affiliates.[25]

Keeping in mind Ike's dedication to his father's ideas and to his own 1898 scheme, his delight fifty years later can be imagined in being able to record that "Our brother Dan came on [into H. Kempner] in 1898, after graduating from the University of Virginia. . . . On entering he in a short time brought valuable economic improvements, especially in the keeping of our business records."[26] Ike described the year 1904 as one "of marked activity . . . [when] Lee, after an apprenticeship of a few years in the [Merchants National Bank in Houston, of which Ike had become the commuting president], became cashier of the Texas Bank & Trust Company; [and] Dan became active in [the] management of the Texas Star Flour Mill, we having . . . [a large] interest in the mill."[27] In addition to training future upper-level managers for H. Kempner, Dan expertly managed its M&P Compress.

Young Stanley Kempner first had some business experience in cotton by-products, Ike recorded, coming into it "without a university education, virtually as an office boy." Stanley ("Pat" to his familiars) found himself assigned eclectically because some H. Kempner loans to local businesses were in trouble. Stanley became H. Kempner's "swing man," Block remembered. The youth monitored conformity to whatever stipulations the Kempner bank imposed on rocky borrowers. And so, having thus become involved successively in a jewelry business and a cattle feedlot operation, Stanley next embarked on the

25. Hyman Block, interview with L. Marchiafava, June 6, 1981, RLA; Robert Armstrong, interview with author, Feb. 10, 1987, in author's possession.

26. IHK, "H. Kempner," p. 8.

27. IHK, *Recalled Recollections*, p. 38; H. L. Kempner, "Beneficiary Interest Report, 1963."

export of cottonseed, cake, and meal in a corporation in which H. Kempner had a majority of the capital stock, and he later became interested in life insurance.[28] "Our firm [H. Kempner] had been the founder of what is now the Texas Prudential Life Insurance Company," Ike wrote. "Under Stanley's direction as president the firm achieved a steady and remunerative growth." Stanley earned his insurance wings when undercapitalized Houstonians, having incorporated the American National Life Insurance Company, in 1903 moved their new company to Galveston, and Ike happily noted that "Stanley Kempner shortly afterward began climbing to the [company's new offices in the] . . . Moody bank building at 22nd and Strand, starting his insurance career."[29]

Dropping out of the University of Virginia, Lee, after assisting the managers of an H. Kempner sugar plantation at Sugar Land (see below, chap. 8), headed for a banking apprenticeship, becoming active in the Island City Savings Bank. After H. Kempner acquired control of this bank in 1902, its name became the Texas Bank and Trust Company (later, United States National Bank). Lee was to be its president for more than four decades. The pattern endured, although the duties of those who desired change changed with the decades, Ike reporting in 1952 that "the cotton business of H. Kempner is under the direct management of Harris L. Kempner, son of I. H. Kempner. . . . The warehousing and shipping of cotton is directed by D[aniel] W[ebster] Kempner. The life insurance business is directed by . . . S[tanley] E[ugene] Kempner. The importing and refining of sugar is handled by I. H. Kempner, Jr. [Ike's son, known as "Herb," who was to die the following year]."[30]

Obviously no Kempner was limited to a particular calling. Rather, with the family's combined resources on tap during these "Years of Acquisition" for H. Kempner, everyone could search for his own way (except for the women, and for Ike's own control over H. Kempner). These ventures outside the H. Kempner cotton business tied together the financial interests of every member of the family and provided

28. Hyman Block, interview with L. Marchiafava, Aug. 1, 1981, RLA.

29. IHK, "H. Kempner," p. 10, and *Recalled Recollections*, p. 39. On the fate of this insurance venture with Moody, see chap. 10.

30. Quotation from memo, June 6, 1952, in file "CG&SFRR – Galveston," #80-003, Kempner Papers; other details, IHK, *Recalled Recollections*, pp. 38, 41, 43; H. L. Kempner, "Beneficiary Interest Report, 1963."

generations of the men, almost as a birthright or marriage benefit, with opportunities for careers.

Most of the external ventures were profitable. If, however, one or another failed to prosper, H. Kempner eventually sold its interest or otherwise disassociated from the unsatisfying venture. Looking backward on eighty years of these procedures, Ike's son Harris L. Kempner stated in 1981 that

> we have never considered that Kempner blood gave them the right to a job! We've always tried very hard to get . . . the business people of each generation to take a place in the family businesses. There's always been more or less a need for them, sometimes more than others, and we have tried very hard to persuade [promising young] people to come to work for us. A number of them went out to work elsewhere and came back to work for us . . . [They] didn't want to come to work for us just because they were related; they wanted to prove themselves elsewhere as a competent executive and then come to work for us. Either they live away or they are engrossed in their own business or profession, or they have inherited businesses from the other side [i.e., their own spouses]. A number of them partake [as board members] in the H. Kempner decisions but they don't work for us.[31]

Business Oligarchy?

Granting that the primary goal of all this activity was family cohesion, was it likely that Kempners joined a tight oligarchy in order to place Galveston's economy and society in metaphorical amber?

Hardly. To be sure, complex relationships existed between business and urban government. The city's chief business leaders, corporate officers, bankers, and lawyers unquestionably did dominate an intimately intertwined kinship and non-kinship network. Leaders of the city government and of diverse business and professional firms mixed public duties and private interests, as in the Wharves and the Deep Water Committee. Alleged conflicts between Wharves policies and civic well-being would become perennially central elements in city politics. Always deriding as unreal "the distinction between civic ownership and Wharf ownership," Ike's son Harris derogated all sug-

31. H. L. Kempner, interview with L. Marchiafava, Aug. 1, 1981, RLA.

gestions that conflicts of interest existed in these interwoven associations. He noted correctly the fact that leading turn-of-century civic reformers viewed such multiple involvements as partnerships in progress.[32] Similar or at least analogous partnerships between bankers, lawyers, transit and utility executives, commodity merchants and other businessmen, and city officials were common in the New South. Since the initiation of Galveston government under the new charter, this formula seemed to promise spoils-free municipal reform along with healthy urban, commercial, and community growth.[33] Ike devoted his talents and energies to both H. Kempner and public service, defining the latter to include the agendas not only of the revenue commissioner and mayor but also concerns shared by the management of the quasi-public Wharves and Deep Water Committee. In such perceptions, government and business interests merged until efforts to separate the two appeared to be irrelevant.

Ike's creative public financing won Galveston the seawall, raised grade, and new bridge plus a rebuilt and enlarged urban infrastructure. It included new schools, water and sewer systems, a repaired city hall and other municipal buildings, resurfaced streets for the business district and several residential sections (including for the first time some predominantly black neighborhoods), modernized police and firefighting equipment, the state university medical college, and the growing commerce brought in on the Intracoastal Canal. He contrived these assets with only modest increases of the pre-storm tax rate and without apparent scandal or even accusations against him.[34]

In addition to Ike's concerns about family cohesion and prosperity, his decades of post-storm involvement in community betterment responded also to exciting contemporary ideas about a city as an organic, dynamic, evolving entity. Perceptions gaining currency then, while ignoring or excusing racial residential segregation, stressed the dangers of urban health posed by ethnic neighborhoods competing for city services. Both the son of an immigrant and a major reformer

32. Quotations in Harris L. Kempner, interview with R. L. Jones, June 16, 1980, RLA. Barker, "Partners in Progress," pp. 54–55, offers a schematic depiction of these connections.

33. Russell, *Atlanta, 1847–1890,* passim.

34. See [IHK], "Kempner Addresses [Tulane University] Economics Society," in DWK Scrapbook, 1894–1915; IHK, *Recalled Recollections*, pp. 56–57; H. L. Kempner, interview with R. L. Jones, June 17, 1980, RLA.

of Galveston's corrupt electoral arrangements, Ike had steeped himself in the literature of urban reform. Cooperation, not competition, was the urban Progressive watchword.[35]

If all this Progressive activity amounted to self-serving self-deception, Kempners had a great deal of company in it. The repairs and improvements in the city's fabric that they helped to initiate had created a cooperative community, the Kempners believed, one that would attract and keep younger relatives as permanent residents. The city had to cope with change, not be an ossified, economically moribund carcass. The new Galveston commission government worked because individuals of probity, commitment, and ethicality served as its officials while simultaneously holding leadership positions in the Deep Water Committee, the Wharves, and other public and quasi-public enterprises, Ike insisted. For all his long life (he died in 1967), Ike remained convinced that the real reform was less the commission structure, valuable as it was, but the interlinked, largely self-perpetuating group that initiated and implemented the reform. So perceived, Ike wrote in 1946, the commission device "is a most dependable instrument, an efficient weapon, a sturdy shield, whose power and worth lie in the hands of the people who have an opportunity to use it."[36] Kempner promoted the commission as a suitable vehicle for ordered urban adaptability to uncomfortable but inescapable changes. He was especially flattered that President Theodore Roosevelt praised the device and that reformers in archrival Houston and nearly a score of other Texas cities adopted variants. Ike became a peripatetic missionary for commission gospel, broadcasting rather than concealing the interwoven pattern of leadership positions in Galveston's reformed government. The openness of these arrangements is suggested also by the fact that Galveston's annual city directory, an inexpensive commercial publication available in libraries, bookshops, and on newsstands, traced them for anyone to read.[37] Such frankness keeps a burden of proof on those who suggest that Kempners and their intimates

35. H. L. Kempner interview with Jones, June 17–18, 1980; Melvin, *Organic City*, passim; IHK, "Galveston Commission Form of Government" (Address to Galveston Historical Society, Feb. 12, 1946), unpaginated, [p. 5]. On Sugar Land as Ike's experiment in a nonutopian but superior city, see below, chaps. 8 and 13.

36. IHK, "Galveston Commission Form of Government," [p. 4]; [IHK], "Kempner Addresses [Tulane University] Economics Society."

37. *Morrison and Fourmy's General Directory of the City of Galveston* (1901–1915).

functioned covertly in intersections of government and business in order to frustrate social change and to gather personal profits.

Ike and the Wharves

To illustrate this balance between public and private, it was, apparently, Kempner among the city officials who reacted negatively when in 1901 the Wharf Company issued bonds to repair and rebuild from the storm, and to continue acquiring new land for additional rail spurs at dockside. Legal questions rose from the company's actions, and Kempner was sensitive to them. The city had not taxed Wharves property acquired since the 1869 Brazoria Decree, and the Wharves Company had paid the city no dividends on profits. Relentlessly searching for new city revenue, in 1905 Kempner initiated lawsuits against the company. In an out-of-court settlement, the only kind that Ike, like his father, favored, the company paid the city sixty thousand dollars, earmarking the money for drainage projects plus two thousand dollars for arrears in fire protection levies, and also paid the city all dividends due to its one-third interest.

Thereafter the Wharves and the city cooperated in acquiring additional bay frontage and building rail freight tracks to be shared with Southern Pacific Railroad. These facilities were assets for the community as well as for the rail company. Such evidence impelled one student of the Wharves to suggest that instead of marking time or looting the city or its commercial customers, the Wharves directors, both private and public, and the municipal officials involved, "concentrated on creating the finest port on the Gulf coast."[38]

So concentrating, Ike became involved more than ever with state and national officials. As part of the Progressive bent toward a more activist government, Texas and federal lawmakers created rate-setting administrative commissions for freight transportation. After lobbying by Deep Water Committee members, the federal rates became lower for shippers routing goods via rail from Chicago, Denver, Kansas City, or Saint Louis to either Houston or Galveston than to New Orleans. Meanwhile construction advanced on the canal across Panama. Galvestonians' hopes increased for new shipping business through the cut. Galveston investors including Kempner encouraged a Nor-

38. Barker, "Partners in Progress," pp. 57–72.

wegian shipping line to initiate Galveston-Mexico freight runs, recruited the Lykes Steamship Company to base operations in Galveston, and launched a Banana and Steamship Company for service to Honduras. With Kempners deeply involved, the "Galveston Movement" for emigrants to America (see chap. 9) inspired a major German shipline, North German Lloyd, to make Galveston one of its primary ports of call. A St. Louis, Brownsville, and Mexican Railroad Company began operations in 1906, and the Seaboard Rice Milling Company opened in Galveston in 1902, by decade's end supplying Puerto Rico with 20 percent of its rice, but further increasing Galveston's export-import imbalance. Rumors of war in Europe became fact in August, 1914, a fact that soon resulted in increased exports through Galveston, especially of grains and cotton.

But, opening in 1914, the same year that the Panama Canal began operations, the Houston-to-Gulf Ship Channel connected deepwater traffic to transcontinental rail trunk lines fifty miles inland from Galveston. Galveston's splendid port facilities became less attractive to shippers. Additional competition developed. Texas City offered free wharf accommodations. Galveston countered by increasing the efficiency of Wharves operations. Then, in 1912–14, the Interstate Commerce Commission approved a $1.75 charge per railroad car of Texas City freight, while stipulating a $3.50 rate for Galveston. Houston also enjoyed a rail rate differential in its favor. The differentials hurt.[39] Worse, Houston's publicly owned port facilities were exempt from price regulations of the Interstate Commerce Commission, and the inland city undercut Galveston tariffs.

Worse still, as noted earlier, by the nature of Texans' concentration on cotton and grains, far more exports than imports, by a 30-to-1 ratio, went through Galveston's port. This imbalance was unhealthy, for it placed the city in an inherently colonial position of increasing its dependency on external centers of rate policy. For example, railroads allowed a reduction for "backhauls," that is, freight cars heading inland laden with imports after unloading commodities at a seaport for export. Because Houston had transcontinental rail trunk lines carrying diverse cargoes in two directions, it profited

39. Ibid., p. 73. See also Houston, East & West Railway Co. *v.* U.S., and Texas & Pacific Railway Co. *v.* U.S., 234 U.S. 342 (1914).

from backhauls. Ironically, both the Panama and Intracoastal canals increased Galveston's export business and thus increased its ultimate disadvantages.

Kempner and others tried to stimulate imports. They succeeded in having the United Fruit Company establish an office at Galveston. But this and similar efforts failed to redress the export excess or to persuade major railroads to route their trains through Galveston rather than Houston.

In sum, a heavy economic hand lay on Galveston.[40] Its visibility may have helped to inspire Ike's almost frantic searches for income alternatives for both Galveston and for H. Kempner. His conviction was that what he was doing served both his and the public's interests. Such mixing of private and public concerns ill suit more democratized and skeptical ways that would prevail in the future. Only if recent standards are applied to the more distant past, however, can the "business oligarchy" and "fly in amber" labels fit Kempner purposes and Galveston's history. In the sense of a united front of selfish, near-conspiratorial spoilsmen, no oligarchy existed. Indeed, even the temporary unity among the city's makeweights inspired by the 1900 Great Storm sundered in its wake.

A notable sunderer was William Moody, Jr., who, having remained largely aloof from Kempner's several relief and recovery efforts, refused to buy seawall securities until risk passed, thus threatening the entire bond issue. Even historian David Q. McComb, who is critical of Kempner, concluded that "the Moody family did not make the transition to social responsibility until the end of the second generation [i.e., the 1960s]."[41]

By the mid-1890s the Kempners had already made the transition to social responsibility, and the unresisting family would travel much further along this path, which is not to endow the Kempners with

40. Potts, *Railroad Transportation in Texas*, pp. 184–89. These basic disadvantages to Galveston shippers deriving from the rail rate structure persisted through succeeding decades, despite ongoing efforts by Ike, other Kempners, and numerous Galveston spokesmen to alter the rate structure. The DWK Scrapbook, 1929–1935, documents such efforts.

41. McComb, *Galveston*, pp. 137–38; IHK, *Recalled Recollections*, pp. 39–41, 49–51, 57, 89–93; Sara K. Weston, interview with L. Marchiafava, Aug. 29, 1981, RLA. See also below, chaps. 15 and 16.

mythic, selfless qualities. But they were more than limited, hyperacquisitive, overthrifty *haute bourgeoisie.* Concern about community quality was an essential cohering element for the family. A primary Kempner commandment was that not even the Great Storm should throttle the city's economic pulse, because an unprosperous, static, decaying community threatened the prosperity of H. Kempner and therefore the family's cohesion.

Family Profits and Prophets

As Moody had noted in his crabbed way, new people and new money encouraged changes. In a manner inharmonious with "fly in amber" motivations, Kempners encouraged new money, new people, and changes. For example, in the depression year 1907 Ike learned that the Cuban cattle market had collapsed. Ships once plying that trade were now surplus. Ike maneuvered to shift their business to the Galveston wharves, himself luring them with H. Kempner's cotton and sugar cargoes. It worked. H. Kempner profited. So did Galveston. Meeting Lee Kempner years later, Mrs. Genevieve Lykes told him that "if it had not been for . . . H. Kempner . . . there may never have been a Lykes Steamship Company [in Galveston]." Perhaps because he was already annoyed by early "fly in amber" gossip, Lee replied, "I'd like to have that in writing." She obliged.[42]

New businesses like the Lykes line or the tourism that Kempners promoted, though not of the labor-intensive, smokestack sort, necessarily required a permanent resident work force. Increased numbers of workers meant more voters who were not addicted to the Kempners' kind of Progressive, "silk-stocking" urban reform politics, if only because those politics affected the most tender of southern sacred cows, race relations.

In 1907 Ike publicly opposed a Jim Crow ordinance for Galveston streetcars. Realizing that the segregationist sentiment in the city council was too strong to sway, he forced the council to publish in newspapers the names of pro-segregationists who had placed the proposition before the voters. Although the ordinance passed, in about one-third of the signers' households the black servants quit, Ike recalled happily fifty years later. But that was the most overt gesture

42. Lykes, *Gift of Heritage*, p. 72.

toward equal race access Kempners were to dare until, in the 1950s and 1960s, Ike, his son Harris, and other Kempners would openly support the Supreme Court's Brown *v.* Board antisegregation decision and oppose efforts to resist its implementation in Galveston restaurants and other places of public resort, in some of which the Kempners had financial interests.[43]

Perhaps father and son took these regionally unpopular public stands primarily in order to persuade blacks that Galveston was a decent place for them to live and work. Nevertheless their forthright positions reflected also family standards of human relationships. Ike summarized them in explaining why he opposed the 1907 Jim Crow ordinance: "Our negro population resented such legislation."[44]

He was far more sensitive to the fact that in the storm's wake, blue-collar America, industrial managers, and investors considered Galveston unsafe.[45] Redefining safety, Ike urged holders of Galveston bonds to buy more of these insecure securities not merely to rebuild the city's damaged infrastructure but basically to improve it with better facilities for providing pure drinking water, quality schools, a modern hospital and medical school, more adequate roads, and sufficient police and firefighting organizations to supplement the seawall, raised grade, and new bridge and make Island life both safe and attractive, thus overcoming mainlanders' fear. That fear, Kempner insisted, was "the sole reason why labor cannot be induced to locate there, and has compelled the closing down of the [pre-storm] cotton mills, the rope mills, and the bagging mills, in fact, [of] almost every manufacturing institution in the city."[46]

Ike's optimism on these matters veneered a justifiable sense of urgency. The 1900 census, taken just before the Great Storm, showed that Houston's population (of approximately thirty-five thousand) had at last crept up to Galveston's, and had surely since surpassed it. Kempner hoped to prevent what did occur—Galveston's relatively flat popu-

43. See chap. 16 and Conclusion, below.

44. IHK, *Recalled Recollection*, pp. 47, 52; on Harris in 1954, Robert Allbright, interview with Steve Wapen, June 8, 1977, RLA. See also Rabinowitz, *Race Relations in the Urban South;* Doyle, "Segregation and Social Change in the Cities of the New South" (Organization of American Historians, 1986).

45. McComb, *Galveston*, pp. 67–68.

46. "To Holders of . . . Bonds . . . of Galveston," unidentified and undated (ca. June, 1902) clipping in DWK Scrapbook, 1894–1915.

lation growth that by 1980 would only double the 1900 figure while Houston's soared to two million. But Galveston's insular character proved to be as intractable a natural obstacle to prosperity as the Great Storm. All island cities are cramped for building space and, as a result, real estate costs are high. But by contrast with Galveston, New York City had diverse light manufacturing and smokestack industries, and the many immigrants who became their skilled and semiskilled work forces swelled tax bases and consumer populations.

Despite all efforts, Galveston attracted few large on-site industries. Its population, talent pool, and tax base increased relatively slowly. Most immigrants debarking at Galveston moved inland, a process that, ironically, the Galveston Movement was itself to encourage (see chap. 8, below). Any substantial new residential, commercial, or industrial developments in Galveston's less expensive, sparsely settled western portions required costly utilities beginning with fresh water and new automobile and train roads from the Island's populated eastern section to San Luis Pass on its western tip. But such roads would lead to nowhere until a bridge spanned that pass to Freeport on the mainland, allowing a rail bypass around Houston. Construction of this essential, costly, seven-thousand-foot span across turbulent San Luis Pass to Brazoria County was to wait, however, till the late 1960s. And by then Houston had become by far the dominant city.

Historian Harold Platt's judgment is sound: "What years of intense lobbying [by Houston's apostles of a deepwater Gulf-to-Houston ship channel] failed to achieve, one terrible storm accomplished."[47] Rarely sitting on their hands, Ike and his colleagues were to broadcast the fact that Galveston suffered only modestly in major storms of 1901 and 1905 and that competing Gulf cities also endured natural afflictions. But, as with earlier rumored or real epidemic diseases, promoters of other Gulf ports effectively claimed that Galveston was cursed with peculiar vulnerability, arguments that these backers "emphasized very vigorously," Ike grumbled later.[48]

At the century's turn and for twenty years after it could not be anticipated that Galveston water wells would be inadequate even for a slowly rising population, much less for incredibly thirsty new in-

47. Platt, *City Building in the New South*, p. 177.

48. IHK, *Recalled Recollections*, p. 34; Sibley, *Port of Houston*, pp. 125–26; McComb, *Galveston*, pp. 150–51; Goodwin, *Lone-Star Land*, p. 160; Barker, "Partners in Progress," pp. 39–40.

dustrial processes, or that majorities would vote to reject municipal bond issues and so let basic urban facilities decay. But failure as a seer is not equal to willful stagnation of a city's economy and society. Available data plus the Kempners' imperatives toward family cohesion made it reasonable for them to try to energize, not immobilize, the Island's economy.

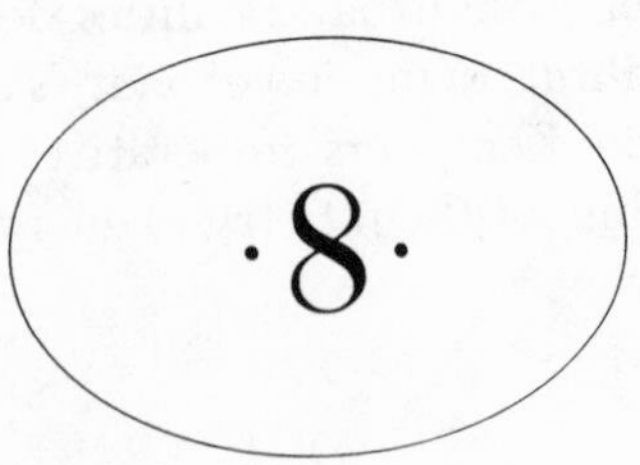

Cotton, Oil, and Sugar

In later years Ike offered autobiographical details to a local chronicler who labeled him correctly as a "Civic Builder and Humanitarian."[1] The writer noted that, like all Galvestonians, Ike had waited for nature to test the soundness of the seawall, raised grade, causeway, and the reformed city government, which he continued to serve until 1915 as revenue commissioner, to prove themselves. Simultaneously, he was rationalizing H. Kempner's cotton operations into a vertical, farmer-merchant-spinner process.

Company Culture

Implemented, the Kempners' goal of family cohesion illuminates detailed relationships between cultural values and economic behavior.[2] Wide-ranging generalizations about capitalism and culture want illumination by historical examinations of "company culture," that is, the effects of individuals' social values on business decisions and the attitudes of people in business as distinguished from a society's attitudes to business. A 1987 interpretation argues properly that "the ethos of a firm, far from peripheral to its performance, directly influences its success or failure."[3] So defined, efforts by the Kempners to create an H. Kempner company culture harmonious with their un-

1. J. D. Claitor, "Personality Sketch of Isaac Herbert Kempner: Civic Builder Emeritus and Humanitarian" (manuscript), RLA, p. 6.

2. Max Weber's *Protestant Ethic and the Spirit of Capitalism* is a broad, classic analysis of such relationships.

3. Dellheim, "The Creation of a Company Culture," *American Historical Review*, pp. 13–14.

folding vision of family cohesion, deserve description. As a result of these efforts, as noted earlier, they established on Galveston the M&P Compress and Warehouse Company, invested off-Island in the oil boom at nearby Spindletop, and more significantly, risked capital in sugar growing and refining at then-distant Sugar Land.

As if all this were inadequate for an agenda, in the 1905–14 decade Ike was also actively supporting the "Galveston Movement" (see chap. 9). Like the movement, Sugar Land involved social visions perceived as benefiting Galveston in both economic and humanistic terms, which echoes the central argument: Galveston, their core community, remained the Kempners' first concern even as they pursued off-Island ventures. Ironically, none of these efforts ever generated the on-Island mass-employment smokestack industries that Galveston needed for its continued regeneration.

The M&P

Ike believed that in-house compressing of raw cotton and attendant processes (grading, bagging, warehousing, and shipping) were essential if he was to realize his plans to reorganize H. Kempner into a cotton merchant with vertical control of the commodity from farm to mill. In 1898 H. Kempner acquired a foreclosed Galveston cotton press. Its extensive acreage near the wharves sprawled over two and a half city blocks, and it was, Ike noted, "a very effective compress." H. Kempner paid fifty thousand dollars for the stock of the defunct company, then contributed it at an inflated valuation to the new firm Ike created, the M&P. Soon with Dan as manager, M&P began to modernize its facilities at great expense, although, the historian of the compress industry has noted, that was "not a propitious time to enter the cotton compress business in Galveston."[4]

4. IHK, *Recalled Recollections*, p. 26; Ellis, "The Cotton Compress Industry" (Ph.D. diss.), p. 361, provided detail. See also "Keys Report, 1964" (manuscript), Kempner Papers, p. 2. The title of the report is derived from the crossed-keys logo on the cover. Kempners composed these reports to aid reporting to family trust shareholders (see chap. 11). This item will hereafter be cited as "Keys Report," and unless otherwise specified, reference is to the 1964 text, which was most useful in preparing this account. Keys Reports of the past two decades were written by Harris L. ("Shrub") Kempner, Jr., and Leonora Thompson's son, Edward ("Tim") Thompson, Jr., perhaps as part of their on-job training in H. Kempner enterprises, then "edited . . . firmly" by Harris Senior and Arthur

Indeed not, at least in terms of immediate profits. From 1898 through 1914, M&P lost money, its managers received no salaries, and dividends to shareholders were only sixty-five hundred dollars in 1900 (before the Great Storm) and ten thousand dollars in 1905.[5] But the investment served longer-range purposes, keeping cotton farmer-clients loyal to H. Kempner as their first-choice purchaser of crops.

Compressing and warehousing were parts of cotton farming that frequently spilled over into politics. Increasing in value dramatically since Appomattox, by 1900 cotton was the state's primary money crop. But while the output of cotton farmers soared, during the Galveston career of Ike's father, ca. 1870–95, the price they received per pound plunged, from thirty-one to nine cents. Meanwhile the rates they paid to railroads, bankers, and factors increased. This squeeze helped to inspire legislation on railroad rates enforced by a regulatory commission. By the mid-nineties, when Ike succeeded his father at the helm of H. Kempner, commission rulings were accepted, if unhappily at times, as mandates.

Attempting to moderate those rulings, Ike and other Galveston cotton dealers echoed their farmer-customers' complaints but from commercial perspectives. They sponsored inconclusive conferences with railroad and commission officials and testified frequently before the federal Interstate Commerce Commission, especially about rate discriminations and quality standards for cotton, the latter affecting price schedules for carriage, insurance, and handling.[6]

Kempners hoped that Galveston might be Texas' premier cotton processing center, market, and port. To that end coastal cotton merchants, Ike in the van, encouraged vast changes (now called "modernization") in relevant transportation, communications, and financial technologies. But each year an increasing number of mainland cotton growers built and/or used local inland presses instead of forwarding crops to Galveston. Some of the very "terminus merchants" that Galveston cotton dealers like Kempner subsidized themselves became local bankers, establishing competing inland facilities.

Galveston was never able to reclaim its early primacy as the loca-

Alpert. Tim Thompson's memo to Leonora Thompson, copy to author, dated Aug. 18, 1988. On finances, see "50 Years Ago" column, *Galveston Daily News*, May 3, 1950.

5. Ellis, "Cotton Compress Industry," pp. 373–76.
6. Ibid., chaps. 5–8.

tion of the state's sole substantial compresses. Worse for Galveston, after compressing, cotton owners or agents, using what were known as "through bills of lading," increasingly shipped via rail or rail-boat combinations at specially discounted rates set by the railroad commission, directly to East Coast and European spinners. Even if such cargoes went through coastal ports, little save warehousing and reloading income stayed there. Galveston cotton dealers were so anxious to retain adequate shares of the trade that H. Kempner and others sometimes assumed compressing costs.

M&P could not restore the domination over cotton processing that the pioneer generation had enjoyed. Instead, for what stretched into decades, M&P was part of H. Kempner's ultimately successful struggle to retain a substantial share of the income from compressing, warehousing, and reshipping. Of all Texas cotton ports, only Galveston survived the change to inland compressing and rail shipping. "Uncle Dan early took over its [M&P's] supervision and management," Ike's son reported in 1963, "and all these years it has been an important and profitable part of our cotton business." Which meant, of course, that Dan settled down in Galveston for a lifetime career in an H. Kempner enterprise, and acquired the latest machinery for M&P. H. Kempner's reputation for honesty, its credit sources, and its intimate direct connections with European spinners attracted steady customers. The Kempners gambled that these repeaters would overweigh the stubbornly higher costs on freight to Galveston, and in this sense they succeeded.[7]

But as measured by the family's larger purposes, M&P's success enlarged the perils for their community that they would have wished it to avoid. Chief among these hazards was the fact that despite all efforts toward diversification, Galveston remained virtually a one-industry city. The swelling trade in wheat, hides, and wool migrated to shipping centers inland. Without adequate new non-cotton, labor-intensive industries on the Island, a drastic decline in compressing or shipping meant a moribund, dependent community, one potentially unattractive as a place for Ike and his bright, ambitious younger brothers to spend their whole lives and careers.

Now compress owners, Ike and Dan had to wrestle not only with

7. H. L. Kempner, "Beneficiary Interest Report, 1963," p. 2; Ellis, "Cotton Compress Industry," pp. 366–68, 375.

problems in and questions about the cotton marketplace but also its industrial processes. For example, what was the proper density of compressed, baled cotton? Ike had welcomed the state railroad commission's 1895 standard (of 22½ pounds per cubic foot) but not the assignment to the compress of financial responsibility for recompression if railroad inspectors discerned variant densities. Nor did he appreciate the "Galveston differential," which had arisen because of competition for cargoes to be moved between Houston and Galveston, by rail or water. But few interior points had competitive carriers, and higher inland rates reflected this lack. The commission "equalized" the situation in a manner that disfavored Galveston.[8]

Another commission ruling granted to Texas ports concentration privileges that attracted several large compress and warehousing firms to Galveston. To meet the competition and adjust to onrushing technology, H. Kempner further modernized M&P, financing the improvements by selling M&P's land, excluding machinery and improvements, to the Southern Pacific for $180,000, temporarily leasing back the land. The sale exceeded the assessed value of the property by $20,000. With this money Ike liquidated the outstanding bonds and the sinking fund, bought new land, and built a plant equipped with up-to-date machinery.[9] By 1917, M&P had two Webb high-density compressors in operation. The best available, they could compress 200 bales an hour. M&P now boasted automatic sprinklers, a fleet of electric trucks and trailers for drayage, and fireproof warehousing for 100,000 compressed bales.

Hardly had the new plant started when, in 1915, perverse nature unleashed another massive storm on Galveston. Advising Ike, who was away on one of his now-frequent lobbying expeditions in Austin, Dan noted happily that M&P's concrete construction

> [with]stood the storm without any danger whatsoever. The wooden shed that we erected last year, at a cost of about $30,000 is about one-half destroyed. We had 15,000 bales of cotton in the press, all of which is more or less damaged by ground water, but we are already at work trying to dry this out. About 1,000 bales . . . [of] ours in all have floated away, but we will salvage about 500. . . . All other

8. Ellis, "Cotton Compress Industry," chap. 3.
9. IHK, *Recalled Recollections*, p. 100.

presses in town have suffered more severely than we did. Moody['s], we understand, will lose 4,000 bales which floated away, although their concrete warehouse stood as well as ours.[10]

The seawall proved itself by blunting the great waves, and the hurricanelike winds that sent water across the island did far less damage than had the monster of 1900. The 1915 storm cost only twenty-five lives. Damage to structures was largely confined to the unprotected western portions of the Island. Downtown Galveston suffered, not from gulfside winds driving deep water in but from eccentric northwest winds that drove bay water through the central business and residential streets. Merchants suffered losses from the flooding and the temporary inconvenience of disrupted rail, telephone, and water lines. But without the seawall and raised grade, Dan wrote very soon after the event, "there would hardly have been a building left in Galveston or a life safe." True, the causeway bridge was destroyed. But "we will do as we did after the 1900 storm – go to work and re-build our property and city; and be thankful that we have all escaped harm and so few lives lost."[11]

All the Kempners pitched in to repair damages. At the Kempner private bank in Galveston, Ike's son Harris, working there during a summer vacation apprenticeship, "went down and ironed wet currency – high executive positions like that."[12] Then World War I greatly affected all of H. Kempner's operations.

World War I

The United States remained neutral from 1914 to 1917. "At first both sets of belligerents furnished an active market for our cotton," recalled Harris, "but, unfortunately, through the unconscious violation of some [trade] regulations or other, we were . . . put on the British blacklist [in 1915] for trading with the enemy." While H. Kempner remained excluded from the rich Allied commerce, "a number of our . . . competitors built up large fortunes, . . . [but] we had to spend a

10. Ibid., pp. 54–55.

11. Ibid., pp. 53–56; DWK letter, Aug. 20, 1915, in "Texas Prudential Insurance Co." file, Kempner Papers.

12. H. L. Kempner, interview with L. Marchiafava, June 6, 1981, RLA.

good deal of our time and energy in getting ourselves removed from the blacklist before we could trade again with the allied nations."[13]

H. Kempner had allegedly shipped cotton to blockaded Germany. Britain's Admiralty controlled convoys to England and Europe and, through licenses (called "navicerts"), dominated available shipping space and convoy assignments. The family never learned why the British were hostile to the firm.[14]

Once released from the blacklist, H. Kempner's business and M&P income rose. The efficiency of the new plant accounted for part of the increase, a Texas Railroad Commission ruling favorable to Galveston helped matters, and decisions of the War Industries Board allowing a 50 percent increase in compression charges, from ten to fifteen cents per hundred pounds, plus wartime shortages of shipping space, resulted in higher prices for bales compressed to the highest density. M&P profited from recompressing bales that less modern inland presses could squeeze no further.

But by 1920 Houston, not Galveston, was the largest spot cotton market and compress center in America. Well served by its trunk rail web, Houston's cotton chiefs benefited also from the federally funded and state-subsidized farm-to-market road network developed from the 1920s through 1940s. Synthetics were increasing competition with cotton. Cotton, and Galveston, faced dour futures.[15]

Elusive Oil

An elusive source of wealth for Galveston, petroleum initially took Kempner money off-Island, although Ike and Dan pursued "black gold" both on and off Galveston. Indeed, storm-battered Islanders were keenly interested in the petroleum frenzy gripping America, one centered not in distant gold-rush locales but only ninety miles east of Houston at the once-undistinguished hamlet of Beaumont.

Within weeks of the Spindeltop gusher, forests of new wells sprouted and spouted there and in other boom communities lying in an arc seventy miles from Galveston. "The speculation was beyond imagina-

13. H. L. Kempner, "Beneficiary Interest Report, 1963," p. 3; Milner, *Cotton Contraband; New York Times*, Aug. 21, 1915.

14. H. L. Kempner interview with Marchiafava, June 6, 1981.

15. Ellis, "Cotton Compress Industry," pp. 304–49.

tion," recalled H. Kempner clerk Hyman Block. A feverish rush almost daily produced reports of instant millionaires and began an eighty-year regional obsession with oil.[16]

Unlike any other commodity Galvestonians handled in their businesses or for which their city served as port, oil puzzled and frustrated the Kempners. Accustomed to success both as officials and entrepreneurs, they failed to garner for their city large shares in the new oil wealth. Houston, not Galveston, became the major technological and financial center of the petroleum industry.[17] The fact that the oil boom became a failed opportunity for the public interest of Galveston, but, as we shall see, less so for private investors like the Kempners, fed the tradition that they shortsightedly or deliberately resisted chances for the city to profit, thus justifying "fly in amber" imagery.[18]

To balance, the Great Storm made the oil boom brutally ill-timed for Galveston and Kempner interests, which were focused on storm relief and recovery. When Galvestonians did try for oil wealth, they moved sluggishly in contrast to the quick inventiveness they displayed in other, less exotic business endeavors and in pressing relief and recovery work. Their normal sensitivity to opportunities for economic gain seemed blunted.

Oil, they were to learn, was strange stuff. It profited extractors and refiners only under favorable conditions, especially cheap transportation for both the raw or refined commodity. Further, in this pre-automobile time, oil gushing from a wildly increasing number of wells so outpaced demand and lowered prices as to enrich only the most favored speculators, a corps that did not necessarily include extractors and processors. Yet oil was touted as a new revenue source for the city from increased port traffic and enlarged resident work forces. And so, despite their public-sector work and various private enterprises, beginning in 1901 Ike Kempner and some of his associates tried fitfully for shares in the bonanza.

In early 1901 the Galveston city council authorized a survey of the Beaumont fields before risking public funds in modifications to the

16. DeGolyer, "Anthony F. Lucas and Spindletop," *Southwest Review*, p. 83; Hyman Block, interview with L. Marchiafava, Aug. 1, 1981, RLA.

17. Platt, *City Building in the New South*, p. 175; Kelly, " 'Twixt Failure and Success" (MA thesis), pp. 102ff.

18. Gunther, *Taken at the Flood*, p. 18.

Galveston port that would enable it to handle oil.[19] The course of action bears the Kempner mark of prudence, but Galveston's deliberate official pace stands in sharp contrast to the speculative atmosphere prevailing in Houston. News leaked that, as result of the survey, oil drilling would begin on Galveston Island. Speculative boomlets developed almost immediately. Charters were issued for more than three dozen oil companies with Galveston head offices. Some newborn Texas petroleum exchanges indulged daily in paper transactions out-totaling those of Wall Street. Directors of Galveston paper enterprises issued shares totaling $8.6 million, and announced that the capital would be spent to build wells and other refineries on the Island plus pipelines to Beaumont and other producing fields.[20]

But the 1915 storm, added to the 1900 monster, defined in chokingly narrow terms the benefits that Galveston was to earn from oil. As Ike recalled unhappily, "but for the public appraisal of future menace of similar occurring conditions, Galveston would have been the logical point of location of the main offices of several oil companies which had been previously contemplated, but which instead as a psychological effect of the storm damage recurring, were domiciled in Houston and Beaumont."[21]

Ike tried to reverse the drift. In June, 1902, as Galveston's recovery efforts were gaining momentum, he predicted to edgy holders of the city's bonds that "by reason of . . . [Galveston's] proximity to the oil fields of Texas . . . a new impetus will be given to [Island] manufacturing and development." A professional well driller, Ike's "new impetus," brought in only dry holes or effusions of mud from his borings.[22] Thereafter the speculative shares went begging. By 1906, not one of the Galveston refining companies that, on paper at least, had sprung up since 1901, existed. Instead, by 1914 when the Houston Ship Channel opened oceanic traffic to that inland city, refinery complexes tapping producing fields decorated its sinuous course. Railroad tank cars and pipelines soon linked these fields and complexes to trans-

19. Barker, "Partners in Progress" (Ph.D. diss.), p. 3.

20. Block interview with Marchiafava, Aug. 1, 1981.

21. Barker, "Partners in Progress," pp. 39–40; McComb, *Houston*, pp. 115ff.; *Galveston City Directory 1901–1902* (1902), on the oil companies.

22. IHK in undated, unidentified clipping headlined "To the Holders of the Bonds of . . . Galveston . . . June 1902," in DWK Scrapbook, 1894–1915; on the oil exploration, *Galveston Tribune*, July 8, 1902.

continental carriers and national and international customers. And the wealth from oil, and, later, natural gas flowed into and through Houston, not Galveston.[23]

Galveston's deprivation from oil wealth was neither initiated nor perpetuated by the Kempners or their associates among the Island's leaders. But neither was Galveston's failure to glean oil or gain wealth overcome by them.

In efforts to have H. Kempner share in what a family member recalled as "Texas's [oil] heritage and future wealth," Ike was occasionally fortunate. He joined in late 1901 with what a journalist described as "some of the big men of St. Louis and Galveston" in the International Development Company, capitalized nominally at $2.5 million. "It was revealed that the company had bought eight wells in Spindletop and also more land in the proven territory," the journalist continued.[24] What happened to this investment remains unclear. Presumably it soured. Ike ignored the incident in his valuable memoir set down a half century later.

One invitation to a success in oil came from Harris Masterson, a prominent Brazoria County judge. Masterson had an option on ten mainland acres located near Beaumont. Pooling surnames and funds, Masterson and Kempner formed the Maskemp Oil Company, which "put down a well to the same depth as the discovery well on Spindletop," Ike wrote, "[and] struck a gusher, producing 10,000 barrels of oil a day[!]"[25]

Dan became on-site secretary of Maskemp (the oil venture preceded his M&P job). The brothers' initial jubilation at news of what Ike's son Harris was to describe as "prolific oil on a small acreage," soon lessened, however, then gave way to disappointment. Maskemp's isolated land lacked access to commercial transportation and thus found no market, Ike later confirming that the Maskemp well was "not adjacent to any pipeline or railroad sidings, so we were unable to market profitably our production and hence were forced to sell to those who could install pipe lines."[26]

23. Barker, "Partners in Progress," pp. 39–40.

24. E. R. Thompson, Jr., "History of H. Kempner" (manuscript), Kempner Papers, p. 21, and see Melosi, *Coping with Abundance; Galveston News*, Nov. 1, 1901.

25. IHK, *Recalled Recollections*, p. 35.

26. Ibid.; Thompson, "History," p. 21.

Raw crude oil then sold at such isolated wellheads as Maskemp's for the now almost unbelievable price of three to ten cents a barrel. Even this price allowed the investors a slim profit, but only while the well flowed at its initial vigor and volume and if the producers had access to rail or pipelines. Maskemp's output quickly diminished, and the partners decided to sell out. They got a reasonable price for their well, but almost everything about this venture deterred Ike from further hazardous, time-consuming oil speculations of this sort. Instead Ike leased and subleased potential oil and gas lands for H. Kempner throughout Texas and Oklahoma. With the Maskemp access lesson in mind, he invested in a rail line from Wichita Falls to Frederick, Oklahoma, and the line brought in more revenue than the oil properties did. "I feel sure it was a very healthy investment," office employee Block recalled. Ike joined also with Herman Nussbaum, a frequent associate in cotton contracts, in oil properties between Waco and Dallas and in New Mexico.[27]

In 1909 Ike became treasurer and a director of the Lone Star Gas Company, the state's first natural gas firm, H. Kempner being one of the original shareholders. Until this time drillers either burned off the gas escaping with upwelling petroleum or let it merge with the atmosphere. But industrializing, urbanizing America needed illuminants and fuels. Natural gas was becoming profitable. Much to the benefit of H. Kempner, though not directly of Galveston, Ike held on to Lone Star securities through the many changes in its corporate structure and ownership that it endured in oncoming decades.

Indeed, he could have controlled Lone Star and its successor entities at enormous profit to H. Kempner. Family lore has it that Ike was approached by representatives of the eastern-run Magnolia Oil Company. They offered him the direction of the burgeoning Magnolia enterprise if he helped them to acquire Lone Star. Ike refused. Perhaps regional prejudices played a part. He disliked the style of his visitors and they his. Ike feared also that, if Magnolia acquired Lone Star, the interests of Texas investors, managers, and workers would suffer. Ike's son recalled seventy years later "he felt that our loyalty to Lone Star would prevent our servicing these new people who didn't

27. Block interview with Marchiafava, Aug. 1, 1981; Thompson, "History," p. 21.

like the Lone Star Gas people." The son remembered also "a family story that we watched a Magnolia Oil man go from . . . [Ike's office] down to George Sealy Jr.'s office to invite him to take a position we had refused which turned out very well for Mr. Sealy."[28]

Sealy, like Kempner, was devoted to Galveston. In 1923 he had Magnolia drill a well on the Island's western portion so that the city might share in direct oil wealth. But, as before, the borings oozed only salty, silt-laden water. Even if oil had gushed, it could not have been refined on Galveston Island because of the lack of the large supplies of fresh water needed in refining. Sealy abandoned the attempt, and in 1925 he died. Except for the construction of large oil tanks on the Island's eastern tip later in the 1920s, Galveston's petroleum flirtations were ended. For Galveston as a whole, they never reached profitable climaxes. For H. Kempner the story was different, Ike's son reporting in 1979 that the firm was "one of the founding stockholders of the Lone Star Gas Company, and these holdings we have preserved throughout the years to our substantial gain."[29]

Sugar Land

Denied by nature the chance to develop oil interests and, in turn, their community's interests on Galveston Island, Ike, his brothers, and some of their descendants took advantage of the H. Kempner investment at Sugar Land to advance both their fortunes and their ideas on company culture.[30] Sugar almost inevitably attracted their attention. Certain engaging parallels existed between it and cotton. In Texas at least, sugar, like cotton, was a product of many small farmers. They crushed cane in crude mills on their plantations. A few also built small refineries primarily for their own use. By the century's turn improving technology encouraged construction of larger, costlier local or regional refineries to which area growers brought cut cane to be processed for a fee. Still a trade in which ox-drawn wagons outnumbered

28. H. L. Kempner, letter to author, Apr. 8, 1986.

29. H. L. Kempner, "Beneficiary Interest Report, 1979." See also John McCullough, interview with R. L. Jones, Dec. 4, 1980, RLA; Hidy and Hidy, *Pioneering in Big Business, 1892–1911; Galveston Daily News*, Apr. 25, 1923.

30. For simplicity the place-name Sugar Land will be rendered as two words, to signify both the refinery and the community.

steam-propelled railroads, refiners could transfer few risks from themselves to farmers or to sugar's major consumers, food canners. Instead, refiners were vulnerable to all vagaries affecting growers, including nature's caprices, erratic labor forces, and the international and domestic markets in money, freighting, and cane or beets. Stored and milled cane, molasses or other syrups, and unrefined sugar spoiled quickly. Refiners could neither delay processing nor withhold products until markets improved. Therefore refiners operated at the mercy of money lenders, common carriers, and, increasingly, foreign producers. Conversely, the few refiners with assured supplies of cane from their own or local farms and mills or, after 1898, from Cuba, Hawaii, and the Philippines, plus stable labor forces, advantageous credit sources, and favorable transportation rates, might prosper against all odds.[31] Impressed by sugar's potential profits, anxious also to implement the inseparable goals of Galveston's rehabilitation and family cohesion, soon after the century's turn the Kempner brothers began what was to become an eight decades–long family devotion at Sugar Land, Texas, to nurture a corporate and civic culture congruent with these goals.

Initially, the Kempner effort at Sugar Land aimed solely at profits. A second pattern of paternalistic development and control of both the industrial processes of sugar refining and the community of mill workers soon appeared. This community originally included leased convict workers and paid employees of both races. In later phases (ca. 1915–1960s) modern entrepreneurial techniques mixed with the Kempners' increasingly idealistic aspirations to create a model company town, one incorporating ideas labeled "welfare capitalism."

The essential element in welfare capitalism, wrote a close student of the subject, was "any service provided [by employers] for the comfort or improvement of employees which was neither a necessity of the industry nor required by law."[32] An extensive scholarly literature, often contentious yet consistently illuminating, has grown up about various ideas on industrial democracy after Appomattox and on management-labor tensions in the decades since 1900. A constructive recent suggestion, by John Higham, is that "in a long-term perspective,

31. Shlomowitz, "Plantations and Smallholdings," *Agricultural History*, pp. 1–17.

32. Brandes, *American Welfare Capitalism, 1880–1940*, pp. 4–6.

the distinctive feature of [welfare capitalism] . . . is not the preeminence of democratic ideals or of bureaucratic techniques, but rather a fertile amalgamation of the two."[33]

What brought Kempners to essay this "fertile amalgamation" at Sugar Land? How was it that they escalated practices from that of an employer of contract convict labor to one employing only paid workers? Further, what brought the family to provide workers (initially, primarily only the white workers) with company-built and financed homes, shops, schools, churches, and medical facilities, all of high quality and at nonusurious rates and without the coercive monitoring by company police so common in other analogous developments? Last, why did the Kempners pour money into what became a substantial industrial-civic project over a half century and yet encourage community self-government by its residents, eventually (in the 1960s) giving up all the family's claims to municipal governance?

Answers to these questions require a preliminary sketch of the crisis existing in American labor-management relations around 1900. To soften it, policies of the sort developed at Sugar Land, if only as inspirations for heightened production, were touted in information that flowed through business channels familiar to Ike and Dan. Ike's own work in redeveloping storm-shattered Galveston had a substantial place in this literature as an application of sound business methods to both civic rebuilding and entrepreneurial values.

Sympathetic writers of this time rarely doubted that ethical, philosophical, and religious values inspired the social experiments of an Andrew Carnegie, Henry Ford, and John D. Rockefeller, Jr., or, on a more modest scale, an Ike Kempner. In this literature such men were high priests of individualism whose methods and goals merged private profit with public progress.[34]

In the very early 1900s Ike invested in relatively small sugar farms

33. Higham, "Hanging Together," *Journal of American History*, p. 24. See also Derber, *The American Idea of Industrial Democracy, 1865–1965*, pp. 206ff; Williams, *The Contours of American History*, pp. 360, 416, 428, 438–39, 470; Kolko, *The Triumph of Conservatism;* Weinstein, *The Corporate Ideal in the Liberal State;* Wiebe, *The Search for Order, 1877–1920;* Galambos, "The Emerging Organizational Synthesis in Modern American History," *Business History Review*, p. 280.

34. See Hoover, *American Individualism*, esp. pp. 1–31; Carnegie, *Problems of Today*, esp. pp. 121–42; Adams, *Big Business in a Democracy*, esp. chaps. 4–8.

in or near Fort Bend County, southeast Texas' "sugar bowl."[35] Roughly sixty miles from Galveston and half that from Houston, the area lay within an endurable if wearying day's travel time from the Gulf.

Overseeing H. Kempner's interests in these properties while learning the sugar business, brother Lee proved himself to be, like Dan, a quick study. Dissatisfied with their on-site farm managers, Lee learned that Edward H. Cunningham's nearby plantation of twenty thousand acres and L. A. Ellis's of five thousand acres, were financially distressed. Cunningham especially was trying to create in sugar analogs to what Ike sought in cotton: substantial cost efficiencies from a vertical in-house organization linking farm, mill, refinery, and freight carrier to trunk railroads and ports, to improve producers' leverage against banks, bulk carriers, and canners.

Straddling major roads from Galveston and Houston to San Antonio, Cunningham's plantation also enjoyed lengthy frontage on Oyster Creek. Conscious of their island's problems caused by inadequate water supply, the Galvestonians were impressed that Cunningham's pumping station twelve miles up the Brazos River stabilized the flow into Oyster Creek, ensuring a year-round water supply for his plantation, mill, and refinery. Additionally, Cunningham had built the Sugar Land Railroad, known as the "Sugar Road." Ike and his brothers were learning from their misadventures in oil at this very time the essentiality of access to cheap, dependable bulk freighting. Serving Cunningham and his neighbors, the Sugar Road traversed the region's best cane fields and connected to long-haul carriers. This diversity in routing often afforded Cunningham advantageous rates from carriers. Perhaps the Sugar Road might become a conduit further nourishing the traffic of the Kempners' export-heavy port city.

Cunningham's farm also attracted them because it boasted the state's largest sugar mill and only mechanized refinery. The latter was a tall wooden structure overtopped by several endlessly smoking chimney stacks. Huddled around it were a paper mill for making bags from cane fiber waste, plus maintenance shops, stables, and housing for eight hundred workers. Of the last, substantially more than half were convicts Cunningham leased from the state. Neither Cunningham nor

35. IHK, *Recalled Recollections*, p. 42; DWK, "History of Imperial Sugar" (manuscript), #80-002, Kempner Papers. These plantations included the Palo Alto (also known as the Darrington or Arrington), the Cheenango in Brazoria County and the Belvedere, near Dewalt.

neighbor Ellis had been able to recruit and keep enough free workers, and Ellis leased from the state the labor of two hundred convicts. They worked the fields while free laborers did the processing.

The Hell-Hole of the Brazos

Cunningham's and Ellis's workers, convict and free, lived in a scabrous shantytown-plus-tent city that had grown Topsy-like between the two properties. Known as "Sugar Land," its conditions were "appalling," recalled a veteran employee.[36] Poorly drained, Sugar Land's farms, grazing lands, the living areas were spotted with swamps and ponds. Frequent downpours unleashed unpredictable floods. Often over its banks, the Brazos River swept crops, topsoil, buildings, beasts, and sometimes people to destruction and created breeding ponds for myriads of insects and other pests. Interruptions of production schedules were frequent.

In short, in the early 1900s Sugar Land was a dreary, ugly, jerry-built, jumbled settlement of perhaps one thousand people, with convicts numbering from five hundred to seven hundred of this fluctuating total. Isolated in a rural county, to workers Sugar Land was "the hell-hole of the Brazos." Except for the owners and very few supervisors, life in this mudhole of a settlement was miserable. A gaggle of ratty company stores offered the free workers scant and overpriced comforts. One restaurant and a boardinghouse for the small clerical staff and guards adjoined stables and kennels for the draft animals and hounds whose accumulated noises and odors filled the atmosphere. Although the state stipulated minimum housing standards for the racially segregated leased convicts, conditions in their wooden barracks were bleak. Almost no housing existed for the free workers, however, who, except for the few supervisors, had to content themselves with scant comforts. Indoor toilets and sewers were unknown. All sanitation was rudimentary. Drinking water was often "off." Insects and rodents had infested everything. There were neither churches nor schools to offer wider horizons.

36. R. M. Armstrong, "History of Sugar Land, Texas, the Imperial Sugar Company and Sugar Land Industries" (draft manuscript, 1986), privately held, II [8]. Bracketed numerals denote temporary pagination in Armstrong's draft. See also Johnson, "A Short History of the Sugar Industry in Texas," *Texas Gulf Coast Historical Association Publications*, pp. 1–52.

The Brazos River flood of 1913. The initial phase of improved housing for Sugar Land workers is visible in the foreground. (Courtesy Imperial Sugar Company)

Virtually no married men brought families to live in this grim, almost totally male society. Even in a depressed economy the owners could recruit free labor primarily only from among sailors deserting ships at Galveston, discharged military and railroad personnel, ex-convicts, and drifters.

Unincorporated, Sugar Land had no firefighters or physicians. A senior refinery supervisor of the century's turn, L. H. Rayner, reported that it "was a place without order or law." In addition to the state's guards and tracking dogs watching over the convict workers, a "labor boss" deputized by the county and toting revolvers and heavy canes attended to such community peacekeeping as occurred beyond persuading wholly undesirable vagrants and union organizers to move on. Little recorded attention went to individuals' rights of any sort.

Injuries and diseases among workers were common. Respectable amenities were few. Workers stole off to "Mexico," a squalid squatter settlement a mile away where intoxicants, prostitutes, and gambling were available. Fistfights, knifings, and shootings enlivened payday weekends. On any following Monday almost half the free work force might be ill, injured, or in the county jail in Rosenberg. To sum up this unsavory matter, whether in Texas, Hawaii, or on a Carribbean

The hell-hole of the Brazos (Courtesy Imperial Sugar Company)

island the awful description applied: "Sugar is made with blood."[37]

The chronic problem of a stable labor supply meshed poorly with the unalterable rhythm of sugar farming and the fact that consumer demand for sugar was far outstripping the capacities of domestic growers. A single annual crop, sugar culture left workers idle for half the year unless they could be assigned to other income-producing tasks.[38] But costs were not idle. Alternative uses for labor and fresh sources of both labor and raw sugar were needed.

Concerning the latter, Cunningham especially had ventured in ways Ike admired, borrowing heavily to buy "off-shore raws" (i.e., Cuban and West Indian cane) to supplement inadequate local crops and winning rebates from trunk railroads for carrying the imported commodity from Galveston to the Sugar Road. The prospect of new imports at Galveston was always engaging to the Kempner brothers. But both Cunningham and Ellis indulged in notorious personal extravagances and were often absent. By the early 1900s their plantations

37. Armstrong, "History," II [56]; Paquette, *Sugar Is Made with Blood*, passim.
38. Armstrong, "History," I [1–50], II [9].

Mules pulling rail cars loaded with sugarcane stalks (Courtesy Imperial Sugar Company)

exhibited ravages from inadequate on-site management. Physical deterioration of the buildings and equipment was evident. Bad weather, depressed crop prices, and adverse federal tariffs compounded their problems.

In 1903 creditors forced a receivership on Cunningham. Becoming a member of the receivers' board, Ike proposed an expensive rehabilitation of the plant. His ideas rejected, he resigned from the board but remained convinced that the property deserved repair. A full-time effective resident manager, loans from H. Kempner, more stable free labor supply to replace the inefficient leased prisoners, and major modernizations of the refinery and the Sugar Road, especially the connection to Galveston, were the keys. Ellis's property was a natural one to join with Cunningham's. But, exhibiting again the family's habitual respect for the expert, Ike, though anxious to keep Lee occupied and to find a permanent career for Dan, withheld bids on both until he located a competent resident manager for the combinable spread.[39]

39. Ibid., I [54–55]; IHK, *Recalled Recollections*, pp. 42–43; Cronholm, "The Kempners," *The Imperial Crown*, pt. 1 (unpaginated).

Enter William T. Eldridge

Ike found such a manager in William T. Eldridge. In his mid-forties when he and Kempner met, Eldridge was a shrewd, semiliterate, Texas-scale promoter. Bare of formal education, burly and occasionally truculent, as a youth Eldridge, like Ike's father, had been a peddler, and perhaps Kempner found the parallel appealing. Thereafter Eldridge had traded in commodities, freighted goods, and bossed successively a grocery, clothing store, bank, restaurant, sugar plantation, and mule-drawn railroad. He was, Ike wrote later, a "self-made man with considerable vision, though at times his ambitions triumphed over his judgment."[40]

Perhaps Eldridge had also studied Ike, for in conversations he emphasized the efficiencies gained from joining the Kempners', Ellis's, and Cunningham's properties and from recruiting and keeping a stable free labor supply. A handshake sealed agreement.[41]

How dissimilar Eldridge and Ike were! A longtime employee of the partners asserted that Eldridge was "ruthless" in his business dealings. Eldridge's earlier ventures had ended in deadly shootouts with one partner and with a relative of the dead man. He successfully pleaded self-defense in ensuing murder prosecutions. Thereafter, fearing vendettas, Eldridge never sat with his back to an open window. Not a family man though he married three times, fathered four children, and acquired two stepchildren on the way, Eldridge dismayed Kempner's mother. Ike recorded that Eliza "was extremely concerned about our association with Eldridge, who she feared would not hesitate to shoot one of us." Her fears were groundless. "Eldridge and the Kempners . . . had no trouble or serious difference of opinion in our business affairs and attendant personal relations," Ike wrote of their unlikely amity that endured until Eldridge's death in 1932.[42]

In 1905 Ike and Eldridge bought out Ellis's creditors. Despite the

40. IHK, *Recalled Recollections*, pp. 43–44; Armstrong, "History," II [11–19].

41. Sixty years later the president of a corporate descendant of this informal agreement complained that for the whole period 1905–1919, company records "are very sketchy" (Armstrong, "History," II [2–4], and see [HLK?] "Sugarland Industries, Inc., and Its Subsidiary and Affiliated Companies" [1964], in Kempner Papers [cited hereafter as "Sugarland Industries"]).

42. IHK, *Recalled Recollections*, p. 43; Armstrong, interview with author, Feb. 10, 1987.

W. T. Eldridge, Sr., 1904 (Courtesy Imperial Sugar Company

economic strains of the nationwide panic of 1907, in that year they acquired also Cunningham's controlling interest in his Sugar Land plantation and then incorporated Imperial Sugar as a holding company. Ike named it after a fine New York City hotel where he had stayed. In 1919 they were to form another holding company, Sugar Land Industries (known as "The Industries"), a complex of service, agricultural, and industrial entities that was in legal form a Massachusetts trust.[43] Equal owners H. Kempner and Eldridge remained the united policy center for all Sugar Land, Imperial, and Industries

43. Probably Ike became acquainted with the advantage of this form for H. Kempner's undivided assets from this Imperial adventure. On the H. Kempner Trust of 1920, see chap. 13.

developments. This enduring centrality nurtured a persisting identity between ownership and management. Technical legal changes in Imperial's corporate forms were to be frequent after 1907, but so enduring was the owner-manager relationship that according to one hyperbolic but relevant comment, these changes required only altered labels on company ledgers.[44]

Dan became Imperial's first president and Eldridge, its general manager. Now Ike's basic purpose of family cohesion seemed a large step closer to implementation. He had the pleasure of seeing two of his brothers engaged in complementary H. Kempner enterprises, overseeing potentially lucrative sugar properties within reasonable commuting distance of Galveston. Soon, however, both Lee and Dan would opt for apprenticeships in Galveston itself, as mentioned earlier. This occurring, Ike himself bore the weight of close work with Eldridge. He relished and retained the task until his son Isaac Herbert Kempner, Jr. ("Herb," b. 1906) became Imperial's president after World War II. Virtually until his death in 1953, Herb further improved both Imperial's industrial capacities and the Sugar Land community, especially the quality of housing for nonwhites, and won company recognition of labor unions. But with his death, non-Kempners trained in the sugar industry, usually at Imperial, became its executives, until in 1966 Ike's grandson, Isaac Herbert ("Denny") Kempner III, assumed the chairmanship of Imperial's board. At this writing in 1989 Denny held that position, but it had now grown greatly through the merger of the Imperial and Holly companies, which he helped to engineer. In 1988, Denny's brother James Carroll Kempner (b. 1939), after a career in non-Kempner investment banking at Lehman Brothers and in other financial administration, became Imperial's executive vice-president, chief financial officer, and a director. Also during those decades, other Kempners served (as some do now) on Imperial's board. They included Ann Hamilton, Daniel Oppenheimer, Daniel K. Thorne, Mary Jean Thorne, and Harris Kempner Weston. All, of course, were also shareholders in H. Kempner.[45]

In the pre-World War I decades, Ike's son Harris began to accom-

44. Johnson, "Sugar Industry," pp. 65–69.

45. See chap. 16 and Conclusion; Cronholm, "The Kempners," pts. 1 and 2; Armstrong interview with author, July 14, 1988.

The Imperial Sugar Company Board of Directors, 1965. *Back row:* R. Lee Kempner, Harris L. Kempner, R. M. Armstrong, George Andre. *Front row:* Mary Kempner Thorne, W. H. Louviere, I. H. Kempner, Homer Bruce, O. R. Armstrong, Walter Woodul. (Courtesy Rosenberg Library Archives, Galveston, Texas)

pany him on frequent (often biweekly) monitoring trips to Sugar Land and seven decades later recalled the "adventurous trip it was in those days . . . Getting to Sugar Land . . . was not quite as easy as it is today." Harris remembered also how he and his father would board the big interurban trolley from Galveston to Houston, then

> we took a taxi cab across town to the Southern Pacific Station, and then we got on the train to Los Angeles—the Sunset Limited. There was a railroad at Sugar Land and [it] had a gate there. When they knew we were coming, they shut the gate, the train stopped, my Father and I got off, they shut the Pullman car door, raised the gate, and off they went. Mr. Eldridge was there to meet us and took us to his big country-style house right in the middle of the sugar company property.

He also recalled being terror-stricken one night by a "huge Monster getting into the room making an awful noise"—a passing freight train that sounded close enough to be right in the bedroom with him.[46]

All the Kempners seem to have dealt successfully with what young Harris remembered always as "formidable and crusty people connected with us at Sugar Land," while avoiding serious clashes over Eldridge's unusual demands for salary and other benefits. Initially Eldridge received a five-thousand-dollar annual salary (subsequently raised to twenty-one thousand), 5 percent of the net profits over his half-ownership shares, free housing and furnishings to his own specifications, and all household expenses.[47]

Ike amassed funds for long-range, large-scale redevelopment of Imperial, partly by selling some Ellis and Kempner holdings to the state, which soon established a major prison on this land. Many inmates became contract labor to Imperial, and Texas assigned prisoners on other state-owned farms to grow cane that it sold to Imperial. In addition, the state committed itself to continue growing cane on its new property for ten years and to sell it to Imperial at a low fixed price per ton. In these profitable if exploitative initial ways, Imperial eased the nagging problem of uncertain labor supply and further stabilized its sources of raw cane.[48]

The Kempner-Eldridge Agenda

The unlikely partners developed a remarkable agenda. It suggests that in 1907 Ike already perceived Sugar Land as an arena for aspirations he was unable to realize on Galveston Island, and that he was able to carry Eldridge with him toward goals seemingly foreign to that ruggedly self-centered individualist.[49] All parts of this agenda

46. H. L. Kempner interview with Jones, June 17, 18, 1980; HLK, "The Kempners of Galveston and Sugar Land" (manuscript; speech to the Harvard Business Club of Houston, Sept. 27, 1981), RLA, pp. 10–11.

47. H. L. Kempner interview with Jones, June 17, 1980. By terms aimed not at Kempner but at Cunningham, who soon disappeared from the scene, Eldridge was to have complete management control "of the entire . . . properties of the company . . . and is not to be under the control or supervision of anyone" (Johnson, "Sugar Industry," p. 67; IHK, *Recalled Recollections*, p. 43; Armstrong, "History," II [6]).

48. Johnson, "Sugar Industry," p. 67; Armstrong, "History," II [6, 7]. See also Walker, *Penology for Profit*, p. 159.

49. His own domestic history being so stormy, Eldridge, impressed also by the Kempners' solidarity, caught their family cohesion fever. In 1914 he had his son and namesake made vice-president of Imperial and president of the com-

proceeded simultaneously if at differing and sometimes sluggish paces. That program aspired to

(1) improve living conditions at Sugar Land, initially primarily for white workers and managers, in order to attract reliable, permanent "family-type" permanent employees; drain and level the entire Sugar Land–Imperial acreage and build levees against floods, thereby providing reliable water for homes, sugar operations, grazing cattle, and truck produce gardens for workers and their families;
(2) refit the refinery for year-round operations by using foreign sugar during periods when domestic cane was unavailable, and increase excess agricultural non-sugar production.[50]

This agenda, Ike's son recalled, "started our [family's] years of building up the [Sugar Land] companies, building up the land, and building up the community. And all [through] these times, reinvesting everything they had in Sugar Land."[51] The Kempners volunteered to deny themselves quick profits and to bear these costs for decades. They had to if the Kempner-Eldridge agenda was to become more than a pious statement. Almost no other taxable entities except the sugar refinery existed in Sugar Land until the success of the agenda attracted rent-paying tenant businesses and farmers.

Almost as if to prove that, like the Old South, the New South was a mixture of often contradictory elements, the Kempners leased contract convict labor at Sugar Land until Texas disfavored the practice in 1914. Convict leasing arose after Appomattox from the odious heritages of slavery, the needs of industrial capitalism, and the confusions of the post–Civil War American life. Long defended as a means of stabilizing social order, especially concerning blacks and Hispanics, convict leasing unsalubriously mixed greed, bigotry, and humanitarianism.[52]

Ike Kempner was fifteen years old when in 1888 his father decided to garner some of the profits that leased convict labor was report-

---

munity's bank and then an Industries trustee. But, a later Imperial president recorded, "in spite of every opportunity, Bill failed to make the grade." Finally his father could no longer overlook the son's drinking and gambling. Stripped of all substantive Sugar Land and Imperial offices, he committed suicide in 1931 (Armstrong, "History," II [7]).

50. See Armstrong, "History," II [9].

51. H. L. Kempner interview with Jones, June 17, 18, 1980.

52. Ayers, *Vengeance and Justice*, pp. 192, 222.

The sugar refinery, 1906 (Courtesy Imperial Sugar Company)

edly making for many other businessmen. So when, twenty years later, Ike and Eldridge contracted for a supply of prisoners, they were following not only regional custom and formal state law but Kempner family habit. Indeed, white Texans' reluctance to build and maintain costly prisons (an attitude still prevailing in the 1980s), since the 1870s had led to semiprivatization as an alternative way of coping cheaply with criminals. Although the practice is properly criticized as exploitative if not worse, white Texans' fondness for prison labor, if inexcusable, was not, however, seen then as wholly self-serving. Useful work for inmates was widely hailed as a penological reform. It got them out of moldering cells and exposed the inmates to some new skills while reducing costs to the state.[53]

Then as later, however, a disproportionate percentage of the inmate propulation was nonwhite, for race bigotry infected penology.[54]

53. Walker, *Penology for Profit*, pp. 159–62 and passim; McKelvey, "The Prison Labor Problem, 1875–1900," *Journal of Criminal Law, Criminology, and Police Science*, p. 254.

54. The reformist state constitution of 1869 specified that "the adoption of any system of peonage, whereby the helpless and unfortunate may be reduced

Whether black, brown, or white, convicts the state leased to private contractors, often by auction, were commonly poorly housed, ill-fed, and outrageously exploited. Farmers and manufacturers conspired with corruptible local judges and police to arrest and convict needed labor, particularly blacks, on false charges or none at all. Contractors squeezed profits from the meager amounts Texas allowed for their charges' food, bedding, and shelter. Convicts had few avenues of protest and fewer advocates. Labor unions were particularly weak in southern states. Their members feared convict competition and felt little solidarity with incarcerated workers. Private associations to protect civil rights lay in the future, and officials' commitments to these rights were weak and sporadic. With few defenders or remedies, convict laborers often fell victim to industrial accidents and epidemic diseases, and medical help was rarely available. Their vulnerability and sufferings were usually invisible to respectable society, however, since the Texas contractors for prison labor were most often those engaged in isolated turpentine, lumbering, and sugar operations, as at Sugar Land.

The contract that Harris Kempner signed with Texas in 1883 was much like the one Ike executed for Imperial Sugar twenty years later. Texas furnished the prisoners, tools, and guards plus their horses and tracking dogs. The Kempners provided food and housing for the laborers, guards, and animals and paid the state a nominal amount per day per convict. Unlike most contractors, the Kempner father and son both stipulated that they, not the state, choose on-site managers to oversee operations, a stipulation reflecting their distrust of absentee supervisors and probably also awareness that other employers exploited convict laborers.[55]

The Kempners were unsecretive and unembarrassed about using prison laborers. Employing convicts was merely one factor among

---

to practical bondage, shall never be authorized, or tolerated by the laws of this State; and neither slavery nor involuntary servitude, except as a punishment for crime whereof the party shall have been duly convicted, shall ever exist within this state." But triumphant white "redemptionists" omitted this clause from the 1876 revision.

55. Cf. Harris Kempner, letter to J. T. Jerrad, undated (ca. July, 1883), AJA/HUC; Tinsley, ed., "Select Letters of Harris Kempner," *Gulf Coast Historical Association Publications*, p. 10; Armstrong, "History," II [8]; Gildermeister, "Prison Labor and Convict Competition with Free Workers in Industrializing America, 1840–1890" (Ph.D. diss.).

many affecting the supply and quality of labor, Harris advised a candidate for a job as site superintendent. This seeming insensitivity coexisted with a softer facet: "The undertaking is a big one and we should go into it right," Harris advised the applicant.[56]

Going into it "right" included, remarkably for the time and place, a policy both he and his sons followed, of treating prisoner-workers relatively decently. Perhaps they did so because greater efficiencies resulted and because their contracts with the state called for decency. Yet many other Texans ignored such contract stipulations.

A state investigation of the conditions that leased convicts endured, begun in 1883, the year of initial Kempner venturing into these murky waters, reported venality, whippings, mutilations, sexual oppression, and overworking by owners. In 1909, soon after the Kempner brothers invested in sugar, another state inquiry concluded that brutality, mismanagement, and inefficiency remained as commonplace as it was in 1883. During that quarter century, however, increasing if sporadic protests at excesses were voiced by Christian and Jewish ministers, with Rabbi Cohen in the van of the latter. Cohen became a member of the Board of Prison Visitors. Fearless and sometimes impolitic, he publicly chastised employers of convict labor who allegedly overtasked or abused their helpless charges. Neither published rosters nor his private memoranda lists any Kempners. Instead two generations of Kempners quietly supported Cohen in his investigative reporting.[57]

The Kempners could hardly hide from the zealous rabbi any excesses committed upon leased convicts, or oppress him into silence. Did the Kempners' relatively uncruel administration of leased prisoners reflect another self-interest of the family, one surfacing in Kempner-Eldridge lawsuits against the state begun in 1908?

Early that year, to cope with the growing inflow of convicted felons, Texas proposed to lease or buy for a reported $650,000 all Sugar Land acreage, leaving the mill and refinery to Kempner and Eldridge. In anticipation, the partners contracted with the state for an increased

56. Harris Kempner, letter to Curran & Woolf, July 31, 1885, no. 13, Kempner Letterpress Book; ibid., to H. Seeligson (?), July 23, 1883, no. 20, Kempner Letterpress Book; IHK, *Recalled Recollections*, p. 42.

57. Walker, *Penology for Profit*, pp. 206–208; L. M. Oppenheimer, letter to Cohen, Oct. 22, 1897, Box 3M220, Cohen Papers; Dreyfus, comp., *Henry Cohen, Messenger of the Lord*, pp. 26–30.

number of leased prisoners to run the mill and refinery. Then the deal hung fire.

The state had paid Kempner and Eldridge primarily in Board of Penitentiary bonds. But in the backwash of the 1907 financial panic the bonds became virtually valueless. The partners initiated a lawsuit against Texas for substantially violating the contract. Prevailing legal doctrines of "sovereign immunity" protected Texas from such claims, but lawmakers passed a special bill allowing the suit. For five years the litigation climbed the state court hierarchy. Then in 1912 Texas repudiated leases on Kempner-Eldridge land that the partners had depended on for income. In 1913 a Texas appeals court decided that the state had indeed breached its contracts but that Kempner's lawyers had erred technically in the form of plea, and so a new trial was necessary. Smarting from this Pyrrhic victory, the Kempners paid the lawyers' large fees and settled out of court, which left them and Eldridge back where they had begun. They were still possessed of all the Sugar Land real estate, including the mill and refinery, plus an increasing distaste for prisoner labor and for lawsuits.[58]

Every year during the protracted lawsuits Texas cut the number of convict laborers that planters and refiners could bid for. Then in 1910, a statute, to take effect in 1914, altogether forbade convict leasing, monopolizing for state prison farms and industries all inmate labor. Supporting the discontinuance of private contracting, Kempner and Eldridge nevertheless joined other producers in warning state authorities that sugar output must necessarily decline.[59]

The partners prepared for this eventuality. Their approach was to improve further Sugar Land's physical facilities for free and convict labor while the latter was available, and to attract and keep free labor. Thus in 1907, even before the aborted sale to the state, Eldridge announced that Imperial would erect "the best building in Texas for . . . housing . . . the convicts used on the place." It would have a hospital and two "natatoriums arranged for hot or cold plunges." Indeed, Eldridge continued, "the attempt will be made to make this plantation . . . model in every respect." A journalist concluded

58. Walker, *Penology for Profit*, pp. 200–201; Texas Prison Commission *v.* Imperial Sugar (1908–13), in file 5, Box 32, #80-002, Kempner Papers; many newspaper accounts, in DWK Scrapbook, 1894–1915.

59. Texas Legislature, *Journal of the Senate, 3d & 4th Called Session . . . July 19 and Aug. 10, 1910* (Austin, 1910), p. 228.

that the "guiding genius" of Eldridge and Kempner justified confidence that these plans would actually be carried out. In 1908 Imperial did build the new, vastly more comfortable barracks for its convict workers.[60]

Which suggests that the Kempners applied to convict labor standards of honest dealing and respect for contracts that characterized their other business relationships. As gentlemen of decency, property, and standing, the Kempners, possessed of the powerful political leverage of the purse, saw to it that Eldridge treated their convict workers fairly, as they did the tenant farmers and day laborers, some parolees among them, who after 1914 replaced inmates in Imperial's fields.

Making a Model Company Town

What required the Kempners and Eldridge to elevate conditions for free laborers? Ideas then rising among enlightened large-scale industrial managers included these: that what they perceived to be the regrettable fecklessness of industrial labor required employers to shape not only the workplace but the community, and that rote assembly-line activities deadened pride in workmanship. Sugar refining was an assembly-line process. Many industrial workers turned to liquor and/or labor unions for relief from speed-ups. Industrial employers wished to control the inflow of liquor, in some instances by providing organized religion, education, and culture. Single-industry company towns offered opportunities for social control. In the few benevolently inclined company towns, at least theoretically, managers might better tie workers' interest to those of their employer and foster an anti-union cult of obedience, often by undemocratic means.[61]

A spawning of exploitative company towns occurred, where jaded, speeded-up laborers could look forward not to the finished product of their exertions but only to the end of their shift. What awaited outside factories was little better than what they left inside: squalor, crowding, and the foreman's (or landlord's) unrelenting pressures.

Ike and Eldridge opted against this way. Perhaps Rabbi Cohen stressed the increasingly bad press that some company towns were receiving. A literature was growing that condemned company towns

60. *Galveston News*, May 25, 1907; Armstrong, "Imperial Sugar Co.," II [2].
61. See Montgomery, *The Fall of the House of Labor*, passim.

as overwhelmingly unsalubrious, dangerous, dismal, dead-end environments for workers and their families. In the worst company towns, as in mining, located in isolated rural areas like Sugar Land, owners' and managers' excesses were usually invisible to the general society, and the dominant industry owned and manipulated virtually all physical facilities and human relationships. The "hell-hole on the Brazos" could easily have become one of many company towns in Dixie that historian Frank Tannenbaum ranked among the darker phases of the South.[62]

Critics of such communities insisted that they increased employer-employee tensions, triggered violence, inspired industrial sabotage, and corrupted local justice. Price-gouging and rack-renting by employer-landlords gave rise to laborers' refrains that "I Owe My Soul to the Company Store," reflecting common requirements in company towns that workers buy only in overpricing shops where no competition was permitted.[63] Workers were further victimized by required use of company scrip and by store managers "cooking their books" in the employer's favor. Workers were permitted to live only in company housing, itself overpriced, and, by terms of anti-union "yellow-dog contracts," were subject to swift eviction for many reasons apart from job performance and regardless of the number, ages, and health of family members. Usually poorly maintained, company houses exceeded rents that competitive markets allowed, and home ownership with the resulting independence from the company was almost unheard of. Few company towns encouraged independent shops and factories, for they too might encourage independence among employees. Medical, educational, and recreational facilities were rarely adequate if present at all. Industrial injuries were uninsurable and legal remedies for injured workers a fiction or a travesty.[64]

If agriculture was part of the usual company town, as in Sugar Land, ruinous tenancy arrangements were common, often aggravated by fraudulent weighing, grading, and pricing practices. Like rents, interest rates for loans or credit were usurious. Few tenant farmers or industrial workers in such environments could escape strangling debts that grew from payday to payday, harvest to harvest, season

62. Tannenbaum, *Darker Phases of the South*, passim.

63. Fishback, "Did Coal Miners 'Owe Their Souls to the Company Store'?" *Journal of Economic History*, p. 1011.

64. On a far western example, see Hyman, *Soldiers and Spruce.*

to season. Hireling private detectives and corrupt company police, commonly deputized by a county and often in collusion with local judges, blacklisted troublemakers and enforced prohibitions against labor organizing. Especially where owners of a major industry and community authorities were the same persons, as in Sugar Land, nonconformists might have outstanding debts called in for immediate payment, be fired from factory jobs, have farm tenancy terminated, and/or face eviction from company housing. When neither community nor external restraints existed, corporate power oppressed resident teachers, ministers, journalists, and physicians, who also lived under censorious, sometimes brutalizing company town administrators.[65] But not in Sugar Land.

The same kind of Progressives who had praised Ike's contributions to Galveston's resurrection and reform government were calling for industrial towns "fit to live in" and asserting forcefully that "good homes make good workmen." So-called "model company towns" were controllable, closed communities that stole the thunder of allegedly socialist-oriented labor union organizers by creating safe working and decent living environments and that lured and kept productive, stable, reliable workers. Lecturers at businessmen's meetings, ministers like Rabbi Cohen, and many academics concurred that idealism and self-interest must mix for a thriving capitalism.[66]

Ike and Eldridge were susceptible to this message. Their own agenda of 1907 aimed at keeping workers, not driving them off. Ike, but probably not Eldridge, knew something about Karl Marx, Henry Bellamy, Henry George, and other class-focused social critics, and perhaps Kempner acquainted his partner with contemporaries' ideas on the duties employers owed to labor, especially nonunion labor. Ike certainly rejected all anticapitalist preachments. But Sugar Land's policies suggest that he and Eldridge also rejected vicious coercions and gross exploitations.

Harmony between labor and capital was a perennially attractive vision to many turn-of-the-century Americans, an elusive yet persis-

65. Allen's *The Company Town in the West* is useful but scants Texas. See also Reiff, "Pullman and Paternalism" (Social Science History Association, 1987).

66. Tarbell, "Good Homes Make Good Workmen," *American Magazine*, p. 39; Wright, "Industrial Town That's Fit to Live In," *American City*, p. 388; [anon.], "Model Company Town: Benevolent Landlord," *Saturday Night*, p. 30. For an interesting analog, see Petersen's *Company Town*.

tently alluring reform. To achieve this harmony Ike was willing to try to build a one-industry town into a decent small city with a viable economy. Initially this economy would depend on one industry, sugar. But diversity in both industrial and agricultural pursuits quickly became part of the patient vision.[67]

Ike's pride in the profits that improvements to Imperial generated became overmatched by his satisfaction in the changes he and Eldridge initiated in the Sugar Land community. To Ike Sugar Land was more than the source of labor for the refinery or a profitable investment. Instead, by World War I Sugar Land had already become for Ike an expression of idealism, one that, as we shall see, he and other Kempners would translate into homes, health services, schools, and shops. Sugar Land, in short, became Ike's almost-romantic substitute for the kind of smokestack industry–based company and community culture that he yearned to develop on Galveston Island.[68]

Improving the Sugar Land Community

It took from 1907 through 1917 for the Kempners' and Eldridge's labors, funds, and determination even to begin to transform this grimy, repellent settlement into a livable community and longer than that to rate the "model" label that it ultimately achieved, deserved, and kept. While work continued on the new barracks for the convict workers, the partners set other gangs to clearing fields, draining tens of thousands of acres, and building levees. Flood control achieved also the diminution of insect pests and poisonous reptiles, and ensured a water supply adequate for present work forces, future homes, shops, schools, and hospital, and for fighting fires, in addition to the refinery's thirsty operations and such ancillary or independent manufactories or shops that soon developed. Cleared land not dedicated to sugar (and each year the owners ordered that less and less land be planted in cane in deference to surer year-round supplies available abroad and the rising domestic demand for the refined product) was turned to grazing cattle and diversified truck produce both for anticipated resident Sugar Land consumers should they appear and for the ballooning consumer markets of Houston, Galveston, and San An-

67. Walker, *Reform in America*, p. 206.
68. Abbot, *Seeking Many Inventions*, esp. chaps. 6–8.

tonio. But all this adaptation and land preparation took time and cost money while generating little immediate income.[69] Over decades no Kempner protested at Ike's unwavering, years- and then decades-long monetary devotions to the place. Substantial industrial and community improvements involved even greater cash outlays and longer deferment of profits than those the fields required.

Kempner family decisions to commit the money and wait for income dated back to 1907. Ike and Eldridge proposed then to modernize Imperial's seriously deteriorated production facilities in a manner to make breakdown-free, year-round operations possible. Profits might thus be wrested from more efficient free labor when and if the state ended prisoner leasing and from the owners' plans to rely increasingly on imported cane and raw sugar.[70] Thereafter refinery rehabilitation advanced (as did housing and other community improvements; see chap. 13). New sugar-house machinery, storehouses, rail spurs to the Sugar Road and the Southern Pacific, another spur up the Brazos River valley—all became real. Recruiting specialist mechanics, managers, and foremen, especially from Louisiana, and lodging them in new dormitories and houses that Imperial's artisan teams were building also for paid laborers, the Kempner-Eldridge partners exhibited logistical skills like those Ike displayed in Galveston's seawall and grade raising.

Once resident in Sugar Land, the sugar specialists kept cadres of Imperial artisans busy refurbishing the mill and refinery. In 1907 these facilities had processed 500,000 pounds a day but operated only half the year because the antiquated, poorly maintained machinery broke down frequently for long periods and because domestic producers could supply stock only for a half year, so swiftly was demand rising. But by 1910 Imperial processed 750,000 pounds daily, 850,000 in 1915. Ike saw to it that enough Cuban, Philippine, and Jamaican raw sugar to run Imperial eleven months a year came in through Galveston, adding to the port's viability. Imperial used the remaining weeks for annual cleaning and adjustments.[71]

Eldridge and Kempner became proud, indeed vain, about their early accomplishments at Sugar Land/Imperial. During a 1913 visit

69. Armstrong, "History," sec. on Imperial Sugar Co. [2].
70. Eldridge interview, *Galveston News*, May 25, 1907.
71. Armstrong, "History," sec. on Imperial Sugar Co. [1–6].

of state officials to Sugar Land, Eldridge lectured them, declaring publicly and with "evident feeling" that "if it had not been for the financial ability and confidence of . . . I. H. Kempner, . . . who backed me, the prison commissioners of Texas would have destroyed these enterprises which you see here."[72]

Memory of the prison-labor years did not end with the formal termination of the system. In 1929 state senator Walter Woodul informed Texas Prison Board member Rabbi Cohen that "some prejudice" remained "against the Imperial brands of sugar on the mistaken grounds that this sugar was [still being] manufactured by the prisoners at the State Penitentiary." True, the "Imperial State Farm" had deserved "occasional notoriety" in the distant pre-Kempner/Eldridge past. But Imperial had proved itself to be a fine taxpaying "citizen," the legislator continued, and should no longer suffer from unjustifiable public ill will. He suggested that Imperial's owners change the firm's name.

Cohen sent his copy of the report to Ike, who, thanking the rabbi, implied that no name change would occur. None did.[73]

Ike was simply too proud of what Sugar Land was becoming as a community and of Imperial as a trade name associated with his family, to alter the label. Ike usually nursed his pride discreetly. He exhibited it openly, however, in commissioning his fellow-Galvestonian turned motion picture director, King Vidor, in 1915 to produce a film of the refinery and company town.[74]

Chapter 13 will sketch developments at Sugar Land as a community and an industry after World War I. Central in Ike's affections during these exceedingly busy World War I years was another humanitarian effort, this one unconnected to possibilities for profit. This effort, the Galveston Movement, now wants attention.

72. *Galveston News*, May 22, 1913.

73. Woodul, letter to Prison Board Members, and I. H. Kempner, letter to Cohen, Mar. 12, 1929, Mar. 9, 1929, respectively, Box 3M246, Cohen Papers.

74. No copy of the film survives. See H. L. Kempner, letter to author, Nov. 9, 1982.

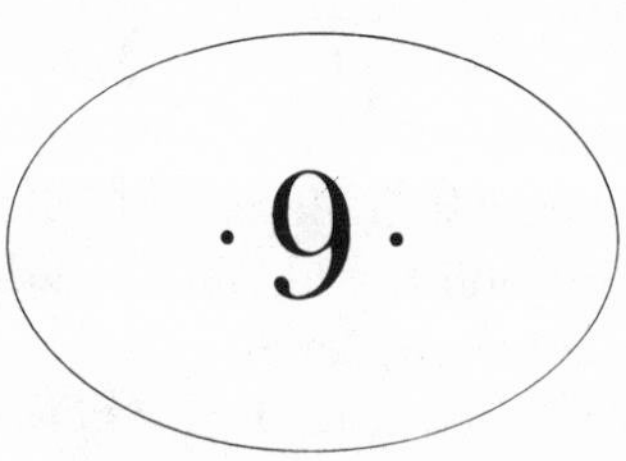

The Galveston Movement

WITHIN THIRTEEN YEARS after Harris Kempner's death, Rabbi Cohen and Ike Kempner had expanded the meaning of his life. Employing it as one model among many, by 1907 they justified Galveston becoming the primary port of entry into America for a planned multitude of emigrating eastern European Jews fleeing new and ever more severe official anti-Semitism. Galveston would also be the transition environment between the two cultures. In it, Texas donors of money and myriad social services, like the Kempners and Rabbi Cohen, would ease the immigrants' integration into their strange new land.

This complex immigration-acculturation-resettlement effort had its headquarters in New York City but became known internationally as the Galveston Movement. Arising out of the sometimes diverging purposes of many persons, especially Israel Zangwill, the English writer, playwright, and Zionist, and Jacob Schiff, the non-Zionist American banker and philanthropist, the Movement connected Zangwill and Schiff with Rabbi Cohen and, through him, with Harris Kempner as a model and with both Cohen and Ike Kempner as essential on-site implementers.[1]

Ike perceived the Movement in several connected ways. As civic booster and businessman Ike welcomed newcomers and their dispersion on the mainland, a process reflecting his father's career. This increased traffic through the port and the resulting enlarged consumer demand would encourage a larger permanent Island City popula-

1. Marinbach, *Galveston,* chaps. 1–2 and passim. On more modest contemporary efforts, see Hartmann, *The Movement to Americanize the Immigrant,* pp. 38–97; Lissak, "Liberal Progressives and the 'New Immigrants'," in *Studies in American Civilization,* p. 79.

tion and more imports, all to Galveston's benefit. And Ike, like Rabbi Cohen, saw the Movement also as an implicit tribute to the essence of his father's history: success, ethicality, adherence to Judaism, and intense American patriotism.[2]

More generally, the Galveston Movement reflected a perception that at least some Jews in the South and West had discernible advantages over coreligionists elsewhere in America. Instead of a Jewish nation-state the Movement promised emigrants a new secular home and unrivaled opportunities to realize dreams for their childrens' futures.[3]

The Movement did indeed come to aim at ways of life and labor that Harris Kempner and others like him had traced: individual rather than community emigration from Europe and dispersed resettling in inland cities and towns rather than in the northeast's ghettos or, as some advocated, on communal farms. By the time the Movement took form in the first years of the twentieth century, Harris Kempner's career in America was well known in the city, state, and region, and also among many central European Jews, so that when agents of the Movement were asked, "Who . . . ever heard of Galveston?" the recruiters had convincing replies.[4] A specialist on immigration history noted: "In nearly every aggregation of [earlier] immigrants a group of successful store owners, small bankers, and political leaders emerge to serve as models of individual mobility and to reinforce the notion that personal striving could be reinforced in the United States. . . . Immigrants also had concrete definitions of what America meant in both historic and contemporary times. In neither period did they move aimlessly or randomly into some vague 'land of opportunity.' Rather, they almost always moved into specific cities and jobs."[5]

Almost every phase of Harris Kempner's life fit perceptions of the Movement's American and foreign prime movers and intended beneficiaries. He was one of the relatively small number of German-speaking immigrants of the 1850s who had moved from the north-

2. Hyman Block, interview with L. Marchiafava, June 6, 1981, RLA; IHK, *Recalled Recollections*, p. 58.

3. Dinnerstein and Palsson, eds., *Jews in the South*, passim.

4. Henry Cohen, "History of the Jews of Galveston" (manuscript), Cohen Papers; Brown, *Indian Wars and Pioneers of Texas*, pp. 278–80; Clark, *The Texas Gulf Coast*, pp. 97–100; Mondell and Mondell, "West of Hester Street," *Texas Humanist*, p. 3.

5. Bodnar, "Symbols and Servants," *Journal of American History*, pp. 144, 146.

eastern cities of their initial settlement to smaller cities and towns, favoring particularly the broad midwestern and southern expanses, there often to win substantial successes, especially as owners of businesses.

With such careers as his helping to define the Movement's goals, its strategists, staff, and supporters aimed to scatter the new wave of immigrant Jews in largely non-Jewish, smaller urban communities, where practical alternatives existed to dead-end labor in "eye of the needle" sweatshop garment trades and subsistence retail shops.[6] Further, diffusion would, it was hoped, defuse renascent anti-Semitism, not diminish allegiance to Judaism.

On the religious adhesion issue, difficulties in preserving ancient ways obviously faced isolated Jews. But on this score, too, Harris Kempner offered a reassuringly positive example. He was both successful and religiously observant yet elicited respect, not bigotry. To established German Jews who (perhaps forgetting their own rude treatment by the earlier, Sephardic immigrants) simply assumed that they would tutor Russian and other eastern European Jews, the Kempner way led to the good life in the United States and in Texas.

No doubt this patronizing view was deplorable.[7] But it was kindness itself when contrasted to the bigotry of numerous defenders of "true" American values who wished to limit immigration, or at least to keep Jews, once here, out of public preferments and private associations. These views were based on beliefs that Jews were unassimilable in terms of mores and ethics, questionable in terms of allegiance to America, and undesirable as voters, much less as officeholders, jury members, or business or professional associates. Such detractors neither realized nor likely would admit the possibility that the religious "outsiders" they deplored possessed immense force for the strengthening of values that were emphatically American.[8]

Harris Kempner had needed to struggle against few such barriers, and his story was thereby the more compelling and engaging to fence-sitting potential recruits for the Movement. But Movement organizers knew that since the 1880s, as the influx of Russian and Balkan

6. Waldinger, *Through the Eye of the Needle.*

7. Rischin, "German versus Russians," in *The American Jewish Experience*, p. 120.

8. Moore, *Religious Outsiders and the Making of Americans;* Higham, *Send These to Me*, chaps. 2, 7–10.

Jews ballooned, virulent anti-Semitism had resurfaced, seriously undercutting the earlier sense of identity between American Jews and non-Jews. Leading barrier breakers among established American Jews of German origin worried that the highly visible newcomers excited discriminations and even violence against all Jews by their very numbers, unfamiliar dress, and devotion to Hebrew liturgy and vernacular Yiddish. Less self-protectively, they resisted also the growing inclination of congressional representatives to restrict immigration by legislation. Such restrictions inevitably increased the distress of millions of coreligionists in Russia, Poland, and the Balkans.[9] Because the Movement embraced divergent perceptions of a happier Jewish-American future as well as of relief in a troubled present, its significance transcended the geographical shift to the Texas port of entry.

Galveston ca. 1907

Was Galveston a fit stage for these purposes? Kempner and Cohen had to convince Schiff, Arthur Hays Sulzberger, and other founders of what became the Movement that the affirmative reply was justified. Though hardly devoid of sensual and often sordid attractions, Galveston paled next to New Orleans's lurid reputation and sad epidemiological history while yet exhibiting a rich cultural texture and a diverse ethnic, racial, and religious population. European emigrant aid societies had resettled whole German farming communities in the interior of Texas through Galveston, a precedent that in both positive and negative terms interested the Schiff and Zangwill organizations. And in 1905 Ike was beginning to plan the improved community at Sugar Land.

No one involved in these several efforts deceived themselves that everyone in Texas, Jew or non-Jew, was a success. The least upwardly mobile group of the Island City were blacks, who totaled perhaps 10 percent of Galveston's population. They were locked into inferior jobs and, with rarest exceptions, lacked opportunities to improve their situations.[10] Many earlier Jewish-German arrivals had either failed in businesses and jobs or scratched out bare subsistence. But some

9. Higham, "Anti-Semitism in the Gilded Age," *Mississippi Valley Historical Review*, p. 559; Leonard, "Louis Marshall and Immigration Restriction," *American Jewish Archives*, p. 6.

10. Taylor, *The Distant Magnet;* Rice, *The Negro in Texas.*

Texas Jews of German origins had achieved brilliant successes, among them Kempner. Before 1900 some Russian Jews reached Galveston after traveling overland from New York[11] or came by ship, as did Louis and Leah Sakowitz, for example, from Kiev, in the early 1880s. Sakowitz opened a hole-in-the-wall dockyard store to sell clothing to merchant sailors. The shop did not thrive, and Sakowitz's sons took to peddling sailors' clothes and comforts on the Galveston docks. By the nineteenth century's last decade they had escalated from denims to expensive clothing and were on their way to developing a long-lived department store.[12]

The business and social worlds of the Kempners and Sakowitzes rarely meshed, but intersection did occur in their shared temple. Through Rabbi Cohen, Kempner probably aided hard-luck new immigrants financially. If the Sakowitzes' hardscrabble early situation confirmed prejudices held by German Jews about Russian coreligionists, the Russian latecomers, as a group, were to prove the doomsayers to be spectacularly wrong. By the 1920s, sociologist Milton Gordon concluded, "The rise in socio-economic status of the Eastern European Jews . . . [was to be] the greatest collective Horatio Alger story in American immigration history."[13] Which is, of course, exactly what the fabricators of the Galveston Movement had dared to hope for.

Even as Harris Kempner's career prefigured aspects of the Galveston Movement, it helped also to shape attributes of that city which attracted the Movement's leaders. As a Cold Springs peddler-shopkeeper, as Marx's partner in wholesale grocering, and as solo cotton factor and risk-taking investor in a hundred enterprises, Harris Kempner created closely interwoven networks of farmers, retail merchants, and bankers throughout the state. His links to northern and eastern credit sources and cotton spinners both at home and abroad were re-

11. One such newcomer from Russia informed an American official at Ellis Island that he was looking for a relative who lived on Houston Street in the city's famous Lower East Side. "The next thing he knew . . . he was on a train bound for Houston, Texas. Seeing New York . . . he was very glad they had sent him to Texas" (*New York Times*, Nov. 24, 1985).

12. Cook, "The Fraying Empire of Bobby Sakowitz," *Texas Monthly*, p. 132, errs in suggesting that the Sakowitzes were aided in the early 1880s by the Galveston Movement. See also Tenebaum, "Immigrants and Capital" (American Historical Association, 1985).

13. Gordon, *Assimilation in American Life*, p. 185; Cohen in *Galveston Daily News*, Apr. 16, 1894, on Kempner's benefactions.

sources that the Movement's officers hoped also to exploit. And Ike's decade of achievements since his father's death encouraged all supporters of the Movement.

Harris Kempner, American and Jew

Especially through Rabbi Cohen, Movement makeweights Zangwill, Schiff, and others knew that Harris Kempner and his family were consistent and enthusiastic secular acculturationists. As noted earlier, Harris Kempner, like Schiff and other successful American Jews of English and German origins and Reform inclinations, had identified wholeheartedly with their chosen land as a generally welcoming and benign society.[14] "I came to America to be an American," Kempner had written in 1893, "and I tried to adapt my ways to American ways. I was young, and the right to participate in all phases of American life—political, social, economic, even military—was as wonderful to me as the right of a people to govern themselves as they thought best. I knew what it was like not to have that right, either individually or collectively." That same year, in a striking parallel to then-ailing Harris Kempner's testament, Cohen identified loyalty to America with Judaism. "Americanism . . . has become a passion with us [Jews]," Cohen preached soon after World War I, a sentiment evoking warm concurrence from Eliza Kempner and all her children.[15]

Of course by then Harris Kempner was long dead. But he had taught Americanism to his family well. The lessons were both explicit, as in his 1894 statement on Americanism and acculturation, and implicit.

Immigrant Utopias

High among implicit lessons was Harris Kempner's stress on rural lands for capitalist ventures, not for Jewish communal settlements. He appears to have been almost wholly uninterested in reports that came to Galveston about the small number of Jewish farming communities then existing or planned in the United States. Most of these

14. Block interview with Marchiafava, June 6, 1981.

15. In E. R. Thompson, Jr., "History of H. Kempner" (manuscript), Kempner Papers, p. 13. Typescripts of this 1918 essay of Cohen's, and another of 1923, in Box 236, Cohen Papers, and see also Dreyfus, comp., *Henry Cohen, Messenger of the Lord*, pp. 23–24; IHK, *Recalled Recollections*, p. 58.

communities reflected Zionist aspirations, and, even less palatable to many Jewish Galvestonians, also expressed utopian, vaguely socialist purposes.[16]

Harris Kempner's probable disapproval of these communities was an implicit posthumous context in the Galveston Movement.[17] In this sense Harris Kempner indirectly influenced the Movement toward urban, artisan, merchant, capitalist, non-Zionist goals for the immigrants, an influence that, through Ike, became evident in 1917.[18]

By then mayor of Galveston, Ike was serving on war-emergency committees aimed at increasing America's food supplies. Rabbi Cohen officiated that year at the dedication of a memorial to deceased Galvestonian Morris Lasker at a Jewish farming community in Pennsylvania. Asked to contribute to the memorial, Ike, for one of the few times on record, took issue with his rabbi. Doing so, Ike both reflected his own large knowledge of agricultural economics gained from what was by then a decade of experience with the farming phases of Sugar Land, plus his concern that though the Movement had by then been aborted, its memory should continue to reaffirm his father's life.

Any movement "for the colonization of Jewish farmers [in America] is ill-timed and premature," Ike stated. Few Jewish immigrants had farming experience. It was a "practical futility" to turn amateurs loose on the land. That part of the scheme "calling for . . . experts to assist by advice about the cultivation of the soil, . . . assist in marketing their crops, etc., is excellent," he wrote. But "the fact remains that such expert direction cannot and will not make a successful farmer out of a tailor, shoemaker, or a garment worker, who is not inured to the physical and climatic demands that farming in our Southland entails." If, however, Cohen could produce enough veteran Jewish farmers who aimed at profits, not social change, then Ike was unworried about financing.[19]

Cohen's wartime praise of the agricultural experiment was an aberration. As a major figure in the Movement noted in 1907, the rabbi

16. Reps, *The Forgotten Frontier;* Herscher, *Jewish Agricultural Utopias in America, 1880–1910;* Brandes, *Immigrants to Freedom;* and Goldberg, *Back to the Soil,* offer details.

17. Historians and biographers often link incomplete chains of evidence with logic or even intuitions. See Bentley, *The Process of Government,* p. 152.

18. The Movement terminated, of necessity, on the outbreak of World War I.

19. Ike, letter to Cohen, Jan. 15, 1917, Box 3M235, Cohen Papers.

otherwise kept agricultural, communal projects "apart from our . . . [Galveston Movement] work."[20]

Potential Divisiveness

It was well that avoidance of some issues and compromise on others were possible and that Movement activists Kempner and Cohen shared with Zangwill and Schiff unwavering dedication to the effort's central purpose—the rescue of hundreds of thousands of eastern European Jews from the increasing perils of life there. For, as noted, Zangwill and Schiff were at sharp odds on other, near-top-of-the-agenda alternative goals for the Movement.

Zangwill was an ardent secular Zionist who aimed first at establishing the emigrés *somewhere* as pioneers of a wholly Jewish nation-state. He was simultaneously and somewhat paradoxically also an ardent Americanophile (although he never visited the United States) and author of a play, *The Melting Pot.* The play preached that wholesale intermarriage in America would quickly erase anti-Semitism by blending all races and faiths into a new, amalgamated people in which credal distinctions would be meaningless—an unattractive result to Harris and Ike Kempner, Cohen, and Schiff.[21] For his part, Schiff became convinced that the dispersion of immigrants throughout America's heartland, and thus swift acculturation in Schiff's own manner and that of a Harris Kempner, was the necessary and proper course.

Schiff would come to this judgment in some substantial part through counsel he received from Rabbi Cohen, his "close friend . . . [who] was largely responsible for the success of that philanthropist's Galveston Immigration experiment," Rabbi Stephen Wise would inform the publisher of *Time* magazine.[22] The early sharp divisions of purpose and perceptions between Zangwill and Schiff threatened the chances for cooperation in aiding the harassed Jews of Russia and the Balkans. But masters of mediation, including Cohen, were able to bridge the gaps, eventually swaying Zangwill to accept the largely secular goals and American environment that Schiff advo-

20. Morris Waldman, letter to Cohen, Mar. 12, 1907, Box 3M225, Cohen Papers.

21. See "Around City Hall," *The New Yorker,* Sept. 14, 1987, pp. 116ff.

22. Wise, letter to Henry Luce, Mar. 16, 1933, Box 2M255, Cohen Papers.

cated. Cohen had enduring, warm links to Zangwill, his boyhood friend in England, where Zangwill had recruited his rabbinically inclined schoolmate into a Zionist youth organization. But upon coming to Galveston, Cohen had altered his views.[23] Disagreeing sharply about Zionist timing and tactics perhaps analogous to pre–Civil War abolitionists' discord about immediate emancipation, American Jews like Cohen and the Kempners would argue such questions for decades to come, while yet supporting some form of Jewish presence in what in 1948 would become Israel, but not necessarily as a Jewish nation-state.[24]

Zangwill's cooperation was essential. He commanded the only European and British apparatuses capable of directing multitudes of emigrants away from America's northeastern cities, where support societies were already dangerously overstrained, to Galveston. There, as suggested, the Kempners and other locals would house and feed the newcomers and instruct them in the ways of their new country. Acting thereafter as resettlement administrators, the Texans would then direct the immigrants toward permanent habitations and livelihoods in small towns and cities of the Gulf, Rocky Mountain, and West Coast regions, aiding them further with direct loans from locally funded, low- or no-interest revolving accounts. Aimed to accommodate tens of thousands of newcomers, it was an expensive and ambitious program.[25]

Schiff, Cohen, Ike Kempner, and other American leaders of the Movement were intent on "Americanizing" the beneficiaries of this novel social engineering effort. They shared a pervasive belief that Harris Kempner's story, including the late cotton factor's successes in business, fidelity as congregant, and generosity as philanthropist locally and abroad, was deservedly a model of the achieving, responsible American Jew, a model that architects and implementers of the Galveston Movement tried to replicate. Further encouragement existed in the shared comprehension of the Movement's backers that

23. See Cohen, letter to J. Schiff, Jan. 30, 1945, Box 3M286, Cohen Papers.

24. Friesel, "The Influence of American Zionism on the American Community," *American Jewish History*, p. 130; Urofsky, "Zionism," in *The American Jewish Experience*, p. 211.

25. Cohen, *The Galveston Movement, 1907–1914;* Cohen, "Israel Zangwill: An Appreciation" (manuscript), Box 3M326, Cohen Papers.

small towns and cities had tamed — were still taming — the enormous American West.[26] Precisely in the Movement's vulnerable formative years Ike was performing central roles rebuilding Galveston after its Great Storm and, as noted, systematically rehabilitating Sugar Land.

Organizers and Ramrods

The Texas cotton merchant and his rabbi were a team helping to shape and implement the Galveston Movement, its "active . . . organizer and ramrod," a journalist noted. Cohen was the indefatigable Movement gadfly who touched donors' consciences and wallets. Additionally, in close concert with Kempner, Cohen exploited rabbinical and business contacts in interior Texas and elsewhere in order to aid "graduates" of the Movement's Galveston phase who took up new careers on the mainland. In terms applicable also to Kempner, Cohen's family would describe the rabbi as becoming "so completely an integral factor in the work of the . . . Bureau that the people of Galveston, Zangwill in England, and . . . Schiff in New York came to think of the Galveston end of the Movement in terms of him."[27]

By 1905 Galveston was the only Texas city with significant advantages to the Movement. Still one of Texas' largest population centers, Galveston possessed facilities to cope with armies of immigrants upon arrival and then to disperse them inland. From the wharves to the Strand the city's business leaders, stevedores, physicians, lawyers, bankers, and their wives, educated by the Great Storm to deal in large categories of human needs, could provide new arrivals with the skilled services that were essential for transitions. An expandable charitable and emergency apparatus in Galveston existed in the form of hospital and church-related social service agencies, largely run by women, at a time when government offered virtually no such aids.

26. Cohen, "Additional Notes on Jews in Texas" (manuscript), Box 3M326, Cohen Papers; Rochlin and Rochlin, *Pioneer Jews;* Stanley, "Merchandising in the Southwest," *American Jewish Archives*, pp. 86–102; Day, "The Americanism of Harris Kempner," *Southwest Review*, p. 125; Moore, "Jewish Migration to the Sunbelt," in *Shades of the Sunbelt*, pp. 42–43, discusses the Industrial Removal Office, a B'nai B'rith effort to settle skilled male immigrants in appropriate cities, and compares it with the Galveston Movement.

27. See *Houston Chronicle*, Dec. 27, 1936; Nathan and Cohen, *The Man Who Stayed in Texas*, p. 201, and see pp. 189–209.

Galveston's phenomenal bootstrapping since the 1900 storm was known internationally, as were Ike Kempner's contributions to the city's survival and revival. The web of public and private associations such as the Deep Water Committee and the boards of the temple and several hospitals, were precisely the kind of in-place service structure with links to governments' resources that the Movement's backers needed. Charitable, social service, educational, and moral uplift associations and agencies in which Galveston's women as well as men were active and effective were peculiarly relevant to the planned mass movements of whole families.[28]

Highest-level matters, especially the Europe-to-Texas phases, were in the hands of Zangwill and Schiff. The Movement would flourish or wither on the Texas front, however. The Galvestonians involved in implementing it had to plan and pay for the arrivals' temporary but often extended transitions once landed at the wharves. Housing, food, clothing, medical and dental care, and forced-draft tutelage in English formed part of the Texans' catalog of concerns. Additionally, the on-site "old" Texans assumed responsibility for scouting inland communities to which the immigrants might eventually move. Both the transition and relocation efforts required substantial financing for domiciling and educating the newcomers about possible vocations or businesses and then for proffering loans to seemingly worthy aspirants in order to start them toward independence.

In all this Ike played several essential roles. He exploited on behalf of the Movement H. Kempner's peripatetic cotton agents on the Texas mainland, plus all the manifold banking, business, and farming connections that his father and he had developed since the 1870s. Additionally, Ike monitored the sophisticated transition effort on Galveston itself, an exceedingly delicate and difficult task, considering the variant personalities and approaches of numerous volunteers and professionals in social work, education, finance, and public health. Ike was also a largely behind-the-scene primary fundraiser for the Movement's costly Texas operation, all during years when he was simultaneously Galveston's revenue commissioner and advancing H. Kempner's interests, including the Sugar Land enterprise. In sum,

28. Turner, "From Benevolent Ladies to Civic Women" (Southern Historical Association, 1986).

the still-young businessman seemed almost to have been prepared for the grueling humanitarian effort in mass social engineering that the Movement became.

In 1906 Cohen had persuaded Ike to accept membership in a new nationwide committee of "representative" successful Jews to coordinate Jewish charity across the country for the first time.[29] But the congruence of the new committee's continental scope, personnel, and timing, with the Galveston Movement, suggests that the committee was to overcome what Ike and other supporters of good causes had long deplored about Texas parochialism. Galveston's Jews "apparently do not have much influence with our fellow [Jewish] citizens in Dallas or Houston or San Antonio," he complained. Fundraisers for national and international Jewish charities agreed with Ike that Texas Jews exhibited an insular, inward-dwelling "lack of deep interest in . . . national Jewish charities." Ike Kempner and his family had led an earlier shift toward "deep interest," and not only to aid Jews. Sufferers from San Francisco's earthquake and the Russo-Japanese War as well as Jewish victims of Russian pogroms received aid from Galveston, a particularly impressive record since it was Texas' only city with a substantial Jewish population and yet was itself still recovering from the Great Storm.[30]

Ike, Morris Lasker, and Kempner family lawyer John Neethe also accepted appointment in 1907 by the Galveston Temple B'nai Israel congregation to a committee to oversee the "secret charity fund" of the Hebrew Benevolent Society. Whereupon the trio assigned Rabbi Cohen to be their disbursing arm, with apparent intention that the minister spend the augmented budget especially for the oncoming immigrants of the Movement. Ike also "represented Galveston in the [Movement's] meetings in New York where they [Schiff et al.] were raising funds," Hyman Block recalled. Ike, Cohen's behind-the-scenes troubleshooter and on-site emergency fundraiser, in effect held the key to America's southern golden door. Block remembered that if Schiff or others in the Movement's New York or Cincinnati headquarters needed "$100,000 they would wire Mr. I. H. Kempner and before the

29. *Galveston News*, Oct. 24, 1906.

30. Ike, letter to Morris Waldman, Secretary, American Jewish Committee, Nov. 30, 1928, Box K-10-11, File: Texas Prudential Insurance Co., Kempner Papers; manuscript in undated Donation Record File, Financial Records, Box 3M334, Cohen Papers.

ink was dry [on the telegram] Mr. Kempner would inform [Galveston fellow-merchants] Mr. Heidenheimer or Mr. Lasker how much they must contribute."[31]

In persuading the ultimate policymakers that Galveston should be the Ellis Island of the West, Cohen and others had referred frequently to Harris Kempner's accomplishments. As Rabbi Stephen Wise and, on another occasion, Ike Kempner noted, Cohen's several widely popular essays on the history of the Jews of Texas in general, and of Galveston in particular, illuminated connections between Harris Kempner and other Jewish Texans and the Cincinnati activists of the Movement. These connections held the Movement together and made it work.[32]

But it fell to Ike to overcome sharp concerns about the financial burdens that Texas Jews must anticipate once the immigrants filled the paltry number of mercantile and industrial jobs that the state's overwhelmingly agricultural economy could offer. "Later on the hardship will fall on Galveston and on all Jewish Texans," warned one Waco merchant.[33]

History, however, was in one of its grimmest moments. The Movement began operations in 1907. By 1914, having already directed ten thousand Europeans to and through Galveston, it was only shifting from low gear. Then the guns of August sounded. Europe's warring governments closed off emigration, thus sealing the fates of an uncertain but vast number of thwarted potential beneficiaries of the Movement. By a terrible geometry, the descending curtain of World War I thereafter increased the hazards that bigotry imposed on the trapped Jews. The Movement's leaders were correct, however, to believe that self-improvement by many of the immigrants who did reach the United States would occur once Europe's constraints were lifted. This optimism derived in part from such careers as that of Harris Kempner, and Ike was adding to that reputation. But Ike's very successes in the Movement were to recoil on him in the 1919 Galveston municipal elec-

31. Block interview with Marchiafava, June 6, 1981; resolution, Nov. 27, 1907, Box 3M225, Cohen Papers; Cohen, "The Galveston Movement," in *Western States Jewish History*, pp. 114–19.

32. Cohen, "Settlement of Jews in Texas," *American Jewish Historical Society Publications*, p. 139; Cohen, "History of the Jews of Galveston" (manuscript, undated), Box 3M326, Cohen Papers. See also Wise, letter to Cohen, May 18, 1900, Box 3M221, and I. H. Kempner to same, July 19, 1902, Box 3M223, Cohen Papers.

33. Louis Weigel, letter to Cohen, Mar. 11, 1907, Box 3M225, Cohen Papers.

tions when he ran unsuccessfully for a second term as the city's mayor.[34] Leading to that reversal were tenacious rumors concerning his motives in supporting the Movement.

Allegations against the Galveston Movement

Was the Galveston Movement only a cruel swindle benefiting primarily anti-union owners of industries like the Kempners' M&P cotton compress on Galveston Island and mainland refinery at Sugar Land? Did Ike and other regional implementers of the Movement aim to force displaced eastern European women, Jews and non-Jews alike, into ill-paid neo-peonage, since contract prison labor was evidently on its way out in Texas, or worse, into prostitution? First to the prostitution question.

Organized international "white slavery" in the early twentieth century was a peril of passage that claimed many victims among poor eastern European females. According to some accusers, they became prostitutes in America in part as result of collusions between employers and gangsters, the latter sometimes intriguing in turn with owners of bail-bonding businesses, brothels, saloons, pawnshops, or gambling dens. No disproportionately large numbers of Jews, however, have ever been identified in the prostitution trades. Indeed, a peculiarly Jewish opposition existed to prostitution. This antipathy is rooted both in the Talmud and in a secular environmentalist view popular among Jewish Progressives, that prostitutes (like many convicts) were less evil offenders than victims who deserved more remedial help than contumely.[35]

Some allegations about Galveston Jewish business leaders encouraging prostitution among immigrant women brought in by the Movement perhaps had origins in a prewar effort of one special interest to exploit Jews' concerns about anti-Semitism. Shortly before the initiation of the Movement, in 1905, lawyers from Houston serially approached Galveston banker Bertrand Adoue, Rabbi Cohen, and Ike.

34. See below, chap. 10.

35. White, "Prostitutes, Reformers, and Historians," *Criminal Justice History*, p. 203; and see Bristow, *Prostitution and Prejudice*, and Connelly, *The Response to Prostitution in the Progressive Era;* Nadell, "Perils of the Passage" (Social Science History Association, 1987).

They reported insinuations that important Galveston Jews headed prostitution and other organized vice there.[36]

Apparently the Houston lawyers warned Ike and the others that schemers aimed to broadcast further allegations of prominent Galveston Jews importing Jewish prostitutes under some humanitarian cloak and pressuring into prostitution respectable resident Jewish and non-Jewish recent immigrant women and innocent females from the mainland. Their major supporting evidence derived from the fact that some Galveston Jews owned or leased structures used for bordellos, gambling halls, and unlicensed saloons and that some Jewish pawnbrokers allegedly "fenced" stolen goods, often collusively with pimps, prostitutes, pawnbrokers, gamblers, bail-bond agents, and bartenders. The lawyers concluded that the allegations had their source in some Texas beermakers who were anxious to lessen the public's identification of them with saloons, corrupt politics, prostitution, and other social evils. Militant Protestant women were then trying to shut down saloons. The brewers hoped to deflect this effort into a crusade with anti-Semitic undertones aimed at running prostitutes out of the city, by conducting "a peculiar fight, carried on for the most part in the dark in order to make it successful." This can translate into blackmail or even violence. The targets of this "peculiar fight" were to be owners (especially, it appears, any Jewish owners) of the "palaces of joy," saloons, casinos, and pawnshops, plus the supposed importers of Jewish prostitutes.

To this time "a general campaign against [Galveston] prostitution could not be successful," one of the lawyers acknowledged. But, he continued, "the Jewish prostitute has none of the affiliations [i.e., protection in high places] that the Gentile woman of the town has." Notwithstanding, some agents of the brewers had approached Ike directly, perhaps to threaten publicity about Jewish prostitutes if he did not curtail anti-saloon militants and fatten the agents' fees. But after meeting with Ike, one of the agents admitted to a lawyer: "we do not suppose that it [i.e., Ike's cooperation and larger fees] will come from that source."[37]

36. John T. Wheeler, letter to Bertrand Adoue, Oct. 19, 1905, Box 3M224, Cohen Papers.

37. Ibid.

Although the devious plotters failed to lever money from Galveston's leading Jewish businessmen, including Ike, the rumors they generated resulted in heartbreak for some would-be immigrant women. Canards were then common in white, Protestant America about the sexual immorality of the most numerous, visible, and "exotic" immigrants, chiefly Jews and Roman Catholics. The essence of these canards was that crime flourished where Jews were, and that the importation of prostitutes, or, worse, the enticement of "Americans" into the trade, was among the most lucrative of these highly organized crimes.

Galveston Movement executives in New York, London, and Galveston learned that from 1907 to 1913, four times (i.e., forty-three per one thousand) the number of female Jewish immigrants were denied admission at Galveston as morally defective and swiftly deported than at New York City (eleven per one thousand). Almost all the Galveston deportees were alleged prostitutes.

From London, Israel Zangwill expressed his concern to Schiff about the "unjustifiable deportation of Galveston immigrants." Zangwill's staff in Europe and England had screened the Galveston-bound emigrants. He implied that if any of the women were prostitutes, they had joined that sisterhood of misery only after landing in Galveston.[38] In essence Zangwill credited ideas that corrupting influences were indeed at work in Galveston.

Such notions widened gaps already growing between Orthodox and Reform Jews in Galveston. A distressing public exchange between spokesmen for the two congregations occurred in 1913, when Rabbi Cohen accused the Orthodox congregation of harboring a "so-called white slave trafficker," and then, upon the death of the accused, of refusing to give the corpse burial space in the Orthodox cemetery. According to Cohen, the dead man had come to America under the auspices of an Orthodox aid society, not the Galveston Movement. Once on the Island, the ghettoizing tendency of Orthodoxy insulated the immigrant in question from "the influence of the melting pot process . . . the assimilation policy and the mission idea," and so he fell prey to evil. Reminded by the lay head of the Orthodox synagogue

38. Zangwill, letter to Schiff, Dec. 5, 1913, in "Immigrants and Immigration" file, AJA/HUC. Zangwill intended to complain about this matter to President Wilson as a "fellow-author."

that "We are not more responsible for the . . . bad Jew than you or your congregation," however, Cohen withdrew his charges.[39] But the sores festered and would erupt again in 1919, to Kempner's political detriment.

Labor and the Galveston Movement

Suggestions also appeared in major Yiddish-language newspapers in New York City, Chicago, and Europe, that the Galveston port-of-entry scheme had other sinister purposes related to the Kempners' anti-unionism in their use of convict laborers. Generally reflecting varieties of socialist thought, the journalists insisted that newcomers would be dumped in Galveston and nearby, at M&P and Sugar Land by implication, not scattered across interior America as promised. Thereupon the local Texas police, described as mere tools of rich Galveston employers, would arrest the immigrants as vagrants. Like blacks, these hapless newcomers would then find themselves contracted out by the state as convict labor.[40]

Such innuendo from coreligionists galled Ike and all Movement activists. To counter them, Schiff, through President Theodore Roosevelt, had Terence V. Powderly, the former head of the Knights of Labor and United States commissioner-general of immigration (in 1907 the head of its information division), visit the Movement's Galveston facilities. In his report, Powderly commended all the Movement's Galveston activists for the facilities and procedures they had developed for the immigrants. After his site visit Powderly wrote that everything was "homelike" but efficient. The large Galveston staff had agents (including H. Kempner field staff lent to the Movement) in many inland communities to keep track of the newcomers after their departure from Galveston. "In addition to all this," Powderly marveled, "they extended a helping hand to the needy who are not Jews and as cheerfully guard the welfare of the friendless Gentile as the Jew." After addressing the Galveston Cotton Exchange as well as labor union assemblies, Powderly reported that the Movement "was held in the

39. Secretary, Executive Committee (name illegible), letter to Cohen, Feb. 25, 1913, Box 3M230, Cohen Papers.

40. Typescripts (trans. from the Yiddish) of unidentified newspaper articles, in "Immigrants and Immigration" file, AJA/HUC.

highest esteem by all classes," and he extolled Rabbi Cohen and the city's foremost business leaders.[41]

Perhaps the tenacious rumors helped to persuade Kempner to quit leasing prisoners. In any event, times were changing. Ike's curt statement in his memoirs on the matter—"Political and sentimental opinion was becoming assertive in prohibiting by law such hiring"—likely reflected sentiments against the practice from members of his family, their rabbi, and their associates in Galveston society, business, and philanthropy. Ike would end the practice before the state's revised laws of 1914 required its termination.[42]

No evidence ever implicated any Kempners or persons close to them in the prostitution traffic or in a desire to create a new source of industrial peons. Nevertheless, these unsavory and unsettling matters help to explain why Ike chose to play behind-the-scenes roles in much of the Movement's tragically foreshortened lifetime.

As it was, Ike wore himself almost into illness by his simultaneous exertions. By late summer 1911 he was under a physician's care, with the rabbi nagging him about the need for recuperative rest. "The fact remains, Doctor," Ike wrote the rabbi, "that I am physically and mentally better off when I have both my hands and brain active. I have no particular ambition for wealth or power, but I do admit that my chief pleasure is to be actively and energetically at work at some thing or many things, however the exigency may arise." Nevertheless Ike promised that he would "gradually work if not to a more passive at least to a less strenuous goal, and your words will not be without their effect in helping me to arrive at a means of doing it."[43]

His good intention went the well-known way. When the European war started in 1914, hopes continued in America for a while that the Movement scheme might endure. To that end, and more generally to aid the Jewish War Relief organization, Cohen conducted special fund-raising campaigns among his Galveston congregation, extending it statewide in part by conscripting H. Kempner's field agents among others. Ike became unpaid state treasurer for this special drive, "receiving all sums collected in the state." He accepted no reimbursements for his own expenses or those of his employees. In the

41. Powderly, letter to Schiff, May 13, 1908, Box 3M226, Cohen Papers.
42. IHK, *Recalled Recollections*, p. 52.
43. Ike, letter to Cohen, Sept. 9, 1911, Box 3M229, Cohen Papers.

last prewar year Texas Jews had contributed roughly $25,000 to national sectarian relief agencies. In 1914 Texas alone provided the Jewish War Relief Agency with $500,000. Galveston oversubscribed its quota in part because Ike reversed the tradition among its Jewish residents of not dunning Christian Islanders for contributions, he himself visiting all "business houses, warehouses, factories, etc." These visitations alone consumed a full month.[44] But World War I would affect Ike and his family in more ways than these.

44. Cohen, letter to Milton R. Gutsch, director of the University of Texas war records archives, June 20, 1919, Box 3M237, Cohen Papers.

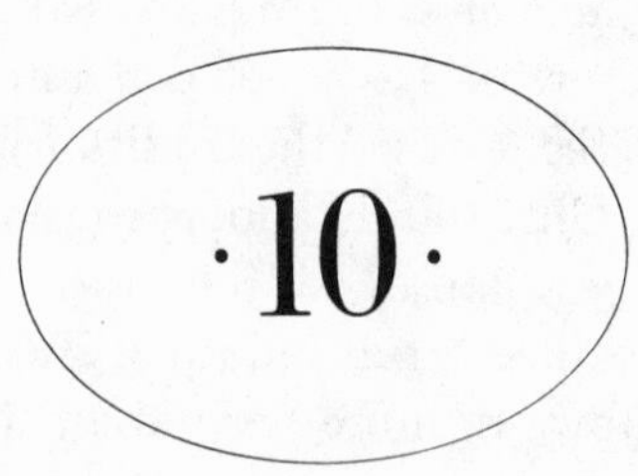

World War and Local Skirmishes

The Decline of Urban Progressivism

WORLD WAR I was to become a pivot of global history and a crossroads of liberalism in America. By the time of the November, 1918, Armistice the prewar urban Progressive impulse was severely blunted, its adherents in disarray, their earlier passion to improve withered. Many one-time reformers went on to newer crusades, including female suffrage or liquor prohibition. Some retreated the whole distance and thereafter opposed efforts to curb social evils, monitor the conduct of public officers, or crusade for a better society. To such rearward marchers, further public-sector exertions on behalf even of the defenseless or the inarticulate were futile and efforts to unearth the venal or to punish the corrupt, useless.[1]

Ike's generation had believed in laws of nature that governed the affairs of men and nations. Optimism about the inevitability of human progress derived from mixes of Newtonian and Darwinian notions that seemed to be self-evident truths. Such estimates made little claim to total philosophical coherence or inclusiveness. In Kiplingesque imagery, Europeans and Americans assigned themselves the task of lighting whole "dark continents" of interior Africa, Australia, Asia, western North America, and elsewhere, by military force if necessary. But before 1914, granting such exceptions as major civil wars, the expansion of Europe and America seemed to be largely if not wholly benign.

1. Link, "What Happened to the Progressive Movement in the 1920s?" *American Historical Review*, p. 833; and see Schlesinger, *Cycles of American History*, and Fussell, *The Great War and Modern Memory*, both passim.

Then came August, 1914. Thereafter, industrial technology applied to weaponry created meat-grinding trench warfare, the suffering of whole civilian populations, the erosion of once-stable economies, and disequilibriums of dynastic empires.[2]

The United States entered World War I in 1917 on what became the militarily victorious side. Like Europeans, many Americans suffered an accumulating decline of confidence in the inevitability of progress. Essayist Randolph Bourne hit the mark in his perception that American prewar Progressive activists realized that they were subject to "the same process that shocked us abroad."[3]

A generation of prewar improvers, including academics and practical reformers like Ike Kempner and his family, had enthusiastically supported the war and expected an improved world as the outcome. But wartime barbarities and domestic excesses and venalities diminished both enthusiasm and expectation. A new "gilded age" was in the wings. Americans were emphatic about their right to pursue happiness in largely materialistic and hedonistic terms.[4]

World War I through Kempner Eyes

Eliza, Ike, and his now-adult siblings shared in the redemptionist sense of mission that was supposed to lead both to the world's regeneration and to quick improvement of community.[5] The dream becoming nightmare, Ike was to follow the Progressives' exodus from elective public service, although not willingly.

By 1917 he had already devoted more than fifteen years to such service, as Galveston's elected revenue commissioner (1899–1915), then as the city's wartime mayor (1917–19). Upon defeat in his bid for a second term, Ike never again sought elective office. He saw his 1919 defeat as repudiation, a personal insult, and an expression of inadequate public gratitude for his services. Ike told an interviewer that he, having "done his part in the way of public service," chose

2. Patterson, *Toward a Warless World*, esp. chaps. 1–2, 10; De Benedetti, *The Peace Reform in American History*, chaps. 3–5; Kuehl, *Seeking World Order*, chaps. 3, 7–8.

3. Introduction to Bourne, *War and the Intellectuals*, p. 7.

4. Cook, "Academicians in Government from Roosevelt to Roosevelt" (Ph.D. diss.), chap. 4; May, *The End of Innocence*, passim.

5. Harrington, *The Dream of Deliverance in American Politics*, chaps. 1–3.

to become thereafter a "civic builder emeritus and humanitarian."[6]

"Humanitarian," undoubtedly, but "emeritus" was a premature label. On Galveston Island and in Sugar Land, Kempner civic building and benefactions were to be numerous and lasting. Abandonment would too sharply swerve family habits from cherished ways and so greatly risk its cohesion as not to be dared. In both locations entrepreneurship mixed with humanitarian purposes persisted among Kempners in post-Armistice decades.[7]

Galveston Politics, 1900–1917

Ike's political problems predated World War I. Those problems were reflected in what a contemporary journalist called "the hectic electioneering epoch" begun in Galveston in the wake of the Great Storm.[8]

Among the reformers of the century's turn a primary article of faith was the corrupting nature of permanent, entrenched municipal political organizations. Despite this dogma, Kempner and his associates in Galveston's post–Great Storm recovery and reform efforts felt impelled themselves to organize standing party apparatuses, at first to win popular approval for financing the seawall, raised grade, and other monumental public works. Allying especially with the Sealy family in these efforts, they learned that despite the new charter's apolitical stances, a permanent political organization was wanted in order to police incumbents, to develop new policies and candidates, and to reenergize popular interest at each biennial election. For, once built, the seawall and raised grade might protect the city and port. But the question remained: what kind of city, what quality of port?

The Kempner-Sealy coalition developed a consistent reply to such questions. The city and port must regularly and systematically improve both wharf facilities and civic amenities. Therefore, voters should consistently accept higher taxes to fund municipal bond issues for effecting these ongoing civic improvements and moderniza-

6. J. D. Claitor, "Personality Sketch of Isaac Herbert Kempner: Civic Builder Emeritus and Humanitarian" (manuscript), RLA, p. 67.

7. Ike's brother Lee became Galveston city treasurer in 1926 and held the post for thirty years. His daughter-in-law, Ruth Levy Kempner, became the first female city council member (1961–63). IHK, *Recalled Recollections*, pp. 58–60, is relevant.

8. Brackman, "Galveston's Gulf," *Houston Gargoyle*.

tions in the urban and port infrastructures. To Kempners this theme complemented their ways in Sugar Land—that is, to defer immediate returns of capital in order to build a more durable, attractive, and prosperous community.

Enter the Moodys

Equally consistently, the Moody family opposed higher taxes. Extremely parsimonious, Moody so passionately hated the higher property taxes that municipal bonds required that he would prefer to let depopulation occur. Thereafter, Moody told his son, William Lewis Moody, Jr., fishing and hunting would improve for themselves. According to black Galvestonian John Clouser, young Moody grew up to be "everybody's enemy," a man increasingly difficult for Ike to work with yet one difficult to avoid in the Island's clubby context.[9]

So polarized by the chemistry of personality and the emphases of upbringing, it was perhaps inevitable that the Moodys and Kempners, the latter with Sealy allies, should clash in both business and politics. Their skirmishes began with the senior Moody's turn-of-the-century refusal to buy seawall bonds. Thereafter a Kempner-Sealy platform and slate of candidates for mayor and commissioners vied with Moody competition almost every two years. Both the Kempner-Sealy and the Moody organizations felt it wise to avoid the regionally dominant Democratic party label or less widespread Republican, partly in order to exhibit fidelity to the principles of the 1902 charter reform and because Galveston, unlike most of the South, harbored unusually vigorous labor unions and black voting blocs. Therefore the parties invented a bewildering variety of names for themselves. Usually the Kempner-Sealy organizations were labeled some variant of "City Club" or "City Party." Moody organizers preferred such names as the "New City Party," the "Galveston Party," or, increasingly by the late twenties, the "Popular" or "People's" party.

A journalist asked: Was this "just another local political wrangle, . . . a [mere] colorful, picturesque, and in some ways humorous little

9. John H. Clouser, interview with R. L. Jones, Apr. 22, 1980, RLA. Kempner sources were the basis for this and all following accounts of the family's relationships, both public and private, with the Moodys. Neither available manuscript nor printed sources deriving from Moody materials balance estimates better. A study of the Moody family is needed.

fracas worth [only] nine minutes and eight seconds of any South Texan's reading time[?]" Or were these Island City party battles, extending over decades, an "Odyssey of the Oleanders . . . [which], for intricacy and ramifications need take second place to . . . the annals of few American cities[?]"[10]

On this essential matter of motivation, lawyer-politician Adrian Levy and historian David McComb agree: The Kempners, in opposing the Moodys, were more than a rival clan obsessed with status and power. These battles existed not only for personal self-gratification but also for Kempner family solidarity, it requiring in turn a diverse, prosperous, stable business and living community. As noted earlier, by the 1890s the Kempners had made a transition to social responsibility. The Moodys waited until the 1960s.[11]

Additionally, Ike and his family nursed decades-long pocketbook grievances against the Moodys. In 1903 Ike and Moody associated in the purchase of a Houston-based insurance company, the American National. They moved the headquarters to Galveston, and, as noted earlier, a younger Kempner started work there. The company's course was troubled. Ike learned of a junior agent's "cupidity and duplicity" in an illicit "pyramid" scheme whereby policyholders became a commission-earning sales force. He fired this miscreant. The company's impressive growth nevertheless attracted the attention of a state examiner who recommended to Moody, Ike being away on business, that the firm hire a full-time manager to prevent similar excesses among agents. Moody apparently misrepresented the recommendation to Ike as a requirement that either he or Ike had to be that full-time manager. Unwilling to commit himself further, Ike sold out to Moody. Two years after the sale, the state examiner, by then an assistant secretary of the U.S. Treasury, explained to Ike what he had actually told Moody, and admitted that "he . . . had wondered why . . . the Kempners sold."[12]

An alternative version exists. It is that an aggressive Island City agent of a New York insurance company borrowed fifty thousand dollars from H. Kempner and Moody jointly, in order to start his own

10. Brackman, "Galveston's Gulf."

11. McComb, *Galveston*, pp. 137–38; Adrian Levy, interview with R. L. Jones, Sept. 30, 1980, RLA.

12. IHK, *Recalled Recollections*, pp. 39–41.

company in Galveston. The firm prospered. Ike and Moody each wanted to buy it for himself. Local folklore has Moody saying to Ike: "Now, Kempner, you know more about life insurance than I do. I'm a cotton man myself. What do you say if we let you take over this business. You know so much more about it. However, I think it only fair that we each place a sealed bid on the table and I'll just bid to protect my interest."[13] But instead of making only a symbolic low bid, Moody knowingly outbid his partner and thereafter owned the very prosperous American National Insurance Company.

Either way, Kempners neither forgot nor forgave the alleged duplicity and cupidity. Sixty years after the event Ike's son noted to family members: "We are all familiar with the episode of our participation in the founding of the American National Insurance Company and of the way we were euchred out of it."[14]

To add to their anger and discomfort, as decades passed Moody not only parlayed the American National into the South's largest insurance company but also, in a thinly veiled manner, mocked the Kempners for letting slip that prize.[15] Moody's underhanded triumph (as Kempners measured the insurance "euchre") became Galveston gossip. The Kempners were both angry and embarrassed by being left "out in the cold" in the insurance scheme. Ike's marketplace humiliation "is strictly pertinent to the matter at hand," decided an investigative journalist who tried later to untangle Galveston political history for Houston readers.[16]

Joined to all other reasons for Kempner antipathy to Moody politics, this "strictly pertinent" one nourished what became Ike's consistent aim. It was "to prevent Shearn Moody from obtaining absolute political control" of Galveston. And so Kempners and Sealy allies became involved in what developed into a third-of-a-century-long holding action against what they termed "Moodyism." Moody tacticians

13. Sara Ellen Stubbs, "Galveston Was Their Home: Genealogy of the Kauffman-Stubbs-Brotherson Families" (typescript, 1977), RLA, p. 68.

14. H. L. Kempner, "Beneficiary Interest Report, 1963" (manuscript), p. 2. The Kempners later created a competitor to the American National, the Texas Prudential. But an unwise choice of a manager "certainly left a great deal to be desired," and the Kempner firm was destined to remain less profitable than Moody's.

15. Brackman, "Galveston's Gulf."

16. Don Hinga, in *Houston Chronicle*, Apr. 11, 1950.

discerned in what they called the Kempner-Sealy "Wharf monopoly" one of two promising avenues of attack.[17] The other involved sustained criticism of the life-styles of elite Galveston families, especially the Kempners.

Ike as Wartime Mayor

In 1917, responding to patriotic appeals, Ike "was persuaded to become a candidate for mayor. I agreed on condition that I would personally ask no one to vote for me and [that] the family not contribute a penny to the campaign," he wrote. Once elected, by his own stipulation Ike served without even the modest salary the position offered under the charter he had helped to create fifteen years earlier. "Not bound to any party or person," wartime mayor Kempner had to deal with growing problems.[18]

They were not personal or family financial problems. In April, 1917, when the United States declared war on Germany, the recently elected mayor told his longtime colleague in Galveston charities, Roman Catholic bishop Kirwin, that "the house of H. Kempner would not realize a dollar out of the war, but would give both men and money to the utmost. This the family lived up to," Kirwin declared years later.[19] Nevertheless, H. Kempner did profit financially from wartime demand for cotton, sugar, and related services. But the war also upset both the H. Kempner firm and the Kempner family.

Lee and Stan both obtained Army commissions. Later decorated by the British government for his services, Dan shifted substantial portions of his time to the Red Cross and other homefront war work, as did the adult Kempner women, including Eliza and her daughters-in-law.[20] Ike picked up his brothers' workloads. But he sorely missed their energy and insights. Nevertheless, he devoted time and energy to the Red Cross and to Jewish war relief agencies, perhaps finding

17. Adrian Levy, interview with R. L. Jones, Sept. 30, 1980, RLA; Brackman, "Galveston's Gulf."

18. IHK, *Recalled Recollections*, pp. 58–60.

19. Quoted in undated, unidentified newspaper article, ca. 1933, headlined: "Galveston Banker Receives Birthday Congratulations," DWK Scrapbook, 1914–1935.

20. IHK, *Recalled Recollections*, p. 58, on official recognition of their several wartime services.

in them substitutes for the now defunct Galveston Movement. And all H. Kempner workers, including those of the family's satellite enterprises, who entered the military service either through volunteering or the draft enjoyed job security and salary continuation.

Ike was still smarting from the prewar rumors about his family's alleged support of the Galveston Movement as a front for importing prostitutes and/or cheap labor for Sugar Land. Had these rumors been factual, the cutoff of emigration by European nations in 1914 should have decreased the number of prostitutes in Galveston. Instead the number soared. The ranks of potential Galveston customers for sin also soared as military camps sprouted in southeastern Texas, workers in a new oil boom became unprecedentedly prosperous, cotton presses and warehouses went on double shifts, and the Wharves recruited stevedores and longshoremen by the hundreds. Vacationers poured in. All attracted prostitutes, gamblers, and bootleggers to the Island City.

All cities experienced analogous wartime growths in vice, but Galveston's increase was probably unequaled. One 1916 estimate was that the Galveston prostitute-to-population ratio was already roughly twice that of Shanghai, four times Chicago's, and nine times London's.

Galveston had a traditional red-light district, with isolated establishments elsewhere. An eclectic mix of transient women served all customers, except that race segregation prevailed. Some prostitutes were Jews, or at least were popularly identified as such. On occasion enough women so labeled concentrated on Church and Twenty-eighth streets as to prompt the area's being called "Port Said in miniature." Otherwise, except for race, the prostitutes' religious and ethnic backgrounds are unknowable. Further, the ownership and management of Galveston prostitution was in the hands of the resident madams, not of local or absentee vice lords of any particular faith.[21] Nevertheless, rumors revived that pimping Galveston Jews, including Ike himself, either controlled or at least profited by all or much of this traffic in vice, if only as the landlords of buildings used for such businesses.

Many associated urban and rural antivice reformers were convinced that purity in civic politics would result only from the elimination of liquor, barrooms, brothels, and gambling rooms, but, lacking such

21. McComb, *Galveston*, pp. 155–57.

purgatives, America would continue "leaking at the [moral] seams."[22]

Wartime America escalated such concerns from the question of who profited, to who suffered. Soldier-sufferers became Washington's primary concern, a shift in focus that lifted traditionally municipal responsibilities about vice to the federal level. Everywhere, patriotic imperatives made policy alternatives about heretofore-unspeakable topics such as vice and venereal disease, fit for respectable people to argue.

When the United States entered World War I, the War Department ordered cities to close brothels, saloons, and gambling casinos near military camps or face the economic consequences of those cities being declared off limits. In the 1917 Lever Act, Congress and executive agencies virtually ended liquor production.[23] All of which seemed to all the Kempners to be an unprecedented attack on private property, and naive as well.

Progressive approaches to social problems, including the control of vice and alcohol, were familiar topics at the Kempners' few-holds-barred family meals. Considered as a form of anti-epidemiology, laws limiting access to liquor and prostitutes should be approached clinically, not moralistically, the socially conscious Kempner men and women agreed. They likely also championed a heavily "environmentalist" position, one popular among Progressive women of their religion, class, and time, that preventive or therapeutic medicine and social rehabilitation for *nafkehs* (Yiddish for prostitutes) and drunkards were superior to punishment. And so Mayor Kempner publicly criticized the wartime federal regulations as unimaginative and unproductive.[24]

He preferred San Antonio's more scientific social innovations. Relying on the state's delegated "police powers," San Antonio's ordinances had long restricted bordellos to specified locations and required prostitutes to submit to frequent medical examinations. City boosters published trolley-car route maps for the convenience of visiting males in search of the famed vice district, with appropriate directions for differing races, rates, and services. Galveston had contented itself with

22. Teaford, *The Twentieth-Century American City*, chap. 1; Richard Hamm, "Leaking at the Seams" (American Historical Association, 1986), pp. 1–3.

23. Hamm, "Leaking at the Seams," pp. 2–4.

24. IHK, *Recalled Recollections*, pp. 58–60. See also Joseph, "The *Nafkeh* and the Lady" (Ph.D. diss.).

sporadic police raids on peculiarly offensive centers of vice. With the war this sluggishness fed rumors of high-level protection for miscreants and of police corruption.[25]

To Ike, the wartime attack on brothels and barrooms could lead only to uncontrolled dispersion of prostitutes, to freelance prostitution, bootlegging, and distilleries, to the accelerating corruption of adolescents, and to soaring rates of venereal disease and alcoholism. In Washington on both city and cotton business, Kempner advised his former schoolmate, Secretary of War Newton D. Baker, that "we could better control . . . vice and the incidence of disease if we licensed a limited but adequate number of such places." Agreeing, Baker replied, however, that "too many women['s] and church and reform organizations, whose combined numerical (and hence political) influence was enormous, were behind this ruling." On his way home to Galveston Ike visited with New Orleans's mayor. They agreed that antivice regulations "could never diminish the practice or make the sport unpopular." New Orleans defied Baker's order. Galveston obeyed, "with the only result that houses of prostitution were officially closed, but the inhabitants and patrons so spread over the city that the War Department after six months closed their eyes to the city's proven inability to close such places," Ike reported. Thereupon the Galveston commissioners, Ike concurring, ordered a mild imitation of the controls used in San Antonio.[26]

Discord among Galveston's Jews

Ike's irritation with government antivice policies added to the concern he felt about the persistent rumors that leading Galveston Jews profited from illicit sex. Such rumors re-raised issues about Jews as "hyphenated Americans" who allegedly were sources of disease and crime and were unassimilables unworthy of citizenship.

The Island City's Jewish community was also disturbed, but in different ways, by news of Palestine's emergence from Turkish rule, Turkey being allied with Germany, and Britain's Balfour Declaration in support of a "Jewish homeland" in Palestine. Heated arguments

25. Mackey, *Red Lights Out*, esp. chaps. 2–3, 6.

26. IHK, *Recalled Recollections*, pp. 58–60. See also Brandt, *No Magic Bullet;* McComb, *Galveston*, p. 155.

were renewed among Galveston's Jews about the appropriateness of support for a future Israel.

Numbering slightly more than one thousand persons by 1910, by 1918 Galveston's Jews were trifurcated into the major doctrinal and liturgical camps—Orthodox, Conservative, and Reform. Sharp disagreements concerning Zionism as allegedly opposed to secular acculturation in America helped to exacerbate those divisions.[27]

Back in 1885, a then-infant association of American Reform rabbis in the so-called "Pittsburgh Platform" had insisted that "we consider ourselves no longer a nation, but a religious community, and therefore expect neither a return to Palestine, . . . nor the restoration of any . . . Jewish state."[28] Cohen would always abide by this principle, and in 1917 he and other Reform rabbis, in convention in Chicago, reaffirmed it. As elsewhere in Jewish America, in Galveston such continuing differences about acculturation had troubled administration of the Galveston Movement. So intense were disagreements that, for example, one passionate Texas Zionist, though himself a recent emigré from czarist Russia, advised Rabbi Cohen in 1906 not to "breathe a word about [the possible] emigration [of large numbers of eastern European Zionists] to Texas," because, allegedly, "the American Jew unfortunately holds himself aloof from a cause which the great majority of his kith and kin regard as the only solution to a dreadful situation. He (the American Jew) does not dwell in a land where official pogroms are the order of the day."[29]

A Waco correspondent of the rabbi's, "an old Galvestonian," opposed the Galveston Movement on other grounds. He directly contradicted Ike's publicized arguments to inland Texas Jews that the immigrants, once resettled in small communities state- and region-wide, would cost older residents nothing. Instead the critic insisted that later phases of the transition from immigrant to citizen would fall heavily on established earlier comers. However good-willed, organizers of the Movement in New York City and Galveston were mistaking their insular situations with inland realities.[30]

27. Analogous situations are described in Howe, *World of Our Fathers*, pp. 96–99.

28. In Stern, "The Role of the Rabbi in the South," in *Turn to the South:* Nathan Melvin, p. 28.

29. J. Friedland [?], letter to Cohen, Jan. 18, 1906, Box 3M225, Cohen Papers.

30. L. Weigel [?], letter to Cohen, Mar. 11, 1907, Box 3M225, Cohen Papers.

During the years 1905–14 many such crosscutting expressions of concern received close attention from Cohen and Ike. For example, they both troubled to reply to the Waco complainant, and in such effective manner as to evoke from Movement headquarters in New York congratulation on the effect of "[y]our last letter and that of Mr. Kempner . . . to the Waco people [which] has been stronger than I anticipated. The Rabbi of Texas surely controls his people most effectively."[31]

World War I had initially unified Galveston's Jews. Aborted, the Galveston Movement no longer served to sunder them, and humanitarianism and patriotism were mighty coagulants. Before and after the United States became a combatant in 1917, Galveston's Jews, with Kempner and Cohen always in their van, contributed heavily to Jewish, transsectarian, and secular relief causes. President Wilson proclaimed a Jewish Relief Day in early 1917, and Kempner was the Texas-Oklahoma treasurer for contributions. With America in the war, Kempner joined with Jacob Schiff and Henry Morgenthau in a direct appeal for contributions to a Jewish War Sufferers Fund, themselves providing large initial "seed" contributions.[32] All of which suggests that by the time Ike became mayor in 1917, Galveston's Jews were apparently reweldable into a community, one composed of "every Israelite who has a spark of Jewish feeling," to quote one of Ike's favored fundraising phrases.[33]

Throughout World War I and for long after, Kempner and Cohen remained convinced secular assimilationists and anti-Zionists. In 1914, Cohen's basic position was this: "I am more convinced than ever that Political Zionism is not good for the Jewish People." And ten years later he wrote that American Jews "cannot tolerate any other political affiliation but that of the United States."[34] But most of Galveston's Orthodox Jews and some of Kempner's Reform coreligionists were ardent Zionists. Such persons were a group that Ike had never before

31. Morris Waldman, letter to Cohen, Mar. 12, 1907, Box 3M225, Cohen Papers.

32. Waldman, letter to Cohen, Aug. 28, 1907, Box 3M225, Cohen Papers.

33. "Every Israelite" quotation in ibid. Other data, all in Cohen Papers: A. Godcheaux to Cohen, Jan. 13, 1913, Box 230; IHK, "Jewish War Sufferers Fund" circular letter and mass meeting calls, Dec. 20, 1914, and Nov. 5, 1915, Boxes 232–34; Hyman Block, letter to Cohen, Jan. 18, 1915, Box 233; Cohen, letter to J. Billikopf, May 25, 1917, Box 235; also, *Galveston Tribune*, Jan. 25–27, 1916.

34. Cohen, letter to J. Swiff, Jan. 30, 1944, with carbon copy to Ike reviewing these matters since 1916; and see I. H. Kempner, letter to Cohen, Jan. 11, 1945,

needed to court, one that, after the Balfour Declaration, found his and Cohen's stances increasingly unpalatable.

Then in the midst of the Armistice celebration, a delegation of Galveston Jews, including in its number some of Ike's Reform co-congregants, asked him to have the Star of David flag raised on the City Hall staff during what he called "some celebration in Palestine" to mark the Balfour Declaration. He refused, saying that "only the Texas flag and the flag of the United States had [ever] flown from our City Hall." Ike wrote: "Particularly as a Jew I decline to make the exception requested." But he had to pay a price for his stand.

In early 1919 Ike decided to seek a second term as mayor. Until that time he had exhibited consummate political skills appropriate to the urban arena, the only one in which he was ambitious. He anticipated that his second bid for the Galveston mayorship, coming so soon after the Armistice, would be a celebratory "shoo-in" for himself, the incumbent in that year of martial victory. But his political antennae had become desensitized. So had Rabbi Cohen's.

Caught up in wartime good works, both he and Cohen grossly miscalculated the political climate. Overwork plus, on Ike's part, irritation at the further demands on him caused by the antivice policies in which he disbelieved, led him into errors and insensitivities that left him bitter about fellow Jews of Galveston. Ike grumbled later that "if there is such a thing as an orthodox Jewish vote, it was in this election effectively invoked against me and contributed to defeating my aspiration (if any) for a second term as mayor." He was dismayed when all "those who favored independence and honesty in government . . . were defeated."[35]

The 1919 split among Galveston's Jews was a new phase of the older schism about acculturating into secular American life that had produced the Orthodox-Conservative-Reform factions and would fester even into the decades of Nazism's rise, the Holocaust, and the subsequent establishment of Israel. Nazism later tempered Ike's and Cohen's anti-Zionist stands. "We wish to contribute to the Youth Aliyah [i.e., return to Israel] Movement all that our funds will permit," Ike,

---

Box 3M286, Cohen Papers, and typescripts of Cohen's 1918 and 1923 essays on Americanism, with both quoted phrases, in Box 3M236, Cohen Papers. See also Dreyfus, comp., *Henry Cohen, Messenger of the Lord*, pp. 23–54; IHK, *Recalled Recollections*, p. 58.

35. IHK, *Recalled Recollections*, p. 57.

as chairman in 1943 of Galveston's chapter of the United Jewish Welfare Association, would write to the president of the national Jewish women's organization, Hadassah.[36] But nothing transformed him or Cohen into important Zionist activists.

More generally, a journalist's perceptive suggestion deserves attention: The years 1917–1919 were unfavorable politically almost everywhere to people who, like Ike, were "imbued with a reasonable philosophy that their own advancement is not incompatible with [their society's] progress.[37]

During those years, family disequilibrium increased dangerously with Fannie's insistence on marrying a non-Jew, a determination that brought to a head her mother's uncertain legal status as administratrix of the H. Kempner estate, still undivided a quarter century after his death. And simultaneously, in 1919 Ike and his brothers were feeling the goads of renewed commitment to developing Sugar Land further and the torsions of what would develop into a half-century-long series of negotiations, litigations, and frustrations, known collectively as the "spinners'" lawsuits.

This history turns now to these substantive distractions tugging at Ike and his family in the post-Armistice season.

36. I. H. Kempner to Irma Lindheim, June 3, 1943, Box 3M284, Cohen Papers. See also Kolsky, "Jews against Zionism" (Ph.D. diss.); IHK, *Recalled Recollections*, p. 57. In later years as interest increased in Israel as a Jewish nation-state, Ike became upset during service on a charity board when a majority of its members decided to send all its funds there one year rather than to a Jewish-supported hospital in Arkansas (Block interview with Marchiafava, June 6, 1981).

37. Brackman, "Galveston's Gulf."

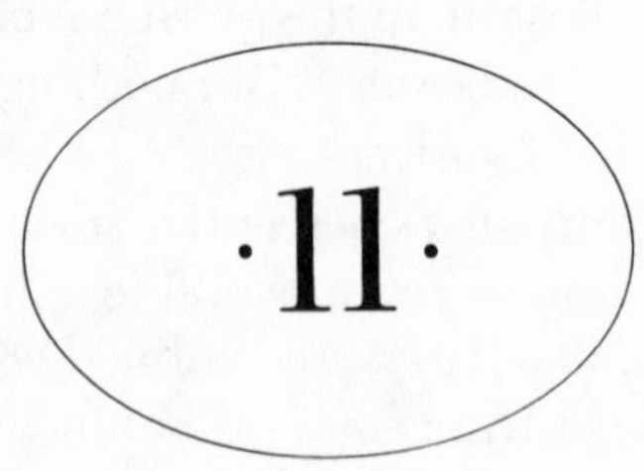

The 1920 Massachusetts Trust

Family Expansion

BY 1914 the Kempner family had grown considerably. Ike had married Henrietta Blum in 1902. He and "Hennie," a BOI, had known each other since childhood. She was twice engaged to marry before 1900 but ended both relationships. Many young bachelors courted her, Ike and Lee Kempner among them, "as well as a good looking New York chap, introduced to me by Ike," she recalled. Engaged in turn to the visitor, she professed surprise late one evening when Ike showed up at her home and proposed marriage. It was too late, she replied. "Nothing daunted, he called the New Yorker and told him the news," Hennie recalled. "He accepted the decision very graciously." Their wedding in December, 1902, was "a large and magnificent affair," of considerable social importance."[1]

But the honeymoon was less grand. Exploiting the Kempners' connections among rail executives, Ike had arranged for other newlyweds to enjoy private railroad cars for their honeymoons. But he failed to indulge himself and his bride similarly. "I'm not sure I want to come on this trip," Hennie told him. He persuaded her to accept merely first-class train accommodations to California, but, upon receiving there news of a business crisis in Texas, Ike canceled their planned next leg, to Hawaii. Returning to Galveston, they established a separate apartment in his mother's already-large household, and

1. *Galveston News*, undated, in DWK Scrapbook, 1894–1915, and, on "magnificent affair," Henrietta Blum Kempner, "The Blum Saga" (manuscript, 1968), both in Kempner Papers.

Henrietta Kempner, with sons Harris and Herbert, ca. 1907 (Courtesy Leonora K. Thompson)

in 1906, they set up their own luxurious home at 1502 Broadway.[2]

Henrietta's family, of French background, had sent her to school in Germany. Her command of foreign languages, an asset in the port city, seemed to confirm the wisdom of the Kempner stress on broad cultural educations even for women. Cotton merchant Ike frequently brought home important foreign merchants and consular officers, impecunious medical students, campaigning politicos, visiting lecturers (including Norman Thomas and "O. Henry"), and other interesting guests. She was prepared to entertain frequently as well as graciously.

2. Henrietta Blum Kempner, "Blum Saga"; IHK, *Recalled Recollections*, pp. 35–36.

Hennie's at-home receptions were Island and regional social events. But relatives were the center of the mealtime rituals: Every Kempner by birth or marriage "who was in town came for the lunch gathering," son Harris remembered in 1980: "That was an important part of life too."[3]

Five children were born to Henrietta and Ike within a dozen years after their marriage. They were Harris Leon in 1903 (every Kempner branch that produced sons named one Harris) and Isaac Herbert, Jr., in 1906. Then came daughters Cecile in 1908, Lyda in 1911, and Henrietta Leonora in 1913 (a big year for all Kempners in terms of marriages and births). Dan married Jeane Bertig of a prominent Arkansas merchant family in 1906, and their daughter Mary Jean also arrived in 1913. Hattie's marriage to Henry Oppenheimer, a San Antonio banker, occurred in 1903. Eliza and Ike provided Hattie with "the most elaborate wedding in the history of the city of Galveston," according to a *Galveston Tribune* reporter, who thought also that the bride's sisters Fannie and Sara gave Hattie competition for center stage.[4] Three children followed Hattie's marriage to Oppenheimer: Frances in 1907, Dan in 1908, and another Harris Kempner in 1913. Sara became Mrs. David Weston of Cincinnati in 1913, their union producing tragically short-lived David, Jr., in 1915 and still another Harris Kempner in 1918. To anticipate, Fannie married Louis A. Adoue, the son of Ike's banker associate, in 1918. Their daughter Frances was born in 1919. Ike's brothers Robert Lee and Stanley and sister Gladys did not marry.

These maturings, marryings, and birthings from 1902 to 1919 suggest how increasingly pressured Ike must have felt as the person primarily responsible, if only from his own sense of prime responsibility, for the well-being of this swelling corps, one whose legal stability became threatened by a romance.

Religion and Eliza's Legal Status as Administratrix

In technical legal terms Eliza's status since 1895 as the executrix of Harris Kempner's undivided survivor-in-community estate left that

3. Quotations and date in H. L. Kempner, interview with R. L. Jones, June 17, 18, 1980, RLA; IHK, *Recalled Recollections*, pp. 72, 116, 121.

4. *Tribune*, Dec. 19, 1903.

Eliza ("Granny") Kempner with grandchildren, ca. 1914. *On floor:* Harris K. Oppenheimer. *In chairs:* Lyda Kempner (Quinn), Frances Oppenheimer (Ullman). *On lap:* Mary Jean Kempner (Thorne), Leonora Kempner (Thompson). *In back:* Cecile Kempner, Herbert Kempner, Eliza, Dan Oppenheimer, Harris L. Kempner. (Courtesy Leonora K. Thompson)

increasingly valuable property vulnerable. The local court retained a right, albeit one it left unexercised, to examine "her" books, that is, H. Kempner's. No one could foresee how long H. Kempner would enjoy its treasured business privacy. Further, the estate was disturbingly vulnerable to estate taxes and later to income taxes, and to potentially ruinous lawsuits initiated in the course of business or inspired by intrafamily discords, all leading to possible partitions of assets.

Like most states, Texas had created the survivor-in-community status in order to liquidate quickly the estates of intestates, not to continue them undivided over decades or to encourage their undivided enlargement by the kind of collegial family that the Kempners were.

Eliza Kempner, ca. 1910 (Courtesy Leonora K. Thompson)

From 1895 to 1920 the Kempners continued treating their inheritance as undivided capital.[5]

Law-trained, Ike was sensitive to threats of involuntary partition of the estate through adverse litigation. A discontented or resentful heir, or, later, their spouses or children, might seek division by suit. A resulting contest, even if won, meant the attenuation of the still-pooled capital, the immobility or faulty operation of H. Kempner and its increasing number of affiliated enterprises, and expensive fees. Some disgruntled business associate or client might claim that H. Kempner had no right to contract or that Ike's signature lacked adequate lawfulness because of Eliza's shaky legal status.

When the question of her status did rise seriously it was to come from within the family, not outside. Until then, Ike marked time on the matter of Eliza's legal situation. His decision not to decide, however, prolonged the estate's uneasy vulnerability.

5. See IHK, *Recalled Recollections*, pp. 61–62, 111. Ike's son Harris believed theirs was "a record for the length of time that an unsettled estate stayed in being" (HLK, "The Kempners of Galveston and Sugar Land" [manuscript, speech to Harvard Business Club of Houston, Sept. 27, 1981], RLA, pp. 10–11).

Eliza's legal status was questioned. Back in 1898 when Ike organized M&P, questions arose concerning the legitimacy of the chartering. Was Eliza, the signatory for the purchase as survivor-in-community, exceeding the lawful bounds of her function? How long should a survivorship last?

In order to avoid a need to acknowledge such questions much less answer them, Ike saw to it that the stock certificates in M&P were issued not to Eliza as executrix, but to himself, Dan, and uncle Joseph Seinsheimer. They then assigned their certificates to H. Kempner (i.e., to Eliza), which now became the owner of M&P. No discernible illicit purposes have come to light about the legal tactic, and no one challenged it in court during the fifty years of the M&P's charter.[6] But no one knew that it would not be challenged or what else might be challenged.

Ironically, in 1904 Ike himself brought to public attention the fiction that his mother legally directed its assets. He was then concentrating on H. Kempner's affairs, on Galveston's post-Storm resurrection, and on early phases of the Galveston Movement and of Sugar Land. At the height of all these efforts, Galveston County sued Eliza.

The county's complaint alleged that she had failed to meet her (i.e., H. Kempner's) commitment to pay for $50,000 worth of seawall bonds out of a total of $400,000 that the county had issued for its share of that construction. Of course it was revenue commissioner Ike, not Eliza, who had nonperformed so embarrassingly, if nonperformance was a fact. The only defaulter among eight major subscribers (the other seven being Ike's city council and business associates), H. Kempner faced the prospect of paying out not only the stipulated $50,000 but additional substantial damages plus interest and court costs.

Ike was able to prove that "many months ago" H. Kempner had paid in $5,000 of the total as an earnest money deposit, a fact forgotten by the complaining, part-time county officials, men perhaps as fatigued as he in the Great Storm's backwash. Ike's check for an additional $14,000 plus pledges for the remainder accompanied his response to the county attorney, who acknowledged publicly that it had been he who was at fault and who, dropping the lawsuit, stated that

6. Ellis, "The Texas Cotton Compress Industry" (Ph.D. diss.), pp. 366–68.

"the matter could have been settled without suit and that a suit was unnecessary to collect the subscription."[7]

No similar external threat to the undivided estate appeared. But neither Ike nor his mother could anticipate future good fortune in this regard. Almost ten years later, in 1913, the youngest girl, Gladys (b. 1893), reached her majority. Whereupon Dan appeared in a local court with a petition for the removal of her legal disabilities deriving from her minority.[8] Then in 1915, with the world war engulfing Europe and H. Kempner and its subsidiaries belatedly sharing in the general prosperity then nourishing neutral America, Ike further accommodated the firm's legal form to his family cohesion goal by altering it to a partnership of all his father's heirs. Eliza's continued status as administratrix remained equivocal, however, and simple partnerships, though blessed with in-house privacy and control, burdened their principals with unlimited personal liability and uncertainties about succession upon a partner's death or incapacity. These hazards magnified during that turbulent decade, especially as the girls matured. What today is labeled as gender discrimination magnified the strains the Kempner family endured in the World War I period.

Ike's Brothers and Sisters

A crisis developed about sister Fannie's romance with a non-Jew. Odds are that had one of Ike's brothers rather than a sister been involved in such a romance, less difficulty would have arisen. Therefore it is in order to look first briefly at Dan, Lee, and Stan.

By the new century's first decade, each of Ike's brothers had opted in turn against further higher education, independent businesses, or professional careers and, upon returning to Galveston, had begun apprenticeships in one or another H. Kempner business. Ike had sometimes become impatient about what he saw as his brothers' lingering adolescences. Eliza and Ike had also felt some concern that the younger boys, too conscious of the family's growing wealth, were becoming snobs. It was seemly to take pride in the family's climb since Harris Kempner's travails as a peddler in Cold Springs. But it seemed

7. *Galveston News*, Oct. 22, 1904, plus, for quotes and additional facts, an unidentified, undated clipping, in DWK Scrapbook, 1894–1915, Kempner Papers.
8. Unidentified clipping, DWK Scrapbook, 1894–1915.

less good that Ike should have to break up a shoving match between his pugnacious younger brother Lee and one of the Lasker boys. According to a gossipy columnist decades later, the youths "were throwing punches and abuse at each other. . . .'Your father,' said [Lee] Kempner, bitterly, 'is a millionaire. That's what he is.' . . . 'Yeah, and your father,' countered Lasker, also with bitterness, 'is a BIGGER millionaire.'"[9]

For a while Dan and Stanley seemed like incurable playboys to Ike. Dan's banjo and Stan's guitar were more in evidence than ledgers, textbooks, or technical manuals. Red-haired and freckled Stanley (nicknamed "Pat") delighted younger sister Sara. He looked like a "typical Irishman," she recalled: "The others were more serious. But he really enjoyed life." So did their brother Lee.[10]

Recruited in his turn for a summertime apprenticeship at H. Kempner, "Stan was kind of foot-loose and fancy free," Hyman Block recalled, and at first "didn't cotton much to all this . . . work. [He] would stay out a little late at night instead of showing up in the office." On such occasions Ike would telephone their mother and rather forcefully demand that she wake her laggard son and send him to work. Ike had Block, a multipurpose employee, serve as office sentry over the youngster.[11] Lee may have enjoyed life as much as Stan, but he was quieter about it.

Local gossip colored Stan and Lee as lady's man and good catch, respectively, but neither gave up bachelorhood.[12] They did, however, settle into unfrivolous ways that Ike admired. But until Ike was confident that his brothers were as devoted as he to life's labors, their seemingly overextended adolescences added to his "constant worries," Ike's wife recalled. She adopted "a 'pollyanna outlook' in what became a half-century long effort to lighten his burdens," Hennie reminisced, "but I'm afraid he saw through me."[13] She saw through him, too.

By the early 1900s Dan and Lee had emerged from youthful fri-

9. Leonard Lyons, in *Indianapolis News*, Aug. 13, 1948, clipping in DWK Scrapbook, 1945–1948. Stress is original.

10. Sara Kempner Weston, interview with L. Marchiafava, Aug. 29, 1981, RLA; typescript dated Jan. 21, 1924, DWK Scrapbook, 1924–1929.

11. Hyman Block, interview with L. Marchiafava, Aug. 29, 1981, RLA.

12. From a satirical tribute to Lee on his thirtieth birthday printed Jan. 21, 1924, in *States National Weakly*, a burlesque of the house publication of the bank Lee served. Copy provided by H. L. Kempner.

13. Henrietta Blum Kempner, "Blum Saga."

Sara Kempner (Weston) and Fannie Kempner (Adoue), ca. 1914 (Courtesy Leonora K. Thompson)

volities, and World War I proved that Stan too had ended his playboy phase. President Wilson recognized Dan's homefront volunteer work for the Red Cross with a citation. Lee and Stan both became Army captains.[14]

By the time the "boys" came marching home in 1919, they were ready to shoulder family duty. Youthful excesses forgotten, Dan, Lee, and Stan were now, like Ike, diligent in work and concerned about family cohesion and community.

As for the sisters—theirs were different stories. Eliza and Ike governed the upbringing, schooling, and social horizons of the Kempner girls far more tightly than they did those of the boys. First Fannie

14. *The Texas Gulf Coast: Its History and Development, Family, and Personal History* (1955), 3:99.

Gladys Kempner, ca. 1925 (Courtesy Leonora K. Thompson)

and then Sara attended Mrs. Hopkins's private school for the children of the Island elite. Then, unstereotypically, Eliza sent them to Galveston's public high school. Perhaps because Fannie was already receiving attention from Louis Adoue, an Episcopalian, the son of an Island banker and family friend of long standing, she suddenly found herself boarding at the Ogontz School, near Philadelphia, an exclusive "finishing" establishment housed in the former mansion of millionaire Jay Cooke. Adoue proved persistent even at long distance. Since Eliza and Ike assumed that, like the boys, his sisters should acquire wide cultural horizons, they sent Fannie to board in Germany for a year. But unlike the boys, she went chaperoned, as did her sisters and other female relatives in their turns.

Sara, meanwhile, graduated from high school and yearned to go to Vassar. Eliza insisted on Ogontz for her as well, and there Sara went.[15] Home for every possible summer vacation and school recess, Fannie and Sara, as debutantes, accepted chaperonage while occasionally eluding it. "The [Kempner] brothers were very solicitous about us," Sara remembered. "They were very careful that . . . the girls were going with the right boys." But even chaperoned beach parties were fun. They were held in secluded portions of the western beaches reached on donkeys. Succulent barbecue and copious fresh seafood were enlivened by Dan's banjo and Stanley's guitar.

To add to Eliza's worries about Adoue and Fannie, younger sister Sara's first serious suitor turned out to be another likable non-Jew. Eliza "didn't want that to happen," Sara remembered. But young David Weston (then, Westheimer), a Jew, came along, and "the entire family agreed upon him, so I knew that was right." He and Sara married in 1913 and remained so for over fifty years, to his death.[16]

As for Fannie, however, Galveston socialites kept encountering her with Adoue: at the Ladies' Morning Musical, the Men's Choral Society, and the theater when traveling troupes played the Island. The wife of the Lykes Steamship line owner noted that "I met many attractive people," especially the Kempners, "a large and interesting family. . . . [We] always had a round of parties together . . . Fannie Kempner was there with Louis Adoue, who led me in one of the Cotillions."[17]

Fannie and Louis were in love. Intent on marrying, they faced Eliza's and Ike's strong opposition. The Kempners liked Louis – everyone did. But, Eliza's grandson recalled in 1986, "Granny objected because she did not want non-Jews to marry into the family and she was the type of matriarch who had her way without raising her voice."[18]

Not this time, however. After a dozen frustrating years of further family obstacles placed between her and Adoue, in 1917 then-thirty-year-old Fannie determined to wed. Knowing that Rabbi Cohen opposed intermarriages, she confided her decision to him, pleading also for both his understanding and for temporary secrecy from her family.

> A friendship that I have always valued most highly [she wrote Cohen] . . . after twelve years of loyalty and devotion has ended very

15. Fannie Kempner Adoue and Sara Kempner Weston, interviews with L. Marchiafava, Aug. 1 and Aug. 29, 1981, respectively, RLA.
16. Sara Kempner Weston interview with Marchiafava, Aug. 29, 1981.
17. Lykes, *Gift of Heritage*, p. 70.
18. Harris L. Kempner, letter to author, Mar. 12, 1986.

> much like a romantic novel or fairy tale where the . . . hero and heroine fall in love, marry, and "live happily ever after." Such has been the happy ending of my friendship with Louis Adoue. I wonder if my engagement comes at all as a surprise to you? For years Louis and I have been struggling with this very serious matter, realizing the difference in religious beliefs and trying very much to fight off the love that has been so closely connected with our friendship. . . . [But] our deep love for one another has been stronger than our faith. . . . I know you do not approve of intermarriages, but I know you *do* approve of Louis. . . . I cannot feel that I am committing such a sin. . . . I intend to help him respect his faith and religious principles and I should want, and know, he will respect mine.[19]

She realized her intention in February, 1918, in a ceremony conducted by a judge, not the rabbi, in her family's home.

But at year's end Fannie's husband died, a victim of the worldwide influenza epidemic. In mid-1919 she gave birth to their daughter Frances Louise. "The tragic event [of Louis's death] shocked everybody, particularly Granny and others who held themselves partially responsible for preventing the marriage that many years," Ike's son remembered. "Since that time, there have been objections to individual suitors, but on the account of personality rather than religion," he added.[20]

Ike praised Eliza's "indomitable and gratifying efforts to keep the family intact, united [and] respectful of each other's rights." One of these rights was apparently that of the males to make all business decisions. Ike congratulated his mother and the other women in the family for having "accepted the judgment of the managing males." This "absence of dickering or bickering," he continued, "the acceptance of some errors as inevitable, their appreciation of resulting accomplishments, all contributed to clear judgments and inspired renewed efforts on the parts of my brothers and myself."[21] Ike's son Harris repeated the theme in later years: "The girls have always been interested, but there was never any particular thought of their go-

19. Fannie Kempner, letter to Cohen, July 15, 1917, Box 3M235, Cohen Papers; IHK, *Recalled Recollections*, p. 59. Stephen Birmingham, *"Our Crowd,"* p. 342, notes that record numbers of Jews entered into mixed marriages beginning in the early 1920s and that doing so became suddenly fashionable. All evidence suggests that Fannie's was a love match.

20. Harris L. Kempner, letter to author, Mar. 12, 1986. Fannie never remarried.

21. IHK, *Recalled Recollections*, p. 63 and see pp. 64–66.

ing into the business as such. . . . They stay on the outside and give suggestions."[22]

Eliza contributed fundamentally, however, with respect to binding her children, their spouses, and her grandchildren into a cohesive unit. Six of her grown children, including all the males, established permanent residence in Galveston. The three bachelors, Gladys, Lee, and Stanley, plus Fannie after widowhood, with her child, lived with Eliza, who continued almost until her death in 1947 command-performance Friday night and Sunday meals at their home. Well attended, these occasions became almost domestic annexes to the H. Kempner offices, one of the cores of the planetary Kempner business system whose members enjoyed having their paths cross on a regular basis.

With Eliza's social gatherings staffed by a large number of both black and middle-European servants, it seemed to the Kempner youngsters that culture more than any other factor except race determined social standing. Race was a different matter. Although the black choir of Saint Paul's United Methodist Church, situated catercorner across the street from Ike's house, woke Harris and Herb every Sunday morning, and though neighborhoods were incompletely ghettoized racially on this narrow island, whites and blacks did not mix socially. "You can't pretend that it was a raceless society, because there were distinctions and clear ones," Harris stated in 1980. Being Jewish, however, was not one of the distinctions for the Kempner children: "It really didn't interfere with Galveston life very much," according to Ike's son.[23]

Jewishness did "interfere," however, when the question of the family's religious affiliation and degree of commitment became linked to Eliza's legal status as administratrix of the Kempner estate.

It appears arguable that the apprehension of future non-Jewish inlaws moved the Kempners to review the legal condition of the H. Kempner estate. This was not so, according to family lore. The Kempner tradition is that in 1920 the "unusual arrangement of a Massachusetts trust was formed only because of the growing number of heirs, because Texas law then prevented corporations from engaging in multiple businesses, and because of changing tax laws."[24] Similarly,

22. H. L. Kempner interview with Marchiafava, June 6, 1981.

23. H. L. Kempner interview with Jones, June 17–18, 1980. For a black perspective see Pitre's *Through Many Dangers, Toils, and Snares.*

24. E. R. Thompson, Jr., "History of H. Kempner" (manuscript), Kempner Papers, p. 40.

in 1987 Ike's son Harris, as noted, excluded religion from reasons impelling the formation of the 1920 trust. Fannie's marriage to a non-Jew "was entirely unrelated to and independent of the family decision to review Eliza's status as executrix," he insisted.[25]

But the Massachusetts trust form was not an "unusual arrangement." As mentioned earlier, H. Kempner's lawyer, certainly privy to the family's aim for cohesion and to Fannie's desire to wed Adoue, the year before that wedding had arranged a Massachusetts trust for the family's half-interest in Imperial–Sugar Land. He had then, "in thoroughly amicable intent and approach," Ike wrote, warned the family about each member's monetary vulnerability under the existing survivor-in-community form of 1895 as amended by the 1915 partnership.[26] A quarter century's usage had dangerously overextended a legal device intended for brief employment. This warning was given thrust by the fact that recently Dan had been a surety for a local banker who defaulted, and H. Kempner—that is, all Kempners—covered the amount. Last, the still-novel federal income tax plus Texas' estate taxes did indeed require accommodation by H. Kempner if the family capital was to remain pooled. Accommodation required that holdings be more liquid than had been the case so that upon a shareholder's death survivors might avoid crushing tax burdens. The Massachusetts trust for H. Kempner promised all these advantages. But it was Fannie's defiance that triggered the question, the fears, and the response.

H. Kempner remained (and remains) unincorporated, and so the Texas corporation law referred to above was inapplicable. The tax motive was valid, but determinative? Something more than chronological coincidence seems to have linked Fannie's intense determination to marry Adoue and the Kempners' decision to search for a better legal vehicle for H. Kempner than the creaky 1895 survivorship or the flimsy 1915 partnership.

If the religious issue was indeed inseparable from, or even central to, the decision to seek a legal form for the estate that would retain it undivided and yet preserve the family's collegiality, then orthodoxy became the casualty of these imperatives. The family thereafter ac-

25. H. L. Kempner, letters to author, Jan. 8, Mar. 12, Sept. 1, 1987; IHK, *Recalled Recollections*, p. 98.

26. IHK, *Recalled Recollections*, p. 58; "Keys Report, 1964," pp. 5–6.

cepted religious heterodoxy, thus easing strains generated by Fannie's long romance and tragically foreshortened marriage.

Religion aside, fears were common then among leaders in family businesses that future in-laws might be unpredictably greedy or importunate. The girls' marriages, especially Fannie's, increased Ike's concerns about the estate's stability. It made sense for Ike to worry that a male in-law, controlling his Kempner wife's share, might try to force himself into top H. Kempner management. If denied entrance or for other, perhaps venal reasons, such an in-law might provoke a partition of the undivided estate or at least jar the cordial entrepreneurial center that Ike was developing. Disruption of this center occurring, the unrecallable dispersion of assets spelled an end to the dream of family cohesion along with the marketplace clout that the amassed estate offered.

On this point, a Kempner family member insisted that the preceding argument "does not hold against the fact that all of the sisters (including Gladys, whose spinsterhood was not then foreseen) were given full control of their portion of the estate without restriction." That is, each sister could have theoretically elected to do with her share what she wished, as she could marry as she pleased with respect to religion. Indeed so. But, continuing, he notes also that the 1920 trust "concentrated authority in the Trustees [i.e., the Kempner brothers plus Seinsheimer], making permanent a tenure which was already 20 years old." Perhaps this habit of unprotested deference to the "managing males"—Ike's phrase—sustains the intuition that the trust's formation and Fannie's marriage were linked.[27] Further, the pooled estate was profitable to the equal shareholders, complex in organization from inception, and consistently illiquid. The easier way was to let the golden goose alone.

Yet perhaps the Scottish verdict, "not proved," is best concerning the relationships of religion to the shift in the Kempner family's legal status in 1920. What is provable is the smooth transition the members of this remarkably cooperative group made that year, to a legal form better suited to their immediate needs and to the continuing aspiration to maintain family collegiality and cohesion. For more than a half century to come, Kempners old and young would agree on the

27. Mr. Thompson's notes, in Leonora K. Thompson, letter to author, Aug. 18, 1988; IHK, *Recalled Recollections*, p. 128.

essentiality of this pooling. Their agreement built on the 1920 legal change from the "survivor-in-community" to the Massachusetts trust.

The 1920 Massachusetts Trust

Nineteenth-century New England shipmasters, merchants, and industrialists tended to be outlived by female kin, so lawyers specializing in ways to preserve estates developed the dynastic trust to insulate allegedly credulous females and minors against unscrupulous males. The dynastic trust form known as the Massachusetts trust, named after the state of its origin, accommodated neatly both the imperative to keep the estate undivided and the fact that H. Kempner had become the core of diverse cotton and noncotton businesses. It legitimized the Kempners' long-term pooled business assets, a stabilization needed in light of a common-law "Rule against Perpetuities" that forbade indefinite prolongation of trust estates.[28]

A flexible legal contrivance, the Massachusetts trust form was well suited to serve large numbers of family relations linked by financial interests. It fit precisely Ike's 1898 goals, for "it can simultaneously serve the family as an investment trust, a voting trust for blocks of shares in corporations, a coordinating directorate for the close management of several businesses, and a holding company for . . . controlling interests in a number of corporations," concluded one recent analyst.[29] The Massachusetts trust expedient allowed the Kempners to look forward more confidently than before to extended years of private control of the family's increasingly diverse businesses. Sixty years later, Ike's son Harris recalled that "a Massachusetts trust was picked upon because it was the only vehicle they could find which would enable them to carry on with the multiplicity of businesses they had under the same roof. It had many disadvantages. It was taxed as a corporation. It had individual liability as if it were a partnership. But it did permit them to operate the thing as a unit."[30]

28. Friedman, "Dynastic Trust," *American Jewish Historical Publications*, pp. 547–50; IHK, *Recalled Recollections*, pp. 98–99, and see pp. 61–62; Alexander, "The Transformation of Trusts as a Legal Category, 1800–1914," *Law and History Review*, p. 303.

29. Marcus, "Law in the Development of Dynastic Families," *Law and Society*, pp. 877, 872, respectively.

30. HLK, "Kempners of Galveston and Sugar Land," p. 11. He added: "A Mr.

The 1920 trust was to run for twenty years and to be renewable thereafter. It was destined to be renewed in 1940 as scheduled, again in 1948 thence to 1968, and then to 1988 when it received extension to 2008. The trust embraced all H. Kempner property except shareholders' "homesteads" (primary residence as defined by Texas law). By deed of gift to her children Eliza added her share to theirs, so that now they owned eight-ninths of the estate, plus her undivided one-ninth, all represented by the five thousand "beneficial" shares that each received of the forty-five thousand total. The value of each share was a portion of the pooled enterprises.

As suggested earlier, the five "original" trustees became, in effect, an executive board with Ike as chairman, and Dan, Lee, Stan, and Eliza's brother Joseph Seinsheimer as members. When death or disability diminished the original incumbents, replacements were selected by the remaining trustees. As intended by its creators, the trust's self-perpetuating board remained for a long time the preserve of the Kempner brothers plus Seinsheimer, and, later, of the succeeding generations of Kempners. Subsequent trust amendments and indentures called for by state laws requiring periodic renewals basically preserved the 1920 process for filling vacancies. But, as will be detailed in subsequent chapters, by the 1950s too few qualified blood Kempners were available or ready for a board seat. Therefore non-relatives were selected whose fidelity had been proven by long and effective service to H. Kempner. Able managers of the central H. Kempner office proved to have the inside track for selection as trustees with only one selectee (R. I. Mehan, a tax consultant for the firm) being recruited in the 1950s from outside that thin rank.

Thus, Seinsheimer was both H. Kempner office manager and a trustee until 1932. Ike's son Harris filled his uncle's vacated trusteeship beginning in 1940 except during his military service in World War II. Meanwhile office management had devolved on A. H. Blackshear, a graduate of Dan's tough mentorship in H. Kempner procedures and purposes, and he was escalated to a trusteeship in 1955. In 1957,

---

George Marcus [professor of anthropology, Rice University] wrote a paper which says 'shared hereditary wealth is given some business capital through the creative use of legal instruments when managed and maintained by legal specialists and family leaders.' That is a very highbrow way of saying we found this vehicle, we used it, and it was really quite a success."

Mehan succeeded Blackshear, serving until 1964, when A. M. Alpert rose to the board, to serve until the mid-1980s.[31]

However selected, trustees were required by state law to be prudent and were barred from speculating with trust funds, both agreeable precepts to Kempners. In most Massachusetts trusts only the trustees might terminate the instrument before the specified date. The Kempner trust provided for early termination by unanimous vote of the trustees plus written agreement by two-thirds of the shareholders. Massachusetts trusts commonly contained "spendthrift clauses," included to prevent the squandering of shares and to shield assets from creditors. But the Kempner men wanted also to limit the capacities of their sisters, and eventually, of the next generation, to alienate shares indiscriminately by external sales. Therefore the Kempner Trust required shareholders to offer their shares first to the trustees at existing value. Should the trust elect not to buy, other individual shareholders might do so. Only after all refused might a shareholder sell externally. Shares in the trust remained within the family except as some bequests occurred during succeeding decades to the Harris and Eliza Kempner Fund, a separate legal entity created in the late 1940s for supporting charitable, cultural, and scholarly endeavors.[32]

Building the H. Kempner Trust

Almost at once with the death of Fannie's husband in 1918 and the creation of the H. Kempner Trust in 1920, strains within the family caused by her break from religious orthodoxy ebbed. Under the shield of the trust the Kempner males and their mother guided the clan toward consensus and successes in diverse businesses during H. Kempner's years of acquisition and consolidation, as Ike's son described the period.[33] Granting exceptions, such as the spinners' lawsuits (see chapter 12), Ike and his brothers wielded the H. Kempner tool with marked effectiveness.

31. The Declarations of Trust, beginning in 1920, are in Kempner Papers. A. M. Alpert, letter to Leonora K. Thompson, undated, ca. July, 1988, copy supplied to author, and H. L. Kempner, letter to author, Sept. 1, 1987, clarified these points.

32. The trust was silent about alienation by gift. On the fund, see below, chaps. 15–16.

33. "Years of Acquisition," in HLK, "Beneficiary Interest Report, 1963."

From 1920 until the firm divested itself of the cotton trade in the late sixties, H. Kempner's cotton operations, in addition to its merchant banking, remained the core of the trust. "We are probably the oldest cotton exporting firm in America," Ike boasted in 1954 to an Australian spinner, "doing business nearly everywhere in the world and are members of the principal cotton exchanges throughout the world!"[34]

All the Kempners had their assets in the trust. Its relationship to H. Kempner's manifold interests may be depicted as follows:

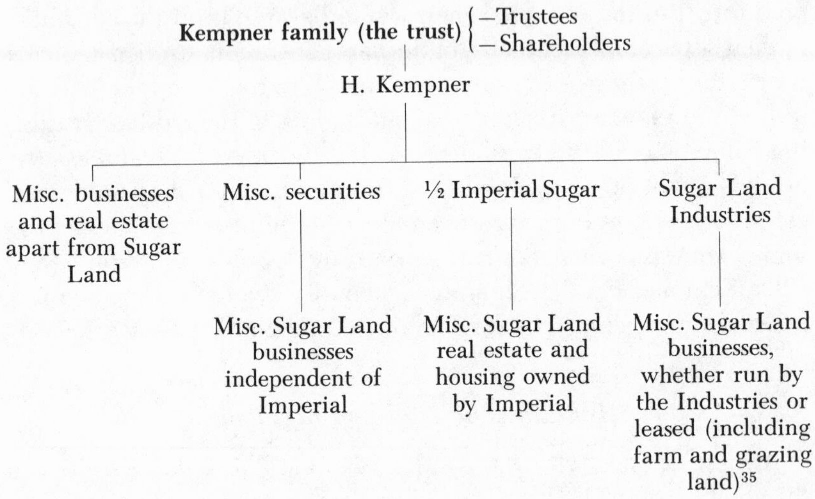

The Kempner Women

With their status, and incomes, further stabilized as equal shareholders in the trust, Kempner women felt able more than ever to select satisfying life-styles. Some would remain content with the vigorous social life that the family's rank and wealth provided. But other Kempner women greatly enlarged their commitments to community good works.

Later described accurately as the "head . . . and ruling spirit" of

34. Letter to R. Robson, Dec. 17, 1954, file 1, Box 119, #80-002, Kempner Papers. The antiquity boast is repeated in in-house manuals translated into several languages that the Kempners prepared to inform clients and new staff about the firm.

35. Derived from various items in the Kempner Papers, especially H. L. Kemp-

the extending family, Eliza contributed financially to Rabbi Cohen's trans-sectarian and often color-blind welfare activities and encouraged her daughters and daughters-in-law to participate in the temple's secular and sectarian good works.[36] Until 1910 or so, Eliza's daughters and daughters-in-law, Hennie and Jeane among the latter, were too young to participate, enmeshed in maternity, or, like Fannie, away at school.

Cohen was ever a rabbi. His first duty was to guide all his congregants through the wide yet puzzling ways open to Jews in America. Kempner generations recorded his able, effective, affectionate tutoring. Cohen appealed to and helped to link Kempner generations to themselves and each other.[37] But more than to any other Kempner, the rabbi attended to Eliza. A respected matriarch in her adopted city, like Cohen, Eliza was a veteran in a community of transients. Deeply committed to faith and family, she, Hennie, and then other Kempner women as they matured were hubs of the temple's crowded charity and cultural activities. With good reason the rabbi hoped for more generations of women like them, motivated to religious, civic, and private good works.

Hennie's entrance into the Kempner family as Ike's wife in 1902 exposed her to the tutelage of Eliza and the rabbi. Self-described as a typical, politically unaware debutante of a wealthy family, bearing five children between marriage in 1902 and 1913, she was, Hennie recalled, "never allowed to come downstairs until 30 days after [each] delivery!" But she found herself fascinated by the dynamics of community welfare, a fascination defined by the Great Storm's catastrophic effects. As quickly as maternity allowed, Hennie redefined and enriched her own life and Eliza's as well.[38]

Cohen, Eliza, Ike, Hennie, and Dan had developed confidential arrangements to get H. Kempner money to needful recipients, Jews and non-Jews, black and white. These arrangements would extend into mid-century. Ike's veteran office staffers were necessarily privy

---

ner's "Beneficiary Interest Report, 1963." Further details on trust development are in chaps. 11, 13, and 14.

36. Mimeographed press release, Sept. 26, 1947, and other sources too numerous to mention, DWK Scrapbook, 1945–1948, Kempner Papers.

37. Confirmation list in Box 3M228; Frances Adoue, letter to Cohen, misdated Mar. 11, 1929, Box 3M246, Cohen Papers.

38. Henrietta Blum Kempner, "Blum Saga."

to these arrangements. "Our rabbi had authority to come into the [H. Kempner] office and go to our cashier and say—Ben, give me $2,000," Block recalled, "and without question Ben gave him the $2,000, took his receipt for it, and nobody ever found out what that money was used for. That's how much faith they had in the rabbi."[39]

That faith built partly on the Kempners' desire to continue a practice their late father had begun in the 1880s, of disbursing regular stipends to needy European relatives (a practice that endures in the late 1980s). When soon after 1900 Ike and Dan visited their father's family in Poland, these beneficiaries lauded this "champion family from golden America" as personified kindness, filial love, [and] . . . every virtue existing."[40] But thereafter the American Kempners felt harassed by pleas for funds from Europeans claiming relationship, whose links to the family seemed dubious. Dan took the problem to Cohen. Through him, when in Paris on their "Innocents Abroad" trip, Dan and Ike employed a French lawyer and a Paris rabbi to ease genealogical research in both Poland and Germany. So aided, the brothers "dug back to the year the Ark landed," as Block recalled. They carried a family tree back to Galveston that included "the name of every 979th cousin, aunt, and uncle, . . . and if somebody [from Europe] wrote in and [said that] they needed money or was dying, if any of them wasn't on the list, they would investigate . . . [before] they would give."[41]

Indebted to Cohen for such practical aids, Cohen and Eliza recruited Kempner females by blood or marriage as patrons and executives of the temple's charity and education programs. Later, Hennie's work with the Red Cross and the Parent-Teacher Association eased Cohen's task of linking the temple's community programs to those of non-Jewish churches and to the city's welfare, public health, and education hierarchies.

First Eliza, then Hennie, then Jeane managed the temple's lecture series. With fees often subvented by Kempners, carefully chosen visiting lecturers in effect lobbied for the post-storm charter reforms and

39. Block interview with Marchiafava, June 6, 1981.

40. Rose Anspach, letter to Dan Kempner, May 14, 1944, in DWK Scrapbook, 1929–1935.

41. Block interview with Marchiafava, June 6, 1981. For an analogous later genealogical effort by the Herbert Lehman family in the 1930s, see Birmingham, "*Our Crowd*," pp. 366–67.

attendant bond issues. Like the Kempner men a supporter of the Equal Suffrage Association, Cohen used both genders' networks to lobby for the Nineteenth Amendment. It achieved, he encouraged newly enfranchised middle- and upper-class women not to revert only to gracious voluntarism or social whirligigs. Cohen was particularly concerned that all Kempners, female and male, "carry on the [family] tradition of civic duty," in Hennie's apt phrase.[42]

She became an active member and sometime administrator of the Red Cross, helped, as noted, to form and direct a Parent-Teacher Association local, served in the council of Jewish Women, and ran as well as subvented Galveston's Little Theater and other organized good causes, especially those that were run essentially by women. To cope with the ballooning budgets, Hennie raised funds from private sources and through lobbying in the city hall and state capital. In short, she became an experienced, able manager in diverse community enterprises, one with access gained both by reason of women's own tough demands for ingress and because the storm has forced many doors open. Even when in New York City awaiting an ocean liner to Europe in 1921, Hennie recruited other Texas women there who "seemed very bright and much interested in Galv[eston] politics."[43]

Other Kempner women remained interested primarily in more genteel projects, including reviewing books in newspapers (Leonora's occasional task), beautifying the reemerging Island City with mass plantings of shrubs, and reviving the Little Theater, the last also one of Hennie's lifelong interests.

Perhaps no woman of the family was totally uninterested in public service. Elected to the Galveston school board in 1919, the year Ike suffered defeat in his bid for a second term as mayor, Hennie won reelection through 1925. Perhaps her political victories were too easy, consequent duties too light, and popular appreciation too scant. Like Ike and other Kempners, Hennie wanted significant work to do, plus recognition of her efforts. She "found the [school board] job to be one of indifference . . . [to] the public and resigned," Ike wrote. Fannie replaced her sister-in-law on the school board. Even more quickly than Hennie, Fannie became fatigued. Adopting Hennie's rationale

42. Henrietta Blum Kempner, "Blum Saga"; Wygant, "A Municipal Broom," *Houston Review*, p. 117.

43. Henrietta Blum Kempner, "Blum Saga," and letter to Rabbi Cohen, Apr. 24, 1921, Box 3M238, Cohen Papers.

of public indifference, after only one year in that post Fannie too resigned, to nurse a vexing, erroneous memory that hers was ever a "sort of selfish life."[44]

Fannie herself forgot that throughout these decades she and her women relatives devoted time, thought, passion, and money on behalf of many public and private good works. She overlooked also the fact that she herself, her daughter, and the whole next generation of Kempner children residing in Galveston, learned from their grandmother, parents, and rabbi to avoid merely selfish lives.

For example, on her tenth birthday (1923), Dan and Jeane Kempner's daughter Mary Jean asked the rabbi to "enroll me as one of your co-workers in charity and accept this small donation [amount unspecified] to charity with the provision that it be used to keep one little boy or girl of my age, who is not as fortunate as me." Her parents had promised Mary Jean that their future birthday presents to her would be similar, "and until I am old enough to dispose of it myself I will ask you to let me send it to you [so] that with your help I may make one little child who is growing up in this world more comfortable and happy."[45]

Between her marriage to Dan in 1906 and Mary Jean's birth in 1913, Jeane, in addition to temple welfare activities, had concentrated her civic devotions in a low-budget clubwomen's volunteer effort, one for which she recruited Eliza and Hennie: running the Galveston office of the American Merchant Marine Library. The busy port produced enough sailors with literary thirsts or empty between-payday wallets to keep library volunteers busy. But not busy enough. Jeane expanded her civic activities, energizing the city's League of Women Voters local and then becoming statewide president in 1927, and helping to build Texas' perennially insubstantial Progressive-Democratic party coalition.[46]

What emerges from this overview of the women's post-storm involvements in community good works, both secular and religious, is the fact both of the enlargement and diversity of these involvements.

44. Fannie Kempner Adoue interview with Marchiafava, Aug. 1, 1981; IHK, *Recalled Recollections*, pp. 58–60.

45. Mary Jean Kempner, letter to Cohen, misdated Feb. 5, 1913 (should be 1923), Box 3M320, Cohen Papers.

46. On the library, Mrs. B. Sproul, letter to Cohen, June 13, 1930, Box 3M249, Cohen Papers.

Ancient barriers to opportunity collapsed or sagged. Combined with women's access also to the vote beginning in 1920, the modern phase of Kempner history became one in which the family's goal of cohesion over generations would be affected by the increasing freedom of choice the women enjoyed in ordering their lives, whether in good works, in choosing mates and careers, or in adhering to Judaism.

The Galveston women's large successes in unprecedented responsibilities from 1900 to 1920 helped to convince Kempner males to support the Nineteenth Amendment and, after its ratification, to encourage female candidates for elective and appointive public offices.

By more recent notions, paradoxes or worse existed in the men's gender attitudes. Ike's generation of males responded to its rhythms, not ours, which is description rather than excuse. While patronizing even females of their own family, the Kempner males were also honest with them financially, encouraged their post–Great Storm civic activism, and were enthusiasts for woman suffrage. But Ike's generation of Kempner men abandoned few if any Edwardian notions about gender, notions justifying to themselves the masculine monopolies they treasured in the management of H. Kempner businesses and the off-color jokes Ike liked to tell at all-male gatherings of businessmen and politicians.

When chips came down, however, Ike preferred the more open ways of the 1950s and 1960s to those of the century's turn. Odds are that his wife Hennie and daughter-in-law Ruth Levy Kempner, Harris's wife, were especially important mentors in his transition. The latter recalled in 1981 that "every one of us [female family members] . . . down here have had absolutely individual lives of our own, and we've all done things." By which she meant not only charity work but activist politics. Her insight is the most emphatic by its artless reference to the Kempners who remained "down here" in Galveston. This is precisely what the first Harris Kempner had dreamed of in 1894, as had Ike, who conveyed the dream to Dan in 1898.[47]

Sexism notwithstanding, Kempner men perceived clearly that their mother, wives, and sisters helped to repair the family's storm-eroded hopes for cohesion in a decent, improved, thriving community. They were a far cry from women who, according to Ike, held the "introduction of debutante daughters . . . [as] a zenith of social achieve-

47. Ruth Kempner, interview with L. Marchiafava, June 5, 1981, RLA.

ment." Therefore he and his brothers encouraged the women from private benevolence to civic activism and never expressed surprise or displeasure when some females refused to retreat and others preferred not to advance. Ike and Hennie supplied their daughter Cecile (b. 1908) with a sound secondary education at the Baldwin School, near Bryn Mawr, on Philadelphia's Main Line. In 1924 and again in 1930, Cecile, who would have a successful career as a buyer for a major New York City department store and who would never marry, joined Ike and Hennie to watch her sisters graduate, Lyda (b. 1911) from the Mary Lyon School and Lenore (b. 1913) from Baldwin. Without demur from parents Lyda aimed for Columbia and Lenore for Vassar, where, according to her father, she "major[ed] in a policy to be married." But that choice was hers.[48]

Selecting Faiths and Mates

Institutionalized in the 1920 trust, family cohesion took precedence over fidelity to Reform Judaism, although all the then-adult Kempners remained its faithful adherents. Religious pluralism thereafter became a greatly lessened threat to the warp of family assets and the woof of family unity that Eliza and Ike were laboring to weave. Nevertheless Fannie's marriage was a breach, how well repaired or permanently no one knew. The Kempners' heartfelt acceptance of the secular society's values helped Eliza and Ike to accept Fannie's marriage and prepared them for other matches, including religiously pluralist ones, that they thought impended.[49]

No one could foresee in 1920 that Fannie's was to be the last marriage in chronological order among Eliza's children, since Lee, Stan, and Gladys remained bachelors. What Ike's wife Henrietta called the "wedding march" of Eliza's grandchildren did not begin until ten years after Fannie's wedding, clustering in the 1930s and 1940s. Between Eliza's and her sons' new tolerance of religious heterodoxy (for others, not themselves) and the effects of time's passage, the passions that Fannie's marriage had raised in the family cooled. Senior Kempners made it clear to the younger that though the overall goal of family

48. IHK, *Recalled Recollections*, pp. 46, 63, 82, 85. See also *Galveston News*, Oct. 5, 1924; *Galveston Tribune*, May 23, 1935.

49. Cf. Tuchman, "The Assimilationist's Dilemma," in *Practicing History*, pp. 210–12, and IHK, *Recalled Recollections*, pp. 58, 94–95, 116–17, 115–16.

cohesion was undimmed, all substantive choices, including those of education, vocation, political candidates, or permanent locations, were up to the individual. Further young Kempners of both genders understood that they were also in charge of their own religious destinies. Even in 1981 Sara, who had dated a non-Jew but married in the faith, recalled how she and her brothers and sisters, when young, then their children, burdened Ike with demanding questions about alternative religious life-styles as well as a hundred other matters. Ike's reply concerning religion: "Every man for himself . . . [After] you're 14 you can make up your mind. If it's too far out, then we'll tell you." She concluded that Ike was "very fair."[50]

Among the now-adult first American-born Kempners, Fannie had most resisted direction by their mother and Ike. Ike became less a father-figure to her than "a wonderfully understanding man" who, happily, was never stern with his own children. "Now my mother was pretty stern [with hers]," Fannie recalled. "Now that I look back on it, I must confess that I didn't blame her because she had the responsibility to bring us [girls] up practically alone. Every day she had to make decisions [about her daughters] that my brother couldn't make."

After her husband's death, Fannie, restless, had asked her brothers for advice about a gift shop she might buy into. All except Ike tried to dissuade her. He, feeling that decisions were hers to make, offered both advice and financial aid. She ventured briefly and unsuccessfully into retail commerce. Sara too always remembered Ike's "personal concern for all the family. . . . We consulted Brother Ike when we wouldn't have consulted any of the others. It wasn't that they weren't interested, but they knew the last word was from Ike." In questions most pertinent to the girls, their mother "definitely . . . had the last word in making a decision. . . . Brother Ike was a wonderful man."[51]

Perhaps he had to be. Many weights burdened him. Ike seemed to ask for them, indeed, to demand them. "He had to take over everything," Fannie recalled in what, despite her seemingly critical tone, was a warm and loving reminiscence.[52]

By the time Ike's own children and those of his siblings readied

50. Henrietta Blum Kempner, "Blum Saga"; Sara Kempner Weston interview with Marchiafava, Aug. 29, 1981.

51. Fannie Kempner Adoue and Sara Kempner Weston interviews with Marchiafava, Aug. 1 and Aug. 29, 1981, respectively.

52. Fannie Kempner Adoue interview with Marchiafava, Aug. 1, 1981.

for marriage in the 1930s, little in the way of religious affirmations or complete areligiosity was "too far out." By then the Kempner parents exerted only "very little" pressure on the children concerning religious expression. "It was really a question of letting [each of] us make our own decisions," Harris recalled. "I don't remember Mother being as concerned about it as Dad was. My Grandmother [Eliza] was concerned. She used to take me to Temple . . . relatively regularly with her in those days."

For himself, young Harris didn't mind attending temple, for Rabbi Cohen was so "very learned . . . in a number of extraordinary things." Harris and his brother Herb were bar mitzvah and in 1980 Harris mused, "How should I put it [?] I am a dues-paying member of the Temple and . . . so I am for all purposes a Jew except that I am not a very good one."[53]

No Kempner protested overtly when in 1932 Ike's son Herbert married Mary Carroll in a ceremony conducted by a Baptist minister, Rabbi Cohen attending "only as a guest." Two years later Cohen officiated at Ike's daughter Henrietta Leonora's (known always in Galveston as "Nonie") wedding to Edward Thompson, an Episcopalian. Later that busy connubial year a Roman Catholic priest conducted the marriage service for her sister Lyda to Arthur Quinn. Then in 1939 Harris and Ruth Levy faced Rabbi Cohen for their Jewish wedding. "If this seems quite a mixture of creeds and ceremonies," Ike suggested, "it is above all an exhibition of tolerance of faith differences in which increased practice would find merit." To dinner guest Norman Thomas, Ike boasted on one occasion: "Oh, I've got one child married to a Jew, one . . . to a Baptist, one . . . to an Episcopalian, and one . . . to a Catholic, and I am President of the Synagogue."[54]

Harris had delighted the Kempner BOIs when in 1939 he married another "native," Ruth Levy, whose vigor, education, intelligence, and forthrightness matched any Kempner's. Ruth felt that "either you end up being more of a Kempner than the Kempners or you find that they make you feel inferior and you resent them and you fight them. This has happened in the case of some of the men who have married into the family," she noted. Able to give as good as she took, Ruth "got

53. H. L. Kempner interview with Jones, June 17, 1980.

54. IHK, *Recalled Recollections*, pp. 72, 116, 121; H. L. Kempner interview with Jones, June 17–18, 1980.

along fine with Eliza, Ike, and Hennie. As far as I'm concerned, there never was a family that I could admire more, but I really do think that they have to live up to me."[55]

Ruth and the Kempners did indeed live up to each other. Self-described in an autobiographical sketch as a "housewife and trouble-maker," Ruth listed herself further as "Government Official, Clubs, Dissent/Reform. Active in League of Women Voters (1950s). . . . Active in many reform movements."[56]

In 1961 Ruth adapted her commitments from reforming the 1902 city charter to running for and then filling a council office in the resulting government, the first woman so to serve. Fellow reform candidates took Kempner-like positions. They "would not even invest in . . . [paper?] clips because . . . [they] wanted to prove that any man [or woman] could afford to run for the [City] Council." The reform committee hoped "that many people would express the responsibility of serving without pay and that the turnover would be frequent so that the City would hear from all people."[57] Paylessness limited elective incumbency primarily to the well-off. Whatever the merits of the idea, it echoed far back into the Kempners' story, and was brought forward in time to the present by Ruth and other Kempner women.

For example, Nonie, a longtime activist in Galveston's Community Chest and United Way organizations, beginning in the 1950s also became a trustee of the Harris and Eliza Kempner Fund, then its secretary-treasurer, and, as the 1980s closed, its board chairman. Similarly, Lyda Quinn successfully ran her late husband's oil and gas business after his death in 1978.[58] And the boards of Kempner corporations had long been open to women of the family who wanted such tasks.

In brief, Galveston offered its privileged females who wanted the burdens unusually rich opportunities for on-job education in public service and activist politics. Women included, Kempners were always well represented among both tutors and learners, and Kempner men among their supporters. "Ruth has been so busy with her civic duties,"

55. Ruth Kempner interview with Marchiafava, June 5, 1981.

56. Winegarten, ed., "Finder's Guide to the Texas Women" (typescript; Texas Woman's University Library, 1984), p. 109.

57. Sara Ellen Stubbs, "Galveston Was Their Home: Genealogy of the Kauffman-Stubbs-Brotherson Families" (typescript), RLA, p. 154.

58. H. K. Weston, letter to author, Aug. 19, 1988.

her husband would note, "that we have not seen as much of . . . [her] as we would have liked."[59]

By 1948, Dan's daughter Mary Jean Kempner (b. 1913) was a globe-trotting *Vogue* magazine staff writer and internationally syndicated photojournalist, already widely known for her wartime dispatches and 1946 articles on a famine in India. Independent in spirit and with income from her H. Kempner shares, Mary Jean, like Cecile, established permanent residence in New York City. All Kempners were proud of her and encouraged her passionate search for independent self-expression and career. Her choice of residence was her own, even though it involved amendment to the family cohesion imperative so far as residence in Galveston was concerned.

With exceptions, over three generations most Kempner women, like the males, preferred lifetime Galveston residency and options about participating in civic affairs. Such participation advanced the Kempners' family cohesion by helping to keep Galveston attractive and its economy dynamic.

Hardly alone among acculturated American Jews to make choices like the ones they did in 1920 and later about accommodating religious heterodoxy, the Kempners' strategic retreats on this front served to protect the cohesion of the growing, increasingly secularized family, and preserved the claims of Eliza and her sons to run H. Kempner's diverse affairs.[60]

Despite apostasies and intermarriages the Kempners served Rabbi Cohen in ways transcending but never ignoring charity. For fifty years their names headed the rabbi's lists of contributors for the temple's special fundraising drives, and the twentieth century was to be depressingly rich in its calls for urgent assessments. Cohen estimated that every Island City Jew contributed at least $100 annually to special fund drives throughout the wearying decades, every adult Kempner giving ten to fifteen times more, often secretly, as with Cohen's arrangement with H. Kempner. After 1920 the H. Kempner Trust gave additionally as an entity. Like a meter of global distress, the trust's offerings increased from approximately $1,500 annually in the early

59. H. L. Kempner to S. Lacerda, Oct. 21, 1961, Box 177, File "K Camp," #80-002, Kempner Papers.

60. IHK, *Recalled Recollections*, pp. 116–17.

1920s to $2,000 yearly 1936–38, to $27,500 in 1949. From such evidence, Cohen concluded that fundraisers for Jewish causes were wrong to assert that Galveston coreligionists were provincials concerned only about local ills. Instead, he wrote, the problem was that "the same few cannot lend their interest to [so] many fine institutions."[61]

Dan and Rabbi Cohen conceived and implemented a search for Galveston Movement veterans and beneficiaries, in part to document the program's successes and also to tap them for charitable donations. Since their relocations inland Cohen had overlooked these people as sources of funds for temple benevolences. Ike learned that priests and ministers were successfully dunning immigrants resettled by the Movement on behalf of Christian charities. He encouraged the rabbi to repair the omission, and Dan regularized what became a systematic outreach effort of the Galveston Reform temple for funds from these new, welcome donors, some of whom wondered why they were overlooked earlier. For this relief, Galveston's small Reform congregation gave much thanks.[62]

In the early 1930s Jeane, a League of Women Voters official, at Cohen's suggestion specialized in immigration matters. At that time American Jews focused concern about immigration primarily on refugee European coreligionists who, fleeing fascism, had slipped into the United States from temporary Latin American havens and had since been apprehended by American authorities. Visiting a local detention center, a former Movement facility, Jeane was horrified at its conditions. She tried to have the Texas LWV lobby Congress for money to improve the place, to hasten admission procedures, and, most politically tender, to admit more refugees. The league refused and she resigned. Thereafter she and Cohen pressured Ike and Dan to travel to Washington several times a year as necessary to testify on behalf of would-be immigrants before federal immigration boards, Dan reporting sadly after a particularly exhausting trip and session that "in not one of these cases has anything been achieved." Other times, the Kempners' commitments to employ individual refugees won their conditional admissions. In several such instances, despite depression con-

61. Memo, undated, Box 3M334, Cohen Papers. The above figures ignore changes in taxation and inflation rates.

62. Exchanges, H. Miller and Cohen, Jan. 25–29, 1925, Box 3M234, Cohen Papers.

straints, one or another Kempner enterprise made work for the harassed newcomers.[63]

Nazism in Europe inspired aspirations—tragically, never consummated—for systematic mass resettlements of Jewish refugees in the United States, on the Movement model. Working closely with Cohen, Ike was elected director of the Texas branches of the American Jewish Committee and the United Jewish Appeal. Themselves reaching middle age as the 1940s ended, Eliza's children retained their caring ways about each other as a family and about their community.

All this looks very far ahead from the stabilizing of the estate by means of the 1920 trust. Very soon after the crafting of the trust but long before its beneficial effects were clear, major new threats to H. Kempner's survival had to be endured, most notably the so-called spinners' litigations. They were precisely the kind of long-drawn-out, expensive, and enervating lawsuits that the Kempners traditionally avoided.

63. D. W. Kempner, letter to E. Baruch, Aug. 27, 1942, and IHK, to Cohen, Aug. 27, 1942, Box 3M282, Cohen Papers. On LWV, see letters, File 8, Box 34, #80-002, Kempner Papers.

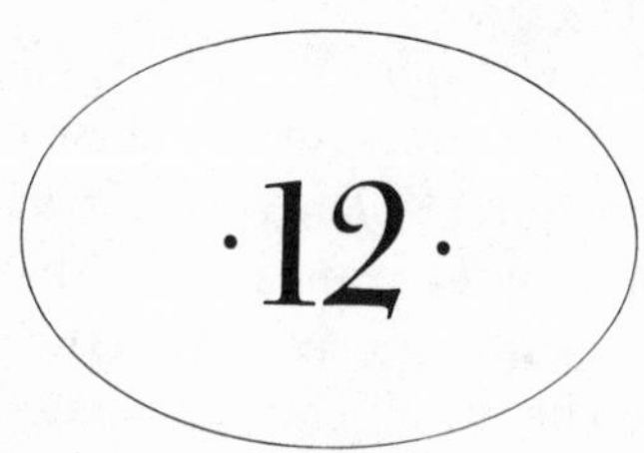

12

The Spinners' Litigations

Describing the cotton-exporting business in the 1930s, Harris L. Kempner told an anecdote concerning a professor's inquiry to students about sex: Which is better, dreaming about sex or actually experiencing it? One student preferred the dream because "I meet a much nicer class of people." "So," Harris continued, "I say that's the cotton business. You're screwed by a very nice class of people!"[1]

The near-destructive, frustrating, and unending spinners' litigations may have provoked Ike to such a wry description. Those lawsuits had their origins both in the economic swirls of the immediate post–World War I scene and in Ike's ongoing efforts to improve H. Kempner's bargaining position with European millers (i.e., spinners).

To the latter end, as soon as possible after hostilities ceased Ike contracted with Ernest Heller, an Austrian-born naturalized Englishman, to open an H. Kempner office in Zurich, Switzerland. Ike's son Harris remembered admiringly that Heller "spoke nearly all commercial languages." Among Heller's manifold tasks was "the intricate, cumbersome thing [of] hedging our currency and operations . . . to be sure to convert [German] marks into Swiss francs and back into dollars." Currency trades were and are part of commodity marketing. H. Kempner agents in foreign countries could give the firm competitive advantages in these endless daily transfers. Heller also oversaw other H. Kempner offices subsequently opened in Europe. Harris re-

1. H. L. Kempner, interview with L. Marchiafava, June 6, 1981, RLA; and see IHK, letter to H. R. Cullen, Mar. 5, 1945, IHK Correspondence file 1, #80-002, Kempner Papers.

called also the "daily exchange of cables [from Galveston] with practically all these people."

Meanwhile, in 1919, a German, Waldemar Hapke, a self-employed agent in America both for European spinners and American factors, "a great salesman" according to Harris, contracted not with Kempner but with a minor New Orleans factor, the Lighter Company.[2] Its president, George Lighter, specialized in the peculiarly aggressive "spot" market, in which he was already associated with Herman Nussbaum, also a Galveston spot specialist and a longtime family friend to the Kempners.

H. Kempner handled only futures, not spot cotton, but of course Ike understood both modes. Keeping in mind how he treasured and trusted fellow Islanders, and that most cotton exchange transactions were made on the basis of a nod, handshake, or telephoned commitment, Ike was impressed that his friend Nussbaum had entered into a partnership with Lighter, with Hapke now as their joint agent in European spinning centers. Lighter/Nussbaum invited Ike to join the partnership, primarily, it appears, to be their private banker in the sense of being a source of quick and generous credit.[3]

Although already a veteran investor in diverse enterprises, by 1919 Ike, except for directing H. Kempner itself and for short stints on boards of directors, had associated in long-term partnerships involving active management and risk capital only in the Maskemp effort in oil and at Sugar Land. Maskemp had died early. In 1919 Sugar Land was developing into one of the most engaging projects of Ike's life. His partnership there with Eldridge was destined to be amicable, profitable, and enduring for both parties. Probably the early triumphs and sturdy concord of the partnership with Eldridge at Sugar Land inclined Ike and the other senior Kempners to judge other, superficially similar opportunities less searchingly than they might otherwise have done.

Ike knew Nussbaum well, and Lighter had his sponsorship. Lighter was a former Cincinnatian (always a plus to a Kempner). Having once studied for the Roman Catholic priesthood Lighter later opted for a classicist's career, abandoned that, and had begun factoring cotton

2. H. L. Kempner interview with Marchiafava, June 6, 1981; and see IHK, *Recalled Recollections*, p. 62.

3. See IHK, letter to Tom Connally, Jan. 13, 1931, in DWK folder, Box IHK, (1952), #80-002, Kempner Papers.

in New Orleans in 1898. Lighter/Nussbaum had spinners anxious to order at unusually high price levels, or so Hapke, their agent, claimed. But the spot operators lacked capital and a surer supply of raw cotton than the spot market was likely to provide. Further, as Ike was to learn, Lighter/Nussbaum never quite agreed on internal management aspects of the operation, whether of bookkeeping, commodity standards, or responsibility to monitor agents.

For his part Ike was still unsure of H. Kempner's own, still largely untried European agents. He bit the bait of an alternative on-hand agent already possessed of spinners' large orders for Texas cotton at high prices. By terms of a 1919 contract between H. Kempner, Lighter, and Nussbaum, later extended, Ike eased his new partners' shortage of capital by having H. Kempner buy 60 percent of their operations and delegating to them H. Kempner's New York and Chicago exchange seats. Lighter/Nussbaum agreed to buy only from H. Kempner any spot cotton their European spinners needed.

The Conversion Contracts

In "conversion contracts" that the new partnership signed with European spinners through Hapke, the Americans refined traditional "hedging" techniques long common in cotton wholesaling. The refinement permitted the American partners to take advantage of the monetary inflation then plaguing European nations where the textile spinning industry was significant both economically and politically, including Germany, France, Italy, and the Netherlands. Spinners there yearned for Texas cotton. But the strong American dollar impeded trades, and most American middlemen hesitated to risk commitments out of uncertainty about the drift of currency rates.[4] The conversion contracts allowed both parties, presumably, to take advantage of international currency oscillations rather than be obstructed by them.

Conversion contracts allowed buyers (i.e., spinners) to (1) accept the cotton as committed, or (2) move the delivery date forward in hopes of a favorable price fluctuation, or (3) liquidate the contract at a loss or profit. These options permitted spinners to contract for more cotton than they needed.[5] With the excess they could choose

4. Guidry, "Twisted Threads" (Ph.D. diss.), chap. 2.

5. Memorandum, Jan. 13, 1931, DWK folder, Box IHK (1952), #80-002, Kempner Papers.

advantageously in the inflating market between converting or liquidating and thus gain hard currencies for future purchases from suppliers like H. Kempner. Meanwhile, H. Kempner needed to advance little or no credit in the form of cash, and the brokerage fees gave the American investors substantial windfalls.

Lighter/Nussbaum could not themselves deliver the volume of cotton Hapke committed; the amounts were "too big for them" according to Harris. Instead Lighter/Nussbaum bought additional cotton in New York at fixed prices. H. Kempner then "covered" or "hedged" by buying an appropriate amount of futures, or options, at a still-undetermined price. If the market continued to rise, then Lighter/Nussbaum, with H. Kempner behind the scenes, shared in the profits deriving from their purchases at a lower price. If their earlier estimates of the volume of cotton the spinners would buy fell short, then, at worst, the Lighter/Nussbaum/Kempner partners could buy more, though at the newer, higher price, by exercising H. Kempner's option, and still make money. "We could in effect write our own ticket for that part of the contract," Harris reminisced. He recalled also that Hapke had apparently convinced his father and Lighter/Nussbaum that conversion commitments to deliver "spot" cotton were worth risking, that is, that the partners could anticipate and profit from fluctuations in the supply of cotton, not inflationary currency rises, by exercising a "sort of . . . option."[6]

But in retrospect it is clear that Ike should have heeded warning signals. The loudest was the fact that H. Kempner and its subsequently "vanished subsidiaries" (i.e., Lighter/Nussbaum) were probably the only cotton merchants in America to enter into such conversion contracts in a large way and to stick with them after their hazards were apparent. Ike's son admitted later that "I'm certain we were the only ones [i.e., cotton merchants] that did it on such a scale. . . . [T]here was no one else that we could find, with whose company we could share our misery." Ike did offer America's largest cotton-exporting firm, that of Anderson Clayton, an old friend to his family, a share in the H. Kempner conversion contracts. It declined, preferring only to supply Ike with in-house data he requested on Anderson Clayton's own very brief and minor experience with such contracts. It appears, however,

6. H. L. Kempner interview with Marchiafava, June 6, 1981.

that the Anderson Clayton firm shared Ike's basic assumption that the conversion approach was merely a variant of the trade's traditional "hedge position."[7]

Commitments in these conversion contracts ballooned quickly, by 1924 involving over thirty-five thousand bales of cotton for spinners concentrated in Germany and France, and H. Kempner money interests in excess of $3.3 million.[8]

As Ike later noted to Texas' Sen. Tom Connally, "For one reason or another, the [German and French] mills delayed conversion of the futures into actual cotton, and, finally, after the very disastrous [price] decline [beginning in 1924] refused to take the cotton or pay the losses, acting in concert in what actually seems to have been a conspiracy."[9]

The great cliché of contract disputes is that all was well until a party defaulted on obligations. The European spinners may or may not have colluded to avoid paying the now-swollen contracted prices for Texas cotton or to accept further deliveries from Galveston. But viewed from Galveston's Strand, H. Kempner was "holding the bag of a bunch of high priced conversion contracts" at a time when M&P and Sugar Land were gobbling up the firm's liquid capital.[10]

Gambling or Hedging?

In 1924 market manipulations by some American commodity brokers (a clique from which even an account unsympathetic to this aspect of the Kempners' career omits them) triggered the swift decline in the price of cotton.[11] This decline inspired spinners to search for ways out of contracts like those with Kempner. Exits existed if the conversion contracts were proved not to conform to prescriptions of the New York Cotton Exchange, where the contracts were executed, and/or to the law of relevant European nations which now forbade gambling in commodities and made speculative contracts unenforce-

7. H. L. Kempner interview with B. Guidry, Aug. 16, 1982, RLA.

8. Deposition by Dan Kempner, Mar. 1, 1941, in DWK folder, Box IHK (1953), #80-002, Kempner Papers.

9. IHK, letter to Tom Connally, Jan. 13, 1931.

10. H. L. Kempner, "The Kempners of Galveston and Sugar Land" (manuscript, speech to Harvard Business Club of Houston, Sept. 27, 1981), RLA, p. 12; and see H. L. Kempner interview with Marchiafava, June 6, 1981.

11. Guidry, "Twisted Threads," pp. 51–56.

able. Were the spinners' options in certain Kempner conversion contracts speculations or gambling?[12]

Imprecisions and overlaps existed in the contracts, in the laws of Germany and other milling nations, and in the rules of the New York Cotton Exchange. All future contracts were speculative by nature. Intent governed. A futures contract aimed at ensuring an adequate supply of a commodity was a legitimate "considered risk" as defined in the leading contemporary American business "bible." One aimed at riding price waves was gambling, an "excessive hazard."[13] But little precision existed anywhere (a condition still true in the 1980s).

Everything in these intermingling relationships began to unravel. To then-young Harris apprenticing in the H. Kempner office, "it was quite a . . . story. They [the spinners] wanted to dishonor the [conversion] contract[s] and wouldn't pay us for the margins or anything else."[14]

In retrospect, Ike was to blame himself for "foolishly" guaranteeing "terms [in the conversion contracts] which guaranteed the [European] purchasers against declines in the market, but gave them the benefit of any advances." It was all to result "in an enormous loss" to H. Kempner.

Dan Kempner added to his other tasks, especially the management of M&P and the recruitment and training of future top management, the protection of the family's interests in resulting lawsuits. Probably out of respect for Ike, Dan refused to cut losses for far longer than proved to be prudent.[15] But however extended and expensive, imprudence is neither felony nor misdemeanor.

Were the Kempners tainted with worse than imprudence in these contracts? Skeptical about their purposes, one author concludes that Ike intended to gamble (i.e., speculate), thus sustaining the defaulting spinners' primary defense that this intention made the contracts unenforceable according to the laws of relevant European countries. Further, this author suggests that Ike's intention in joining with Lighter and Nussbaum was to monopolize cotton exporting in the Gulf re-

12. Ibid.
13. Hubbard, *Cotton and the Cotton Market*, pp. 430–32.
14. H. L. Kempner, "The Kempners of Galveston and Sugar Land," p. 12.
15. IHK, *Recalled Recollections*, p. 62.

gion. If provable, this monopoly purpose violated American antitrust laws that labeled such goals as white-collar felonies.[16]

These were absurd canards, Harris Kempner insisted in 1984: "We [H. Kempner] were too small to even think of such a thing [i.e., a monopoly] and if we had thought of it, we would have had sense enough not to try it," he wrote then.[17]

Perhaps the aforementioned conclusion that a monopoly was intended arose from a misreading of Ike's simultaneous efforts to reorient H. Kempner's cotton operations vertically, efforts that do not, however, reflect an intention to create monopolies through the European conversion contracts. For its part, the American government never initiated an antitrust prosecution of H. Kempner during the forty-plus years of the spinners' litigations, which frequently received wide publicity. It is therefore plausible that in the conversion contracts Ike was trying to liberate his entrepreneurial capacities from confining, obsolescing marketplace practices.[18]

More positively, the evidence suggests that the Kempner/Lighter/Nussbaum trio indeed lacked either intent or capacity to monopolize. Recall that Ike always claimed that H. Kempner's primary role in the association with Nussbaum and Lighter was that of private banker, this being a time when the H. Kempner letterhead proclaimed that the firm's dual primary interests were indeed "Cotton and Banking."[19] By the most generous estimates H. Kempner could not finance a corner on cotton. Lighter and Nussbaum associated with Ike because they needed H. Kempner capital even for futures trades. Ike was serving as banker in order, as always, to have H. Kempner profit. Beyond this, he envisaged the Lighter/Nussbaum association as a parallel on the European side for what he was attempting domestically: that is, a part of a vertical farmer-merchant-spinner process. Unless so considered, the partnership with Lighter/Nussbaum was jarringly untypi-

16. Guidry, "Twisted Threads," pp. 51–56 and chap. 2, passim. See also B. Guidry, letter to H. L. Kempner, Aug. 3, 1984, copy supplied to author by H. L. Kempner.

17. H. L. Kempner, letter to B. Guidry, July 17, 1984, copy supplied to author by H. L. Kempner.

18. Cf. McGerr, "Confinement, Liberation, and Social Class" (American Historical Association, 1986), p. 5; Guidry, "Twisted Threads," chap. 2.

19. On the claim, and the letterhead, IHK, letter to Tom Connally, Jan. 13, 1931.

cal for H. Kempner. But so evaluated, it fits into a pattern of intended rationalization, one ultimately thwarted to be sure, but hardly one of intended restraint of trade.

Hapke: Villain in the Piece?

Waldemar Hapke appears to have played a primary role in bringing on the troubles everyone endured. Commodity dealers' and spinners' agents like Hapke were not timeclock-punching employees. Instead, agents were themselves commission-earning entrepreneurs, middlemen for middlemen. Agents active in international commodity dealing were commonly accomplished in diverse languages and had connections with both spinners and merchants. No one shook such webs casually. Disgruntled agents could exact fearful retributions for what they perceived as wrongs done to them by principals, as, for example, by accepting a place (as Hapke was to do) with a former principal's adverse litigant or competitor and divulging trade secrets or giving damaging courtroom testimony.

Evidence about Hapke's misdeeds unfolded incrementally. Ike worried that H. Kempner's own resident agents in Europe, upon learning of Hapke as agent of the Kempner/Nussbaum/Lighter partnership, might resent being faced with competition from their own principal. Hapke nevertheless represented himself to German mills as serving H. Kempner, not the three-way partnership. Dan wrote Lighter: "We resent these bragadoccio [*sic*] remarks. . . . They are wholly unnecessary for our business; they reflect upon our own agents and make them dissatisfied. . . . Mr. Hapke's remarks are wholly not true."[20] Hapke must cease using the H. Kempner name or the Galveston firm might sever the partnership, Dan warned.

Noteworthily, Dan threatened Lighter, not Hapke, for the latter was Lighter's long-term agent, not H. Kempner's. Hapke proved to be irrepressible. In 1923 and 1924 he contracted on his own with some European spinners in a speculation in which Hapke exploited the Kempner/Nussbaum/Lighter conversion contracts as security, all "without Ike's or Dan's knowledge and probably without Lighter's," concluded a diligent untangler of these twisted threads. Ike wrote a "very

20. DWK, letter to Lighter, Apr. 8, 1922, quoted in Guidry, "Twisted Threads," pp. 54–55.

strong letter" of complaint about Hapke to Lighter in late 1924, suggesting that H. Kempner would never again take "one bale of [cotton] futures [the basic ingredient in the conversion contracts] if we ever get out of the mess we are in now."[21]

No one could quell the obstreperous German. And until the price collapse of 1924–25, Hapke, however disagreeable, was making money for the partners and himself. But while waiting for upturns that failed to happen, and while allegedly serving his principals, he speculated for his personal profit on their accounts, exploiting insiders' advantages in manner not then illegal. Apparently he also forged, stole, and lied to the principals. Hapke orally extended contracts with spinners beyond the twelve-month limits allowed by American law and promised certain spinners reductions in handling fees below the levels set by the New York Cotton Exchange. Kempner and the others felt obliged to honor their agent's promises. They deducted resulting losses from his commissions. But they never carried out threats to bring him to arbitration before the Bremen Cotton Exchange or to fire him. Why? In the least generous estimate, "The shaky legal status of the [conversion] contracts necessitated this approach."[22] But the evidence allows alternatives. Among them is the fact that in the 1920s, as in the 1980s, commodity exchanges were relatively free-wheeling arenas. Standards of conduct were uncertain. Ever since 1899, Ike himself, though rising swiftly to the peak of exchange officialdom, had been complaining to fellow brokers about the exchanges' distressing looseness. As a result the commodity marketplaces tended to attract individuals "of utter disregard of any interest save for private gain," Ike had stated. Exchanges did offer "the ponderous machinery of the factory" for self-policing. But the complex business and legal relationships present in every commodity transaction necessitated speed among potential contractees. Thus, though valuable, the most the exchanges could provide was "a restrained hand."

Ike's effort to develop his own resident agents abroad in part reflected the exchanges' deficiencies.[23] Since these new agents were still unproved, Ike stayed also with Hapke, a veteran of the existing ways, which further explains why Ike chose not to tell his own European

21. Guidry, "Twisted Threads," pp. 63–64, 68.

22. Ibid., p. 71.

23. See unidentified clipping on Ike's address on the utility of exchanges, in DWK Scrapbook, 1894–1915, Kempner Papers.

agents about Hapke and the H. Kempner connection to Lighter and Nussbaum. No principal must tell agents what he chooses to keep from them. Such reticence may be unwise. Only outcomes determine foolishness or wisdom.

Contemporary business literature and the Kempner family's own history with unsquelchable relatives warned against runaway agents and the need for top management to control them. But from 1919 to 1926, when Hapke generated more profits than complaints, the extent of his transgressions was still unknown. It was the price slide of the mid-1920s that transformed irritation with Hapke into knowledge of his double dealings. For Ike to have repudiated Hapke in advance of this knowledge calls for prescience.

Further Accusations

As 1924 advanced, Ike, pondering the grim news of the price slide, learned that his limited partners, Nussbaum and Lighter, might fail in ventures wholly unconnected to H. Kempner. But every shareholder in the unincorporated H. Kempner 1920 trust was subject to unlimited personal liability.

Back in 1919, when contracting with Nussbaum and Lighter, Ike had withheld agreement unless they agreed to use H. Kempner's bookkeeping forms and procedures (which were more advanced and detailed than those the other employed), and agreed also to incorporate, with H. Kempner as majority shareholder in both new entities. Ike stored the controlling shares, already endorsed by Nussbaum and Lighter, in H. Kempner's safe. In extreme circumstances Ike could limit the H. Kempner portion of liability to its investment amount or even divest H. Kempner of connection with the new partners.

This reservation on Ike's part can seem to be part of a duplex pattern, as one analyst so views it.[24] But the divestment possibility makes sense also in the context of the unincorporated status of H. Kempner and the unlimited liability of the trust shareholders. Prudence on Ike's part was warranted. In its absence the threats to family cohesion could multiply.

Ike never concealed H. Kempner's acquisition of majority shares

24. Guidry, "Twisted Threads," chap. 2, passim.

in the Lighter firm. As private banker to his associates, Ike was following prudent contemporary lending practices in taking physical possession of the borrowers' assets as security. The spinners' lawsuits themselves suggest that the association hardly gave H. Kempner effective control over Lighter and that the association with Nussbaum was a personal joint venture, not a joining of entities. Nussbaum and Lighter gained no place on the board of the then-new H. Kempner Trust which in 1920 Ike was perfecting in order to keep strangers out, not to get Nussbaum and/or Lighter in.

Last in this catalog of alleged faults, Ike signed on with Nussbaum/Lighter in his own name rather than as H. Kempner. Was he apprehending exposable irregularities or illegal activity and so by this flimsy disguise trying to shield the pooled family assets? Or was the personality of Ike's signature so well known in the trade as the equivalent of H. Kempner as to make the fact of which one he used of no substantial significance?

It may well have been the latter. Even "in 1957 when A. M. Alpert joined H. Kempner as office manager, everyone [on the staff still] signed checks and letters as 'H. Kempner,'" Alpert noted. The "bold signature 'H. Kempner'" was known and respected in cotton and banking circles nationally and internationally, but the senior Kempners simply had to delegate authority to trusted subordinates to subscribe the firm's name in order to keep the unending, sometimes tumultuous paper flow moving.[25]

Perhaps Ike used his own name (though on H. Kempner stationery) to retain more confidentiality about this venture even with respect to his longtime office staff than he or Dan usually sought. Or, equally possible from the evidence, Ike was merely behaving idiosyncratically. What is certain is that he shared information about the venture with the H. Kempner Trust's board, if only because he had to. Neither he nor any of his siblings then had "venture capital outside the [H. Kempner] firm," recalled Ike's son. None of them "made an outside investment without putting it up to the firm [i.e., H. Kempner] first." In short, Ike, extending H. Kempner capital to Nussbaum/Lighter over his own signature, *was* H. Kempner so far as the com-

25. A. M. Alpert, letter to Leonora K, Thompson, undated (ca. July, 1988), copy supplied to author by Mrs. Thompson.

mon understanding of the family and business community was concerned.[26] No veiling could have succeeded anywhere in the global cotton or banking patches even had it been intended.

The Spinners' Litigations

As usual, Ike tried to avoid lawsuits. In 1926 Galveston lawyer John Neethe, long the Kempners' local counsel, in company with Lighter toured Germany and France to confer with defaulting spinners.[27] Encountering a "united front" by the defaulters against specific performance within one year of executing the contract, Neethe recommended to the Kempners that "avoidance of litigation" was advisable. The Americans successfully proposed to the spinners a mutual extension of the one-year delivery stipulation to five years. But within a year the European spinners were again evading commitments under the extended contracts. Then Dan, with Harris and Neethe in tow, retraced the would-be mediation circuit across Germany and France.

After one unfruitful tour, the Americans found themselves on the same westering steamship as the American ambassador to France, Myron T. Herrick, himself a prominent lawyer-banker-diplomat with special competence in private international debt settlements. Along with the American ambassador to Germany, Fred Sackett, and every relevant United States commercial attaché and legal counselor, Herrick had already advised Dan to sue the defaulting spinners. Now the ambassador, according to Dan, "promised immediate attention to these claims on his return to France."

But once the Kempners went to court in France, even American ambassadors proved to be unable to spur the French courts' glacial pace, especially when the plaintiffs were foreigners. Herrick died in 1929. A decade later Dan offered this estimate of French justice: "Political influences in France have so delayed the French suits that ten years have elapsed without final decision in any one case." Meanwhile

26. For example, about the time of these events (1925), Lee brought to an H. Kempner board lunch meeting "a proposal to join in the establishment of the first movie chain in Texas, which we turned down, but in which he invested personally because we had already turned it down, which was of course very wise of him as it was very profitable" (H. L. Kempner, interview with L. Marchiafava, Aug. 1, 1980, RLA).

27. On Neethe, see Resolution, Nov. 27, 1907, Box 3M225, Cohen Papers.

Nazi Germany had reannexed the Alsace-Lorraine provinces, where all the French spinning mills were located.[28]

Ike remained reluctant to initiate suits. At his request Dan had assumed charge of everything concerning the spinners. Germany remained the major arena for the spinners' lawsuits. Dan and Ike pored over the recommendations for specific resident attorneys provided by American diplomats and colleagues in cotton. Dan hired as lawyer in Germany the diplomats' choice, Alexander Lifshutz of Bremen.[29] Endlessly optimistic and energetic, Lifshutz had a fine reputation among European lawyers, but he was not a specialist in commodities litigations. By his own wishes Lifshutz agreed to represent H. Kempner on a contingency basis, with expenses to be paid by the client.

Among the earliest lawsuits blossoming on the dockets of German courts beginning in 1925, one by Kempner against the defaulting spinner George Hochgreve set a pattern. At Lifshutz's instruction, Dan collected statements from America's leading cotton dealers such as Anderson Clayton and officers of the major cotton exchanges, supporting the Kempner position that the contested conversion contracts were for actual deliveries of the commodity, not for gambling speculations.[30] Hochgreve provided a grim resolution. Claiming to have been swindled himself, in May, 1929, he committed suicide. A German court thereafter awarded Kempner a $7,000 settlement from Hochgreve's estate. Far from reflecting the size of the Texans' claims, the award was an arbitrary share to creditors of the estate's assets. H. Kempner lost something like $115,000. But it had won the verdict, and perhaps this victory influenced Ike and Dan to persevere with other delinquents.[31]

Another German spinner, Otto Schoen, had become desperate and defaulted. Kempner's lawsuit against him involved details similar to Hochgreve's until Hapke appeared as witness for Schoen. Lifshutz tried to get German cotton brokers to testify on behalf of his clients. But many were connected with Schoen or Hapke, and none appeared.[32]

In mid-1929 Schoen won the verdict, then, six months later, an appeal. Dan authorized still another appeal, to Germany's highest court

28. Deposition by Dan Kempner, Mar. 1, 1941.
29. IHK, letter to Tom Connally, Jan. 13, 1931.
30. In ibid., Ike summarized the early legal maneuvering to Sen. Connally.
31. On the verdict, Guidry, "Twisted Threads," pp. 69–88.
32. Ibid., pp. 94–101.

(the Reichsgericht). In late 1930 its decision sustained those of the lower courts. The Kempners were out over $260,000 in futures losses and $22,000 in direct court costs, and other lawsuits impended.[33]

Perhaps the Kempners took some minor comfort from the vociferous but ineffective protests against the Schoen verdicts by Germans in the trade and Americans as well. Somewhat tardily from the Kempners' viewpoint, the German cotton trade journal editorialized that conversion contracts were indeed genuine transactions with an insurance feature, not gambling or speculation, and that the German courts were relegating the industry to medieval warehousing procedures. Similar statements issued from European and American chambers of commerce, cotton exchanges, and the American Bankers Association.[34] U.S. secretary of state Henry L. Stimson instructed Ambassador Sackett to protest the Schoen decisions through diplomatic channels, and Texas senator Connally criticized the German high court's ruling as imposing harsher standards of proof on alien plaintiffs than on native litigants, an argument that Ike had carefully spelled out to the senator after prior coaching from Lifshutz, one to which other German judges awarded seals of merit. The Schoen decision did violate standards of international comity that American courts had sustained by enforcing rules of the Bremen Cotton Exchange against U.S. citizens, for example.[35]

Every German cotton exchange and those abroad stripped Schoen of membership. Unable to purchase cotton, he closed his mill. Opening another, Schoen found German lending sources closed to him. Bankrupted, like Hochgreve he chose suicide. And so, by the end of 1931, the spinners' litigations had already cost two lives, several careers, and almost $400,000 of the Kempners' money.[36]

The Transaction Slips

Here a digression is necessary. Sometime in the early 1930s Ike and Dan became aware that their firm's reputation was in trouble as a result of the spinners' litigations. Rumors circulated in European cot-

33. Ibid., pp. 94–105.
34. *Textil Zeitung*, Nov. 15, 1930, cited in ibid.
35. IHK, letter to Tom Connally, Jan. 13, 1931; see Birge-Forbes *v.* Heye, 251 U.S. 317 (1920); *New York Times*, Jan. 30, 1930.
36. Guidry, "Twisted Threads," pp. 101–105.

ton centers that the quality and quantity of Kempner shipments were questionable. Thereupon collections slipped or ended from other spinners. Like Schoen, the delinquent spinners retorted to Kempner calls for payment that the disputed contracts were illegal or unenforceable and demanded proofs from H. Kempner's books of the actual grade and volume of cotton shipped to each spinner. These not forthcoming, the spinners would repudiate their contracts.[37]

Thus the question of physical evidence of contract execution became central. Had Lighter/Nussbaum sent short shipments but allowed central bookkeeper H. Kempner to charge for full ones? If so, was H. Kempner a dupe or co-conspirator?

A considered response focuses on Dan. He refused to send H. Kempner books for audit, arguing the impropriety of hazarding the interests of uninvolved clients. Instead Dan agreed to supply the original transaction certificates or slips. These, filed at the New York Exchange, confirmed the actual volume of H. Kempner's cotton shipments.

Would Dan have requested the exchange to supply the certificates if he knew that they revealed shortages? Exchange officials, however, concurring with the Kempners that the word of reputable dealers sufficed in normal trade practice, decided that they would provide the certificates only in instances of formal complaints lodged in the exchange against a member. The German spinners preferred lawsuits in Germany to complaints in America.[38]

Thereupon H. Kempner clerks began the huge, wearying task of searching tons of company files for the in-house copies of confirmation slips on futures trades. H. Kempner sold to many middlemen. Confirmation slips did not indicate the spinner being served. But if the slips' totals during a sales period equaled the Lighter/Nussbaum shipments to spinners, a presumption of adequate authentication seemed reasonable. Dan also asked other merchants from whom H. Kempner had supplemented supplies of the commodity to search their files, at H. Kempner's expense, for relevant records. Much, but not all, was recovered.

Although H. Kempner was famous for meticulous bookkeeping, in that preelectronic time easy or quick data retrieval in the cotton industry did not exist. It was almost never needed. Warehouses were

37. Ibid., pp. 104–19.
38. Ibid., pp. 119, 172–73.

full of largely unindexed $3 \times 5''$ confirmation slips. Until Dan started his search through them the industry had contented itself with derivative ledger entries.

Dan's search for these slips was either an honest one confirming the view that "finding one, or even several, slips was a nearly impossible, task," or a sham.[39] The latter charge derives weight from Lighter's use of H. Kempner letterheads bearing Dan's coded symbol, to create, and, by implication, to alter copies of transactions. But Dan apparently never used these blanks for any purpose. The idea for the letterheads appears to have been Lighter's, who was developing a reputation for instability. Odds are that Dan simply stored the unused bogus blank forms. Thereafter, Dan and Ike began to disassociate from Lighter, and in 1928, completing the severance, assumed all interests in the spinners' contracts. For the first time in a decade they were free of Lighter's erratic ways, and so, though mistakenly, felt less vulnerable.[40]

Back to German Courts

Meanwhile lawyers for the European spinners argued that Kempner/Lighter/Nussbaum never intended to send all the promised cotton, and thus would not produce the transaction slips. The Americans held that the spinners never intended to pay. Convinced that German courts would void any contract in "any business in which a taint of gambling is in evidence," Dan proposed to settle with the spinners. Encouraged by Hapke's inside information about his former principals in America, the spinners refused the tender.

Dan also told Ike that H. Kempner should abandon the claims against the spinners, swallow its losses, and avoid similar entanglements, arguments he repeated often but fruitlessly during the next quarter century. Ike refused. Deferring to Ike, Dan asked Texas congressional representatives to delay releasing German properties America had seized in World War I until the spinners settled, but this effort failed.[41] Nevertheless, perhaps because of Lighter's exit, the Kempners exhibited new steadfastness. So did the spinners.

39. Ibid., p. 121.

40. Ibid., pp. 119–23, offers alternative interpretations, and pp. 123–34, full details.

41. Ibid., pp. 127–30.

None of the latter paid when in March, 1928, the Kempners' lawyer in Germany demanded that delinquents settle all debts or face suits. Whereupon the Kempners sued the Kolbermoor and Stadtbach companies. Encouraged by Schoen's victory in the Reichsgericht, the defendants stressed the gambling defense and the Kempners' delay in supplying transaction slips. But Schoen's subsequent suicide weakened the spinners' gambling defense.

Begun in 1928, the suit against the Kolbermoor mill was for $160,000 plus interest. The defense lawyer stated that Lighter/Nussbaum (and H. Kempner as holder in due course of their interests) did know or should have known of their agents' gambling purposes. H. Kempner's lawyer argued the plaintiff's innocence of illicit intent or procedural negligence. Kolbermoor executives, not the Americans, had intended to defraud, Lifshutz insisted.[42]

Kolbermoor won in both lower and intermediate German appeals courts. Nevertheless, the opinion, if not the verdict, in the latter encouraged the Kempners. It was that conversion contracts were legal in Germany if any commodity exchange recognized them.

Dan agreed to appeal the case to the Reichsgericht, a step requiring H. Kempner, as an alien in Germany, to post a $20,000 bond, a peculiarly heavy burden at the time. Losses in Germany were adding to the depression's effects at home.[43] The recourse to the Reichsgericht seemed justified, however, by two remandings (in 1931 and 1933) of the case back to the intermediate (Oberlandesgericht) court.

Other German spinners wearied the Kempners by at last filing complaints against them in the New York Exchange. One account concluded that Ike responded (on March 23, 1931) reluctantly to complaints concerning H. Kempner's relationships with Lighter and Nussbaum with "a mixture of obfuscation, half-truth, and outright falsehood."[44] This conclusion, however, derives partially from Ike's withholding of in-house information until the exchange officers promised not to divulge it to the German spinners who, Ike argued, were on a self-serving fishing expedition. The exchange officials agreed with him.

Whereupon Ike supplied them with lists of transactions. Some

42. Ibid., pp. 134–36; pp. 143–46 summarize Lifshutz's report on Lighter-Nussbaum *v.* Kolbermoor, in Kempner Papers.

43. Guidry, "Twisted Threads," pp. 143–48.

44. Ibid., p. 152.

were fictitious, the same critic charged, conceived to cover collusive, substandard, and/or short deliveries to the foreign spinners, and mere speculations. But the exchange's investigating committee members, each a veteran cotton marketer, concluded that H. Kempner "has made a full and satisfactory reply to the matters under investigation; . . . the committee therefore considers the investigation closed."

Nevertheless Ike failed in informal efforts to get from the exchange board a public exoneration of H. Kempner from any unethical or improper conduct. Perhaps this failure meant that the exchange officers, though allegedly an "old boy" network, nevertheless believed the Kempners to be tarred. Perhaps, too, the Kempners' controversy with the spinners involved shadowy practices common among depression-plagued exchange members, who therefore cleared H. Kempner of the technical charges and declined to provide the requested exoneration.[45]

The evidence sustains many possibilities, but that of the Kempners' essential rectitude in unprecedented situations is enhanced by the favorable 1931–32 decisions of the Oberlandesgericht and the Reichsgericht, respectively, in the suit against the Stadtbach spinning firm. Both decisions registered that the conversion contracts were not gambling and that tangible proofs of the Kempners' meticulous execution of the contracts exceeded the industry's norms. Whereupon, if only to act within Germany's four-year statute of limitations, the Kempners initiated suits against six other spinner firms: Bayerlein, Forchheim, Hornschuch, Kuchen, Kulmbacher, and Leuze.

By this time the Nazis ruled Germany. The spinners' lawyers immediately tied up $55,000 of H. Kempner's cash by having the German government rule that required bonds must be in hard currency, not the usual form of commodity certificates. Further, the spinners got their government to apply new prohibitions against the exportation of any damages the Kempners might win, and had the court disbar Lifschutz, the Kempners' lawyer, as a Jew, by terms of the April, 1933, "Hitler Decree," thus unsettling the Texans' legal operations.[46]

Ike and Dan again prodded Texas congressmen. Pressured in turn,

45. Ibid., p. 115, and see pp. 151–54, 156; *Galveston News*, July 12, 1931.

46. Guidry, "Twisted Threads," pp. 156–60. Lifshutz's maternal grandmother was Jewish, but he was a Lutheran. His firm continued to act for the Kempners, with Dan supplying a stipend after the lawyer's disbarment.

Secretary of State Cordell Hull ordered the American ambassador to Germany, Lawrence Groves, to protest against the effects of the Hitler Decree not only on the litigating Americans but on all cotton exporters to Germany, many of whom were Jews and/or whose German representatives were Jews. These protests were futile. In mid-December, 1933, Kolbermoor and Dan settled that suit out of court. H. Kempner was to receive $90,000 (U.S.) and pay its own lawyers' fees and court costs.[47] But the Texans did not yet appreciate the obstacles building in Germany against Jews.

They learned. In 1933, revisiting France and Germany soon after the favorable outcome of this suit, now in company with nephew Harris, Dan, fearful of the barely hidden anti-Semitism of French officials and the overt anti-Semitism of the German, asked the State Department for a document "that would permit me to travel in Germany and France without molestation." Then Dan received a happy wire from Galveston: The Austrian spinners had settled the Texans' claims. But a second, drearier wire followed: The Austrian government, already tending toward policies espoused by Germany, had forbidden the export of capital.[48] The next year, in Germany once more, Dan met with both American ambassador Sackett and the head of the German Divisenstelle (Exchange Control Bureau), a Dr. Hartenstein. The latter arranged to have the agreed amount of marks transferred to the Guaranty Trust Company in New York, and, according to Dan, promised that in the event of future verdicts favoring the Kempners, dollar-mark transfers would be made in the same manner. Favorable verdicts followed. The money did not.

Collecting on Judgments

In Nazi Germany's escalatingly anti-Jewish environment, the Kempners found that collections were as difficult as winning judgments. The Nazi's Finanzamt agency generally disregarded the legal rights of alien owners of property in Germany, especially of Jewish aliens. If issued, the funds commonly took the form of a fiat currency usable only in Germany. The economics ministry created a confusing spec-

47. Ibid., pp. 160–65.

48. DWK, letter to U.S. senator M. Sheppard, June 30, 1933. It and all telegrams are in files 26 and 27, Box 46, #80-002, Kempner Papers.

trum of fiat currencies including "blocked credit marks," applicable to export-import businesses. This scrip depreciated quickly abroad but alien creditors had to accept it as legal tender. German law also forbade the export of capital, so that victors in lawsuits had either to invest the awards in Germany or somehow get what hard money they could to safer havens.[49]

The State Department got the Kempners the privilege of using 170,000 blocked marks for legal expenses in Germany and to export 10,000 marks a month—but only for three months. Thereafter a new application leading to another round in the slow administrative process was required. In early 1934 the Kuchen spinning firm settled with the Kempners, adding more blocked marks to the unusable mass. Not yet fully aware of how limited and sporadic the flow of money from Germany would be, Dan contracted to sell 110,000 of his firm's *Sperrmarks* (i.e., German funds obtained from judicial verdicts or settlements) at heavy discounts to an American bank, which resold the marks. Unable to lever the promised marks out of Germany, the Kempners themselves supplied the U.S. equivalent, $16,000, to the bank.[50]

Then in 1937 Dan revisited Germany. The American ambassador arranged an interview for him with Hjalmar Schacht, Hitler's economics minister and Reichsbank president. Schacht agreed that the Texans "had been shamefully treated both by the Spinners and by the Divisenstelle," Dan stated, "and that he would endeavor to see that . . . [the Americans] would receive the preferential treatment theretofore promised by Dr. Hartenstein."[51]

The Germans were playing cruel cat-and-mouse games with claimants like the Kempners. They belatedly understood their own essential helplessness but kept struggling. Responding to events in Germany, the Kempners settled claims against Kuchen (1936), Forchheim (1938), and Leuze (1939). The Reichsgericht decided against the Kempners in two: Hornschuch (1934) and Bayerlein (1936), and favorably in the suit against Kulmbacher (1938). Four suits (against Bourcart, Jacquel, Keiner, and Marchal) pended when, in September, 1939, World War II began.

Probably the Kempners lost the Hornschuch and Bayerlein litiga-

49. Guidry, "Twisted Threads," pp. 175–79; Hamburger, *How Nazi Germany Has Controlled Business*, pp. 99–101.

50. Guidry, "Twisted Threads," pp. 179–90, 196.

51. Deposition by Dan Kempner, Mar. 4, 1941.

tions because the spinners testified self-servingly that they had entered into the conversion contracts in order to gamble. German judges concluded that the spinners' intention tarred the Kempners with the gambling brush and that the Americans deserved to lose the total amount of at least $150,000 involved.[52]

Happier for the Kempners, after seven years of suing, the Reichsgericht held in the Kulmbacher suit that gambling had not motivated these contracts, that H. Kempner need not produce those vexing transaction slips, and that Kempner deserved roughly $210,000 plus interest from 1930. But the mark had deteriorated greatly since the decade's beginning. Dan initiated an appeal for the real difference. Kulmbacher settled, adding more than $25,000, perhaps $40,000 less than the court's award, in dollars. Predictable legal fees made more litigation unwise, Dan and Ike decided, and, accepting Kulmbacher's offer, they closed that file—they thought. They settled also with the Kuchen, Forchheim, and Leuze firms, losing a total of approximately $1.2 million.[53]

From late 1934 until the outbreak of World War II in 1939, Dan, trying to get the blocked funds out of Germany, had explored complex conduits in Italy, the Vatican, Albania, and Holland. All fell through. The efforts kept Dan, Ike, and Harris shuttling between Galveston, Washington, and Europe in the late 1930s and even in early 1940, the period of United States neutrality in the conflict. Dan described one such visit to Germany in April, 1938:

> Dr. Schacht recalled his conversations and promises of the previous year, but stated that he had been shorn of most of his powers and was "not as big a man as he was the year before"; that he was no longer Minister of Economics, but simply Reichsbank President; that he had been unable to accomplish the promises that had been made because of the opposition of his successor as Economics Minister, Dr. Walter Funk, but that he would arrange a meeting with Dr. Funk or Dr. Brinkman, then head of the Divisenstelle. Dr. Schacht at this meeting again repeated his statement that Lighter and Nussbaum had been shamefully treated, and used the German term "Du arme Kerl," the equivalent of "you poor devil" in speaking to Mr. Kempner.[54]

52. Guidry, "Twisted Threads," p. 171, 172.
53. Ibid., pp. 172–73.
54. Deposition by Dan Kempner, Aug. 8, 1941, DWK folder, Box IHK (1953), #80-002, Kempner Papers.

The Kempners asked to see the new head of the economics ministry, Dr. Landwehr. He surprised the American party, which included Robert Stephenson, the American commercial attaché and a personal friend of Dan, by becoming "very abusive of the United States and its policies" because of a recent unofficial boycott of German goods at home especially popular among American Jews. "Mr. Kempner," Landwehr stated to Dan, "if you lived in the Argentine, you would have had your money before this, but as a citizen of the United States of America we will do nothing for you." Stephenson "showed extreme surprise at such statements, and asked Mr. Kempner to immediately return with him to the Embassy and verify such statements to the Ambassador. This was done."[55] But this and Dan's additional trips overseas were fruitless.

Confiscated Assets

The outbreak of war in Europe opened an opportunity for the Kempners partially and incompletely to redress matters at home. In December, 1939, learning that a British cruiser in the Caribbean had chased into a Florida port a German freighter, the *Arauca*, laden with sugar bought from the Kempners' own Imperial refinery, the Kempners, who had an earlier unsatisfied claim against the freighter's owners, filed suit against the owners in a federal court in Fort Lauderdale. Their swift moves lifted morale on the Strand, irritated German authorities, and eventually brought in some money.[56] But the amount hardly redressed losses from the spinners' defaults.

During the remainder of World War II the German and French governments suspended the processes in which the Kempners' claims were involved. Whereupon the Texans turned attention to German assets the United States had seized in World War I, since held in a German Special Deposit Account (GSDA), controlled by the Alien Property Custodian.

Washington lawyers Carl von Zielinski and Harold Aron specialized in pressing Americans' claims to restitution from GSDA funds.

55. Ibid. On Stephenson, see D. W. Kempner, letter to Rabbi Cohen, Dec. 14, 1938, Box 3M371, Cohen Papers.

56. *Houston Post*, Dec. 21, 1939. Seeking approximately thirty-seven thousand dollars, the attachment, or "libel," eventually brought Imperial Sugar that sum, minus costs. See DWK Scrapbook, vol. III, Kempner Papers.

In 1941 the H. Kempner Trust became their clients, on a mixed fee–plus–contingency basis. A special relief bill in Congress was the best tactic for the Kempner claim, the attorneys advised, a recourse involving more lobbying than litigating. Congress had first to restore GSDA funds (the Kempner claim alone was for more than $1.8 million) and in this the State Department's support was essential. Meanwhile the lawyers explored complex alternatives.[57]

One option involved the assumption of H. Kempner of a Philippine cigar manufacturer's claims against the United States in exchange for the latter's assumption of the Texans' claims against Germany. The Asian cigar maker, another client of Aron's, had supplied Admiral Dewey's wardrooms with cheroots in 1898, and thereafter sought payment from the United States without success. Aron believed further that $1.2 million in the GSDA never belonged there, for it was the Kaiser's "spy money," not businessmen's assets. He wanted it paid directly to the Kempners, who would then turn over to the cigar manufacturer all the Texans' claims to blocked funds in Germany plus proceeds from future claims. No American funds would be involved, and other claimants for impounded German funds were not bypassed.

Following Aron's script, in August, 1941, Dan saw the secretary of commerce, fellow Texan Jesse Jones:

> He tried to rush me, but at our request agreed to telephone Under Secretary [of State] Sumner Welles that he knew Kempner, that [H.] Kempner was an honorable and upright firm, and that when this matter came to the State Department he would appreciate Welles giving it serious consideration. Jones also . . . [had Dan see] Daniel W. Bell, Under Secretary of the Treasury. . . . Bell . . . was responsible for having wrongly, as we claim, put these ["spy money"] funds into the German Special Deposit Account, and was expected to resist any request on our part to restore this money to the Undisclosed Enemy Account. . . . [Bell] . . . did show resistance to this, and further stated that the Undisclosed Enemy Account had only a few hundred [thousand?] dollars remaining. Aron says that . . . there is a million or more dollars in the fund. We saw [Senator] Connally. . . . He seemed to shy off from the problem, fearing that Congress might consider that a special favor was being shown to

57. Harold G. Aron, counsel, "Memorandum in Support of S. 1072, 81 Cong., 1st sess., for the Relief of the Trust Association of H. Kempner, July 5, 1950." Copy in Kempner Papers.

> Kempner, and money that properly belonged to other claimants . . . would be used. Connally finally said to Aron "You seem to know your way around, so get the State Department and Treasury Department to agree to a bill and I will consider offering it." . . . I saw . . . Lyndon Johnson . . . but made no special mention of the matter . . . , stating that it had not yet advanced far enough. . . .[58]

But the scheme floundered. Secretary of State Hull opposed it, alleging the unavailability of evidence from Germany. Thereafter matters lagged until, in May, 1944, Senator Connally introduced a relief bill in favor of H. Kempner. But he did so only in a "by request" mode indicating that Connally, though the bill's sponsor, was not invoking Senate privilege, that is, deference to him in a home state matter. The bill died in committee.

In 1945–46 another such relief bill survived the committee and passed unanimously in both houses of Congress. It followed Aron's idea of a trade of funds with the Philippine cigar maker. "I am going to see LBJ sometime this week," Herb advised his father in April, 1945, a happy time of visible military success in Europe: "The man who could really help me, perhaps, more than anybody else is Big Jesse [Jones]." But Connally proved to be a more useful ally for the Kempners. For the first time in his long career Connally specifically asked the president to sign a bill. Celebrations in Galveston proved to be premature, however. Probably advised by Hull and Bell, President Harry Truman unexpectedly vetoed the bill, criticizing its contrived connection between the Philippine cigar maker and the Kempners and the fact that the Texans initiated their claim too late to qualify under terms of the 1917 Trading with the Enemy Act.[59]

Senator Connally attributed Truman's veto to the opposition of the State Department.[60] Other, successful corporate claimants on the GSDA funds, including Standard Oil, International Harvester, and the Chase National Bank, had joined in a formal association to press

58. Deposition by Dan Kempner, Aug. 8, 1941.

59. Herb Kempner, letter to IHK, Apr. 12, 1945, folder 16, "I. H. Kempner, Jr.," #80-002, Kempner Papers; Guidry, "Twisted Threads," pp. 203–208; veto in *Congressional Record*, Aug. 12, 1946, App. p. A5252.

60. Connally, telegram to D. W. Kempner, Aug. 12, 1946, in DWK Scrapbook, 1945–1948; Dan Kempner, telegram to Sara Weston, same date, Sara Weston file, Personal Letters, #80-002, Kempner Papers; *New York Tribune*, Aug. 10, 1946.

their claims, and judgments in their favor were depleting the GSDA. The Kempners had no such allies.

They were encouraged again, however, when in mid-1948 Truman approved a bill creating a World War II compensation fund like its World War I predecessor, but far larger. In late February, 1949, for the fourth time, Senator Connally introduced a private bill favoring the Kempners' claim. Upon request of the Senate Judiciary Committee, the Justice Department commented on the claim, and, to the Kempners' distress, unfavorably. The government should reject it, the government lawyer wrote, because it bypassed the federal Court of Claims. Whereupon the Judiciary Committee tabled Connally's bill.

Dan was ready to quit. But Aron had worked without fee (H. Kempner paying his expenses) for more than fifteen years on H. Kempner's behalf, and urged further effort. Dan agreed to let the lawyer push on. In 1950, with avowedly pro-business President Dwight Eisenhower in office, the auguries appeared brighter.[61] Ike and Dan lent themselves to lobbying as never before. At their request business associates nationwide supported the Kempners' cause with home congressmen while the Texans concentrated on their own state's delegation. The tactics worked in the House, where a relief bill passed in mid-February, 1953.

But it stalled in the Senate. There Sen. Lyndon Johnson praised the family publicly but admitted privately that their concentration on this issue wearied him. Worse, their attorney irritated the temperamental Texas senator. Aron, Johnson groused to Dan in late March, 1954, "knows more about how I ought to run my office than I do. If the effect he [Aron] has on the other Senators is the same as he has on me, then I don't think you are going to get a very sympathetic hearing."[62]

Nevertheless, Johnson helped to guide a Kempner relief bill through the Senate despite adverse lobbying by Dean Acheson. A former secretary of state in Truman's cabinet and now a prominent Washington attorney, Acheson, Dan wrote to Texas governor Allan Shivers, "had an interest contrary to ours in the funds from which we are seeking reimbursement."

61. Aron, "Memorandum in Support."

62. Quotation in Guidry, "Twisted Threads," p. 213, and see pp. 203–13; IHK, *Recalled Recollections*, p. 99.

Acheson was reinforced by Attorney General Herbert Brownell, who echoed to the president the negative views of his predecessor. Anticipating Brownell's position, Dan had tried to swerve him. "Who in Houston knows Herbert Brownell very well?" Dan had inquired earlier of his nephew, Ike's son Herbert, by now president of Imperial Sugar: "We are not seeking influence peddling [but only] an opportunity to explain the situation."[63]

But though in early October, 1954, the Kempner relief bill passed the Senate, was harmonized with the House version, and went on to the White House, on October 13 Eisenhower vetoed it, basically for the same reasons that had inspired Truman's veto.[64]

And so ended the sapping litigations, endless negotiations, and fruitless legislation. During three-plus decades, the spinners' controversies so occupied the senior Kempner men that, year after year, on every working day they generated an average of five pages of interoffice and external correspondence on this frustrating topic plus unrecorded telephone calls and mealtime and corridor conversation. These vexing matters had consumed more than thirty-five of Dan Kempner's seventy-nine years. He was to die two years after the Eisenhower veto. Although involved in the successes of the close-to-home M&P and Imperial Sugar/Sugar Land ventures, in the spinners' controversies more than any other Kempner venture Dan "managed" a major family failure. Ike, however, always accepted primary responsibility, writing later about his own "poor judgment" and "folly" both in negotiating the spinners' contracts and in persisting in the lawsuits.[65]

63. D. W. Kempner, letter to Shivers, Sept. 1, 1945, Parten-Swann file, and Dan, letter to Herb Kempner, Mar. 9, 1953, DWK folder, Box IHK (1953), both Kempner Papers.

64. Guidry, "Twisted Threads," p. 214, and see IHK, *Recalled Recollections*, pp. 111–12.

65. IHK, *Recalled Recollections*, pp. 45, 111–12, and see Guidry, "Twisted Threads," pp. 221–24.

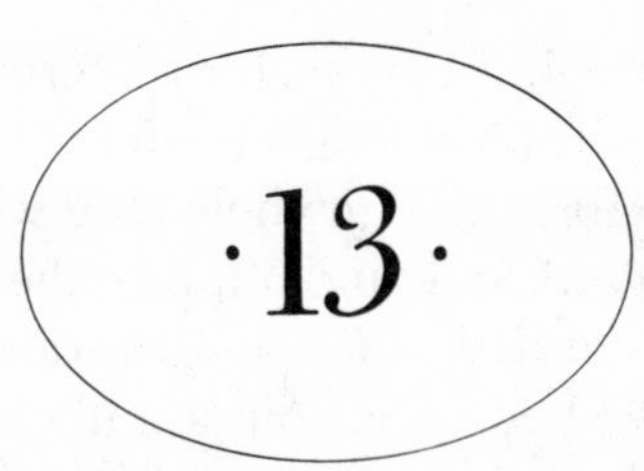

The Kempner Conglomerate

STABILIZATION of the family's legal and religious situations in 1919–20 occurred none too soon. By the early 1920s all the younger Kempner brothers were back from war and as committed as Eliza and Ike to family cohesion. Upon completing their formal educations in the late 1920s and early 1930s, Ike's sons Harris and Herbert would join their father and uncles in adjusting H. Kempner businesses to conditions of peace, newer technologies, and modes of competition. Unlike the ill-fated cotton conversion contracts, this search for newer ways evoked constructive responses to hazards and opportunities.

Wealth continued to swell the undivided estate. In 1927 H. Kempner's "capital and surplus" was approximately $5.7 million. As always with the firm, this estimate was based on very conservative below-market valuations. Ten years later, despite global depression and market upsets caused by the lengthening shadows of totalitarian military and trade policies, H. Kempner's "book value" would rise to $7.1 million, while distributions to shareholders were kept at "barely 1%."[1]

Ike continued efforts to transform the cotton factorage he inherited into a cotton merchant operation. It sustained in turn increasingly diverse family-owned businesses and investments, and they also fed profits into the capital pool. For a happy while H. Kempner's profits came easily. Goods-hungry consumers here and abroad bid for America's cotton and sugar. But the removal of wartime regulations also created volatile oscillations in commodity prices. Those for cotton soared; for sugar, they plummeted in a brief period from twenty cents per pound to less than two.

1. "Keys Report, 1964" (manuscript), Kempner Papers, p. 7.

Imperial Sugar, Sugar Land, and The Industries

Alert competitors smelled trouble for Imperial in sugar's descending price. Could Imperial survive the effort to modernize its antiquated machinery, reform the unwholesome working and community conditions at Sugar Land, and improve the inefficient, unstable labor force? Gossip had it that Ike and Eldridge were at odds, because in 1920 Imperial had to pay out a million-dollar judgment in a lawsuit caused by the failure of Eldrige's chief assistant to keep up with the wildly swinging sugar prices, thereby committing Imperial to contracts "with too-broad terms," Harris recalled sadly. This adverse verdict "hurt like fury," he remembered vividly sixty years later. In order to cover the judgment Kempner and Eldridge had to sell Sugar Land oil lands and the farm railroad. To balance, the painful episode confirmed for the Kempners the wisdom of having chosen for Galveston the Massachusetts trust form that was already serving them in Sugar Land.[2]

In the late 1920s promoters announced plans to construct a competing up-to-the-technological-minute sugar refinery on Galveston Island, an industrial development of a sort Ike loved to see there. Planners for the Island City firm hired away from Imperial a promising young production line supervisor. Eldridge wanted Imperial to outbid the salary offer that had levered this able employee from Sugar Land. Ike discouraged the effort. Later encountering the former Imperial worker on Galveston's seawall, Ike asked why H. Kempner had not been solicited to invest in the competing refinery. Replying, the former Sugar Lander predicted that the "Galveston refinery would put . . . [Imperial] out of business." Unnettled, Ike subscribed for twenty-five thousand dollars' worth of the new company's shares, once they were issued, "and said that he was doing it for Galveston and not for . . . [H.] Kempner."[3] But the Galveston refinery was never built; its shares were never issued.

Having thus satisfied his sense of responsibility to encourage Island

2. HLK, "Beneficiary Interest Report, 1963" (manuscript), Kempner Papers, p. 4; H. L. Kempner, interview with B. Guidry, Aug. 6, 1982, RLA; "Keys Report," p. 4.

3. R. M. Armstrong, "History of Sugar Land, Texas, and Imperial Sugar Company, and Sugar Land Industries" (draft manuscript, 1986; privately held), I [7]; R. M. Armstrong, interview with author, July 14, 1988.

City industry, Ike saw to it also that Sugar Land, a community that was becoming his "other city" as it were, and Imperial Sugar, its economic reason for being, fought back against a competitor that did come into being in Texas City, up the Houston Ship Channel. After seven years of intense competition with Imperial, the new sugar plant was shuttered. Imperial and Sugar Land survived because Ike and Eldridge had decided not "to rock along just as they were [before World War I]," in the phrase of a rising Imperial manager.[4]

Indeed not. Instead, the partners had been planning for further improvements to both refinery and community once peace broke out. The 1919 adverse court judgment caused by Eldrige's slipshod assistant delayed the initiation of these plans. Meanwhile, costs were rising in the wake of the Armistice. Leased convict labor was no longer lawful, and Imperial's payroll necessarily fattened. To balance, Imperial's work force was already more efficient than in convict-cursed years. Once Ike and Eldridge further enlarged and modernized the refinery in a manner to make it the state's most efficient as well as largest, Imperial produced sugar at a profit even while the price of refined sugar was decreasing so sharply.

In 1919, despite the costs of the continuing improvements to refinery and community, Imperial showed a net profit of $478,000 and in 1920, $1,863,000. By 1920 Imperial's refining capacity was one million pounds daily. It shipped out thirty-five carloads of near 100 percent refined sugar each day, each carload weighing thirty thousand pounds. Meanwhile carloads of raw sugar from external sources unloaded at Galveston's wharves for transshipment to Sugar Land, thus feeding the economy of the Island City. And so these lures drew the Kempners and Eldridge to improve still further the Imperial refinery far beyond regional standards.[5]

In 1924 they drew up a plan "to increase refined sugar production by 50 %, from 1,000,000 pounds per day to 1,500,000 pounds per day." To cost more than $1.5 million over the next three years, the plan initiated further improvements, including an eight-story brick "char filter house" and almost equally huge satellite buildings for additional boiling pans, warehousing, packaging, and shipping. Connecting every-

4. Johnson, "A Short History of the Sugar Industry in Texas," *Texas Gulf Coast Historical Association Publications*, pp. 71–72; Armstrong, "History," II [5].
5. Armstrong, "History," II [4–56].

thing, mechanized conveyor belts stacked the daily output of refined sugar in layers of hundred-pound sacks forty-two feet high, ready for shipping when taken on other belts to the improved freight yard and rail spur. Alert Imperial executives toured the plant frequently and allowed little waste at any step in the process.[6] It all paid off in terms of industrial production. What of the human environment?

The Company Town

When, forty years after the Armistice, Ike was asked to sketch the lifetime accomplishments of which he was proudest, he stressed not his "civic and business connections or . . . my career with Imperial." He said instead, "I have in mind such things as . . . the building of new [owner-occupied] homes on attractive sites that is taking place at Sugar Land, [and] the expense . . . of opening up new areas for the sale of [residential] lots," Imperial's strikeless record, and the huge import duties Imperial paid for raw sugar (an amount equaling that year the total federal outlay for navigation improvements in Texas), which to him were contributions to society in general and the community infrastructure in particular.[7]

The easiest way to profits was to do nothing for the community and simply modernize the refinery. Indeed, improvements to the refinery alone to make the company's product "almost unchallengeable" among competitors depended on the owners plowing back earnings for years.[8]

The huge sums needed for physical improvements to both refinery and community were clear to trust shareholders because improvements began long before World War I. Back in 1908 Eldridge had chosen as a site manager for the refinery, community, and fields a then-twenty-six-year-old craftsman, Gus Ulrich, from Schulenburg, a Texas city settled predominantly by Czechs and Germans. Ulrich had proved himself first as a foreman of a crew assigned to demolish the noisome shanties of "Mexico." Reinforced by county deputies, the Imperial

6. Sharon et al., "Cane Sugar Refining," *Industrial and Engineering Chemistry*, p. 552; and R. M. Armstrong, interview with author, Feb. 10, 1987, offer details.

7. IHK, letter to Max Jacobs Advertising Agency, May 13, 1954, Folder "Jenkins," Box IHK (1954), #80-002, Kempner Papers.

8. "Beneficiary Interest Report, 1963," p. 7.

employees had driven out the squatters and, using mules, axes, and battering rams, razed the flimsy structures, all without resistance or known complaints by the unsalubrious residents.

This done, Ulrich had set gangs of unskilled laborers (contract prisoners among them until their use stopped in 1914) to dredging Oyster Creek and draining the major potentially arable fields on Imperial's almost twenty thousand acres, a massive undertaking. Between 1919 and 1932 the workers removed over five million cubic yards of earth from Oyster Creek and from the borders of fields, using the excised soil for protective levees, filling in insect-breeding lowlands, grading residential streets and lots, and establishing firm beds for automobile and truck roads. This arduous labor diminished fears of floods and insect-borne diseases and encouraged increasingly diversified agriculture in place of the earlier concentration on sugar.[9]

Meanwhile, Ulrich busily recruited skilled building trades craftsmen from the Schulenburg area. So many of them chose later to settle permanently in Sugar Land as Imperial workers, farmers, and shopkeepers, that the growing settlement these men built around the Imperial refinery was known for a while as "Little Schulenburg."[10]

Ulrich assigned these workers to construct what became a new small town. By 1918 the whites' section of Sugar Land was already transformed. Instead of former foul warrens and dusty or muddy tracks strewn with animal droppings and garbage, the new town's three main streets were now well graded, drained, and paved with gravel and ground oyster shells from the creek. Street cleaning was a company responsibility. There were now streetlamps, and even a few traffic lights at the major business intersections testified to the vigor of a new small city. All the rotten shanties, tents, and barracks for the refinery work-

9. [Anon.] "Sugarland Industries, Inc., and Its Subsidiary and Affiliated Companies" (typescript, 1964), Kempner Papers, p. 4 (hereafter cited as "Sugarland Industries").

10. Armstrong, "History," II [3, 56]. All Sugar Land population statistics before 1950 are approximate. It remained an unincorporated Kempner property until 1959 and was therefore not surveyed for the U.S. Census. In 1950, residents numbered approximately 2,285; in 1960, 2,802; in 1970, 3,318; in 1980, 8,826; and, in 1988, perhaps 17,000. The pre-1980 figures do not reflect the large numbers of those who worked at Imperial and elsewhere in Sugar Land but commuted from Richmond and elsewhere. The booms of 1980 and 1988 reflect the expansion of Houston's exurbs into Fort Bend County. In 1900 Fort Bend County's population was 16,538; in 1980, 130,846 (U.S. Census, *Characteristics of the Population, 1900–1980*).

Improved residences and facilities for white members of Sugar Land's labor force, ca. 1918 (Courtesy Imperial Sugar Company)

ers under the old dispensation were gone. In their place Ulrich's crews had erected over a hundred comfortable frame houses. A year after the 1924 plan's implementation, more than five hundred such structures existed. They were homes for more than two thousand white residents. The streets in this section now had concrete sidewalks and covered sewers. Water, electric, and gas utilities graced every residence, amenities rare in rural Texas.

The whites-only residential section lay both north and south of the railroad tracks, on the east side of town. Streets were paved with gravel or shell, and later macadamized. The houses had from one to three bedrooms, screened porches, indoor plumbing, and sheet-metal roofs. Many home sites had sizable lawns and some boasted garden plots. By regional standards these were high-quality accommodations for salaried workers. The houses followed a small hierarchy of sizes, numbers of rooms, and elevations. Rentals paid by worker-tenants to their employer-landlord reflected the differentials.

Conditions remained far less salubrious and the improvements more modest in the racially segregated area known as the Quarters, located north of the tracks on the town's west side. It sheltered the black and Hispanic laborers and their families, the two groups being fairly equal in number and totaling roughly half of Sugar Land's population. The filthy, miserable shanties that had sprawled randomly there from the Cunningham years were replaced with one- or two-room tarpaper-covered "shotgun shacks" that whites of the region deemed to be fit for nonwhite tenants. Although greatly improved over what they replaced, residences in the Quarters had, instead of indoor plumbing, a single water faucet in each front yard and a backyard privy. Streets in the Quarters lacked sidewalks, and roadways were less well graded and surfaced than in the whites' area. The measure of the Kempner-Eldridge improvements is in the fact that blacks and Hispanics eagerly sought the new Imperial housing.

The Quarters would endure through the 1950s, until the next Kempner generation, represented by Ike's son Herbert, took command at Sugar Land. Initiating then a second costly phase of improvements both to the refinery and the community, Herb roughly equalized housing conditions for whites and nonwhites and more truly than ever made Sugar Land deserve the "model" company town label.

The many tenant farmhouses, most of which had nonwhite inhabitants, were the least and last improved. Each was isolated on its petty parcel of Imperial's vast acreage, and therefore the unit costs of improvement were highest for these dwellings. Further, the near-invisibility of the tenants' scattered sites in this sparsely settled rural county, plus the nomadic habits of many tenant tillers, left that population with little economic or political clout. This condition persisted until New Deal and post–World War II government policies, plus, as in the Quarters, the enhanced social consciousness of the younger Kempners, such as Harris and Herb, illuminated deficiencies. Like those in the Quarters, however, Imperial's tenant farmhouses were favored regionally by transient agriculturalists. The Eldridge-Kempner partners were reputed to be fair-dealing and Sugar Land was said to have become a blessedly better environment than any others in the region concerning schooling for residents' children, medical facilities, and pricing policies in shops.[11]

As noted earlier, in Galveston Ike and other Kempners had sporadically championed more sensitive treatment of black residents, at least concerning equal access to public transportation and the distribution of charity. Still, Ike's insistence after the Great Storm on

11. Armstrong interview with author, July 14, 1988.

A Sugar Land farm tenant's dwelling, among the last to be improved (Courtesy Imperial Sugar Company)

equitable supplies to nonwhites as well as whites and the fact that his grade-raising and other infrastructural improvements included the homes of blacks were no small matter. In addition to simple justice, this concern with equities reflected the fact that Galveston blacks had vigorous champions, sometimes among political enemies of the Kempners.

Sugar Land blacks and Hispanics had no equivalent advocate group in their inland rural island. Enjoying no tradition of self-assertion and restricted overwhelmingly to menial, dead-end jobs in the refinery or to subsistence tenant farming, they nonetheless benefited from the Kempner-Eldridge improvement agenda, but for far too long only in minor ways. Yet, to be dealt with honestly by landlords, employers, and shopkeepers was itself a vast elevation in their life-styles. But even if brave by regional gauges, Ike held to race hierarchy almost as long as did the rest of white America.

Home sites of blacks as well as whites had lawns and gardens. Silt from the dredged creek and systematically collected manure (an increasing resource as cattle grazing and truck farming leavened the area's economy) from the stables and farms nourished the plantings. An unending water flow supplied by the faithful old pumping station upriver kept plantings green. Flower beds presented spectrums of color, and shade trees soon provided respite from summer sun. Each day a garbage wagon attended by a black Imperial employee collected refuse along every residential and business street. First a rooming house and then a hotel, both built by Ulrich's crews, accommodated bachelors, newcomers, and transients. Thereafter Imperial's crews maintained all these structures on calendared rotations and were on call for emergencies. Some of these buildings remain sound and usable seven decades after their construction.[12]

As Sugar Land grew into a small city, it became orderly and family-oriented, no longer attractive to the overtly idle, vicious, or rootless. Unlike the Pinkertons and deputies who patrolled other company towns, Sugar Land's "police force" consisted for a long time of one man, Jim Guyer, a picturesque holdover from the Ellis years. A Stetson-hatted western type on horseback, he patrolled Imperial's acreage and the city streets accompanied by noisy but undangerous hounds. Apparently his major task was ensuring that probable undesirables, chiefly freeloading vagrants riding railroad freight cars, kept going out of Sugar Land.[13] He seems to have been more picturesque than officious. Recruited from among both Imperial white- and blue-collar workers, a volunteer firefighting company supplemented this slim law-and-order arrangement. Imperial paid for the equipment and negotiated with nearby county and state prison authorities for mutual aid in emergencies.

In the early 1920s Ulrich built also a retail and service street adjacent to the Imperial refinery. Soon a food market, barbershop, and hardware and dry-goods stores flanked the north face of the rail line. They flourished, and Ulrich busied his crews in constructing a second and then a third phase of commercial buildings. The additions included a bank, telephone exchange, motion picture theater, beauty shop, real estate sales office, restaurant, and appliance and furniture stores. A third surge of commercial construction, ending in the mid-twenties, produced a lumberyard, automobile-truck dealership, drugstore, and ice-cream parlor.[14]

Almost at once upon the opening of these retail facilities, Sugar

12. Armstrong, "History," sec. on "The Company Town" [1–3].

13. Sims, "Childhood on a Sugar Land Prison Farm," *Southern Exposure*, pp. 35.

14. "Sugarland Industries," pp. 1–11. In 1952 a modern shopping center, since further modernized, located south of the tracks, replaced this strip.

Land became both the favored shopping as well as population center of this agricultural county. On Saturdays crowds filled the lengthening main street facing the refinery, railroad tracks, and station. Horse- and mule-drawn wagons, Model-T autos, and chain-driven Mack trucks competed for parking and travel space while pedestrians promenaded on the new sidewalks that insulated users from mud, dust, and animal droppings. Refinery hands, tenant farmers, independent agriculturalists drawn from throughout the huge rural county; Houstonians and Galvestonians attracted by opportunities to buy fresh produce and, in some instances, to visit relatives or friends in the nearby state prison; and traveling salesmen in Sugar Land to sell to refinery officials and shopkeepers—all mixed in a busy, multiracial bustle, one sharply contrasting with the dreary, crude atmosphere of the decades before Kempner and Eldridge came to Sugar Land.

Until 1918 or 1919 the partners may have issued to worker-residents company scrip in lieu of cash, good only for purchases in community shops. This was a common and commonly exploitative practice in company towns. But Harris, who accompanied his father to Sugar Land very frequently in those years and whose curiosity and memory about that period were remarkable, could not remember its existence.[15]

Imperial both owned and operated the early retail commercial facilities, at first assigning as managers and clerks some superannuated employees, convalescents from illnesses or injuries or those whose full time was not occupied by mill or agricultural labors. In addition, perhaps as part of Rabbi Cohen's several rehabilitation programs, some prisoner-trusties whose sentences had expired and who wished to settle in Sugar Land, either as salaried refinery workers, tenant farmers, or in a mix of both, seem to have been favored also for employment as clerks in a kind of "halfway house" arrangement.

The increase of urban facilities became possible financially because Imperial/Sugar Land successfully kept its labor force and increased refinery efficiency. Meanwhile, the demand for sugar kept rising, and the Kempners kept pumping money into both refinery and community improvements.

Domestic sources of raw sugar could not keep pace with demand,

15. H. L. Kempner, "The Kempners of Galveston and Sugar Land" (manuscript), RLA, p. 22; Armstrong interview with author, July 14, 1988.

and an insect infestation in the late 1920s decimated domestic cane fields, further impelling refiners to look abroad, especially to Hawaii and the Caribbean, a search in which Imperial had the advantage of the pioneer. Sugar Land's tillable acreage for noncane production grew due to Ulrich's extensive improvements in drainage and irrigation. As acreage became available for production, nonsugar farming and grazing at Sugar Land became more attractive and profitable. In the early 1930s Imperial would dismantle its raw sugar mill, selling it for scrap, thereafter depending on external sources of raw sugar.[16]

Growth and Diversity

As planned, the decent housing and other urban amenities attracted increasing numbers of women and children to Sugar Land. This increase of families inspired Ike further to encourage new sources of work-force stability for Imperial. The results were early decisions against an Imperial monopoly of jobs, housing, farms, wholesale or retail merchandising, or credit. Instead, diversity of legal relationships as well as competition for trade developed. Third parties bought or leased some shops, Imperial eventually retaining only a relative few. Ulrich's crews built also some industrial-type buildings for lease to independent manufacturers such as Sealy Mattress. Of course Imperial profited from the rentals, leases, and sales. Simultaneously, however, the presence of alternative employment necessarily diminished residents' dependence on Imperial.

This diversification created more burdens for Kempner and Eldridge. As Harris recalled, by the early 1920s "Sugar Land wasn't only sugar [any longer]. It was agriculture, cattle-raising, cattle feed processing, as well as human feed, a telephone company, [and] a bank."[17] Increasingly, Imperial assumed management tasks, as in developing leases allowing different periods and conditions of farm tenancy suited to varied crops and animal husbandry. Tenants now grew cotton, fruit, vegetables, and grains, and carried on feedlot grazing of livestock that irrigation made feasible. They sold livestock and truck produce in the nearby urban markets of Houston and San Antonio, thus also increasing their independence. These diverse activi-

16. Sitterson, *Sugar Country*, pp. 318, 344.
17. H. L. Kempner interview with author, July 14, 1988.

ties justified Kempner and Eldridge in constructing a feed mill, cotton gin, cottonseed oil mill, and a freight warehouse in the growing mercantile-inudstrial center of the little city.

An increasing number of refinery workers and farm tenants wanted to become future owners rather than renters of company houses and land. Imperial opened a real estate management and sales office. Over the years several company-owned stores, mercantile properties, houses, and farms were first leased then sold to third parties, primarily to tenant-occupiers. Imperial's managers encouraged such ambitions with favorable loans from the local bank and invited in competition in the form of an independently owned bank (later, two banks) in Sugar Land. Borrowers were free to contract locally or elsewhere.[18]

Whatever formal changes occurred in Imperial's corporate forms and in the owners' relationships to Sugar Land as a community, as landlords and real estate promoters the Kempners early established and maintained certain policies favoring residents. Among them storekeepers, whether managers for Imperial, renters, or independents, did not gouge customers. Similarly, except for rare disturbers of the community's placid ways Imperial seems almost never to have evicted a renter of a house, shop, or farm, even defaulters of rents or payments, a policy that received severe tests in the depression decade of the thirties. Store prices were kept roughly at the Houston level, and house rents and utility rates, much lower. Assessments in lieu of taxes for civic improvements were always less than tax rates for similar services elsewhere. Local schoolteachers, journalists, and preachers were not harassed, textbooks not censored, and private detectives not employed. To be sure, for a long time union organizers were unwelcome. But, it appears, neither were they assaulted.

Until 1921 members of all Christian denominations in Sugar Land met in an improvised "union" church. That year, Kempner and Eldridge donated four downtown lots to as many Protestant congregations and one to a Roman Catholic body. The Imperial-owned bank provided loans to these congregations to build churches, on very favorable terms.[19]

A small school building becoming inadequate, in 1916 Kempner and Eldridge sent Imperial's chief engineer to California to study in-

18. Armstrong, "History," sec. on Imperial Sugar Co. [2].
19. Armstrong interview with author, July 14, 1988.

Houses for white Sugar Land workers, ca. 1926 (Courtesy Imperial Sugar Company)

novations in pedagogic architecture, and in 1917 construction began. When completed, Sugar Land's new school had eleven buildings of one classroom each plus washrooms. Arranged in a "covered-wagon" semicircle, the buildings' outer faces were linked by paved and roofed walkways offering shelter from sun and rain and separate access to each room. Every classroom opened also to the inner courtyard created by the circling form where a five-hundred-seat auditorium became both a school and community facility for plays, concerts, and special lectures. In the mid-thirties Imperial built a second half circle of eleven buildings, and its courtyard housed a gymnasium and indoor pool. The school enjoyed quick accreditation and a rising reputation. Although also accredited, far less imagination and funds went into the two other schools that Imperial built for black and Hispanic children.[20]

No medical facilities existed in the area when Kempner and Eldridge took over. Convict laborers "enjoyed" the services of a state physician

20. Ibid. In Sept., 1988, the I. H. Kempner Senior High School opened in Sugar Land. During his lifetime, Ike forebade having his name attached to the school.

The new school at Sugar Land, ca. 1918 (Courtesy Imperial Sugar Company)

at the nearby prison at Ellis, who, by arrangement, also treated such Sugar Land residents as were too hurt or ill to make the rail trip to Houston. Then, funded by both The Industries and the Sugar Railroad, in 1920–21 the Laura Eldridge Hospital Association opened a modern thirteen-room hospital plus an annex for nonwhites and staff; in 1957 a thirty-one-bed replacement came into being. Beginning in 1924, employees enjoyed a strikingly advanced, comprehensive medical insurance "package." For $1.50 per month, deducted from the employee's pay, in the early years workers enjoyed full medical and surgical coverage, up to a year of hospitalization and generous outpatient terms, plus discounted medicines, prosthetics, and eyeglasses.[21]

"The Industries"

This growth and diversity strained even the Kempners' energies and abilities to focus. Eldridge attended primarily to the refinery and Ike,

21. Armstrong, "History," II, sec. on "The Company Town" [2–9]; "Sugarland Industries."

to the community both as a residential environment and as a business and government, since it lacked status as a municipality. In person and by frequent visits and telephone calls, Ike tried to keep control of every aspect of this large-scale action. But the details of leases, mortgages, and house repairs were less attractive. Nor would any Kempner slight H. Kempner's cotton affairs. The spinners' litigations and Galveston's politics demanded attention.

During the 1920s major American corporations were indulging in early visions of the "merger mania" so prominent again in the 1980s. Among Kempners, the urge existed to merge all their diverse holdings. But such impulses were countered by other imperatives derived from the family cohesion tradition. This impulse generated a desire to shield H. Kempner Trust shareholders from unlimited liability in the event of adverse judgment in lawsuits, a concern deepened by the 1919 courtroom reverse and the spinners' litigations, and by the need to keep individual Kempners' assets liquid to pay income and/or estate taxes.[22]

In 1919 Ike and Eldridge split off from Imperial all subsidiary Sugar Land business assets. The nonrefinery entity the partners chartered, The Sugarland Industries Trust, known colloquially as "The Industries," was a holding company, in legal form a Massachusetts trust (as H. Kempner itself would become a year later). In formal terms Imperial became The Industries' subsidiary. Then in 1924 a new Imperial Sugar corporation came into being. It was legally separate from The Industries. But the latter's owners owned all the Imperial shares. Ike, Dan, Eldridge, and Ulrich were The Industries' trustees while Eldridge and H. Kempner remained the equal owners of Imperial's shares.

Responsibility for day-to-day management of these increasingly numerous and diverse properties by the mid-twenties lay with The Industries. But since overall decisions were up to The Industries' trustees, who included the Eldridge-Kempner partners in Imperial plus an additional close relative and trusted subordinate, in essential terms, policies for The Industries conglomerate complemented those for Imperial, and vice versa. In subsequent decades the legal relationships

22. Kantrow, *The Constraints of Corporate Tradition*, and Sklar, *The Corporate Reconstruction of American Capitalism, 1890–1916*, both passim, deserve attention. On taxes and liquidity, see "Keys Report," passim.

of Imperial and The Industries would undergo change, but the basic harmony of the interlocking directorates endured.[23] The Industries' "General Departments" would soon administer also a feed mill, dehydrating plant, cotton gin, cotton-buying office, cottonseed office, a bulk freighting agency, two small railroads, the canal and pumping facilities, and miscellaneous farm and grazing acreage. Thus Sugar Land and The Industries' general departments simultaneously embraced extractive, industrial, agricultural, mercantile, and service businesses plus the expectable civic institutions of a bustling small city that, with its agricultural and cattle-grazing hinterland, spread across much of a substantial county.[24]

While animal power remained important, The Industries' "Agricultural Departments" included a blacksmith shop. Other Industries employees were responsible for monitoring the financial records and productivity of day laborers, the company's feedlot for calves and the cotton acreage, and the growers of alfalfa, corn, Johnson grass, and pecans. Noteworthily, cultivators of sugarcane are absent from this listing by the mid-1920s.

Among The Industries' "Wholly Owned Subsidiaries," the Sugarland Motor Company sold and serviced automobiles, ran two gasoline stations, a truck line, and a warehousing company. "Affiliated Companies" came to include the Alcorn Farms, the Belknap Realty Company, the Fort Bend Cattle Company, the Foster Farms, and the Sugar Land Telephone Company.

Sugar Land agricultural and industrial "exports," like the produce and manufactured goods produced by independent firms attracted to Sugar Land, increased revenues for the Sugar Land Rail Road, which carried them to long-haul trunk lines and to the Galveston wharves. In this manner the Kempners balanced better Sugar Land's analogue to export-import rates in ways unachievable at Galveston, while yet

23. H. L. Kempner interview with Marchiafava, June 6, 1981; H. L. Kempner, "The Kempners of Galveston and Sugar Land," pp. 11–12.

24. "Sugarland Industries," pp. 1–4, 11, which lists tenants, including small retail and service businesses, some belonging to "The Industries," others to rent-paying independents, plus truck farmers and cattle feedlot grazing operators. Larger tenants were to include the Brazos Valley Irrigation Company, Sealy Mattress, Sugar Land Manufacturing, Allied Imperial Mercantile, Imperial Bank, Sugar Land Railway, Faber Mercantile, Uvalde and Northern Railway, Port Isabel and Rio Grande Railway, and the Sugar Land Oil Field.

trying to steer new transshipping business toward the Island City.[25]

All these incremental developments diminished both the Kempners' dynamics of control and residents' dependence on Imperial. Ultimately these policies transformed the erstwhile one-industry hellhole based on convict labor into a small, comfortable, prospering city, one since self-governing, one that is mindful of its past, conscious of present needs, and hopeful for its future.[26]

Imperial/Sugar Land, M&P, and Organized Labor

Nationally, relatively few entrepreneurs of the early twentieth century voluntarily deferred profits in favor of improving workplaces and life-styles for employees. Paradoxically, while Kempners encouraged improvements at Sugar Land, they resisted repeated requests for analogous elevations of laborers' conditions in the cotton trade.[27]

Perhaps the difference is partially explicable by Ike's antipathies both to labor unions on what he discerned as the left and to the Ku Klux Klan on the right. Klan strength never amounted to much at Sugar Land, and angry KKK spokesmen attributed their flaccidity to "that rich Jew Ike Kempner [who] had insisted that any [Imperial] workman found a member of the Klan should be summarily fired and his man Friday, W. T. Eldridge, was promptly carrying out [Ike's] orders."[28] It is impossible to fit Eldridge into a "man Friday" category, and arbitrary firings were so foreign at Sugar Land as to demand absolute proof for belief, which is lacking. What of M&P?

In 1914 a shrewd union representative had maneuvered Dan into a union-members-only construction contract for a new M&P warehouse by noting that a concurrent Moody-owned compress enlargement employed unionized Mexican "rat labor." In another instance, however reluctantly, Ike accepted arbitration by a local "labor council" composed of both employers' and workers' representatives.[29]

25. Armstrong, "History," sec. on "Imperial Sugar Co." [2].

26. *Houston Chronicle*, Feb. 21, 1988, sec. 3, p. 8.

27. Ellis, "The Texas Cotton Compress Industry" (Ph.D. diss.), pp. 381, and see 350–80.

28. IHK, *Recalled Recollections*, pp. 63, 80.

29. Both incidents are described in an unidentified clipping dated July 24, 1914, and another, undated and unidentified, both in DWK Scrapbook, 1894–1915, Kempner Papers.

Neither experience encouraged Kempners' affection for labor unions.

Concerning even the conservative American Federation of Labor (AFL), Ike and Dan fended organizers off from both Sugar Land and Galveston as long as they could, but in differing ways. To use recent jargon, in both industries the Kempners were trying simultaneously the better to synthesize operations in order to lessen the vagaries of international commodity markets, including oscillations caused by speculators, cartelists, and public regulations. In sugar the appropriate way they discerned was that of imaginative, dynamic welfare capitalism. But in cotton they kept H. Kempner and M&P operating on the industry's static standard of channeling profits among owners and managers rather than among workers.[30]

In one sense this dichotomy reflects basic differences in the two commodities, cotton and sugar. Cotton grew in the region in huge quantities. But, increasingly, it had to be exported for conversion into textiles and faced growing competition from foreign sources and from synthetic fabrics. By contrast raw sugar had to be imported because of insatiable domestic demand. Refineries like Imperial, if well staffed and technologically modernized, had customers to spare. Efficient, skilled, stable labor was essential at Sugar Land. Swift replacement of any substantial number was to be avoided. Although skilled cotton graders would prove to be virtually irreplaceable, unskilled gang labor in a cotton press could more easily supplement or replace departees than was true in rural Sugar Land. Therefore, the Kempners and Eldridge consistently forestalled labor problems for Imperial by anticipating workers' needs both in the refinery and community.

By contrast, at Galveston in 1920 a dockworkers' strike, one of a wave of stoppages spreading from Boston and Seattle, hurt cotton merchants, including H. Kempner, and soured labor relations in the region for decades to come. The 1920 strike also inhibited Kempner political fortunes in Galveston and distracted Ike and Dan just when the spinners' conversion contracts were on their desks. Ike led cotton dealers and Wharves executives, the Island City's major employers, in opposing the strikers.

The 1920 strike failed. AFL leadership in Texas appeared to be chastened. Actually, union strategists had decided to encourage in-

30. Galambos, "Technology, Political Economy, and Professionalization," *Business History Review*, p. 471; Ellis, "Cotton Compress Industry," p. 381.

dustrial reforms by cooperating with educable management (like the Kempners at Sugar Land, but not at Galveston) rather than by strikes, boycotts, or other economic persuasions. But many businessmen, including Kempners, saw AFL quiescence as weakness.[31]

M&P Prosperity

For years thereafter M&P prospered. Despite huge outlays for improvements to its machinery and plant, in December, 1921, M&P paid its first dividend since 1905, totaling 600 percent of its stock value. Unlike Imperial's profits, which H. Kempner shared 50 percent with Eldridge, all of M&P's profits went into the Kempner family pool. As at Sugar Land, Kempner business diversity increased at Galveston, but by a far smaller rate, Harris noting that on the Island in the 1920s "there was the [H. Kempner] cotton business, the bank, the landholdings, stock portfolio, [and] the life insurance company." Also as in Sugar Land, Ike and Dan preferred to plow most profits back into improvements. From 1930 through the 1960s, however, M&P's accumulated cash reserves would help to balance outflows of money so that, retrospectively at least, even the depression "just pinched us," according to Harris.[32] Surpluses remained available for other investments.

For example, in the early 1920s Ike and Dan launched an imaginative venture, one analogous to their earlier dispatchings of agents to railheads to drum up consignments among mainland farmers. M&P bought three powered deepwater barges. This little fleet cruised Texas' long Gulf coast and shallow bays and rivers in search of cotton cargoes. It did not succeed. Cutting losses, H. Kempner bought the boats from M&P, then sold them at a loss. M&P expanded nevertheless, in 1925 adding a new large warehouse plus another improved high-density press, three years later purchasing a competitor in Galveston, the Liberty Press, and in 1937 creating another, the Galveston Cotton Company.[33]

31. Angell, "Controlling the Workers," *East Texas Historical Journal*, p. 14; Hurvitz, "'Union-Management Corporation,'" in *Religion, Ideology, and Nationalism in Europe and America*, p. 277.

32. H. L. Kempner interview with Marchiafava, June 6, 1981, and with Guidry, Aug. 6, 1981.

33. Ellis, "Cotton Compress Industry," pp. 380–84. "The Galveston Cotton

Meanwhile in 1931, while the spinners' litigations were going poorly and early constraints of the depression were being felt, a Texas appeals court ruled that Dan had to pay Galveston over $170,000. He had stood as surety for another Galveston private banking firm, Ed McCarthy & Co., long the city's fiscal depository, since bankrupted. Among other defaults the McCarthy company had failed to pay interest due to holders of the very seawall bonds that Ike had promoted a quarter century earlier. No taint adhered in all this to any Kempner. But as a McCarthy surety Dan was liable and H. Kempner paid Galveston that considerable sum.[34]

Still, among Kempners "there were no recriminations, and nobody hurled invectives at Dan or anyone else," Harris marveled.[35] Instead, the Kempners' interwoven business and family culture exhibited its resilient strength. Ike had H. Kempner assume "some real estate holdings from the other bond signer, and thanks to Dan Kempner's handling, the real estate was ultimately liquidated to close to the amount paid out under the bond," Harris stated. He noted equally proudly that all H. Kempner's property had "always been carried [on the account books] on a very conservative basis and some holdings have always been worth more than the book value." Even so the assets had risen from approximately $1.5 million in 1895 to $5.75 million in 1927 to $7.2 million in 1938, despite the need in the last year to write off more than $1 million as bad debts due primarily to the spinners' litigations.[36]

But weaknesses existed also. The depression revealed them.

Pressed for Money

No pockets were bottomless. Dan's payout, the running sores of the spinners' lawsuits, the decline in agricultural prices through the 1920s,

---

Company acts for corporation tax purposes as an intermediary between H. Kempner, who owns the Liberty Press and the Merchants and Planters Compress and Warehouse Company, who leases it" ("Keys Report," p. 7).

34. Sullivan et al. *v.* City of Galveston, 34 *Southwest Reporter*, 2d. (1931), 808. See also "Keys Report," pp. 5–7; *Galveston News*, undated clippings in DWK Scrapbooks, 1929–1935. The state Commission on Appeals lowered Dan's liability from the $238,000 imposed by a lower court (*Galveston News*, May 1, 1929).

35. H. L. Kempner interview with Guidry, Aug. 8, 1981.

36. "Keys Report," pp. 5–7. These estimates are substantially confirmed by more than thirty years' accumulated relevant data, 1922–56, in Box 44, labeled "H.K./D.W.K.," #80-002, Kempner Papers.

and then the depression required the Kempners to reevaluate agendas. In the early thirties Harris noted that "to cope with all these difficulties, both internal and external, was almost a superhuman job, but we had certain assets."[37]

Sugar Land remained the brightest of the "certain assets." But the depression worsened its luster as tenants defaulted on residences, businesses, grazing land, and farm rents, mortgages, and other long-term commitments. Instead of invoking penalties, including foreclosures and evictions, or deducting portions of affected Imperial workers' salaries, Ike (Eldridge, declining in health, was decreasingly active), through The Industries, as noted earlier, let almost all defaulting tenants and mortgagors stay in place. The Industries deferred rents and mortgage payments, eventually forgiving many. Imperial fired few refinery workers. Instead, its management conjured up new or supplemental jobs for those becoming fully or partly superfluous in refining processes. Obedient to a systematic plan, Imperial turned redundant workers to further modernizing the refinery and the community's infrastructure. Imperial suffered no strikes, lockouts, or boycotts, although it cut laborers' wages. Workers whose wages had been cut received first chance at "moonlighting" jobs in local factories, shops, and farms, plus cheap and often free produce from community fields. Ike and Eldridge imposed food relief distribution duties on "Sheriff" Guyer, who replaced his long-unused pistol with a clipboard. A rising young Imperial manager, who had recently been a factory hand himself, recalled that there was "never a vacant house in Sugar Land, no evictions, and no starvation."[38]

Who was responsible for this impressive record? All the Kempners, in the sense of agreeing to these policies; Ike, who was retaining his particular warm interest in his "pet project" of Sugar Land; and his son Herbert, whose influence was the most direct.

Enter Herb Kempner

Herb, three years younger than Harris, upon his return from Harvard and travel abroad, in the late 1920s had plunged happily into

37. H. L. Kempner, "Beneficiary Interest Report, 1963," p. 5.
38. Armstrong interview with author, Feb. 10, 1987; Armstrong, "History," sec. on "Imperial Sugar Co." [2–4].

Imperial–Sugar Land on-job training for management, as a plant engineer and then as an assistant treasurer. Married in 1930 to Mary Carroll and with a new son, Isaac Herbert Kempner III, born in Sugar Land in 1932, Herb learned the sugar business and the manifold concerns of The Industries from his father, uncles, the ailing Eldridge (who was further depressed in spirit because of the recent suicide of his son), and former carpenter Ulrich, now high on the Imperial ladder. Herb was a willing pupil of these able if disparate mentors.

Upon Eldridge's death in 1933 Ulrich, not Herb, became Imperial's general manager. But this succession reflected no lack of confidence in Herb, Ike assured inquisitive Rabbi Cohen. Instead, the decision for Ulrich reflected in part Herb's preoccupation with his infant son plus the fact that Eldridge's death required an experienced helmsman, not a relative novice, to shoulder Imperial's weighty burdens, if only because the firm was just then seeking a financial transfusion from a New Deal agency. Perhaps, too, Ike, though now nearly sixty years old, was already exhibiting a stubborn inability to drop any reins. He would himself be Ulrich's behind-the-scenes but omnipresent monitor, a supervision that Herb, now in his thirties, apparently found unpalatable.[39]

Ike is faultable for considering himself to be indispensable. But Eldridge's death was an actual and imminent peril for the entire Imperial/Sugar Land enterprise, one that again illuminated the advantages of the Kempners' solidarity as a family.

Back in 1925 Eldridge and his wife had divorced. The legal proceedings were protracted, bitter, and expensive. Mrs. Eldridge and their daughters might already have drained his half of the liquid assets of the partnership with H. Kempner. Ike and his brothers had supported Eldridge in the divorce action. Eldridge wrote to his lawyer: "Had it not been for Mr. [Ike] Kempner, I would have been wiped off the slate a long time ago." Additionally, Eldridge had borrowed substantial sums from Ike to cover extravagances by his then-wife and daughters. These debts made Eldridge's partnership interest vulnerable to demands from H. Kempner for repayment when due, had such demands been made. On this, Eldridge wrote, "had

39. I. H. Kempner, letter to Cohen, Aug. 29, 1932, Box 3M253, Cohen Papers.

the Kempners forced payment, all of [my] . . . equities would have been wiped out."[40]

Through the stressful depression and World War II, Eldridge's survivors occasionally questioned the amounts due to them as half-owners of Imperial/Sugar Land. Such implications of unfair divisions of funds must have been exasperating to the Kempners, and ill-phased, coming in the depression when, according to a company writer, "both Imperial and . . . [Sugar Land] Industries were just a step away from receivership." It must also have been personally offensive to Ike, whose personal fondness for the picturesque Eldridge had grown through the decades.[41]

Given free choice Ike would likely have had H. Kempner at once buy out the half-interest of Eldridge's irksome survivors. But he had to wait until 1946 to become sole owner. Meanwhile, the more immediate need for Imperial/Sugar Land was survival.[42]

Its peril became evident as farm and business tenants defaulted. Imperial's competition with the Texas City sugar refinery in effect erased a freight rate differential long favoring Imperial. Additionally, Imperial had been selling large amounts of sugar on credit to a resident fig-canning company, plus advancing it funds for new machinery, bottling glass, and payrolls. The loans seemed prudent when made, for America was indulging then in a health fad involving figs. But the fig fad ended abruptly, the cannery closed, and Imperial/Sugar Land was the loser by perhaps $2.5 million.[43]

"Once again," an Imperial journalist would write, "the Kempners pulled together to face the crisis squarely and do what had to be done." Tightening all Kempners' belts, Imperial sold more Sugar Land oil acreage, the town newspaper, and grazing and truck farmland. These sales brought in "substantial . . . badly needed cash," Harris recalled.

40. Eldridge's memo, Mar. 10, 1925, in file 58, and lawyer George King's, May 25, 1923, file 15, both in Box 70, "Eldridge Family Letters," #80-002, Kempner Papers.

41. Cronholm, "The Kempners," *The Imperial Crown*, p. 3; Herbert Kempner, report on Sugar Land (typescript), Apr. 24, 1951, DWK Folder, #54, Kempner Papers.

42. Dun & Bradstreet, "Analytical Report" on H. Kempner (typescript, Oct. 26, 1950), Kempner Papers. On lack of adequate funding, see H. L. Kempner, "Beneficiary Interest Report, 1963," p. 4.

43. Armstrong interview with author, Feb. 10, 1987.

But more was needed. A portion came as loans from H. Kempner and from "some of our old banking connections," one, the Bank of New York, dating from his grandfather's initial business ventures in the 1870s. Meanwhile, lawyer Homer Bruce of Houston worked out a "life saving loan" for Imperial from the federal Reconstruction Finance Corporation.[44]

Begun under Herbert Hoover and greatly expanded by the New Deal, among other functions the RFC existed to lend money to distressed but rehabilitatable businesses. Intensive conferences in Washington with RFC head Jesse Jones, a Texan and major investor in many regional enterprises, resulted in a $1.2 million loan on terms that Harris described as "a solution acceptable to Mr . . . Jones and yet at the same time possible for us to live with." That solution gave the RFC a mortgage on Imperial and all Sugar Land including the town sites and The Industries, each Kempner brother signing a personal note for $1.2 million.[45]

And despite Dan's own problems at M&P (see below), he also supplied relief from its long-undistributed surplus, which, allowing for cotton plant modernizations, M&P now paid out as dividends to H. Kempner. Trust shareholders then lent sorely needed funds to Imperial/Sugar Land.[46]

This lifesaving from government and family was "so essential that . . . [it] spelled the difference between operating or practically closing the [Imperial] plant," Ike recalled ten years after securing the RFC loan. By 1942 Imperial was fully in the black again because, back in the mid-1930s, encouraged by the confidence exhibited by the RFC and the family, the president of the Republic National Bank, overriding the negative verdict of its staff analysts about Imperial's prospects, "largely on personal grounds . . . entered the picture," Ike reminisced in gratitude to the banker. Now Imperial boasted a cash balance of over $1 million on deposit, especially in the Republic. "We [now] owe no bank a dollar and have not owed anything for several months," Ike continued. Since 1940 Imperial had accumulated cash enough to liquidate all its long-term bonds and was reducing that

44. Cronholm, "The Kempners," pp. 3–4; "Keys Report," pp. 5–6.

45. H. L. Kempner, "Beneficiary Interest Report, 1963," p. 5; Armstrong, interview with author, Feb. 10, 1987.

46. H. L. Kempner, "The Kempners of Galveston and Sugar Land," p. 12.

obligation. Its stock of refined sugar was large, demand was increasing, and the sale of the current production would cover all accounts payable.

Concerning The Industries, then Imperial's "parent company," it had not been a borrower for "many years," Ike jubilated. Taken together, by 1942 Imperial and The Industries had not only repaid the RFC but also paid all The Industries' current bills and still had a cash balance of $400,000. Only the problem of securing adequate supplies of raw sugar was a serious and persistent difficulty, one exacerbated by wartime shipping shortages and uncertainties.[47]

Triumph and Tragedy at Sugar Land

Survival achieved and balance sheets improving by the late 1930s, Herb became Imperial vice-president as well as treasurer, a trustee of The Industries, a manager of Fort Bend Utilities, and a director of the Imperial-owned bank in Sugar Land. And, having proved his worth, Herb opted for new policies concerning labor.

Many Texas employers resisted New Deal laws requiring recognition of unions. Some close associates of the Kempners advised creation at Sugar Land of a company union in the classic puppet pattern. But, Harris recalled, Herb insisted on "disentangling [Sugar Land] from [any taint of] the company town aspect." Arguments continued about recognizing unions until 1939 when Herb, now vice-president, negotiatied Imperial's first contract with a union, a local of the CIO's United Sugar Refinery Workers. As Harris noted, Herb "generally showed a very farsighted and enlightened view . . . of . . . community responsibility."[48]

Herb's social sensitivities derived in part from his upbringing, including Rabbi Cohen's influence. In the mid-1930s Cohen had organized a Galveston unit of the national Committee on Social Justice, which originated in Cincinnati. He was able quickly to report that in Galveston "Jewish members on the strike . . . and labor disputes

47. Ike, letter to Fred Florence, Jan. 11, 1943, copy supplied to author by H. L. Kempner.

48. H. L. Kempner, "The Kempners of Galveston and Sugar Land," p. 12; Cronholm, "The Kempners," p. 4.

[subcommittees helped to resolve] . . . matters that embrace social justice [which were] very well managed in Galveston."[49]

Another nurturer of Herb's social conscience was a then-youngish Imperial technician, one destined to become its president, W. H. ("Bill") Louviere. A southerner, he had become an advocate of the need to improve workers' conditions, especially those of black workers. Probably Herb's World War II naval service further sensitized him to social warts that might earlier have been invisible to him. Like Harris a Legion of Merit medalist as a wartime Navy officer, Herb in 1946 became the company's and the community's chief executive official. Forty years old in the mid-1940s, educated, a veteran of industrial and military administration, Herb made it clear that he no longer intended to play a junior's role. While in the Navy stationed in Washington, he had kept current with Imperial/Sugar Land developments. In effect, Herb performed as an effective activist for Imperial as his Navy duties permitted, especially concerning repayments on the RFC loan and matters of rationing, space allotments on railroad and shipping lines, and manpower controls.[50]

In 1947, at Herb's urging H. Kempner bought the Eldridge heirs' 50 percent of Imperial/Sugar Land, after what Harris described as a very "difficult negotiation." With sole ownership now in the H. Kempner Trust and with the RFC loan repaid, Herb was "free from . . . [the] tutelage of banks." Thereafter the Imperial/Sugar Land industrial-residential complex "progressed rapidly in all directions and laid the foundations for the remarkable setup . . . which exists there."[51]

Now fully automated, Imperial employed three eight-hour shifts, seven days a week. Profits and dividends reached records. Imperial produced two million pounds of refined sugar a day. Unsatisfied, Herb and Louviere planned and launched an expensive, long-range pro-

49. Cohen, letter to Adolph Rosenberg, Dec. 17, 1935, Box 3M263, Cohen Papers.

50. Herb, letter to I. H. Kempner, Apr. 12, 1945, folder 16, "I. H. Kempner, Jr.," and see also I. H. Kempner, letter to D. Weston and D. Oppenheimer, July 5, 1945, in folder 24, "Weston, Sara K.," and "Wartime Washington Correspondence & Personals," folder 3, all #80-002, Kempner Papers.

51. "Keys Report," p. 8. Imperial's repayment of loans from the Bank of New York apparently helped to elevate to the bank's presidency its agent for the Imperial/Sugar Land account. We "gave him a good reputation," Harris recalled (H. L. Kempner, interview with R. L. Jones, June 17–18, 1980, RLA).

gram of further improvement. Soon, Imperial boasted a virtually "no-hands" refining procedure ending in the industry's only air-conditioned packaging room. Imperial also simultaneously refurbished Sugar Land's numerous shops and houses in the whites-only section, for maintenance had been deferred during wartime.[52]

And, at last, improvements were undertaken for the disgraceful Quarters. The racially segregated housing there had suffered from diminished maintenance during the depression and war. Beginning in 1955–56, almost as a response to the U.S. Supreme Court's Brown *v.* Board of Education decision, a root-and-branch equalization program in housing got under way in Sugar Land. Imperial assumed responsibility to build wholly modern brick homes, each with indoor plumbing and served by paved streets and sidewalks. A first phase of 150 units was followed by several more. In order to create this minor effort in urban renewal, Imperial first temporarily rehoused the black and Hispanic tenants, one street at a time. Square by square the decrepit shanties were demolished, and sewers, electric, gas, and telephone conduits installed. Then, street after street, the former residents moved into the spanking new residences while, in a manner reminiscent of the Galveston regrading, the process advanced to the next street of the Quarters. Saving only—if "only" is the right word—the preservation of racial segregation in the Quarters, the improvements greatly benefited the same people it had displaced, a rare achievement in city rehabilitations.

With its own funds plus guarantees from the Federal Housing Authority, Imperial extended fifteen-year mortgages to would-be nonwhite buyers on a no–down payment, below-market interest rate basis, with payments deductible from salaries. Imperial never foreclosed on even one of these contracts, although some became delinquent.

Herb and Louviere together conceived this plan and Herb convinced the Kempners that it was both imperative in terms of justice and a reasonable business proposition. But Herb was not to see it fully executed, the successful implementation falling to Louviere, who succeeded Herb as Imperial's president.[53]

52. Armstrong, interview with author, Feb. 10, 1987; *Houston Press*, Apr. 25, 1947, p. 1.

53. Armstrong interview with author, July 14, 1988.

Herb's Death

In 1952 Ike and Henrietta celebrated their fiftieth wedding anniversary and a year later, Ike's eightieth birthday. He had been involved in Sugar Land for as many years as his marriage. With the depression conquered, the war won, and his sons and brothers set in prospering family businesses, it was time to celebrate. And so, unaware of impending tragedy – Herb made everyone promise to keep a dark secret from his parents – in early 1953 Henrietta and Ike started a half-century-long deferred honeymoon to Hawaii.

Herbert had lung cancer. His parents away, he endured surgery. But the malignancy spread. Aware that he had only weeks of life remaining, he fended off suggestions from Dan and others that they relieve him of all Imperial responsibilities. While he could, his wife Mary drove him daily from Galveston or from a Houston hospital, to Sugar Land. They planned for her situation as a widow and for the education of their children. And, as a company testimonial recorded, "up to five days before his death, knowing that his span of life would shortly culminate, . . . [Herbert] planned [also] the policies of this Company, [and] the range and duties of its new officers."[54] The family mourned. But Herb's aspirations and directions for Imperial/Sugar Land would outlive him.

H. Kempner, Dan Kempner, and M&P

Meanwhile, at M&P, Dan had also been coping with the effects of the depression. By the end of 1932 he had reluctantly cut salaries. White-collar staff accepted month-long unpaid vacations to avoid layoffs. Maneuvering to accommodate the New Deal's price-support programs for cotton, Dan shifted M&P from a business which in the 1920s received 39 percent of its income from compressing and only 24 percent from warehousing, to one which in the 1930s obtained 56 percent from storage and 13 percent from compressing. The change resulted from government policies that subsidized reduced acreage for the crop and provided loans to farmers to withhold cotton from the market, not to merchants for freight costs of warehousing. Com-

54. Quotation in G. Andre file, Box IHK, A–J (1954); Dan, letter to Herb, Mar. 9, 1953, German Spinners folder, Box IHK (1953), both in #80-002, Kempner Papers; IHK, *Recalled Recollections*, pp. 106–107.

bined with the freight rate differentials, this policy hurt Galveston interests. But cooperation in New Deal programs was better than alternatives.[55]

Determined to land warehousing business for M&P, Dan borrowed heavily from the United States National Bank. With the loan he sent a reinforced corps of agents throughout interior Texas, offering advances to producers who committed their cotton to M&P. But he obtained so little cotton that he quickly abandoned the effort.[56] In 1935 he contracted with the government's Commodity Credit Corporation (CCC) to store cotton on which federal loans had been taken. M&P's responsibility was to insure the stored cotton against loss by fire or damage for its full market value. In return, the CCC paid M&P twenty cents a bale for weighing, sampling, tagging, and receipting the received cotton, plus a daily storage fee per bale. If M&P compressed or recompressed, the CCC paid it fifty cents a bale, but M&P had to deliver recompressed cotton to dockside. Any cotton loosened from bales was to be the CCC's property. M&P promised to recondition cotton it damaged. Drawn from the industry, government cotton buyers knew that sampling and grading were always troublesome matters. M&P had to deliver to the CCC samples from each side of every bale in anticipation of a standardized government grading system which never came. Its nonappearance was caused in part by the insistent lobbying of the Galveston cotton merchants, including H. Kempner, against any grading except by traders.[57]

The cotton merchants' complaints were not mere self-serving. Even well-run M&P had its gross income more than halved in the 1930s compared to the 1920s, from $4 million to less than $2 million, with the net income dropping from close to $1 million to less than $250,000. Yet M&P showed an absolute loss only in 1930, and from 1935–39 it paid H. Kempner dividends.[58]

Dividends were possible because in 1937 H. Kempner had secured incorporation for the Galveston Cotton Company, primarily to warehouse private cotton assigned to the federal government under New Deal parity programs. M&P remained largely dedicated to handling

55. Whisenhunt, "Huey Long and the Texas Cotton Acreage Control Law of 1931," *Louisiana Studies*, p. 142.

56. Ellis, "Cotton Compress Industry," pp. 382–87.

57. *Galveston Daily News*, Dec. 23, 1938.

58. Ellis, "Cotton Compress Industry," pp. 388–90.

H. Kempner's grower-clients. The new Galveston Cotton Company came into being "to provide a duplicate channel through which to sell cotton to individuals or in areas where it seemed to our advantage not to mention . . . connection with H. Kempner," according to an in-house statement. In the same depth-of-depression year, 1937, H. Kempner formalized earlier decades of connections with a large-scale West Texas ginner, J. C. Wilson, by incorporating the Texas Cotton Industries Company. In turn, H. Kempner as banker "made advances in large amounts which were used by the Texas Cotton Industries to finance farmers and gins in the [West Texas] area."[59]

M&P and Labor

Unlike nephew Herbert, Dan responded unsympathetically to New Deal laws encouraging or requiring employers to treat with labor unions. In 1935 the Supreme Court's Schechter decision and employers' refusals to bargain collectively triggered vast, often violent strikes. These chaotic conditions were destined to last until the Fair Labor Standards Act of 1938 restabilized management-labor relationships.[60] In mid-1937, laborers in Galveston's cotton industry, though demanding collective bargaining, displayed both unprecedented militancy and interracial cooperation by affiliating with the International Longshoremen's Association (ILO) and aiding Galveston blacks and Hispanics to form locals (racially segregated ones). The cotton employers, M&P included, in contrast to automakers and mine operators, created a negotiating committee of their business group, the Galveston Compress and Warehouse Association (GCWA). Avoiding both violence and demands for strikes, ILO spokesmen asked for union preference in hiring, an eight-hour workday with an overtime scale, a base wage of sixty cents an hour, and, for workplace safety, a minimum number of workers for the "specified gangs," that is, the weighers, tier makers, banders, bale sewers, bucklers, hoisters, truck loaders, and markers – an ongoing issue between workers and management.

The GCWA rejected this overture, claiming that Galveston presses already paid more than their Houston competitors. Accepting the

59. "Keys Report," p. 7.
60. 295 U.S., 495 (1935); Bernstein, *The Lean Years*, chap. 15.

GCWA counteroffer, the union reaffirmed the existing wage level of thirty-five to fifty cents an hour but won a nine-hour workday and the specified gang minimum.[61]

America's entrance into World War II once again illuminated contrasts between cotton and sugar. Importation of raw sugar from Cuba, Hawaii, and other protectable sources was possible all through the war. Indeed, because military shipping sailed to the western Pacific fully laden but were largely empty-hulled on eastward legs, authorities encouraged them to take on cargoes like Hawaiian sugarcane for delivery to Imperial and other refiners. Therefore, as an H. Kempner internal report noted, "The Sugar Company was very active during this period, as indeed were all operations in Sugarland." By contrast, cotton was "on a stand-by basis and did very little business. . . . As a result the [H. Kempner Trust] capital surplus went down from $7,156,000 in 1938 to $4,875,000 at the end of 1945."[62]

Nevertheless cotton was declared an essential industry in Washington. Male M&P workers were fixed to their jobs and their modest pay scales unless drafted or otherwise released to other war industries that billed the government on "cost plus" bases and enticed M&P skilled labor away with high hourly wages plus overtime. By 1945 M&P was importing Mexican laborers to ease the shortage. The war ending, government agencies freed mountains of baled cotton (of which thirty thousand bales were M&P's) to domestic and foreign users, including Lend-Lease and United Nations relief agencies.

Themselves now released from wartime regulations, in April, 1946, union members asked M&P for a forty-cent per hour across-the-board wage increase. This would beggar the firm, Dan insisted. The greater wartime flow of cotton through M&P had not meant equivalent profit increases because the M&P's expensive, high-density presses were technically efficient but uneconomical. Compression now brought in only 7 or 8 percent of the firm's revenue while labor ate up more than 50 percent.

Denied its requested wage increase, the union struck M&P. The nonviolent strike lasted until late June, 1946, when a compromise restored production.

Ike and Dan concluded in 1947 that M&P must alter nearly half-

61. Ellis, "Cotton Compress Industry," pp. 389–94.
62. HLK, "Beneficiary Interest Report, 1963," p. 7.

century-old policies. No longer would it concentrate almost exclusively on H. Kempner's clients but instead would reach out for the general warehousing trade, thus duplicating the purposes of the Galveston Cotton Company. To attract the trade, M&P temporarily reduced its rates roughly 25 percent.

M&P's original incorporation authority expired in 1948. Its new charter of 1948 was to run for fifty years. The company's forty-five thousand shares of capital stock were valued nominally at one dollar a share, all owned by H. Kempner. Since M&P was incorporated, the recharter allowed arms-length separation of M&P from the personal assets of the incorporators (Ike, Lee, and Harris) and the merged assets of unincorporated H. Kempner. These separations were desirable because M&P issued warehouse receipts for cotton it stored. Such receipts circulated freely as commercial paper. H. Kempner was M&P's banker. M&P's warehouse receipts for H. Kempner cotton, deposited with H. Kempner's bank, could mean that M&P was issuing these receipts to itself. Now that M&P was beating the bushes for clients apart from H. Kempner's it seemed better to separate the two entities.[63]

Then in mid-1950, a large Memphis cotton firm, Cook & Co., bought M&P for $1 million, with M&P backleasing part of the property and use of a press for five years. Almost simultaneously by charter amendment Harris, his brother-in-law Arthur Quinn (Lyda's husband), and Blackshear chartered a new entity, the Pelican Compress Company, and renamed it M&P. Announcing the deal to the press, Ike stressed its historic meaning: "Kempner interests will continue to use the port of Galveston for handling cotton as has been done for more than 70 years." Further, "Cook & Company, one of the foremost and progressive cotton houses in the country, . . . will . . . definitely locate in Galveston . . . together with other parties that may be associated with them." Last, the new M&P would return to purposes to which Ike had long held its predecessor: the company "would be restricted to the handling of cotton for his firm [H. Kempner] only."[64]

Anxious further to ensure stable inflows of raw cotton and to benefit from Mexico's lower wage scales and more tractable labor, by the

63. Ibid., pp. 394–99, 400.
64. *Cotton Trade Journal*, June 9, 1950 (unpaginated). Apparently the new M&P absorbed the Galveston Cotton Company; see Dun & Bradstreet, Oct. 26, 1950, report on H. Kempner, in misc. file, Kempner Papers.

mid-fifties H. Kempner was investing heavily there. It created for the purpose a new company, Algodones Universales, S.A., which bought gins and warehouses in Guymas, Matamoros, Mexicali, San Miguel, and Sonora. In a poignant reversal, the Mexican investments returned H. Kempner to factoring functions involving not ownership but handling of the commodity, that for fifty years Ike had been replacing with the merchant's ownership pattern.[65]

In Galveston, M&P and the Wharves shared the costs (nearly $1 million) of constructing a new compress and warehousing building on the latter's piers. M&P's new plant included sprinkler systems and the most modern available grading and testing devices. But M&P continued to earn more from storing cotton than from pressing it. Ostensibly for these reasons the Kempners, through the GCWA, though offering employees a pay raise, in 1954 resisted ILO demands for renewal of the "specified gangs" stipulations.

After two months of increasingly heated and fruitless negotiations on the issue, M&P locked its workers out. Two workless months followed before the union surrendered about specified gangs. Work resumed. But salaried workers were displeased by the fact that from 1942 through 1954 M&P hourly wage rates rose only a dollar an hour. Then in 1957 a retirement plan inspired by Harris, who like Herb insisted on progressive changes in dealing with labor, mollified salaried workers. In 1960 Harris merged this plan with the older H. Kempner retirement plan for office staff, with himself as trustee.[66]

Meanwhile, through mechanization M&P tried to hold down costs of labor and frequency of workplace accidents. From 1940 through the 1960s forklift attachments permitted lone M&P drivers to move heavy bales with relative safety, from rail cars or warehouses onto ships. Cotton racks allowed fewer workers to "break out" (i.e., to assemble ordered lots of) stored cotton more systematically. These expensive innovations plus the inflating costs of bagging supplies and labor increased overall operating budgets. Fluctuations in government purchasing and storage programs resulted in wide variations in M&P income from warehousing, while income from compressing remained

65. E. R. Thompson, Jr., "History of H. Kempner" (manuscript), Kempner Papers, p. 62a.

66. Ellis, "Cotton Compress Industry," pp. 400–405.

relatively constant but a lower percentage of the total business. Nevertheless, looking at M&P in 1963, the sixty-fifth year of its operation, its historian concluded:

> The[se] years, other than the period from 1915–1932, have not been easy. At one time or another, storms, wars, depression, freight rates, government regulations, and inflation have placed a strain on . . . the company. Yet . . . the company has improved its position over the years. However, if any feature can be said to characterize the company . . . , it is that of uncertainty, as reflected in the dissolution and organization of companies and the selling and building of plants. Such uncertainty . . . is a reflection of the larger shadow that hovers about the entire cotton industry.[67]

Dan, and cotton, never escaped that shadow. Sugar suffered from far fewer equivalent limitations on sensibility or talent.

67. Ibid., pp. 407–408.

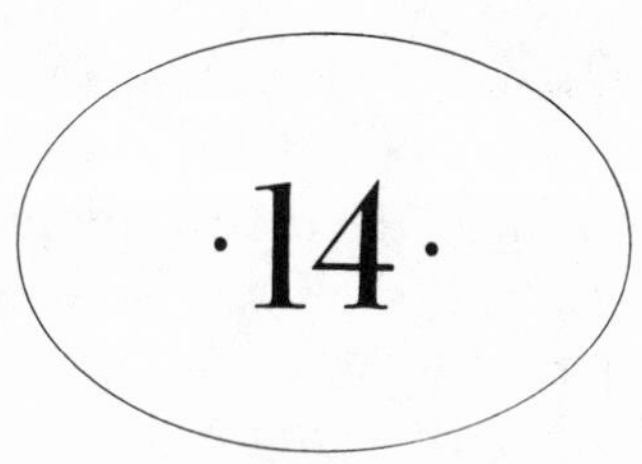

14

A Pool of Talent and Trust

IKE'S REPUTATION ROSE strikingly in the 1920–70 half century. Summing up this consensus, a nationally syndicated journalist described him in 1933 as a "Texas genius in Finance and Industrial Life," and repeated Lone Star State gossip that he "is the richest man in Texas, if not in the South. Certainly he is one of the ablest."[1]

Another journalist familiar with Lee's work in banking concluded that the Kempners deserved collective rather than individual praise: "All those who are enlivened by family solidarity, whose feeling of exaltation is quickened by brothers and sisters getting along harmoniously, undivided, without the usual bickering, dissension, and cross-purposes, should hearken to the story of the Kempners of Galveston." Upon reading this estimate, Kempner lawyer Homer Bruce wrote Ike:

> This is the most remarkable family history that I have ever known. Aside from the many outstanding and constructive accomplishments, in both private activities and public affairs, of your father and mother and all of their children, I know that this long and continued family solidarity, with its daily intimate associations, has ever been a source of joy to your mother and you and all of your brothers and sisters, and should serve as an example for other families to strive to emulate.[2]

John W. Davis, Ike's university classmate and once a presidential candidate, praised "the extraordinary history of your family." Davis won-

1. Spillane in *Philadelphia Public Ledger*, reprint in unidentified Houston newspaper, n.d., in DWK Scrapbook, 1894–1915, Kempner Papers.

2. *Texas Bankers Record*, Apr., 1944, p. 22; Homer Bruce, letter to I. H. Kempner, May 14, 1944, in DWK Scrapbook, 1929–1935, III, Bk. 1, Kempner Papers.

dered at Ike's transformation from "the skinny little fellow that I knew at Washington and Lee in 1893 . . . [to the] rather portly and dignified gentleman in a photograph of the Kempners that accompanied an article about them." In a tribute from a younger relative, Hattie's son Dan Oppenheimer echoed the theme, adding: "I could have told them many more things . . . besides your business ability—your ability to be good, kind, and generous at all times and to all people." Rabbi Cohen concluded a public praise of Ike in the mid-1920s with the wise injunction that appreciations "are not due to him alone, but to the whole Kempner family."[3]

If reasons existed to judge Ike as preeminent, the evidence leans also to a judgment that by the early 1900s he was first among equals. For example, in the formal organization of the H. Kempner Trust from 1920 to 1950, all the brothers were trustees in addition to their executive or board positions in many other trust interests. Other evidence affirms the judgment made in an H. Kempner in-house retrospective of the 1960s that "there is virtually no limitation on the powers of these trustees and there is no specific limitation on the types of businesses . . . which may be undertaken."[4] As an example of this elasticity in the trust and of sharings of duties and authority among the brothers, Ike, as noted earlier, had risked trust capital to buy the Island City Savings Bank, largely because it alone among Texas banks had a pre-1907 charter allowing it to handle both time-deposit savings and trust accounts. Lee had encouraged the acquisition, and, years later, after himself taking charge of the bank, was to say, "The charter was broad enough to run a funeral home."[5]

So, too, was the H. Kempner Trust. Under its clauses the Kempners, as trustees, in endlessly varying patterns bought, invested in, managed, and/or served on boards of so many businesses that efforts to recreate the roster fully have failed.[6] Many represented monetary commitments of risk capital by the H. Kempner Trust, like those made

3. Davis, letter to I. H. Kempner, May 2, 1944, and Dan Oppenheimer, letter to Lee Kempner, undated, both in DWK Scrapbook, 1929–1935; Cohen quoted in *Houston Chronicle*, Mar. 22, 1925.

4. "Keys Report, 1964" (manuscript), Kempner Papers, p. 11.

5. E. R. Thompson, Jr., "History of H. Kempner" (manuscript), Kempner Papers, p. 22.

6. I. H. ("Denny") Kempner III, letter to H. L. Kempner, Feb. 10, 1986, supplied lists, copy provided to author by H. L. Kempner. It is partial because searches of both H. Kempner office records and the Kempner Papers failed to turn up

The Kempner brothers, ca. 1945: Ike, Dan, Robert, and Stanley. A portrait of their father, Harris Kempner, is on the wall above. (Courtesy Leonora K. Thompson)

by any investor. But others, like Imperial/Sugar Land or M&P, reflected huge, ongoing commitments of both H. Kempner money and of the males' lifelong careers as executives.

No individual, however talented or energetic, could run such a burgeoning, dynamic mélange of a holding company. A quartet or quintet might be able to cope. Other owners in like situations resorted to professional managers. As stressed earlier, the Kempner brothers, deeply committed to their family cohesion ethic, preferred to recruit from among themselves, their sons-in-law, and sons.

Reality would set limits. Only Ike's two sons would choose H. Kemp-

---

records or mention of other enterprises that were once affiliated. Private investments and non-trust board positions were not included.

ner careers, and Herb's untimely death left Harris alone of the second American-born generation of Kempners in command of a family firm, albeit the central one of H. Kempner. Their few male cousins preferred professions or independent businesses.

Several male in-laws of the 1920–70 decades did, however, express interest in top H. Kempner positions. But each of these few aspirants were deemed unsuitable. If recoverable at all, the reasons offered for their exclusion range from inadequate initial on-job performances to failure to fit in.[7] The result of the exclusions is clearer than the reasons for them: No in-law achieved a top H. Kempner management position. Therefore, nonfamily managers were recruited, often after rising from humble in-house jobs.

Was the extended success of the Kempner conglomerate due to Ike or to the collegial talents of all the brothers, or even of the whole family? Several points want making. First, success existed, both financially and in terms of family cohesion. Second, success was achieved on commendable levels of marketplace standards. And, third, over decades, though Ike appeared to have overshadowed his brothers, not to mention his mother and sisters, the judgment favoring the collegial contribution is reasonable.

All these intertwined points are illuminated by attending to trust operations.

Ike: General Overseer

Both at home and at work Ike did seem to be a center of decision-making. "He had to take over everything," Fannie recalled in what, despite her seemingly critical tone, was actually a warm and loving reminiscence. Longtime H. Kempner office staffer Hyman Block judged that Ike made himself "the general overseer of everything, . . . the brains, you might say, from which all knowledge flowed." Among Eliza's adult children Ike was clearly "No. 1," Block continued, "To this day [1981], the average person . . . [when] you talk about the Kempners, they think of Mr. I. H. Kempner. . . . He greatly overshadowed his brothers."[8]

7. Harris Kempner Weston, interview with author, July 5, 1986, notes in author's possession.

8. Fannie Kempner Adoue and Sara Kempner Weston, interviews with L. Marchiafava, Aug. 1, 1981, and Aug. 29, 1981, respectively, RLA (perhaps

Such an opinion by the "average person," even by a longtime H. Kempner employee, failed, however, to appreciate subtler interrelationships. Ike's apparent primacy was largely a matter of deliberate style and long habit among the Kempner managing males.

A habitual posture of deference to Ike developed during years when then-immature siblings and, later, sons took cues and instructions from him. Probably Eliza encouraged this posture. Ike was the breadwinner for the large brood, bringing it safely across hazards opened by their father's death. But siblings aged. None were ciphers. Time and the strong personalities of both birthright Kempners and many spouses required the sharing of leadership. By 1900 Ike's once solo mastery of H. Kempner was already evolving painlessly into shared accountability and amiable collegiality.

Consider an early pre-trust venture that Ike and Dan made on behalf of H. Kempner. Soon after the century's turn the brothers bought rural real estate near Wichita Falls. Dan became excited by possibilities for growing rice in this semiarid land by damming a creek. Commitments to Imperial/Sugar Land were then under consideration plus the brothers' other activities. Yet when Dan took to his brothers his ideas about growing rice, a thirsty crop, in a dry area, if costly investments were made for irrigation, "Agreement was reached within the [H. Kempner] firm to test Dan's theory," a family chronicler noted. "This agreement was in actuality simply the result of informal conversations [among the brothers]."[9] The rice-growing venture yielded no profits.

To be sure, the trust's executive group, the trustees, made business decisions. But the fact of all shareholders' equality received frequent and respectful attention from the managing males. In sum, in the H. Kempner Trust Ike was no autocrat. His brothers and Seinsheimer were coleaders as named board trustees and as the executives of specific H. Kempner businesses, and neither they nor the shareholders were shy or complaisant or interested only in "bottom lines." They were equal also in other, more intimate senses configured by imperatives of heart as well as of law or ledgers, senses defined by

Fannie's judgment here suggests the deliberate separation of Kempner females from management); Hyman Block, interview with L. Marchiafava, June 6, 1981, RLA.

9. Thompson, "History," pp. 23–24.

mutual respect and trust as well as by the technicalities of the trust.

What developed in the trust was what existed in the Kempner family: less a hierarchy that anyone controlled than a substantially collegial body of decision makers, primarily the males but with the females active both in calendared shareholders' assemblies and in less formal but far more frequent family occasions. In the daily management of H. Kempner's diverse affairs the on-site men—Ike, Dan, Lee, and Stanley—performed as executives must, each nominally in charge of specialized or "pet" businesses. But over decades their performances resembled a skilled chamber music quartet more than solos, a quartet playing to a beloved constituency.

Quartets need first violinists. Gregarious, a collector of jokes, aphorisms, news items, and quotations more or less apt for businessmen's luncheon audiences,[10] and boundlessly energetic, Ike's very busyness fed the idea that he dominated everything, an idea his brothers willingly fostered. They preferred less public roles. If he was a workaholic, so were they, and they functioned contentedly in shadows he cast. Behind this façade consensus governed significant trust decisions.

The very structure of the 1920 trust mitigated against anyone's automatic dominance. Instead of a managerial monopoly for one Kempner, the trust, combined with the Kempners' habits, strong wills, and aspirations, nurtured debates and sharings of interests, profits, losses, decisions, and affection. This unusual mutuality and accord imposed special burdens on trustees.[11] But they were also shared by these cultured and toughened risk-takers.

Ike's reputation as family leader developed in part also because for decades he chaired the annual meetings in Galveston of H. Kempner Trust shareholders, an enlarging tribe as marriages and births grew numerous in the 1930s. His headship of H. Kempner made him a natural center of trust affairs. Recall that the named trustees of the H. Kempner Trust functioned not only as its formal "board of directors"—Hyman Block's imagery—but also as an informal board for all H. Kempner enterprises.[12] In turn, H. Kempner held all the trust's

10. See Ike's pocket journal, supplied by H. L. Kempner, 1980.

11. Henrietta Blum Kempner, "The Blum Saga" (manuscript, 1968), Kempner Papers.

12. Block interview with Marchiafava, Aug. 1, 1981.

diverse and pooled assets in which all Kempners were equal shareholder-beneficiaries. Therefore Ike's reports as head of H. Kempner were the heart of the trust's annual meetings.

He ran them well, year after year, decade after decade.[13] On Ike's death (1967) the chair passed to his son Harris. With the death of his brother Herb (1953), Harris was the only second-generation American-born Kempner who by training and desire had already earned this top billing in the Kempner business conglomerate. And in 1987, on Harris's death, this distinction of chairing passed to his son and namesake, Harris Leon, Jr.[14]

This succession suggests that what prevailed in trustee meetings was less a tight-paced business agenda than an intimate, filial, clubby atmosphere that pleasantly enveloped nonrelative cotrustees of later years as well as kin. Ike helped to create this atmosphere in part by intruding humor if levity was appropriate. He was good at the tactic, one he had been developing for decades.[15] For example, perhaps the "genial commissioner" retrieved some credit with his wife for having had to interrupt their honeymoon in Hawaii in 1902 by having her join him in 1907 on what he insisted was a three-month pleasure trip to Germany. A journalist interviewed Ike soon after his return to Galveston, finding him "back at his desk . . . hard at work . . . his coat and collar off and . . . trying to make the best of a warm afternoon." Replying to questions about the trip, Ike suggested ingenuously that its high point was the midnight delivery to their hotel bedroom of a wagon-load of vegetables. A porter had mistaken Ike for another guest, a wholesale produce merchant en route to market.[16]

Not quite. As in his and Dan's "Innocents Abroad" expedition years earlier, Ike and Hennie's seemingly indulgent 1907 sojourn overlay busy visits with German textile spinners and cotton exchanges that for business reasons he chose to disguise.[17]

13. H. L. Kempner interview with Marchiafava, Aug. 1, 1981.

14. A. M. Alpert, letter to Leonora K. Thompson, undated (ca. July, 1988), copy to author.

15. *Galveston News*, undated clipping (ca. Dec. 7, 1902), in DWK Scrapbook, 1894–1915.

16. Unidentified, undated newsclipping, DWK Scrapbook, 1894–1915; IHK, *Recalled Recollections*, pp. 35–36, on the honeymoon.

17. See telegram, P. F. Lenz, vice-president, Bremen Cotton Exchange, June 17, 1907, DWK Scrapbook, 1894–1915.

Shareholders in the Trust

So few major companies now remain family-owned that, as Harris Kempner Weston, an Imperial director and prominent lawyer, suggested in 1981, "There's not even a Ford running Ford anymore." Increasingly divorced from ownership "the running is in the hands of professional managers and the directors are usually professional managers."[18] But not in the Kempner family. Its members owned all the shares and were its trustees and executive board.

The practice in the majority of trusts is for boards of trustees to meet infrequently, having delegated to professional managers the actual operations of trust enterprises and the uses of trust funds. When trustee boards do meet, it is usually for ceremonial purposes. Not so H. Kempner trustees, who "were a [substantive] meeting . . . whenever and wherever they were together," Harris noted.[19] The brothers and other trustees were together almost every day, often several times a day, thus further fusing business and family relationships and realizing the cohesion aspiration.

Persons who knew the Kempners understood that their seemingly casual daily ingatherings were parts of a carefully knit and nurtured complex that housed both business and family interests. Most often the men gathered in the H. Kempner office suite where Ike presided and where Dan, in charge of M&P, of recruiting and training potential executives and managers, and of the Kempner side of the spinners' claims, and much else, also had rooms. Lee and Stanley usually joined Ike and Dan there. Hyman Block recalled Lee arriving in Ike's office "with a sack of papers and his pencil, and he would sit down with Mr. Ike . . . [who] would then advise him on bank matters and [then] he [Lee] would then advise . . . [Ike] on . . . [H. Kempner] matters, and of course Stanley was just across the street. . . . It was as informal as it could be. It was just plain family, not 100 but 100,000 percent."[20]

Joined in early decades also by Seinsheimer and later by non-Kempner successors, these informal "somewhat collegial" exchanges of views, as Harris, an attentive and informed future participant, de-

18. Harris Kempner Weston, interview with L. Marchiafava, Aug. 29, 1981, RLA.

19. H. L. Kempner, letter to author, Sept. 1, 1987.

20. Block interview with Marchiafava, June 6, 1981.

scribed them, the trust board members surveyed together their individual concerns—banking, insurance, cotton, sugar, real estate, cattle-grazing, investment opportunities, etc.—and the ways these affected each other. Again to quote Harris:

> Dan was always in charge of the care-taking part [of the H. Kempner cotton business as part of which he] . . . ran the [M&P compress &] warehouses; he was responsible for the building [in 1924] of the U. S. National Bank Building [in Galveston], he was in charge of a number of the [H. Kempner-owned] ranches and plantations. . . . My uncle Lee . . . went into the . . . Island City Savings Bank . . . from a lowly place to become president. . . . Later on, when we formed the Texas Prudential Insurance Company, Pat . . . became head of that. . . . My father [Ike] ran the [H. Kempner] cotton export business and was in constant conference [by telephone, telegram, and mail] with Mr. Eldridge in Sugar Land. . . . But the . . . four [Kempner] brothers met almost on a daily basis . . . [in Galveston.][21]

Everything the trust did or failed to do was up for discussion. They talked out differences of opinion. Formal votes were almost never taken. "If somebody really objected to a course of action," Harris stated, "it was very likely that the others would not pursue it even though they might have favored it." Ike enjoyed no final say in disputes, and there were disputes. Sometimes one family enterprise suffered in order that others might benefit. For example, H. Kempner might assume a certain employee's salary or special expense of one of the other enterprises, something "which might fall between the lattices and didn't really belong to anybody." Other times the head of a Kempner enterprise would ask merchant bank H. Kempner (Ike) or commercial banker Lee, for credit. But "this didn't seem to cause any problem. Nobody was going to ask the [Kempner] bank to make a loan to the [H. Kempner] cotton company which some other bank wouldn't make."[22] Criticism was candid. No individual had a formal final veto or approval, which means that everyone did but apparently rarely if ever exercised it nakedly. "There were lots of things that they [the brothers] didn't like, but once they agreed, they stayed together," Block

21. H. L. Kempner interview with Marchiafava, Aug. 6, 1981, and June 6, 1981.

22. Ibid., Aug. 1, 1981.

recalled. Let one of them report error, however, and "Lo and behold, . . . then all the rest of them let him know what a mess he was." But "mess" or not, once a policy had been agreed to, the brothers pursued it "without bickerings, or any attempt to change the color of the cards after the game was . . . played. They stayed through the bitter end. They either won or they lost. . . ."[23]

Apparently it rarely mattered if a business policy being criticized was the "pet project" of one or another Kempner. Nothing was exempt from review. And for decades even the most seemingly acrimonious exchanges of views failed to erode the rare cohesive quality that flavored Kempner assemblies. Reflecting on this, Harris Kempner Weston in 1981 could recall no occasion when Imperial's affairs, for example, came out in trust meetings "as a family fight."[24]

Advantages of Proximity

An advantage in the Kempners' close physical proximity was that competent, aware, trusted substitutes were available when one or another brother was ill or away. Of the brothers, Ike traveled the most frequently and for the longest periods, a reflection of his energies and of the several "front-man" roles he played. Dan was next in frequency of absences, while Lee and Stan chose to be less mobile. Dan carefully comonitored H. Kempner and M&P business even while he was abroad, responding with keen observations about political and economic developments in the several European nations he visited on cotton affairs.

Banker brother Lee, who took on general monitorship over widespread family real estate and mineral interests, sometimes replaced Ike as the family spokesman even for Sugar Land operations. Lee exhibited the Kempner trait of scrupulous care for minute details.[25] For example, in 1959 he inquired of The Industries' president, Thomas L.

23. Block interview with Marchiafava, Aug. 1, 1981.

24. Harris K. Weston interview with Marchiafava, Aug. 29, 1981.

25. See boxes 1948 and 1953, #80-002, Kempner Papers, for numerous pertinent documents. Lee was both bank president and executive chief of the United States National Company, a "land holding vehicle" controlling the USNB building and other real estate and oil assets ("Keys Reports," p. 5; Alpert, letter to Leonora K. Thompson, undated [ca. July, 1988], which details USNC–USNB–H. Kempner Trust connections).

James, about progress on a civic beautification program for Sugar Land including mass plantings of wildflowers on roadsides and lawns. Where, Lee asked further, was the washateria to be located in the new, Kempner-built shopping center then rising across the railroad tracks from the refinery? And where was James's promised report on school district consolidation in Sugar Land? Lee noted also that he and his brothers (not Ike alone) had decided against having the brand-new Sugar Land high school bear the family name as residents had suggested and state education officials had approved, because future generations of students would likely prefer war heroes or athletes.[26]

Perhaps the brothers kept such sharp watch on James because, they thought, the year before he had undervalued Kempner acreage that the state purchased for a freeway. Unlike Ulrich before him, James had not come to management from the Imperial refinery production line. A former stenographer to Ulrich, James was a feisty and able defender of his actions. He argued correctly that the Kempners might have made a few thousand dollars more had he held out, but the freeway would raise the value of Venetian Estates, a Kempner-financed residential subdivision then under construction, one unconnected to the refinery housing area, more than the disputed amount.

Another time James wanted authority and money to build a new factory adjoining the Imperial refinery in which to produce animal feed from sugar and truck-farm by-products. The Kempners decided against it. They had determined during the depression to avoid illiquid credit or capital squeezes. "We may be termed conservative along these lines," Dan wrote James, "having had experience in the 1930s when our debt was very heavy and burdensome, at which time we vowed that we would never get in this position again!"[27]

The depression left many deep memories among the Kempner brothers. Dan's father-in-law, Joseph Bertig, an Arkansas banker and industrialist, had died in 1927. First Dan, then, as years passed, all the Kempner men, advised Bertig's widow concerning her assets and investments. In early 1929 Dan's advice on stocks quintupled her

26. T. L. James file, Box 162, #80-002, Kempner Papers. In 1988 Isaac H. Kempner High School opened in Sugar Land.

27. All in "Sugarland" files, esp. DWK and IHK exchanges with T. L. James, Apr.–Aug., 1958, in Box 156, #80-002, Kempner Papers. On the Venetian Estates, see comment by L. K. Thompson, in letter to author, Aug. 18, 1988.

wealth, on paper. But all evaporated in the market crash and ensuing depression. Amidst all their other expenditures of energy, thought, and time, the Kempners took responsibility for the management of the extensive Bertig properties (and debts), successfully it appears, without taint of self-serving or arguments among themselves or any member of their families.[28]

Often discussions became arguments that the men carried on at lunchtime in one or another of their offices, although usually each lunched in his Galveston home. Additionally, all of them plus their wives and children dined at Eliza's each Friday Sabbath eve, at her insistence. On all occasions trust affairs were likely to flavor conversations, sometimes rowdily, Block remembering how "every Friday night even after all [the boys] were married, they met at Mrs. [Eliza] Kempner's house and they decided over . . . supper whether they were going to buy one cent stamps or two cent stamps, whether they were going to fire you or hire him—all the business—like a Board of Directors."[29]

The U.S. National Bank

Perhaps both for vainglory and to create more efficient stages for their interactions, in 1923 H. Kempner trustees financed the high-rise U.S. National Bank Building in Galveston. Its origins lay in events two decades earlier, when Lee was a trainee in H. Kempner's newly acquired Island City Savings Bank. A senior cashier absconded with fifteen thousand dollars, but Ike reassured depositors and named Lee to replace the miscreant.[30]

The new bank building, Galveston's tallest, was completed in 1925, and Lee became bank president in 1930. Kempner brothers, except for Stanley, had offices throughout the new building. Stanley continued to run Prudential Insurance Company from a succession of rented offices in Galveston. When the old Ball High School building became available in the 1950s, the Kempner trustees bought and

28. File 1, Box 43, #80-002, Kempner Papers.
29. Block interview with Marchiafava, Aug. 1, 1981.
30. *Galveston Tribune* clipping, undated (ca. 1904), DWK Scrapbook, 1894–1915.

transformed it into a luxurious office building to house Stanley and Prudential.[31]

Stanley did not live to see the opening of his lush new quarters. His death in 1954, followed bruisingly soon by Dan's in late 1956, lent weight to long-standing concerns felt by Stanley's brothers about the fact that his performance as insurance executive left the Texas Prudential "unfortunately a one-man concern." That is, though respected among his business peers, Stanley had failed to develop his own successor, nor had Dan, Ike, Lee, or other trustees repaired the lack. It led to the decision, one uncontested among H. Kempner Trust shareholders, to sell the insurance company. But Stan was a full participant in all H. Kempner Trust affairs and family gatherings; a participant no less important than his older brother.[32]

As in most states, Texas required trustees to report at scheduled intervals to a trust's shareholding beneficiaries. The generally happy mood at shareholders' formal annual meetings reflected also the trust's prosperity that Ike was able to report in the many good years, which meant income for shareholders. Profits from some trust enterprises helped to offset reverses, or, as in Sugar Land, decisions to defer profits.

In most businesses, especially substantial corporations, relatively few shareholders trouble to attend calendared meetings. H. Kempner Trust shareholders were disinclined to proxies or to being orchestrated. The trustees "let them [shareholders] voice any opinion they wish [on a policy]," Harris recalled, "and then the trustees, who are business people,. will decide on whether or not to do it." Harris recalled further that the management of the H. Kempner Trust was in the hands of "a self-perpetuating board, and nobody [on it] has ever been replaced until he died."[33] Which lends an unabashedly autocratic if benevolently paternalistic flavor to H. Kempner Trust policymaking not only at annual meetings but every workday.

But the Kempner meetings were different. First, the trustees' job was "to let them [the other shareholders] know *all* about what's go-

31. IHK, *Recalled Recollections*, pp. 120–21.

32. "Keys Report," p. 10; H. L. Kempner, "The Kempners of Galveston and Sugar Land" (manuscript), Kempner Papers, p. 14; *Houston Chronicle*, Mar. 22, 1925; H. L. Kempner, letter to author, Sept. 1, 1987.

33. H. L. Kempner interview with Marchiafava, Aug. 1, 1981.

ing on." Honoring this commitment to candor and completeness in reporting, the Kempner men found places in their meeting agendas for full disclosures about the spinners' lawsuits and the need to carry on costly improvements at Sugar Land, as examples.[34]

Second, as Rabbi Cohen discerned and most Kempners never forgot, the trust shareholders' assemblies were family ingatherings as well as forums, and a primary purpose of all the efforts was family cohesion. Sharing the Kempner trait of strong-mindedness, and responding also to Eliza's careful nurturing of the family's bonds of affection and trust, for many years the Kempners came to the trust's annual meetings with few chips on shoulders and left without rancor, recrimination, jealousy, or distrust.

Third, profits were not uncommon. Many tendencies toward argument and even obstruction might have been blunted or diverted by the pressure favoring accommodation and approval of the managers' policies that dividends generated.

Fourth and probably most important, Ike was able to report not only profits but equal sharings in profits. Equality of interest among all shareholders likely generated reciprocal interests between the managing males, their non-managing siblings, and the widening circle of spouses and a new generation of children. Let other families break up over unequal, inequitable divisions of profits. Not the Kempners. Harris expressed the shared perception: "It didn't make any difference what happened to the [pooled] income; it all belonged in the same pot."[35]

Sharing Alike

Equal sharings among Eliza and her eight matured children remained a core adhesive of the H. Kempner Trust. This continuity is the more remarkable in light of the fact that three of Eliza's and Harris's eight children who reached maturity never married and died childless, while the others produced heirs. Eliza distributed her widow's share equally to her children. But by the 1950s when death began to claim some members of Ike's generation, inequalities of in-

34. Ibid.; memo, June 6, 1952, in "Gulf Coast & Santa Fe Railroad—Galveston," #80-002, Kempner Papers; IHK, *Recalled Recollections*, pp. 38–39.
35. H. L. Kempner interview with Marchiafava, Aug. 1, 1981.

heritances inevitably resulted among their children. Ike and Henrietta had five children, Dan and Jeane one, Hattie three, Fannie one, and Sara one. Yet the Kempners escaped for a long time the expectable feuds, bitterness, schisms, and lawsuits between cousins who received less than others did. Commenting, Harris suggested in 1981 that part of the explanation lay in the legal principle of *per stirpes* (i.e., the joint taking of deceased parents' shares in property by children).[36] What occurred was that all eight of Eliza's children—Ike, Dan, Hattie (Oppenheimer), Robert Lee, Stan, Fannie (Adoue), Sara (Weston), and Gladys—would leave their shares to their descendants if they had any and, if they had none, then equally to all the descendants of their siblings. The result was that rough equality of shareholding would eventually prevail among the descendants.

Thus Ike's five children received a larger gross amount but not larger individual amounts of the estates of the childless aunt and uncles than did their cousins whose parents produced fewer offspring. "But it evened out" beyond eventual inheriting when Ike's generation died, Harris noted, as, of his childless aunt and uncles, one left his shares to all the nieces and nephews, one to grandnieces and nephews, and one to a combination of both. Further, before any of the first American-born generation died, its members established in 1947 the Galveston Fund, renaming it in 1950 the Harris and Eliza Kempner Fund, a charitable and educational foundation.[37] It too received shares of the three siblings' estates.

"So," continued Harris, "per estate stirpes, there was an exactly even division among the eight [children of Eliza and Harris and their children] whether they were running . . . [an H. Kempner] business or not." Harris marveled that the practice as well as the principle of equal sharing endured for by far the better part of a century, from 1898, the year of the Spanish-American War, through the nation's celebrations of the Constitution's bicentennial. He concluded that "it has probably been one of the great sources of strength and family solidarity as long as the memory of it lasts to realize that everyone was treated alike even though the burden of running this complex of businesses rested on the four boys and the people they recruited."[38]

36. Ibid.
37. See chap. 16.
38. H. L. Kempner interview with Marchiafava, Aug. 1, 1981; H. L. Kempner, "Beneficiary Interest Report, 1963" (manuscript), Kempner Papers.

Ike too had been so proud of this fact that in 1952, when he was preparing a new statement for inclusion in a biographical dictionary, he stressed that H. Kempner's "various business activities, separate and varied though they may be, are equally for the account of all." He repeated the theme in 1958, in the context of his own recalled recollections about 1898 and of his father's vision of 1894.[39]

What held it all together for so long? The basic glue must have been trust in one another and reciprocal affection. Another adhesive was the Texas law that led Eliza and her advisors to shape the estate in ways encouraging both efforts to increase its mass and to retain it in undivided form, though all heirs owned equal shares. The happy factor of longevity was another tie. Eliza lived until 1947, and Ike until 1967.[40] While they lived it was difficult, though hardly impossible, for serious squabbles to develop or persist over management policies, adequacy of dividends, or recruitment of future executives from among the rising generation(s), all being banes of other family businesses.

Ike especially sometimes irked his juniors, their spouses, and children. But his relatives, including most in-laws, respected him and one another, a quality reflected in an insight of Harris Kempner Weston, Sara's son, a law clerk to U.S. Supreme Court Justice Harold Burton and a Cincinnati legal practitioner and resident. His father was also part of a family business. Differences between it and the Kempners' impressed Weston. In the Weston family business, he realized, intergenerational discordances and discontinuities alienated close relatives, even siblings, from one another, "and there's nothing that brings us together." But all the Kempners "go down to Galveston . . . at least once a year . . . [for H. Kempner Trust] meetings so we keep up a personal relationship as well as a business relationship that is not found in other families."[41]

Eliza

Eliza's role remained central until her death in 1947, eight months after her ninety-fifth birthday. On that occasion journalists and the

39. Quotation in memo, June 6, 1952, file "GC and SFRR – Galveston"; IHK, *Recalled Recollections*, pp. 38–39; IHK, "H. Kempner: The First One Hundred Years," *Gulf Coast Historical Association Publications* 1 (1958): 13.

40. Stanley died in 1954, Dan in 1956, Hattie in 1958, Lee in 1966, Ike in 1967, Gladys in 1968, Sara in 1983, and Fannie in 1987.

41. H. K. Weston interview with Marchiafava, Aug. 1, 1981.

writers of publications for Kempner businesses and benefactions paid tribute to her, as they did later in her obituaries. The obsequies took note of more than her happy longevity. One obituary declared that "Mrs. Kempner became the head of, and the ruling spirit over, a family whose large accomplishments in our City and beyond its borders are proverbial."[42]

Was it merely conplimentary to describe Eliza as the "head . . . and ruling spirit" over her family? As a young bride in the early 1870s, she had learned quickly how to traverse the web of southern social, religious, and racial relations. Traditionally leery of all but fellow BOIs, native Islanders had nevertheless welcomed this impressive woman, warmly and forever.[43]

The very intensity of her husband's and her own devotions to family, work, and community encouraged a deep sense of religious obligation. Even before her husband's premature death Eliza was a veritable matriarch at home, and afterward she ruled as matriarch the enclaves of a persistently patriarchal family domain. Although the Kempners' Jewish tradition stressed the males' preeminence, it also assigned significant roles to the wife and mother, and Reform Judaism further emphasized those roles. True, in Galveston society and under Texas inheritance laws Eliza was primarily Harris Kempner's wife and widow, and she would spend much of her life in that metaphorical enclosed garden. Nevertheless, the enclosure of Kempner women was only as complete as they wished it to be, because the idiosyncratic Galveston situation encouraged involvement of women not only in private charity but also in the "municipal housekeeping," that is, in the same urban Progressive reform movement so compelling to men.[44]

Eliza's own heritage and strong personality were essential strengths in her marriage and long widowhood. Growing up in the Reform-oriented Jewish community of Cincinnati, she was surrounded by labor's early efforts to unionize and by the declamations of abolitionists and Union patriots. By the time she married, Cincinnati reform

42. Mimeographed press release, Sept. 26, 1947, and other sources too numerous to mention, DWK Scrapbook, 1945–1948.

43. See for example, unidentified clipping dated Jan. 25, 1899, DWK Scrapbook, 1894–1915.

44. See, generally, Beard, *Woman's Work in Municipalities;* Hoy, "Municipal Housekeeping," in *Politics and Reform in American Cities, 1870–1930,* pp. 173–98.

efforts had bridged long-divided ethnic, religious, class, and racial groups and neighborhoods. The message in Cincinnati (which Eliza visited at least annually most of her life) was that merely moral suasion by women was moral balderdash.[45]

Eliza, however, chose never to interfere directly in the administration of the H. Kempner Trust or the H. Kempner business. Throughout her life she made her home a center for all Kempners residing in Galveston and for those who traveled there for the calendared assemblies of the trust shareholders. Friday night meals were "musts" for her adult children and their spouses and children. Few were loath to enter the boisterous arguments about almost anything, and young Kempners learned early to interrupt, to defend themselves from hecklers once attention was gained, to out-argue, and to recognize and applaud logic, wit, and humor. Eliza made the first admission of a young Kempner to the adults' table and to the discussions there, an honor that both boys and girls aspired to as a rite of passage.[46]

Although Hattie and her family lived in San Antonio and Sara and hers displayed a regrettable but excusable lapse in taste by living as far away as Cincinnati, Eliza would welcome all to the shareholders' meetings in Galveston and expand these annual midwinter events into family reunions and celebrations. Formal trust business might consume only one day, but the socializing, including birthday celebrations for Ike, Eliza, and Lee, often spread over a week.

Recruiting the Next Generation

Annual meetings of trust shareholders were training environments for future Kempner executives. Harris recalled fondly how every assembly of the family was enlivened by "fantastic arguments in which everybody interrupts everybody else." Young Kempners and later their spouses and children had to learn that "being able to speak your piece requires great agility in the Kempner family, particularly at the dinner table." His elders always encouraged all the children "to state our views and to be able to defend them."[47]

This dynamic family environment had the H. Kempner Trust board

45. Ross, *Workers on the Edge;* Melvin, *The Organic City*, both passim; Ginzberg, "'Moral Suasion Is Moral Balderdash'," *Journal of American History*, p. 601.
46. H. L. Kempner interview with Marchiafava, Aug. 1, 1981.
47. Ibid.

at its hub. Vacancies on that central, self-perpetuating board were to be slow in occurring. Death waited thirty-four years after the creation of the 1920 trust to claim a Kempner brother (Stanley, in 1954). But long before that, however, Kempners had reached a consensus: "We've always taken [on the board only] those [maturing aspirants, whether blood kin or in-laws] who we thought had demonstrated their ability and knowledge of the family business," Harris stated in 1981.[48]

On-job apprenticeships in the core family businesses — H. Kempner, M&P, Imperial/Sugar Land, the U.S. National Bank, and Prudential Insurance — leading to top management if deserved, were the routes to places on the trust board. Ike, then Dan, Lee, and Stanley traced those routes, as Ike's sons Herbert and Harris did in their turns. But, as noted, three of Eliza's children (Lee, Stanley, and Gladys) remained bachelors. Hattie and Sara had sons but none chose careers in H. Kempner enterprises. The unanticipatable result was that of blood kin only Ike's sons Harris and Herbert enlisted for such careers and proved that they deserved them.

Enter Harris ("Bush") and Other Branches

Chief among the pleasures of these decades for Eliza and Ike was the sight of the younger Kempner men shouldering H. Kempner weights. Known forever in the family as "Bush" because of his mop of unruly hair (a nicknaming that began a horticultural labeling tradition), Harris, like his brother Herb, even when in the early teens, had, as noted, exhibited intense interest in H. Kempner's core cotton and sugar businesses, respectively.[49] After private secondary school educations, each went in turn to Harvard. Harris graduated *cum laude*, and then, as in family tradition, he spent a year (1923–24) in Paris at the Sorbonne doing advanced work in European history. While there Harris toured much of Europe, visiting especially textile mills and agents connected with H. Kempner. Returned, Harris seized every

48. Ibid.

49. H. L. Kempner interview with Marchiafava, June 6, Aug. 1, 1981. Thus Harris's son and namesake became "Shrub" and his oldest son, "Branch." Because, according to Shrub, this "horticultural *shtik* [comedy routine] happens only once in a generation, only Branch, in 1985 eighteen years old, or Shrub's other son Randall, then sixteen, can determine whether there will be a Rose or a Petunia someday" (Long, "The Wizard of Galveston," *Ultra*, July, 1985, pp. 60–64).

opportunity to shadow his father during the latter's frequent visits to Sugar Land and other mainland family properties. But cotton interested the boy more than sugar, cattle, or anything else. The procedures involved in acquiring, grading, and selling cotton so fascinated Harris that sixty years later he recalled happily how he had "worked in the [H. Kempner] sample room learning to distinguish between the qualities of cotton, which is a highly recondite art."

Herbert, also a Harvard liberal arts graduate (1928), "was always fascinated by what went on in Sugarland," Harris remembered. Harris noted proudly that Herbert "went into the Sugarland picture [as a blue-collar production line engineer] and became president of the major organizations up there. . . . That's the division [of work] we sort of fell into naturally." But behind the seeming structurelessness were the hopes his grandparents and parents had nourished since the 1880s. Harris recalled his own eagerness to return to Galveston in the mid-1920s as his Sorbonne year neared its end: "It [Europe] didn't cast any doubt on my devotion to Galveston. That [i.e., the option of not returning] never came up."[50] That it "never came up" in the then-youth's own agendas was the best compliment that Harris's grandparents and parents could have received.

They returned the compliment in the form of the careful, extended tutelage in H. Kempner ways and means that Dan especially provided to him, Herb, and other aspiring Kempners and in-laws in their turns. Dan continued as the family's primary instructor almost until his death in 1956, and Harris succeeded him in this duty until his own death in 1987.

The copious Kempner archive does not specify how the spouses of Eliza's daughters learned about their new family's arrangements concerning career opportunities and equal sharings in the pooled trust assets. Apparently much of this tutoring was left to informal connubial occasions. In any event, the Kempner trustees early differentiated between shareholding (including voting rights) by in-laws who received their beneficiary interest from Kempner spouses or parents as gifts or bequests, and the access of male in-laws as matters of right to management of H. Kempner businesses.[51] Shareholders, yes; managers and future trustees, not necessarily. As an unintended result,

50. Long, "Wizard."
51. H. L. Kempner interview with Marchiafava, Aug. 1, 1981.

Herb and Harris Kempner, 1952 (Courtesy Leonora K. Thompson)

"no relative except blood descendants of I. H. K. ever independently managed anything that I. H. K. or his brothers started or invested in," Harris stated.[52]

An illustration of the recruiting process exists for a cherished "blood relative," Ike's grandson and namesake, nicknamed "Denny." As noted, in the mid-1950s death claimed Denny's father Herbert, who had been Imperial's president, plus great-uncles Dan and Stanley. Himself ailing and no longer able to monitor Imperial and The Industries plus the community, Ike appointed able non-Kempners to run both: Bill Louviere as Imperial's president and Thomas James in charge of The Industries.

During Herb's truncated but fruitful years in Imperial's manage-

52. H. L. Kempner, letter to author, Sept. 1, 1987.

ment he had encouraged Sugar Land's residents to move toward political independency from Kempner control and toward full legal status as a city. Ike yearned to see a Kempner on track one day to continue Herb's policies, including a self-governing Sugar Land, collaboration at Imperial with labor unions, and further improvements to The Industries, refinery, and community. When in 1960 Ike wrote to then-twenty-eight-year-old Denny, who had been testing banking waters in Houston and finding them uncongenial, these purposes and hopes infused his letter. Tom James "needs an understudy, or a sub-executive, which we must seek for prompt trial," Ike stated. Denny should try Sugar Land. "There would be no nepotism involved . . . nor in placing you on the road to earn promotions. . . ." An emergency existed in the family due to death's grim tally. The situation "could easily become a matter of urgency, which could defeat the great pride we should have in the efforts and success of another Kempner at Sugar Land."[53]

But voices raised also in opposition to the proposed move for Denny. His mother advised against it. Not wishing to retire and apprehending Denny as an advance agent of a forced retirement, Louviere held on until his seventieth birthday in 1964 forced his retirement. Once R. M. Armstrong succeeded Louviere, however, obstruction ended from this quarter. Welcomed by Armstrong, Denny took on The Industries, later becoming board chairman at Imperial as well, as noted earlier. In both capacities he made good his kinship claim on leadership of family enterprises, in the process advancing further his late father's progressive plans for the community as well as the plant and commercial properties.[54]

In 1959 Sugar Land received state incorporation as a city. Working closely with Imperial staff, the new municipal officers began the complex process of assuming obligations and functions the Kempners had borne for so long. Almost every official and employee of the new city was also an Imperial or Industries employee. Kempner management gave them generous paid time off during the transition. Once Imperial/Industries subsidiaries, the now-private utility companies kept residents supplied with water and energy. A city marshal replaced

53. Ike, letter to "Denny," Oct. 12, 1960, in IHK Personal file #21/24, #80-002, Kempner Papers.

54. Memo by Robert Armstrong, undated, in Leonora K. Thompson, letter to author, Aug. 18, 1988.

I. H. ("Denny") Kempner III, ca. 1980s (Courtesy Imperial Sugar Company)

the old Imperial labor foreman and a modern peacekeeping department has since come into being, as with firefighting, sanitation, and other essentials. The Kempner-built schools became incorporated into the Fort Bend Independent School District, still a bellwether in the state. The Kempners provided to Sugar Land all physical assets—land, buildings, vehicles, equipment—without cost, the city thereafter maintaining them, for which purpose its first revenue bond issues appeared in 1961–62.[55] And in all this, as well as in his Imperial re-

55. R. M. Armstrong and William A. Little, interviews with author, July 14,

finery duties, Denny proved his worth. He has since ascended to the chairmanship of Imperial's board, the post he fills at this writing.

Under all the legal forms that succeeded the survivor-in-community contrivance of 1895, the principle prevailed that all Kempners were "treated alike, even though some devoted all their time to running the business for the benefit of others," Harris wrote in 1963, prideful like his father of the fact that his family had learned how to avoid the common shirtsleeves-to-wealth-to-shirtsleeves pattern. "It [the equality principle] sounds very unusual and really very impractical," Harris stated later, "but it worked pretty well for some time."[56]

It would stop working well. When it did, the family had to accommodate less trusting and patient temperaments among trust shareholders (see chap. 16). All America was changing, and the Kempners were not immune from the need to alter ways.

1988. Little was an Imperial employee, a member of Sugar Land's first city council, and mayor.

56. H. L. Kempner, "Beneficiary Interest Report, 1963"; H. L. Kempner interview with Marchiafava, Aug. 1, 1981.

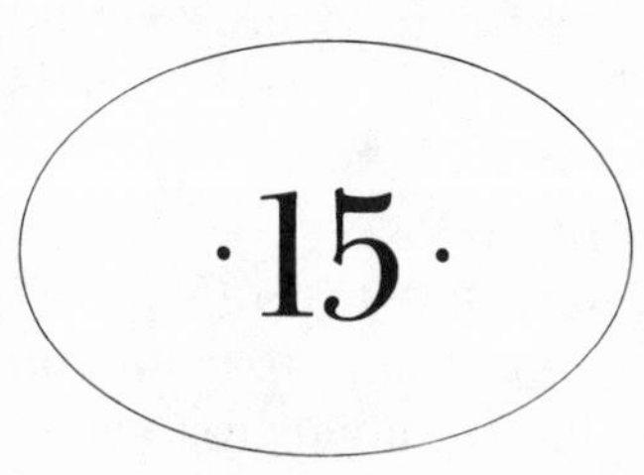

Politics and Moralities

AFTER A PARTICULARLY VICIOUS city election in 1939, Ike and a comrade of many municipal political battles, George Sealy, told outgoing mayor Adrian Levy, Sr., "Well, alright, we've had enough. They [the voters] don't appreciate our work here and the ownership . . . and . . . operation [of the Wharves]; we will divest ourselves and let the city take it over and get through with it." Their disgruntled decision to divest themselves from further direct civic political involvements had roots in what a journalist called the "hectic electioneering epoch"[1] begun in the wake of the Great War.

Then, as in many American generations, warnings became common that self-indulgence was eroding society's moral fiber. Visible extravagances of the wealthy generated demands for reform from horny-handed "populists" and elite social critics, both insisting that wealth justify itself. Throughout the 1920s and early 1930s the Kempners' increasingly lavish consumerism, including their frank enjoyment of prohibited liquor and toleration of nightlife, though common nationwide, provided ammunition for the family's foes, who included anti-Semites.[2]

As a region the South both admired the rich and criticized their antics, yet in this as in many matters southerners marched to slightly differing beats from those other Americans heard. Regional commit-

1. Adrian Levy, Sr., interview with R. L. Jones, Sept. 30, 1980, RLA; Brackman, "Galveston's Gulf," *Houston Gargoyle*, May 5, 1929.

2. Cf. Lapham, *Money and Class in America;* Horowitz, *The Morality of Spending;* Bloom, *The Closing of the American Mind*, all passim; IHK, *Recalled Recollections*, p. 63, and see Greene, "Guardians against Change," *Houston Review*, p. 3 and passim.

ments to order, continuity, tradition, and hierarchy combined in a durable sense of self. These comforting continuities helped southern makeweights like the Kempners to escape what historian Richard Hofstadter called "status anxiety" induced by critics of their ways and by changes in American life.[3]

Calm about status, Kempners accommodated criticisms. The family had moved early beyond claims to community leadership tied to a planter-industrialist-banker alliance, to claims based also on sustained, fruitful public service. Entrenched civic and commercial leader Ike Kempner could lose elections yet retain influence, primarily because of this civic and humanitarian activism. Despite Ike's declared intention in 1939 of retreating to "emeritus" status, neither he nor most relatives abandoned habits of and fondness for civic preeminence. For example, Lee enjoyed a long (1925–61) tenure in that Kempner near-fief, Galveston's treasurer, a tenure itself reflecting the family's reputation for prudence and probity.[4]

High Living and Low Life

Nevertheless, during the 1920s and 1930s the family found itself increasingly out of phase with community paces. One cause of this disharmony was Texas' perennial concern about vice.

After World War I, Texas' religious fundamentalists in politics retained concerns about prostitution, liquor, vice, and civic corruption. Guardians of rural values seized control of reform politics from predominantly urban Progressives who in Galveston had achieved so much.[5] Between 1919 and 1939 antivice activists, reinforced in the Galveston instance by the Kempners' critics, especially the Moodys, with increasing effectiveness mixed morality questions with issues of the Wharves management and ownership, until this mix became so

3. Hofstadter, *The Age of Reform;* McWilliams, *The New South Faces the World*, all passim.

4. *Galveston Daily News*, Sept. 17, 1963; IHK, *Recalled Recollections*, p. 63; and, generally, Cobb, "Beyond Planters and Industrialists," *Journal of Southern History*, p. 45.

5. Timberlake, *Prohibition and the Progressive Movement, 1900–1920*, chap. 1; Hobson, *Uneasy Virtue*, passim; Stevens, "What Made Grandpa Blush" (Organization of American Historians, 1988); Greene, "More Than a Thimbleful," *Houston Review*, pp. 45–56.

potent that Ike withdrew from Galveston's political power structure. Nevertheless except in politics the family retained what one mayor, a Kempner ally, described as "some clout when they came to see me."[6]

The Moody offensive built incrementally, taking advantage especially of the fact that the Kempners did not champion endorsement by Texas for the proposed Eighteenth ("prohibition") Amendment to the U.S. Constitution. When the war ended the state was already "dry," legally at least. Galveston immediately found itself a natural port for smugglers from Latin America, the Caribbean, and Canada. By 1919 a "rum row" of large foreign-flag ships lay anchored in the Gulf outside United States territorial waters, their holds stuffed with illicit liquor. A new Galveston "mosquito fleet" of smaller boats lightered wholesale lots of bootleg potables onto the island. Some "rum-runners" unloaded brazenly at the Wharves or at private boat clubs.

Once landed, illegal liquor was reportedly often stored in major cotton warehouses where experienced work gangs stacked cases of liquor onto cotton bale mattresses in rail freight cars with other bales cushioning the sides and a top layer further insulating and concealing the illicit cargo. Thereupon it moved comfortably to customers nationwide except for the fraction (amounting to far more than a thimbleful) staying in Galveston for home use and for sale in the flourishing number of bordellos, casinos, and speakeasies.[7]

The question resurfaced: Could mass evasions of local, state, and federal antivice and liquor prohibition occur without corruption at every level of government and in the cotton industry, the Wharves, and the railroads? Were elite miscreants enjoying protections by the Galveston police, county sheriffs, and state attorneys and judges? The statement of a black jazz musician who performed in many otherwise racially segregated speakeasies reflects the popular notions about Galveston vice from the 1920s to the 1950s: "The Jews owned it, the Italians ran it, and the Blacks enjoyed it."[8]

In the spring, 1919, mayor-council elections, Moody spokesmen depicted themselves as torchbearers of a new reform crusade, thereby feeding an increasing cynicism about the operations of local govern-

6. Levy interview with Jones, Sept. 30, 1980.

7. McComb, *Galveston*, pp. 159–66; Lender and Martin, *Drinking in America*, passim.

8. Leon Banks, Sr., interview with R. L. Jones, May 2, 6, 1980, RLA.

ment, an attitude that Ike condemned as "the usual civic indifference of Galveston as a whole." Moody gauged the postwar political winds better than Ike did. He imported from New York an advisor "schooled in political lore and practice," who relabeled the Moody party organization as "independents," thereby suggesting that Kempner-Sealy people were dependents, chiefly upon the Wharves. By contrast, the Moody "New Galveston Party" managers were willing to cultivate bravely "the very important labor and Negro vote (Galveston having grown to be a powerful union center, with the dollar-an-hour organized wharf workers as a backbone)," wrote a journalist. When Ike lost his 1919 bid for a second term as mayor, again to quote the journalist, "The New City [or Galveston] Party [was] swept into office, on a platform of breaking up the Sealy[-Kempner] monopoly of the . . . [W]harves and obtaining municipal control of the one-third portion of the shipping docks owned by the city."[9]

Lacking a calendar or budget for the change, the election was not followed by a transformation of the Wharves to a wholly public organization. Instead, for twenty years Kempners resisted implementation of the sense of the 1919 vote as they did the resurrecting allegations that they controlled or condoned vice in their community. Criticisms of the high-living Kempners, who allegedly transgressed public laws with impunity, increased. Although able for two decades to impede Moody progress toward the coveted Wharves buyout, the Kempners gradually found themselves in unfamiliar defensive roles. Kempners kept emphasizing business boosterism-plus-clean municipal government for Galveston. But the Moody spokesmen were more adept in sensing and exploiting the antiliquor evangelical morality and in tying it to the emotional issue of Wharves policies.[10] Other topics ranging from the seemingly trivial to the obviously major became subsumed in Wharves alternatives.

Taking advantage of distresses from the 1920 dockworkers' strike, in 1921 Moody candidates were again victorious in the municipal elections. They made it a two-pronged "fight for the people" by opposing

9. IHK, *Recalled Recollections*, pp. 50–51; Brackman, "Galveston's Gulf." The Moody manager of 1919 was Frank Anderson.

10. Bailey, "Business Boosterism and Evangelical Morality" (Texas State Historical Association, 1987).

a one-cent increase in trolley fares that Mayor Kempner had initiated and by proposing to implement the 1919 vote against the existing Wharves management. Wharves officials sued successfully to prevent the implementation, and voters supported the trolley fare increase.[11]

Kempners learned too and were willing to find teachers where they could. Referring to the Popular Party's defeat in 1921, Hennie, in New York City, commiserated with Rabbi Cohen about deferred reform hopes: "I know just what a mean time you all had over the election. I think the efforts of the Popular party were fine only as usual we started too late. I have met a man here . . . [who has] a fine [urban reform political] organization. . . . He promises to give me some data and working details, so maybe next time we will be ready too."[12]

Leaders of Texas' Democratic Party had long resented Galveston's maverick independence in politics. They smelled opportunity to align the Moody faction with the regular statewide organization. By 1925 Democratic Party regulars and Moody workers had unofficially combined into what Kempners called "Moodycrats."

Though misfiring in 1925–27, the Moodycrats caught the public mood in the 1928 national election. As in other southern states, in Texas the Roman Catholic religion of the Democratic presidential candidate, Alfred E. Smith, broke the "solid South." Galvestonians applauded a Moody spokesman who opposed Smith because the New Yorker was "a Catholic, a damned Catholic, and a God-damned Catholic."[13] By this time Shearn Moody had taken charge of his family's political interests. Branding as "damnable lies" Kempner charges of subservience to mainland political bosses, "Mr. Moody took pains to assure the writer [a journalist] that the [state] Democratic party is 'merely using his office as [a local] headquarters.'" Moody indicated further that though he would keep the Wharves ownership issue as the highest priority, he would continue swinging his organization away from the anti-development positions of his father, and toward more eclectic, populist-flavored appeals for votes.[14]

11. Angell, "Controlling the Workers," *East Texas Historical Journal,* p. 14.
12. Henrietta Kempner, letter to Cohen, Apr. 24, 1921, Box 3M238, Cohen Papers.
13. *Galveston News,* May 7, 1939, on the 1928 diatribe.
14. Brackman, "Galveston's Gulf."

Anti-Semitism in Galveston Politics

Political rhetoric in Galveston sometimes had anti-Semitic undertones. Kempners professed to believe that little bigotry existed and that when it surfaced it was easily scotched. Joined by Eliza and Ike, back in 1906 Rabbi Cohen had protested against a public school production of *Merchant of Venice*, noting, however, that "I do not know of a single outspoken instance of religious prejudice in school life, in this city." Such an instance did occur in 1915, however, in the vicious, unpunished hazing of a Jewish high-school student.[15]

Meanwhile, as noted, wartime liquor prohibition and antivice efforts increased rumors of Jews profiteering from both sources. As in Sugar Land, the Ku Klux Klan surfaced in Galveston. During the 1920 longshoremen's strike, Billie Mayfield, the provost marshal of the Texas National Guard sent to Galveston to contain violence, soon became the Klan's regional mainspring. Belatedly but ineffectively discredited for his excesses during the strike, Mayfield settled in Houston, where he published fulminations against Jews, Roman Catholics, race-mixing, divorce, and labor unionists.[16]

On business trips to New York City, Ike met with Louis Marshall, director of the B'nai B'rith Anti-Defamation League, and exchanged data on Klan activities nationally, in Texas, and in Galveston. So armed, Kempner helped to expose local Klansmen, a task eased because Rabbi Cohen's son had become an editor of a Galveston newspaper and H. Kempner an investor in a local radio station. The rabbi aligned the city's leading Catholic and Protestant clergy in an antibigotry front. He and Ike were "alive to the possibilities and . . . taking quiet precautions," Cohen advised Marshall. All Klan candidates lost in the 1922 Galveston city election.[17] One careful Galveston-watcher noted that in 1925 and again in 1927 "the Moody-supported outfit lost . . . [the city elections, taking only two commission portfolios] only after

15. Cohen, letter to Dr. J. W. Hopkins, Superintendent of Galveston Schools, May 16, 1906, Box 3M225 Cohen Papers; Cohen, letter to W. A. James, Principal, Ball High School, Dec. 6, 1915, Box 3M234, Cohen Papers; IHK, *Recalled Recollections*, pp. 63, 80.

16. Greene, "Guardians against Change," pp. 3, 12.

17. Cohen, letter to Louis Marshall, with attachments, Oct. 5, 1922, Box 3M239, Cohen Papers; Nathan and Cohen, *The Man Who Stayed in Texas*, pp. 249–61.

the Klan bogey had been invoked and swung the Catholic, Jewish, and Negro vote over to the [Sealy-Kempner] City party."[18]

But bigotry had been blunted, not vanquished. The story that the Kempners were suppressing Klan recruiting at Sugar Land resurfaced repeatedly in the 1920s.[19] Another persistent anti-Semitic rumor was circulated by a self-styled Protestant "reverend." He implied (to Rabbi Cohen) that he was on the staff of Rice Institute (now Rice University); that "wealthy Jewish men of leisure pursue gentile girls in the attempt to wreck their lives"; that "the Russian and Polish Jew is a notorious liar"; that "the Jew has a hard name morally"; and that organized prostitution in the Galveston-Houston region was "in the hands of Jews" and Roman Catholics. It all referred clearly to the Kempners.

Cohen demanded public retraction of the charges. The rabbi revealed that for two decades prominent though unnamed Galveston Jews had been financing Island City antivice efforts and related rehabilitation and resettlement enterprises for repentants among offenders and victims, especially prostitutes. No retraction issued. Not an ordained minister but a Rice Institute undergraduate and student YMCA officer, the accuser never provided proofs of significant Jewish participation in, much less domination of, Galveston prostitution, bootlegging, narcotics, or gambling.[20]

No Galveston Jews were important in the "downtown" and "beach" gangs that came to run Island City liquor, gambling, and prostitution during Galveston's "gaudy decades" from 1920 through the 1960s. Bootleggers might well have bribed public officials and work-crew chiefs at the wharves, cotton compresses, and rail yards. But nothing implicated Kempners in these transactions. Like most Jews, they abhorred the fact that even a tiny number of coreligionist criminals were fouling their American haven and home.[21]

Ike knew that federal and Texas laws were ambiguous about per-

18. Brackman, "Galveston's Gulf."

19. IHK, *Recalled Recollections*, pp. 63, 80.

20. Cohen, letter to "Rev." James Ludwell Davis, May 1, 1922, Box 3M229, Cohen Papers; information on Davis from Woodson Research Center files, Rice University.

21. McComb, *Galveston*, pp. 159–66; summarizes this body of research. Data on Jewish gangsters in Howe, *World of Our Fathers*, pp. 96–99, and Karp, *Haven and Home*, passim.

sons who harbored vice innocently. Uncertainties abounded concerning an owner's responsibility for uses to which tenants put rented, leased, or subleased buildings. Some Jews owned buildings where bootleg liquor, gambling, and sex were the merchandise. Innocently or not, pawnbrokers, some of whom were Jewish, did "fence" stolen goods. Intent to commit or nourish crime was difficult to prove. Texas' legal environment emphasized the sanctity of private property, especially real estate, and of (white) individuals' derivative right to use it largely as they wished. Federal and state constitutions restricted arbitrary searches and seizures and self-incriminations while stressing due process.[22]

Kempner Life-Styles as Political Targets

Long recovered from the 1900 Great Storm, the Kempners, especially the women, reemphasized cotillions, balls, and Galveston's increasingly lavish annual Mardi Gras festivities, while the men found the sailboat regattas to be engaging pastimes. These activities, however, did not lessen the senses of responsibility for the community and family.

Like millions of other Americans, Kempners frequently violated the prohibition amendment to the Constitution and federal and state implementing laws. Although the forbidden liquor was for their personal use, its unsecretive importation and consumption left the Kempners vulnerable to critics who mixed issues of private morality with such public policies as management of the Wharves. Increasingly the Kempners regarded the "noble experiment" as a symbolic crusade at best, one whose monetary and social costs outweighed benefits.[23] Throughout prohibition the Kempners had wine on their tables for the older children and harder potables for adults. Ike remembered always the "wine storage space: off the separated kitchen in the M Street house in which he grew up, and similar facilities graced all Kempner households. To them wine was a table beverage. Returning from a European vacation in 1924, Dan grumbled to a reporter that

22. On legal points, Mackey, *Red Lights Out*, chaps. 3–5; and see Hobson, *Uneasy Virtue*, passim.

23. Gusfield, *Symbolic Crusade*, chap. 6; Timberlake, *Prohibition and the Progressive Movement, 1900–1920*, chap. 5.

"there are today more things 'verboten' in the United States than were ever 'verboten' in Germany before the war." Dan became an activist in a Galveston unit of a national anti-prohibition amendment association.[24]

Until prohibition was repealed in 1933 bootleggers supplied the wines and liquors for the Kempners' homes and clubs, and for the speakeasies, restaurants, cabarets, gambling casinos, and bordellos for which Galveston remained regionally notorious. Summing up their nightlife styles during prohibition, on one occasion Ike wired the absent wife of a party-giving Galveston host, "After bathing and dining at the Country Club, [and] dancing at the Tokio [Club], . . . [the] guests and the Tokio orchestra . . . completed a wonderful evening."[25]

The Kempners came to justify their nightlife participation from their growing disbelief in democratically mandated morality. Besides, they enjoyed the cabarets and dining rooms where, as Galveston lawyer and later mayor Adrian Levy remembered, "one could go and gamble and see beautiful shows . . . without admission—somewhat along the lines that you find . . . in Las Vegas." Galveston was always an "open city," Levy noted.[26]

Islanders could go directly to offshore sources of alcoholic supplies. When the champagne stock failed at a family wedding, Harris and friends sailed out on the Gulf to a convenient rum-runner, took on several cases, unloaded them openly at the family's boat slip and transported them undisguised through the city streets to the reception, attracting no police interest and troubling no assembled Kempners or guests.[27]

Kempners rarely needed themselves to smuggle. Galveston bootleggers had regular clients and routes. Bootlegging minions bossed by "Big Jim" Clark, George Musey, Ollie Quinn, or "Dutch" Voight

24. *Galveston Tribune*, June 28, Sept. 16, 1924; H. L. Kempner, interview with R. L. Jones, June 17, 18, 1980, RLA. On wine storage, I. H. Kempner, letter to Beverly Harris, Feb. 29, 1965, "Curtis Hall" file, Box 1956, #80-002, Kempner Papers; announcement of association meeting, dated Apr. 19, 1927, Box 3M243, Cohen Papers.

25. Lykes, *Gift of Heritage*, p. 113, has the telegram.

26. Levy interview with Jones, Sept. 30, 1980.

27. H. L. Kempner interview with Jones, June 17, 1980. Reflecting the common family attitude, Henrietta Kempner became president of the Galveston local of the Women's Organization for National Prohibition Reform in 1932.

brought in wholesale cargoes regularly. These careerists, not the Kempners or other Jews, connected the underworld to respectable society.

The clubs that most prominent merchants enjoyed were downtown in the city's heart, while newer cabarets clustered first on the then-distant western fringe of the city, on county land. Then Sam and Rosario Maceo built an elaborate in-city establishment, the Balinese Room, on a pier at Twenty-first Street and the Seawall, in old Galveston's heartland. The Maceos and the others almost always could guarantee themselves and their customers safety from both criminal violence and police arrest even though rum-running speedboats moored just beneath the Balinese dining room and unloaded cargoes directly onto their pier, implying regular subornings of justice officials. Under such protection, Maceo slot machines, lottery tickets, dice or card games, and punch boards displaced others from barbershops, hotel lobbies, garages, and grocery stores. Occasional violence erupted between these competitors.[28]

Insulated from this sordidness, in the 1920s and 1930s the Kempners exhibited wealth and status as never before. Coming-out parties for debutantes, graduations, engagements, weddings, and births were celebrated lavishly. Kempner residences and, for some, chauffeured automobiles, reflected their owners' prominence and affluence. H. Kempner's annual shareholders' assemblies brought relatives to Galveston for well-reported social activities that supplemented business agendas. City, state, and regional newspapers frequently featured articles and likenesses of Kempners prominent at the time. The press described Lee chairing conventions of Texas bankers, Ike hosting assembled cotton merchants and taking his first airplane flight, Dan's reception for journalists covering a Democratic Party nominating convention, and costumed family participants at Galveston's annual Mardi Gras festivals, especially when a Kempner girl (Cecile, in 1928) was "given" (i.e., crowned). Frequent social whirligigs developed around exchange house parties, "galas" at private clubs, sailing regattas, Little Theater productions (one of Hennie's favorite benefactions), tennis tournaments, shopping trips to New York, and Ike's fiftieth (1923) or Eliza's ninety-fifth (1947) birthdays. Departures or returns from

28. McComb, *Galveston*, pp. 157–87.

excursions to Europe achieved special attention from journalists and from critical political foes.[29]

Harris Kempner and Prohibition Agent Al Scharff

One nonviolent liquor-centered incident involved Ike and Harris with a picturesque—almost picaresque—federal revenue agent, Al Scharff, stationed in Galveston. Himself a nonobserving Jew, Scharff, a former cowboy, had rustled Mexican livestock and served as a United States secret agent there. He married a sister of prominent Galveston businessman Herman Nussbaum, a close friend to the Kempners.

Scharff's record of raids, seizures, and arrests was exceptional. But as his biographer admitted, "Scharff's unorthodox methods not only stirred Galveston's anger but lifted a few brows in Washington."[30] Circulating in Galveston's highest society, Scharff won otherwise unobtainable leads for what came to be called "sting" operations, one of which involved the Kempners.

Dining one evening with his Nussbaum in-laws, Scharff overheard a remark about Antonio Campdera, a wealthy resident agent for Spanish cotton mills. Campdera was planning next morning to relocate inland, Scharff heard, and Campdera's "big automobile" would be laden with bootleg liquor.

At dawn next day Scharff had Campdera stopped on the causeway bridge. The Spaniard's car contained no liquor. Released, Campdera complained to the Spanish ambassador to the United States, whereupon this hot-potato issue passed from the American secretary of state to the secretary of the treasury, and then down bureaucratic lines to Galveston. Scharff fended off thunderbolts from Washington. But his Galveston friends, including Ike, were furious with him for violating family privacy. "Didn't he know everybody had a bottle or two?" prominent businessmen asked. How, they persisted, "could they be sure he wouldn't stop and search *them* on the highway?"[31]

Scharff learned that the Galveston Cotton Exchange (Ike was president) was preparing to petition the secretary of the treasury to dis-

29. DWK Scrapbooks, 1924–1929, and the Kempner Papers document these matters, too voluminously to cite individually.

30. Roark, *The Coin of Contraband*, p. 276 and passim.

31. Ibid., p. 278 (italics added).

charge him. Why, Scharff wondered, this local pressure? Had Campdera had warning of the secret roadblock and so carried no liquor?

Scharff's brother-in-law, Nussbaum, provided answers. He had left the dinner with Scharff for cards with Ike, Henrietta, and Harris. "Ike, Campdera is in for one hell of a mess tomorrow morning," Nussbaum had said: "Campdera is taking his whiskey with him to Dallas, and Al [Scharff] will grab him." Harris "went straight to Campdera with what he had heard, and Campdera went out and unloaded his whiskey."

Learning this, Ike interrupted exchange action on the removal petition. Confiding to colleagues that "my son [Harris] tipped him [Campdera] off," Ike asked, "Now, . . . who's going to be in trouble? Me, the president of the Cotton Exchange, that's who, because Al Scharff is going to tell the truth about it."

Scharff suffered only a mild reprimand. Campdera later confessed to criminal possession of the untaxed liquor of the anecdote.[32] The incident slid by. But corrosions among Galveston's officialdom allegedly because of prohibition did not diminish.

As the quality of public life eroded, the rhythm and tone of private pleasures, at least on the level the Kempners knew, seemed to become enhanced. Not so the speakeasies and "blind pigs" that serviced less-favored Galvestonians. Long after national prohibition ended in 1933, grimy and sometimes dangerous environments attracted merchant sailors, stevedores, cotton press laborers, and plebeian tourists with whom the Kempners had nothing to do socially.

In the late 1930s persons involved in this traffic contested ever more bitterly, violently, and overtly for larger shares in illegalities, finally straining public tolerance too far. State prosecutors and tax officials belatedly began to break up long-immune Galveston gambling and vice establishments. Squeezed and irritable, gang members lost restraint. In 1938 a well-known underworld underling killed an innocent bystander in a tavern dispute. Witnesses of the murder disappeared or lost memories. It appeared that because of corrupt and inept police officers the brazen killer might get off. Notions spread in the city that domestic communists, by insinuation chiefly Jews, ac-

32. Ibid., pp. 279–80; confirmed by H. L. Kempner in telephone conversation with author, May 11, 1986.

tive in the militant longshoremen's union, were behind both the murder and the corruption of the officials.[33]

Moody spokesmen made the most of these itchy sentiments, leading to Ike's 1939 decision to get out of politics. But in their now-traditional behind-the-scenes way, Lee Kempner and George Sealy met as private citizens with the long-incumbent police chief. That official suddenly resigned, whereupon witnesses equally suddenly recalled events. Found guilty, the convicted murderer later died in the electric chair. But the most recent historian of Galveston concluded that "there was no [real] anti-vice reform . . . and the power structure remained in place."[34]

Tourism

However seemingly inconsequential a topic compared with those of the port facilities or vice, tourism then as since represented one of Galveston's major chances for economic survival, according to business booster Ike and other Kempners. Encouragements to tourism were nothing new in this family. The seawall, bridges, major hotels, commuter rail lines, and autobus causeways and roads—all had long been identified with Kempner enterprise and enterprises. Yet in tourism lay another source of Kempner-Moody friction.

Even before the Great Storm, Ike had touted tourism. Then, in rebuilding the city, Ike perceived accurately that the seawall was likely to attract tourists, and he partially justified the accompanying new causeway as an essential supplemental facility for the visitors he hoped would substitute for the smokestack industries that stubbornly refused to locate there. Like most Islanders Ike wished to attract wealthier tourists, not plebeian day-trippers, rough-housing stevedores, and grimy oilfield roustabouts. To that end, he invested H. Kempner money and a great deal of his own time and energy in a consortium that planned and funded the posh new Galvez Hotel. It opened in 1911. But Ike found to his dismay that his major consortium colleague, William Moody, was unwilling to share the burdens of overseeing the

33. McComb, *Galveston*, pp. 164–66; see also *Galveston Daily News*, Jan. 22, 24, 1937 on communists; Max Nathan, letter to Henry Cohen, July 24, 1938, Box 3M274, and Maceo Steward to Cohen, Aug. 13, 1938, Box 3M270, Cohen Papers.

34. McComb, *Galveston*, pp. 164–66.

management of the Galvez. This was, Kempner wrote, "a tremendous job to make the project merit the admiration and approval of all Texas." He, not Moody, did the "tremendous job."[35]

Meanwhile, the success of the beaches and seawall as lures for mass tourism altered Ike's views. Relatively impecunious tourist masses would come if attracted. The Kempners argued that they should be lured. Even day visitors constituted retail traffic, and some number should logically become besotted with the Island's beauties and become permanent taxpaying residents.[36] In the 1920s the Moodys generally opposed any tax-supported improvements in public recreation facilities that Ike and other boosterish businessmen asserted were essential to attract crowds of lower-income tourists. For their part, until Shearn Moody shifted positions on this matter at decade's end, the Moody concern expressed little interest in the city's recreational amenities. To the Moodys, the seawall alone adequately supplemented nature's bounty. Parks, playgrounds, and toilets for day visitors (or for black Galvestonians, for that matter) were excessive.

Perhaps from concerns about resulting racial tensions, revenue commissioner Lee Kempner, in the city council, proposed new public parks and playgrounds for black and white visitors, respectively, as well as residents. The issue became part of the party battles of the decade. It bobbed up frequently on the city's agendas, often introduced by Lee, but was tabled until Shearn Moody, himself altering course, made it one of his causes. Black Galvestonians felt both bitter at the delay and the manner and timing of the resolution's passage.[37]

With Houston's ballooning permanent population in mind and Galveston's static one distressingly apparent, Ike persisted in efforts to make the seaside a means of redressing this imbalance, financially at least. In the 1920s and 1930s automobiles were beginning to fall within pocketbook range of most Americans. To attract blue-collar masses and auto-riding Texans to the Gulf shore, Ike and his colleagues sought state funding for a new causeway to the mainland, one able to carry buses and interurban trolleys as well as autos from Houston and more distant points.[38] In addition to the fine new Galvez, other

35. IHK, *Recalled Recollections*, pp. 50–51.
36. Clark Thompson, interview with R. L. Jones, Jan. 24, 1980, RLA. Thompson was Moody's brother-in-law and a future congressman.
37. Ibid., and John Clouse, interview with R. L. Jones, Apr. 22, 1980, RLA.
38. IHK, *Recalled Recollections*, pp. 47, 50–51; Kaplan, "Interurban Memo-

more modest hotels served this growing traffic, and soon after the Armistice early "auto courts" so encouraged automobile trippers as to make traffic lights, parking meters, and lane markers into political issues.

To build tourist numbers, back in 1918, as mayor, Ike had sponsored a Mardi Gras festival including a bathing beauty contest, and it became an annual Galveston event. Again with Kempner support, other beauty pageants, fishing competitions, automobile and boat races, and visits of naval vessels became part of the city's calendared attractions.[39]

Moody spokesmen argued that too few tourists became taxable residents to justify tax hikes for them. Instead, facilities for tourists increased residents' tax burdens while degrading the Galvestonians' life-styles, in part because tourism also allegedly attracted criminals, bootleggers, and prostitutes, adding to vice, crime, and the corruption of officials.[40] Brown-bag tourists did indeed overextend themselves in saloons (later, barrooms and cocktail lounges), and in gambling halls and bordellos.

As the decade of the 1920s progressed, Ike fell prey to nostalgia about prewar years, writing an essay of the period entitled "Our Hearts Were Young and Gay." He perceived that time as one of civility, neighborliness, mutual help, and decent if static race relationships; a time when adventurous entrepreneurs were ready and willing to imagine bravely and take the kind of big risks that his family was assuming in Sugar Land.[41]

Great Lakes to Gulf

Sometime in the late 1920s Ike conceived a Sugar Land–scale plan for Galveston, one that hearkened back to his 1899 vision of Canada-to-Gulf commerce to enrich the Island City. He envisaged an improved

ries," *Houstonian*, June, 1986, p. 92; other details in *Houston Post*, Oct. 20, 1957, sec. 1, p. 9; *Galveston Daily News*, Nov. 28, 1937.

39. Undated, unidentified clipping, DWK Scrapbook, 1929–1935; IHK, *Recalled Recollections*, pp. 47–51.

40. See Ike's open letters, to W. L. Moody, Jr., George Sealy, et al., *Galveston Tribune*, Jan. 21, 1927 (cited hereafter as IHK, "Open Letter, 1927"), and to the city council, *Galveston News*, Apr. 3, 1931.

41. IHK, *Recalled Recollections*, pp. 63–66.

automobile roadway connecting wintry Winnipeg to sunbelt Galveston, thus making the Gulf city the primary route for central North America, potentially further enhancing exports to the Caribbean, Latin America, and Europe. Ike, inspired in part by Lee's love for automobiles, foresaw the growth of their private ownership and of consequent mass mobility. He aimed to tap the large motor bus traffic, especially in the long north-south stretches in the Midwest from southern Canada to the Gulf. When such travelers graduated to their own autos, Ike wanted them to be in the habit of visiting Galveston. Therefore he proposed that the Winnipeg-Galveston improved highway should have standardized signs containing reliable information not commonly available then, including local speed limits and intercity distances (with mileage to Galveston always to be added), plus roadside rest facilities for people and maintenance facilities for vehicles.[42] The whole proposal was advanced for its pre-freeway time, and the fact that it came from a businessman rather than a "World of Tomorrow" urban architect or brainstorming civil engineer is the more impressive.[43] Ike became chairman of a city commissioners' advisory advertising committee in 1926, which proposed a modest feasibility study for his large plan. It was to advertise Galveston all along the still-unimproved Winnipeg-Texas corridor "as a summer and winter resort and to develop the city industrially." (The smokestack mirage still beckoned.) The necessary "seed money," as it would be described today, for billboard posters and newspaper advertisements would come from the city. Thereafter, Galveston merchants benefiting from resulting business upturns would bear the costs of a greatly expanded nationwide advertising effort. But anti-tourism forces among the commissioners blocked the requested initial appropriation.

Irked, Ike lashed out publicly at the negative voters in an open letter in Galveston newspapers:

> If the Galveston spirit manifested in disaster can be invoked to help us in prosperity, in letting the world know us from information furnished by ourselves not by our enemies; If civic and individual cooperation has a value beyond mere words and boasts; If a broad vision of visible accomplishment is to rise above the selfish policy of watchful waiting for the other fellow to carry the burden—then,

42. IHK, "Open Letter, 1927."
43. "World of Tomorrow" was the theme of the 1939 New York World's Fair.

> and only then, can Galveston permanently challenge the attention of the business and tourist world.[44]

Ike offered $35,000 from H. Kempner over five years, to initiate the publicity fund that the commissioners had refused to supply, and he asked for equal contributions from Moody, Sealy, and a few other "large interests." The immediate goal was $70,000 to $100,000. Additional amounts would come from "the general public . . . if we light the way," Ike asserted. The Galveston Painters Local was already ready to contribute $100. If coveralled artisans understood the need, could Galveston's major businessmen do less than provide a representative share? With pointed reference to Moody, Ike offered this challenge: "That . . . the firms and corporations in which the Kempner interests own a controlling interest, or in which they are the active officers . . . will pledge $7,000 a year for a period of five years, if you, Mr. Moody, for the interests that you control will pledge a similar amount; . . . if you, Mr. Sealy, will pledge a similar amount for the Galveston Wharf Company,—the largest interests on the wharf front."

Probably with the Galveston Movement experience in mind, Ike argued further that once the tourist numbers grew as a result of the planned advertising "investors are readily [to be] found to supply needed facilities once it is believed that the demand for them will be permanent." And, again criticizing Moody, if obliquely, Ike asserted that "there is much . . . that Galveston should and must do to meet such a future, but the greatest stimulus to general action will be the investment example of those of us who . . . have our hearts as well as our interests here."[45]

As Ike anticipated, Sealy matched the Kempner contribution. Moody did not. Ignoring his own stipulation that a noncontribution in effect voided the H. Kempner offer, Ike commenced using the on-hand money (approximately fourteen thousand dollars). His committee had billboard posters, leaflets, and other information materials printed and distributed. Accusations circulated that Ike was, without authorization, committing the city to large future expenditures in these advertising contracts.

Again resorting to an open letter, Ike, angry, in early 1931 proved from committee records that he had consulted about budget implica-

44. IHK, "Open Letter, 1927."
45. Ibid.

tions with the mayor and council and received their approval. "Not one penny can be spent until the board of commissioners approve what we are doing," he insisted. But he would not take every preliminary cost estimate, artist's sketch, or sloganeer's idea to the commissioners for advance approval and decisions about options. Such a procedure rendered the committee superfluous. Better that the city dismiss its busy members.[46]

Neither dismissed nor further enriched as to budget, the committee limped along. Its ambitious program marked time, then faded.[47] Later in the mid-1930s, Ike and Mayor Levy lobbied Galveston voters to approve tax increases for a bridge to nearby Pelican Island and another, longer one to Bolivar Peninsula to replace the picturesque but commercially inefficient ferries. Levy remembered that the bridge proposals were "soundly and roundly defeated because the steamship interests up in Houston and some [interests] in Galveston considered that . . . [a] bridge might fall down and block . . . the Galveston-Houston Ship Channel and prevent ships from going up to Houston." Kempner and Levy tried to counter such charges with the fact that New York and San Francisco bridges overarched the highest ships, but, Levy mourned, "You can't convince the people of Galveston of that." And so "the ships go [to Houston] where the cargo is."[48]

A Last Hurrah?

Because these ships were going there, early in 1935 "a quartet of the leading citizens in Galveston" had visited Levy, then in private law practice, at his office. The four were Ike, George Sealy, Walter Kelso, and Sealy Hutchings. They asked him to run for mayor, promising to underwrite all campaign expenses. The lawyer for some of

46. *Galveston News*, Apr. 3, 1931.

47. Encouragements to tourism in the 1970s and 1980s by George Mitchell's redevelopment of the Strand, by the Galveston Historical Foundation, and by an anti-gambling casino coalition in which Harris L. ("Shrub") Kempner, Jr., is prominent suggest the accuracy of Ike's vision in the 1930s. See Conclusion, below.

48. Levy interview with Jones, Sept. 30, 1980. A Galveston-Pelican Island bridge was not built until 1955, too late to capitalize on the industrial growth on Pelican in World War II by Todd Shipyards. A Galveston-mainland bridge over San Luis Pass was not built until the late sixties. No Galveston-Bolivar bridge has been built.

the quartet's largest interests, Levy was sensitive to the "clout" of these men. Nevertheless, he was close to a decision to refuse. Then, once home, Mrs. Levy, a close coworker with Henrietta Kempner in Galveston good works, persuaded him to run.

Once committed, Levy fought vigorously against allegations that he was a Kempner puppet and that the Wharves' mixed form of ownership invited ineffective and corrupt management. The Moodys spent "untold millions of dollars," even courting blacks' votes, which, Levy recalled ironically in 1980, "in those days wasn't as strong as it is today."[49]

But numbers from the federal census would change Ike's pleasure at Levy's narrow victory to gloom about Galveston's long-range prospects as a viable community and port. Just before the Great Storm in 1900, federal census-takers counted approximately 38,000 Islanders. Ten years later Ike's efforts had helped to rebuild that number almost to the 1900 figure. In part because of the World War I boom and Ike's encouragement of tourism, in 1920 Galveston boasted more than 44,000 residents, and he delighted in the swelling number of newcomers during the next decade that in 1930 brought the head count to 62,938. But thereafter that rise faltered, until in 1940 federal counters would register a decrease from 1930, to 60,862.[50]

True, bulk exports through Galveston increased every year from 1918 through 1940. But imports did not notably increase, and so the traffic flow through the port remained lopsided. Galveston's port charges increased compared to Houston's primarily as a result of aging equipment but also because of the export imbalance, for much port machinery became underused in import phases.

Levy's victory notwithstanding, Galveston balloters opted consistently for the Moody mode of constrained city budgets during the 1930s and later. Even minimal urban housekeeping and social services were curtailed. Port facilities began a process of deterioration that nearby Houston and other burgeoning cities along the Ship Channel took pains to avoid for themselves. Waterborne traffic shifted increasingly to Houston. Pipelines began to encroach on wheeled trans-

49. Ibid.

50. U.S. Bureau of the Census, *Census of Population Reports, 1790–1980.* The 1980 figure (61,902) is virtually the same as that of 1940.

port for petroleum and agricultural commodities, a shift that auto-truck roads of the sort Ike had sketched for the Winnipeg-Galveston route might have delayed, as freeways would do later.[51]

Ike concluded that programs he and others favored might have slowed the downward drift if not reversed it. Ironically, the very persistence of Ike's efforts and those of his family and other close associates to reverse this pattern lent credence to propagators of "fly in amber" imagery, which anti-Kempner spokesmen exploited.

Except at Sugar Land the times were out of joint for Ike. However self-indulgent the Moodys' policies appeared to him, the voters liked them.

Retreat from the Wharves

Striking longshoremen shut down the wharves in 1931. Cotton production declined, and with it Galveston's mainstay, export shipping, in four years of "dust bowl" drought. Competition from synthetics and foreign producers further depressed cotton prices. From 1932–36 no grains at all passed through Galveston's port facilities. The Wharves' directors skipped dividends as deficits followed deficits.[52]

Kempner fretted. In his opinion, both Hooverian and New Deal relief measures failed to ease Galveston's problems. The 1930 Smoot-Hawley tariff law discouraged trade with Europe, and the 1933 Agricultural Adjustment Act and its successors reduced acreage devoted to cotton and other staples, thus diminishing export traffic further. This diminution was to last until Europe's and Japan's preparations for war and America's preparedness efforts from 1940 on increased orders.[53] But for the Wharves' directors the economic upturn was to be too late.

Many of Ike's business colleagues professed to see socialism lurking behind all New Deal policies, including the acreage reduction and subsidy programs. For a time, Ike supported these programs. He later turned against them, wanting the cuts in production to become part of a regionally coherent effort to raise the quality of Texas cotton.

51. McComb, *Galveston,* pp. 166–74.

52. Barker, "Partners in Progress" (Ph.D. diss.), p. 143; *Galveston News,* June 29, 1939, Jan. 11, 1940.

53. I. H. Kempner, "Foreign Trade" (Address at Washington and Lee University, Nov. 5, 1948), Kempner Papers, pp. 1–8.

Once armed with an improved product, American cotton farmers would again be able to compete effectively in cheap-labor foreign markets. Until then, however, Asian, African, and Latin American producers would undercut the American.[54]

So far as the Wharves were concerned, Ike remained convinced that the familiar, mixed public-private ownership and control arrangements were better than the wholly public-ownership mode that Moody endorsed. His steadfast position left him increasingly isolated. Longtime anti-Moody stalwarts, including even his brother Lee, were observed paying duty calls at Moody–Democratic Party offices. Pressures grew favoring conciliation with "Moodycrats." George Sealy and E. R. Cheesborough referred to the Wharves as a dead issue, implying that Moody was winning. New Deal tax laws were impelling Sealy toward trimming Wharves' sails in the Moodys' direction, perhaps because when the Wharves distributed profits to private shareholders, surtaxes on dividends applied. Nationwide, the Wharves was the only port entity so affected.[55]

The 1939 Election

In early 1939, an advertisement in Galveston newspapers, signed by the mayor and four city commissioners, "vehemently" denied that Lee Kempner "has dominated or in anywise or to any extent, controlled the activities of the Board or any members thereof, nor has any attempt been made by him to do so."[56] Behind this unprecedented statement by a supposedly apolitical board of commissioners lay charges by the Moody–People's Party 1939 candidate for mayor, George Fraser, that Lee Kempner had "more power than any man has a right to have over a democratic community." At a public meeting, Fraser asserted further that Lee ran a "dictator government" on behalf of the Kempners. The Kempners and their allegedly hand-picked mayoral candidate of 1939 to succeed Levy, Brantley Harris, were aim-

54. IHK, *Recalled Recollections*, p. 140; see "Cut in Acreage Is Urged by Kempner," *Galveston News*, Mar. 29, 1930; cf. Lamar Fleming, Jr., "Speech to South Carolina Cotton Manufacturers Association," May 4, 1956 (manuscript), file 6, Box 134, Kempner Papers. See also Barker, "Partners in Progress," pp. 143–82.

55. Levy interview with Jones, Sept. 30, 1980; Barker, "Partners in Progress," p. 183. Pro-conciliation tendencies as early as 1928 are described in Brackman, "Galveston's Gulf"; McComb, *Galveston*, p. 183.

56. *Galveston News*, May 9, 1939.

ing to keep Galveston's economy and society static, thus retaining their privileged positions. The Kempners' "reactionary political machine" had offered voters only decades of pipe dreams about economic stimulants for Galveston. But results were always sparse, and this disappointing pattern was intentional on the Kempners' part, Fraser claimed.[57]

Attacks grew wilder as election day neared: The family was developing further its supposed links to organized crime. Controlling city money as treasurer, Lee had allegedly co-opted Galveston's police, fire, and sanitation departments as "political shock troops" in his behalf. It was said that Lee was Ike's link between city hall and the H. Kempner offices and that his hands had to be greased before any requested action was likely from municipal officials, especially in matters of property-tax assessments. But Galveston was too intimate an environment for excessive exaggeration or outright lying. Stephen McCarthy, the People's Party candidate for Lee's position as city revenue commissioner, offered a poignant footnote that softened the tone of this unprecedentedly vicious campaign. McCarthy "expressed his appreciation to the good men and women who had aided his mother on the death of his father and prevented them [the McCarthy children, including himself] from going to an orphanage." Among the "good men and women," McCarthy listed Eliza Kempner, all her sons, and Rabbi Cohen.[58]

In an election eve response to all charges and accusations, Lee joined incumbent Mayor Levy and the sitting commissioners on the platform at a City Party public rally. Every political incumbent had a "dictator," Levy acknowledged: "For [himself and for] each man [on the board of commissioners] that dictator has been the voice of his own conscience." Mayoral candidate Harris rebutted allegations that Lee Kempner had ousted George Sealy and W. A. Kelso from the City Party: "You see Mr. Sealy and Mr. Kelso on this platform; do they look like they have been eliminated?" Had the Kempners, as charged, "tried to run the colored people off the [Galveston public] beach?" The local Lion's Club had tried to have the city formally segregate the city beaches, then segregated by custom. Neither Lee

57. Ibid., May 7, 1939.
58. Unidentified, undated clipping, DWK Scrapbook, 1924–1939.

nor Ike Kempner were Lions. Both had successfully opposed the proposed ordinance (though not the custom). Suggestions about the supposed anti-Catholicism of City Party leaders had to mesh with the fact that two of its candidates for commission portfolios were themselves Catholics.

Harris was followed in turn by popular Adolph Suderman, a man who had clawed his way from blue-collar dock laborer to the ownership of a tugboat and stevedoring firm and to the waterworks commissionership. "About this dictatorship charge, I have been in office since 1929 except for two years," Suderman stated. "I have yet to have Mr. Kempner come to me to ask for any favor. I can't understand how people can get up on a platform and say such damnable lies."[59]

Civic Builder Emeritus

Although candidates that Ike favored won in 1939, he was depressed by the spectacle of his beloved city ripping itself apart at every biennial election and agreed to a mutual cease-fire among the major political combatants. Early in the 1939–40 winter, a meeting of Kempners, Moodys, and Sealys took place at the invitation of Congressman Clark Thompson, a Moody relative, and the Galveston Chamber of Commerce, which traditionally looked on the Kempner-Sealy duo as its standard-bearers. The three families agreed henceforward to remove themselves from city politics.[60]

In 1940 Galveston purchased the Wharves' outstanding private shares for $6.25 million, bringing the company wholly into the public realm. By terms of the 1940 agreement, the mayor, a city commissioner, and three representatives of Sealy's Galveston Corporation would constitute the new management, with Sealy retaining executive control until the city called in all Wharves bonds for purchase.[61]

Ike saw the majority decision about the Wharves as a verdict of failure on himself. Agreeing sadly with Sealy that the voters never understood "our work here," Ike's faith dimmed in the reliability and

59. Ibid.
60. Clark Thompson, interview with R. L. Jones, Jan. 24, 1980.
61. McComb, *Galveston*, p. 169. The last private Wharves securities were bought by the city in 1947. John Sealy had died in 1944.

soundness of majoritarian decisions. To Ike, the fact that his beloved city for which for forty years he had worked so hard was better off if he did not serve it, could only gall. And so he determined henceforward to be a "civic builder emeritus and humanitarian."[62]

62. Levy interview with Jones, Sept. 30, 1980; J. D. Claitor, "Personality Sketch of Isaac Herbert Kempner: Civic Builder Emeritus and Humanitarian" (manuscript), RLA, p. 6.

16

Not Running Out of Family

As World War II neared its conclusion in Europe, the Kempner brothers met informally one day, as was common, in Ike's office. While "just sitting around and discussing things," they reached one of their consensuses.[1] It was that the time had arrived to divest H. Kempner of some—perhaps many—of its holdings, to consolidate the presumably more manageable remainder the better to accommodate the family's growing number of shareholders, and to systematize the Kempners' Topsy-grown commitments to eclectic charities. The spinners' litigations were still unsettled, and the fate of many European textile men and firms was unknown.

Lee announced suddenly his intention to retire in 1948, when he would be sixty-five years old and the 1920 trust charter would require renewal and revision. His "statement [was] hardly believed by his brothers and nephews whose attachment to their work precluded the thought of a life without the challenges and responsibilities of business," noted a family chronicler.[2] Disbelief notwithstanding, time had crept up on them. In 1945 their mother was ninety-three years old; Ike, seventy-two; Dan, sixty-eight; Lee, sixty-two; and Stanley, sixty. Their sister Hattie was sixty-five; Fannie, fifty-seven; Sara, fifty-five; and Gladys, fifty-two. As a family, the Kempners had thus far been exceedingly lucky concerning demises. In the present century, except for Fannie's husband in 1918 and uncle Joe Seinsheimer in 1938, death had bypassed its closest members. But many warm friends and trusted

1. H. L. Kempner, interview with R. L. Jones, June 17–19, 1980, RLA.

2. E. R. Thompson, Jr., "History of H. Kempner" (manuscript), Kempner Papers, p. 51.

business associates had died. Now Eldridge's protégé at Imperial, Gus Ulrich, was himself ailing. Additionally, wartime casualty lists and awareness of the Holocaust, to which Kempners were privy early through their activism in Jewish causes, made obituaries a too-common topic in 1945 and ensuing years.

In the midst of these trials, in 1955 Ike fainted at his desk. Surgeons excised much of his stomach, and his recuperation was fitful but eventually substantial save for an understandable decline in his total energy. Nevertheless, in 1961 his daughter Lyda Quinn noted on a photograph taken that year of Ike and Lee: "Ike looks younger at 91 than Lee [at 78]. Ike [has] no stomach [but] has his two Martinis and Bar-Be-Que." But even in 1945 Ike was wearying. Yet despite the evident ability of his son Harris to head H. Kempner, Ike would prove to be exceedingly reluctant to let go of its reins.[3]

The Eldridge Heirs

Also forcing the Kempner brothers to take stock, the Eldridge heirs had been giving them unwanted lessons almost since his death in 1932 about the miseries that unhappy survivors of a deceased partner could inflict on business associates. Perhaps rumors of possible Kempner retirements beginning in 1945 were unsettling the Eldridge beneficiaries. Their demands for accountings increased, sometimes with barely veiled threats to sue. At the 1945 meeting the Kempners agreed to either buy the Eldridges' 50 percent interest in Imperial or themselves sell out.

Empowered by his brothers to act, Ike, reinforced by Dan and soon by Harris and Herb, entered into the difficult negotiation with the Eldridges. It derailed in the face of their unyielding demands and misperceptions concerning the original partnership and its evolution. Since forty years earlier Ike and Eldridge had sealed their partnership only with a handshake, differences of interpretation were to be expected, but the Eldridges' suggestion of four decades of self-serving on the part of the Kempners was not.

3. Photograph courtesy Mrs. Quinn; IHK, *Recalled Recollections*, pp. 113–17; D. W. Kempner, letter to Sam Hubbard, "Holbrook" folder, Box IHK, A–Z, #80-002, Kempner Papers. In 1963 Ike had surgery for ulcers not removed in 1955 (Henrietta Blum Kempner, "The Blum Saga" [manuscript], RLA). Henrietta Kempner died in 1970.

In order to minimize protracted, costly contract litigations, Texas law allowed state judges, upon petition, to decide disputed commercial relationships. Assigning its interests to a trustee, the U.S. National Bank, H. Kempner chose this route. Whereupon in early 1947 the Eldridge heirs agreed to sell their interest in Imperial/Sugar Land to H. Kempner for $2.5 million, a sale not, as a journalist reported, consummated with "perfect good feelings" among all parties.[4]

Now the lucrative Imperial/Sugar Land development was all H. Kempner's, and Herb and then his son Denny began lifetime careers there.

Spinning Off

By the time H. Kempner bought out the Eldridges, the original nine principal Kempner shareholders (already reduced to eight by Eliza's precedent gift of her portion to her children) had grown to more than three times that number, and a larger new generation was in the wings. Advantages of privacy deriving from the firm's unincorporated status were still treasured. But specialist lawyers had the aging men convinced that pitfalls yawned both for themselves and their heirs. Principally, Harris stated, the hazards concerned widows who faced large tax bills and resulted "from the personal liabilities involved [in H. Kempner's unincorporated status and] in the heavy speculative nature of the cotton business." H. Kempner's trustees and perhaps shareholders were vulnerable to unlimited liability in the event of adverse judgments in lawsuits, and the spinners' litigations still shadowed the firm in the late 1940s. How ironic if H. Kempner, an entity dedicated to preserving the family wealth and cohesion, should itself be the instrument of its impoverishment and disruption. The solution, Harris was to write, was an "ingenious operation, masterminded by Mr. [Homer] Bruce," a Houston lawyer. It was to split off [not to sell] and to incorporate separately all H. Kempner holdings except H. Kempner itself, with H. Kempner retaining controlling shares in the spun-off corporations.[5]

Additional justifications existed for the spin-offs. More mobile than

4. *Houston Press*, Apr. 25, 1947; IHK, *Recalled Recollections*, p. 91; "Keys Report, 1963," p. 9.
5. "Keys Report," pp. 8–10.

ever because of their World War II experience, younger Kempners might be disinclined to live by the Galveston residence–family cohesion ethic. With notable exceptions like Harris and Herb, seemingly qualified blood kin were not evidencing ardent interest in Kempner career ladders. Perhaps the now half-century-old pooling of assets had overcentralized the family's interests in the aging Galveston male seniors. The cotton trade was chaotic and the Imperial/Sugar Land complex alone was overtasking any individual's capacities.

Therefore, in 1946, perhaps as a toe-in-the-water test of the strategy, Imperial had gone public in a modest way. A minority block of shares was sold outside the family, and Sugarland Industries assumed more direct control over the diverse enterprises, rural real estate, and residential areas. An oversimplified sketch of the relationships suggests these configurations:

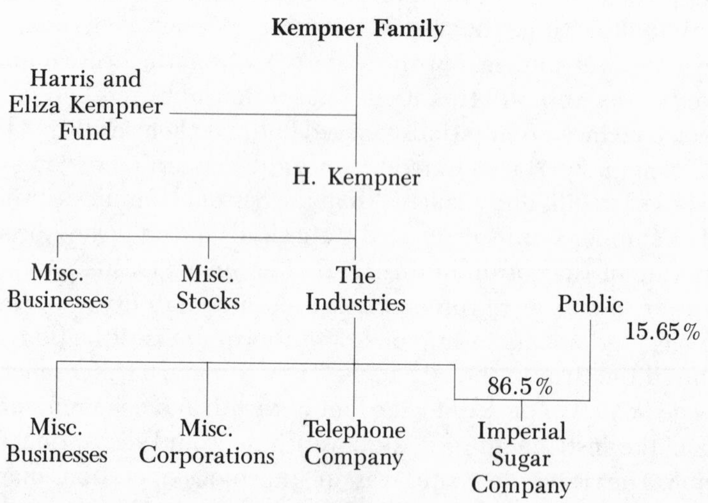

A subsequent reorganization placed H. Kempner even further to the side from central formal axes of authority where the brothers had officiated since the century's dawn. All shareholders in H. Kempner received a proportionate share of the securities of the spun-off companies, and some shareholders, especially the females and in-law males, were invited onto the new corporations' boards of directors. Harris noted that these arrangements left "the Kempner family . . .

the dominant owners of each of these companies."[6] In other words, the individual shareholders of the family, not H. Kempner, owned the companies. This revision can be sketched in this manner:

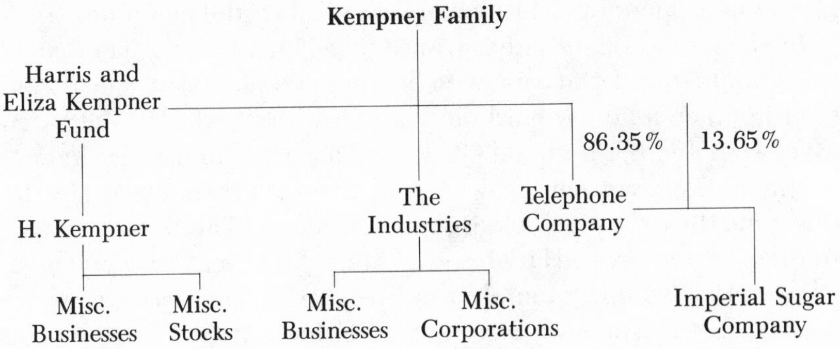

A Chink in the Armor

This emphasis on individual shareholders rather than on H. Kempner's "managing males," plus Harris's 1963 plea to shareholders to continue "the long history of working for the group and not for self alone," reflected the first major outbreak since 1894 of ambitions, tensions, and incivilities among Kempners.[7] Ike had always insisted on and obtained at least overt civility at H. Kempner shareholders' meetings. Picking up reins that his aging father only reluctantly let drop, Harris in the 1950s unexpectedly found himself the unhappy target of accusations of ineptitude or worse in carrying out fiduciary responsibilities to shareholders. Recalling the outbreak of recriminations that Kempners had so long prided themselves on avoiding, Harris remarked: "It was unpleasant because we weren't used to disagreements at that level."[8]

For reasons wholly outside his control, especially the weddings, births, deaths, and others' career decisions, Harris, now nearing his fiftieth year, was the only male Kempner of his generation in the central family business. While coping with the crotchets of an aged fa-

6. H. L. Kempner, "The Kempners of Galveston and Sugar Land" (manuscript), RLA, p. 13.
7. H. L. Kempner, "Beneficiary Interest Report, 1963" (manuscript), Kempner Papers, p. 9.
8. H. L. Kempner, interview with L. Marchiafava, Aug. 1, 1981, RLA, p. 12.

ther he was trying also to control the H. Kempner conglomerate and to survive the turbulent cotton trade. And Harris was assuming also his late Uncle Dan's role of recruiter-teacher of future leadership for H. Kempner, with special attention to his son Shrub, to Herb's sons Denny and James, and to Leonora's son Edward Thompson, Jr.

By the 1950s several relatives wished to sell their H. Kempner shares, many times in order to cope with death and estate taxes. The major such instance followed hard on Dan's death in 1956. His daughter Mary Jean and her husband Oakleigh Thorne, who held H. Kempner shares as gifts from his wife, wanted to sell them externally, to that time the only shareholders opting to do so. The Kempner men resisted. Whereupon, Harris noted, Mary Jean went to "very good lawyer[s] . . . , and we found a way, we gave her some cash and some [shares] of our [spun-off] assets, and we think both of us came out advantageously." Lawyer-cousin Harris K. Weston had warned Harris that Mary Jean threatened an "ugly situation." Avoid a "business battle," Weston pleaded. After a conversation with Mary Jean, Weston passed on to Harris her several concerns: "But above all she considers 'the cotton business is speculative' and while not doubting your *ability* sees little reason to make possible or probable sacrifices or speculation to gratify *your* inclinations [to stay in cotton]."[9]

Mary Jean's concerns about the instability of the cotton business were accurate readings of that market. Further, although in Galveston her actions and known purposes were "not looked on very kindly at the time, . . . it [the crisis] was ultimately handled in . . . a reasonably satisfactory way," Weston thought.[10]

Less satisfactory was the fact that by the mid-1960s the annual meetings of H. Kempner shareholders became decreasingly amiable and cohesive, due especially to Lyda Ann Quinn Thomas, the daughter of Ike's daughter Lyda. Born in 1936, Lyda Ann and her husband Jerry made themselves the voices of the new generation, at least in their own view. The Thomases expressed grievances with increasing vehemence and frequency at H. Kempner annual meetings. They insisted that they and all trust shareholders had received less than they should have from the sales of Sugarland Industries assets. Notwith-

9. Ibid.; H. K. Weston, letter to Harris L. Kempner, Nov. 21, 1957, Kempner-Lipowski file, Box K-9/1957, #80-002, Kempner Papers; H. K. Weston, interview with L. Marchiafava, Aug. 29, 1981, RLA, p. 19.

10. H. K. Weston interview with Marchiafava, Aug. 29, 1981, pp. 19, 33.

standing the fact that the sale of The Industries' assets was determined formally by its board, not that of H. Kempner, the Thomases focused on Harris, now in his father's place, as guilty of misfeasance and malfeasance.[11] His ascent was another evidence of the results of the overlong inbreeding in both H. Kempner and The Industries, the Thomases claimed, a position perhaps reflecting the H. Kempner trustees' unwillingness to open their ranks to Lyda Ann's father, Arthur William Quinn. He, according to one recollection, "never really fit in [with the Kempners]." Neither had her husband, whose "hostility during this thing [according to Harris] derived from Jerry's feeling of insecurity and . . . inferiority . . . about everything that went on with the Kempners. He always thought he could do it better and never proved any of it. We even offered him a [nonmanagement?] job at one time, but he wanted such outrageous conditions that we didn't accept him."[12]

Lyda Ann later divorced Jerry Thomas, but in the 1960s they were an outspoken, formidable duo at H. Kempner gatherings at Galveston. Her Aunt Sara, always peppery, recalled that she, a Cincinnati resident since her marriage in 1913, felt freer than the Texans to respond to the Thomases "because . . . I leave the next day [after a meeting and] . . . nobody can get mad at me." But Sara became increasingly irritated with Lyda Ann and her husband. Learning on one occasion that Lyda Ann was "going to start confusion" at an imminent annual meeting, Sara "got mad at her." The older woman insisted to Lyda Ann that Harris was owed an apology, "and if she doesn't give that apology," her vigorous aunt would defend him before the assembled family. Lyda Ann chose not to attend that meeting.[13]

Instead Lyda Ann and her husband went to lawyers. Since The Industries was chartered as a Delaware corporation, the lawyers initiated, first, a petition in a federal court for an injunction to halt further sales of Industries and Sugar Land assets, on the grounds that the price Harris had negotiated with the buyers was inadequate and that the Thomases and their four minor children, as shareholders in

11. This composite reconstruction is derived from several interviews: H. K. Weston with Marchiafava, Aug. 29, 1981, p. 14; H. L. Kempner with Marchiafava, Aug. 1, 1981, pp. 13–17; and Sara Kempner Weston with L. Marchiafava, Aug. 29, 1981, all RLA.

12. Interviews: H. L. Kempner with Marchiafava, Aug. 1, 1981, p. 14; H. K. Weston with author, July 5, 1986, in author's possession; Hyman Block with L. Marchiafava, Aug. 1, 1981, p. 7, RLA.

13. Sara K. Weston interview with Marchiafava, Aug. 29, 1981.

The Industries, would suffer.[14] The judge issued the injunction, and the criticized sale stopped at Sugar Land.

The Kempners thought both the suit and the injunction to be unfair. Concerning the aborted sale, Lehman Brothers' staff had set the asking price, $24 million. Through a different broker the Thomases found a new buyer willing to pay $27 million. The $3 million differential was fine with Harris, except that he doubted the ability of the higher bidder to carry out the contract, and events proved him correct. Worse, Harris and the other Industries directors learned that the new buyer had "a side deal with the Thomases that they would retain a certain amount of the property, a deal which was not offered to other members of the family. This was anathema to us. We have never given any part of the family that type of preference over others. So we [had] resisted this [sale]."

As ordered by the court, the Kempners initiated a new sale of the real estate. Whereupon windfall piled on windfall, for Houston's suburbs and exurbs were then extending toward Sugar Land. One of Houston's most aggressive real estate developers, Gerald Hines, years earlier had negotiated fruitlessly with the Kempners about other Sugar Land acreage. Hines now came in with a bid not $3 million but $13 million higher than the first, controverted one. Contracts were signed. Then, underscoring the Kempners' concern about buyers meeting obligations, Hines, though associated in this venture with the Ford Foundation, encountered difficulty. The Kempners amended their contract with him, "and Mr. Hines with his skill and adroitness has gotten another partner," Harris recorded, "and the thing is now going great guns." The Thomases were right about the value of the land, he admitted, "but they were wrong about the way they wanted to cure it. We were all very lucky with the ultimate outcome."[15]

But the Thomases, still unhappy, initiated a second lawsuit. In it they charged Harris and the other Industries directors with having "done a variety of things that they shouldn't have and hadn't done certain things they should have, and asked for money damages from

14. H. L. Kempner interview with Marchiafava, Aug. 1, 1981, pp. 11–14.

15. Ibid., p. 15. Harris estimated that the Ford Foundation lost $10 to $15 million because of Hines's problem in meeting the mortgage. H. L. Kempner, "Beneficiary Interest Report, 1963," p. 9, on inflation of real estate due to Houston's exploding suburbs.

those directors," stated lawyer Weston. The litigation ended in a settlement without money damages or payments to the plaintiffs but requiring an appraisal of H. Kempner by a professional valuator, and that shareholders wishing to sell should be free to do so with H. Kempner undertaking to buy the shares at the appraiser's valuation.[16]

Not yet satisfied, in 1973 the Thomases sued to have The Industries assume all their attorney's fees. Estimating them as excessive, Harris refused. Resulting litigation dragged on to 1981. As Harris recalled, "the interesting thing is the $3 million that they set out to get [through the original injunction] was almost exactly what we ended up paying their attorneys. So they as [Industries'] stockholders lost as much to the payment of their attorneys as they would have gained if we had taken their sale price."[17]

It was all too much for the Kempners. Harris expressed their consensus by stipulating in the settlement that if the Thomases wished to sell their shares they must sell all of them, including those of their four children, also plaintiffs in the suits, to H. Kempner. "I *wanted* them to sell because they [the parents] were trouble-makers and I wanted them out," he concluded.[18]

Agreeing that the Thomas litigation was "the only really major controversy in the family that I know of," Harris's lawyer-cousin Weston concluded that H. Kempner had responded usefully if belatedly to these pressures from within the family, pressures that rose, he noted, from younger female relatives and their spouses.[19] Since then H. Kempner has avoided such situations, in part by regularizing stock repurchases. H. Kempner trustees have occasionally offered shareholders opportunity to sell their shares to the trust association. Thus, shareholders wishing to disassociate from the family investment pool would need only patience. Further, a valuation technique like that imposed by the court in the Thomas litigations became a consistent H. Kempner process. It involved having H. Kempner assets appraised, as called for in the Thomas settlement, by an evaluator drawn from H. Kempner's staff. Informed of the price thus set for H. Kempner shares, hold-

16. H. K. Weston interview with Marchiafava, Aug. 29, 1981, p. 19.

17. Ibid., pp. 16, 14, respectively (emphasis original). See also Block interview with Marchiafava, Aug. 1, 1981, p. 6.

18. H. L. Kempner, "The Kempners of Galveston and Sugar Land," p. 15.

19. H. K. Weston interview with Marchiafava, Aug. 29, 1981, pp. 19, 33.

ers would have the opportunity to sell at that price, with first refusals to H. Kempner itself. Referring to the appraisal and sale procedures resulting from the Thomas litigation, Harris later estimated that "less than five percent of the stockholders took advantage of the opportunity to sell, principally the [Thomas] family of plaintiffs."[20]

Another, unofficial policy, established in the 1970s, aimed to avoid the situations that arose with Lyda Ann's father and husband when they failed to win access to high H. Kempner positions. Henceforward, more relatives, especially younger ones, would be invited into active participation, beyond shareholding, in H. Kempner businesses, usually as members of boards of directors.[21]

By the 1980s, with exceptions noted earlier (especially the prosperous Foster Farms real estate firm and the telephone company at Sugar Land), the Kempners were out of The Industries. Sugar Land had become a self-governing, thriving, comfortable small city well equipped with urban amenities. The Industries "is now a dissolved corporation," Harris reported: "It doesn't exist anymore." But Imperial Sugar has continued as a Kempner property. It is, he continued, "an active ongoing concern, spending large amounts of money on refurbishing and building up the plant and [it] has prospects that run into the indefinite future."[22]

There would be other, lesser frictions among blood Kempners and spouses, but except for the tensions attending the spin-offs and buyouts these clashes proved to be matters more of style than of substance. Galveston Kempners sometimes wondered at the ways of non-resident cousins and in-laws, some of whom offered not only able technical advice but also criticism of some of the Galvestonians' business decisions.[23] But such minor burrs in human relationships were easily accommodated. There were more important business concerns, cotton chief among them.

20. H. L. Kempner interview with Marchiafava, Aug. 1, 1981, pp. 8, 13–14. An earlier stock repurchase eased problems faced by Dan's widow due to unanticipated estate taxes. A policy ensued that allowed heirs to sell shares to H. Kempner, thus avoiding the illiquidity that is a common problem in closely held companies (H. L. Kempner, "Keys Report, 1964," p. 11; H. K. Weston interview with Marchiafava, Aug. 29, 1981, p. 27).

21. H. K. Weston interview with Marchiafava, Aug. 29, 1981, p. 27; and see H. L. Kempner, "Keys Report," p. 11.

22. H. L. Kempner interview with Marchiafava, Aug. 1, 1981, p. 22.

23. Block interview with Marchiafava, Aug. 1, 1981.

Spinning Off Cotton

Mary Jean's wish to sell her H. Kempner shares and those of her mother stemmed from well-grounded fears that cotton was too volatile a commodity for investor safety in the postwar world. Although consistently admitting the problems facing American cotton merchants, Ike and Harris also expressed unfailing confidence, both to H. Kempner shareholders and to possible buyers of cotton abroad, that the industry would revive. Yet in a private moment in 1945, Ike, writing to another of the region's major businessmen, had referred to himself semijestingly as an "aged and feeble-minded" holdfast who "35 or 40 years ago, remained in the cotton business at the time you left it."[24]

The cotton trade was eroding. Gluts swelled American stocks, foreign competition and affection for synthetics multiplied, tariff walls soared, and legal problems frustrated American middlemen. New Deal farm policies helped growers but not exporters by diminishing plantation output and raising the price of American cotton internationally.[25]

Ike and Dan had generally applauded prewar New Deal commodity price support policies. But during World War II the government had necessarily curtailed cotton exports almost to nothing. Warring governments subsidized production of synthetics, and the international trade's skilled financiers, agents, and workers were scattered or worse.[26] Only the Marshall Plan for Europe and, later, equivalents for parts of Asia, resuscitated the American industry, a revival that allowed for profits until the end of the Korean War in 1953. Then a decline in the cotton trade again set in. Attempting to mitigate it, Ike and Harris lobbied, lectured, published articles in trade magazines, and participated in government missions, one, ironically, to Japan to resurrect the textile industry there. Despite these exertions and public assertions all efforts to resurrect the cotton export trade

24. To H. R. Cullen, Mar. 5, 1945, IHK Correspondence file 1, #80-002, Kempner Papers; see also IHK, *Recalled Recollections*, p. 93.

25. Buenger and Pratt, *But Also Good Business*, p. 109.

26. H. L. Kempner interview with Jones, June 17–18, 1980; see also Harris L. Kempner, "Report to Foreign Affairs Committee of American Cotton Shippers Association," Apr. 14, 1961, Box 176, #80-002, Kempner Papers, plus the association's lobbying program in which he participated, 1946–54, Box 121, Files 1–3, #80-002, Kempner Papers; IHK, *Recalled Recollections*, pp. 95–96.

failed. By 1962 an "atmosphere of black depression" shadowed historic cotton offices on Galveston's Strand. That year, for the first time since H. Kempner began eight decades earlier, it went on a five-day workweek because business was so sluggish in Texas and abroad.[27]

If reluctantly, Harris began then to pressure his father to take H. Kempner out of the cotton export trade. America had become "a residual supplier [to global spinners, but] a supplier of last resort. They only turned to America when they couldn't buy elsewhere in the world," he had concluded. To be sure, Japanese and other "Asian rim" spinners were large consumers. But overall the trade was choking. He had always felt a "sentimental preference" for the cotton business, since his early days of "gofering" in the H. Kempner offices.[28] Nevertheless, even he privately admitted that it was time to get out.

Reports spread of Ike's decline and of Harris's bent toward taking H. Kempner out of the cotton trade and of consolidating its other investments. Hearing such rumors, then fifteen-year-old Marion ("Sandy") Kempner, Harris's son, at prep school in Pennsylvania, wrote to his grandfather with a concerned inquiry about the reasons for selling H. Kempner properties. Ike replied:

> Personally I was very reluctant to sell, but we faced the fact that the economy had grown beyond the ability of your father . . . or myself to supervise it and it was not doing as well as it should have done. We could not hope to have the company progress as it should without one of . . . us giving virtually all of his time to it. I could not do it because of my age; Lee could not do it because he is very busy at the bank and the handling of Uncle Pat's . . . and Uncle Dan's estate[s]; and your father could not do it because the operations of H. Kempner and . . . our Sugar Land interests is all, if not more than, he could undertake.

And in the didactic Kempner style so reminiscent of letters Ike had received from *his* father and had himself echoed to Dan and other brothers, he admonished Sandy: "Keep up your hard work because never in our history has there been greater need of scholars who knew

27. Quote and data on office closings, in memos, Mar. 28 and Apr. 26, 1962, Box 188, Kempner Papers; Shulman, "The Wages of Dixie" (Organization of American Historians, 1988); IHK, *Recalled Recollections*, pp. 95–96, 104.

28. H. L. Kempner interview with Marchiafava, Aug. 1, 1981, pp. 22–34.

the depth of knowledge and not try to get along on a mere smattering of it."[29]

Though no Lear-like monarch in name only, by the early 1960s Ike no longer took "a very forceful part" in making decisions, Harris recalled. Increasingly weighty evidence, including a parallel decline of an H. Kempner cotton venture in Mexico, favored exiting from cotton.[30]

Looking around, Harris saw that cotton factors and merchants as ancient as H. Kempner, some long associated with it in the trade, were closing. And how old so many of H. Kempner's most skilled and irreplaceable employees were! The firm's "head classer," that basic functionary who established the commodity's value, was about to retire, and no replacement was in sight. H. Kempner's general European agent "came over and told us [that] he had a chance to do something else and he suggested we might want to terminate the business. So now was the time to do it," Harris remembered. "But it was a decision that had been growing on us for several years. We didn't do it overnight."[31]

Knowing how illusory the idea was, Ike and Harris sometimes imagined a new cotton organization, one echoing what Ike had built up so painstakingly beginning a half-century before only to see it eroded by the venal European resident agent Hapke, by the spinners' lawsuits, and by World War II. No, a successful organization still required "the proper talents to carry it on," Harris stated, probity being preeminent among those talents:

> You need a buyer, someone who is willing to stay up half the night and to talk to people from the country about buying cotton and you need someone who is an expert salesman, a general agent abroad to visit your specific agents and talk to the mills and distinguish between the white hats and the black hats among your customers. You need someone who has an intuitive or instinctive knowledge of cotton campaigning, which is really the key thing. . . . You might have to try three or four people for each job before you got the one unless you're really lucky. That's an expensive way to proceed.

29. I. H. Kempner, letter to Sandy Kempner, Nov. 15, 1957, file "Kempner-Lipowski," Box K-9/1957, #80-002, Kempner Papers.

30. Benito Longoria, letter to H. L. Kempner, Nov. 10, 1968, copy provided by H. L. Kempner.

31. H. L. Kempner interview with Marchiafava, Aug. 1, 1981.

It was also too risky. Besides, what Harris called "the facts of economic life" overcame his sentimental preference to remain in the cotton business.[32]

This lack of ready replacements among trustworthy foreign agents, skilled cotton supervisors, and family trainees for top Kempner management did not reflect inattention to the need on the part of Ike, Dan, or Harris. But credible agents were desperately few, and the falling markets for cotton never justified the initiation of extensive training programs for H. Kempner cotton workers. And, concerning family recruits for top jobs, other than Herbert and Harris, only one, Harris's nephew Edward R. ("Tim") Thompson, Jr. (b. 1935), an earlier victim of a grievous automobile accident, had seemed both interested and qualified. Thompson, Harris recalled, had "spent some time in the same stages in Europe that I had learning the cotton business on the spot there and would have been available [to carry it on], but he had settled down into the banking business. [Tim] . . . was willing to come [into H. Kempner] if I needed him, but he wasn't chafing at the bit. Even so . . . I'd have to help him build an organization."[33]

Economic facts added up to this: Many of H. Kempner's noncotton ventures were prospering, and the sales of The Industries, of the Texas Prudential Insurance Company, and of other family properties, had ballooned the nominal wealth of the conglomerate holdings, at least for purposes of valuing the securities of the spun-off corporations. In 1963, Harris reported that H. Kempner capital and surplus in 1945 was $4,875,000, and at the end of 1961, was $24,654,000. Earnings for this period averaged nearly 10 percent of the capital and surplus. But this appreciation was partly artificial. Before the spinoffs the H. Kempner properties were simply reflected in the firm's books, but appreciation, as distinguished from earnings and payouts, was not part of the accounting picture.[34]

And so the Kempners' consensus grew against a futile last-ditch battle to stay in the cotton trade despite its historic significance to the family. This consensus was congruent to the family's overall aim of liquidity and stability, especially "to protect the younger share-

32. Ibid., pp. 35, 34, respectively.
33. Ibid., p. 36. See also IHK, *Recalled Recollections*, p. 104.
34. H. L. Kempner, "Beneficiary Interest Report," p. 9.

holders of the Trust Association from the personal liabilities involved in the heavy speculative nature of the cotton business." Further, Harris noted in 1964, the split-off from cotton as well as in other former H. Kempner enterprises occurred "to allow the individual stockholders, whose numbers grew as the generations proliferated, a chance to receive directly profits from these businesses, and also to permit them to profit directly from any sales of stock that might take place."[35]

Discontinuities

Two unending sadnesses marred Harris and Ruth's long catalogs of achievements and joys. The ailments and deaths of senior Kempners and of other relatives, friends, and associates in the 1940–67 quarter century were normal though painful parts of life. A different sadness was evoked by Herb's death from cancer in 1953. His life so cruelly foreshortened, his death left both a lingering sense of an unfair lack of symmetry and of respect for the dying man's valiant efforts to advance improvements at Sugar Land/Imperial. Perhaps even less bearable was the death in 1966 of Ruth and Harris's twenty-four-year-old Sandy. A 1964 graduate of Duke University, Sandy was admitted to the University of Texas law school and expressed a Kempnerian attraction to public interest law. But the tensions of the Vietnam War tore at him. Though a self-described "pessimist and confirmed cynic," Sandy volunteered for the Marines, was commissioned a lieutenant, and took command of a rifle platoon, traditionally the most hazardous position.

Sandy believed pragmatically that the United States had to fulfill the obligations it had made. He wrote to his father that "we must fight where the confrontation is, despite its cost, infeasibility, and possible illegality, and physical and mental toll upon the participants," and to other relatives that "we are doing, if 'right' is the word unusable when describing international politics and/or war, a 'righter' thing by being here trying to give these people a chance and a choice." In early November, 1966, Sandy and his platoon were guarding farmers in the rice fields. One of his men tripped a land mine, and the explosion killed Sandy. Condolences from his superiors were lauda-

35. "Keys Report, 1964," p. 10.

tory, his captain reminding the grieving parents that "he was on a mission to help and not destroy. . . . [He was] both very brave and compassionate."[36]

Combined with Ike's evident weakening in 1966 (he died the next year), Sandy's death was coincident with the exit of the H. Kempner Trust Association from its long concentration on cotton exporting. Along with every other woe, the too-proximate loss of a revered father and a beloved son who might one day have succeeded the parent in guiding H. Kempner was too much.

However justifiable, the deemphasis on cotton "was a real blow to me," Harris admitted.[37] Obeying family consensus and his own sense of business trends, Harris, now senior trustee of the H. Kempner Trust, continued the process of spinning off some trust properties in cotton into separate corporations and of selling others.

Advised by lawyer Homer Bruce, Harris had already engineered the creation of the H. Kempner Cotton Company, becoming president of this new incorporated entity distinct from H. Kempner. He distributed its stocks, valued at $4.5 million, *pro rata*, to shareholders in the trust. Then in 1967 Harris surrendered his shares in the H. Kempner Cotton Company for an agreed equivalent of shares in a new corporation formed in New York: Schwabach, Kempner, Perutz, Inc. All the other stockholders in the H. Kempner Cotton Company were offered and accepted cash for their shares. In essence, after eighty years H. Kempner was out of the cotton trade, so far out that despite the corporate title of one of its side investments in a Texas Cotton Industries, it was actually a real estate enterprise.[38]

Rearrangement and Fruition

Described as a period of "the fruition of many seeds planted in the past," during the 1960s and especially the 1970s the H. Kempner

36. Marion Lee Kempner, "Letters from Sandy," *The Jewish Veteran*, pp. 13–15; "Memorial Service for Marion Lee 'Sandy' Kempner, Temple B'nai Israel, Nov. 17, 1966" (typescript), copy in author's possession.

37. H. L. Kempner, "The Kempners of Galveston and Sugar Land," p. 14.

38. A. M. Alpert, letter to Leonora K. Thompson, undated (ca. July, 1988), copy supplied to author; IHK, *Recalled Recollections*, p. 131; Certificate of Consolidation of Schwabach, Perutz & Co., Inc., and the H. Kempner Cotton Company, into Schwabach, Kempner, Perutz, Inc. (1967), typescript supplied by H. L. Kempner; "Keys Report," p. 17.

Trust Association identified and advanced toward two primary goals. They were, first, the liquidity to repurchase "at any time" $2 million in shares from the remaining original shareholders or their survivors. The second, derivative goal was to shift H. Kempner's investments from risky, usually illiquid enterprises to stabler ones, while seeing to it that the shareholders enjoyed "steady income."

By late spring 1964, H. Kempner substantially met these goals then surpassed them. Instead of $2 million H. Kempner had close to $5 million in cash, readily convertible securities, and demand loans. Reviewing steps toward this comforting liquidity, the trustees applauded especially Herb's achievements at Imperial and Sugar Land. "The 'real prosperity' there . . . was built up by plowing back earnings for years . . . [so that it is] now almost unchallengeable."[39]

To keep profitable Imperial Sugar totally under H. Kempner ownership, as noted earlier H. Kempner split off the Sugar Land Industries into a separate corporation and subsequently sold them, except for the Foster Farms real estate operation and the community telephone company. Sugar Land itself began the process of achieving civic autonomy from Imperial/Industries at this time. Further cementing the Kempners' interests in Sugar Land despite the spin-offs and autonomy, H. Kempner bought the American Canal Company, "primarily as a protective investment in natural resources" there. That company owned Sugar Creek and other Sugar Land waterways, thus controlling the future of that Houston exurb for both residential and industrial growth. A private bank in Richmond, the county seat that was a few miles from Sugar Land, also became an H. Kempner property. The Gulf Coast Bank was, Harris wrote, an "extremely well managed institution" that did "a large loan business in Sugarland and . . . recently cooperated in financing Imperial Sugar's new housing development."[40]

The Texas Prudential Insurance Company was then sold, and with that, but for a few noted exceptions, H. Kempner no longer operated businesses. The exceptions then included an uninsured private bank, 90 percent of whose business was the service of family shareholders. In its place, H. Kempner incorporated a bank holding company in 1969.[41] The latter was a response to new federal regulations which

39. "Keys Report," pp. 9, 12.
40. Ibid., pp. 10–11, 17.
41. Ibid., pp. 10–11; H. L. Kempner, "The Kempners of Galveston and Sugar

would likely have defined H. Kempner's majority shares in the U.S. National Bank as themselves constituting a bank holding company. This done, H. Kempner would have become subject to the federal controller of the currency, "and we couldn't possibly operate under the regulations of the Controller," Harris decided. "So we formed the bank holding company in which the sole asset was the . . . controlling stock [H. Kempner owned] of the U.S. National Bank. Later we added to it the [H. Kempner] stock of the Sugar Land State Bank and the [Apple] Computer Company. And recently we have agreed to merge with the Cullen/Frost banking system."[42] In effect, H. Kempner was evolving swiftly toward what it remains—something "very close to an investment trust or [closed end] mutual fund" composed of diverse assets, Harris stated. Among them were a large portfolio of common stocks and some real estate including a large amount of mineral interests in both North and West Texas from which H. Kempner derived substantial revenues.

Increasingly "a pool of venture capital, partially invested," H. Kempner under Harris's direction did indeed venture beyond the spun-off major corporations that for so long had constituted its primary concerns. Family lore pointed both to prudence in taking risks and to the penalty of excessive timidity, the latter concerning H. Kempner's refusal decades earlier to agree to Lee's suggestion of investing in what became Texas' first motion picture theater chain. Lee invested personally, and his independent sortie enriched him. And so, Harris recorded, "We are always indulging in new ventures. One or two of them out of five or ten come in, and we feel very happy about it."[43]

In some instances H. Kempner had, as noted, acquired oil interests or rights as part of its real estate holdings. Increasingly Harris and his fellow trustees looked on such investments not as his father and grandfather had, as long-term or permanent commitments, but, except for retaining mineral rights, as short-term risks. Further, Harris stated in 1981, "We are stockholders in a number of oil companies, some of which are smaller ones which we think we have special knowl-

Land," p. 14. After the Kempner bank closed, the only uninsured private banks in Texas were the D. & A. Oppenheimer Bank in San Antonio (closed in 1988) and the E. L. Price Bank in Galveston (closed in 1989).

42. H. L. Kempner, "The Kempners of Galveston and Sugar Land," pp. 16–17; H. K. Weston interview with Marchiafava, Aug. 29, 1981, p. 11.

43. H. L. Kempner interview with Marchiafava, Aug. 1, 1981, pp. 22–23.

edge about." In those pre-depression-in-the-oil-patch years, Harris acted on "chancy" opportunities in petroleum on the basis of information from good "advisors and friends."[44]

The pursuit of profitable investments meant that unprofitable ones had to be sloughed off, sometimes to the dismay of co-investors. One unamiable relationship developed when H. Kempner pulled out of a stubbornly dry oil-gas exploration, allegedly without adequate warning to a partner, a picturesque "wildcatter." She complained to an H. Kempner office staffer: "As many things as [the] Kempners control, . . . they could have given us something to do, instead we worked like dogs and were left away off up here [Durango, Colorado] and we have suffered for two years. . . . I paid H. Kempner everything I owed [&] they would not even give me 10% off. . . . We worked for them but all we got was a kick in the pants."[45]

Though the number of H. Kempner's shareholders exceeded sixty by the 1970s and eighty a decade later, with residences as scattered as their careers were diverse, Harris insisted on distributing the largest practical amounts in annual dividends. Federal tax policies sustained his choice. H. Kempner's growing stress on "passive" investments rather than commodity merchandising exposed shareholders' dividends from the trust to especially high rates unless profits were all paid out annually. Therefore the trust required payouts to shareholders larger than they could reasonably expect to obtain elsewhere, if cohesion was to be retained.

Times had changed. With rare exceptions like Lee's venture in motion picture theaters, Ike's and Harris's generations had kept H. Kempner as their virtually sole market conduit. But, Harris understood, the succeeding generations "felt free . . . to use their money wherever they like." Most had chosen residences far from Galveston and elected careers wholly apart from H. Kempner or any business.[46] To be sure, the Kempner core that he and others represented remained in that city and in H. Kempner. But the core's durability depended upon its capacity to accommodate shareholders' independence from both tradition and change.

44. Ibid., pp. 20, 24.

45. Fay ("Mom") Hunsacker, letter to Curt Lewis, Mar. 3, 1956, File 1, Box 137, #80-002, Kempner Papers.

46. H. L. Kempner interview with Marchiafava, Aug. 1, 1981, p. 17.

The Harris and Eliza Kempner Fund

A significant portion of H. Kempner attention and income became devoted to another kind of spin-off, this one a charitable trust incorporated in 1947: the Harris and Eliza Kempner Fund. Its story too requires a return to 1945.

During World War II, Ike, though overtasked and irked by failing eyesight, accepted the chairmanship of the Galveston Community Chest fund drive. Despite his efforts the chest failed to reach its goal, a modest $166,000, evoking his grumble about his neighbors' "parsimony of spirit and impulse."[47]

For decades the Kempners had listened sympathetically to Rabbi Cohen's arguments that charities and other deserving entities, including their temple, required reliable, systematic contributions supplemented by occasional donations. Cohen partly repaid the favors by nagging the overworked Kempners, especially Ike, about their health.[48] In the midst of World War II, Ike, still in close association with Cohen, reversed that concern. The rabbi chaired the Galveston unit of the United Jewish Welfare Association. In another echo of the Galveston Movement, the association was then still trying to lever Jews out of Nazi Germany and to resettle them in Central America. It was all overtasking Cohen, Ike complained to one group: "I regret particularly that you saw fit to write Rabbi Cohen, whose strong sense of duty prompted him, on receipt of your letter, to run around in our tropical summer heat for the better part of two full days, with its attendant effect on a man of his age and frail body; viz., almost physical exhaustion and personal worry and disappointment that he could not increase the remittance to you."[49]

Now, with World War II just won, the Kempner brothers, concerned with their own aging and the consequences of estate taxes on their heirs, were increasingly cynical about the dedication to charity of their fellow Islanders. The brothers began to seek ways to stabi-

47. IHK, *Recalled Recollections*, p. 93; see also pp. 117 and 91, for Dan's analogous frustration on appealing for fifteen thousand dollars and receiving only ten thousand. He apparently made up the difference himself.

48. Ike, letter to Cohen, Sept. 9, 1911, Box 3M229, Cohen Papers; and File 62-3, Box 8, #80-002, Kempner Papers.

49. Ike, letter to Dominican Republic Resettlement Association, July 14, 1942, Box 3M324, Cohen Papers.

lize and systematize for the future the numerous traditional benefactions of individual family members as well as to encourage new ways to return benefits to the society that had so benefited them.[50]

In 1946 the Kempners organized a "Galveston Fund" in honor of their nonagenarian mother. Fears were common in the mid-forties and fifties of another cataclysmic depression. If it occurred H. Kempner might distribute lower dividends or none at all and its shareholders' diverse charities would suffer.[51]

Upon Eliza's death in 1947, her survivors reorganized the Galveston Fund, restyling it the Harris and Eliza Kempner Fund. This new charitable trust was financed initially with contributions of $5,000 each by Ike, Dan, Lee, Stanley, and Harris, plus additional endowment from H. Kempner and its subsidiary corporations, for a total of slightly less than $300,000. In the subsequent forty years additional donations and bequests by Kempner companies and by individual Kempners, in cash, stock, and real estate, would, in addition to the escalated market value of these properties, loft the fund's endowment dramatically, to almost $15 million.[52]

The fund made its initial contributions in 1951, happily in time for Rabbi Cohen to know of this fruit of his ministry (he died in 1952). In addition to honoring the founding Kempner generation, the fund helped to stabilize the temple's income and that of other Kempner beneficiaries.

Permanent donations to good works by wealthy individuals, either by gift or will, was an ancient practice. Donations to charity, education, and the arts by businesses, however, often by endowing their own securities, as with the giant Ford Foundation, was a young practice. Indeed, in the Harris and Eliza Kempner Fund lesser wealthy like the Kempners pioneered in "creative grant-making, . . . well in advance of the trend," leading "to a wide range of innovative as well

50. IHK, *Recalled Recollections*, p. 126.

51. H. L. Kempner interview with Jones, June 17–18, 1980; IHK, *Recalled Recollections*, pp. 102–103; File "Harris and Eliza Kempner Fund, 1951–9," in Family Personal Papers, 1957–1963, #80-002, Kempner Papers.

52. Harris and Eliza Kempner Fund, "1985 Report and Application Guidelines" (courtesy Leonora K. Thompson); see also the fund's "1987 Report." Eliza and her three childless children willed shares of their estates to the fund, a habit that Kempners with children followed: interviews, H. L. Kempner with Marchiafava, Aug. 1, 1981, p. 7; with Jones, June 17–18, 1980; H. K. Weston with Marchiafava, Aug. 29, 1981, p. 7; IHK, *Recalled Recollections*, p. 126.

as traditional programs for the enhancement of the local community and for students seeking formal education," Harris asserted in 1985.[53]

In addition to honoring their ancestors and better institutionalizing concerns about the community, the fund provided Kempners also with a chance to reaffirm their general fidelity to Judaism and diverse individual decisions concerning religion since 1920. From the fund's beginning its directors substantially supported Galveston's nonsectarian United Way and its United Jewish Welfare Association. Indeed, these are the fund's only two permanent institutional beneficiaries. But, reflecting basic, ongoing changes in American life, especially with respect to race relations, changes that Herb, Harris (the latter a member of the fund's initial board of trustees and its chairman from 1966 to his death in 1987), and other Kempners favored, the fund contributed "also . . . [to] a large variety of other minority causes," Harris wrote proudly in 1985.[54]

As was true of the H. Kempner Trust, the fund's trustees were virtually unrestrained by the terms of its charter, Harris noting that "we are on the small side, we are informal, we are diverse (practically anything is grist for our mill) and we continue to devote ourselves and our resources to objectives that will honor our two eponyms." But, though the charter was "drawn as broadly as possible, with no specific limitations," nevertheless from the late 1940s through the 1980s a tilt exists toward the support of "local projects."[55]

Relatively early in the fund's history the trustees chose to concentrate its "General Fund" on an annually changing roster of local, national, and even international beneficiaries, aiding them and some further afield with relatively small "seed money" grants. Roughly one hundred such grants, selected from among some five hundred applications, are made each year, to inspire larger commitments from other sources. These seed-money awards were akin to H. Kempner's decades-long risking of venture capital in diverse enterprises.[56]

Seed money institutional grantees represented a wide spectrum of interests and aims, although there developed a trend of interest in minority institutions and those concerned with global overpopula-

53. Harris and Eliza Kempner Fund, "1985 Report"; and see Bremner, *American Philanthropy*, passim.

54. Quotation in ibid.; idem, "1987 Report," p. 10.

55. Harris and Eliza Kempner Fund, "1985 Report."

56. H. L. Kempner interview with Jones, June 17–18, 1980.

tion.[57] In 1987, for example, $660,000, or 15 percent of the fund's grants, went to arts and humanities institutions, including Galveston's symphony orchestra, Houston's Children's Museum, and Ohio's Humanities Council (for a film on Cincinnati, that second city in Kempner affections). Nine percent ($60,000+) aided civic and environmental projects, including Galveston's Carter Colored Methodist Church, the Historical Foundation, and the National Trust for Historic Preservation. A slightly lesser total (7 percent, or $46,000) went to health-care organizations and institutions, including Galveston's St. Mary's Hospital. A substantial 37 percent ($250,000) aided social services, a category embracing the region's Boy Scouts Council, Jewish Welfare Association, Texas' Special Olympics, and the statewide League of Women Voters.

Given his preferences, in 1987 as in other years Harris would have devoted more of the fund's resources to its education programs. That year education grants consumed $211,700 (32 percent) of the awards, the grantees including three Israeli universities, Cincinnati's Hebrew Union College, Galveston's Rosenberg Library lecture series, the United Negro College Fund, the Vietnamese Children's Project, and a new Jeane B. Kempner Fellowship at the state university medical branch on the Island.

Closest to Harris's heart was the additional program he championed, to help worthy students, primarily local residents, regardless of race, faith, or gender, to complete their educations. The idea had roots in a student loan fund the Kempners had established at Sugar Land in Herb's honor. Perhaps the Kempners gained substantial credibility among Galveston minorities by their nondiscriminatory stance in the loans, a credibility that may have helped the city escape the violence common elsewhere in the 1960s and 1970s. The loan fund, Harris reported happily,

> enabled people to go to Harvard Medical School, to classic studies at Edinborough [*sic*], to remedial reading in San Antonio, to study stage design and ballet. . . . You see some bright kid come up and his Mother is a checker at some store and you wonder how he even got through high school. The only way he could get to college would be something like [these loans]. The problem has been since this

57. Harris and Eliza Kempner Fund, "1987 Report," pp. 11–19.

is not the [only chartered] purpose of the foundation, . . . we have to do other things besides that.[58]

The 1963 student loans of $90,000 rose to $600,000 in 1985 and to $800,000 in 1987, assisting 200 students. Renamed the Harris L. Kempner Scholarship Fund that year upon his death, the program provided interest-free loans until five years after the student's graduation, by which time repayment is expected. The inconsequential default rate has kept this revolving fund healthy.

Some fellow trustees thought that Harris had said "Yes" too often to scholarship applicants, and they imposed a cap on loans. But Harris often found ways around such constraints, he confided, "because it gave me such enormous personal satisfaction to be of this help." Once, to his astonishment, the federal Internal Revenue Service asserted that the no-interest arrangement made the repayments of these awards taxable. Harris explained the "very simple" fund guidelines: "One—that we had the money to make . . . [awards], and Two—that we hoped the guy would stay in school. They [I.R.S.] seemed to accept that."[59]

Since its establishment with $25,000, the fund has grown to "the present corpus" (1988) of more than $15 million. This increase has resulted in part from the trustees' prudent financial management and from further gifts and bequests by family members, the latter (numbering more than eighty) being able to augment contributions by means of a matching gift program. Within the fund, Kempners established three endowments for specified purposes. One derived from Dan's wish to honor his wife, Jeane Bertig Kempner. His will endowed funds that produce roughly $100,000 each year to aid students deemed worthy by the faculty of the University of Texas medical school in Galveston. The Stanley E. Kempner Fund supports maintenance of Galveston's Kempner Park (the former Garten Verein). And the third endowment, honoring Jennifer Leonora Ezell (Ike's great-granddaughter; b. 1976), sustains special education efforts. Further, upon the death in 1987 of Dan Oppenheimer, Hattie's son, the fund's trustees funded a molecular biology laboratory in his name in San Antonio at the Southwest Foundation for Biomedical Research.[60]

58. H. L. Kempner interview with Jones, June 17–19, 1980.
59. Ibid.; Harris and Eliza Kempner Fund, "1987 Report," passim.
60. Harris and Eliza Kempner Fund, "1987 Report," p. 4.

Among Kempners, Ike, Dan, and Harris were especially vigorous champions of the University of Texas' medical school on Galveston Island, often serving as its standard-bearers in the frequent appropriations wars in Austin. With fund support in 1956 the school authorities created the Medical Research Foundation. Kempner funds helped also to subvent professorships in the mid-1970s, including one in medical humanities honoring Harris, appropriately aimed to lessen narrow professionalism by attracting and keeping superior faculty. Of these faculty lines Harris in 1980 noted with satisfaction that "these [positions] are all paid for [i.e., funded] now."[61]

Unlike many larger, more professionalized foundations, the Kempner Fund consumed only a relatively small share of its liquid assets in administration. Daily accounting and secretarial chores were coped with by "one part-time employee," Harris noted. Financial records required by law were maintained, for fees, by the trust department of a Galveston bank. The upshot was that a very large share of contributions and endowments was spent for the purposes set down in the 1946 instrument creating the fund and in the 1949 indenture further detailing its purposes and limitations.[62]

In later years Harris alleged that decisions on spending were actually made "more or less by me." Which oversimplified matters. To be sure, Harris was a trustee from 1946 to 1987 and chaired the fund's board of trustees from 1966 to 1987. But other trustees included strong-willed relatives and other emphatic individuals who did not likely permit Harris or anyone else to perform solo.[63]

By asserting his preeminence in fund operations, perhaps Harris was misremembering the frequent round-robin letters, many followed by similar circuitous telephone exchanges of views, that preceded agreements with fellow trustees in many matters that cropped up in intervals between the board's calendared meetings. Originally the board met once a year, but by the 1980s it was convening thrice an-

61. H. L. Kempner interview with Jones, June 17–18, 1980; Harris L. Kempner, "Remarks on the Announcement of the Harris L. Kempner Professorship of Humanities at the University of Texas Medical Branch," *Texas Reports on Biology and Medicine* (1974): 31.

62. Copies of the 1946 and 1949 documents supplied by Leonora K. Thompson. For Harris's description, see H. L. Kempner interview with Jones, June 17–18, 1980.

63. Ibid.; H. K. Weston interview with Marchiafava, Aug. 29, 1981.

nually.[64] Those regular assemblies coincided with those of the H. Kempner shareholders. On site every day as a trustee and chairman, Harris surely played a basic role in giving direction and velocity to fund benefactions. But as had become habit in H. Kempner government since the century's turn, consensus outruled decree.

64. H. K. Weston interview with Marchiafava, Aug. 29, 1981.

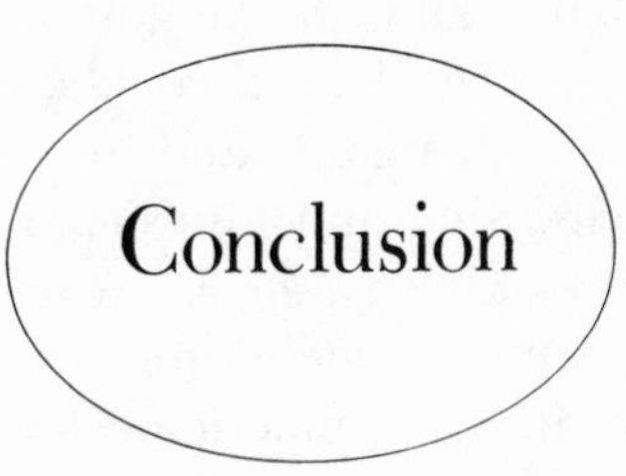

Conclusion

SINCE 1920 the family had preserved collegiality in business matters, at least partly at the cost of religious orthodoxy. Although several Kempners deny to the present that orthodoxy was the price of collegiality, nevertheless it is demonstrable that by the 1940s that price seemed to some then-seniors, including Ike, to have been high.[1] Looking backward, as he and his brothers aged they began to reconsider many aspects of life, decisions, and consequences. As with numerous acculturated American Jews, the Holocaust thrust them away from the anti-Zionism, which in 1919 had helped to cost Ike reelection as mayor, and turned their thoughts to the religious intermarriages that many Kempners had made since then. As noted earlier, Ike had been moved to boast to distinguished dinner guests about his descendants' "mixture of creeds and ceremonies . . . [as] an exhibition of tolerance of faith differences in which increased practice would find merit." Yet, thirty years after these weddings occurred, Ike questioned not the merit of these unions or of secular assimilation, but their effects on Judaism: "I wonder whether such inter-marriages would have taken place had the choice and decision rested with me. My doubts as to my decision as I witness the adoption by my grandchildren either of religious beliefs which I do not share or of no training or indoctrination in fundamentals of our Jewish creed. It has ever been a source of real regret to me that not one of our grandchildren was either 'bar Mitzvah' or confirmed in the synagogue ritual."[2]

1. IHK, *Recalled Recollections*, pp. 94–95.
2. Ibid., pp. 72, 82. The more recent arguments that assimilation is a betrayal would likely have been unappealing to Kempners. See Fein, *Where Are We?*, and Cohen, *American Assimilation or Jewish Revival?*

In 1942 the Passover week embraced Easter Sunday. Ike rose at dawn to shepherd his Roman Catholic grandchildren to early mass. Later that morning he escorted his Episcopalian grandchildren to their services, then to the Easter parade and to a fashionable party. He fretted at the lack of Jewish grandchildren. "Regretfully," Ike wrote in the 1960s, "I have never been able, as my parents were, to impress *my* children much less my grandchildren with the pride and privilege they should have in being practicing Jews and Jewesses."[3]

Evidencing his increasing interest in nurturing Jewish practices among young adults, in the latter 1940s Ike had very quietly begun what became a two-decade devotion to the youth organization Hillel at the University of Texas. He became its "first chairman and did a magnificent job for us . . . I greatly admired and respected him," wrote a national Hillel official on news of Ike's death.[4]

In 1945 Ike "yielded to Rabbi Cohen's blandishments" and spoke from his pulpit on Yom Kippur, the Day of Atonement to Jews, a high honor for a layman. Two years later Cohen called on Ike again to address the temple congregation on that most solemn of days for Jews, Ike employing the opportunity to inveigh against anti-Semitism in America as an unjustifiable closure of access to persons who would otherwise grace science, business, and the arts. Moved emotionally in 1951 when the Harris and Eliza Kempner Fund began its donations to the Women's Home and to the temple, institutions his parents had supported, Ike reflected that the fund was "a tribute to their faith and evidence of their belief in Judaism. Regretfully in my family (children and grandchildren) this nobility of faith and pride in religion is not an accepted part of their inheritance."[5] Then in 1955 Ike, though himself ill, insisted on attending the dedication of the new Temple B'nai Israel building to which all Kempners had contributed, because, he stated, "Temple B'nai Israel is close to my heart. It represents and recalls the devotion to our faith of our Mother and Father; also accentuates [my] regret that adherence to Judaism or Jewish tradition was not inherited by our children or grandchildren. I feel keenly and frequently the difference, between my respect for

3. IHK, *Recalled Recollections*, p. 9; I. H. Kempner's Passover-Easter comments, "Letters to Cecile, 1940–53," Box 72-0111, Kempner Papers.

4. Milton Smith, letter to Morris Polsky, Aug. 19, 1967, Jewish Institute of Religion, AJA/HUC.

5. IHK, *Recalled Recollections*, pp. 91, 94–95, 103, 110–11.

and influence of religion, instilled in me by my parents, and the shallow respect for Judaism that I instilled in my children."[6]

A half year later Ike again offered the Yom Kippur address. He dwelt on what he called "the present day retrogression of United States Jews . . . [into] schisms and quarrels between various branches . . . orthodox, conservatism, reform, which was damaging to both the attacked and the attacker." Surprisingly, considering his own attachment to Reform ways, Ike, though crediting its adherents' accomplishments, doubted their warmth and fidelity:

> We reform Jews live too frequently . . . on a diet of excuses for lack of participation in, and alibis for, non-attendance at synagogues. . . . Reform Judaism . . . is being gradually swept from the ancient moorings of the Torah and the Talmud. While we may minimize the value of adherence to ancient (or outmoded) rites in the ritual, or deprecate special garb on the pulpit, we need not by reason of our views cancel attendance at divine services or fail to help our poor, support our temples and our rabbis with our attendance, not solely by paying annual dues to our congregation.

Concluding, Ike repeated the late Rabbi Cohen's admonition that congregants should attend services more frequently than on Yom Kippur, for that was like "leaving an annual visiting card on God Almighty." Memorializing Cohen ten years after the rabbi's death, Ike in 1961 said of the late minister and friend: "He [Cohen] emphasized to his adult congregants . . . our failure to appreciate or pass on our religious heritage to our children." And Dan Kempner, who exhibited a similar, almost puzzled wistfulness about religion, specified in his will that he was to be buried as a Jew.[7]

In these intimate, tender, sometimes bruised ways, as a family and as individuals, the first American-born Kempners made their peace with religion. Each in his and her own ways, members of succeeding generations came to grips with their root Judaism, if even by inattention. These were and are not uncommon pressures, decisions, and nondecisions among American Jews.[8] What deserves stress is that such

6. Ibid., p. 113.

7. Ibid., p. 116–17; Dan's will in "Last Wishes," DWK folder, Box 1891–1965, Kempner Papers; I. H. Kempner on Cohen in Dreyfus, comp., *Henry Cohen, Messenger of the Lord*, p. 133.

8. Meyer, *Response to Modernity*, passim.

torsions have not sundered the Kempners either as a family or an economic entity.

Civic Reform

By mid-century Ike was questioning also assumptions about the improvability of his beloved city's government. Urban ills were endemic in post–World War II America, and the Progressive ethic seemed everywhere to be unraveling.[9] Many of the Kempners' closest personal friends and business comrades were turning rightward in political-ideological terms. In some matters the senior Kempners swerved with them. An earlier admirer of Franklin Roosevelt's courage and vigor, Ike, for example, had become disenchanted with certain New Deal policies, chiefly in commodity pricing.

In 1945 Ike was pleased that one journalist described him as a reactionary; another, as a communist.[10] Concerning academic and other First Amendment freedoms, frequently warm topics in Texas from the 1940s to the present, Ike supported an open forum–style discussion and lecture series in Galveston that Harris organized. It brought in controversial speakers, often over vehement conservative protests. To be sure, in the 1940s Ike, then chairman of the University of Texas' Medical College Committee, also supported reactionary university regents in their successful effort to oust President Homer Rainey, less perhaps from ideology than because Rainey wished to remove the Galveston medical campus to Houston or Austin.[11] Still, both Ike and Dan publicly criticized the far-right positions espoused in the 1950s that condemned all New Deal social legislation, the United Nations, the Supreme Court, and most academics.

Kempners were educable on race matters. Back in 1942, Ike, when irritated at the lack of a Jewish grandchild, had grumbled privately: "All that is needed now is for Cecile [his daughter] to marry a Jap." His wartime passion would fade. Increasingly throughout the South in the 1950s rabbis like Cohen and congregations like B'nai Israel pondered race segregation. First a few then a large proportion came

9. Danbom, "*The World of Hope*"; Kahn, *Cosmopolitan Culture*.

10. I. H. Kempner, to George Seldes, editor of *In Fact*, Nov. 14, 1945, folder 14, IHK Correspondence, #80-002, Kempner Papers.

11. See Ike's reaction to Rainey's address to faculty, file Kempner personals, 1944, #80-002, Kempner Papers.

out publicly against its perpetuation and against resistance to steps toward desegregation.[12] In 1958, after the historic Brown *v.* Board of Education desegregation decision, Ike congratulated Lyndon Johnson for thwarting the "various Bills . . . attacking the Supreme Court and attempting to curb its functions":

> I cannot imagine how any responsible member of a society based on democratic principles could endeavor to be disrespectful to the body charged with the final interpretation of our laws. . . . There are few, if any, laws or . . . interpretations which could be pleasing to our entire nation . . . with its diversified interests and philosophies. If, however, those who are dissatisfied with specific laws or interpretations attack our whole governmental philosophy in an effort to make their view prevail, they are obviously digging the grave of the government of laws on which our nation was founded and has flourished.[13]

By the late 1950s Ike, Harris, and Ruth were not only publicly supporting the Supreme Court's desegregation positions, but, perhaps more importantly, frustrating attempts to impede its implementation in Galveston. "I was just a busybody" about race equality under law, Harris reflected. Concerning Galveston's first and only pro-integration sit-in, Harris recalled that "I was very active in it. I thoroughly approved of the objectives of the sit-in people. I managed to get numerous small gatherings of drugstore and restaurant owners and then told them that . . . they could [not] preserve . . . segregation . . . that it was just not going to endure; that it was so much better to give in gracefully." Harris and other Kempners helped to establish a rapport among Galveston bankers, lawyers, medical school administrators, ministers, union and business leaders, TV station and newspaper staffs, and leading blacks. The one sit-in, happily unviolent, sufficed to collapse Galveston's segregationist structure of dual, unequal public facilities.[14]

12. Undated, in "Letters to Cecile," Boxes 72-0111 to 72-0308, Kempner Papers; Krause, "Rabbis and Negro Rights in the South, 1954–1967," in *Jews in the South*, pp. 360–85.

13. IHK, letter to Johnson, Aug. 28, 1958, in file Walker City, Box 154, and see Davis-Richberg folder, file IHK, both #80-002, Kempner Papers.

14. H. L. Kempner, interview with R. L. Jones, June 16–17, 1980, RLA; see also McComb, *Galveston*, pp. 209–15; *Houston Post*, Sept. 25, 1987.

The 1962 City Charter Reform

The constant in the Kempner scale of values was that individual selfishness should play second fiddle to intelligent general interest. Even in the 1930s Ike, employing this gauge, was privately worried that the 1902 commission reform he had helped to conceive and nurture had lost its "force and value." Ike blamed taxpayers' reluctance to keep the city and port in adequate repair and the decline of the commissions into bickering baronies.[15] Nevertheless cities of any size should benefit from commission operations, he mused to a grandson who for a college term paper in 1953 inquired of this living source: "The Commission form of Government should succeed [even] in larger cities [than Galveston] . . . for the authority concentrated permits ability to be exerted or inability to be discovered. . . . I still believe in municipal government by a small board; not, however, as . . . automatic or perfect, nor a prescription that is a panacea to cure all buck-passing bellyaches or other inevitable chronic complaints."[16]

Even members of his family, however, chiefly Ruth and Harris, had differing estimates by the 1950s and 1960s. Instead of rationalizing city government, successive Galveston administrations had become as inefficient, corrupt, and partisan as the aldermen before the century's turn, they concluded. Contractors again kicked back to officials to overlook shoddy work or nonperformance. Twilight zones between departments were again fertile areas for vice to fatten in, often in concert with spoilsmen. Frances Kay Harris, who was to play a leading role in trying to end these abuses, described machinations of the once proudly reformed city administration:

> It had evolved into probably one of the worst forms of government that there is. There were no checks and balances. Each commissioner was a czar in his own particular field. . . . If the other commissioners didn't try to take from his budget he wouldn't try to take from their budget. Therefore, the budgets could go sky high, but there was no one to do an audit, there was no one to find out how the money was being spent . . . and no one was really responsible

15. IHK, *Recalled Recollections*, pp. 30–31, 56–57.

16. I. H. Kempner, letter to "Timmy," Oct. 26, 1953, IHK folder 1953, Box 154, #80-002, Kempner Papers.

to anybody, except seeing that whatever they wanted to do was done.[17]

By the 1950s such ways were reflected in the city's deteriorating infrastructure. Persons seeking sites for new businesses recoiled at the visible signs of inept public administration. Even near the important wharves district, cracked major streets imperiled trucks and cargoes. Lesser streets were absolute hazards. Many traffic signals and fire alarms were inoperative or erratic. The fire department's mobile pumpers and ladders and the police department's vehicles were ancient and unreliable, all with more than 100,000 miles on odometers. Storm and sanitary sewers frequently overflowed, burdened excessively by users who had bribed water department personnel in order illicitly to tie their plant, shop, or house into overtasked mains. Fines seemed somehow not to flow into the treasury.

Unpunished thefts of goods from warehouses, rail freight cars, and retail stores were part of a covert tax that swelled from wide-open gambling, prostitution, and liquor. Almost every cotton compress, shop, and freight yard housed slot machines and lottery boards. Taxi drivers, bellhops, storekeepers, and foremen directed inquirers to high-stakes gambling, to penny ante shares in out-of-state lotteries and rigged punchboards, or to bordellos, all protected. Work-force reliability suffered as did the city's effort to be known as a safe family resort. Everyone seemed to wink at the payoffs, kickbacks, and other misfeasances. Complained to, state lawmakers were indifferent because, as representatives of overwhelmingly rural, "moralistic" constituents, they did not want to be tainted politically by working with the representatives of urban, "disreputable" Galveston, not even to stop corruption.

Robert Albright, a Chicagoan transplanted to Galveston, and his wife became activist critics of these matters and was himself elected to the council under a second reformation of the city charter in the 1960s. He recalled that under the 1902 charter "commission meetings were a kind of free for all, particularly when budgetary matters were concerned; he who yelled and screamed the loudest got the most money . . . [I]t was government by who you knew, by who you were.

17. Frances Kay Harris, interview with Jane Kenamore, Dec. 1, 1976, RLA.

It was not government on an equal basis for all concerned . . . [but] on the basis of favor."[18]

The Glorious Revolution of 1962–63

Newcomers like the Albrights and BOI Kempners, including Harris and Ruth, beginning in the mid-1950s allied in a new reform coalition. World War II and the GI Bill had elevated the aspirations and resources of a generation. Like stagnant Jim Crow race relationships, urban corruption had become unacceptable. Reform again became the new game in town.

Galveston's League of Women Voters had become a training ground for reform activists. Its members had agendas ready-to-hand: simultaneously to avoid violence while the city moved toward race equality; to rehabilitate urban services; and by a new charter to modernize fundamentally Galveston's government.

After years of study, public education, and politicking, in 1962 the 1902 charter was revised. The commissioners gave way to a council that was policy-making rather than operational. It would elect a president-mayor from among its members and choose a professional city manager to oversee the work of city departments.[19] Meanwhile, as noted, official race segregation collapsed. So encouraged, Harris's wife Ruth, who was "on the board [of the League of Women Voters] forever," she recalled, devoted three years of her life and substantial amounts of money to research on municipal government and to giving speeches on the theme, even in such male preserves as union hiring halls and businessmen's fraternal lodges. Going further, Ruth committed herself to be a candidate for the council, in the police slot, if the voters in a referendum approved a new city charter.

At league headquarters one day assignments were made for gaining residents' signatures and money contributions for the referendum and campaign. Ruth received the list for the red-light center. The only woman among the league militants willing to enter bordellos, she "drove down [to] the hiring halls across the street from the whore-

18. Robert Albright, interview with Steven Wapen, June 8, 1977, RLA.

19. McComb, *Galveston*, p. 214; Harris, "The Women Do It Again," *National Civic Review*, pp. 326–27.

houses, and . . . was beautifully received in all of them," she recalled. A genteel madam and her prostitutes offered Ruth coffee:

> I told them what . . . I needed the money for. . . . And I raised more money . . . from that district than had ever been raised before. . . . [I]t really didn't hurt me one damn little bit! And when I was campaigning, an interview was arranged with one of the madams . . . by the name of "Big Tit Marie," . . . a woman taller than I with sort of a shelf bosom. . . . There was Mrs. Kempner in . . . the simplest of cotton dresses, and Miss Marie was in a blue brocade dress, hat, jewelry, makeup, everything. And I said to her, . . . as far as I'm concerned, but for the Grace of God I would be in your house, and I believe that people in your profession have . . . always had a place in our civilization, and I'll do everything in the world I can to protect you, but I . . . intend to have an honest police department, and the first time a policeman is paid off, heads are going to have to roll . . . [B]ut if you find that you have to pay off the police, I want to be told about it . . . [W]e were elected to office . . . they [the prostitutes] voted for me too. . . . I think everybody was intrigued . . . that I'm a woman; I'm a Kempner; I'm a Jew; and I'm proud of all three of them. You may think they're not assets. I think they are.

Elected to be Galveston's pioneer woman city councillor and assigned to oversee the police department, on her first day in office Ruth called in the top police officers and told them, "The first one of you that takes it out in trade . . . five dollars worth and I hear about it, I'm telling you right now, we are instructing the City Manager to fire you. You don't belong here."[20]

There were strains in Kempner households. "We [Harris and Ruth] spent an interesting two years not discussing . . . [the 1962 commission reform proposal with Ike] while I was trying to get it adopted," Ruth recalled. But Ike understood that the political-business network of his lifetime could no longer exclude either blacks or women. Besides, the women like Ruth refused any longer to be excluded and kept pushing very hard indeed. In the 1980s in Galveston, "lace" won over "steel," and a woman became mayor. Ruth would monitor her

20. Ruth L. Kempner, interview with L. Marchiafava, June 6, 1981, RLA.

Ruth and Harris Kempner, ca. 1970 (Courtesy Leonora K. Thompson)

performance and that of all incumbents, gender and race notwithstanding, critically and consistently.[21]

Ike was never convinced, however, that all he had favored and fought for was flawed and all that replaced it was superior. One day in 1957, when Ike was eighty-four years old but spry and jaunty in his red bow tie and belt, he gazed intently out of his top-floor office window. Asked at what he was peering, Ike replied: "I see trees. Hundreds and hundreds of trees . . . and they've been planted by many people here. When I was a boy on this island, there weren't any trees."[22] No one planted metaphorical trees any longer in the sense of long-term commitments of capital and unselfish devotion to the city.

Some Galvestonians suggested that Ike's own efforts since the early 1900s to solve their city's economic problems had created other en-

21. Ruth L. Kempner, letter to author, Aug. 20, 1986; Belkin, "'Lace over Steel'," *New York Times Magazine*, p. 41; *Galveston Daily News*, Nov. 13, 1987, p. 4-a.

22. *Houston Post*, Oct. 20, 1957, sec. 1, p. 9.

during woes. Automobile-based tourism, one of Ike's goals, had become the most visible offender. But, as of 1989, no one has yet devised a way superior to tourism, broadly defined, plus the medical school campus, for reviving the torpid economy of the Island City. Indeed, many Galvestonians continued to employ their perceptions of Kempner civic behavior as the best benchmark. For example, in 1950 one letter-to-the-editor writer recalled Ike's interest-free loan to the city a half-century earlier to advance seawall construction, a generous act but, assertedly, only one of "many . . . [by] our prominent citizens who served not . . . for any personal gain but for civic betterment. They felt that if they could give a part of their time and efforts for two or four years to make Galveston a better place to live it was their civic duty to do so. . . . How times have changed!"[23]

Persons closest to Ike understood the ambiguities in his attitude toward the changes in the city's government that Ruth was then championing so effectively. After all, stated Frances Kay Harris, Ruth's comrade in the 1962 charter reform effort, the superseded city charter on which he and the comrades of his youth had lavished so much energy and inventiveness, was "his baby and it's very difficult to see anything happen to your baby."[24]

Continuities

H. Kempner's five trustees as of 1981 were Harris as chair, Shrub, Denny, Dan Oppenheimer (Hattie's son, a San Antonio banker, who died in 1987), and Arthur Alpert, another longtime H. Kempner office manager. As of 1988 Denny was board chairman at Imperial Sugar, and Shrub, a director of Imperial as well as chair of the H. Kempner Trust board, has become known as the "Wizard of Galveston" for the acuity of his investment policies.

Born in 1940, Shrub had joined the long line of Kempners who had followed paths their ancestors blazed. Unsure which career options to follow, in 1969, diplomas from Harvard and Stanford in hand, he was working for the family bank when its manager of "a very small pooled equity fund" quit. Shrub filled in and in this typically Kemp-

23. *Galveston Daily News*, May 8, 10, 1950.

24. Frances Kay Harris interview with Kenamore, June 1, 1976; IHK, *Recalled Recollections*, pp. 30–31, 56–57.

ner manner discovered his own way. He acknowledges that Kempner connections eased his access. His assured income from H. Kempner shares and his job security allowed him the luxury of making long-term decisions. They proved to be remarkably good. In 1982, Shrub formed Kempner Capital Management, Inc., independently of H. Kempner, whose investments he also manages.[25]

It would have delighted Harris further to know that in late 1987 and early 1988, Denny arranged Imperial's purchase of Holly Sugar, a refining corporation based in Colorado with plants also in Wyoming, Montana, and California. Like earlier arrangements that had assured Imperial of Hawaiian raw stock, this one with Holly added to the Kempner refinery's dependable sources of the commodity. Imperial processed cane and Holly, sugar beets. Holly enjoyed federal price supports not available to Imperial and had long-term contracts with its grower-suppliers that promised further to rationalize refinery operations. Despite popular concerns about calories and a shift toward non-sugar sweeteners, the market for sugar remained huge. Holly was either the nation's third or second-largest beet sugar refiner, depending on which financial reporter one read. The 1988 acquisition would reportedly make Imperial the second-largest American refinery, outsized only by a Georgia firm, Savannah Foods. Considering the severe competition for Holly by an investment conglomerate (whose leader allegedly received death threats during the negotiations), Denny, a novice at buy-outs and mergers, acquitted himself admirably. He assisted Imperial's president, non-Kempner Robert C. Hanna, both being aided by Shrub's presence on Imperial's board and by the line of credit extended by that old Kempner source of risk capital since the 1870s, the Bank of New York.[26]

Hoping for such triumphs and that the generational cohesion would continue, in 1963 Harris had addressed his relatives, all fellow-shareholders in H. Kempner about "my thinking and training for many years":

> [Y]our management were [not] supermen! . . . There have been many mistakes and some of them quite serious ones. Further, . . . the social and economic progress made by the nation, the state, and

25. Long, "The Wizard of Galveston," *Ultra*, July, 1985, pp. 60–64.

26. See *New York Times*, Oct. 13, 1987, p. 20; Dec. 25, 1987, p. 25; *Galveston Daily News*, Dec. 29, 1987, p. 1; *Houston Chronicle*, Jan. 5, 1988, sec. 3, p. 2.

> the areas in which we operate, greatly favored our growth. What is perhaps unique in the Kempner history and . . . certainly most remarkable, . . . is the long history of working for the group and not for self alone. . . . As the family grows larger and stems further and further from the root, one can only hope that this spirit of joint endeavor will be continued by the management and recognized by the stockholders.[27]

Reviewing Kempner history to fellow Harvard alumni in 1981, Harris concluded, "We hope to do better in the succeeding generation." Similar aspirations were becoming illusory for other generation-spanning family businesses, including some owned by close friends and even relatives to the Kempners. For example, in 1988 Henry Oppenheimer's descendants decided to close the family's private San Antonio bank. Explaining their decision, Jesse Oppenheimer acknowledged that his sons "were not in it [the bank]. We've run out of family." Besides, he continued, "It's not like yesterday, when things were done on trust and confidence. Today it's all balance sheets and statements."[28]

The Kempners had already closed their family's unincorporated, uninsured private bank. But unlike the Oppenheimers, they had not run out of family. Instead, with good reason they could echo Harris's hope that the family would do better about recruiting from within its ranks in the succeeding generation. As noted, in 1988 Denny recruited his cousin James Carroll Kempner to be Imperial Holly's executive vice-president and chief financial officer, an impressive and suitable choice based on the latter's experience with other firms.

But if Kempners will indeed carry on together, Harris will not know the results. In September, 1987, while playing tennis the eighty-four-year-old tripped and fell to the hard-packed court, incurring a swiftly fatal neurological injury. One obituary observed that "sprays of oleanders were placed on the doors of the many historical . . . properties that Kempner helped to preserve through his family's charitable fund."[29]

Nor would Harris know the outcome of acrimonious ongoing public debates in Galveston about proposals to develop Atlantic City–

27. HLK, "Beneficiary Interest Report, 1963," pp. 9–10.

28. H. L. Kempner, "The Kempners of Galveston and Sugar Land" (manuscript), Kempner Papers, pp. 22–23.

29. *Houston Chronicle*, Sept. 25, 1987.

and Las Vegas–scale gambling casinos on the island. With Harris, Ruth, Shrub, and Leonora Kempner Thompson in the van, from the initiation of the proposals Kempners had prominently and consistently opposed it. They professed disbelief in promoters' claims that the casinos would return prosperity to Galveston, increase city tax and franchise revenues, and generate jobs for substantial numbers of residents of the economically depressed community. The Kempners' opposition revived "fly in amber" accusations against the family, especially the charge of insensitivity to the needs of the poor, especially Galveston's blacks.

Shrub denied that the proposed casinos would reinvigorate the Island City and said that instead, taxes and living costs would rise. Healthier, more truly wealth-generating projects, including several encouraged by Kempners, were under way, especially those involving the medical campus, a Navy proposal to increase its presence in Galveston (a project since scuttled due to federal budget constraints), and ambitious non-gambling residence and recreation developments for second homeowners, long-term vacationers, and day trippers. Shrub then indicated that his great-grandfather's ambition of 1894 remains in 1988 a central theme to many members of this family. Asserting that the pro-casino promoters were acting wholly in self-interest, he defended the motives of the opposition: "The people who are opposing it [the casinos] are people who tend to have families here or who want to continue bringing their families here."[30] The August, 1988, referendum went against the casino-gambling initiative, the third such popular verdict against it in the 1980s. But the pressures favoring reentrance of legal gambling sometimes depressed even peppery Ruth Kempner. Her poem "Devices Out of Place" admitted to near despair about the prospects for the Kempners' beloved community to remain livable:

East and West:
  Thirty miles of beach — rock and sand and sparkling water
North and South:
  Three miles of grid-patterned, oleander bedecked streets
And its symbols?

30. Ibid., Aug. 7, 1988.

A pair of dice, an automatic, a spoon,
a match, a sprinkling of snow that isn't snow
Even the gulls wheel in fear and despair—
their bread turned into paper.[31]

Though far from ended, with the deaths of nonagenarians Sara (1983) and Fannie (1987), the last surviving children of Harris and Eliza Kempner; and, in 1987, of Dan Oppenheimer and Harris Leon Kempner, the Kempner family's oleander odyssey reached new crossroads. Paths from the present remain open to many futures for members of this clan. But unriven links to the family's past extend back to the 1850s when young, ambitious Harris Kempner reached Abraham Lincoln's America. T. S. Eliot's advice in his *Quartet* closes this unclosed story: "The end of our exploring will be to arrive where we started and see the place for the first time."

31. *Galveston Daily News*, July 27, 1988, p. 7-c.

Bibliography

The very large (three hundred or more archival boxes on deposit at the Rosenberg Library, Galveston, Texas) Kempner Family Papers are the primary sources for this book. Many footnotes refer to this collection's holdings of essays, drafts of speeches, business correspondence, transcripts of oral history interviews, and personal letters, etc., by generations of Kempners and their associates. These individual items are far too numerous to cite again here in detail.

Manuscripts

Armstrong, R. M. "History of Sugar Land, Texas, the Imperial Sugar Company, and Sugar Land Industries." Draft manuscript, 1986. Privately held.

Cohen, Henry, Papers. Eugene C. Barker Texas History Center, University of Texas at Austin, Austin, Texas.

Congregation B'nai Israel Executive Committee Minute Books, 1868–1902. American Jewish Archives, Hebrew Union College, Cincinnati, Ohio.

Dreyfus, A. Stanley. "A Hebrew Benevolent Society." Manuscript of speech delivered October 30, 1966. American Jewish Archives, Hebrew Union College, Cincinnati, Ohio.

Dun Reports. R. G. Dun Collection. Baker Library, Harvard Graduate School of Business Administration, Cambridge, Mass.

Heidenheimer, Sampson, Collection. Eugene C. Barker Texas History Center, University of Texas at Austin, Austin, Texas.

Kempner Family Papers. Rosenberg Library Archives. Galveston, Texas.

Kempner Letterpress Book. American Jewish Archives, Hebrew Union College, Cincinnati, Ohio.

McDonough, Elinore M., comp. "Building the Santa Fe." Unpublished manuscript. Rosenberg Library Archives, Galveston, Texas.

Stubbs, Sara Ellen. "Galveston Was Their Home: Genealogy of the Kauffman-Stubbs-Brotherson Families." Typescript, 1977. Rosenberg Library Archives, Galveston, Texas.

Winegarten, Ruthe, ed. "Finder's Guide to the Texas Women: A Celebration of History Exhibit Archives." Typescript, 1984. Texas Woman's University Library, Denton, Texas.

Books

Abbot, Phillip. *Seeking Many Inventions: The Idea of Community in America.* Knoxville: University of Tennessee Press, 1987.

Adams, James Truslow. *Big Business in a Democracy.* New York: Scribners, 1946.

Aldrich, Nelson W., Jr. *Old Money: The Mythology of America's Upper Class.* New York: Knopf, 1988.

Allen, James B. *The Company Town in the American West.* Norman: University of Oklahoma Press, 1966.

Allen, Michael P. *The Founding Fortunes: A New Anatomy of the Super-Rich Families in America.* New York: Truman-Talley Books, 1988.

Allen, Ruth. *Chapters in the History of Organized Labor in Texas.* Austin: University of Texas Press, 1941.

Appleby, Joyce. *Capitalism and a New Social Order: The Republican Vision of the 1790s.* New York: New York University Press, 1984.

Ashkenazi, Elliot. *The Business of Jews in Louisiana, 1840–1875.* University, Ala.: University of Alabama Press, 1988.

Atherton, Lewis Eldon. *The Southern Country Store.* Baton Rouge: Louisiana State University Press, 1949.

Ayers, Edward L. *Vengeance and Justice: Crime and Punishment in the 19th Century American South.* New York: Oxford University Press, 1984.

Bainbridge, John. *The Super-Americans.* Garden City, N.Y.: Doubleday, 1961.

Baritz, Loren. *The Good Life: The Meaning of Success for the American Middle Class.* New York: Knopf, 1989.

Basch, Norma. *In the Eyes of the Law: Women, Marriage, and Property in Nineteenth-Century New York.* Ithaca: Cornell University Press, 1982.

Beard, Charles A. *American City Government: A Survey of Newer Tendencies.* 1912. Reprint. New York: Arno, 1970.

Beard, Mary Ritter. *Woman's Work in Municipalities.* 1915. New York: Arno, 1972.

Bender, Thomas. *Toward an Urban Vision: Ideas and Institutions in 19th Century America.* Baltimore: Johns Hopkins University Press, 1982.

Bentley, Arthur. *The Process of Government: A Study of Social Pressures.* 1908. Reprint. Cambridge, Mass.: Belknap Press, 1967.

Bernstein, Irving. *The Lean Years: A History of the American Worker, 1920–1933.* Boston: Houghton-Mifflin, 1960.

Beverley, Mary Frances. *Cowbells and Coffins: The Old General Store.* Austin: Eakin, 1987.

Birmingham, Stephen. *"Our Crowd": The Great Jewish Families of New York.* New York: Harper and Row, 1967.

Blackford, Mansel G., and K. Austin Derr. *Business Enterprise in American History.* Boston: Houghton-Mifflin, 1986.

Bledstein, Burton. *The Culture of Professionalism: The Middle Class and the Development of Higher Education in America.* New York: Norton, 1976.

Bloom, Allan. *The Closing of the American Mind.* New York: Simon and Schuster, 1987.

Bork, David. *Family Business, Risky Business: How to Make It Work.* New York: AMACOM, 1986.

Bourne, Randolph S. *War and the Intellectuals: Collected Essays, 1915–1919.* Ed. Carl Resek. New York: Harper and Row, 1964.

Brandes, Joseph. *Immigrants to Freedom: Jewish Communities in Rural New Jersey since 1882.* Philadelphia: University of Pennsylvania Press, 1971.

Brandes, Stuart D. *American Welfare Capitalism, 1880–1940.* Chicago: University of Chicago Press, 1970.

Brandt, Allan M. *No Magic Bullet: A Social History of Venereal Disease in the United States since 1880.* New York: Oxford University Press, 1985.

Bremner, Robert. *American Philanthropy.* 2d ed. Chicago: University of Chicago Press, 1988.

Brenner, Marie. *The Bingham Family of Louisville.* New York: Random, 1988.

Bristow, Edward J. *Prostitution and Prejudice: The Jewish Fight against White Slavery, 1870–1939.* New York: Schocken Books, 1983.

Brown, John Henry. *Indian Wars and Pioneers of Texas.* Austin: Daniell, 1890.

Buenger, Walter, and Joseph Pratt. *But Also Good Business: Texas Commerce Banks and the Financing of Houston and Texas, 1886–1986.* College Station: Texas A&M University Press, 1986.

Carnegie, Andrew. *Problems of Today: Wealth, Labor, Socialism.* New York: Doubleday, Page, 1908.

Carosso, Vincent P. *Investment Banking in America: A History.* Cambridge: Harvard University Press, 1970.

Carosso, Vincent P. et al. *The Morgans: Private International Bankers, 1854–1913*. Cambridge: Harvard University Press, 1987.
Castells, Manuel. *The City and the Grassroots: A Cross-Cultural Theory of Urban Social Movements*. Berkeley: University of California Press. 1983.
———. *The Urban Question: A Marxist Approach*. Cambridge: MIT Press, 1977.
Chafets, Ze'ev. *Members of the Tribe: On the Road in Jewish America*. New York: Bantam Books, 1988.
Chandler, Alfred D., Jr. *The Visible Hand: The Managerial Revolution in American Business*. Cambridge, Mass.: Belknap Press, 1977.
Chandler, Alfred D., Jr., and Stephen Salsbury. *Pierre S. DuPont and the Making of the Modern Corporation*. New York: Harper and Row, 1971.
Chandler, David. *The Binghams of Louisville: The Dark History behind One of America's Great Fortunes*. New York: Crown, 1987.
Cheesborough, E. R. *Galveston's Commission Form of Government: Its History, Details and Practical Workings*. Galveston: Hunter, 1910.
Clark, John, et al. *Three Generations in Twentieth Century America*. Rev. ed. Homewood, Ill.: Dorsey Press, 1982.
Clark, Joseph Lynn. *The Texas Gulf Coast: Its History and Development*. New York: Lewis Historical Publishers, 1955.
Cochran, Thomas C. *Challenges to American Values: Society, Business, and Religion*. New York: Oxford University Press, 1985.
———. *Railroad Leaders, 1845–1890: The Business Mind in Action*. Cambridge: Harvard University Press, 1953.
Cohen, Henry. *The Galveston Movement, 1907–1914*. Rev. ed. Galveston: privately printed, n.d.
Cohen, Steven M. *American Assimilation or Jewish Revival?* Bloomington: Indiana University Press, 1988.
Collier, Peter, and David Horowitz. *The Fords: An American Epic*. New York: Summit Books, 1987.
Connelly, Mark T. *The Response to Prostitution in the Progressive Era*. Chapel Hill: University of North Carolina Press, 1980.
Danbom, David B. *"The World of Hope": Progressives and the Struggle for an Ethical Public Life*. Philadelphia: Temple University Press, 1987.
Daniel, Pete. *Breaking the Land: The Transformation of Cotton, Tobacco, and Rice Cultures since 1800*. Urbana: University of Illinois Press, 1985.
De Benedetti, Charles. *The Peace Reform in American History*. Bloomington: Indiana University Press, 1980.
De Cordova, J. *Texas: Her Resources and Her Public Men*. 1858. Reprint. Waco: Texian Press, 1969.

Derber, Milton. *The American Idea of Industrial Democracy, 1865–1965*. Urbana: University of Illinois Press, 1970.

Dethloff, Henry C., and Keith L. Bryant, Jr. *Entrepreneurship: A U.S. Perspective*. College Station: Texas A&M University, 1983.

Dinnerstein, Leonard, and Mary D. Palsson, eds. *Jews in the South*. Baton Rouge: Louisiana State University Press, 1973.

Dreyfus, A. Stanley, comp. *Henry Cohen, Messenger of the Lord*. New York: Bloch Publishing, 1963.

Drucker, Peter. *Innovation and Entrepreneurship: Practice and Principles*. New York: Harper and Row, 1985.

Eisenhower, Virginia, ed. *Alexander Sweet's Texas: The Lighter Side of Lone Star History*. Austin: University of Texas Press, 1986.

Ellis, L. Tuffly. *The Texas Cotton Compress Industry*. Dallas: Southwestern Compress and Warehouse Assoc., 1962.

Evans, Eli N. *Judah P. Benjamin: The Jewish Confederate*. New York: Free Press, 1988.

———. *The Provincials: A Personal History of Jews in the South*. New York: Atheneum, 1973.

Evans, Sara, and Harry C. Boyte. *Free Spaces: The Sources of Democratic Change in America*. New York: Harper and Row, 1986.

Fehrenbach, T. R. *Lone Star: A History of Texas and the Texans*. New York: Macmillan, 1968.

Fein, Leonard. *Where Are We?: The Inner Life of America's Jews*. New York: Harper and Row, 1988.

Fite, Gilbert. *Cotton Fields No More: Southern Agriculture, 1865–1980*. Lexington: University Press of Kentucky, 1984.

Fussell, Paul. *Class: A Guide through the American Status System*. New York: Summit Books, 1983.

———. *The Great War and Modern Memory*. New York: Oxford University Press, 1975.

Galambos, Louis. *The Public Image of Big Business in America, 1880–1940*. Baltimore: Johns Hopkins University Press, 1975.

Goldberg, Robert A. *Back to the Soil: The Jewish Farmers of Clarion, Utah, and Their World*. Salt Lake City: University of Utah Press, 1986.

Goldwasser, Thomas. *Family Pride: Profiles of America's Best-run Family Businesses*. New York: Dodd, Mead, 1986.

Goodwin, Frank. *Lone-Star Land: Twentieth Century Texas in Perspective*. New York: Knopf, 1955.

Gordon, Milton. *Assimilation in American Life: The Role of Race, Religion and National Origins*. New York: Oxford University Press, 1964.

Grantham, Dewey. *Southern Progressivism: The Reconciliation of Progress and Tradition*. Knoxville: University of Tennessee Press, 1983.

Green, George N. *The Establishment in Texas Politics: The Primitive Years, 1938–1975.* Westport, Conn: Greenwood, 1979.

Greene, Victor. *American Immigrant Leaders: Marginality and Identity, 1800–1910.* Baltimore: Johns Hopkins University Press, 1986.

Gunther, John. *Taken at the Flood: The Story of Albert D. Lasker.* New York: Harper, 1960.

Gusfield, Joseph. *Symbolic Crusade: Politics and the American Temperance Movement.* Westport, Conn.: Greenwood, 1963.

Hamburger, Ludwig. *How Nazi Germany Has Controlled Business.* Washington, D.C.: The Brookings Institution, 1943.

Handlin, Oscar. *Adventure in Freedom: Three Hundred Years of Jewish Life in America.* New York: McGraw-Hill, 1954.

Harrington, Mona. *The Dream of Deliverance in American Politics.* New York: Knopf, 1986.

Hartmann, Edward. *The Movement to Americanize the Immigrant.* New York: Columbia University Press, 1948.

Harvey, David. *Social Justice and the City.* Baltimore: Johns Hopkins University Press, 1973.

———. *The Urbanization of Capital.* Baltimore: Johns Hopkins University Press, 1985.

Hayes, Charles W. *Galveston: History of the Island and the City.* Vol. 1. Austin: Jenkins Garrett, 1874.

Hays, Samuel P. *Response to Industrialization, 1885–1914.* Chicago: University of Chicago Press, 1957.

Hearden, Patrick J. *Independence and Empire: The New South's Cotton Mill Campaign, 1865–1901.* Dekalb: Northern Illinois University Press, 1982.

Herberg, Will. *Protestant-Catholic-Jew: A Sociology of American Religion.* 2d ed. Garden City, N.Y.: Anchor Books, 1960.

Herscher, Uri. *Jewish Agricultural Utopias in America, 1880–1910.* Detroit: Wayne State University Press, 1981.

Hidy, Ralph W., and Muriel E. Hidy. *Pioneering in Big Business, 1892–1911: The History of Standard Oil Company.* New York: Harper, 1955.

Higham, John. *Send These to Me: Immigrants in Urban America.* Baltimore: Johns Hopkins University Press, 1984.

Hobson, Barbara M. *Uneasy Virtue: The Politics of Prostitution and the American Reform Tradition.* New York: Basic Books, 1987.

Hofstadter, Richard. *The Age of Reform: From Bryan to F. D. R.* 1955. 2d ed. New York: Random House, 1965.

———. *The Progressive Movement, 1900–1915.* Englewood Cliffs, N.J.: Prentice-Hall, 1963.

———. *Social Darwinism in American Thought*. Rev. ed. New York: G. Braziller, 1959.

Holmes, Richard. *Acts of War: The Behavior of Men in Battle*. New York: Free Press, 1986.

Hoover, Herbert. *American Individualism*. Garden City, N.Y.: Doubleday, Doran, 1934.

Horowitz, Daniel. *The Morality of Spending: Attitudes toward the Consumer Society in America, 1875–1940*. Baltimore: Johns Hopkins University Press, 1985.

Howe, Irving, *World of Our Fathers*. New York: Simon and Schuster, 1976.

Howe, Mark A. DeWolfe. *Justice Oliver Wendell Holmes: The Proving Years, 1870–1882*. Cambridge, Mass.: Belknap Press, 1963.

Hubbard, W. Hustace. *Cotton and the Cotton Market*. New York: D. Appleton, 1923.

Hyman, H. M. *Soldiers and Spruce: The Loyal Legion of Loggers and Lumbermen*. Los Angeles: Institute of Industrial Relations, 1963.

Jacoby, Sanford M. *Employing Bureaucracy: Managers, Unions, and the Transformation of Work in American Industry, 1900–1945*. New York: Columbia University Press, 1985.

Jick, Leon. *The Americanization of the Synagogue, 1820–1870*. Hanover, N.H.: University Press of New England, 1976.

Jones, Charles A. *International Business in the 19th Century*. Brighton-Sussex, England: Wheatsheaf Books, 1987.

Jones, Fred M. *Middlemen in the Domestic Trade of the United States, 1800–1860*. Urbana: University of Illinois Press, 1937.

Kahn, Bonnie M. *Cosmopolitan Culture: The Gilt-edged Dream of a Tolerant City*. New York: Atheneum, 1987.

Kaler, Samuel P., comp. *History of the [David and Cornelia] Kerr Family, from 1708*. Columbia City, Ind.: privately printed, 1898.

Kanin, Garson. *Moviola*. New York: Simon and Schuster, 1979.

Kantrow, Alan M. *The Constraints of Corporate Tradition: Doing the Correct Thing, Not Just What the Past Dictates*. New York: Harper and Row, 1988.

Karp, Abraham. *Haven and Home: A History of Jews in America*. New York: Schocken Books, 1986.

Kempner, Isaac H., *Recalled Recollections*. Dallas: Egan, 1961.

Kirkland, Edward Chase. *Dream and Thought in the Business Community, 1860–1900*. Ithaca, N.Y.: Cornell University Press, 1956.

Kolko, Gabriel. *The Triumph of Conservatism: A Reinterpretation of American History, 1900–1916*. New York: Free Press of Glencoe, 1963.

Konvitz, Josef W. *Urban Millennium: The City-building Process from the Early Middle Ages to the Present.* Carbondale: Southern Illinois University Press, 1985.

Kuehl, Warren F. *Seeking World Order: The United States and International Organization to 1920.* Nashville: Vanderbilt University Press, 1969.

Lacey, Robert. *Ford: The Men and the Machine.* Boston: Little, Brown, 1986.

Lane, Robert. *Political Life: Why and How People Get Involved in Politics.* Glencoe, Ill.: Free Press, 1959.

Lapham, Lewis. *Money and Class in America: Notes and Observations on Our Civil Religion.* New York: Weidenfeld and Nicolson, 1987.

Larsen, Lawrence H. *The Rise of the Urban South.* Lexington: University Press of Kentucky, 1985.

Lazarou, Kathleen. *Concealed under Petticoats: Married Women's Property and the Law of Texas, 1840–1913.* New York: Garland, 1986.

Lefebvre, Henri. *La révolution urbaine.* Paris: Gallimard, 1970.

Lender, Mark E., and James K. Martin. *Drinking in America.* New York: Free Press, 1987.

Levine, David O. *The American College and the Culture of Aspiration, 1915–1940.* Ithaca, N.Y.: Cornell University Press, 1986.

Lykes, Genevieve P. *Gift of Heritage.* N.p.: privately printed, 1969.

McComb, David G. *Houston, a History*, Rev. ed. Austin: University of Texas Press, 1981.

———. *Galveston: A History.* Austin: University of Texas Press, 1986.

Mackey, Thomas. *Red Lights Out: A Legal History of Prostitution, Disorderly Houses, and Vice Districts, 1870–1917.* New York: Garland, 1987.

McWilliams, Tennant S. *The New South Faces the World: Foreign Affairs and the Southern Sense of Self, 1877–1950.* Baton Rouge: Louisiana State University Press, 1987.

Marcus, Jacob R., and Abraham J. Peck, eds. *The American Rabbinate: A Century of Continuity and Change, 1883–1983.* Hoboken, N.J.: KTAV Publishers, 1985.

Marinbach, Bernard. *Galveston: Ellis Island of the West.* Albany: State University of New York Press, 1983.

Mason, Herbert M. *Death from the Sea.* New York: Dial Press, 1972.

May, Henry F. *The End of American Innocence.* New York: Knopf, 1959.

Medick, Hans, and David W. Sabean, eds. *Interest and Emotion: Essays on the Study of Family and Kinship.* New York: Cambridge University Press, 1984.

Melosi, Martin V. *Coping with Abundance: Energy and Environment in Industrial America*. Philadelphia: Temple University Press, 1985.

Melvin, Patricia M. *The Organic City: Urban Definition and Community Organization, 1880–1920*. Lexington: University Press of Kentucky, 1987.

Meyer, Michael. *Response to Modernity: A History of the Reform Movement in Judaism*. New York: Oxford University Press, 1988.

Miler, William, ed. *Men in Business: Essays on the Historical Role of the Entrepreneur*. Rev. ed. Cambridge: Harvard University Press, 1962.

Milner, Alfred. *Cotton Contraband*. London: Darling and Son, 1915.

Montgomery, David. *The Fall of the House of Labor: The Workplace, the State, and American Labor Activism, 1865–1925*. New York: Cambridge University Press, 1987.

Moore, R. Laurence. *Religious Outsiders and the Making of Americans*. New York: Oxford University Press, 1986.

Munro, William B. *The Government of American Cities*. New York: Macmillan, 1912.

Nathan, Anne, and Harry I. Cohen. *The Man Who Stayed in Texas: The Life of Rabbi Henry Cohen*. New York: McGraw Hill, 1941.

Norris, James D. *R. G. Dun & Company, 1841–1900*. Westport, Conn.: Greenwood Press, 1978.

Nunn, William C. *Texas under the Carpetbaggers*. Austin: University of Texas Press, 1962.

O'Brien, Gail Williams. *The Legal Fraternity and the Making of a New South Community, 1848–1882*. Athens: University of Georgia Press, 1986.

Ousley, Clarence, ed. *Galveston in Nineteen Hundred*. Atlanta, W. C. Chase, 1900.

Paquette, Robert. *Sugar Is Made with Blood*. Middletown, Conn.: Wesleyan University Press, 1988.

Patterson, David S. *Toward a Warless World: The Travail of the American Peace Movement, 1887–1914*. Bloomington: Indiana University Press, 1976.

Pessen, Edward. *Riches, Class, and Power before the Civil War*. Lexington, Mass.: D. C. Heath, 1973.

Petersen, Keith. *Company Town: Potlatch, Idaho, and the Potlatch Lumber Company*. Pullman: Washington State University Press, 1987.

Pitre, Merline. *Through Many Dangers, Toils, and Snares: The Black Leadership of Texas, 1868–1900*. Austin: Eakin Press, 1985.

Platt, Harold. *City Building in the New South: The Growth of Public Services in Houston, Texas, 1830–1915*. Philadelphia: Temple University Press, 1983.

Pollack, Norman. *The Just Polity: Populism, Law, and Human Welfare.* Urbana: University of Illinois Press, 1987.

Porter, Glen, and Harold Livesay. *Merchants and Manufacturers: Studies in the Changing Structure of Nineteenth Century Marketing.* Baltimore: Johns Hopkins University Press, 1971.

Potts, Charles. *Railroad Transportation in Texas.* Austin: University of Texas Press, 1909.

Proctor, Samuel, and Louis Schmeier, eds. *Jews of the South.* Macon, Ga.: Mercer University Press, 1984.

Pusateri, C. Joseph. *A History of American Business.* 2d ed. Glenwood, Ill.: Davidson, 1988.

Rabinowitz, Howard. *Race Relations in the Urban South.* New York: Oxford University Press, 1978.

Reps, John W. *The Forgotten Frontier: Urban Planning in the American West before 1890.* Columbia: University of Missouri Press, 1981.

Rice, Bradley. *Progressive Cities: The Commission Government Movement in America, 1901–1920.* Austin: University of Texas Press, 1977.

Roark, Garland. *The Coin of Contraband: The True Story of United States Customs Agent Al Scharff.* Garden City, N.Y.: Doubleday, 1964.

Rochlin, Harriet, and Fred Rochlin. *Pioneer Jews: A New Life in the Far West.* Boston: Houghton-Mifflin, 1984.

Rosenwaike, Ira. *On the Edge of Greatness: A Portrait of American Jewry in the Early National Period.* Cincinnati: American Jewish Archives, 1985.

Ross, Steven J. *Workers on the Edge: Work, Leisure, and Politics in Industrializing Cincinnati, 1788–1890.* New York: Columbia University Press, 1985.

Russell, James M. *Atlanta, 1847–1890: City Building in the Old South and the New.* Baton Rouge: Louisiana State University Press, 1988.

Ryan, Mary P. *Cradle of the Middle Class: The Family in Oneida County, New York, 1790–1865.* New York: Cambridge University Press, 1981.

Sarna, Jonathan D., ed. *The American Jewish Experience.* New York: Holmes and Meier, 1986.

Schlesinger, Arthur M., Jr., *Cycles of American History.* Boston: Houghton-Mifflin, 1986.

Schmeier, Louis, ed. *Reflections of Southern Jewry.* Macon, Ga.: Mercer University Press, 1982.

Schuyler, David. *The New Urban Landscape: The Redefinition of City Form in 19th Century America.* Baltimore: Johns Hopkins University Press, 1986.

Shammas, Carole, et al. *Inheritance in America from Colonial Times to the Present.* New Brunswick, N.J.: Rutgers University Press, 1987.

Shore, Laurence. *Southern Capitalists: The Ideological Leadership of an Elite, 1832–1885.* Chapel Hill: University of North Carolina, 1986.

Sibley, Marilyn M. *The Port of Houston: A History.* Austin: University of Texas Press, 1968.

Silberman, Charles. *A Certain People: American Jews and Their Lives Today.* New York: Summit Books, 1985.

Sitterson, J. Carlyle. *Sugar Country: The Cane Sugar Industry in the South, 1753–1950.* Lexington: University of Kentucky Press, 1953.

Sklar, Martin. *The Corporate Reconstruction of American Capitalism, 1890–1916: The Market, the Law, and Politics.* New York: Cambridge University Press, 1988.

Steffens, J. Lincoln. *The Shame of the Cities.* 1904. Reprint. New York: P. Smith, 1948.

Stowe, Steven. *Intimacy and Power: Ritual in the Lives of the Planters.* Baltimore: Johns Hopkins University Press, 1987.

Tannenbaum, Frank. *Darker Phases of the South.* New York: G. P. Putnam's Sons, 1924.

Teaford, Jon C. *The Twentieth-Century American City: Problem, Promise, and Reality.* Baltimore: Johns Hopkins University Press, 1986.

Tiger, Lionel. *The Manufacture of Evil: Ethics, Evolution, and the Industrial System.* New York: Harper and Row, 1987.

Timberlake, James. *Prohibition and the Progressive Movement, 1900–1920.* 1963. New York: Atheneum, 1970.

Trammell, Camilla D. *Seven Pines: Its Occupants and Their Letters, 1825–1872.* Dallas: Southern Methodist University Press, 1987.

Tuchman, Barbara. *Practicing History: Selected Essays.* New York: Knopf, 1981.

———. *The Zimmerman Telegram.* New York: Viking, 1958.

Van Tassel, David, and John Grabowski, eds. *Cleveland: A Tradition of Reform.* Kent, Ohio: Kent State University Press, 1986.

Waldinger, Roger D. *Through the Eye of the Needle: Immigrants and Enterprise in New York's Garment Trade.* New York: New York University Press, 1986.

Walker, Donald R. *Penology for Profit: A History of the Texas Prison System, 1867–1912.* College Station: Texas A&M University Press, 1988.

Walker, Robert H. *Reform in America: The Continuing Frontier.* Lexington: University Press of Kentucky, 1985.

Weber, Max. *Protestant Ethic and the Spirit of Capitalism.* Reprint. New York: Scribner, 1976.

Weems, John Edward. *A Weekend in September.* 1957. Reprint. College Station: Texas A&M University Press, 1980.

Weinstein, James. *The Corporate Ideal in the Liberal State: 1900–1918.* Boston: Beacon Press, 1968.

White, Dana F. *The Urbanists, 1865–1915.* New York: Greenwood Press, 1989.

Wiebe, Robert H. *The Search for Order, 1877–1920.* New York: Hill and Wang, 1967.

Williams, William Appleman. *The Contours of American History.* Cleveland, Ohio: World, 1961.

Woodman, Harold. *King Cotton and His Retainers: Financing and Marketing the Cotton Crop of the South, 1800–1925.* Lexington: University of Kentucky Press, 1968.

Woodward, C. Vann. *Origins of the New South, 1873–1913.* Baton Rouge: Louisiana State University Press, 1951.

Wright, Gavin. *Old South, New South: Revolutions in the Southern Economy since the Civil War.* New York: Basic Books, 1986.

Wyatt-Brown, Bertram. *Southern Honor: Ethics and Behavior in the Old South.* New York: Oxford University Press, 1982.

Wyllie, I. G., *The Self-made Man in America.* New York: Free Press, 1954.

Articles and Essays

Alexander, Gregory S. "The Transformation of Trusts as a Legal Category, 1800–1914." *Law and History Review* 5 (1987): 303.

Angell, William D. "Controlling the Workers: The Galveston Dockworkers' Strike of 1920 and Its Impact on Labor Relations in Texas." *East Texas Historical Journal* 23 (1985): 14.

———. "Vantage on the Bay: Galveston and the Railroads." *East Texas Historical Journal* 22 (1984): 3.

Ashworth, John. "The Relationship between Capitalism and Humanitarianism." *American Historical Review* 90 (1987): 813.

Atack, Jeremy. "Firm Size and Industrial Structure in the U.S. During the 19th Century." *Journal of Economic History* 46 (1986): 463.

Axelrod, Bernard. "Galveston: Denver's Deep Water Port." *Southwestern Historical Quarterly* 70 (1966): 220.

Bates, L. W., Jr. "Galveston: A City Built upon Sand." *Scientific American* 95 (July 28, 1906): 64.

Belkin, Lisa. "Lace over Steel: The Women Mayors of Texas." *New York Times Magazine*, March 20, 1988, p. 41.

Benedict, M. L. "Laissez-faire and Liberty: A Re-Evaluation of the Meaning and Origins of Laissez-Faire Constitutionalism," *Law and History Review* 3 (1985): 293.

Blumin, Stuart. "The Hypothesis of Middle-Class Formulation in Nineteenth-Century America: A Critique and Some Proposals." *American Historical Review* 90 (1985): 299.

Bodnar, John. "Symbols and Servants: Immigrant History and the Limits of Public History." *Journal of American History* 73 (1986): 137.

Brackman, Arthur. "Galveston's Gulf." *Houston Gargoyle*, May 5, 1929.

Bradford, Ernest. "Financial Results under the Commission Form of City Government." *National Municipal Review* 1 (1912): 374.

Brownell, Blaine A. "The Urban South Comes of Age, 1900–1940." In *The City in Southern History*, ed. Brownell and D. Goldfield, p. 152. Port Washington, N.Y.: Kennikat, 1977.

Buenger, Walter. "Secession Revisited: The Texas Experience." *Civil War History* 30 (1984): 293.

Burka, P. "Grande Dame of the Gulf." *Texas Monthly* 11 (December, 1983): 164.

Carosso, Vincent P. "American Private Banks in International Finance, 1870–1914." *Business and Economic History* 14 (1986): 1926.

Clark, Gregory. "Authority and Efficiency: The Labor Market and the Managerial Revolution of the Late Nineteenth Century." *Journal of Economic History* 44 (1984): 1069.

Cobb, James C. "Beyond Planters and Industrialists: A New Perspective on the New South." *Journal of Southern History* 54 (1988): 45.

Cochran, Thomas. "The History of a Business Society." *Journal of American History* 54 (1967): 5.

Cohen, Henry. "A Call to Justice." *Texas Jewish Herald*, September 18, 1930.

———. "The Galveston Movement: Its First Year." *Western States Jewish History*. Reprint. 1986.

———. "Settlement of Jews in Texas." *American Jewish Historical Society Publications* 2 (1984): 139.

Cook, Allison. "The Fraying Empire of Bobby Sakowitz." *Texas Monthly* 13 (December, 1985): 132.

Cronholm, Debra. "The Kempners: First Family of Imperial." *The Imperial Crown* 2 (May, 1980): Pts. I and II.

Danhoff, C. "Business Leadership in the South." *Journal of Business* 29 (1956): 130.

Davis, Christopher. "Life at the Edge: Urban and Industrial Evolution of Texas, 1836–1896." *Southwestern Historical Quarterly* 89 (April, 1986): 443.

Day, Donald. "The Americanism of Harris Kempner." *Southwest Review* 30 (1944): 125.

DeGolyer, E. "Anthony F. Lucas and Spindletop." *Southwest Review* 31 (1945): 83.

Dellheim, Charles. "The Creation of a Company Culture: *Cadburys*, 1861–1931." *American Historical Review* 92 (1987): 13.

Diggins, John P. "Comrades and Citizens: New Mythologies in American Citizenship." *American Historical Review* 90 (1985): 614.

Doyle, Don Harrison. "Urbanization and Southern Culture: Economic Elites in Four New South Cities (Atlanta, Nashville, Charleston, Mobile), ca. 1865–1910." In *Toward a New South? Studies in Post–Civil War Southern Communities*, ed. Orville V. Burton and Robert C. McMath, Jr., p. 11. Westport, Conn.: Greenwood, 1982.

Dugas, V. L. "A Duel with Railroads: Houston vs. Galveston, 1866–1881." *East Texas Historical Journal* 2 (October, 1964): 118.

Ellis, L. Tuffly, "Maritime Commerce on the Far Western Gulf, 1861–1865." *Southwestern Historical Quarterly* 77 (1973): 167.

———. "The Revolutionizing of the Texas Cotton Trade, 1865–1888." *Southwestern Historical Quarterly* 75 (1970): 478.

Fishback, Price V. "Did Coal Miners 'Owe Their Souls to the Company Store'? Theory and Evidence from the Early 1900s." *Journal of Economic History* 46 (1986): 1011.

Fleming, Lamar, Jr. "Growth of the Business of Anderson, Clayton & Co.," ed. James Tinsley. *Texas Gulf Coast Historical Association Publication Series* 10 (1966): 1.

Friedman, Lee M. "Dynastic Trust." *American Jewish Historical Publications* 44 (1954): 547.

———. "The Problems of Nineteenth Century American Jewish Peddlers." *American Jewish Historical Publications* 44 (1954): 1.

Friesel, Evyatar. "The Influence of American Zionism on the American Jewish Community." *American Jewish History* 75 (1985): 130.

Galambos, Louis. "The Emerging Organizational Synthesis in Modern American History." *Business History Review* 44 (1970): 280.

———. "Technology, Political Economy, and Professionalization: Central Themes of the Organizational Synthesis." *Business History Review* 57 (1983): 471.

Ginzberg, Lori. "'Moral Suasion Is Moral Balderdash': Women, Politics, and Social Activism in the 1850s." *Journal of American History* 73 (1986): 601.

Grantham, Dewey. "The Twentieth Century South." In *Writing Southern History: Essays in Historiography in Honor of Fletcher M. Green*, ed. Arthur Link and Rembert Patrick. Baton Rouge: Louisiana State University Press, 1965.

Greene, Casey. "Guardians against Change: The Ku Klux Klan in Houston and Harris County, 1920–1925." *Houston Review* 10 (1988): 3.

———. "More than a Thimbleful: Prohibition in Galveston, 1919–1933." *Houston Review* 11 (1989): 45.

Gurock, Jeffrey. "The Emergence of the American Synagogue." In *The American Jewish Experience*, ed. Jonathan D. Sarna, p. 193. New York: Holmes and Meier, 1986.

Hareven, Tamara. "Family History at the Crossroads." *Journal of Family History* 12 (1987): ix.

Harris, Frances Kay. "The Women Do It Again." *National Civic Review* (1960): 326.

Haskell, Thomas. "Capitalism and the Origins of Humanitarian Sensibility." *American Historical Review* 90 (1985): 547.

Hearden, Patrick. "Agricultural Businessmen in the New South." *Louisiana Studies* 14 (1975): 146.

Higham, John. "Anti-Semitism in the Gilded Age." *Mississippi Valley Historical Review* 43 (1957): 559.

———. "Hanging Together: Divergent Unities in American History." *Journal of American History* 61 (1974): 24.

Hoy, Stephen. "Municipal Housekeeping: The Role of Women in Improving Urban Sanitation Practices, 1880–1917." In *Pollution and Reform in American Cities, 1870–1930*, ed. Martin Melosi, p. 173. Austin: University of Texas Press, 1980.

Hudson, W. S. "The Great Sea Wall at Galveston." *Scientific American* 93 (August 26, 1905): 163.

Hurvitz, Haggai. "'Union-Management Cooperation': A Conservative Retreat or a Drive for Industrial Reform? The Case of the AFL's Policy in the 1920s." In *Religion, Ideology, and Nationalism in Europe and America*. Jerusalem: Hebrew University Press, 1986.

Isaac, Paul E. "Municipal Reform in Beaumont, Texas, 1902–1909." *Southwestern Historical Quarterly* 78 (1975): 409.

Jensen, Richard. "Quantitative Collective Biography: An Application to Metropolitan Elites." In *Quantification in American History*, ed. R. Swierenga, p. 389. New York: Atheneum, 1970.

Johnson, W. R. "A Short History of the Sugar Industry in Texas." *Texas Gulf Historical Association Publications* 5 (1961): esp. chap. 3.

Karp, Abraham J. "Ideology and Identity in Jewish Group Survival in America." *American Jewish Historical Quarterly* 65 (1976): 310.

Kempner, Harris L. "Remarks on the Announcement of the Harris L. Kempner Professorship of Humanities at the University of Texas Medical Branch." *Texas Reports on Biology and Medicine* (1974): 31.

Kempner, Isaac H. "The Drama of the Commission Plan in Galveston." *National Municipal Review* (August, 1937): 410.

———. "H. Kempner: The First One Hundred Years." *Gulf Coast Historical Association Publications* 1 (1958): 1.

———. "My Memories of Father," *American Jewish Archives* 19 (1967): 41.

———. "Their Hearts Were Young and Gay." *Guide Magazine to Galveston and the Mainland* (October, 1947): 2, 14.

Kempner, Marion Lee. "Letters from Sandy." *The Jewish Veteran* (November–December, 1982): 13.

Kliger, Hannah. "Traditions of Grass-Roots Organization and Leadership: The Continuity of *Landsmanschaftn* in New York." *American Jewish History* 71 (1986): 25.

Krause, Allen. "Rabbis and Negro Rights in the South, 1954–1967." In *Jews in the South*, ed. Leonard Dinnerstein and Mary D. Pallson, p. 360. Baton Rouge: Louisiana State University Press, 1973.

Kraut, Benny. "Reform Judaism and Unitarian Challenge." In *The American Jewish Experience*, ed. Jonathan D. Sarna, p. 89. New York: Holmes and Meier, 1986.

Langbein, John H. "The Twentieth-Century Revolution in Family Wealth Transmission." *Michigan Law Review* 86 (1988): 722.

Leonard, H. B. "Louis Marshall and Immigration Restriction." *American Jewish Archives* 24 (1972): 6.

Light, Ivan. "Immigrant Entrepreneurs in America." In *Clamor at the Gates: The New American Immigration*, ed. Nathan Glazer, p. 170. San Francisco: ICS Press, 1985.

Link, Arthur. "What Happened to the Progressive Movement in the 1920s?" *American Historical Review* 64 (1959): 833.

Lissak, Rivka. "Liberal Progressives and the 'New Immigrants': The Immigrants' Protective League of Chicago, 1908–1919." In Vol. 32, *Studies in American Civilization*, ed. E. M. Budick et al., p. 79. Jerusalem: Magnes Press, 1987.

Litwack, Leon. "Trouble in Mind: The Bicentennial and the Afro-American Experience." *Journal of American History* 74 (1987): 315.

Long, Steven. "The Wizard of Galveston." *Ultra*, July, 1985, p. 60.

McKelvey, Blake. "The Prison Labor Problem, 1875–1900." *Journal of Criminal Law, Criminology, and Police Science* 25 (1934): 254.

Marcus, George. "Law in the Development of Dynastic Families." *Law and Society* 14 (1980): 859.

Marcus, Jacob R. "Trailblazers of the Trans-Mississippi West." *American Jewish Archives* 8 (1956): 59.

Mayer, Michael. "German-Jewish Identity in 19th Century America." In *The American Jewish Experience*, ed. Jonathan D. Sarna, p. 45. New York: Holmes and Meier, 1986.

Mondell, C., and A. Mondell. "West of Hester Street." *Texas Humanist* (1981): 3.

Moore, Deborah D. "Jewish Migration to the Sunbelt." In *Shades of the Sunbelt: Essays on Ethnicity, Race, and the Urban South*, ed. Randall M. Miller and George E. Pozzetta, p. 41. New York: Greenwood Press, 1988.

Munro, William B. "Municipal Government by Commission." *Nation* 83 (October 18, 1906): 322.

Muson, Howard. "Generations." *New York Times Magazine – Business World Supplement*, November 29, 1987, p. 25.

North, Douglass, and John Wallis. "Measuring the Transaction Sector in the American Economy." In *Long Term Factors in American Economic Growth*, ed. Stanley Engerman and Robert Gallman, p. 95. Chicago: University of Chicago Press, 1986.

Platt, Harold. "City Building and Progressive Reform: The Modernization of an Urban Polity in Houston, 1892–1905." In *The Age of Urban Reform: New Perspectives on the Progressive Era*, ed. Michael Ebner and Eugene Tobin. Port Washington, N.Y.: Kennikat, 1977.

Rice, Bradley R. "The Galveston Plan of City Government by Commission: The Birth of a Progressive Idea." *Southwestern Historical Quarterly* 78 (1975): 363.

Roberts, Henry M. "Curbing the Sea at Galveston." *Scientific American* 113 (September 25, 1915): 268.

Rosen, Christine M. "Infrastructural Improvement in 19th Century Cities." *Journal of Urban History* 12 (1986): 211.

———. "The Power of Business Elites in the History of the City." *Reviews in American History* 15 (June, 1987): 303.

Schweikart, Larry. "Antebellum Southern Bankers: Origins and Mobility." *Business and Economic History* 14 (1985): 79.

———. "Entrepreneurial Aspects of Antebellum Banking." In *American Business History: Case Studies*, ed. Henry C. Dethloff and C. Joseph Pusateri, p. 122. Glenwood, Ill.: Davidson, 1987.

Shankman, Arnold. "Friend or Foe?: Southern Blacks View the Jew, 1880–1935." In *Turn to the South*, ed. Nathan Kaganoff and Melvin Urofsky, p. 105. Charlottesville: University Press of Virginia, 1979.

Sharon, Will H., Jr.; W. H. Louviere; and R. M. Laperouse. "Cane Sugar Refining." *Industrial and Engineering Chemistry* 4 (1951): 552.

Shlomowitz, Ralph. "Plantations and Smallholdings: Comparative Perspectives from the World Cotton and Sugar Cane Economies, 1865–1939." *Agricultural History* 58 (1984): 1.

Sims, Patsy. "Childhood on a Sugar Land Prison Farm." *Southern Exposure* 14 (1986): 35.

Smith, Timothy. "New Approaches to the History of Immigration in Twentieth-Century America." *American Historical Review* 71 (1966): 1265.

Stanley, Gerald. "Merchandising in the Southwest." *American Jewish Archives* 23 (1971): 86.

Stern, Malcolm. "Role of the Rabbi in the South." In *Turn to the South: Essays on Southern Jewry*, ed. Nathan Kaganoff and Melvin Urofsky, p. 21. Charlottesville: University Press of Virginia, 1979.

Supple, Barry E. "A Business Elite: German-Jewish Financiers in 19th Century New York." In *The American Jewish Experience*, ed. Jonathan D. Sarna, p. 73. New York: Holmes and Meier, 1986.

Suttle, Bruce B. "The Passion of Self-Interest: The Development of the Idea and Its Changing Consequences." *American Journal of Economics and Sociology* 46 (1987): 459.

Tarbell, Ida. "Good Homes Make Good Workmen." *American Magazine* 80 (1915): 39.

Tinsley, James, ed. "Select Letters of Harris Kempner." *Gulf Coast Historical Association Publications* 1 (1957): 3.

Train, John. "Rejuvenating Old Money." *New York Times Magazine—Business World Supplement*, June 8, 1986, p. 90.

Tuchman, Barbara. "The Assimilationist's Dilemma: Ambassador Morgenthau." In *Practicing History: Selected Essays*, ed. Barbara Tuchman, p. 208. New York: Knopf, 1981.

Turner, George K. "Galveston: A Business Corporation." *McClure's*, October, 1906, p. 610.

Urofsky, Melvin. "Zionism: An American Experience." In *The American Jewish Experience*, ed. Jonathan D. Sarna, p. 211. New York: Holmes and Meier, 1986.

Veblen, Thorstein. "The Country Town." *Freeman* 7 (1923): 420.

Wall, Bennett H. "What Is *Not* in Southern History, 1918–1988." *Journal of Southern History* 55 (1989): 3.

Waller, J. L. "Overland Movement of Cotton." *Southwestern Historical Quarterly* 35 (1931): 137.

Wardell, Nancy. "The Corporation." In *A New America?*, ed. Stephen Graubard, p. 97. New York: Norton, 1979.

Wayne, Leslie. "Brothers at Odds." *New York Times—Business World Supplement* (Dec. 7, 1986): 82.

Whisenhunt, D. "Huey Long and the Texas Cotton Acreage Control Law of 1931." *Louisiana Studies* 13 (1974): 142.

White, Louise. "Prostitutes, Reformers, and Historians." *Criminal Justice History* 6 (1985): 201.

Whitfield, Stephen J. "American Jews: Their Story Continues." In *The American Jewish Experience*, ed. Jonathan D. Sarna, p. 284. New York: Holmes and Meier, 1986.

Williams, Joan C. "The Constitutional Vulnerability of American Local Government: The Politics of City Status in American Law." *Wisconsin Law Review* (1986): 83.

Woodman, Harold. "How New Was the New South?" *Agricultural History* 58 (1984): 529.

Wright, J. E. "Industrial Town That's Fit to Live In." *American City* 13 (1915): 388.

Wygant, Larry. "A Municipal Broom: The Woman Suffrage Campaign in Galveston, Texas." *Houston Review* 6 (1984): 117.

Papers at Professional Association Meetings

Alsobrook, David. "Bosses and Businessmen: The Fight for Commission Government in Mobile." Southern Historical Association, 1985.

Clark, Christopher. "Taking Stock of the Nineteenth Century Store." Organization of American Historians, 1985.

Dahlin, Michel R. "Old Age Policy, the Family, and Inheritance in 20th Century America." Organization of American Historians, 1985.

Doyle, Don. "Segregation and Social Change in the Cities of the New South." Organization of American Historians, 1986.

Fabian, Ann. "The Metaphysics of Money Making." Organization of American Historians, 1988.

Fite, Gilbert. "The Agricultural Trap in the South." Southern Historical Association, 1985.

Hawley, Ellis. "The Corporate Component of America's Quest for National Efficiency, 1900–1971." Organization of American Historians, 1986.

Kraut, Benny. "Dissent and American Judaism." Organization of American Historians, 1987.

McGerr, Michael. "Confinement, Liberation and Social Class: Synthesizing Early 20th Century American History." American Historical Association, 1986.

Nadell, Pamela. "Perils of the Passage: Jewish Women Immigrants Enroute to America." Social Science History Association, 1987.

Reiff, Jan. "Pullman and Paternalism: Community Restraints on Corporate Power." Social Science History Association, 1987.

Rice, Bradley C. "Commission Government Adoption in Jackson, Mississippi: Race and Politics." Southern Historical Association, 1985.

Shulman, Bruce. "The Wages of Dixie: The Federal Government and the Reorganizations of Southern Industry, 1933–1945." Organization of American Historians, 1988.

Stevens, John. "What Made Grandpa Blush? Guardians of Local Morals in the 1920s." Organization of American Historians, 1988.

Tenebaum, Shelly. "Immigrants and Capital: Hebrew Free Loan Societies in the United States, 1880–1940." American Historical Association, 1985.

Turner, Elizabeth. "From Benevolent Ladies to Civic Women: Galveston's Female Voluntary Associations, 1900–1910." Southern Historical Association, 1986.

———. "Women, Religion, and Reform in Galveston, 1880–1920." Texas State Historical Association, 1987.

Watson, Harry L. "U.S. Local History and the Possibility of National Synthesis." Southern Historical Association, 1985.

Welter, Rush. "The American Money Mentality after the Civil War." Organization of American Historians, 1985.

Theses and Dissertations

Barker, Thomas Truel, Jr. "Partners in Progress: The Galveston Wharf Company and the City of Galveston, 1900–1930." Ph.D. diss., Texas A&M University, 1979.

Cook, Paul B. "Academicians in Government from Roosevelt to Roosevelt." Ph.D. diss., University of Kentucky, 1982.

Ellis, L. Tuffly. "The Texas Cotton Compress Industry: A History." Ph.D diss., University of Texas, 1964.

Gildermeister, G. "Prison Labor and Convict Competition with Free Workers in Industrializing America, 1840–1890." Ph.D. diss., Northern Illinois University, 1977.

Guidry, Barbara. "Twisted Threads: H. Kempner and the Cotton Spinners Litigations, 1919–1956." Ph.D. diss., Rice University, 1984.

Hinze, Virginia. "Norris Wright Cuney." MA thesis, Rice University, 1965.

Joseph, Judith L. "The *Nafkeh* and the Lady: Jews, Prostitutes, and Progressives in New York City, 1900–1930." Ph.D. diss., SUNY Stony Brook, 1986.

Kelly, Ruth E. "'Twixt Failure and Success: The Port of Galveston in the 19th Century." MA thesis, University of Houston, 1975.

Kolsky, Thomas. "Jews against Zionism: The American Council for Judaism, 1942–1948." Ph.D. diss., George Washington University, 1986.

Mervis, Leonard J. "The Social Justice Movement of the American Reform Rabbis, 1890–1940." Ph.D. diss., University of Pittsburgh, 1951.

Moretta, J. A. "William Pitt Ballinger: Public Servant, Private Pragmatist." Ph.D. diss., Rice University, 1985.

Scoufelis, Aristedes. "The Public Views on Charitable Contributions of American Big Businessmen toward Learning, Culture, and Human Welfare, 1910–1932," Ph.D. diss., Columbia University Teachers College, 1985.

Index

Oleander Odyssey was composed into type on a Compugraphic digital phototypesetter in ten and one-half point Caledonia with two and one-half points of spacing between the lines. Caledonia was also selected for display. The book was designed by Jim Billingsley, typeset by Metricomp, Inc., printed offset by Thomson-Shore, Inc., and bound by John H. Dekker & Sons, Inc. The paper on which this book is printed carries acid-free characteristics for an effective life of at least three hundred years.

TEXAS A&M UNIVERSITY PRESS : COLLEGE STATION